HARRY S TRUMAN

HARRY S TRUMAN

BY

MARGARET TRUMAN

ILLUSTRATED

HAMISH HAMILTON
LONDON

First published in Great Britain 1973
by Hamish Hamilton Ltd
90 Great Russell Street London WC1

Copyright © 1972 by Margaret Truman Daniel

SBN 241 02416 1

Photo Credits:

The Harry S. Truman Library: 1–4, 6, 8, 15, 19, 21, 22, 28, 30, 34, 36; United Press International: 5, 9, 10, 12, 16, 17, 20, 23, 24, 26, 27, 31, 32, 33, 37; *Kansas City Star*: 7; *The Washington Post*: 11; U.S. Army: 13, 25; Acme News: 14; U.S. Navy: 18; *The New York Times*: 29; Oliver Atkins: 35.

Printed in Great Britain by
Redwood Press Limited
Trowbridge, Wiltshire

ACKNOWLEDGMENTS

I WOULD LIKE to take this opportunity to thank the staff of the Truman Library, and in particular the director, Benedict K. Zobrist, for their cheerful and repeated assistance. Rose Conway, who served my father so well as his secretary during the White House years, has been equally helpful in guiding me through his voluminous personal files. I would also like to thank ex-members of the Truman White House staff, in particular George Elsey, Charles Murphy, Donald Dawson, Clark Clifford, Major General Harry Vaughan, and Matt Connelly, for sharing their recollections of the Truman years with me. Others to whom I owe debts of gratitude are James Farley, who shared some hitherto unrevealed recollections of the Roosevelt years with me, and John Snyder, my father's Secretary of the Treasury as well as one of our closest family friends. The staff of the Roosevelt Library gathered together on microfilm a number of documents from the 1930s and early '40s which shed new light on my father's career. Finally, I must especially thank historian Thomas Fleming for his invaluable advice and help in researching and organizing this book.

[CHAPTER]

One

WE WERE in the sitting room of the presidential car, the *Ferdinand Magellan,* racing across Kansas by night. The date was September 19, 1948, and my father, Harry S. Truman, was seated opposite me, reading a speech that he would make the following day in Denver. My mother sat beside me, reading a murder mystery.

It was a typical Truman family evening, unchanged by the admittedly unique circumstances surrounding it. We were hurtling into the climax of the wildest presidential campaign of the century. My father was fighting for his political life, and for something even more important—his political self-respect as a man and President. Yet the atmosphere in the *Ferdinand Magellan* was calm, tranquil to the point of serenity.

We had left Independence, Missouri, earlier in the day, and made a whistle-stop visit to Junction City, Kansas, at 11:05 P.M. As we roared across the immense prairie of western Kansas toward the Rockies, the engineer let the throttle out all the way. Dad was scheduled to speak at noon the following day in Denver, and it was to be broadcast over a national radio hookup. Maybe someone had told the engineer to take no chances on arriving late. At any rate, from the sound of the spinning metal wheels alone, I could tell that we were traveling at an unusual speed.

Then I noticed that Dad's eyes rose from the page he was reading, and he stared for a moment at the wall just above my head. This was very unusual. One of the most remarkable things about my father is his power of concentration. He has always been able to read a book or a memorandum with the radio or the phonograph playing, and my mother and me conducting a first-class family argument. I am convinced that the world could be coming to an end, but he would not look up until he got to the bottom of the page he was reading.

My mother went into the dining room to discuss the menus with Mitchell, the steward who ran the car. Dad let his speech fall into his lap and stared almost grimly at the wall above my head. "Take a look at that thing," he said.

I twisted my neck, remembering that there was a speedometer up there to tell us how fast the train was going. At first I could not believe what I saw. We were hitting 105 miles an hour.

Like most twenty-four-year-olds, I considered myself indestructible, so this discovery only excited me. "Wow," I said, and rushed to the window to stare out at the black blur of landscape whizzing by.

I glanced back at my father and saw something very close to disgust on his face. I had obviously missed his point. "Do you know what would happen if that engineer had to make a sudden stop?"

Only then did I remember that the *Ferdinand Magellan* weighed 285,000 pounds—as much as the biggest engine on the line. It had been built for President Franklin D. Roosevelt during World War II, and its base was solid concrete, reinforced by a section of steel track embedded in it. It also carried three inches of armor plate and the windows were bulletproof. The goal was the safety of the President of the United States. But it made for problems on the right of way.

"If he had to stop suddenly," Dad said in the same calm, matter-of-fact voice, "we would mash those sixteen cars between us and the engine into junk."

He heard the car door opening and quickly added, "Don't say a word to your mother. I don't want her to get upset."

The person coming through turned out to be not Mother but Charlie Ross, the White House press secretary. He wanted to find out what the President thought of the latest draft of tomorrow's major speech. The President said he thought it was fine. Then, almost casually, he said, "Charlie, send someone to tell that engineer there's no need to get us to Denver at this rate of speed. Eighty miles an hour is good enough for me."

This calm, quiet, but authoritative way of dealing with a situation that would have agitated an average person was typical of the man I am writing about in this book, the man who was both my father and President of the United States. In our home he rarely raised his voice, never used profane or even harsh language, and made a point of avoiding arguments. My mother and I love to argue, and one of the great frustrations of our life as a family has been my father's constant refusal to join us in our favorite sport. I am not, of course, claiming that Dad *never* lost his temper, or *never* used salty language when talking man to man. When the circumstances warranted it, he could match his sparks against the greatest temper-losers in White House history, including his hero, Andrew Jackson. But it was very, very seldom that he thought circumstances warranted it. Ninety-nine times out of a hundred he preferred to play the calm peacemaker's role.

Charlie Ross, who had gone through school with him from the third grade to the last year of high school, often marveled at the modesty that characterized Dad's style in the day-to-day operations of the White House. He hated to use the buzzers on his desk to summon a man peremptorily. Nine times out of ten he preferred to go to the aide's office. When he did summon a man, he would usually greet him at the door of the Oval Room office. More often than not the purpose of the call was to get his opinion on one of the many problems confronting the nation. This constant consideration for others, the total lack of egotism with which Dad conducted the day-to-day affairs of the White House was the real source of the enormous loyalty he generated in those around him.

To really understand Harry S. Truman, you must grasp the importance of humility in his thinking. To him humility meant never blowing your own horn, never claiming credit in public for what you did or said, above all never claiming that you were better, smarter, tougher than other people. But this *practice* of humility never meant that Dad downgraded his worth, his accomplishments, in his own mind.

Let me give you an example of what I mean. When Dad visited Bermuda in 1946, he was shown a Masonic Register which George

[3]

Washington had purportedly signed. Some enterprising tourist had ripped out the page and made off with the autograph. The Bermudians asked Dad to sign the register, and he was happy to oblige. "I don't suppose anyone will ever want that signature," he wrote to his mother.

That was his humility speaking. To this day Dad cannot picture himself as a great man, or a great President. But as you shall see in a few pages, when the 1948 campaign was beginning, he wrote to his sister and told her that he deserved to be reelected because most of the decisions he had made were "right." This was the other side of his mind—that calm objectivity which included an amazing ability to stand back and look at himself, even talk about himself as if he was another person. But only in private, in the intimacy of the family circle. He would never dream of making such a statement in public.

"I only wish I could get the public to appreciate the Harry Truman I know," Charlie Ross used to say.

In the fall of 1948 those words had special poignancy. Harry S. Truman was conducting a campaign for the presidency, which most of the nation's political experts considered a waste of time. The Republican nominee, Thomas E. Dewey, seemed to be so far ahead that one of the nation's leading pollsters, Elmo Roper, announced in September that further polling was a waste of time and money. Political leaders ranging from James Roosevelt in California to William O'Dwyer in New York had publicly urged the President not to run. On the left, Henry Wallace was leading the Progressive party on a platform that would hand much of the world over to Joseph Stalin & Company. On the right, Senator Strom Thurmond of South Carolina had led the Dixiecrats out of the Democratic party, in the hope that the South would forget who had surrendered to whom at Appomattox. The Republican candidate was so confident of victory that he barely bothered to mention my father's name in his lofty paeans to unity. "President Truman," said Connecticut's Congresswoman Clare Booth Luce, "is a gone goose."

Everyone in the world seemed to believe it except Harry S. Truman, my mother, me, a loyal little band of White House aides—and the people who came to meet our campaign train. Of that group only Mother and I needed no convincing in advance.

We had seen Harry S. Truman win too many elections after the opposition had counted him out. But in 1948 my father had to convince first his White House staff, then the Democratic party, and finally the American people that he was going to win this election.

In many ways the victory injection he gave the White House staff was most important. It came late in July, when they began discussing the details of the coming campaign. Dad sensed a mood of discouragement, not to say defeat, in the comments that were made. Someone even intimated that there was no chance of winning, and the best they could do was go down fighting. Dad instantly disagreed with this attitude. "We *are* going to win," he said. "I expect to travel all over the country and talk at every whistle-stop. We are going to be on the road most of the time from Labor Day to the end of the campaign. It's going to be tough on everybody, but that's the way it's got to be. I know I can take it. I'm only afraid that I'll kill some of my staff—and I like you all very much and I don't want to do that."

Charlie Ross, who was famous in Washington as a man who never "gilded a fact," was fond of saying that as far as he was concerned the election was won that day in the Oval Room. Charlie knew that wasn't true, of course; he was only trying to emphasize how totally the campaign of 1948 was Harry S. Truman's personal creation.

If, like many people, you wonder where my father found this confidence in victory, you can find part of the answer in this letter which he wrote to his sister Mary earlier in 1948:

> Dear Mary:— Just three years ago tonight at 7:09 P.M. eastern standard time I was sworn in as President. It seems an age and it has been. Two wars were in progress—one in Europe and one in Asia. We were supporting both of them with men, munitions, planes and ships. Just 26 days after that day Germany surrendered. On August 14 Japan gave up and signed the surrender document on board the Battleship Missouri on September 2, 1945.
>
> In the meantime between the two surrenders I went to Berlin to meet Stalin and Churchill. On that trip coming home I ordered the Atomic Bomb to be dropped on Hiroshima and Nagasaki. It was a terrible decision. But I made it. And I'd

[5]

made it to save 250,000 boys from the United States and I'd make it again under similar circumstances. It stopped the Jap War.

Many decisions have had to be made—most of them of world-wide significance—many of them affecting only home affairs. They've almost all been right and when history is written without prejudice it will say just that. I've still a long way to go whether it is to Jan. 20, 1949 or to Jan. 20, 1953. And it will be a rough road. It can't be any worse than the trail behind. So don't worry about it.

Equally important, perhaps, my father believed he *had* to win. He was running because he believed the future of the United States of America literally was at stake. In a letter to his sister earlier in the year, he made this clear:

I'm rather fed up on all the fol-de-rol it takes to be President. If it were not for the world situation and my lack of confidence in the presidential candidates I'd throw the whole works out the window and go home and stay there. But I can't run from responsibility as you know. So I have to face the music.

Europe, China, Palestine, terrible Russia and the special privilege boys here at home.

For me, personally, my father's struggle to revivify the Democratic party was the most moving part of the campaign. You have to understand how profoundly the Trumans identify with the word Democrat to realize how painful it was for him to face the grim fact that major sections of the party, possibly a majority of the leaders, did not think he was worthy of support, after three and a half years in the White House. Yet this was precisely what seemed to be happening.

Over the July Fourth weekend, James Roosevelt, who was serving as the chairman of the California delegation to the Democratic Convention, persuaded eighteen other prominent party leaders to send a telegram to each of the 1,592 delegates to the convention, urging them to come to Philadelphia two days early for a special caucus to select "the ablest and strongest man available" as the party's presidential candidate.

Roosevelt's telegram did not come as a surprise. Earlier in the year, when J. Howard McGrath, the Democratic national chairman, addressed a political dinner in Los Angeles, Roosevelt

[6]

carefully arranged for his followers to pack the affair and boo angrily when Mr. McGrath praised Harry Truman. Then Jimmy, to a storm of predictable applause, seized the podium and made a rousing speech on behalf of Dwight Eisenhower as the best Democratic candidate. At the same time Jimmy's brother Franklin D. Roosevelt, Jr., was working equally hard in New York to persuade the Democrats to draft Ike.

My father had reacted forcefully in response to this earlier threat. When General Eisenhower left the army in 1947, Dad had asked him bluntly if he intended to enter politics. Eisenhower had firmly and categorically said no. Dad had praised the wisdom of this decision. He pointed out how General Ulysses S. Grant had tarnished his great reputation by blundering into politics. The moment the Eisenhower boom began in 1948, Dad ordered Defense Secretary James Forrestal to call the General and advise him to make a statement that he was not available. At Forrestal's request Ike had called FDR Jr. and told him he was not in the running.

But the Roosevelts had ignored that statement and continued to keep alive the Draft Eisenhower movement. Professional liberals under the banner of Americans for Democratic Action began picketing Eisenhower's New York home with signs reading, "Ike You Favor the Draft, We Favor It For You." Not even a public statement which Eisenhower made on July 5 declaring he would not accept nomination for any public office stilled these anti-Truman voices. John F. Bailey, the Democratic leader for Connecticut, suggested that the party should nominate Eisenhower anyway and run him for President even if he refused to campaign. Senator Claude Pepper of Florida went him one better and suggested that the party abandon the name Democratic and draft Ike as a nonpartisan candidate. "The Democratic party's rewards would lie in the tribute it would gain for its magnanimity in a time of crisis," intoned Senator Pepper.

When Eisenhower remained unavailable, the ADA, led by Leon Henderson, attempted to switch its support to Supreme Court Justice William O. Douglas. "The Democratic party must choose Douglas or invite a disaster that will imperil the future of progressivism in America," said Henderson.

Fortunately not all the Democrats lost their heads. One of the

[7]

best, David Lilienthal, former director of the Tennessee Valley Authority, a man with impeccable liberal credentials, wrote the following words in his diary around this time:

> July 5, 1948
> I am simply aghast at the unfair way in which President Truman is being "judged," if the current lynch law atmosphere can be called "judging." And the attitude of liberals and progressives, so whooping it up for Eisenhower or Douglas, is the hardest to understand or be other than damn mad about . . . my God! What *do* these people want? . . .

Watching this bizarre circus, I began to appreciate for the first time Dad's dislike of what he calls "professional liberals." On the eve of the Democratic National Convention, he had yielded to the pleas of the national chairman, J. Howard McGrath, who was trying to placate the liberals, and agreed to call Douglas and ask him if he would consider running on the ticket as vice president. Here, from Dad's private papers, is a memorandum telling what he really thought about this idea:

> I call him [Douglas], tell him I'm doing to him what FDR did to me. He owes it to the country to accept.
> He belongs to that crowd of Tommy Corcoran, Harold Ickes, Claude Pepper crackpots whose word is worth less than Jimmy Roosevelt's. I hope he has a more honorable political outlook. No professional liberal is intellectually honest. That's a real indictment—but true as the Ten Commandments. Professional liberals aren't familiar with the Ten Commandments or the Sermon on the Mount.
> Most Roosevelts aren't either!

Ironically, my father received unexpected—and completely unintentional—support from Strom Thurmond, the Dixiecrat candidate, around this time. Someone asked Mr. Thurmond why he had broken with the Democratic party over the Truman civil rights program. Hadn't President Roosevelt run on platforms with almost the same promises of justice and equal opportunity for America's black citizens?

"I agree," said Thurmond grimly, "but Truman really means it."

The antics of the younger Roosevelts inspired Dad to make

[8]

some interesting comments on party loyalty to his sister Mary. Dad mentioned an ex-governor and said:

> He was a fine old man but a sort of Bill Southern [the publisher of the Independence *Examiner*] Democrat, one that apologizes for his Party most of the time and knocks it the rest; then takes all he can get from it if it profits him personally. The word "sacrifice" is not in their dictionary, especially if it means personal sacrifice for Party good. We have immense numbers of Democrats like that.
>
> Then we have them whose definition of loyalty is loyalty to themselves—that is it is a one way street.
>
> Take the Roosevelt clan as an example. As long as Wm. Howard Taft was supporting Teddy he was a great man—but when Taft needed support Teddy supported Teddy. The present generation of Franklin's is something on that order. Although it looks as if Eleanor & Anna are not going along with Elliott & Franklin Jr.—at least *not yet.*
>
> Anyway we'll attempt to beat the whole works when it comes down to brass tacks.

As a result of this fratricidal feuding, the Democratic Convention opened in an atmosphere of appalling gloom. I think it will be clear from the following notes, written by my father on July 12, how badly the party needed his leadership:

> Douglas says he can't quit the Supreme Court. Says the family are of the opinion that his lack of political experience would cause trouble in the campaign. Says no to my request that he take second place on the ticket with me. I'm inclined to give some credence to Tommy Corcoran's crack to Burt Wheeler that Douglas had said he could "not" be a No. 2 man to a No. 2 man.
>
> Call old man Barkley and soothe his feathers so he'll go ahead and make the keynote speech.
>
> McGrath calls me and suggests I call Barkley again and say I am not against him. I don't do it.
>
> Barkley makes a real keynote speech. Ends up at midnight. I can't get him by phone. My *"good"* friend Leslie Biffle spends all his time as sergeant at arms of the convention running Barkley for President. I watched the demonstration on television. Having been in on numerous demonstrations I'm not

fooled. I can see everything taking place on the platform. The "actors" forget that.

Barkley in his good speech mentions me only casually by name.

Perhaps I should identify more completely some of this cast of characters. Tommy Corcoran, often known as "Tommy the Cork," was an old Roosevelt brain truster. Burt Wheeler was Burton K. Wheeler, the Democratic isolationist senator from Montana. Alben Barkley was, at this time, the senator from Kentucky and the Democratic majority leader of the Senate. Leslie Biffle was the secretary of the Senate and one of Washington's shrewdest politicians. It was a good index of how demoralized the Democrats had become, that someone as normally loyal and dependable as Mr. Biffle would try to double-cross the President of the United States.

The following day, my father was back at work, quietly taking control of the party:

> I called Barkley and smoothed him down again. Tried to call him last night after his good speech but can't get him.
> Call McGrath and tell him I'm coming up tomorrow on the train and accept.
> He is not very happy over it.
> Talked to Hannegan, Ed Flynn and Frank Walker. All disgruntled as has-beens always are with a new chairman. It means not one thing. The result is what counts.
> Platform fight this afternoon, postponed until tomorrow. But they have a good fight on credentials. A Negro alternate from St. Louis makes a minority report suggesting the unseating of Mississippi delegation. Vaughn is his name. He's overruled. . . . Congressman Dawson of Chicago, another Negro, makes an excellent talk on civil rights. These two colored men are the only speakers to date who seem to be for me wholeheartedly.
> Snyder calls and says Jimmy R., Leon Henderson and Wilson Wyatt are running Barkley for President. Maybe so, but Barkley is an honorable man. He won't give me the double cross, I'm sure.

Bob Hannegan, Ed Flynn, and Frank Walker were all former Democratic national chairmen. As Dad said, like most ex-officeholders, they had nothing to offer but criticism. Snyder is John Snyder, Dad's Secretary of the Treasury, and one of his closest friends. Thanks to him and other Truman loyalists, my father knew exactly what was happening at the convention, from the inside.

On Wednesday, July 14, Dad continued making notes on the convention, as he saw it:

> Take the train for Philadelphia at 7 P.M. Eastern Daylight Time, arrive in the rain at 9:15. Television sets at both ends of trip. No privacy sure enough now.
> Hear Alabama & Mississippi walk out of the convention. Hear Gov. Donnelly nominate me. Both on the radio. Hard to hear. My daughter & my staff try to keep me from listening. Think maybe I'll be upset. I won't be. . . .

Philadelphia on that night of July 14 seemed to be wrapped in a huge suffocating blanket of heat and humidity. Mother and Dad and I were led to a small airless room beneath the platform, used as a dressing room when actors were performing at Convention Hall. We had to sit there for four long hours while the convention recovered from the civil rights wrangle and got down to the business of nominating my father for President and Alben Barkley for vice president.

Once Dad had deflated his presidential boomlet, Barkley had passed the word that he was available for the vice presidency. He had been doing this at nearly every convention since 1928, and now, at the age of seventy, he was rather touchy on the subject. "It will have to come quick," he told his friends. "I don't want it passed around so long it is like a cold biscuit." Dad admired Alben's abilities as a speaker and respected his long career in the Senate, where he had served as majority leader for both him and President Roosevelt. So he promptly passed the word that the senator had his support and telephoned him in Philadelphia. "Why didn't you tell me you wanted to run, Alben?" Dad said. "That's all you had to do."

Never have I seen so much smoke without a fire as I saw that humid night in Philadelphia. I thought sure I was going to expire. Oxygen was my only thought. Dad, apparently bothered neither by the heat nor the pollution, went right on politicking.

[11]

He sat in a nearby room, greeting delegates, congressmen, senators, and assorted Democrats who streamed in to shake hands and assure him of their backing. He had a particularly pleasant visit with Senator Barkley.

Occasionally, in the rare moments when he was not being besieged by visitors, Dad stepped out on a little balcony and looked down on Philadelphia, where the nation's political history began. He thought about the task to which he was committing himself, and about the wily, determined foe he was fighting—Joseph Stalin. My father felt we were very close to war with Russia. Even as we sat there, waiting for the Democrats to stop debating and orating, American planes were flying tons of food and clothing and other necessities of life into beleaguered Berlin. On June 24, 1948, the Russians had cut off all land access to Berlin, as part of an attempt to force the United States and our allies to withdraw from this symbolic city. On June 26, Dad ordered all the available planes in the European theater to begin a massive airlift of supplies. Twenty-five hundred tons of food and fuel were being flown into the city every day by 130 American planes. My father had made this decision against the advice of many of his closest aides and Cabinet members. "We will stay in Berlin," he said.

Later Dad recalled that he also thought about some of the presidents to whom he felt close. One was John Tyler, to whom we are bound by blood as well as history. Dad's grandfather, Anderson Shippe Truman, married a direct descendant of John Tyler's brother. Tyler was the first vice president to become President on the death of the Chief Executive—in his case, William Henry Harrison. Daniel Webster, his Secretary of State, and Henry Clay, the leader of the Whig party in Congress, thought they were going to run the government but they soon found out that Tyler was planning to be his own President. When Dad is willing to admit that he has a stubborn streak (which is seldom), he humorously attributes it to his Tyler blood.

Finally, at 1:45 A.M., my father was escorted to the convention floor. He had been officially nominated, beating Senator Richard Russell of Georgia, 947½ votes to 263. But the South was in such a truculent mood that Sam Rayburn, the chairman of the convention and one of Dad's staunchest friends, did not dare call for the usual extra round of voting to make the nomination unanimous. While the band played "Hail to the Chief," Mrs. Emma Guffey Miller, sister of the senator from Pennsylvania, released a flock of doves from inside a floral liberty bell. She and her brother were part of the professional liberal bloc that was trying to convince the Democratic party and the country that peace with Stalin could be won by appeasement. The doves were an incredible disaster. One almost perched on Sam Rayburn's head as he was trying to introduce my father and Alben Barkley. Another blundered into an upper balcony and plunged to the floor, dead or unconscious. In the pandemonium, a reporter said he overheard a delegate from New York comparing Harry Truman to the dead pigeon.

Ignoring this idiocy, my father strode to the lectern and opened a small black loose-leaf book in which he carried the notes of his speech. He never looked more like a leader, as he waited for the soggy, weary crowd to settle down and listen to him. He was wearing a crisp white linen suit, and he exuded a vitality which practically no one else in that muggy cavern of a convention hall felt, at that moment. He knew they needed an injection of his vitality, and he gave it to them with his first sentence.

"Senator Barkley and I will win this election and make those Republicans like it—don't you forget that."

An incredible current of emotion surged through the crowd. People who thought they were too tired even to stand up again were on their feet, shouting their heads off.

For the next twenty minutes he told them why he was going to win. He listed the failures of the Eightieth Congress, and pointed out the tremendous gains that families and workers had made under the Democrats. It was one of the toughest, most aggressive speeches ever made by a presidential candidate. He brought the crowd to their feet again and again, roaring their approval.

But only Mother and I and a handful of White House aides were ready for the totally unexpected climax.

My father's thirty-five years in politics, and his constant study of American history, had made clear to him the key to victory in any political campaign—take the offensive, not only in words but in action. As he put it later, "I . . . had made up my mind

[13]

that I would spring my first big surprise of the campaign in that speech. "

> On the 26th day of July, which out in Missouri we call Turnip Day, I am going to call Congress back and ask them to pass laws to halt rising prices, to meet the housing crisis—which they are saying they are for, in their platform.
>
> At the same time, I shall ask them to act upon other vitally needed measures. . . .
>
> Now, my friends, if there is any reality behind that Republican platform, we ought to get some action from a short session of the 80th Congress. They can do this job in 15 days, if they want to do it. They will still have time to go out and run for office. . . .

For two solid minutes the convention hall was drowned in total pandemonium as the delegates roared their support of this daring move. Even liberal columnist Max Lerner, who had been writing "this has been the Convention of the vacuum—the only ruling passion of empty men is the feat of looking foolish," did an abrupt about-face and reported: "It was a great speech for a great occasion, and as I listened I found myself applauding. . . ."

The following day my father brought himself up to date with more notes on his desk calendar:

> Arrived in Washington at the White House at 5:30 A.M., my usual getting up time. But I go to bed at 6:00 and listen to the news. Sleep until 9:15, order breakfast and go to the office at 10:00.
>
> I called a special session of the Congress. My, how the opposition screams. I'm going to attempt to make them meet their platform promises before the election. That's according to the "kept" press and the opposition leadership "cheap politics." I wonder what "expensive politics" will be like! We'll see.

The following day he was even more pleased by the reaction he was getting:

> Editorials, columns and cartoons are gasping and wondering.
> None of the smart folks thought I would call the Congress. I called em for July 26th; turnip day at home.
> Dewey synthetically milks cows and pitches hay for the cameras just as that other faker Teddy Roosevelt did—but he never heard of "turnip day."

[14]

I don't believe the USA wants any more fakers—Teddy and Franklin are enough. So I'm going to make a common sense intellectually honest campaign. It will be a novelty—and it will win.

While he was standing the Republicans and their publicity men on their ears, my father had to continue coping with the horrendous world situation. On July 19, 1948, he made the following notes on a meeting with Secretary of State George Marshall and Secretary of Defense James Forrestal:

> Have quite a day. See some politicos. A meeting with General Marshall and Jim Forrestal on Berlin and the Russian situation. Marshall states the facts and the condition with which we are faced. I'd made the decision ten days ago to *stay in Berlin.*
>
> Jim wants to hedge—he always does. He's constantly sending me alibi memos, which I return with directions and the facts.
>
> We'll stay in Berlin—come what may.
>
> Royal Draper & Jim Forrestal come in later. I have to listen to a rehash of what I know already and reiterate my "stay in Berlin" decision. I don't pass the buck, nor do I alibi out of any decision I make.

Fighting as he was to keep the world from blowing itself up, there were times when my father found the situation almost unbearable. On July 10 he poured out his feelings in a hitherto unpublished letter to Winston Churchill. The great British leader, out of office, had written him a letter wishing him well in the election and voicing his fear that the Kremlin might begin a war in the autumn. "I greatly admire your conduct of international affairs in Europe during your tenure of the most powerful office in the world. I only wish I could have been more help," Mr. Churchill wrote.

Here is Dad's reply:

> My dear Winston:—
>
> I was deeply touched by your good letter of June 7. I am going through a terrible political "trial by fire." Too bad it must happen at this time.
>
> Your great country and mine are founded on the fact that the people have the right to express themselves on their leaders, no matter what the crisis.

Your note accompanying "The Gathering Storm" is highly appreciated, and I have made it a part of the book.

We are in the midst of grave and trying times. You can look with satisfaction upon your great contribution to the overthrow of Nazism & Fascism in the world. "Communism"—so called, is our next great problem. I hope we can solve it without the "blood and tears" the other two cost.

May God bless and protect you

Ever sincerely your friend

Harry Truman

On this same crowded July 19 Dad had to play another important presidential role—the ceremonial presence at solemn occasions.

Went to Pershing's funeral in the marble amphitheater in Arlington. The hottest damn place this side of hell and Bolivar, Mo. An impressive ceremony. This is the fifth time I prepared to attend the General's funeral. . . .

The reference to Bolivar was inspired by a recent visit we had made to that little town in southwest Missouri, to assist the president of Venezuela in dedicating a statue of the great South American liberator after whom it is named, Simón Bolívar. It was a scorching July day, and we practically melted. In spite of the heat, General Pershing's funeral was one ceremony that my father would not have missed, no matter what was happening elsewhere. There were few Americans he revered more than General of the Armies John J. Pershing, whom Dad called "my old commander." He had served under him in World War I, and he knew what Pershing had achieved, against terrible odds. One of the first things Dad did, in the hectic days after he became President, was pay a call on the General, in his room at Walter Reed Hospital.

My father ended his notes to himself on July 19 with a personal lament. Mother and I had returned to Missouri, leaving him alone in the White House.

Bess & Margaret went to Mo. at 7:30 EDT, 6:30 God's time. I sure hated to see them go. Came back to the great white jail and read the papers, some history, and then wrote this. It is hot and humid and lonely. Why in hell does anybody want to be a head of state? Damned if I know.

[16]

Dad's only escape from this pressure was the yacht *Williamsburg*. On July 26 he wrote to his sister Mary:

> I went down the river on the yacht Friday at noon and slept almost around the clock. I sure needed it. And I'll need some more before November.

Still in a gloomy mood, he added:

> It's all so futile. Dewey, Wallace, the cockeyed Southerners and then if I win—which I'm afraid I will—I'll probably have a Russian war on my hands. Two wars are enough for anybody and I've had two.
>
> I go to Congress tomorrow and read them a message requesting price control, housing and a lot of other necessary things and I'll in all probability get nothing. But I've got to try.
>
> The weather is fine here. I hope it's not too hot there. I'll be home Sunday to vote on Tuesday.
>
> Then back here to Congress for the balance of August. And then the campaign and the ballyhoo and Nov. 2 will be here in a hurry and my troubles will be over or just beginning however you look at it. But we'll win anyway.

Two days later my father wrote me a letter. I was busy trying to lose weight in Missouri by gardening and painting the kitchen pantry. He combined this knowledge and his worries over Congress in his letter:

> Dear Margie:— I was highly pleased to get your nice letter. And more than glad to get the telegram from you and your mother about the message to Congress.
>
> You seem to have been slaving away at your paint job and your garden. I am hoping to see an excellent result in each instance. I shall expect to be able to pick a nice bouquet from the garden when I come home Sunday and I shall hope to be able to see myself in those slick pantry walls!
>
> I am somewhat exhausted myself getting ready for this terrible Congress. They are in the most awful turmoil any Congress, I can remember, ever has been. Some of them want to quit right away some of them want to give the Dixiecrats a chance to filibuster and the Majority are very anxious to put the Pres in the hole if they can manage it.
>
> It will take a few days for the message to sink in completely. In the meantime I shall take it easy and let 'em sweat.

On July 31 Dad flew to New York to make a speech. There he saw the first proof that he had knocked some of the defeatism out of the Democratic party. He noted it on his calendar in the following words:

> Great reception in N.Y. O'Dwyer, mayor of N.Y., met me for *the first time!* He's either been sick, out of town or too busy before. It's good sign because he's a bandwagon boy.

Unfortunately, the same day my father flew on to Missouri to vote in the Democratic primary. There his spirits plunged again. The Democratic party in his home state, and even in his home county, was in terrible shape. He noted glumly on his calendar:

> Saw Rufus Burrus, candidate for Congress in the 4th Mo Cong district which I had way in 1933 set up for myself. Didn't get it. Went to the Senate instead—and became President. Some change I'd say. Rufus has not a chance.

The local politicians had let Dad down badly. Instead of capitalizing on the prestige of having a Missouri man in the White House, they had taken to cutting each other's throats

> and mine too [he noted in his calendar]. My brother Vivian . . . told me all about the situation politically, in my home county. I don't see how it can be so bad—but it is.

My father voted and flew back to Washington. Very few pro-Truman Democrats fared well in the Missouri primary. From the White House he wrote to his sister Mary: "The election in Missouri was disappointing but I still hope we can carry the state in the fall." He was consoled by the Tennessee elections, in which Boss Ed Crump of Memphis had been beaten badly. Mr. Crump was one of the first Democratic leaders to come out against Dad, earlier in 1948. "Old Man Crump received a well deserved beating in Tennessee," Dad wrote. "He has always been against me. Even in 1944, that delegation never did make my nomination [as vice president] unanimous. So I'm not sorry for him."

Then he turned to the special session of Congress which was accomplishing nothing. The Republicans were too busy fulminating against the idea of the special session, as a "last hysterical gasp of an expiring administration."

Although Dad expected them to do nothing, he had sent them

a legislative package crammed with vitally needed bills on control of inflation, housing, on civil rights, aid to education, and similar national problems. He asked for an increase in the minimum wage, a meaningful national health program, an extension of Social Security coverage, and funds to bring cheap electricity to the rural parts of the nation. He would have welcomed action on any or all of these recommendations, and his disgust is evident in the comment he made to his sister:

> My special session has turned out to be a dud as I was sure it would. They are just fooling around doing nothing as I expected. It is a crying shame for them to act like that when the country so sorely needs action.

When Congress adjourned on August 12, my father was able to denounce their performance as a "do-nothing" session of a "do-nothing" Congress. Dad told his sister:

> The Congress ran off and left everything just as I expected they would do and now they are trying to blame *me* because they did nothing. I just don't believe people can be fooled that easily.

Meanwhile, the day-to-day work of the presidency had to be done. Apologizing to his sister Mary on August 18 because he hadn't written to her, Dad explained:

> My writing hand doesn't work as well as it used. Signing documents and memos at the rate of 600 to a thousand a day has worn down my control to some extent. But I do as best I can.

Most of the time, Dad was philosophical about it. On September 2 he told his sister:

> I've had as usual a very hectic week, seeing customers [his word for White House visitors], writing speeches, signing documents and making decisions, national and international. But there's no use crying about it. I'm here and the job has to be done.

Then, in the teeth of statements from pollsters and pundits that he did not have a chance, he calmly prophesied victory:

> It looks now like another four years of slavery. I'd be much

better off personally if we lose the election but I fear that the country would go to hell and I have to try to prevent that.

The Republicans may have supplied us with plenty of political ammunition, but one thing they did not supply was that equally vital ingredient for political campaigns—money. For a while it did not look as if the Democrats were going to do very much in that department either. The lack of money in the party war chest was literally terrifying. Not until September 14, three days before we started our first major campaign tour, did the Democrats even have a finance chairman. Colonel Louis A. Johnson, former Assistant Secretary of War, took on the thankless job and proceeded to accomplish miracles.

The first major crisis came on Labor Day, when we went to Detroit to make the traditional kickoff speech in Cadillac Square. Typically, Dad managed to convert it into a mini-whistle-stop tour going up and back, beginning with speeches in Grand Rapids, Michigan, at 8:15 A.M., and ending with another rear platform performance in Toledo, Ohio, at 11:55 P.M. Everywhere, people were astonished by the crowds—there were 25,000 in Republican Grand Rapids in spite of a heavy downpour. But the speech in Cadillac Square was the heart of the trip. It was aimed at working men, not just in Detroit but throughout the United States on a national radio hookup. On Saturday morning Oscar Chapman, who was handling the advance planning for the campaign, was coolly informed by radio network executives that they wanted to see the $50,000 fee by the end of the day or they were going to cancel the Monday broadcast. The local Detroit labor unions did not have that much cash on hand, and only a frantic appeal by Chapman to Governor Roy J. Turner of Oklahoma raised the money from wealthy Democrats in that state. Thus Dad was able to go ahead with a speech that galvanized numerous lukewarm labor leaders, such as AFL president William Green, CIO president Philip Murray, and Teamsters' president Daniel Tobin—three who had been conspicuously absent from the Democratic National Convention.

There were times when my father had to step in and do his own fund raising. In mid-September, as we were packing to board the campaign train for our first national swing, party treasurer

Louis Johnson called a group of wealthy Democrats to the White House and Dad got up on a chair in the Red Room to inform them that if they did not come through with $25,000, the "Truman Special" would not get beyond Pittsburgh. Two men immediately pledged $10,000, and that is how we got rolling.

More than once, Howard McGrath, the Democratic party chairman, or Jack Redding, the publicity director, carried $25,000 or $30,000 in cash to broadcasting studios, to pay for radio time. While candidate Dewey was delivering long, exquisitely polished radio addresses without an iota of trouble, my father was frequently cut off in mid-sentence because the radio networks would not allow him to speak a single second beyond the paid-for time. Louis Johnson became philosophic about this harassment. He decided it was actually helping Dad, because people were annoyed by such insulting treatment of the President.

In Oklahoma City on September 28, the cash shortage struck again. We found that we did not have enough money to get the train out of the station. Once more, Governor Roy J. Turner was the miracle man. He convened a fund-raising party aboard the train and raised enough cash to pay for the rest of that tour.

None of this in the least fazed or, as far as I could see, even momentarily discouraged my father. He was absolutely and totally convinced that he was on his way to victory, and he let other people worry about the details. What I like to think of as his finest unknown or private moment came on October 11, 1948, when one of the White House aides jumped off the train and bought the latest issue of *Newsweek*. The magazine had polled fifty veteran political writers around the country. Huge black type announced the results: FIFTY POLITICAL EXPERTS UNANIMOUSLY PREDICT A DEWEY VICTORY. You could almost see the morale sag all around us. Dad stared at the magazine for a moment and then grinned. "Oh well," he said, "those damn fellows—they're always wrong anyway. Forget it, boys, and let's get on with the job."

Sometimes nature itself seemed to be against us. The first major speech of the fall campaign came at Dexter, Iowa, at the National Plowing Contest. It was a hot, humid September day. The plowing plus the feet of 75,000 farmers and their families stirred up a huge cloud of choking dust, which simply hung there between the sky and the earth, as dust clouds are wont to do in the mid-west. Ignoring the dirty air and the heat, Dad gave a rousing, scorching speech, which almost tore his throat apart. For at least a week, Dr. Wallace Graham, his personal physician, had to spray his throat before every speech. Dad was the only man on the train who was surprised by this particular bit of damage.

His attitude is visible in his comment on his throat to his sister Mary: "Dr. Graham just sprayed, mopped and caused me to gargle bad tasting liquids until the throat gave up and got well."

The big speeches were extravaganzas in which all of us—except my father, I suppose—felt almost superfluous. Big crowds have an almost numbing effect. You feel like you are being swallowed in a maelstrom of roaring voices, waving hands, and swirling faces. For all of us—and I know this included Dad—the whistle-stops were the heart of the trip. A President can always fly to Detroit, or Denver, or Los Angeles to make a major speech. But he can't get to Pocatello, Idaho; Clarksburg, West Virginia; or Davis, Oklahoma—at least he is not likely to go there—unless he's whistle-stopping.

The whistle-stop routine seldom varied. As we pulled into the station bands would blare "Hail to the Chief" and the "Missouri Waltz." Dad, usually accompanied by three or four local politicians, would step out on the back platform of the train, and they would present him with a gift—a basket of corn, a bucket of apples, or some item of local manufacture. Then one of the local politicians would introduce the President, and Dad would give a brief fighting speech, plugging the local candidate, and asking the people for their support. But the heart of these little talks was a local reference, sometimes supplied by Dad spontaneously, more often by careful advance research on the part of the staff.

Whenever possible, my father preferred to say something that he knew or felt personally. He told his listeners in Clarksburg: "I've always had a warm spot in my heart for Clarksburg. I have been a student of the War Between the States, and I remember that Stonewall Jackson was born here in Clarksburg." At Hammond, Indiana, where many of the tanks for our World War II armies were produced, he drew on his knowledge of our war effort, which he had scrutinized intensively, as head of the Truman Committee in the Senate. "Our armies all over the world

[22]

were grateful for the high quality of work you turned out," he told the crowd. This was authentic. It was not just something he was reading off a card. He knew and felt these things.

I have always believed that the great difference between Harry S. Truman and Thomas E. Dewey in 1948 was Dad's uninhibited refusal to be anyone but himself. At Dexter, Iowa, I think he won thousands of farm votes with an impromptu talk he gave after his formal speech. "I can plow a straight furrow," he said, "a prejudiced witness said so—my mother." He told his farmer audience how he used to "sow a 160 acre wheatfield without a skip place showing in it." Then, bragging as only a Missourian can brag, he added that he did it all with only four mules and a gangplow. There were few tractors around during the eleven years before World War I, when he was a farmer.

After his whistle-stop talks, Dad would introduce first my mother and then me. Mother was introduced as "the boss," and me as "the one who bosses the boss." We never did get him to stop introducing us this way in spite of numerous demands. He was equally stubborn about other routines. Hitting hard at the Republican Congress's failure to do something about the housing shortage, he often included himself in the problem. In Ogden, Utah, for instance, he suggested that if the voters did the right thing on the second of November, "That will keep me from suffering from a housing shortage on January 20th, 1949." In Colorado Springs he told the crowd: "If you go out to the polls . . . and do your duty as you should, I won't have to worry about moving out of the White House; and you won't have to worry about what happens to the welfare of the West."

Frantic memorandums and letters from White House staffers and friends in the sophisticated East warned that these housing remarks did not "help create a picture of strength and confidence." My father ignored them. He knew that the people were delighted to find their President talking their language, on this and all other points.

By this time, even in formal speeches Dad was working with nothing more than an elaborate set of notes. At the beginning of his career even his best friends admitted he was a very mediocre speaker. Ted Marks, one of his old battery mates from World War I, often told the story about one of the first speeches my father ever made, when he was running for county judge in Missouri. "We were all sitting at the top of the hill when Captain Harry started to talk. By the time he finished, we had slid all the way to the bottom."

In succeeding years, Dad taught himself to speak effectively in his own Missouri way. Whenever possible, he always preferred to speak off the cuff. That was when his natural dry wit came through, along with his sincerity. But during the first three years in the White House, he was so acutely conscious of the historical importance of what a President said, he hesitated to use anything but prepared texts. The result was continuous erosion of his public support. He read a speech badly, always seeming, as one man said, to be "rushing for the period."

On April 17, 1948, a time when his statistical popularity had sunk to an all-time low—George Gallup said only 36 percent of the people approved of his performance as President—he gave a speech to the American Society of Newspaper Editors in Washington. His prepared address drew no more than a flicker of polite applause from the crowd. But instead of sitting down, he started telling this very important and influential group of men exactly what he thought of the national and international situation, in his own vigorous down-to-earth language. Charlie Ross, a man never given to overstatement, said, "The audience went wild."

"The old philosopher," as everyone in the White House called Charlie, talked the experience over with his lifelong friend, and they both decided it was a major discovery. Henceforth, every speech my father made, from there to the end of the campaign, was off the cuff to some extent at least. For major speeches he had carefully worked out phrasing for key statements on foreign or domestic policies. But even in the major speeches there were long passages which were only outlined. The wording, the facts, were up to the President to supply. This meant, along with the already enormous amount of reading and absorbing my father had to do, he voluntarily added the extra burden of cramming his mind with material for the speeches.

On May 7 Dad wrote to his sister Mary explaining why he was willing to make the effort.

I've been experimenting with "off-the-cuff" or extemporaneous speeches. The one yesterday was really off-the-cuff [at the National Conference on Family Life in Washington].

There has been much talk that my prepared speeches don't go over but that when I talk without notes they go over. Well I don't know or care very much. What most of the commentators are interested in is something to fill out their own comments, and of course the politicians are interested in winning an election on Nov. 2 and I happen to be interested in the welfare of the country as a whole and very few in fact an infinitesimal number of people are really interested in that except when their own special interest happens to coincide with the general welfare. But I must keep trying and the Republicans have no program and no interest in the little fellow.

On May 1, 1948, after Dad had experimented with another off-the-cuff speech which "seemed to go over big," he noted on his desk calendar: "Suppose I'm in for a lot of work now getting my head full of facts before each public appearance. If it must be done I'll have to do it." Ever a realist about himself, he added, "Comes of my poor ability to read a speech and put feeling into it."

A few days later, my father made an even riskier experiment— an off-the-cuff radio and television speech on family life.

The audience gave me a most cordial reception [he noted on his desk calendar-diary]. I hope the radio and television audiences were half as well pleased.

I may have to become an "orator." I heard a definition of an orator once—"He is an honest man who can communicate his views and make others believe he is right." Wish I could do that.

Because I think I've been right in the approach to all questions 90 percent of the time since I took over.

Then he added a fascinating recapitulation of his experience in becoming President:

I was handicapped by lack of knowledge of both foreign and domestic affairs—due principally to Mr. Roosevelt's inability to pass on responsibility. . . . The Palace Guard was the cause. . . .

The objective and its accomplishment is my philosophy and

[25]

I am willing and want to pass the credit around. The objective is the thing, not personal aggrandizement. All Roosevelts want the personal aggrandizement. Too bad. Byrnes and Baruch also have that complex.

My father's speeches reflected his dislike of big words and flowery language because they gave the audience the impression the orator was showing off—and they also interfered with the communication of the facts. When it came to deciding how to phrase something, he had only two rules. No "two-dollar words" and make the statement as simple and understandable as possible. "Let's not weasel-word it," he often said to Clark Clifford, Charles S. Murphy, Matt Connelly, and Charlie Ross, who worked on speeches with him in the dining room of the *Ferdinand Magellan*.

The simplicity was another reason why my father loved the whistle-stops best. There was no need to get into elaborate discussions about foreign or domestic policy. There simply wasn't time. So he could tell the crowd what he thought of the Eightieth Congress in the plainest, bluntest terms. At a whistle-stop he also got the kind of feedback that he loved. "Give 'em hell, Harry," someone invariably yelled, and Dad would beam and promise to give them exactly that.

He had his share of hecklers, but they never bothered him. He would let them shout for a few minutes, and then he would say, "Now give me a chance to be heard." Fair play took over and in another sixty seconds he had the crowd with him. Once some twelve- and thirteen-year-olds got really raucous and ignored this approach. Dad waited another minute for them to shut up, and then he pointed to them and said, "I think it's time you boys went home to your mothers." The crowd roared, and they did a sheepish vanishing act.

Our biggest concern—and my personal nightmare—in all of these whistle-stops was the possibility of someone getting hurt. A railroad train is a very odd, very dangerous contrivance. The average person has no idea that it operates under mysterious laws of physics which are uniquely its own. For instance, when a train brakes in a station, the cars bunch together, and then slowly roll back the length of their couplings. On a seventeen-car train, this means the last car may roll back as much as three or four feet.

[26]

Invariably, as we stopped, people would crowd around the rear platform and frantic efforts had to be made to keep them at a safe distance, until the *Ferdinand Magellan* had completed its rollback. For a while, a Secret Service man broadcast a warning through the loudspeakers as the train rolled into a station. "For your own safety, keep back; six feet at the sides, thirty feet at the rear. For your own safety, thirty feet." But no one paid any attention to him. They would surge right up under the wheels. Once I tugged on an emergency brake that was on the rear platform to prevent a rollback. I was quietly reprimanded. Dad pointed out I was liable to start a panic in the crowd.

If you think it's fun trying to stop a 285,000-pound railroad car, I can assure you that it isn't. We were particularly sensitive about this problem, because Mr. Dewey's train had rolled back at Beaucoup, Illinois, and in a fit of pique he publicly suggested shooting the engineer, thereby probably costing himself several hundred thousand labor votes. Dad would never have said anything so heartless.

At another stop in Oklahoma, a young man on a very skittish horse was among the crowd. The train terrified the animal, and he was obviously close to bolting. There was a real danger that he might have hurt or killed the rider, as well as many other people in the crowd. While White House aides and Secret Service men wondered what to do, my father stepped down from the rear platform, strode over to the jittery animal and unsteady rider, and seized the bridle. "That's a fine horse you've got there, son," he said. He opened the horse's mouth and studied his teeth. "Eight years old, I see." Calmly, he led the animal over to one of the Secret Service men, who escorted him a safe distance from the train.

Dad never hesitated to kid himself in public. After a whistle-stop speech in California, a lady called up to him, "President Truman, you sound as if you had a cold."

"That's because I ride around in the wind with my mouth open," Dad replied.

In Shelbyville, Kentucky, he had everyone howling as he told the story of how his grandfather, Anderson Shippe Truman, had run off with President Tyler's descendant. The bride's mother was so furious she refused to recognize the marriage. Facetiously

Dad added that I had come down to Shelbyville a few years ago, to see if my great-grandparents "were legally married." I had in fact paid the town a visit, and had been shown the marriage documents, on the way to the Kentucky Derby. The crowd loved it.

What I loved most was when Dad turned his humor on the Republicans. That was his own idea. He saw that Dewey, with his fondness for platitudes that said nothing, was presenting a perfect target. My favorite, I suppose, is the imaginary dialogue between Mr. Dewey and the American people that Dad conducted in Pittsburgh. He described Mr. Dewey as "some kind of doctor with a magic cure for all the ills of mankind," and asked his listeners to imagine that "we, the American people" were visiting him for "our usual routine checkup which we got every four years."

"You been bothered much by issues lately?" asks the doctor.

"Not bothered, exactly," the patient replied. "Of course, we've had a few. We've had the issue of high prices, and housing, and education, and social security, and a few others."

"That's too bad," says the doctor. "You shouldn't have so many issues."

"Is that right?" replied the patient. "We thought that issues were a sign of political health."

"Not at all," says the doctor. "We shouldn't think about issues. What you need is my brand of soothing syrup—I call it unity."

Dad twirled an imaginary mustache, and the doctor edged up a little closer and said, "Say, you don't look so good."

"Well, that seems strange to me, Doc," the patient replied. "I never felt stronger, never had more money, and never had a brighter future. What is wrong with me?"

"I never discuss issues with a patient," the doctor replied, "but what you need is a major operation."

"Will it be serious, Doc?"

"Not very serious. It will just mean taking out the complete works and putting in a Republican administration."

In Cleveland, Dad called the public opinion polls "sleeping polls" and said that he was sure the people were not being fooled by them. "They know sleeping polls are bad for the system, they affect the mind. An overdose could be fatal." Again twirling that imaginary mustache, he said he knew the name of a doctor who was passing them out. It was also fun when he pictured Dewey as an aristocrat having "a high-level tea party with the voters." But Harry Truman insisted on dragging "that old reprobate, the 80th Congress, out of the back room to disclose him to the guests as the candidate's nearest and dearest relative."

My father seemed to gain rather than lose energy as the campaign built. On October 5 he wrote proudly to his sister Mary after returning to the White House from our first swing through the West:

> We made about 140 stops and I spoke over 147 times. Shook hands with at least 30,000 and am in good condition to start out again tomorrow for Wilmington, Philadelphia, Jersey City, Newark, Albany and Buffalo. Be back in Washington Saturday night and start again the following Monday, finally winding up in KC Sunday morning October 31.
>
> It will be the greatest campaign any President ever made. Win, lose or draw, people will know where I stand and a record will be made for future action by the Democratic Party.
>
> We had tremendous crowds everywhere. From 6:30 in the morning until midnight the turnout was phenomenal. . . .

Most of the reporters simply tried to explain away the constantly growing turnouts for a candidate that they in their political wisdom had dismissed before the campaign began. Richard Rovere of *The New Yorker* admitted the crowds were big, but said they were unenthusiastic. He said the people received Dad like "a missionary who has just delivered a mildly encouraging report on the inroads being made on heathenism in northern Rhodesia." James Reston of *The New York Times* sighed that the President was not conveying "the one thing he wants to convey, a conviction that something really fundamental is at stake in his campaign."

The reporters may not have noticed the change, but politicians did. They were not as likely to be mesmerized by public opinion polls. One of our more amusing converts was Frank J. Lausche, who was running for governor in Ohio. We were told quite candidly by people close to him that he had bipartisan appeal, and he could see no point in linking his name with a sure loser like Harry S. Truman. Only after considerable verbal arm-twisting did Lausche agree to board the *Ferdinand Magellan* at all. He joined us a few miles outside Dayton, Ohio, but made it clear that he was getting off as soon as we reached that city. Then we hit our first whistle stop of the day. It was only a small city, but 7,000 persons were roaring their approval of Harry Truman there in the middle of the morning. Mr. Lausche could not believe his eyes. Then came Dayton. People were practically standing on each other's shoulders in the station and they spilled out of it to stop traffic in all directions. "Is this the way all the crowds have been?" Mr. Lausche asked cautiously.

"Yes," Dad said, "but this is smaller than we had in most states."

Mr. Lausche swallowed hard. "Well," he said, "this is the biggest crowd I ever saw in Ohio." When we pulled out of Dayton on the way to Akron, Mr. Lausche was still aboard.

Of all the thousands of people who climbed on and off the campaign train during these hectic weeks, there are two men who stand out in my mind. One was Jake More, who captured the state of Iowa, almost single-handed. He was not an officeholder. He was, quite simply and in the plainest terms, a Truman believer. My father stirred something deep in him, which convinced him that a victory was possible when everyone else said defeat was a certainty. He appeared with us on the campaign train, and then after we left the state, he never stopped working for the ticket. As a result Iowa went Democratic for the first time in years.

The other man was Aaron H. Payne, a Chicago lawyer whose clients included Joe Louis. He was the first black man to address a national Republican Lincoln Day dinner (in 1940). He paid his way aboard the train with his own money, and he campaigned for Dad throughout the Midwest in September and October the same way. He told Martin S. Hayden of the Detroit *News:* "Harry S. Truman has done more for my people than Franklin D. Roosevelt ever did." His goal was to replace every dollar and every vote that the Dixiecrats cost the party with a black dollar and a black vote. Later, we found out that Mr. Payne had had tremendous influence in helping us carry four predominantly black wards in Cleveland. Since we won Ohio by a little more than 7,000 votes, it is no exaggeration to say that his influence was crucial.

In Los Angeles my father decided to deal with the attack from the left. By this time it was clear that the Progressive party was dominated by hard-core Communists. Mr. Wallace did nothing to diminish this impression with his almost unbelievable naïveté. "I would say that the Communists are the closest things to the early Christian martyrs," he said at one point, and at another time, he said that he thought the American Communist party platform for the campaign was at least as good as the Progressive platform.

But instead of lambasting the Progressives as agents of a foreign power, Dad spoke out of his deep respect and affection for the two-party system. In one of his greatest speeches, he urged California's liberals to return to the Democratic fold. "The simple fact is that the third party cannot achieve peace, because it is powerless. It cannot achieve better conditions at home, because it is powerless. . . . I say to those disturbed liberals who have been sitting uncertainly on the outskirts of the third party: think again, don't waste your vote."

My father's speeches undoubtedly had a great deal to do with bringing the state into the Democratic column, but the immediate reception we received was cool. Jimmy Roosevelt's negative influence was still strong in the California Democratic party. Although he had accepted Dad as the Democratic nominee, his enthusiasm was invisible and the state party reflected this fact. The low point was reached on September 23, when Dad spoke in Gilmore Stadium in Los Angeles. In spite of the fact that Ronald Reagan—considered a rather left-wing Democrat at the time—and other Hollywood notables were on the platform, only about 10,000 people showed up. Thomas E. Dewey had attracted almost twice that number the previous night at the Hollywood Bowl. The problem was lack of advance planning.

These days candidates send swarms of advance men into every city before they arrive. They are equipped with lavish amounts of money and every known publicity device. In 1948 Oscar Chapman was trying to do it all alone. It was simply too much for one man to handle, especially when he was getting no co-operation from the local Democratic organization. Dad decided to call for reinforcements. In the middle of the night he ordered Matt Connelly, his appointments secretary and one of the shrewdest politicians aboard the train, to find someone fast. In a few days we would be in Texas—where the local Democratic organization was even more unsympathetic than they were in California.

An hour later Don Dawson, a big, handsome ex-army air force

[31]

officer who had recently joined the White House staff, was jolted out of bed by a phone call from Matt. He was told to get on a plane immediately and head for Texas. It was a very good choice. Don had just the right combination of energy and daring to pull things together down there. As Dad had foreseen, the party regulars were sitting on their hands. But Don quickly put together a team of Truman loyalists, including Sam Rayburn's brother, the brother of Attorney General Tom Clark, and two old friends of Dad's, publicist Bill Kittrell and businessman Harry Seay. They began working on each town and city on our schedule. "We knew who the right people were in each community, and we just called them on the telephone and literally told them what to do," Don said. "We told them when the train would arrive and how to get the people down there."

While this vital groundwork was being laid, Don was confronted with a major decision. Where was the President going to speak in Dallas? The local Texas Democrats thought he should speak right in the railroad station. "They didn't want to take the chance of going into a big stadium or a ball park," Don says. "They didn't think they could produce the crowd." Don took one look at the station area and decided it was hopeless. Swallowing hard, he informed the local Democrats that the President would speak in the Rebel Stadium. This was a big ball park on the outskirts of the city. Grimly Don and his team tackled the job. "We got loudspeaker trucks at work, and we got the schools to let the pupils out," he said.

Most important, he called in black leaders and told them that their people would be welcome at the stadium and there would be no segregation. Don knew Dad would give him complete support on this decision, but it was *very* daring in Texas in 1948.

That is the behind-the-scenes story of how Dad spoke to the first integrated rally in the South. Proudly—and just a little ruefully—Don Dawson recalls, "It worked so smoothly that the black newspaper reporters who were on the train didn't even notice it. We had to go to them later and tell them all about it so that they would print it." The meeting in Dallas was a tremendous success. Rebel Stadium was packed and the crowd roared their approval of the tongue-lashing Dad gave the Eightieth Congress.

We followed the same integration policy all the way across

Texas. In Waco there was a tense moment when he shook hands with a black woman and the crowd booed. But my father refused to back down and boldly told them that black citizens had the same rights as white Americans. "In some towns," Don Dawson says, "they didn't even want the black voters to come down to the train. We just told them they were going to come. The President wanted them there."

In San Antonio a different kind of confrontation took place. People wanted to know what Dad was going to do about the Russian threat. He proceeded to give them what I consider his greatest foreign policy speech. It was completely off the cuff, completely impromptu, and completely candid. He told them what the Russians had already done—all the agreements they had broken—all the details of their arrogant thrust for world power. Then he told them what he was prepared to do to achieve world peace. Perhaps the most startling part of his plan was to persuade Joseph Stalin to come to the United States. There was much more to this speech—he spoke for almost a half hour—but to my everlasting regret, it has been lost to history. Jack Romagna, the White House shorthand reporter, who was usually on hand to take down all Dad's off-the-cuff speeches, had not been told to come, and there were no reporters present. Not one word of that speech was preserved.

There were two other high points in our tour of Texas. The first one was a reception arranged for us by Sam Rayburn and his people in Bonham. Governor Beauford Jester, who had not long before accused Dad of stabbing the South in the back, was on hand to take part in the festivities, but it was Mr. Sam who ran the show. Dad spoke first at an outdoor meeting, in bitter cold, and then we stood for literally hours on an indoor receiving line to greet what must have been a majority of the inhabitants of that part of Texas. It was an old-fashioned Southern house, with a central hall that ran from the front door to the back door. The handshakers streamed through the front door and out the rear door. Suddenly Mr. Sam exclaimed, "Shut the door, Beauford, they're comin' by twice." But that didn't discourage anybody. People just kept on streaming out the back door and in the front door again.

On Sunday, September 26, we paid a "nonpolitical" visit to one of Dad's favorite friends, John Nance Garner, FDR's first vice president. Throughout the campaign my father usually refused to make any speeches on Sunday, but there was no harm—and plenty of political value—in paying a visit to "Cactus Jack." He was adored by the conservative wing of the Democratic party in Texas. At 5 A.M. we were greeted by a high school band, at least 4,000 citizens, and an Angora goat wearing a gold blanket lettered DEWEY'S GOAT. Dad bounced off the train and posed for pictures with the beast, and then jovially declared, "I'm going to clip it and make a rug, then I'm going to let it graze on the White House lawn for the next four years." He meant it, too, but he found out that one thing our campaign train was not equipped to carry was a goat.

After this public greeting, former Vice President Garner sat us down to the most tremendous breakfast in the history of the Truman family, and, I suspect, in the history of any American family. There was white wing dove, bacon, ham, fried chicken, scrambled eggs, rice in gravy, hot biscuits, Uvalde honey, peach preserves, grape jelly, and coffee. Dad responded by giving Cactus Jack a present, carefully concealed in a small black satchel. It was, he solemnly told him, "medicine, only to be used in case of snakebites." It was the same medicine that Senator Truman used to share with the vice president when he visited his Capitol "dog house" in the 1930s—some very good Kentucky bourbon.

Outside, where the crowd was still waiting, Mr. Garner called Dad an "old and very good friend." My father called him "Mr. President" explaining that was the term he used when he addressed him in the Senate. My mother was so moved by the vice president's hospitality that she broke her usual public silence, and thanked everyone for coming out to greet us at the incredible hour of 5 A.M.

Along with the pressures of the campaign, the sheer physical challenge of making as many as sixteen speeches in a single day, my father had to cope with the worsening international situation. The Berlin airlift went on, making it clear that he meant what he said when he declared, "We are in Berlin to stay." His Secretary of State, General George Marshall, was in Paris, trying to negotiate the Berlin crisis through the United Nations. Meanwhile Dad had to fend off demands from Secretary of Defense Forrestal to authorize the use of the atomic bomb. From the left Wallace hammered away with his message of appeasement. In mid-September Dad wrote a gloomy memorandum to himself:

> Forrestal, Bradley, Vandenberg [the air force general, not the senator], Symington brief me on bases, bombs, Moscow, Leningrad, etc. I have a terrible feeling afterward that we are very close to war. I hope not.

On October 3 my father made a daring decision. As President George Washington had done in an earlier crisis (with England), Dad decided to send the Chief Justice of the Supreme Court on a personal mission to rescue the peace. The Chief Justice was his old friend, Fred Vinson, for whom my father had enormous respect. "I hoped that this new approach would provide Stalin an opportunity to open up," he said. He wanted to convince the Russian dictator that the United States was sincere in its desire for a peaceful world, but Dad had no intention of attempting to prove this sincerity by disarming or surrendering at any point on the globe where the Russians were challenging us.

If Mr. Vinson could have been launched on his mission immediately, a great initiative toward world peace might have been created. But my father felt that it was important to explain the government's intentions to the American people. So he asked Charlie Ross to get him a half hour of network time to make this explanation. In the course of negotiating with the networks, Charlie had to explain the purpose of this speech.

Charlie was fond of picturing the White House as a gigantic sieve and this time the metaphor was all too exact. In a matter of hours the Vinson mission was leaked to the newspapers and flung into the political arena, before my father could even begin to defend it. The opposition denounced it as a political gesture, and Secretary of State Marshall, in Paris, was more than a little unsettled to discover that Dad was making such a major departure in foreign policy without consulting him. Of course he had no intention of doing any such thing. He had planned to brief General Marshall thoroughly on the mission, before announcing it to the public. But now he had to consider the General's feelings, and the allegations floating around Washington that the President had lost confidence in him. So he summoned General Marshall home for a personal conference and then, with deep regret, announced to the nation that the Vinson mission was canceled.

The decision was in line with my father's fundamental philosophy of the presidency. He never undercut a subordinate or let one down. He always backed the man he had chosen to perform an important job (unless of course he failed to perform it). He considered General Marshall one of the greatest men in American history, and so he deliberately chose, at the height of this searing campaign, to accept what seemed at the time the public humiliation of withdrawing the Vinson proposal rather than embarrass his Secretary of State.

Throughout October the crowds continued to grow in size. A few of the reporters began to comment on this fact. Charles T. Lucey of the Scripps-Howard chain wrote on October 15: "The polls and the pundits say Harry Truman hasn't a chance to be returned to the White House, but you'd never guess it from the way people come out to see him. . . ." Like most of the reporters, however, Lucey attributed this phenomenon to the President's high office, and his "entertainment value."

By now we had gone back and forth across the country once and were in the midst of our second swing. Dad had spoken to almost four million people. He had talked with politicians and plain citizens just about everywhere. On October 13, as the "Truman Special" was thundering from Duluth to St. Paul, he gave George Elsey, one of his aides, a state-by-state breakdown of the results as he now saw them. He predicted he would win with 340 electoral votes, 108 for Dewey, and 42 for Thurmond. As we shall see, the prediction was amazingly accurate—and it was done without the aid of a single pollster. He even went through the nation, state by state, predicting how each one would go. He was right on eight out of ten. But he did not reveal this detailed bit of prophecy to the press. In their mood, it would have only made him the butt of more ridicule. When the reporters asked him if he thought he was winning, he would reply, "That's your job. That's what you're along for. I am the candidate. The candidate is not going to comment. He's optimistic."

In the closing days of the campaign the crowds grew from large to stupendous. In Chicago they swarmed around our motorcade, slowing it to a crawl and almost giving the Secret Service men

[36]

apoplexy. The Chicago Democratic organization pulled out every political stop known to man. The coup de grâce, as far as I was concerned, was a fireworks display which went off just as we were crossing a bridge. I hate noises. I thought the bridge was coming down. Above us a tremendous series of explosions created a fiery image of the candidate. As an old artillery captain from World War I, Dad was not bothered in the least—in fact he loved every bang.

From the Blackstone Hotel Dad told his sister Mary that "former Mayor Kelly and the present Mayor Kennelly . . . both said that the demonstration was better than any ever held here. . . ."

In Boston the crowds literally engulfed us. Police estimated that 250,000 people stormed the parade route. Crowds were equally—or proportionately—huge along the line of a motor tour we took of the Bay State's industrial cities. In Albany, New York, thousands stood in the pouring rain to hear Dad speak.

In New York City the crowds were huge but the Democratic party was practically inert. It did not have enough money to rent Madison Square Garden, and the tiny Liberal party had to bail them out. Even with this help, the Wallace influence was still so strong among the liberals that they were able to sell only 10 percent of the tickets for Dad's Garden appearance. So they threw the doors open and let anyone who followed our motorcade inside, ticketholder or not. A crowd of about 16,000 cheered when Dad came out for "a strong, prosperous, free, and independent" Israel and roared with laughter when he told them how he had complained to Dr. Graham that he had the constant feeling somebody was following him. Dr. Graham told him not to worry about it. "There is one place where that fellow is not going to follow you—and that's in the White House."

By now more than a few old New Dealers were returning to the fold, just as my father had predicted they would. Harold Ickes, whom my father had fired as Secretary of the Interior in 1946, endorsed him and described Dewey as "the candidate in sneakers. . . . For unity, Alice in Wonderland and Grimm's Fairy Tales, to say nothing of home and mother." Hollywood, where Wallace influence had been strong, suddenly produced and distributed free a campaign film urging voters to support the President. They charged the Republicans $30,000 to make a similar film.

Eleanor Roosevelt made a six-minute pro-Truman address from Paris via shortwave radio. Mrs. Roosevelt, after some early hesitation—she conspicuously declined to support Dad during the draft-Eisenhower embroglio—became a staunch pro-Truman Democrat once she saw Dad's fighting campaign. She did her utmost to persuade her sons to join her, in vain. At one point, she had a meeting with Jimmy, Franklin, and Elliott, and they had a long telephone talk with Dad. With great exasperation she told him that she could not do anything with her three sons—but she was ready to go all out for a Truman victory.

We ended the campaign in St. Louis. En route from New York all of the speech writers got together and pooled what they called "their gems"—their best and brightest phrases—and poured them into a speech that they considered the campaign's masterpiece. Meanwhile my father for the first time showed he was at least *capable* of getting tired, and took a long afternoon nap before this climactic performance. When he woke up, the train was almost in St. Louis. Only then did the writers present him with their wit-encrusted, diamond-bright, verbal tour de force. Dad glanced through it, and then said, "I'm sorry, boys, but I just haven't got time to get all this into my head." He threw it aside, and went out on the platform in St. Louis's Kiel Auditorium to give a completely extemporaneous address.

> Of all the fake campaigns, this one is the tops so far as the Republican candidate for President is concerned. He has been following me up and down this country making speeches about home, mother, unity and efficiency. . . . He won't talk about the issues, but he did let his foot slip when he endorsed the Eightieth Congress.

Then he spoke to them as one Missourian to another:

> I have been all over these United States from one end to another, and when I started out the song was—Well, you can't win, the Democrats can't win. Ninety percent of the press is against us, but that didn't discourage me one little bit. You know, I had four campaigns here in the great state of Missouri, and I never had a metropolitan paper for me the whole time. And I licked them every time!

[38]

People are waking up to the fact that this is their government, and that they can control their government if they get out and vote on election day. That is all they need to do. . . .

People are waking up, that the tide is beginning to roll, and I am here to tell you that if you do your duty as citizens of the greatest Republic the sun has ever shone on, we will have a government that will be for your interests, that will be for peace in the world, and for the welfare of all the people, and not just a few.

Everyone, including the White House writers whose pearls had been tossed aside, agreed it was one of his greatest speeches of the campaign. A reporter for the Washington *Post* said that if the election was close, and Harry Truman won, he would give the credit to his performance that night in Kiel Auditorium.

So we came home to Independence, to our familiar and much loved house on North Delaware Street. We had traveled 31,700 miles, and Dad had given 356 speeches—an average of ten a day. Between twelve and fifteen million people had cheered or at least seen us.

We three Trumans voted at 10 A.M. on November 2, in Independence's Memorial Hall. It was my first vote for a President, and it pleased me enormously that I was able to mark my ballot for Harry S. Truman. Reporters asked Dad for a final prediction, and he said, "It can't be anything but a victory."

"Are you going to sit up for the returns, Mr. President?" someone asked.

"No," he said, "I think I'll go to bed. I don't expect final results until tomorrow."

This astonished everyone—except Mother and me—almost as much as his prediction of a victory. Most of the reporters simply did not understand that my father believed there was no point in worrying about whether you succeeded or failed at a job, as long as you were sure that you had done your best.

Meanwhile, back in Washington, Drew Pearson was writing that Dewey had "conducted one of the most astute and skillful campaigns in recent history." In the column which Pearson filed for the day after election, he surveyed for his readers the "closely knit group around Tom Dewey who will take over the White House eighty-six days from now." Walter Lippmann, the Alsop brothers, and Marquis Childs saw a Democratic disaster of such staggering proportions that we were in danger of becoming a one-party (Republican) country. *The New York Times* gave Dewey 345 electoral votes. *Life's* November 1 issue carried a picture of Dewey and his wife which was captioned, "The next President travels by ferry boat over the broad waters of San Francisco Bay." Messrs. Gallup and Crossley continued to insist that there was no contest.

That afternoon my father pulled his neatest trick of the campaign. He went to lunch at the Rockwood Country Club, where he was the guest of honor at a party given by the mayor of Independence, Roger Sermon. There were about thirty old friends at this hoedown, and they gleefully connived in his plan. While the hapless reporters lurked outside, Dad excused himself, supposedly to go to the men's room. Then, with three Secret Service men in tow, he went out the back door and drove to the Elms Hotel at Excelsior Springs, about twenty-five miles from Independence. There he had a Turkish bath, ate a ham sandwich, drank a glass of milk, and proceeded to do exactly what he had predicted he was going to do that morning—go to bed.

This was very shrewd from his point of view, but it left Mother and me alone to cope with squadrons of frantic reporters. I am not using that word "frantic" loosely either. It became more and more apropos as the votes began to come in. At first everyone was told that there would be a Dewey victory message at nine P.M. But Harry Truman seemed to be winning at nine P.M.—as a matter of fact, Dad never was behind—and this historic Republican event was postponed. By midnight we were 1,200,000 votes ahead. But commentator H. V. Kaltenborn kept insisting that there was nothing to worry about, the Democratic candidate was a sure loser. At the Elms Hotel, Dad woke up and heard this prediction, couched in Mr. Kaltenborn's slightly Germanic tones. The candidate chuckled and went back to sleep.

On Delaware Street, meanwhile, reporters were practically storming the house. Again and again I was forced to go out on the porch in my best black dress and ballet slippers (great for weary feet) to assure them that my father was not in the house. When they finally believed me, they began trying to wheedle out of me exactly where he was. That was one night when I was grateful for my native Missouri stubbornness. I sometimes wonder if I could have resisted the terrific pressure those reporters put on me, without it.

As the night wore on, Dad continued to hold that million-vote lead. I began getting calls from various members of the Cabinet. They were stunned to discover that the President was not home and that he was not available to talk with them. I did arrange for Alben Barkley, our vice presidential candidate, to get through to him. My mother went to sleep and so did my grandmother, but I stayed up, knowing that sleep was impossible for me anyway.

Long before the night was over, I knew that we had won. I was in constant touch with Bill Bray in Washington. He had handled a lot of the advance planning on our trips and was a shrewd, canny politician and public relations man. I would call him up, and he would say, "Okay, now we'll go to Ohio," and we'd go through all the districts. In five minutes we could see which way the state was going. We didn't bother to listen to the radio or television. My mother turned on the radio for a few moments, but they were so far behind the data we were getting from Washington, D.C., that we soon saw it was a waste of time.

At 4 A.M. down in Excelsior Springs, Jim Rowley, one of the Secret Service men who was guarding my father, could not stand the suspense any longer. He woke Dad up. Mr. Kaltenborn was still predicting Truman's defeat, although he was two million votes ahead. "I don't see how he can be elected. The election will be decided in the House," said Kaltenborn. Dad listened to this nonsense with Rowley and the two of them laughed. At 4:30 Matt Connelly called from the penthouse at the Muehlebach Hotel in Kansas City, where most of the campaign staff and friends from Independence were already celebrating well past the point of sobriety. Dad told them he would join the party around 6 A.M.

He was there, fresh and smiling, to face the haggard reporters when Dewey finally conceded at 11:14 A.M. (10:14 Missouri time). By then we knew that we had carried California, Illinois, and Ohio, giving us 304 electoral votes (one elector later defected, giving us 303). This was only 36 (or 37) votes away from Dad's October prediction. When the word reached Independence, every whistle, siren, and automobile horn in the city seemed to go off simultaneously and then they added the air-raid alarm to the pandemonium. By this time, of course, I had long since known we had won, and, in my semi-comatose, sleepless state, I was shopping for stockings to wear back to Washington. My brain was so numb, for a moment I wondered what in the world all the noise was about.

The victory took Independence completely by surprise. There was no planning for a possible celebration. Talk about a prophet not being honored in his own country. Or county. Everyone scrambled around frantically, and some 40,000 people showed up in the main square that night to congratulate their native son.

Dad responded with humility. "I thank you very much indeed for this celebration, which is not for me. It is for the whole country. It is for the whole world."

The next morning we boarded our train, now being called the "Victory Special," to return to Washington. I collapsed into my berth, not having slept for something close to thirty-six hours. I was fast asleep when the train pulled into St. Louis, where somebody gave my father a copy of the Chicago *Tribune* with the huge black headline, DEWEY DEFEATS TRUMAN. I managed to wake up by the time we reached Washington, but I did not escape the usual paternal needling for my inability to get up on time and stay awake when important things were happening. Along the route to Washington, wherever the train stopped, we were invaded by people that we soon began calling "Wednesday Democrats." They were party leaders and big businessmen who had sat on their hands or checkbooks, but now wanted to make it clear that "We were with ya, Harry," all the time. In Washington, our money man, Louis Johnson, was sitting under a blizzard of backdated checks—some $750,000 worth—attributable to the same get-on-the-bandwagon set.

In Washington, at Union Station, the crowd was so enormous they couldn't have squeezed in another human being, if it had been Tom Thumb. My mother and I, who are inclined to hold grudges, could only think about the loyal handful who had come down to see us off on the first campaign swing in September.

At 3 A.M. the next morning, my father wrote his sister Mary the following description of our welcome:

> The reception here was the greatest in the history of this old capital. When the train backed into the station the police band played the ruffles and "Hail to the Chief" and then people be-

gan piling on the train. Barkley and I must have shaken hands with at least five or six hundred—some of them johnnie come lately boys. I finally put a stop to the handshaking. Barkley, Bess, Margaret and Barkley's daughter, Mrs. Max Truitt, stepped into the big open seven-passenger car which belongs to the White House fleet. Mr. McGrath tucked himself between Barkley & me. The seat's rather narrow for three—especially three with Barkley. So Barkley and I sat up on the back of the back seat.

There were about 800,000 people on the street between the station and the White House. Said to be the biggest crowd ever out in Washington. Barkley and I made speeches from the front steps of the great white jail and then went to a Cabinet meeting to decide on the first message to Congress.

I will never forget that ride to the White House. Every band in the world seemed to be playing "I'm Just Wild About Harry." On the front of the Washington *Post* building was a huge sign which read: MR. PRESIDENT, WE ARE READY TO EAT CROW WHENEVER YOU ARE READY TO SERVE IT.

Dad quickly made it clear that he had no desire to make the *Post* or anyone else eat crow. Nor did he pay the slightest attention to the endless analyses of his victory. I have never heard him even take satisfaction in what must have pleased him as a professional politician—he had held Dewey to a smaller proportion of the total vote, 45.1 percent, than Dewey got running against Franklin D. Roosevelt in 1944 (45.8 percent). And Dad carried a Democratic Congress with him, in the bargain. But it would no more occur to him to gloat in victory than it would to gloom in defeat. He expected Mother and me to act the same way.

Still, we could not help feeling and sharing the satisfaction that we never bothered to put into words—satisfaction we shared with everyone in the White House. Now the whole country knew what we had always known. Harry S. Truman was no "accidental President." From the moment he took that original oath of office, he *was* the President of the United States.

[CHAPTER]

Two

I FIRST MET this extraordinary man on February 17, 1924. Naturally, I don't recall very much of this or subsequent meetings. I later found out that I had given him and Mother their start on gray hair by being a very sickly, squally baby. I continued to maintain an amazing susceptibility to germs into the time when my first memories emerge. But it failed to dim the happiness with which I recall these years. My father is at the center of these memories. With some help from my mother's brothers he constantly yielded to the temptation to pet and spoil me, while Mother did her often desperate best to repair the damage. I know now that Dad was going through one of the most difficult periods of his life at this time. But he never allowed the anxiety and political harassment he faced almost every day to cast a shadow in the lovely old house on North Delaware Street, where I grew up.

My childhood memories are rich in love and laughter. But this book is about my father, not about me, so I won't burden it with my reminiscences, such as the time he gave me a baby grand piano for Christmas, hoping to speed my recovery from a bout of pneumonia. I had been hoping for electric trains. I burst into tears and refused to touch the piano. Besides, now that I am an adult, I have developed a kind of second memory about Dad that historians may consider more valuable, and I find more interesting. This second memory is composed of answers I have received to innumerable questions I have asked my mother and my father, my grandmothers when they were living, my father's sister, Aunt Mary, and my Cousin Ethel Noland who was our family historian. From their memories and from not a few yellowed newspaper clippings that I had the Truman Library put on microfilm, lest they crumble away at my touch, I have extended my memories of my father back into the years before Mary Margaret Truman entered his life.

There is really nothing very surprising about this, if you stop to think about it. No one's memories are limited to his own life. When you grow up in a big family as I did, with grandmothers who lived into their nineties, the years before your birth are in some ways as vivid as your childhood years. In that sense my memories go all the way back to the Civil War. My father was even more interested in the family's past than I was, and he often talked to me or prompted my Grandmother Truman—Mamma Truman, as we called her—into talking about her memories of Missouri in those days, when Northern and Southern guerrillas roamed the state, shooting and stealing.

The dominant theme in these family memories is not woe but a wonderfully solid happiness rooted in the peaceful rhythms of a slower, more deliberate time. My girlhood was enriched by the presence of two grandmothers. My father's boyhood was even more profoundly affected by his grandfathers, particularly his mother's father, Solomon Young. A big, hard-muscled man, Grandfather Young had driven cattle and led wagon trains across the plains to California and Utah more than once between 1840 and 1870 and had also run a profitable business outfitting and advising the thousands of pioneers who made the journey during those years. At that time America west of Missouri was described as "the Great American desert"—a supposedly impassable, barren wilderness peopled only by savage, very dangerous Indians. Can you think of a more perfect grandfather to awaken in a growing boy the vastness and the drama of a continental nation?

Interestingly, Grandfather Young was equally taken with young Harry. There is a family tradition, vouched for by my Cousin Ethel, that when my father was only three or four, Grandfather Young could not stop telling people what a remarkable little fellow he was. Dad still remembers with great affection one day when the old man—he was in his seventies when my father's family

[45]

moved to the farm—was ill and Dad cautiously approached his bedside to ask how he was feeling. Grandfather Young transfixed him with those bold pioneer eyes of his and said sternly, "How are *you* feeling? You're the one I'm worried about."

Dad's paternal grandfather, Anderson Shippe Truman, was a gentle, very quiet, reserved man—almost the opposite of outgoing, aggressive Grandfather Young. In 1887 when my father was three, his parents moved to the Young farm. Anderson Shippe Truman sold his own smaller farm and followed his son and daughter-in-law. "He had a bedroom upstairs in the farmhouse," Dad says. "He spent a lot of his time there. Believe me, you didn't go into it without an invitation." Reminiscing about these two men at the age of eighty-six, Dad told me: "To be honest, I didn't like either of the old men very much at the time. But when I looked back as an adult, my respect and affection for them grew with every passing year. Half of everything I became I owe to them." Among more tangible things, Dad owed the middle initial in his name to both grandparents. To placate their touchy elders, his parents added an S, but studiously refrained from deciding whether it stood for Solomon or Shippe.

Anderson Shippe Truman died the same year that the family moved to the Young farm, and it was Solomon Young who was the stronger influence on Dad's early years. He took Dad with him to county fairs and for countless rides in his buggy behind one of his superb, high-stepping horses. Their friendship was one of those mysterious gifts which can only be exchanged by a mingling of the generations, a habit we have lost in contemporary America. Although he died when Dad was only nine, Grandfather Young has in many ways lived on in my father's spirit.

Dad was lucky to have had this added presence in his growing years. He had a problem to face, which might have made him a rather unhappy young man—his terrible eyesight. His mother noticed this affliction when he was about five years old. Oddly, she did not notice it when she was teaching him to read. He was able to make out the large letters in the family Bible without difficulty. But when she pointed out objects at a distance—a buggy coming down the road, a cow or a horse at the opposite end of a pasture—her son could not see them. This worried her. Then came a Fourth of July visit to nearby Grandview. The climax of the celebration was a series of rockets that exploded clusters of stars in the sky. Dad jumped when each rocket went off, but he was utterly indifferent to the showers of fizzing stars that were filling the night. He could not see them. Then and there Mamma Truman made up her mind to take her son to an eye doctor.

Remember this was in 1889 in farm country. Glasses were seldom if ever prescribed for children. Mamma Truman's husband was away on a business trip, but she decided that immediate action was called for, so she hitched up two horses to the farm wagon, sat her son on the seat beside her, and drove fifteen miles to Kansas City. There she discovered that my father was suffering from a rare malformation of the eye, which can best be described (at least I often heard it so described) as flat eyeballs. The Kansas City eye doctor prescribed thick, very expensive glasses and sternly warned Dad not to play any of the popular sports, such as baseball or football, or participate in any kind of roughhousing whatsoever, lest he break the glasses.

This cut my father off from boys his own age. I have never heard Dad complain about this deprivation. As a lover of books, he emphasizes the new world that the glasses opened for him. "I saw things and saw print I'd never seen before," he says. But his glasses made Mamma Truman feel a little sorry for him. I know the feeling, now that I have four boys of my own. It is not easy to control the impulse to protect and even overprotect the one you feel needs the most help.

Dad spent a lot of time helping his mother in the kitchen, caring for his baby sister Mary Jane, even braiding her hair and singing her to sleep at night. Meanwhile, his younger brother Vivian was rapidly becoming his father's favorite.

Not that John Anderson Truman ignored his older son. A story Dad likes to tell demonstrates this, as well as an undercurrent of mild disagreement about how to raise young Harry. "I'd ride with my father on my little Shetland and he on his big horse," Dad says. "He'd lead my pony and I felt perfectly safe, but one day coming down the north road toward the house I fell off the pony and had to walk about a half mile to the house. My father said that a boy who was not able to stay on a pony at a walk ought to walk himself. Mamma thought I was badly mistreated, but I wasn't. In spite of my crying all the way to the house, I learned a lesson."

There was an enormously strong intellectual-emotional bond

between Dad and his mother—the sort of bond which, I have discovered from my delvings into presidential lore, has existed between an astonishing number of presidents and their mothers. No less than twenty-one of the thirty-six American presidents to date have been their mothers' first boy and almost every one of them were the favorite sons of strong-minded women.

That brings us to the other side of Dad's relationship with his mother. Even in her seventies and eighties, when I knew her best, Mamma Truman was a woman with a glint in her eye. She had a mind of her own on almost every subject from politics to plowing. Although she spent most of her long life on a farm, she never milked a cow. "Papa told me that if I never learned, I'd never have to do it," she explained once to her daughter Mary Jane. Something else I learned from my mother only a year or two ago. Mamma Truman hated to cook, and only made one dish that was praiseworthy—fried chicken. In her early years she supervised a kitchen that fed as many as twenty field hands, but servants did the real cooking. In her later years, Aunt Mary handled the stove work. Neither she nor anyone else in the family let me in on this secret all during my girlhood years, when we spent almost every Sunday visiting Mamma Truman and dined on her delicious fried chicken. For a while I was convinced that I was a female dropout, because I loathed the idea of cooking from a very early age, and still do it under protest.

Any boy who spent a lot of time with a mother like Martha Ellen Truman could only emerge from the experience the very opposite of a conventional mamma's boy. This is one among many reasons why my father always bridled when a writer or reporter tried to pin this image on him. The rest of the family, knowing Mamma Truman, simply guffawed at the notion.

But Martha Ellen Truman gave her son much else, besides moral fiber. She passed on to him her strong interest in books, music, and art. This may startle some readers. For too many people, particularly in the East, the word "farm" is synonymous with ignorance and poverty. It conjures up images from *Tobacco Road* or *The Grapes of Wrath*. Missourians are constantly astonished by this cultural parochialism. Martha Ellen Young Truman came from a family that was, if not aristocratic, certainly upper-middle class. Even in the early 1900s, when her father's farm was reduced from 2,000 to 600 acres, it regularly earned $15,000 a year—the equivalent of $50,000 to $60,000 today. She had an excellent education, having graduated from the Baptist Female College in Lexington, Missouri, where she majored—if that is not too strong a word—in music and art. I have already noted that she taught my father to read before he was five; she had him playing the piano not much later.

Mamma Truman was the moving spirit behind the family decision to set up housekeeping in Independence. They had been living on the Young farm for three or four years, but the country schools in nearby Grandview were decidedly inadequate, compared to those in Independence. At this point in time—1890—Independence was by no means the quaint little farming community that some of my father's biographers have imagined. It was a very genteel town, with plenty of what might be called "old money" in it, if we foreshorten the term a little. In its heyday, before the railroad spanned the West, Independence had been the jumping-off point for both the Santa Fe and Oregon trails. There were only about 6,000 people living in the town in 1890, but there was a remarkable number of houses built along spacious Victorian lines.

The Trumans moved into one of these, on Chrysler Street, formerly owned by a wealthy family named Blitz. Kansas City, only a few miles away at the western end of Jackson County, was a roaring boom town of 55,000. But neither the Trumans nor the Youngs would ever have dreamt of living there. That was the "Yankee town." Independence was the stronghold of the old original pioneers in Jackson County, most of whom, like the Trumans and the Youngs, came from Kentucky. The atmosphere in Independence was Southern in the best sense of that much abused word.

The pace was slow and dignified, the people friendly. The word "family" included numerous cousins, and the bond between "kin" was strong. The past was very important. I am sure my father's interest in history was born in his numerous discussions of the Civil War with his mother. She always talked as if the Yankee guerrillas from Kansas Territory—"Jayhawkers" as they were called—had appeared at the Young farm only a few weeks ago to slaughter the pigs and cattle, kill the chickens, and steal the family silver and featherbeds. When she recalled these memories for me, she always seemed to reserve a special resentment for the loss of those featherbeds—something that long puzzled me. Only when I was an adult did I realize that it took months of plucking geese to create a featherbed, and they were extremely valuable.

This absorption in the Southern side of our historic quarrel led my father inevitably to an equally strong interest in politics—on the side of the Democratic party. Democrats were not made by campaign promises and rational debate, in Independence. They were born. As for Republicans, Mamma Truman always talked about them as if, at that very moment, somewhere in Kansas they were all collectively dining off her mother's silver.

My impression of John Anderson Truman is not nearly as sharp as my impression of Mamma Truman, because he died in 1914, ten years before I was born. He exists in my mind as a shadowy figure, lovable and charming in many ways, but without the hard delightful impact that flesh and blood leaves on the memory. He was a small man, and very sensitive about it. For years I was puzzled because in the few pictures of him that were taken with my grandmother, he was always sitting down while she was standing up. He was two inches shorter than she was, which meant that he must have been only about five foot four.

John Anderson was an energetic, ambitious man, who tried to follow in his father-in-law's footsteps, and make a career of cattle and livestock trading. The house he purchased on Chrysler Street in Independence had several acres of ground, and there were many cows, goats and horses in pens in the yard. He was also a born farmer, and had a huge garden where he grew vegetables so remarkably large and fine that the family still talks about them fifty years later. Especially remembered are his yellow tomatoes—"peach tomatoes," he called them. But John Anderson's ruling passion was politics. When Grover Cleveland won the presidency in 1892, returning the Democrats to power, John climbed to the top of the Chrysler Street house and hammered a flag to the cupola, while his admiring sons watched from the ground.

Politics was where Dad and his father had a meeting of the minds. John Anderson Truman was always ready to defend the honor of the Democratic party—with his fists, if necessary. He had a famous temper. Again, it is a puzzling phenomenon, remembering how mild-mannered his own father, Anderson Shippe Truman was. My father remembers this pugnacity fondly, because he was often the benefactor of it. No one ever pushed John Anderson Truman's children around without getting some sharp pushing in return. My grandfather was very Southern in his hot-blooded instinct to defend his family at all costs. Dad never forgot the warm feeling his father's fights on his behalf aroused in him. I suspect it explains not a little of his own hot temper, when he found himself defending his flesh and blood on a more public stage, in later years.

Most of the time, however, my father's world revolved around his mother. A story my Cousin Ethel liked to tell illustrates this fact as well as Mamma Truman's strength of character. The boys along Chrysler Street had, it seemed, a habit of bombarding the local chickens with rocks. One woman neighbor repeatedly accused my father of being involved in this mischief and Mamma Truman steadfastly denied it. Finally, one day the neighbor appeared in a monumental rage.

"Your older boy was in it this time," she said. "Now don't say he wasn't because this time he was."

Calmly Mamma Truman replied, "Well, just wait and we'll see, we'll find out. If he was why we're not going to excuse him but we won't blame him unless he's guilty."

She promptly summoned all the boys within calling distance and asked each one of them if my father had done any rock throwing. Vivian and all the rest of them confessed their guilt, but they unanimously exonerated my father. "The neighbor went home a little crestfallen," Cousin Ethel recalled.

I am sure that it was Mamma Truman who sustained Dad's years of studying the piano, in spite of hoots and sneers from his less artistically minded contemporaries. The fact that he was a very talented pianist helped, of course. Dad's stringent modesty when describing his own achievements has confused a lot of people about his musical ability. At first he studied with Miss Florence Burrus, who lived next door. But he soon outgrew her scope, and Mamma Truman sent him to Mrs. E. C. White, a Kansas City teacher who had studied under Theodor Leschetitzky, a very famous European master of the time, the teacher of Paderewski. Twice a week Dad journeyed to Mrs. White's house for lessons, and practiced at least two hours a day. When Paderewski came through Kansas City on a tour in 1900, Mrs. White took Dad to meet him, and the great man showed Dad how to play the "turn" in his Minuet in G. By this time, Dad was playing Bach, Beethoven, Liszt, and he had acquired what was later called "a good foundation." Mrs. White thought he should aim at a musical career. But when he was seventeen, Dad quit because—he says—"I wasn't good enough." There was another reason, which we will see in a few pages.

My father's glasses did not entirely separate him from boys his own age. During his first years in Independence, the Truman home was one of the star attractions of the neighborhood, thanks to its extensive animal farm. John Anderson Truman built a little wagon and had harnesses especially made for a pair of goats that he hitched to it, and every boy in town was soon begging my father and his brother for a ride. When the boys grew older and turned to sports, my father would occasionally join them, at least during the baseball season as umpire.

But my father spent most of his time reading books that Mamma Truman carefully selected for him. His favorite was a red-backed four-volume set of biographies by Charles Francis Horne, *Great Men and Famous Women*. These were the books that made him fall in love with history. To this day he still insists that reading biographies is the best way to learn history. He is also a firm believer in what some cynical historians have called the great man theory. Dad sums it up more positively. "Men make history. History does not make the man."

My father's second preference, after Mr. Horne's biographies, was the Bible. By the time he was twelve, he had read it end to end twice and was frequently summoned to settle religious disputes between the various branches of the Truman and Young families, who were divided among Baptists, Presbyterians, and Methodists. He also discovered the Independence Public Library, and by the time he had graduated from high school, Dad had devoured all of the books on its shelves that might interest a boy. Included in this diet, of course, were great gobs of history. He remained totally fascinated by all aspects of the past. At one point, he and a group of his friends spent weeks constructing a model of a bridge Julius Caesar built across the Rhine. My Cousin Ethel remembered another season when Dad's big enthusiasm was fencing.

Studious though he was, my father was not the brightest boy in his class. This title went to Charlie Ross, a gangling, rather shy young man who read at least as many books as Dad, and had a talent for handling words that won him the admiration of the school's favorite teacher, Miss Tillie Brown. Charlie was editor of the year book and the class valedictorian. On graduation day Miss Tillie gave him a big kiss. Dad was one of several boys who protested this favoritism. But Miss Tillie refused to apologize. "When the rest of you do something worthwhile, you'll get your reward, too," she said. As we shall see, Dad never forgot those words.

Charlie was one of my father's closest friends. But more than friendship attracted him to another member of the class—a very pretty blonde girl named Elizabeth Virginia Wallace, known to her friends as Bess. They had already known each other for a long time. They had attended Sunday school together at the First Presbyterian Church when they were kindergarten age. My father often says it took him another five years to get up the nerve to speak to her, but this can be partly explained by geography. They went to different grammar schools until the Trumans sold their house on Chrysler Street and moved to new quarters on Waldo Street. When Dad transferred to fifth grade in the Columbian School, he found Bess Wallace in his new class. Everyone in the family seems to agree that he was in love with her, even then. "To tell the truth," my Cousin Ethel said, "there never was but one girl in the world for Harry Truman, from the first time he ever saw her at the Presbyterian kindergarten." This was the voice of authority speaking. Cousin Ethel went all through school with Dad and Mother. In high school they used to meet regularly at the Noland house to study Latin with the help of Cousin Ethel's sister, Nellie, who was a whiz in the language. They apparently spent most of their time fencing, however.

I am sure that Mother was the best female fencer in town, and she was probably better than most of the boys. To this day I find it hard to listen to stories of my mother's girlhood without turning an envious green, or collapsing into despair. She was so many things that I am not. She was a marvelous athlete—the best third baseman in Independence, a superb tennis player, a tireless ice skater—and she was pretty besides. Sometimes I think she must have reduced most of the boys in town to stuttering awe. Mother also had just as many strong opinions at eighteen as she has now, and no hesitation about stating them Missouri style—straight from the shoulder. What man could cope with a girl like that—especially when she could also knock down a hot grounder and throw him out at first or wallop him six love at tennis? Sometimes, when someone looks skeptical about my thesis that my father was always an extraordinary man, I'm tempted to give them the best capsule proof I know—he married my mother. Only someone who was very confident that he was no ordinary man would have seen himself as Bess Wallace's husband.

Although they were frequently together in the big crowd of cousins and friends who picnicked and partied during their high school years, they drifted apart after they graduated. Again, geography was the villain. John Anderson Truman took a terrible beating, speculating on the Kansas City grain market in 1901, and in 1902 the Trumans had to sell their house on Waldo Street and move to Kansas City, Missouri. My father had hoped—in fact expected—to go to college. But that was out of the question now. He tried for West Point and Annapolis, but was turned down because of his bad eyes. So, like most young men his age (seventeen), he went to work. To the great distress of his teacher, Mrs. White, he also abandoned his piano lessons. The long years of preparation necessary for a classical pianist's career seemed out of the question now.

My father worked for a summer as a timekeeper with the Santa Fe Railroad. Then for several years he was a bank clerk. He made considerable progress at this job, going from $35 to $120 a month, and handling a million dollars a day in his cage. One of his fellow fledgling bankers was Arthur Eisenhower, whose younger brother Ike was still in high school in Abilene, Kansas. On Saturdays Dad ushered at the local theaters to make extra money—and enjoy free of charge all the vaudeville acts and traveling drama groups that came to Kansas City.

In 1906, John Anderson Truman asked my father to return to the Young farm and help him run this 600-acre establishment, as well as 300 acres nearby, which belonged to Dad's uncle, Harrison Young, after whom he was named. It was sometime during these years—no one seems to remember precisely the date—that Dad regained Bess Wallace's attention, this time permanently.

My Cousin Ethel Noland was the unchallengeable authority on the occasion, because it was from her home that my father returned the famous (in the Truman family, anyway) cake plate, which enabled him to renew the acquaintance. "Mrs. Wallace was very neighborly," Cousin Ethel explained, "and she loved to send things over to us—a nice dessert or something, just to share it." As a result, there were often Wallace cake plates sitting around the Noland house, waiting to be returned. One Saturday or Sunday my father was visiting, when Cousin Ethel remarked that it was about time someone got around to returning one of these plates. Dad volunteered with something approaching the speed of light, and the young lady who answered his knock at the Wallace door was the very person he wanted to see.

I believe there really are no explanations that completely explain why two people fall in love with each other. But if you live with them long enough, you can see glimpses of explanations, and I will advance one here that throws some light on my father's character at the same time. I think the secret of his success with my mother was his absolute refusal to argue with her—a policy he has followed to this day. From his very early years, my father was known as the peacemaker in the Truman-Young families. Even among his Noland cousins he is still remembered as an expert in resolving arguments. Right straight through his presidential years, he continued to play this role in our highly combative clan. Occasionally he complained mightily to me in his letters about the prevalence of "prima donnas," as he called the more difficult members of the family. But he continued to exercise this gift for peacemaking in private—and in public.

Contrary to her public image, my mother is a very combative person. There is nothing vindictive or mean about her. She just likes to argue. I am the same way. To this day we cannot get together for more than twenty minutes without locking verbal horns. (Whereupon Dad will groan, "Are you two at it again?") Who else but a young man smart enough *not* to argue with Bess Wallace could have persuaded a girl like that to marry him?

By 1914, when my grandfather, John Anderson Truman, died, it was more or less understood that Mother and Dad were paired.

She went to my grandfather's funeral, and my father was a regular visitor at the Wallace house on North Delaware Street. Contrary to some of the biographical legends, he did not commute by horseback from the farm at Grandview. At first he came by train and streetcar and later in a magnificent 1910 Stafford with a brass-rimmed windshield and Prest-O-Lite lamps.

Some people have claimed that he bought the car to impress his future mother-in-law, Mrs. Wallace, who supposedly did not approve of the match. But no one in the family believes that story. Sometimes the tale is embellished, to make my mother the richest girl in Independence and my father some poor disheveled dirt farmer, desperately attempting to hide his poverty behind a high-powered engine. This is plain nonsense. By now I trust I have established as undeniable fact that the Trumans were not poor. They had suffered financial reverses, but they still had those 900 acres of prime Missouri topsoil on the Young farms to fall back on. As my Cousin Ethel often said, "There was always a feeling of security there."

What good times they had in that cousinly, neighborly crowd! Whether my father was commuting from his bank job in Kansas City, where he lived with his first cousins, the Colgans, or from the farm at Grandview, when he got to Independence, there always seemed to be a party in progress. My Cousin Ethel had a wonderful picture of the crowd enjoying a watermelon feast in the Colgan backyard. My mother and her brothers are there, all, as Cousin Ethel put it, "into watermelon up to our ears." *Life* magazine once begged her to let them publish it, but they received a frosty no because Cousin Ethel thought Mother looked undignified.

There were practical jokes galore that kept everyone laughing. No one loves a practical joke more than my father, so it doesn't surprise me that he was deep in most of them. Among the favorites was one Dad helped cook up on his cousin, Fred Colgan, and another friend, Edwin Green. They and the girls in the crowd went picnicking on the banks of the Missouri one day. Fred Colgan and Ed Green decided, just for the fun of it, to put a message in a bottle, toss it in the river, and see if they got an answer. My father and the other young jokers promptly concocted two imaginary girls in Mississippi who wrote deliciously teasing letters to Messrs. Colgan and Green. Pretty soon there was a veritable romance budding, with my father and his fellow jokers fiendishly mailing letters and even phony pictures to friends in Mississippi who remailed them to poor Fred Colgan and Ed Green, who were by now getting desperately lovesick. Finally, one of the older members in the family put a stop to it, lest they have a couple of romantic nervous breakdowns on their hands. Fred Colgan took the news especially hard, and, I have been told, did not speak to my father or the other jokers for months.

With Dad's ability to play the piano, and his love of a good joke, he was often the life of the party. Another story that everyone loves to tell concerns his antics en route to a wedding in 1913. The bridegroom was a highly successful young business-man, and he had a very formal wedding. Dad borrowed a tuxedo from one friend and an opera hat from my mother's brother, Frank Wallace. The hat was collapsible, and en route to the reception, riding in a horse-drawn cab, Dad tried to put his head out the window to tell the driver the address. His hat hit the top of the window and collapsed. Everyone went into hysterics at "the little fried egg thing sitting on the top of his head," to quote my Cousin Ethel. Dad let the hat perch there all the way over to the reception, while the cab rocked with laughter. When they finally arrived, they had to sit outside the bride's house for a good five minutes, recovering their senses. "We were carefree and a little irresponsible, I think," my Cousin Ethel said. Those words are a pretty good paraphrase of the fundamental, almost idyllic happiness that comes through to me in the recollections I have heard and overheard of my father's youth in pre-World War I Independence.

Happy memories are a priceless asset to a man when he becomes a public servant. They deepen and broaden his vision of his country's value and make him more generous, I think, more committed to widening the opportunities for happiness for the generations that follow him.

These years also helped to form in my father his deliberate, methodical approach to problems. From his early twenties to his early thirties, he was a farmer—not a gentleman farmer but a working one, toiling most of the time under John Anderson

Truman's stern eye. Off the political platform, when he talked about learning how to plow a straight furrow, he often added, "It had to be straight. If it wasn't, I heard about it from my father for the next year." These were the years when Dad also developed that sturdy physique which prompted us to snort with indignation when someone called him "the little man in the White House." Riding a gangplow across a field behind a team of four horses or four mules took muscle, and added some every time you did it.

When my father discussed his farming days he made you realize the sheer physical labor involved. "I used to milk cows by hand. I used to plow with a four-horse team, instead of a tractor," he said once during the White House years. "I have two nephews on the same farm that get much more out of that farm than I ever did. But they do it with machinery. They milk cows by machine, and they plow with a tractor and they plant with a tractor and they bale hay with a tractor. I don't think that those boys could follow me up a corn row to save their lives, because they ride and I walked."

But the most important thing about a farmer's life is the steady, methodical nature of his work. Dad could count the revolutions of a gangplow's wheel, and figure out exactly how long it would take him to plow a field half a mile square. Things had to be done on a schedule, but nothing much could be done to hurry the growth of the corn or the wheat. The pace of the farm was reflected in the pace of the era. There was no sense of frantic urgency, no burning need to hurry. As Cousin Ethel said, "Harry was always a deliberate man."

Three

My FATHER WAS even deliberate about courting my mother. Sometimes I think that if World War I hadn't come along, he might not have married her until he was forty or fifty, and I might never have gotten here. He proposed and they became engaged shortly before he left for France. He was thirty-four, she was thirty-three. Mother gave him her picture. On the back she wrote, "Dear Harry, May this photograph bring you safely home again from France — Bess." Dad carried this picture with him inside his tunic, through training days and in the mud and danger of the Western Front. That same picture sat on his desk in the White House, and still sits on his desk in the Truman Library. I didn't really know the man who went to France, but I have heard from his own lips the admission that the war changed him enormously. He is still fond of saying that he got his education in the army.

It was quite an education. Among the teachers were the brawling Irishmen of Battery D of the 129th Field Artillery. Products of Kansas City's toughest ward, they had run through three commanding officers before Dad took charge of them. As many another man was to find in the years to come, they discovered that no one pushed Harry Truman around. But here, as in so many other areas of his life, his toughness emanated not only from his inborn character but from his knowledge of how the job had to be done. As a student of military history, my father had a clear-eyed perception of how an army was supposed to operate. Still, it must have been enormously encouraging to discover that he had the natural ability to make this theoretical knowledge work, with the unruly Irish of Battery D. He came out of the army convinced that if he could lead these wild men, he could lead anyone.

One story I remember from Dad's army days—I have heard it repeated ad infinitum in the family—concerns his lost glasses. There will be other lost glasses stories later in the book. The uncanny luck he has had with his glasses is enough to make one wonder if Martha Ellen Truman did not negotiate some special arrangement with the Deity when she put spectacles on her five-year-old-son. One night early in the Argonne offensive, Dad was riding his horse toward the German lines to take up his usual position, well in advance of Battery D, and sometimes of the infantry, where he could study the German lines and telephone firing instructions back to the battery. As he rode under a low-hanging tree, the branches swept his glasses off his face. The horse, oblivious to the disaster, kept on going, and the road was jammed with marching men and lumbering cannons. Dad had a reserve pair of glasses in his baggage but that was in a wagon at the end of the column. There was no time to go back for it. They were moving on a strict to-the-minute schedule. There he was in the middle of the biggest battle in the history of the world, practically blind. He turned around, frantically trying to catch a glimpse of the glasses on the road. A glint of light on the horse's back—dawn was just beginning to break—caught his eye. There were the glasses, sitting on Dobbin's rump.

Another of my father's favorite soldier stories concerns some post-Armistice antics of Battery D. In these days Irish-Americans held a grudge against England. Some of them still hold it. One day Battery D and the rest of the 35th Division assembled for a review by General Pershing and the Prince of Wales—afterwards King Edward VIII. "As we marched off the field, General Pershing and the Prince of Wales and his staff were crossing a little creek not far from me," Dad says. "And as we marched on the other side of the creek with the General and his staff, one of my disrespectful corporals or sergeants yelled: 'Oh Capitaine. What did the little so and so say about freeing Ireland?'

"If Pershing had decided to hear that remark, I suppose I would have gone to Leavenworth and stayed there the rest of my life. He didn't hear it, thank goodness."

Even before my father came home from France and married Mother, he had made up his mind that he was through with farming. Mother played a role in this decision. She made it clear that she had no desire to be a farmer's wife. Like her mother-in-law, she had—and still has—a strong disinclination for cooking (although she can cook very well), and I doubt if the English language is adequate to describe her attitude toward the other laborious chores that need doing around a farm. But not even Mother could make up my father's mind on anything so fundamental, if he didn't want it that way in the first place. Although he had spent eleven of his best years as a working farmer, and enjoyed them thoroughly, he was eager to tackle bigger, more challenging opportunities.

Everyone over the age of thirty has heard ad nauseam about my father's next adventure—his failure as the co-owner of a men's clothing store in Kansas City. He went into business with Eddie Jacobson, a friend who had helped him run a very successful canteen during their army training days in Oklahoma. His political enemies have endlessly retold the story, as if it was a kind of parable that proved Dad was a gross incompetent. The truth is simple and sad—he got caught in the recession of 1920–21 when business failures tripled overnight. Dad has always insisted it was a Republican recession, engineered by "old Mellon"—Andrew Mellon, the Secretary of the Treasury under Harding.

More important than the failure, in my opinion, is the way my father handled it. He absolutely refused to go into bankruptcy and spent the next fifteen years trying to pay off some $12,000 in debts. Altogether, he lost about $28,000 in this bitter experience.

According to those who misread his career, my father, having failed as a merchant, now turned in desperation to politics. Those who prefer the worst possible scenario have him going hat in hand to Tom Pendergast, the boss of Kansas City, and humbly accepting his nomination for county judge. This version reveals nothing but a vast ignorance of my father—and of Democratic politics in and around Kansas City in the early 1920s. The Pendergasts were by no means the absolute rulers of Kansas City, or of Jackson County, which included Kansas City, Independence, and smaller farming communities such as Grandview. They were fiercely opposed in primaries by a Democratic faction known as the Rabbits. The Pendergasts were called the Goats. No one that I have found, including my father, can explain satisfactorily the origin of these nicknames.

My grandfather, John Anderson Truman, had been a close friend of one of the Goat leaders in Independence and thus Dad always thought of himself as a Goat—that is, a Pendergast—Democrat. But it was not Tom Pendergast, the boss of Kansas City, who came into his mind when the name was mentioned. It was Mike Pendergast, Tom's older, far more easy-going brother who led the Goats in eastern Jackson County. As my father explained it somewhat cryptically —"Tom didn't like the country."

During the war my father had become friendly with Mike Pendergast's son, Jim, who was a fellow officer in the 129th Field Artillery. I should also explain at this point that in Missouri a county judge is an administrative, not a judicial office. The three-man Board of Judges in Jackson County were responsible for building roads as well as running the courthouse and other county facilities. They had command of a substantial political payroll, and this made control of the three-man board of vital interest to Goats, Rabbits, and Republicans. One judge was elected from the western district, which included Kansas City. The other judge came from the eastern district, and the third, the presiding judge, was elected from the county at large.

My father had toyed with the idea of going into politics even before he returned from France. Half playfully, he had written Cousin Ethel that he intended to run for Congress when he returned home. Jim Pendergast knew this and told his father, Mike, about it. In mid–1921 when Truman and Jacobson's haberdashery was flourishing, Mike appeared on the customer's side of the counter one day and asked Dad if he would like to run for judge of the county court for the eastern district. My father politely declined to commit himself. It was obvious to him—and to everyone else—that the Pendergasts needed Harry S. Truman at least as much as he needed them.

On January 9, 1922, the Independence *Examiner* ran a story speculating on who would be the Democratic candidate for judge from the eastern district. This story discussed several men, including E. E. Montgomery of Blue Springs, a banker, and Charles W. Brady, the postmaster of Independence. "Among the younger men, Harry Truman is talked of," the reporter wrote. "Mr. Truman was born and reared in Jackson County and lived forty years near Grandview and his vote in Washington Township would be mighty near unanimous if he should run. He now lives in Independence and is in business in Kansas City. . . . Mr. Truman has not said that he is willing to be a candidate."

The publisher of the *Examiner* was Colonel William M. "Pop" Southern. One of my mother's brothers had married his daughter. This explains, in part at least, the editor's kind words. Note, however, that my father was easing himself into the race, not as a Pendergast man, but as an independent. On March 8, 1922, the *Examiner* headlined Dad's formal announcement of his candidacy. It did not emanate from Mike Pendergast's Tenth Ward Democratic Club. Instead, it came from "an enthusiastic meeting" attended by 300 war veterans at Lee's Summit, one of the small farming communities outside Independence. The story told how Major Harry Truman (he had been promoted in the Reserve in 1920) of Grandview was declared the choice of the ex-servicemen as a candidate for county judge from the eastern district. Colonel E. M. Stayton, the former commander of the 129th Field Artillery, presented Major Truman to the meeting. He urged his fellow veterans to back him in the forthcoming election.

"It was a new method for starting out a candidate for county judge," the reporter wrote. "Usually the factions of the Party in Kansas City agree on a man and the word is sent out to the workers in the county and instructions given to support him for the nomination. The Truman announcement is made without any organizational or factional endorsement whatever." The reporter specified that there were men from Kansas City, Independence, Buckner, Blue Springs, and Oak Grove and they included both Goat and Rabbit Democrats. But we can be certain that there was a solid contingent of old Battery D boys in the crowd, from a description of the entertainment. Mrs. Ethel Lee Buxton of Kansas City, who had sung for the soldiers in France, entertained with songs that included "When Irish Eyes Are Smiling," and "Mother Machree."

This appearance also marked my father's first attempt to become a public speaker. It was a disaster. When Colonel Stayton introduced him, Dad rose and completely forgot the little speech he had intended to make. All he could do was stammer that he was grateful for his fellow veterans' support, and sit down. Fortunately the boys from Battery D were not a critical audience. They cheered "Captain Harry" anyway.

On April 21, 1922, another *Examiner* story on the coming election described the ominous three-way fight that was developing among the Democrats. Along with the usual brawl between the Rabbits and the Goats, there was a faction surrounding Judge Miles Bulger, who was presiding judge of the county court. This meant he controlled some sixty road overseers, powerful allies in the sixty districts covering every part of the eastern half of the county. After speculating on Goat and Rabbit candidates, the reporter noted that one candidate, George W. Shaw, had no promise of support from any organization. "Harry S. Truman is another," he wrote. "He has consulted no political director and has already announced and has received much promise of support. He stands well with the ex-servicemen, being an ex-serviceman himself, and is the youngest man suggested. He is going ahead with his campaign regardless of factional permission."

On April 26 the *Examiner* reported a visit of Mike Pendergast to Independence. He held a meeting at the Eagles' Hall, where about a hundred of "the faithful," as the reporter described them, discussed candidates for eastern district judge, but came to no conclusion as to whom they would endorse. Meanwhile, my father was campaigning vigorously. In Grandview, on May 4, he filled the local movie house at a rally. On May 12 the Men's Rural Jackson County Democratic Club endorsed him in a rally at Lee's Summit. The *Examiner* continued to describe him as "Harry S. Truman of Grandview." Already he was demonstrating an instinctive strategy that was to be a basic part of his political success—an ability to bridge the gap between city and country Democrats.

By June, Mike Pendergast had seen enough of Harry S. Truman in action to convince him that he was a potential winner. He invited him to a meeting of the Tenth Ward Democratic Club and announced that my father had the organization's support. Mike gave a speech, describing Dad as "a returned veteran, a captain whose men didn't want to shoot him"—an interesting comment on army mores in World War I. As my father has said repeatedly, in discussing his relationship with the Pendergasts, he was grateful for this support. He knew he needed every available vote to win the election. There were now no less than five candidates campaigning. But he had already made it clear that he had the backing and ability to run a pretty good race on his own. Thus there never was and never would be any subservience in his relationship with the Pendergasts. But there was another element, which some of Dad's critics have mistaken for subservience—party loyalty.

To my father, being a Democrat was and is an article of faith. He could not run on a Republican ticket if an angel from on high appeared with a flaming sword and ordered him to do so. He supported the Pendergasts because they were Democrats, and they supported him for the same reason. His Missouri blood responded to the idea of loyalty with the same fervor that the idea inspired in the emotional hearts of Pendergast's Irish. I am not suggesting that this made life easy. On the contrary, it involved him in some agonizing conflicts.

Even with Pendergast backing, my father continued his strenuous day and night campaigning. He had shown himself to be a political innovator by his shrewd appeal to the veteran vote—a new force in American politics. Later in the campaign he came up with another innovation. He was one of the first to use the airplane as a political weapon.

One of his fellow veterans, Eddie McKim, persuaded a local flier to take Dad up above the biggest political picnic of the summer, at Oak Grove, and bombard the assembled farmers with Truman leaflets. According to Eddie McKim, the plane was "one of those old Jennies that was held together with baling wire." They circled the picnic grounds and disgorged their pamphlets with no difficulty. But then the pilot tried to land in a nearby pasture. "He had a little trouble stopping the plane and it ended up about three feet from a barbed wire fence," Eddie McKim said. "Our candidate got out as green as grass. But he mounted the rostrum and made a speech."

On the eve of the election an ominous force put in an appearance. Grim-faced men stood outside the doors of several Protestant churches in Independence and handed out pink "sample ballots." When someone asked them what they were doing, they simply replied, "A hundred percent." It was the local slogan of the

Ku Klux Klan and it meant a hundred percent American. Only one man on the county ticket was endorsed by the Klan. Opposite his name they had written, "Church affiliation, Protestant, record good." Opposite the name of Harry S. Truman was written "Church affiliation Protestant, endorsed by Tom and Mike." The Pendergasts were Catholic, of course, and the Klansmen, with their instinctive talent for bad taste and worse judgment, were attempting to inject religious hatred into the campaign. The *Examiner,* reporting the story, went out of the way to point out how unfair this slur was against my father who had been "only supported by the Pendergast faction after he had been out campaigning for some months."

When the Klan appeared in Missouri, no one was especially alarmed. It seemed a fairly harmless patriotic organization at first. The Independence *Examiner* wrote a mild editorial, disapproving of its bed sheets and secret meetings but praising the patriotic aspects of its program. My father even considered joining it. But when he met with one of the organizers, he was told bluntly that he had to promise never to give a Catholic a job, if he won election to the county court. My father was outraged. Most of his boys in Battery D were Catholics, and he told the Klansman he would give any one of them a job, if they needed help. That was the beginning and the end of his relationship with the Ku Klux Klan. By turning the story inside out, his enemies were to convert it into a vicious political smear against him in years to come.

When the votes for eastern district judge were finally counted on August 1, 1922, another Truman tradition was launched. My father won what the Independence *Examiner* called "the hottest primary fight in the history of the county" by a plurality of 300, out of a total of 11,664 votes cast. The next day, thanking those who had supported him, he reiterated his independent stance. "I have made no promises to anybody or organization," he said. "The support I received was wonderful and I appreciated every bit. I shall endeavor to so serve as county judge that no man or woman will be ashamed of having voted for me and to give a square deal to everybody and keep the only promises I have made, which were made in my speeches to the public."

The job he tackled was not easy, and the political situation was not much better. Previous county court administrations, especially that presided over by Miles Bulger, had made a policy of boondoggling away millions and running the county into murderous debt. In 1921 the Bulger court had spent $1,070,000 on roads that were already disintegrating because they had been built by crooked contractors using shoddy, low-grade materials. A long history of mismanagement had enabled the state to seize control of several county institutions. There was a deficit of $800,000 as well as $2,300,000 borrowed against incoming taxes at 6 percent interest.

"I learned a lot about government as she is executed in those two years," my father says of his first term as county judge. "They were invaluable in my education. I learned the machinery of operation and I also found out who really ran things locally." It proved to be a harsh education.

Judge Truman and his fellow Democrat, Presiding Judge Henry McElroy, first concentrated on reforming the county's shaky fiscal structure. Dad went to Chicago and St. Louis to discuss ways to improve the county's borrowing, and found bankers who were willing to loan money on tax anticipation notes at 4 percent. Eventually he got them down to 2 percent. In two years they paid off more than $600,000 of the county's debt. When they stood for reelection in 1924, the Kansas City *Star*, staunchly Republican and a violent foe of the Pendergasts, said one of the few nice things they've ever printed about my father. Citing the improvement in the county's roads and the reduction in the debt, the editorial declared: "The men who did this, Judge McElroy and Judge Truman, are up for renomination. Tuesday the Democratic voters of Jackson County will show whether they are interested enough in good service to renominate the men who were responsible for the remarkable showing made."

But on the political side, Judge Truman and Presiding Judge McElroy overreached themselves. They put only Goat Democrats on the county payroll. This aroused the extreme enmity of the Rabbits. Worse, they tried to ignore the growing power of the Ku Klux Klan.

In their now familiar style, the Klan turned the election of 1924 into a vicious, hate-filled melee. They threatened to kill my father at one point. This only aroused his native pugnacity, and he astonished them by appearing at one of their meetings—not the bed sheet variety, but a political forum where they masqueraded as the Independent Democrats—and calling their bluff to their faces. He told them they were a bunch of cheap un-American fakers, and then coolly walked off the platform and through the crowd to his car. As drama, as courage, it was magnificent, but as politics, it was suicide in the year 1924, the high tide of the Klan in Missouri and in the United States. On the eve of the election, the head of the Klan in Jackson County stated bluntly in the Kansas City *Star*, "We are unalterably opposed to Harry Truman." Meanwhile, the Rabbit Democrats were pursuing their own vendetta. They joined forces with the Klansmen to vote McElroy and Truman into political oblivion in November.

Dad was defeated by 877 votes—the only election he ever lost. The Klan and the Rabbits cast all their votes for Dad's Republican opponent, an aging harness maker named Henry Rummel. He did not even know he was running until the Republican leader of the county called him up and told him that he had put up five dollars to file his name.

My father's defeat and my birth practically coincided. "I spent two years thinking and trying to make some bread and butter for my sweetheart and our small daughter who came shortly before my licking," he wrote, in a memoir of these years. Again, his instinctive modesty plays down the rather impressive scope of his activities while he was out of public office. He reorganized the Automobile Club of Kansas City, and boosted it to over 4,000 members. He became president of the National Old Trails Association, a perfect job for Solomon Young's grandson. He traveled extensively around Missouri and many other states, marking famous roads and urging local governments to see the value of their history as a tourist attraction. He also helped launch a savings and loan association, in which he served as vice president. Simultaneously, he kept up his political contacts. He made speeches at American Legion meetings and at school assemblies. Often his subject was historical.

Along with all these jobs and activities, my father struggled to keep up with a course in law. He had decided that a public official ought to have a law degree, and on October 5, 1923, he had enrolled in the Kansas City Law School. For the next two years he carried a staggering schedule, but managed to earn the following grades:

FRESHMAN YEAR

Criminal Law	84
Contracts	85
Blackstone's Commentaries	96
Torts	87
Kent's Commentaries	85
Sales	77
Agency	93
Domestic Relations	84

SOPHOMORE YEAR

Equity Jurisprudence	83
Damages	92½
Bailments and Common Carriers	82
Common Law & Equity Pleading	89
Roman Law	84
Statutory Rights and Remedies	85

On February 21, 1925, at the Washington's Birthday banquet in the Muehlebach Hotel in Kansas City, my father represented his class, and gave a speech entitled, "Honor in Government." But after his sophomore year he had to abandon the course. Every time he came to Kansas City he was overwhelmed by pleas for advice and help from his Battery D boys. To them he was still Captain Harry, the leader who had taken them through France without a single casualty from enemy fire.

Dad's heart was still in politics. Moreover, he was constantly encouraged to return to the hustings by Mike Pendergast and his son Jim. Mike Pendergast was a simple, direct, uncomplicated man, utterly different from his powerful brother. "I loved him as I did my own daddy," my father said after Mike died in 1929.

In the two years since Dad's defeat, the Democrats had been out of power in the Jackson County government and not doing very well in Kansas City either. They were learning the hard way that their endless feuding was politically ruinous. With Republicans in control of the government in Washington and in the

Missouri State House in Jefferson City, the party was hard pressed in Jackson County. In 1926 they decided to bury their feuds and get behind potentially winning candidates. Early that year Jim Pendergast introduced my father to Tom, the "Big Boss," as Dad always called him.

A stocky, grizzly bear of a man with a massive neck and shoulders and huge hands, Tom Pendergast was a formidable character. Prone to violence, he was known to knock a man cold with a single punch in an argument. He was a kind of natural force, around which other men clustered like pilot fish on a shark.

Tom Pendergast was twelve years older than my father. He was the voice—the very authoritative voice—of an earlier, cruder era in American politics. He had been building power in Kansas City since 1900. Along with his native strength of personality and body, Boss Tom was a very shrewd man. Unlike similar bosses in New York and Chicago, his power was not based on the support of masses of immigrants. Foreign-born voters in Kansas City never numbered much more than 6 percent. Tom Pendergast rose to power by demonstrating a genius for local political leadership, for working with people of all creeds and colors.

Jim Pendergast urged his uncle to back my father for presiding judge of Jackson County. Boss Tom agreed. With a united party behind him, Dad swept to a solid victory at the head of a ticket that put Democrats into almost every available county office. The triumph made Tom Pendergast the most powerful politician in Missouri. Earlier in the year the Goats had won complete control of Kansas City, installing Henry McElroy, the presiding judge in Dad's first term, as city manager.

Elected presiding judge by 16,000 votes, my father was, as he described it "the key man in the county government." He dates the real beginning of his political career from this 1926 election. For the first time he had the kind of authority he needed to build a record that voters could see and admire. He poured all his energy into the job, and he needed every bit of it. The county government was in disastrous shape. The roads, most of them built by Bulger, were called "piecrusts" by two local engineers whom my father hired to survey them. "These men with my assistance planned a system of roads estimated to cost $6,500,000," Dad says. My father then went to Tom Pendergast and persuaded him to back a bond issue to build these roads. Pendergast was pushing a $28,000,000 bond issue for Kansas City, and he was extremely lukewarm to Dad's plan. Boss Tom said the voters would never approve it. There had been so much corruption in the county court system that the voters had become extremely reluctant to hand over any large amounts of money to the judges. Dad argued back—something few men had the nerve to do with Tom Pendergast. He said he was confident he could sell the bond issue to the people, by telling them exactly how he planned to spend it. Pendergast told him to go ahead. The Kansas City *Star* declared editorially that the presiding judge did not have a prayer of winning either the votes or the money. Judging from the fate of other bond issues, the *Star* certainly seemed to be making a safe prediction. Out of $116,410,000 requested by the politicians in the 1920s in Jackson County, the voters refused $83,760,000.

This skepticism only made my father more determined. He launched a Truman-style campaign which once more took him into every corner of the county. He explained how he was planning to award the contracts—on a low-bid basis. He proposed a bipartisan board of engineers to supervise the program. He took the head of the Taxpayers League—his former major in the army —over the county roads inch by inch and convinced him of the necessity for new construction. He even persuaded the local leaders of the Republican party to back the idea.

The vote came on May 8, 1928, my father's forty-fourth birthday. To the astonishment of all the local political experts, his entire program—all $7,000,000 of it—won by a three-fourths majority instead of the necessary two-thirds, while the $28,000,000 Kansas City bond issue was pared by most of the same voters to a mere $700,000.

In a few months the road-building program was under way, run exactly as my father said it would be run. The two engineers, Colonel Edward Stayton and N. T. Veatch, were in charge of the specifications, and they administered the contracts with absolutely unswerving honesty. Firms from outside Missouri—as far away as South Dakota—were awarded major slices of the work, on the basis of their low bids. Meanwhile, Dad was roughing up Democrats throughout the county. In Kansas City there was a tradition of carrying one or two thousand city employees "on the pad" without requiring them to show up for work. Some Democrats thought this principle could be applied with equal ease to the county government. But the moment my father found a man drawing pay without performing his job, he fired him.

Cries of political anguish soon reached Tom Pendergast's ears. Even louder were the howls of rage from the local contractors, who had complacently expected to do most of the work for Judge Truman's $7,000,000 road program. Soon Dad was invited to a meeting in Tom Pendergast's office. There he was confronted by three of the leading Goat Democrat contractors, all in a very ugly mood. There was a ferocious argument. My father insisted that he had made a commitment to the voters and he was not going to back down on it. With his eye on Tom Pendergast, he argued that it was not only good government, it was good politics, to keep his promises to the voters.

Tom was fond of saying there were three sides to every argument, my side, your side, and the right side. He decided my father was on the right side, and, in spite of the fact that Mr. Pendergast was a partner of at least one of these crooked contractors, he threw them out of the office and told Dad to go on doing the job the honest way.

Only in the last five or six years have scholars of my father's career begun to dig behind the myths that have accumulated around these days and discover the truth that we Trumans have known all the time. For instance, Dr. Dorsett W. Lyle, in his unpublished doctoral thesis, "The Pendergast Machine," writes of Dad's nomination, "Desperately wanting to gain his hold on the rich county patronage, and likewise desiring to maintain the hold once he regained it, Tom Pendergast decided that he would be willing to relinquish, if necessary, such assets to his machine as special favors to contractors, in order to be able to hold on to the patronage. This was exactly what Pendergast had to do the minute he selected Harry Truman to become the machine's candidate for county judge." In this relinquishment, Boss Tom also abandoned special favors for himself. Mr. Pendergast owned the Ready-Mixed Concrete Company which in the past had been used almost exclusively by contractors paving Jackson County roads. In Judge Truman's 225-mile road-building program, only three-fourths of a mile were paved with Ready-Mixed.

The road program was completed on schedule, giving Jackson County one of the finest highway systems in the nation. To everyone's amazement, there was not a hint of scandal connected with it. Even the Kansas City *Star* had to admit that Presiding Judge Truman was "extraordinarily honest." To her dying day, Mamma Truman maintained that he was too honest for his own good—or for her good, anyway. When a new road sliced off a piece of her farm, my father refused to pay a cent for the land. She complained about this super-honesty for years. Other aspects of this remarkable road program can be seen in a long-forgotten booklet that Dad published on Jackson County's roads. It reveals him to have been decades in advance of his time. He set aside land for parks and recreation centers. He discussed the problem of keeping local streams pure and preserving the forested parts of the county. Remembering the tree-lined roads he had seen in France during the war, he planted seedlings along every mile of his new roads. The local farmers, indifferent to beauty as well as soil conservation, uprooted most of them. But Dad's insistence that every farm in the county should be within two and a half miles of a hard-surface road won him their undying enthusiasm.

Tom Pendergast, reading the stories in the paper, and hearing echoes of the warm wave of approval from the rural part of Jackson County, realized my father was right—fulfilling campaign promises was good politics as well as good government. In 1929 Mike Pendergast died. Although there was considerable competition from other Goats in the organization, Tom made Dad his official representative, responsible for the eastern part of the county. At this point in his career, Tom Pendergast knew exactly what he was doing, politically, and the results of the following year's elections proved it. Harry S. Truman surged to the top of the party's local ticket, and at the age of forty-five was reelected presiding judge by 55,000 votes.

In four years of hard, continuous effort, my father had accomplished a great deal. He has summarized these accomplishments in his memoirs. But he has never revealed the inner agony he suffered as he struggled to retain his principles and at the same time build a political career within the domain of Boss Tom Pendergast. Unfortunately for history, Dad has never kept a diary. But at times of stress in his life, he has written memoranda in which he wrestled with himself over decisions that confronted him. He has given me one of these documents which he wrote shortly after his reelection as presiding judge:

I have been doing some very deep and conscientious thinking. Is a service to the public or one's country worth one's life if it becomes necessary to give it, to accomplish the end sought? Should a man in public office see that his family and offspring are provided for- even though ethics and honor have to be thrown overboard? One of my predecessors answered that in the affirmative.

Since a child at my mother's knee, I have believed in honor, ethics and right living as its own reward. I find a *very* small minority who agree with me on that premise. For instance, I picked a West Pointer, son of an honorable father, a man who should have had Washington, Lee, Jackson, Gustavus Adolphus for his ideals, to associate with me in carrying out a program and I got—a dud, a weakling, no ideals, no nothing. He'd use his office for his own enrichment, he's not true to his wife (and a man not honorable in his marital relations is not usually honorable in any other). He'd sell me or anyone else he's associated with out for his own gain, but for lack of guts. He worried about the front in the army in 1918 until he made himself sick enough to stay at home.

I am obligated to the Big Boss, a man of his word, but he gives it very seldom and usually on a sure thing. But he is not a trimmer. He, in times past, owned a bawdy house, a saloon and gambling establishment, was raised in that environment, but he's all man. I wonder who is worth more in the sight of the Lord?

I am only a small duck in a very large puddle, but I am interested very deeply in local or municipal government. Who is to blame for present conditions but sniveling church members who weep on Sunday, play with whores on Monday, drink on Tuesday, sell out to the Boss on Wednesday, repent about Friday, and start over on Sunday. I think maybe the Boss is nearer Heaven than the snivelers.

We've spent seven million in bonds and seven million in revenue in my administration. I could have had $1,500,000. But I haven't a hundred and fifty dollars. Am I a fool or an ethical giant? I don't know. The Boss in his wrath at me because his crooked contractors got no contracts, said I was working to

[74]

give my consulting engineers a nationwide reputation and that my honor wouldn't be [worth] a pinch of snuff. I don't care if I get honor, if the taxpayers' money goes on the ground or into the buildings it's intended for.

Several pages of this memorandum describe in detail the terrific fight my father had to wage against corruption on the county court itself. The men he mentions are dead now, and I see no point in printing their names here. So I will tell most of this part of the story in my words. Dad noted sadly that one of his fellow judges, put on the court by Joe Shannon, the Rabbit boss, was instructed "to treat me for what I am in his estimation, that is, the lowest human on earth." But Shannon was soon forced to send his emissaries to see Presiding Judge Truman when he wanted anything. Why? Because his man and the other judge preferred to shoot craps down behind the bench while the court was in session. "When I wanted something done," Dad says, "I'd let them start a crap game and then introduce a long and technical order. Neither of them would have time to read it, and over it would go. I got a lot of good legislation for Jackson County over while they shot craps."

Finally, my father summed up his experience as a county judge:

> I'll go out of here poorer in every way than when I came into office. . . . I hope that there are no bond issues and no more troubles, until I'm done and then maybe I can run a filling station or something until I've run up my three score and ten and go to a quiet grave.

[CHAPTER]

Four

As I HAVE SAID, there was never a hint of this inner turmoil in the man I saw during these years. At home he was the perfect father, full of jokes and a constant tease. For a while he called me Skinny, because I was. He fretted endlessly over my health and one winter early in the 1930s he shipped Mother and me off to the Mississippi Gulf Coast, to see if a miracle could be achieved, and I could get through one year without becoming a case study in walking pneumonia. I had whooping cough, German measles, and a lot of other childhood diseases, but when it came to colds, flu, and the like, I was in a class by myself. Perhaps this was one of several reasons why Dad tended to spoil me, especially in matters of money. He was always slipping me an extra quarter or half dollar, to Mother's vast indignation. She thought I should learn to live on my allowance. More than once, when I found myself struggling as an adult to balance my chaotic checkbook (lately I've given up), I realized Mother was right.

Another argument which I continued off and on for the better part of a year concerned the color of my hair. It grew in snow white, and my father roundly declared that I had inherited it from him. "I was a blond when I was her age," he said serenely. My mother dragged out a picture of him and Uncle Vivian at the age of about four and two respectively. Their hair looked terribly dark to her. That did not bother Dad in the least. He insisted he had been a towheaded toddler. Finally, on one of our Sunday visits to the farm at Grandview, the question was put to Mamma Truman for adjudication.

"Did Harry have blond hair when he was growing up?" my Mother asked.

"Never," snapped Mamma Truman. That was the end of that argument.

Perhaps Dad was worried that I wasn't really a Truman. Perhaps he found it difficult to adjust to being the father of an only daughter. As a natural leader, I suspect he always envisioned himself as the father of a son, whom he could discipline without a deluge of tears. Now that I have become the mother of four boys, I tell him frequently he had a better deal.

Occasionally politicians came to our house on pressing matters. Once one of them, a tall man with a big nose who was running for governor, tried to kiss me. I pulled his nose, to my mother's scarcely concealed delight. Kissing babies, incidentally, was something that Dad himself never felt compelled to do. Most of the time, especially after he became the political leader of the eastern part of the county, he kept politics outside the house, seeing people at an office in the business district of Independence. I was never very conscious of him as a politician, during these early years, but I did know he was a highway builder. He often took me with him on inspection tours of the new roads, and sometimes on longer trips, when he dedicated or inspected an historic road, as part of his still continuing presidency of the National Old Trails Association.

Throughout these early Independence years, my father was haunted by a worry about me which he never mentioned—the possibility that I might be kidnapped. There was still plenty of leftover Klan animosity against Judge Truman in the area, and his insistence on running an honest administration made him enemies by the score in Kansas City. More important, kidnapping around this time was becoming a favorite form of extortion for the underworld. One day when I was in the first grade, an odd-looking character appeared at school and informed my teacher that he was delegated to take "Mary Truman, Judge Truman's daughter" home. I had been christened Mary Margaret, but I had long since abandoned Mary and my teacher, Mrs. Etzanhouser, knew it. Pretending to look for me, she stepped into another room

[77]

and phoned my mother. Dad sent police hustling to the scene. By this time the mysterious stranger had vanished. Thereafter my father or mother—or an available uncle or aunt—drove me to and from school.

Meanwhile, events political and economic were conspiring to deny Dad that impulsive wish he had made, to retire to the simplicities of running a filling station. In his election victory in 1930 he had had the intense satisfaction of running far ahead of the Democratic ticket in general, including his old Rabbit enemy, "Uncle Joe" Shannon, who was elected to the House of Representatives that year. Dad had done more than build a fine set of roads for Jackson County. He had been elected president of the Greater Kansas City Planning Association and in that role proposed—again about thirty years ahead of his time—a metropolitan approach to the planning of the Kansas City area, which would have ignored state boundaries and county lines and included two other Missouri counties and three counties across the river in Kansas.

My father has always been an ardent supporter of urban and metropolitan planning. One day, reminiscing about his experiences in Jackson County, he said, "We haven't done enough planning. There isn't a city in the United States that was properly planned to begin with. I know of only one whose streets were laid out in anticipation of the automobile and that is Salt Lake City. The old man that laid out that city really had vision—in more ways than one."

He was talking about Brigham Young, whom he has always admired.

"I was a great admirer of old D. H. Burnham, who organized the Chicago regional planning," Dad continued, "and he had a motto over his mantel, 'Make No Little Plans.' You can always amend a big plan, but you never can expand a little one. I don't believe in little plans. I believe in plans big enough to meet a situation which we can't possibly foresee now. Back in 1900, we had about 75 million people. In the 1930s we had about 125 million people. It is our business to at least anticipate a population of 300 million, maybe in the next hundred or hundred and fifty years. Maybe it won't take that long."

To drive this point home, Dad told the story of an engineer

who submitted a report to the Appropriations Committee of the United States Senate in the middle of the nineteenth century. "It stated that if a bridge could be built in St. Louis over the Mississippi River, St. Louis now being a thriving village of 300, it was absolutely certain that in fifty years St. Louis would have at least 1,500 people. Well, they built that bridge and St. Louis has got a million people in it. The engineer didn't quite have his sights high enough. You can't get them too high."

Judge Truman's star quality soon had local newspapers suggesting him as gubernatorial timber. The Democrats had lost the governorship race in the Republican landslide of 1928. The Independence *Examiner* and another local paper, the Blue Valley *Intercity News,* both reported growing interest in Truman for governor. The Odessa *Democrat,* in adjoining Lafayette County, made similar remarks. On November 21, 1930, the *Democrat* ran a front page, two column story headlined: TRUMAN COULD BE NEXT GOVERNOR, JACKSON COUNTY JUDGE WOULD BE AN IDEAL DEMOCRATIC CANDIDATE. Even the Kansas City *Star* was still saying nice things about him. "Efficient, unselfish public service is not so common that it shouldn't be dispensed with merely for partisan reasons," the *Star* said, announcing its support of my father for reelection in 1930.

In the spring of 1931 a Truman-for-Governor Club was formed. The men behind it were several National Guard friends such as James E. Ruffin, a young Springfield lawyer who organized support in southwest Missouri. Another enthusiast was my father's cousin, Colonel Ralph Truman. At a Springfield meeting in early May, 1931, fifty-two Democrats from fifteen counties of southwest Missouri endorsed Dad and organized a Truman-for-Governor Club in their region. Ruffin proudly assured potential members that the club included "some of the oldest and most substantial Democratic leaders in southwest and south central Missouri." Alas, the club was doomed from the start.

Perhaps because Tom Pendergast had inherited the political organization from his older brother, Jim, the Big Boss had a penchant for backing older men, such as Senator James Reed, the reactionary who had led the Democratic opposition to Woodrow Wilson and the League of Nations. His unsuccessful gubernatorial nominee in 1928, Francis M. Wilson, was sixty-four and in poor health, yet Pendergast showed strong signs of reendorsing him in 1932. My father appealed to the many Democrats who felt that a younger man, capable of an energetic campaign, was vital for victory.

The Truman-for-governor boom picked up momentum in the spring of 1931. The Kansas City *Star* ran a profile of Dad in a Sunday issue and plans were made for a major rally in Houston, county seat of Texas County in the southern Ozarks. The commander of the Missouri National Guard pledged his support and Dad began making out-of-county speeches in response to numerous invitations. The boom continued, even after Tom Pendergast, on the eve of departing for Europe, declared that the organization would back Wilson once more. My father spoke at the meeting in Texas County and made, in the opinion of a Springfield *Press* reporter, "an exceptionally favorable impression" upon his audience. By this time Dad had mastered a relaxed, down-home style in his extemporaneous speeches. Even more important, perhaps, he kept his speeches short—never more than twenty minutes. This was a rarity in Missouri during those days.

The editor of another local paper, the Houston *Herald,* agreed with the Springfield *Press* about Judge Truman. He was obviously "a clean, conscientious businessman who would render unto the people a real business administration if chosen Governor." Optimism soared in the Truman-for-Governor Club. "If you can get Wilson out of the way," Ruffin wrote to my father, "I think you can win the nomination with very little difficulty."

But Wilson declined to get out of the way. In spite of the very precarious condition of his health, he sensed that 1932 was a Democratic year, and coolly refused to abandon his candidacy. With Tom Pendergast remaining equally immovable, my father, with his instinct for party loyalty, quietly advised his supporters that he was withdrawing from the race. In December, 1931, Dad told Wilson that he could expect his "wholehearted support" for another try at the governorship.

Ironically, everything my father's supporters said about Wilson's health turned out to be tragically true. On October 12, 1932, at the height of the fall campaign, he died, and the Democratic organization had to find a new, last-minute nominee. Although our loyal Independence *Examiner* urged my father as a logical choice, Pendergast had to contend with the growing power of the Democratic nominee for the Senate, Bennett Clark, and a compromise, non-Jackson County candidate was chosen, Guy B. Park.

But the Truman-for-Governor Club had by no means wasted its time and money. It had awakened a great many Missourians outside Jackson County to my father's name and record. Even Francis Wilson recognized Dad's political potential. Not long after he heard my father was supporting him for governor, Mr. Wilson wrote to a friend: "Judge Truman is a mighty fine man. I hope someday to see him elevated to other offices of trust."

Dad had no time to fret over his gubernatorial aspirations. On May 26, 1931, the voters had approved another, even bigger bond issue, for $7,950,000. It was voted for more roads, a county hospital for the aged, and a new $4,000,000 county courthouse in Kansas City. This time, instead of scoffing at Judge Truman's improvement plans, Tom Pendergast used the county's road-building record as the main argument to persuade voters in Kansas City and the rural parts of the county to approve another $31,000,000 in building bonds for Kansas City as well. The proposal was put before the voters as "Kansas City's Ten Year Plan."

By now my father had county road building rather well systematized. But the courthouse was a new challenge. He decided to make it not only the best built, but the best designed public building in the United States. Climbing into his car, he drove 24,000 miles to confer with architects and study county and municipal buildings from Canada to Louisiana. As he drove, he saw grim evidence of the deepening economic depression spreading like a stain across the land.

In Shreveport, Louisiana, he found a courthouse which satisfied him, designed by Edward F. Neild. Dad hired Mr. Neild to design the Kansas City courthouse. (There was another courthouse in Independence which he also rebuilt at this time.) While Mr. Neild was designing his graceful, twenty-two-story building, Dad went off on another automobile journey. This time it was to hire Charles Keck, sculptor of the equestrian statue of Stonewall Jackson in Charlottesville, Virginia. Dad asked Mr. Keck to create an equestrian statue of his greatest hero, Andrew Jackson. Together he and the artist journeyed to Jackson's Tennessee home, the Hermitage, to get the exact measurements of Old Andy's dress uniform. The money for the statue, and an identical statue before the courthouse in Independence, was surplus cash which my father had saved from the bond issue, thanks to his tough economy.

He also demonstrated at this early stage in his career that, while he was a wholehearted backer of the union movement and the rights of the working man, he did not intend to let union leaders push him around. Early in 1934 the construction unions building the Jackson County courthouse in Kansas City went on strike. Dad sent them an ultimatum. Either they went back to work or he would replace every one of them with men from the relief rolls. "I have 3,000 applications for work on my desk," he said. The men went back to work.

During these early depression years my father had to cope with another political disappointment. Missouri, like many other states, redistricted after the census of 1930. My father journeyed to the state capital in Jefferson City and played a leading role in cajoling the legislators into creating a congressional district out of eastern Jackson County and seven eastern wards of Kansas City. His dream was to represent that district in Congress. With his solid backing in the rural part of the county, he was convinced that he could be elected easily. But Tom Pendergast decided that Jasper Bell, a Kansas City councilman whose vote had given the Goats control of the city in 1926, deserved the plum more than Judge Truman. Once more Mr. Pendergast had made it brutally clear that he had no burning affection for my father.

But things were happening in Missouri beyond the boundaries of Jackson County, and in the United States beyond the boundaries of Missouri, that severely threatened Boss Tom's political power. In Missouri Bennett Clark, son of one of the state's greatest congressmen, had won a very big victory in his bid for the Senate and was openly challenging Mr. Pendergast's political control of the state. In Washington, D.C., a new Democratic administration, headed by Franklin D. Roosevelt, was seeking and obtaining unprecedented powers to deal with the Great Depression that was stifling the country. Some naïve political historians have given Mr. Roosevelt credit for destroying Tom Pendergast and thus implied a basic hostility—or at least a difference in political morality—between my father and FDR.

Almost every biographer of my father and every historian of Kansas City and Missouri politics has maintained that Tom Pendergast hated Franklin D. Roosevelt and backed Jim Reed as his presidential candidate in the 1932 Democratic Convention. But insiders in the Jackson County organization knew that Boss Tom was backing Reed for much the same reason that he ran Francis Wilson for governor. Mr. Pendergast was enormously loyal to the friends of his youth, and Reed, vain, egotistic, and utterly isolated from what was happening politically and economically in the country, wanted to run for President and solicited Tom's support. Behind the scenes, however, Pendergast was assuring the Roosevelt forces that they had his wholehearted admiration. Boss Tom told Ike B. Dunlap of Kansas City, a former Roosevelt classmate who was working for FDR's nomination: "If Senator Reed decides to enter the campaign, I would be required to support him. Secondly, and unless something unforeseen occurs, I will be for Governor Roosevelt, whom I greatly admire."

When Jim Farley visited Kansas City on a delegate-hunting tour, state chairman Jim Aylward organized a magnificent luncheon at the Hotel Muehlebach which gave FDR's field general a chance to meet practically every influential Democrat in that part of Missouri. Even after Pendergast took over the state nominating convention and secured Missouri's delegation for Jim Reed, Ike B. Dunlap was writing to the Roosevelt forces, "Pendergast can be relied on." Late in May Tom Pendergast visited FDR in Albany and worked out an arrangement which guaranteed Mr. Roosevelt Missouri's support, any time he needed it, after the first ballot at the convention. Boss Tom followed this procedure to the letter. After the first ballot he released the Missouri delegation to Mr. Roosevelt little by little on succeeding ballots, so that Mr. Reed did not get his feelings hurt while the organization did not alienate the man whom Boss Tom regarded as a sure winner.

Roosevelt's gratitude was demonstrated almost immediately after the election. One of Boss Tom's closest supporters, although he was a Republican, was Conrad Mann, president of the Chamber of Commerce of Kansas City, and a key figure in persuading the citizens to vote into being the Pendergast-Truman $40,000,000 Ten Year Plan. In 1932 Mann was sent to prison for running an illegal lottery. Mr. Pendergast went to Washington personally to intercede for him, and Mann received a presidential pardon in a matter of weeks. When Secretary of Labor Frances Perkins appointed a Republican, Martin Lewis, as state director of federal reemployment, Boss Tom had him fired, and Judge Harry Truman was given the job. My father, with his usual strictness about money matters, refused to accept the $300-a-month salary but took the job, which required twice-a-week trips to the state capital in Jefferson City.

With the Roosevelt Administration in his corner, Boss Tom now turned his attention to Bennett Clark. This was in many ways a thornier problem. Senator Clark had trounced Mr. Pendergast's nominee in the Democratic primary in 1932. Now it was 1934, and the Democrats were facing another senatorial contest for the seat of Republican Roscoe Patterson. Bennett Clark, backed by the aggressive Democratic organization in St. Louis, made it clear that he intended to challenge the Kansas City Democrats again.

Traditionally, Missouri had one senator from the eastern or St. Louis part of the state and one from the western or Kansas City part. If the Clark–St. Louis Democrats could elect two U.S. senators in a row from their bailiwick, they would be able to say with considerable authority that they and not Tom Pendergast controlled Missouri. The 1934 election was thus crucial for the Jackson County Democratic organization. Control not only of a swelling tide of federal patronage but the Missouri State House was at stake. These facts should make it clear that Tom Pendergast did not, as some writers have claimed, nominate Harry S. Truman as an arrogant display of his political muscle. He was desperately in need of a winning candidate.

Two formidable opponents had already entered the race. John J. Cochran, a veteran congressman from St. Louis, announced he was a candidate and promptly received the backing of the city's mayor, Bernard F. Dickmann. On Cochran's heels came Congressman Jacob L. ("Tuck") Milligan, a much-decorated World War I veteran who represented a rural constituency around Richmond, Missouri. Cochran billed himself as the most popular congressman in Missouri. In 1932 when all the congressmen in the state had to run at large because the legislature's redistricting had been vetoed by the governor, he led the Democratic ticket.

Milligan called himself the rural candidate, although his home base was only fifty miles from Kansas City.

Meanwhile, my father had been stumping the state on a completely different mission. The governor of Missouri had appointed him chairman of a committee sponsoring a bond issue to rebuild or replace dilapidated state hospitals, prisons, and other public institutions. Dad had already visited thirty-five counties, and was in Warsaw, Missouri, when he got a phone call from Jim Pendergast, his old army buddy, who asked him to join him and state chairman Jim Aylward in the Bothwell Hotel for a totally unexpected political powwow.

As my father candidly admits, never had his optimism sunk so low as it had in the weeks before he received this call. His term as county judge was on the point of expiring, and by an agreed tradition two terms were a limit in this office. No one in the Jackson County Democratic organization, especially Tom Pendergast, was showing the slightest interest in his future. "I thought that retirement on a virtual pension in some minor county office was all that was in store for me," he said. When he walked into the hotel room in Warsaw and found out that he was being offered the nomination for senator, he was astounded. But he was also shrewd enough to see that the Jackson County Democratic organization needed him, just as much as he needed them. It was a repetition, on a statewide basis, of his first contact with the Pendergasts, when he ran for county judge. Before my father agreed to run, he made it clear that he wanted and expected wholehearted support from the organization. Knowing that Jim Pendergast was speaking for Boss Tom, Dad extracted a declaration that guaranteed him "98 percent of the Democratic support in Kansas City." Satisfied that he had a chance, at least, to win, he decided to make the race.

On May 14, in the Pickwick Hotel in Kansas City, he paced the floor, unable to sleep. He sat down at the desk and wrote another of those intimate letters to himself. "Tomorrow, today, rather, it is 4 A.M., I have to make the most momentous announcement of my life. I have come to the place where all men strive to be at my age." He was fifty years old. What interests me most about this memorandum is its frank implication that he was planning to reach for greatness, with all the strength that was in

[85]

him. He did not feel in the least unqualified to be a senator of the United States. "In reading the lives of great men, I found that the first victory they won was over themselves . . . self-discipline with all of them came first. I found that most of the really great ones never thought they were great. . . ." Dad seemed to sense that he was launching himself in a new direction and concluded, "Now I am a candidate for the United States Senate. If the Almighty God decides that I go there, I am going to pray, as King Solomon did, for wisdom to do the job."

Until this point in his political career my father had been relatively immune from partisan attacks. The Klan had flung mud at him, but not much of it had gotten into the newspapers. His record, his public reputation as discussed in the press, was spotless. Now he found himself being smeared by one of the oldest canards in politics, guilt by association. Bennett Clark solemnly declared: "The fear that lurks in everybody's mind is that if elected to the Senate, Harry would not be able to have any more independent control of his own vote than he had as presiding judge of the county court of Jackson County." One of Cochran's supporters called him a bellboy and someone else called him Pendergast's "office boy." Congressman Milligan said that Dad would get "callouses on his ears listening on the long-distance telephone to his boss" if he went to Washington.

Candidate Truman struck back at these accusations, hard. He pointed out that in 1932, when all the congressmen in Missouri had run at large, Mr. Cochran and Mr. Milligan had both appeared hat in hand to seek the endorsement of Tom Pendergast and the Jackson County Democrats. Now they were alleging that Harry Truman, because he had that endorsement, was de facto corrupt. Milligan brazenly denied that he had sought Pendergast's support and attempted to portray Cochran and Truman as machine candidates. Bennett Clark joined him with a cry that Cochran backers were "beating down the ears of St. Louis employees to keep them in line for their candidate."

It was the hottest July in Missouri's history. The temperature soared above 100 degrees on twenty-one days. But Dad operated at his usual killing pace. He drove through sixty of the state's largest counties, making from six to sixteen speeches a day. Not even a collision that left him with two broken ribs and a badly bruised forehead slowed him down.

[86]

Toward the end of July, just at the climax of the campaign, Dad's foes tried one final dirty trick. The bank which owned one of the notes he had signed when he went into bankruptcy—it had come into their hands at bargain rates, when the previous bank that had owned it collapsed—procured a judgment against him in the Circuit Court for the full amount, plus interest—$8,944. A newspaper clipping from the Kansas City *Star* for July 24, 1934, tells the story the way Dad would want it told—the facts and nothing but the facts:

> Judge Truman was asked about the judgments while he rested here Sunday at Hotel Claridge from the rigors of his campaign. He was shirtless and trying to keep cool under an electric fan when the writer visited him in his room. As the subject was broached, the Senatorial candidate said in a soft voice, "I had been expecting this to be brought up during the campaign but I have nothing to conceal about it and shall be glad to discuss it with you."
>
> He went on to tell the whole sad story of his bankruptcy, and then explained his many efforts to settle this particular claim. "I turned over to the Security State Bank the deed to 160 acres of land I own near Olaph in Johnson County, Kansas," he said, "and felt that I had satisfied this claim. However, after suit was brought against me on the note, I offered to settle for $1,000 but my offer was refused and I have resisted the payment of any more than that and will continue to do so."

None of my father's political enemies seemed to perceive the potential boomerang effect of this smear tactic. The man who had expended some $14,000,000 of public moneys on Jackson County roads and buildings and still did not have the money to pay an $8,944 debt was obviously honest. It was common knowledge that several presiding judges had left the court with half a million dollars in their pockets.

Like all Truman campaigns, this primary fight went steaming to a climax with victory in doubt. Nobody was betting more than even money on Truman, and the St. Louis Democratic machine was confidently predicting a landslide for Cochran. Only Tuck Milligan's fate seemed determined. He was limping far behind, and finished, as predicted, a poor third. "In the whole of Missouri history there have been few such spirited contests within a party," declared the Kansas City *Times*.

On August 9 in St. Louis it was 104 degrees in the shade, yet voters turned out as they had never done before in a Senate primary in Missouri. Cochran rolled up 104,265 votes, while Dad received a mere 3,742. Yet the St. Louis papers, when they fulminated against bossism and the machine vote, always flung their vitriol at Tom Pendergast in Kansas City!

The Jackson County Democrats had a riposte to that mountain of St. Louis votes for Cochran. They reported 137,529 votes for Truman and 1,525 for Cochran. Although my father had a slight lead in this battle of the city machines, it is obvious now that the real decision was made by Missouri's rural voters. Outside St. Louis, Cochran garnered about 130,000 votes; my father collected 135,000. He had won his real victory out there, on the parched, dusty back roads and sunbaked steps of county courthouses where he was greeted as an old friend by local judges and clerks. He had struck hard at the failure of both Cochran and Milligan to support the best interests of farmers in bankruptcy legislation before Congress. Missouri's farmers had listened and found him one of their own. As Richard Harkness, the United Press correspondent in Missouri, said, Truman had defeated Cochran and Milligan "in the creek forks and grass roots."

But Kansas City had beaten St. Louis, and the St. Louis *Post-Dispatch,* one of the nation's most prestigious papers, seethed with dubious moral indignation. The editors called the election a demonstration of "the power of machine politics" and went on to declare, "County Judge Truman is the nominee of the Democratic Party for the United States Senate because Tom Pendergast willed it so." This was not an accurate statement of the facts, but the label of a boss-ruled senator stuck to Dad's name for the rest of the decade. A few years later the *Post-Dispatch* embellished this theory by quoting Tom Pendergast as purportedly saying that he had sent his office boy to the Senate, to demonstrate his political power. If Tom Pendergast ever said such a thing, it only proves that megalomania among other things distressed his later years.

Happily for me, I remained unaware of these attacks on my father's reputation. I was leading the normal life of an energetic ten-year-old, preoccupied with school and games and numerous friends. Our big old house on North Delaware Street was perfect for all sorts of lively activities, from the publication of a neighborhood newspaper, the Henhouse Hicks Secret Six, to my first theatrical venture, a play written by my friend Betty Ogden, about a Mexican bandit called "The Clever One." When Dad was elected to the Senate—he beat his Republican opponent with almost ridiculous ease—I was told that we were going to move to Washington, D.C. I was appalled. For the next two days, every time Betty and I saw each other, we burst into tears, wailing dramatically that we would never meet again. Mother and Dad couldn't make up their minds whether to laugh at me or scold me.

But on December 27, 1934, only a week or so before we departed for Washington, I decided perhaps it was worthwhile to have a politician for a father. This was the day that Jackson County Democrats gathered to dedicate the new courthouse. I led a procession to the shrouded statue of Andrew Jackson and pulled the string which unveiled it. It was my first public appearance with a role to play—even if it didn't have any lines. I decided I liked it.

Less than a week later, I sat in the gallery of the United States Senate in Washington, D.C., and watched my father, barely recognizable to me in a morning coat and striped pants, walk down the center aisle to the dais to take his oath of office. He was escorted by Senator Bennett Clark. Although I didn't really understand what was happening, and I was still morose about the prospect of attending a strange school in a strange city, I was able to perceive that my father—and my mother and I—were starting a new life.

[CHAPTER]

Five

WHEN MY FATHER REMINISCES about his Senate days, he always chuckles over the advice he got from an old judge who had worked with him on the County Court. The judge had once worked for a Mississippi senator in Washington. "Harry," he said, "don't you go to the Senate with an inferiority complex. You'll sit there about six months, and wonder how you got there. But after that you'll wonder how the rest of them got there."

The day after Dad was sworn in, the Democratic whip, Senator J. Hamilton Lewis of Illinois, "a very kindly man," as my father describes him, sat down beside him and gave him exactly the same advice the old judge had given him back in Missouri.

Apartments were expensive in those days, and my father was appalled to find that some wealthy senators were paying as much as $1,500 a month in rent. This was out of the question for him. We had to live on his $10,000-a-year salary. He rented a four-room apartment for us in Tilden Gardens, just off Connecticut Avenue in the northwest part of Washington. It was a shock for all of us to find ourselves crowded into this tiny space, after living in fourteen big rooms on North Delaware Street. By way of consolation, Dad provided us with a piano, which he rented from a local music store. By now I had become fairly proficient on my baby grand, and I enjoyed many an evening of music on that spinet. Dad had little time to play the piano himself. As soon as he was sworn in, he launched a tremendous reading program. Night after night he came home with a bulging briefcase and stacks of books from the Congressional Library on legislation coming before the Senate.

In the Senate he had very little to say. It was a calculated silence, adopted at the advice of John Garner. The vice president took an almost instant liking to Dad. Texans and Missourians have always felt a strong kinship. They play a similar role on the national scene, balanced between Southern and Western loyalties.

There was another good reason for my father's silence during those first months. Democratic senators were hardly a novelty. With the Republican party in disarray, twelve other Democrats had been sworn in with him on that January day. A new tier of seats along the back wall had to be constructed to fit them into the Democratic side of the chamber. With such a surplus of political strength, there was not much interest from the White House.

But my father did not, as some biographers have claimed, spend five months trying to wangle an interview with Mr. Roosevelt. The White House records show that he visited the President in February, 1935, about a month after he arrived in Washington. Dad ruefully recalls that he did not handle the interview very well. "I was practically tongue-tied," he says. He puzzled over this reaction for a long time—and he finally decided it was caused not by awe of Mr. Roosevelt, personally, but of the presidency, and the tremendous role it played in the American republic. "I was before the greatest office in the world," he says. When Dad became President, he noticed that more than a few senators and congressmen were equally tongue-tied when they came to see him. He understood what they were feeling and made an extra effort to put them at their ease.

The most painful part of Senator Truman's freshman year in the Senate was the contempt that various Washington correspondents showered on him, because of his relationship with Tom Pendergast. My father resented the notion that he was Boss Tom's mouthpiece in Congress. He was perfectly willing to admit that Mr. Pendergast sent him telegrams occasionally, but as he told a reporter from the Kansas City *Star,* "I don't follow his advice on legislation. I vote the way I believe Missourians as a whole want me to vote."

He soon proved that he meant what he said. One of the major tests of power in the nation was the Senate vote on the Public

Utility Holding Company Act. These vast and complex financial structures had enabled the Wall Street bankers and a handful of other tycoons, such as Samuel Insull, to dominate a major segment of American business during the 1920s, with disastrous results. The act was aimed at limiting these giants to manageable size, and subjecting them to a reasonable amount of federal regulation, in the interests of all the people. In Kansas City, only one newspaper regularly supported Democrats. This was the *Journal-Post,* which was controlled by Henry L. Dougherty, president of the Cities Service Company in Kansas City, the area's main public utility. The *Journal-Post* editorialized against the bill, and so, of course, did the Kansas City *Star.* Tom Pendergast was equally opposed to it. Not long before, when 11,000 citizens had petitioned to create a municipally owned gas company in Kansas City, Mr. Pendergast's city clerk had thrown out 4,900 of the 11,000 signatures and nullified the petition.

Knowing all this, my father still made it clear that he was voting for the bill. Mr. Dougherty and his cohorts switched to another kind of pressure. In a single day 2,000 telegrams and letters poured into Dad's Senate office. Again he stood firm, and when the bill came up in the Senate, he voted for it. The *Journal-Post* flayed him alive in a two-column front-page article. "Harry S. Truman . . . became United States Senator from Missouri by default, so to speak, getting the Democratic nomination in 1934 because there were no other takers." The editorial writer went on to call him a "tool" of the Roosevelt Administration. They couldn't call him a Pendergast tool, so they called him a Roosevelt tool! Four months before this diatribe was published, this same paper had been calling him one of the best senators from Missouri in over a generation. It is easy to see why he soon became cynical about newspaper criticism.

At the same time, he never blamed the newspapermen who wrote these articles—with the exception of columnists who controlled their own material. Charlie Ross, the bright boy of his high school class, was a rising star at the *Post-Dispatch,* Dad's most vituperative foe, during these years, but my father never allowed this fact to trouble their friendship. He reserved his often ferocious but always private comments for the publishers who set editorial policy and ordered reporters to make the facts fit this policy.

In the case of the *Journal-Post* attack, Dad knew the man who had written the devastating front-page editorial. A few months later he was fired by the paper in an economy wave and could not find work anywhere. Bill Helm, the *Journal-Post's* Washington reporter, who wrote a charming though frequently inaccurate book about Dad, told of having a conversation with Senator Truman about this unfortunate fellow.

"What became of him?" Mr. Helm asked.

"Oh, he has a little job with the County," Dad said, meaning Jackson County.

"A little job with the County?" said Mr. Helm incredulously. "Did you, by any chance get him that job?"

"No, I can't say I did," Dad replied, refusing to take the credit. "All I did was recommend him for it."

Gradually, over the course of the next two years, my father achieved membership in that exclusive inner circle of the Senate, known as "the Club." It is an invisible hierarchy, unknown to most of the voters. Membership is not based upon anything tangible or definable. It requires integrity, of course, but a good personality and an appetite for hard work off the floor of the Senate, in the committee rooms where the real work of government is done—these are far more vital requisites.

One of his first signs of acceptance came when he was solemnly invited to join the "Lowell B. Mason Chowder, Marching and Baseball Club." An attorney for one of the owners of the Washington Senators, Mason had the best box in the municipal stadium and he passed out tickets freely to both Republicans (he was one) and Democrats. Burton K. Wheeler of Montana, Arthur Vandenberg of Michigan, Alben Barkley of Kentucky, and Speaker of the House Sam Rayburn of Texas were among the members. "Membership was controlled entirely by the man's personality, whether or not he was well liked by his colleagues," Lowell Mason said. "It was a very interesting thing that many of the senior senators never got on the invitation list."

On opening day, the journey to the baseball game always began with a luncheon in Arthur Vandenberg's private dining room. As Mason later told it, a few days before this event, in 1935 both Alben Barkley and Sam Rayburn spoke to him about Dad. "Lowell," Mr. Sam said, "we want you to put a new senator on the list because we think he's a comer and we like him per-

[93]

sonally; he's a fellow by the name of Truman, newly elected senator from Missouri. . . ."

My mother is the baseball fan in our family. How she complained when she found out my father was getting one of the best seats in the park! But it should be obvious that baseball was only a minor consideration in Lowell Mason's club. For years my father never missed one of his conclaves. In fact Mr. Mason loves to tell the story of another demonstration of that dominant Truman trait, loyalty. One year Mr. Mason had carefully worked out all arrangements for a luncheon and the trip to the game in cars borrowed from the president of the Senate and the Speaker of the House. Then, to his dismay, he got phone calls from four of his most prominent senators. "Lowell," they said, "we're sorry, but the British ambassador has the Archbishop of Canterbury visiting him and they're going to the game and they would like to have us sit in their box."

In despair at seeing his luncheon fall apart, Mason began calling his other guests. My father was first on his list. "Oh, yes, Lowell," he said, "I was invited by the British ambassador and the Archbishop of Canterbury to eat lunch and sit in their box, and I told them I had already accepted an invitation from you."

My father and Lowell Mason used to play an amusing game, based on their mutual knowledge of Charles Dickens's *Pickwick Papers.* "I remember one day we were standing in the doorway of his office," Mason said, "and a fellow went by, and Mr. Truman turned to me and said, 'Lowell, there goes Alfred Jingle.' " For those who haven't gotten around to rereading the *Pickwick Papers,* Alfred Jingle was the wily villain of several incidents in the story, a man who got others involved in duels, was always trying to seduce wealthy heiresses, and wound up in Fleet Prison.

But this relaxed good humor came in the later years of my father's senatorial career. Even though on a personal level he made rapid progress with his fellow senators, politically he remained on the horns of a dilemma. When he voted with the Roosevelt Administration, the newspapers back home called him a White House tool. When he voted against the administration, the papers sneered that he had done so on the orders of Tom Pendergast, or worse (from my father's point of view) he had surrendered to Bennett Clark, who was building up a name for himself as an anti-Roosevelt Democrat with an eye on the 1940 presidential nomination. No one, it seems, was willing to give Harry Truman credit for voting his convictions.

But the record shows that he established his independence from Mr. Roosevelt, as thoroughly as he did from Tom Pendergast. Throughout the first eighteen months of his term, one of the major political brawls revolved around the veterans bonus. In his campaign for the Senate, my father had repeatedly said he favored a bonus, while his two opponents had denounced the idea as fiscally irresponsible. The Roosevelt Administration took the same position. Yet in vote after vote Dad never wavered in his support of a bonus, because he knew the desperate need for one throughout the nation, and he believed that men who had risked their lives for their country deserved special consideration. He finally voted to override the President's veto of the bill. The St. Louis *Post-Dispatch,* unable to indict him for subservience either to Roosevelt or Pendergast on this issue, decided it proved his "lack of stature."

There were times when my father resented this endless pressure and browbeating. "A Congressman, as you know, is elected by the people," he wrote to one friend, "and most of the people who come to Congress have an honest and conscientious intent to do what is best for the country, but they are pulled and hauled so much of the time that they get to the point where they would just as soon let the country be damned as not." He especially resented the idea that a senator should represent only the wishes of his constituents. He declined to become anybody's Charlie McCarthy. When, later in his senatorial career, the *Post-Dispatch* printed a letter to the editor from a reader who denounced Dad for failing to represent the wishes of the people who elected him in Missouri, he angrily replied, "I voted for what I thought was the welfare of the country and was not governed by threats, pleas or political considerations."

My father was even tougher on this subject with labor leader Otto Maschoff of the United Electrical Radio and Machine Workers of America.

> It doesn't make any difference to me whether you like the
> way I vote or not because I vote for what I think is right, re-

[95]

gardless of what anyone else thinks [he wrote Mr. Maschoff]. You people have a peculiar slant on a man's political career. No matter what he does, if he uses his head and does something you don't like then he is down and out as far as you are concerned. Well, as far as I'm concerned I am doing what I think is right and I don't care what anyone else thinks about it and I don't care whether they like it or not—I can take care of myself while I am doing it.

Another of my father's Senate problems was Bennett Clark. At first the White House gave most of the federal patronage in Missouri to him, in spite of Senator Clark's often violent attacks on the New Deal. Wooing his enemies with gifts was one of Mr. Roosevelt's favorite tactics. My father never believed it was good politics and frequently said so. He thought it discouraged your friends and only made your enemies arrogant. It certainly worked that way with Dad and Senator Clark. Like many sons of famous fathers, Bennett Clark was an unstable, complex man. He felt compelled to seek the presidency, because his father, "Champ" Clark, had been deprived of it, in the 1912 Democratic Convention, by an unexpected surge to Woodrow Wilson. Poor Senator Clark simply lacked the stature for the job. But the desire for it made him an instinctive foe of the Roosevelt Administration.

At first Senator Clark regarded my father with contempt and made no effort to conceal it. But he was also intelligent enough to realize that he needed the help of the Jackson County Democrats, if he was to win reelection in 1938—an absolute necessity for his 1940 presidential hopes. So he began consulting Senator Truman on appointments, and they chose mutually agreeable men. When it came to picking the WPA director for the state of Missouri—probably the most important single federal appointment, from a political point of view—my father had a lot more than half to say. The job went to Matt Murray, a Jackson County Democrat. This meant that the Jackson County organization controlled the thousands of jobs that were handed out by the WPA across Missouri.

While Dad legislated and politicked, my mother and I struggled to adjust to our new way of life. I was enrolled at Gunston Hall, a local Washington girls school in the old Southern tradition. It was a nice school, but I was there only six months of

[96]

the year. At the end of June, we always packed up everything, abandoned our furnished apartment, and went back to Independence for the next six months. There I went to junior high school just a block from home. Then, on the first of January, we packed everything again, and moved to another rented apartment on Connecticut Avenue—I knew every block of Connecticut Avenue before Dad's senatorial career ended. Back I went to sedate, ladylike Gunston Hall.

Our trips to and from Independence were quite an ordeal. The government gave congressmen special boxes to pack the linens, clothes, and other personal effects that they transported back and forth each year. I can still see my father toiling over these boxes in the Washington heat in June or early July. He prided himself on being an expert packer, and he was. My mother and I were hopeless in this department, and still are. Dad can get more things into a box or trunk than anyone I've ever seen.

Among the things he packed each year were the clothes for my Raggedy Ann doll. I was not a great one for dolls. Raggedy Ann was the only one I ever cared for. She had a rather large wardrobe, which my aunts, all experts with the needle, frequently supplemented. One day I was standing around our hot Washington apartment watching Dad toil over a box that was about full. With a sigh, he took the first of Raggedy Ann's wardrobe off her formidable pile and began folding it. Suddenly he looked up at me. I was no longer ten years old. This was '38 or '39, and I was fourteen or fifteen. A Mamma-Truman-like glint came into his eyes. "In the first place," he said, "you're pretty old to be carrying a doll back and forth. In the second place, if you insist on doing it, you're certainly old enough to pack for her." With that, he strolled into the kitchen for some iced tea and left me to finish packing that box. Raggedy Ann soon stopped making the trip from Independence to Washington.

On this semiannual commute, we always went by car. My father did most of the driving, and this always made for interesting family discussions. My mother was convinced that he drove too fast, and she was absolutely right. I don't think Mother ever really saw any of the scenery between Missouri and the District of Columbia. She always had at least one eye on the speedometer.

Our route usually took us through Hagerstown, Maryland, and

over the mountains to Cumberland. In 1938 we came to grief in Hagerstown, and another chapter in the history of Dad's unbreakable, unloseable glasses was written. It was a Sunday morning, and a stop sign at a key intersection was obscured by a parked car. A man in another car plowed into us as we went through the intersection. Our car was completely wrecked. It was almost a miracle that we escaped alive. Dad had a cut on his forehead, and Mother had a badly wrenched neck. Sitting in the back, I escaped with nothing more than a bad fright.

As I was pulled out of the car window, I saw Dad's glasses on the floor, surrounded by upended suitcases—intact. He had flung them over his shoulder at the moment of impact.

First the police were inclined to give the Trumans a very hard time for missing the stop sign. But Dad pointed out that the stop sign was obscured by the parked car. Later we heard that the man who hit us had had two other accidents that month. Dad called his secretary, Vic Messall, and he got dressed in record time and drove down to pick us up. We never did go back for the car. I guess it was towed to the nearest junk heap.

Back in Missouri during those mid-thirties years, my father combined politicking with a continued interest in the army reserve. Almost every summer he spent two weeks on active duty. By this time he was a colonel in command of a regiment. He and his friends had served without pay all through the years since World War I. Along with his enthusiasm for military lore, Dad found the army an invaluable way to maintain friendships with men from many parts of Missouri. Typical of these was an affable St. Louis banker, John Snyder. Two other close friends were Harry Vaughan and Eddie McKim. They were a pair of big easygoing jokers, constantly kidding each other, and Dad.

Eddie McKim was always accusing Dad of owing him $36. He had been a sergeant in Dad's battery. While Dad was away for two weeks at a special artillery school, a replacement captain had busted Mr. McKim to buck private. When Dad returned, Eddie asked for his stripes—or at the very least a promotion to private first class. Dad shook his head. "I was thinking of busting you myself, McKim," he said.

Eddie insisted this was cruel and unnecessary punishment, and he carefully counted each month that he would have earned an extra two dollars as a first class private and insisted that, morally, Dad owed him the money. The accusation, of course, gave Dad an excuse to call him the laziest, most insubordinate soldier in the history of the U.S. Army.

This was a reputation that Eddie never denied. In fact, he was proud of it (although in civilian life he was a demon worker, and rose to head one of the nation's biggest insurance companies). One day at summer camp early in the decade—probably 1930— Eddie was serving as Harry Vaughan's aide. As an ex-enlisted man, he had only recently achieved captain's rank in the reserve. Colonel Vaughan asked him to carry a chair up on a porch. Eddie obeyed, but he muttered that his record was ruined. It was the first work he had done in their entire two-week training tour.

Several years later Eddie and Dad came out to St. Louis by train. Dad wired John Snyder and Harry Vaughan to meet them for an impromptu reunion. They cheerfully agreed and were waiting when the train pulled into the station. Onto the platform stepped a very worried looking senator, and a very very blotto friend— McKim. Dad seemed terribly upset. What would the St. Louis papers say, if they saw their favorite target, Senator Truman, escorted by a drunk? Quickly Harry Vaughan took charge. He sent Dad and John Snyder in one direction and hustled the reeling McKim in the other direction.

Unfortunately, there was only one cab at the taxi stand, and they had to share it. But Colonel Vaughan shouldered McKim through the lobby of the Missouri Athletic Club, where he and Dad were staying, and into the elevator while Dad registered at the desk. On the sixth floor, Eddie fell out of the elevator on his face, and poor Colonel Vaughan had to hoist him onto his back and lug him the rest of the way down the long hall to the room. It was a hot day, and by the time they reached the room, Colonel Vaughan was streaming perspiration. He flung Eddie on the bed and called him a drunken so-and-so.

A moment later Dad and Mr. Snyder walked into the room. Eddie bounced to his feet and took cover behind the couch, a big grin on his face. "You would make me carry that chair up on that porch and spoil my record," he said, to the openmouthed Harry Vaughan.

Eddie and Dad had cooked up the gag on the train, and it had worked beyond their wildest expectations.

This fondness for a good laugh was a universal trait in Dad's good friends. I never found one who was not to some degree a joker. But few had Eddie McKim's talent in this department. Eddie never quit. When Dad introduced him to President Roosevelt at a White House reception, Eddie proceeded to tell FDR in a very serious tone that he ought to do something about the $36 Senator Truman owed him. Naturally the President looked baffled. When Eddie explained, FDR threw back his head and laughed heartily.

Dad's favorite Eddie McKim story recalled the day that his artillery outfit was being reviewed by the commanding general at Fort Riley. Eddie was riding the lead horse of the team that was pulling one of the field pieces, en route to performing an intricate maneuver. Colonel Truman sat on horseback beside the general, making small talk. "Captain McKim was in my outfit during the war," he began. At this point something went wrong with either Eddie or the lead horse, and in a twinkling the gun, the horses, and Eddie were wrapped in an incredible tangle around a tree. The disaster coincided precisely with the end of Dad's remark, and without even drawing a breath, or breaking the rhythm of his sentence, Colonel Truman added, "and he never was any damn good then either!"

This very informal Missouri style was something all the Trumans had to shed when in Washington, D.C. Although there was plenty of room for jokes behind the scenes, on stage a senator had to be very dignified. This was equally true of his wife and daughter. Washington was a small town, or at best a small city, in those days. It had a sedate Southern air, which included a great deal of formality. I can remember driving with mother through the White House gates (without anyone even stopping us!) and up to the front entrance. A butler came out carrying a silver tray, and I reached through the car window, and gravely laid our calling cards on the tray. The butler gave us a solemn little nod, and we drove away. Protocol was still *very* important in pre-World War II Washington. Senators' wives had to be "at home" on Thursday afternoons to pour tea for anyone who cared to visit. Congressmen's wives were at home on another afternoon, and Cabinet wives had their day. Of course, the ladies got together and negotiated mutual assistance pacts, which eliminated the nightmarish possibility of everyone descending at the same time on one hapless woman.

On the afternoons when mother was "at home" or visiting someone else who was wielding the teapot, I rode the streetcar to the Senate Office Building and reported to Dad or his stenographer, Millie Dryden. For the next two or three hours, I was on my own, wandering the corridors or perching in the Senate gallery to watch the action—or lack of it—on the floor. Occasionally Dad introduced me to senators and other politicians who visited his office. Two that stand out in my mind are Vice President Garner and Huey Long.

My father was enormously proud of his friendship with Mr. Garner. It was justifiable pride. Mr. Garner did not make friends casually. Away from the Senate he was practically a recluse, shunning invitations to all parties. Moreover, as a conservative Democrat, he did not agree with many of Senator Truman's New Deal votes in the Senate. I sensed Dad's pride and did my best to be polite to Mr. Garner. He was a small taciturn man, who did not smile easily. Much later I realized that he was immensely powerful behind the scenes in the Senate. He took his vice president's job seriously and seldom left Washington while Congress was in session. But his real work was done not while presiding over the Senate but in his "doghouse" where he huddled with influential senators over legislation and committee memberships. There were ritual pauses to "strike a blow for liberty" with some of the best bourbon served in Washington. Mr. Garner was an artist at soothing ruffled tempers and repairing damaged egos, particularly among Southern and Western Democrats who had no great love for Franklin Roosevelt.

With Huey Long, on the other hand, I could see an opposite emotion in my father's eyes: dislike. This character from Louisiana was upsetting both the Senate and the country in 1935. He dealt in personalities and personal insults on the floor of the Senate in a style that anticipated Senator Joe McCarthy of Wisconsin. He was a raucous critic of the New Deal, offering as a substitute his "Share the Wealth" plan, which was pie in the sky, made with nonexistent apples. All twelve of Dad's fellow freshman senators

[101]

—they called themselves "the Young Turks" because they were the most ardent New Dealers in the Senate—loathed Senator Long and issued a statement denouncing him. I was very cool to Mr. Long—not that it made any difference to him, I am sure. But I must confess, from the viewpoint of an eleven-year-old, I enjoyed his antics on the Senate floor. He added interest to what was usually a rather boring show.

I will never forget a little drama, hitherto neglected by Mr. Long's biographers, I believe, that I saw enacted in the Senate chamber one day. Mr. Long's chair was just a few feet away from swinging doors to the right of the vice president's chair. Huey arose and was obviously about to launch one of his interminable harangues. Senator Joe Robinson of Arkansas, the tall distinguished Democratic majority leader, sprang to his feet and announced, in that remarkably courteous language which almost always prevails when senators address each other, that if the honorable senator from Louisiana said another word, he was going to wipe up the floor with him. My head swiveled from Huey to Robinson, when the senator from Arkansas erupted. Now my head swiveled back to Senator Long. There was no one there. Only the doors swinging in the breeze of his hasty departure.

My father and Huey Long were almost total opposites in their approach to the Senate. Mr. Long spent his time looking for headlines. He never devoted an hour to constructing legislation. This is the real work of the Senate, and it was—and probably still is—done by thirty or forty senators who toiled wearisome hours on the various committees. These workers were the senators whom Dad instinctively joined. His experience running a county government in Missouri gave him an insight into the practical side of legislation. This, plus his appetite for hard work, made him a first-class legislator. Older senators, such as Burton K. Wheeler of Montana, were delighted to see a younger man willing and eager to tackle the many problems the Senate was attempting to solve. To my father's delight, he was put on the Appropriations Committee and the Interstate Commerce Committee, both fields where he had had considerable local experience.

Interstate Commerce was largely involved with transportation, and Dad's intensive study of the Kansas City region's transportation problems, as presiding judge of the Jackson County Court, was an ideal preparation for tackling the transportation woes of the nation as a whole. He was already keenly aware that there was something fatally wrong with the backbone of our national transportation system—the railroads. Before he became senator, the Missouri Pacific, one of the great railroads of the nation, had gone into bankruptcy.

But in the order of urgency, Dad and his fellow committee members decided that the nation's airlines needed the most help. Dad took charge of a subcommittee that began holding hearings on the mess in that department.

As both an ex-soldier and a civilian, my father saw the vital importance of the airplane to the country's future. It was one more example of his ability to peer into the future, and begin planning for it. His hearings brought out the appalling fact that $120,000,000 in private capital had been invested in air transport, and $60,000,000 lost. Addressing the Senate, on July 2, 1937, Senator Truman told them:

> From its very inception air transportation has been a waif in the field of commerce. It has been battered about from pillar to post and it is high time for it to be recognized as a public necessity and given a permanent place in the national transportation system.
>
> England, France, Germany, Russia, all realize what air transport means to national defense. Only poor old Uncle Sam is muddling with civilian air transport. This bill will stop the muddling and inaugurate a real policy—a policy that will make commercial aviation a second line of defense.

Unfortunately, his bill was not passed immediately. It took another year of battling over details in the Senate. One of the big arguments brought on the first—but not the last—of Dad's clashes with strong-willed Senator Pat McCarran of Nevada. My father wanted to create a Civil Aeronautics Authority Board on which the President would have the right to appoint or remove members at his pleasure. McCarran wanted the President's powers limited, a typical senatorial attitude. He insisted that a commissioner could only be dismissed for inefficiency, neglect of duty, or malfeasance in office. Even then, my father did not believe in tying the President's hands unnecessarily. Dad won the argument.

[103]

When the law was finally passed in June, 1938, Arthur Krock praised it lavishly in *The New York Times* as "the product of unremitting and intelligent toil by legislators of ability and character intent upon working out difficult national problems." He singled out my father's efforts as especially praiseworthy, noting his hundreds of hours of listening to witnesses from dozens of different interested groups, from the Reconstruction Finance Corporation to the Airline Pilots Association. Only a handful of experts also appreciated the exquisite care with which Dad had drafted the bill, using terminology already defined by the Supreme Court in its interpretations of the Interstate Commerce Act. An immense amount of time-consuming litigation was thus saved, in advance. Some members of the airline industry were almost stunned by the high quality of the legislation. Edgar Gorrell, president of the Air Transport Association, said: ". . . Now and then democracy takes a great stride forward to catch up with the times."

While my father was writing this law and defending it in the Senate, he was simultaneously conducting hearings on the chaotic state of the nation's railroads. President Roosevelt had called the railroads "the most serious problem of the administration," in 1937. The statistics of their catastrophic decline made this an understatement. In 1926 American railroads employed 1,779,000 men with a payroll of $2,946,000,000. By 1938, 840,000 of these men were out of work and a staggering 10,000 miles of track had been abandoned, with destructive effects on business in uncounted small towns and medium-sized cities. As Dad tried to find out why a business that was handling 75 percent of the nation's traffic (in 1926) could now be tottering into bankruptcy, he became more and more convinced that the answer lay in the manipulations of a small group of greedy men, largely operating in and around Wall Street.

These were not conclusions based on preconceived radical theories. They were reached after endless hours of hearings, and even longer hours of struggling through immensely complex reports on railroads and the holding companies that owned them and played games with their stock. Scarcely a month went by without a new struggle with another group of recalcitrant railroad or investment bank executives. Some railroads tried to refuse Dad's committee access to their books. Others actually presented phony records, under the imprint of some of the nation's biggest accounting firms.

I still remember the grim pleasure my father expressed over a victory he won in an exchange with George O. May, senior partner of Price Waterhouse and Company. In certifying the books of the Missouri Pacific, Price Waterhouse had allowed the company to carry as assets a debt of $3,200,000. This gambit enabled the railroad's executives to misrepresent its financial condition to the public, when it was on the brink of receivership. Mr. May haughtily informed Dad that the assets statement was "misleading in effect but not misleading in intent." My father angrily declared it was misleading in both respects and reported the matter to the Interstate Commerce Commission. This body, whose word is law in railroad matters, immediately ordered the account transferred from special deposits on the assets side to "unadjusted debt."

"That is the way it ought to have been handled in the first place," Dad snapped.

"That is right," Mr. May replied.

It was my father's investigation of the Missouri Pacific that really enraged him and convinced him for all time that "the wrecking crew," as he called Wall Street's financiers, were a special interest group constantly ready to sacrifice the welfare of millions for the profits of a few. The Missouri Pacific was a huge railroad system with no less than seventy-nine subsidiaries under its control. In 1930 the Alleghany Corporation, a holding company formed by some Cleveland manipulators using money supplied by J. P. Morgan, acquired control of the entire eighty-company system. The holding company bosses then proceeded to loot the railroad. They declared dividends out of capital instead of earnings, fired thousands of workers to cut the payroll, reduced maintenance, and abandoned badly needed improvements in the road and equipment. In a few short years the Missouri Pacific was in bankruptcy.

Digging into this mess required considerable political courage for a senator from Missouri. To obtain permission to buy the Missouri Pacific, the Alleghany Corporation had twisted arms and cajoled Democrats and Republicans in the state legislature, as well as almost every other public official in Missouri. One state senator received $1,000 "covering services in the Alleghany-Missouri Pacific matter" which he was never able to satisfactorily explain.

Once more Senator Truman was deluged by telegrams and telephone calls from powerful politicians and businessmen in his home state, urging him to abandon the investigation or at least make it as superficial as possible. My father called Max Lowenthal, general counsel for the investigating committee, and said, "I don't want you to ease up on anything. You treat this investigation just as you do all the others." Not long afterward, he received an anonymous note, warning him that he would die on the Senate floor. Over the next several weeks, the Senate police had extra men on duty in the gallery because, from their analysis of the note, they feared that the would-be assassin would try to shoot Dad from there.

Max Lowenthal told a St. Louis *Post-Dispatch* reporter that he did not know a half dozen senators who could have resisted the kind of political pressure Dad withstood.

Lowenthal was a disciple of Louis D. Brandeis, the great liberal dissenter on the Supreme Court. To be invited to the Justice's apartment on California Street was regarded by many New Dealers in Washington during these days as a great honor. To be invited back was an even greater honor. My father was invited back again and again because, almost on sight, both men recognized they were spiritual brothers. Brandeis had denounced "the curse of bigness" and inveighed against the manipulation of American business to line the pockets of a few financiers. But simply sharing these beliefs was not enough to win a coveted membership in the Brandeis circle. You had to share his patience, skill, and determination to unravel the intricate frauds being perpetrated on the people by the Wall Street bankers. For hours at a time, while other politicians stood watching enviously, Justice Brandeis would talk with Dad about his committee's latest discoveries in railroad wrecking and looting.

Dad agreed wholeheartedly with Justice Brandeis's contention that a company's size should be limited by one man's capacity. Dad proved this point conclusively in his investigation of the Alleghany Corporation. Questioning the man who had bought it, George

A. Ball, my father was able to show that Mr. Ball did not even know the names of several major companies, employing thousands of workers, which he theoretically controlled.

Almost two and a half years after he came to the Senate, Dad was ready to make some major speeches. They were in a style that should have made those with good memories less surprised by his 1948 "give 'em hell" performance.

"Some of the country's greatest railroads have been deliberately looted by their financial agents," he said. Speaking of the Rock Island Railroad, he reminded his fellow senators:

> . . . The first railroad robbery was committed on the Rock Island back in 1873 just east of Council Bluffs, Iowa. The man who committed that robbery used a gun and a horse and got up early in the morning. He and his gang took a chance on being killed and eventually most were. That railroad robber's name was Jesse James. The same Jesse James held up the Missouri Pacific in 1876 and took the paltry sum of $17,000 from the express car. About thirty years after the Council Bluffs holdup, the Rock Island went through a looting by some gentlemen known as the tin plate millionaires. They used no guns, but they ruined the railroad and got away with $70,000,000 or more. They did it by means of holding companies. Senators can see what pikers Mr. James and his crowd were alongside of some real artists.

Dad bluntly accused the Alleghany Corporation of the same kind of railroad robbery.

Later that year, in another speech on the same topic, he inveighed against the curse of bigness and the impersonal financial racketeering it encouraged:

> I believe the country would be better off if we did not have 60 percent of the assets of all insurance companies concentrated in four companies. I believe that a thousand insurance companies with $4,000,000 each in assets would be just a thousand times better for the country than the Metropolitan Life with $4,000,000,000 in assets. The average human brain is not built to deal with such astronomical figures.

Above all he was worried by the erosion of the nation's moral sense, by the awe and brutality engendered by over-concentrated financial power.

One of the difficulties as I see it is that we worship money instead of honor [he said]. A billionaire in our estimation is much greater in the eyes of the people than the public servant who works for the public interest. It makes no difference if the billionaire rode to wealth on the sweat of little children and the blood of underpaid labor. . . .

Reading these forgotten words, perhaps readers can appreciate a little more the sincerity of the President who fought for his reelection in 1948 against a Congress that was trying to give the country back to the control of these same special interests.

At the same time, my father made it clear again and again, during the hearings and in his speeches, that he was not against all businessmen. He went out of his way to praise the courage of many of the executives of the operating railroads, who fought to maintain efficiency and quality while the financial blood was being sucked out of their companies. His answer to the abuses of the Wall Street manipulators was not government ownership, either. More than a few New Deal senators were inclined to see this as the only solution. But Dad insisted that more stringent regulation and severe restrictions on the size of the holding companies would correct most of the abuses.

My father also believed that the time had come for the big financiers on Wall Street to realize that they had better start thinking and acting in the public interest:

It is a pity that Wall Street with its ability to control all the wealth of the nation and to hire the best brains of the country has not produced some statesmen, some men who could see the dangers of bigness and of the concentration of the control of wealth. Instead of working to meet the situation, they are still employing the best law brains to serve greed and selfish interest.

He also sounded a note he was to repeat again and again in later years, in his struggle to attract talented men into the government: "The ordinary government mine-run bureaucratic lawyer is no more a match for the amiable gentlemen who represent the great railroads, insurance companies and Wall Street bankers than the ordinary lamb is a match for the butcher."

His distaste for the way the railroads were being run inclined him to side emphatically with railroad workers in their struggle against their employers. In 1938 the big operating companies asked for the right to cut wages by 15 percent. My father went before a fact-finding board that was conducting hearings and blasted the proposal. He told the board that, as a result of his investigations, he was convinced that the railroads were wasting approximately $667,000 a day: "Banker management should not be permitted to sacrifice railroad labor for their inability to control a situation of their own creation." For the first time, but not the last, union leaders awoke to Harry S. Truman's existence. While other senators opposed the wage cut, no one else could speak with Dad's authority on railroads and their mismanagement.

One amusing by-product of my father's growing fame as a corporate taskmaster was a public confusion between him and Thurman Arnold, the trust-busting assistant attorney general and author of several scathing books on corporate mores, most notably *The Folklore of Capitalism*. Thurman and Truman were similar enough to get even the Washington *Star* confused. The paper once ran a picture of Dad and identified him as Mr. Arnold. There was a constant intermingling of their mail. Since they shared a common philosophy, the two of them decided it was funny and became good friends.

Commenting on one mail mixup, Mr. Arnold wrote: "I can't figure out from the enclosed letter whether this guy thinks I am you or whether he thinks you are me. What is your opinion?"

Dad replied: "I guess he thinks I am you; at any rate, in this instance you are me, or vice versa. From time to time I receive letters addressed to you or to a 'combination' of us. . . . Frankly, I think the writers are giving me entirely too much credit. . . ."

While he was carving out his own niche as an investigator in the complicated world of business and finance, my father also participated vigorously in the turbulent political battles of the middle and late '30s. Most of the time he supported the Roosevelt Administration. Ironically, looking back on his reward for this loyalty in later years, he said:

> I was one of those in the Senate who was called a rubber-stamp senator. Do you know what a rubber-stamp congressman or senator is? He is a man who is elected on the platform of

the party, and who tries to carry out that platform in co-operation with the President of the United States—that's all he is.

These words were spoken by a President who valued every so-called rubber-stamp congressman he could find.

My father was never an unthinking rubber stamp. He supported the administration in perhaps the greatest political brawl of the decade—Franklin D. Roosevelt's attempt to alter the balance of the Supreme Court by obtaining the power to appoint additional justices. This was a battle that almost tore the Democratic party apart. Some of my father's best friends in the Senate were on the other side. Burton K. Wheeler was, in fact, the leader of the opposition, and Vice President Garner was a less vocal but perhaps more powerful opponent of the plan. Bennett Clark was another fierce foe of it. But Dad's investigation of big business had led him to conclude that the tycoons and financiers dominated not only state governments and federal regulatory commissions but the Supreme Court as well. He pointed out there was nothing sacred about a nine-man court. The number of justices had varied from five to ten throughout the nation's history. "The cry," he said, "is that the President wants to pack the Court. . . . I say the Court is packed now and has been for fifty years against progressive legislation."

My father never forgot the lessons he learned from that fight. It was a monumental example of how a President should *not* deal with Congress. Roosevelt had let the "blizzard of 1936"—his tremendous landslide victory—deceive him into thinking that he could get anything he wanted from Congress. With 75 Democrats and 17 Republicans in the Senate and the count in the House 334 to 89 in his favor, it would seem to have been a logical conclusion —for anyone who relied on mere statistics. But human beings are not statistics, and there were many Democratic senators who were already having severe doubts about the ultimate goals of the New Deal. Some of the Senate's greatest liberals, such as George W. Norris, denounced the President's Supreme Court plan with as much fervor as did the conservatives. From February to July the battle raged and only ended when the exhausted Senate majority leader, Joe Robinson, collapsed and died of a heart attack. More than anything else, this Senate revolt forged the alliance between conservative Democrats and Republicans that was to torment Dad and future Democratic Presidents.

Disaster threatened the Democratic program. On the long train ride down to Arkansas for Joe Robinson's funeral, the senators discussed only one topic—who would be the next majority leader? On this choice depended to a large extent the President's ability to lead Congress. From the viewpoint of long service to the party and to Mr. Roosevelt, the choice of most senators was Pat Harrison of Mississippi. Everyone knew that Mr. Roosevelt owed Senator Harrison a debt of gratitude for swinging the Mississippi delegation to him at a crucial moment at the 1932 convention. Jim Farley says that he told Mr. Roosevelt, "If it wasn't for Pat Harrison, you might not be President."

But Mr. Roosevelt feared that Senator Harrison, a Southern conservative, would not support the New Deal with sufficient enthusiasm. So the President swung the weight of his approval behind Alben Barkley of Kentucky. It immediately became obvious that it would be a very close vote. My father liked Mr. Harrison personally, and before Mr. Roosevelt had decided to attempt this unprecedented intervention in the affairs of the Senate, Dad had promised the genial Mississippi senator his vote. Jim Farley recalls the intense pressure that Mr. Roosevelt exerted to swing senators into line. His arm-twisting even extended to Mr. Farley. But he had given the senators his word that he would not intervene in the battle. He adamantly refused to yield to the President's plea to call various political bosses around the country and ask them to browbeat individual senators. "I have no doubt that calls were made, and my name used," Mr. Farley says. In fact, he recalls being visited by a distraught Senator William H. Dieterich of Illinois who told him that he had just received a phone call from Ed Kelly, the boss of Chicago, ordering him to vote for Barkley or forget about reelection. Mr. Farley urged Mr. Dieterich to defy Kelly, but he shook his head and switched his vote.

My father got a similar call from Tom Pendergast. Tom said that the White House had phoned him and asked him to order Senator Truman into the Barkley camp.

"I just can't do it, Tom, and I'll tell you why," Dad said. "I've given my word to Pat Harrison."

Mr. Pendergast assured Dad that he had no personal interest

[111]

in the conflict. "I told them that if you were committed you would stand by your commitment, because you are a contrary Missourian."

To my father's indignation, a Washington newspaper printed a story claiming that he had switched to Barkley on Tom Pendergast's orders. When senators vote for majority leader or whip, they do so by secret ballot. But Dad was so incensed over this smear that just before he handed in his ballot, he turned to Senator Clyde L. Herring of Iowa and showed him the ballot, which he had emphatically marked for Harrison. The vote was excruciatingly close. Senator Barkley won by a single ballot—38 to 37. Senator Dieterich's capitulation to Boss Kelly made the difference. When a Kansas City *Star* reporter asked my father if he had been the crucial switched vote, Dad angrily told him to go see Senator Herring and he would tell him how the junior senator from Missouri had voted.

To make sure everybody got the point, Dad put through a call to Steve Early, the press secretary at the White House. "Listen," he said, "I've got a message for the President. Tell him to stop treating me like an office boy."

[CHAPTER]

Six

WHILE NATIONAL POLITICS and legislative investigations absorbed my father in Washington, he was also deeply involved in Missouri politics. People who wanted jobs or favors sought his help constantly. This was how he came to meet a man who was to give him many a bad hour—Lloyd Stark. One of the owners of Stark Brothers Nurseries and Orchards Company, reputedly the largest apple producers in the nation, Mr. Stark was a millionaire with very strong political ambitions. He had served with distinction in World War I and as early as 1932 had sought the support of Jackson County Democrats for the nomination for governor. But Tom Pendergast had turned him down. Undiscouraged, Stark continued to woo Boss Tom by mail and through every friend who had access to him.

A man of considerable charm, Mr. Stark came to Washington and soon convinced both my father and Bennett Clark to support his bid for Jackson County's votes. Late in 1935 Dad and Senator Clark escorted Mr. Stark to New York where Tom Pendergast was staying, en route to a European vacation. They urged Tom to support Mr. Stark for governor in the 1936 election. Looking back, my father has always ruefully admitted that this was one of the greatest political mistakes he ever made. After much cajoling from Missouri's two senators, Boss Tom reluctantly agreed to back Mr. Stark if he could prove that he had "out-state" —that is, rural—support.

This seemed at first glance an easy thing for Mr. Stark to do. Farmers had been buying Stark's Delicious apple trees from the Stark Brothers Nurseries and Orchards Company for decades. But selling people apples and apple trees and getting their votes are not quite the same thing. Mr. Stark could never have gotten the nomination without the help of Harry S. Truman. Dad sent him a personal list that he had compiled, containing the names of the key men in each county who had worked for him in 1934. Mr. Stark was soon sending Mr. Pendergast a list of out-state names, all of whom were carefully primed to assure Boss Tom that Mr. Stark was strong in their section of Missouri. By October Mr. Pendergast capitulated and guaranteed Mr. Stark Jackson County's Democratic votes. Both Dad and Bennett Clark campaigned vigorously for Mr. Stark in the primary and general election, and he swept to an enormous victory in 1936.

Meanwhile, another Democrat had entered the Jackson County political scene. He was Maurice Milligan, brother of Jacob ("Tuck") Milligan, the congressman whom Dad had defeated in 1934. Bennett Clark, an old friend of Tuck Milligan, had wangled the post of federal district attorney in Kansas City for his brother.

Maurice Milligan launched an investigation of the 1936 election in Kansas City. He was no friend of Jackson County Democrats, and he was emboldened by the absence of Tom Pendergast, who had suffered a physical breakdown in New York earlier in the year—a severe heart attack followed by a serious cancer operation. Soon Milligan was marching Democrats by the dozen into the federal court, where they were tried under a Reconstruction Era statute originally intended to protect Negro voting rights in the post-Civil War South. It permitted the federal government to intervene in state voting practices, if the right to vote was being denied to a substantial number of a state's citizens. This was not the case in Kansas City; the defendants were prosecuted for padding the vote in their districts by using names of citizens long dead, or in some cases totally imaginary. The cases were tried before two ultra-Republican judges; the juries were composed exclusively of people from outside Jackson County.

For two years the trials dragged on, and 259 Democrats were convicted. None of them had previous police records. They were all ordinary citizens, who, if they were guilty at all, had allowed their enthusiasm for the Democratic party to run away with their judgment. Arthur Krock in *The New York Times,* pointing out that the extra votes had not even been necessary to win the election in Missouri, explained the phenomenon: "Any observer of city politics knows the real answer. Each party worker of the professional type is an office seeker. From him results are demanded in exchange for jobs. The better showing he makes, the higher his standing over rival precinct, ward or district workers. This competition has led the boys to be what the boss calls 'over-zealous.'"

Watching this performance from Washington, D.C., my father did a slow burn. He had no love for Maurice Milligan in the first place. Every big city machine in those days padded its voting rolls. The Grundy Republican machine did it in Philadelphia, and the Hague Democratic machine did it in Jersey City. No one was investigating them, under a Reconstruction statute that brought all the latent Southern sympathies in the Truman bloodstream to a simmering boil. Then Dad discovered that Mr. Milligan himself was not simon-pure; he had been accepting fees in bankruptcy proceedings in the Federal Court of Western Missouri, something that no federal attorney should have done. In 1938, when Mr. Milligan's term as federal attorney expired, Dad felt strongly that he should not be reappointed. He was wrecking the Democratic party in Missouri for his own aggrandizement.

When the Roosevelt Administration, with the support of Bennett Clark, reappointed Mr. Milligan, my father made his most controversial Senate speech:

> My opposition to Mr. Milligan began long before vote frauds were brought to light in Kansas City. His morals and political thinking never did appeal to me.
>
> The President has appointed him and the President wants him confirmed because of a situation in Kansas City due to vote fraud prosecutions in the Federal Court. Mr. Milligan has been made a hero by the Kansas City *Star* and the St. Louis *Post-Dispatch* because of these prosecutions.

My father went on to castigate Milligan for accepting bankruptcy fees, pointing out that he had received more money in fees in one case than his federal salary totaled in an entire year.

[115]

The Republican federal judges had smiled sweetly on this practice. Dad also accused these gentlemen of intimidating defending lawyers in the vote fraud cases. Above all Dad deplored the refusal to let a single person from Jackson County—a community of 600,000 people—sit on a jury. Even petit jury panels, he said, were investigated by the Secret Service, and if a man was found to have acquaintances in Jackson County he was barred from service. "I say to this Senate," Dad declared, "a Jackson County Missouri Democrat has as much chance of a fair trial in the Federal District Court of Western Missouri as a Jew would have in a Hitler court or a Trotsky follower before Stalin. . . ."

The St. Louis *Post-Dispatch* ran a Daniel Fitzpatrick cartoon showing a Charlie McCarthy dummy on a knee saying, "Milligan and those judges are railroading the Democrats." The caption reads: "Charlie McTruman does his stuff." The Kansas City *Star*'s comments were, of course, equally caustic, and even the *Journal-Post* said that my father had "done his cause no particular good" by attacking the high-riding Mr. Milligan. No one bothered to listen to the facts in Dad's speech. Everyone assumed that he was simply trying to protect the Pendergast machine. Dad owed Tom Pendergast political loyalty, and he always gave it to him, but never at the expense of his own conscience. In fact, my father recommended to President Roosevelt that Milligan be given a special appointment to continue his prosecution of the vote fraud cases, but some other deserving attorney, more acceptable to Jackson County Democrats, be given the district attorney's job. Nobody except those closest to him shared Dad's point of view or appreciated the courage it took to express it in the teeth of the inevitable disapproval of the two most powerful newspapers in Missouri.

The Senate reconfirmed Milligan. Meanwhile, Governor Lloyd Stark, sensing Tom Pendergast's weakness, entered the battle on Milligan's side. He cut off all patronage for Jackson County Democrats and challenged Boss Tom in a battle for the choice of a Supreme Court justice. Stark won and, together with Milligan, journeyed to Washington and asked President Roosevelt to assign a federal task force to make an exhaustive investigation of Tom Pendergast and his organization. A team composed of FBI and Treasury agents and special investigators from the Attorney

General's office soon descended on Kansas City, with shattering results. Tom Pendergast pleaded guilty to evading more than $1,000,000 in income taxes over the preceding decade, and was sentenced to fifteen months in jail and five years probation. City Manager Henry McElroy resigned and died shortly before he was to be brought to trial for juggling Kansas City's municipal books to conceal huge deficits. Several other high-ranking members of the Jackson County political organization went to jail.

I find it hard to describe how totally stunned my father was by these developments. He knew Tom Pendergast gambled on the horses. But he had no conception of the fantastic mania which eventually obsessed and destroyed the man. Tom reached the point where he gambled on every horse race that was run in the entire United States on a single day. By the mid-'30s his losses were staggering, and he had been forced to indulge in massive fraud to sustain this destructive compulsion.

Numerous Democrats around the state rushed to denounce the fallen leader and did their utmost to pretend they had always been independent of Tom Pendergast. My father remained silent. I remember one day in 1939, being in his office when he received a call from a reporter in Missouri who urged him to condemn Pendergast and point proudly to his record of independent achievement in Jackson County and in the Senate—something Dad could certainly have done. Instead, he became infuriated at the suggestion. "I'm not a rat who deserts a sinking ship," he snapped.

Never before or since can I recall my father being so gloomy as he was in those latter months of 1939, after Tom Pendergast went to prison. Nothing seemed to be going right. The transportation bill, the product of his four years of enormous effort investigating the railroads, was being blocked in the Senate, with Bennett Clark doing not a little of the blocking. Early in 1940, he wrote a friend in St. Louis, "I feel as if my four years and a half hard work has been practically wasted."

Reminiscing in later years about his Senate career, my father wryly remarked that when men first come to the Senate, "they have four years in which to be statesmen. I spent that period myself. Then they have a year in which to be politicians. And one of my good friends from the great State of Washington told me

[117]

that the last year the senator had to be a demagogue if he expected to come back to the Senate. I never heard a statement that is truer than that."

By instinct Dad rejected the idea of being a demagogue. But he did recognize the kernel of truth in that remark—a senator had to make some kind of a splash in his last year to remind the voters that he had not been wasting his time and their money in Washington. The transportation bill was Dad's hoped-for triumph along this line, and it was heartbreaking to see it bogged down in a tangle of objections raised by other senators.

Then came an even more dismaying revelation. Lloyd Stark was in Washington again, visiting the White House. He and FDR had become quite chummy, exchanging notes on a "Dear Lloyd" basis. Stark had come whooping out for a third term for Roosevelt and there was considerable talk, at least in Missouri, about him winning the vice presidential nomination. Vice President Garner had made it clear that he was going to retire. He also made it clear that he did not believe in more than two terms for a President—another Roosevelt innovation that was splitting the Democratic party. My father, with his respect for American political tradition, felt the same way. He made a number of public statements disapproving a third term, but he added that if the Democratic party nominated the President, he would support him. With this for background, you can imagine Dad's anger when Lloyd Stark dropped in to see him in his Senate office and attempted to pull the cheapest of all cheap political tricks.

"Everybody keeps telling me that I ought to run for the Senate," he said with a bland smile, "but don't you worry about it, Harry, I wouldn't dream of running against you."

As a Machiavelli, Stark was almost laughably inept. Dad saw instantly that the governor was trying to lull him into a state of security, so he could catch him flat-footed with the announcement of his candidacy.

The moment Stark left the office, my father said to his secretary, Vic Messall, "That S.O.B. is going to run against me."

The 1940 campaign had begun.

[CHAPTER]

Seven

"I AM GOING TO RUN for reelection, if the only vote I get is my own."

That is what I remember my father saying early in 1940.

According to some reports from Missouri, that was about all the votes he could expect. In spite of the support Dad had given the Roosevelt Administration, Lloyd Stark seemed to have FDR's blessing. The brisk correspondence between the President and the governor, the frequent White House visits, continued. The Jackson County Democrats were in sad disarray, cringing every time the name Pendergast was mentioned.

Late in January my father made a trip to Missouri to see what he could do about rallying some support. He wrote to some thirty friends who he was sure would stick with him and asked them to meet with him in the Statler Hotel in St. Louis to discuss his campaign. Less than half of them showed up, and those who came spent most of their time telling Dad he did not have a chance. He could not even persuade anyone to take on the vital job of finance chairman for the campaign.

One of the few who urged him to run was Harry Easley, an old friend from Webb City in southwest Missouri. He had known Dad since 1932, and he arrived in time to have breakfast with him and report that Senator Truman had a lot of support in his part of the state. Just after breakfast, while Mr. Easley was in one room of Dad's suite and Dad was busy in another room, the phone rang.

[119]

It was the White House calling. Mr. Easley hastily summoned Dad's secretary, Vic Messall, who in turn asked my father if he wanted to come to the phone. Dad shook his head, and Vic took the message from FDR's press secretary, Steve Early. It was an offer from the President. If Senator Truman would withdraw from the race, he could have a seat on the Interstate Commerce Commission, a life appointment at a salary that was a lot more than senators were paid. "Tell them to go to hell," Dad said. "I've made up my mind that I'm going to run."

The St. Louis *Post-Dispatch* found out about the discouraging meeting and chortled over Dad's discomfiture: "Harry Truman, the erstwhile Ambassador in Washington of the defunct principality of Pendergastia, is back home, appraising his chances of being re-elected to the Senate. They are nil. He is a dead cock in the pit."

My father went back to Washington, profoundly discouraged. John Snyder, who was working for the Reconstruction Finance Corporation, joined him in his Senate office for another conference. It was a very depressing talk. Mr. Snyder could do little for him, directly, because he was a government employee. The overwhelming problem was money. As Mr. Snyder recalls the meeting, "The thought came to me that we hadn't even enough money to buy the postage stamps to write to anybody to help us." Not long after he made this glum observation, the meeting started to break up on a note of complete despair. But as Mr. Snyder was leaving, Dad reiterated his determination to run: "I can't walk out on the charges that have been made against me. For my own self-respect, if nothing else, I must run."

Mr. Snyder promised to meet him for another conference on the following day. As he left the Senate Office Building, he met an old friend from St. Louis, Horace Deal. "John, what's happened to you?" asked Mr. Deal. "You look like you've just been run through a wringer."

"Well," Mr. Snyder said, "that couldn't be a better description of how I feel." He told him about his meeting with Dad and their seemingly hopeless economic plight.

"It's pretty bad, isn't it," Mr. Deal said.

"It is," said Mr. Snyder.

"Well, maybe it's not all that bad," Mr. Deal said. Whereupon he took out his checkbook, opened it on the fender of a car, and wrote out a check for $1,000. "I didn't even stop to thank him," Mr. Snyder says. "I grabbed it and ran back into the building, and into Senator Truman's office." He waved the check in front of Dad and said, "Well, at least we can buy postage stamps."

Less than a week later, on my father's orders, Vic Messall drove to Jefferson City and filed the necessary papers to make Dad a candidate for reelection. "I am filing for reelection to the United States Senate today. . . . I am asking the voters of the state of Missouri to renominate and reelect me on my record as a public official and United States Senator," Dad said in a statement from Washington.

Governor Stark had already filed for the senatorial primary. He declared himself an all-out Roosevelt supporter and called for a third term. He also piously declared he was "not planning an attack on any other Democrat in order to win the nomination." This lofty pose was based on his assumption that he was so far ahead he could coast to victory.

For reasons I've already stated, Dad was not an enthusiastic backer of Mr. Roosevelt for a third term. In the statement announcing his candidacy, Dad reiterated this stand and declared himself ready to support Bennett Clark for President at the 1940 convention. By this time Senator Clark had completely broken with Roosevelt and was edging toward the isolationists in Congress, severely criticizing the Roosevelt defense program. War had already begun in Europe, and Dad was a wholehearted backer of the defense program. He and Senator Clark simply did not see eye to eye on this and a host of other issues. But with loyalty to the Democratic party and to Missouri as his cardinal virtue, my father was ready to offer Bennett his support if FDR withdrew or the convention was deadlocked.

Senator Clark did not reciprocate with any statement of support for Senator Truman. That was not his style. But he reacted savagely against Governor Stark's attempt to take over the Democratic party in Missouri and control the delegation to the 1940 national convention. Several voices had already been raised, suggesting Governor Stark as a presidential candidate in his own right. Others continued to say that he would make an excellent vice president on the Roosevelt ticket. The governor did nothing to discourage either of these sentiments.

Even before my father filed for the Senate race, warfare had erupted between Senator Clark and Governor Stark. On January 4, 1940, Bennett, in his inimitably sarcastic style, told a St. Louis *Post-Dispatch* reporter what he thought of Mr. Stark:

> It is hard to estimate the political situation in Missouri just now, since Lloyd's ambitions seem to be like the gentle dew that falls from heaven and covers everything high or low. He is the first man in the history of the United States who has ever tried to run for President and Vice President, Secretary of the Navy, Secretary of War, Governor General of the Philippines, Ambassador to England and United States Senator all at one and the same time.
>
> At the same time that he is running for these offices, Lloyd is apparently trying to control the Missouri delegation and name the whole state ticket. It is rumored that he is also an accepted candidate for both the College of Heralds and the Archbishopric of Canterbury. I understand, too, that he is receiving favorable mention as Akhund of Swat and Emir of Afghanistan.

The story of Lloyd Stark is a classic study of a man overreaching himself. His almost boundless ambition and arrogant style had already split the Democratic party in Missouri down the middle. This fact was dramatized by the holding of two separate Jackson Day dinners—one attended by anti-Stark Democrats, the other by pro-Stark people. My father persuaded Senator Tom Connally to speak on his behalf at the anti-Stark dinner, which was held in Springfield under the sponsorship of the Green County Democratic Committee. Governor Stark did not attend, claiming a conflict in his schedule. When one of his associates rose to say a few words on his behalf, the 700 guests at the dinner booed him so vociferously that the chairman of the dinner finally had to pound his gavel on the lectern and beg for order.

My father was pleased by this news, of course. He wrote to John Snyder that Senator Connally "said enough nice things about me to elect me (if it had been left to that crowd!). The booing of Stark was a rather unanimous affair."

The realization that Senator Truman had some support in Missouri—or at the very least that Governor Stark had some enemies—created near hysteria among the St. Louis *Post-Dispatch* editorial writers. A few days after the Jackson Day dinner, they wrote

an editorial captioned HARRY S. TRUMAN—STOOGE OF
BOSS PENDERGAST:

> The whelps of Boss Pendergast, Harry Truman and Bennett
> Clark, hissed and booed the speaker who rose to deliver the
> greetings of Governor Stark. . . . Truman was one of the
> toasts of the Springfield dinner. He is the stooge whom Boss
> Pendergast lifted from obscurity and placed in the United
> States Senate. He is the stooge who paid off his debt to Pen-
> dergast in the most abject way. He is the stooge who tried to
> prevent the reappointment of the fearless prosecutor, the
> United States Attorney Milligan, because Milligan was sending
> Truman's pals to the penitentiary. Well, Truman is through
> in Missouri. He may as well fold up and accept a nice lucrative
> Federal post if he can get it—and if he does get it, it's a travesty
> of democracy.

Governor Stark's Jackson Day dinner, meanwhile, turned into
a political disaster. The governor of Arkansas, who had agreed to
be the principal speaker, abruptly reneged. When Stark tried
frantically to persuade some prominent New Deal official to come
out from Washington, Dad and Bennett Clark, working together
for once, blocked that move. The governor was reduced to importing a wealthy Kansas cattleman to be the speaker of the evening. This was indeed desperation. Importing a Kansan to address
Missouri Democrats made about as much sense politically as inviting Sitting Bull to address a reunion of the 7th Cavalry Regiment.

Three months later Governor Stark made another mistake in
political judgment. Both he and my father were invited to speak
at a Jefferson Day banquet in Kirksville, Missouri. The dinner
was supposed to promote party unity, and all the speakers were
urged to limit their remarks to lavish praise of Thomas Jefferson
and Franklin D. Roosevelt. Lloyd Stark was the first speaker. To
everyone's astonishment and outrage, he proceeded to make a
searing political speech, blasting the many Missouri Democrats
who did not support a third term for FDR, extolling the achievements of his own administration, and declaring himself practically elected as senator from Missouri. My father threw aside the
speech he had prepared, calling for party unity, and gave Governor Stark the tongue-lashing he deserved. A considerable num-

ber of powerful Missouri Democrats left Kirksville that night professing profound disgust for Governor Stark.

The next round in the mounting struggle was the Missouri State Democratic Convention on April 15. My father wisely remained on the sidelines, while Senator Clark and Governor Stark met head-on in the battle for the control of the delegation. It was really no contest. When Mr. Stark's name was mentioned on the convention floor, he got nothing but boos, and if Bennett Clark had had his way, the governor would not even have been elected a delegate at large to the national convention. My father, with that instinct for playing a peacemaker's role, persuaded his fellow Democrats to give the discomfited Mr. Stark at least that much recognition. But the rest of the delegation was firmly in Bennett Clark's camp, and the senior senator was named chairman.

As my father tartly reminded several of his supporters in Missouri, however, it was not enough to rejoice over these rebuffs to Stark. Something had to be done about getting people to vote for Truman. While carrying his full work load in Congress, Dad struggled to put together an organization. He sent his secretaries, Vic Messall and Millie Dryden, back to Missouri to be the mainstays. But money remained the tormenting problem. Nobody was willing to bet any real cash on Truman. My father still could not even find a finance chairman. He finally persuaded his old army friend Harry Vaughan to take the job. Wryly Mr. Vaughan recalls, "I had a bank balance of three dollars and a quarter."

Millie Dryden, looking back on those hectic days, said, "Many times we had so little money, we ran out of stamps." The few paid employees worked for practically nothing. One young man frequently ran out of gas and had to hitchhike back to the office. "I remember," Millie said, "he lived out south someplace and it was downhill most of the way to where he lived and he used to try to coast as far as he could in order to save his gas because he was making such a small salary." At one time the treasury sank so low that the last few dollars were invested in mailing an appeal to numbers of people asking them to send in a dollar. Two hundred dollars came in, and this was reinvested in another mailing, which raised even more money. But Dad finally had to borrow $3,000 on his life insurance to meet the office payroll and other "must" expenses.

Meanwhile, Stark, with his family millions behind him, was buying up radio time and spending lavish amounts of money on newspaper advertising.

Calmly, methodically, refusing to panic, my father went ahead with the most important task—organizing his campaign. John Snyder, who was present at the first organization meeting, was so impressed by the firmness and clarity with which Dad stated his principles, that he copied them down verbatim. He was kind enough to show me his record of exactly what Dad said at this meeting:

> The Senator will not engage in personalities and asks his friends to do the same. Avoid mentioning the Senator's opponents in any way.
>
> Avoid getting into controversial issues. Stick to Truman—his record as judge, as a senator, as a military man.
>
> While others discuss issues not involved in the primary, each worker will carefully avoid getting into those traps.
>
> The press is a function of our free institutions. If they are wrong in their attitude, try to make them see the true light, but under no circumstances attack them.
>
> Political parties are essential to our republic, our nation and we must not attack them. What we're doing is to show by our actions what we think our party is destined to do. Provide the basic laws for a more abundant life and the happiness and security of our people. Those are the conditions under which I am going to run and those are the conditions I want each of my adherents and co-workers to observe with the greatest of zeal.

In Washington my father did his utmost to get some help from the Roosevelt Administration. He went to see Harold Ickes, Secretary of the Interior, who had numerous employees in Missouri and was highly regarded by farmers and others in the rural parts of the state. Ickes coldly informed him that he supported Governor Stark. Over at the White House Dad did his best to get through to the President and warn him that Stark was wrecking the Democratic party in the state of Missouri. He told him enough about Stark's political style to lower considerably the warmth of the President's letters to the governor.

By April, 1940, FDR was telling my father that personally he would like to see him reelected. The President said he would see

[125]

what he could do about persuading Stark to abandon the race. Charles Edison had recently resigned as Secretary of the Navy, and a few days after this April meeting between Dad and FDR, Mr. Stark called at the White House, and the President reportedly offered him Edison's job. But Mr. Stark refused and later issued a statement denying that the offer had been made. All told, the net result of this tough inside politicking was not too encouraging for my father. But he could console himself that he had eliminated the possibility of a Roosevelt endorsement for Stark.

Back in Missouri, Truman supporters from Jackson County were working out another political maneuver. Several of Dad's good friends, such as Tom Evans, owner of Radio Station KCMO, went to Maurice Milligan and urged that gentleman to enter the race. They pointed out that Governor Stark was taking all the credit for putting Tom Pendergast in jail, when the real work had been done by Milligan and his assistants and the other federal investigators. Milligan already resented Stark's grab for all the glory, and when he saw some of Harry Truman's best friends urging him to run, he decided that the senator was only going to make a token race. Why shouldn't the real slayer of the Pendergast dragon become senator? Mr. Milligan asked himself. So, to Dad's great but carefully restrained glee, Milligan entered the race on March 28.

In Washington my father turned his attention to another source of potential help—labor. Reminding union chiefs of the support he had given their cause in his Senate votes, he asked them to come to his aid now. Multimillionaire Stark had shown himself no great friend of the laboring man while governor. Toward the end of May, Dad's call for help received an enormously heartwarming response. Twenty-one railroad brotherhoods informed him that they were ready to "go down the line for Truman." They had 50,000 members in Missouri. Through their intercession, other Missouri labor groups pledged the support of 150,000 more workers.

But it was the railroad men who provided crucial assistance. Truman-for-Senator Clubs were set up in railroad stations throughout Missouri. Even more important was the chance they gave my father to reply to the smears and slanders being printed about him in most of the state's newspapers. The brotherhoods created a special edition of their weekly newspaper, *Labor*. It was crammed with endorsements from labor leaders and other influential Missourians. The chaplain of the Missouri American Legion, Reverend Father M. F. Wogan, endorsed Senator Truman. Frank J. Murphy, secretary-treasurer of the state Federation of Labor, rated him "one hundred percent perfect" on social and labor questions during his Senate years. President William Green of the AFL applauded Senator Truman's "very favorable record." Dr. William T. Tompkins, president of the National Colored Democratic Association, was listed as general chairman of the Negro Division of the Truman Campaign Committee. He was a Kansas City man, incidentally, and a personal friend.

Most impressive, however, was the gallery of senators who contributed long enthusiastic statements in praise of my father. Alben Barkley of Kentucky, Robert F. Wagner of New York, James F. Byrnes of South Carolina were on the front page, and on inner pages were Burton K. Wheeler of Montana, Kenneth McKellar of Tennessee, Pat Harrison of Mississippi, Elmer Thomas of Oklahoma, Robert Reynolds of North Carolina, Tom Connally of Texas, and Vic Donahey of Ohio. Included in these names were some of the New Deal's best-known spokesmen in the Senate. Anyone reading this list would certainly get the impression that the Roosevelt Administration was backing Harry S. Truman. Lloyd Stark must have shuddered when 500,000 copies of this special edition poured into Missouri. Around the same time the *Labor Tribune* of St. Louis was blasting the governor for ignoring the needs of Missouri's workingmen.

My father was only starting to go to work on Governor Stark. On June 15, at Sedalia, in the center of the state, he kicked off his campaign with a superbly organized rally. Senator Lewis Schwellenbach of Washington was on hand to tell Missourians what his fellow senators thought of their friend Harry S. Truman. On the platform were representatives of Missouri's Democratic party from all parts of the state. Mamma Truman had a front row seat, sizing up politicians with her usual unerring eye. The little courthouse was decorated with huge pictures of Senator Truman and the candidate of the St. Louis Democrats for governor, Larry McDaniel. I sat on the platform with Mother. At sixteen I was able to feel for the first time the essential excitement of American politics—the struggle to reach those people "out there" with ideas and emotions that will put them on your side.

The crowd was big, over 4,000, and very friendly. This was all the more impressive because the day before, Paris had surrendered to the Germans, and most people in Missouri, and in the rest of the country, were glued to their radios, listening to the greatest crisis of the century.

My father's talk that day sounded all the themes that he was to underscore throughout his campaign. He pointed to what the Roosevelt Administration had achieved for the laboring man, he talked about the defense program, for which he had voted and fought in the Senate. Events were now proving it to be vital to the nation's salvation. Above all, he talked about the Democratic party's efforts to achieve equal opportunity for all Americans. By this, he made it clear, he also meant black Americans:

> I believe in the brotherhood of man, not merely the brotherhood of white men but the brotherhood of all men before the law. . . . In giving the Negro the rights which are theirs we are only acting in accord with our ideals of a true democracy. . . . The majority of our Negro people find but cold comfort in shanties and tenements. Surely, as free men, they are entitled to something better than this. . . . It is our duty to see that the Negroes in our locality have increased opportunities to exercise their privilege as free men.

With these words my father was saying what he truly believed. In his years as county judge he had done his utmost to place a fair proportion of black men on the public works payroll. This appeal to black voters also exploited a large chink in Governor Stark's armor. In October, 1939, the United Negro Democrats of Missouri had condemned the governor and refused to back him for United States senator. They accused him of wholesale dismissal of Negroes from public office and castigated his support of a bill in the Missouri Legislature, which purported to create separate but equal graduate school and professional facilities for Negroes at Lincoln University. In reality, the bill was a crude attempt to subvert a U.S. Supreme Court decision which declared that the state was denying Negroes their constitutional rights by refusing them admission to the law school and other graduate schools at the University of Missouri. There were 250,000 Negro voters in Missouri, and it was soon evident that they too were going down the line for Harry Truman.

Much has been made by many of my father's biographers of a cartoon published by the St. Louis *Post-Dispatch* portraying two big trucks, one labeled "Stark for Senator," the other labeled "Milligan for Senator," meeting head on. Scurrying between their wheels was a tiny little truck labeled "Truman for Senator." The caption read, "No place for a kiddie car." Actually, the cartoon is only one more proof that newspaper editors (with certain exceptions) are poor political prophets. By now Milligan was far behind, a poor third in the race. The Truman campaign was building momentum every day. Stark was still in the lead, but my father was confident that he was going to win—every bit as confident as he would be in 1948.

Just as in 1948, he based his confidence on a shrewd assessment not only of his own resources and his determination to get the facts to the public, but also on the deficiencies and weaknesses of his opponent. He knew, for instance, that a sizable number of people disliked Lloyd Stark's arrogance. When the governor approached his car, he demanded a military salute from his chauffeur. Whenever he appeared in public, a staff of uniformed Missouri state colonels made him look like a South American dictator. My father also knew, from his inside contacts with Missouri Democrats, that the governor, the supposed reformer of the state, was "putting the lug" (to use Missouri terminology) on state employees to contribute to his campaign fund. He had done this during the 1938 fight to elect his candidate to the State Supreme Court and it had caused intense resentment throughout the state. Everyone making more than $60 a month had to kick in 5 percent of his annual salary.

My father reported these facts to his good friend Senator Guy M. Gillette, chairman of the Senate committee to investigate senatorial campaigns. On June 20, 1940, Senator Gillette released a report of his investigation. It was a Sunday punch to Lloyd Stark's reformer image. "There is abundance of evidence to prove that many employees were indirectly coerced into contributing, although they may not be in sympathy with the candidacy of Governor Stark for the U.S. Senate," Senator Gillette said. He later

issued a detailed report, citing the names of the governor's assistants who did the arm-twisting, and statements of employees who
said that they had contributed against their wills.

In the middle of July everyone interrupted the primary campaign to journey to Chicago for the Democratic National Convention. Here Lloyd Stark made another blunder—as Dad expected
that he would. With FDR quickly nominated for a third term,
the only office in contention was the vice presidency. Although
Stark had declared only a few days before the convention that
there was "nothing to this talk about my being a candidate for
vice president," he could not resist making a try for the job. He
sent bushels of his family's Delicious apples (to this day I don't
like them—McIntosh taste better) to dozens of influential delegates, opened a headquarters, and organized a demonstration on
the floor of the convention, waving "Roosevelt and Stark" ban-
ners. Then came word from on high that the President's choice
was Henry A. Wallace. A chastened Stark hastily withdrew, but
not before Bennett Clark sank a barb into his posterior. "A man
can't withdraw from a race he was never in," Senator Clark gibed.
To complete the governor's humiliation, Senator Clark ordered
the Missouri delegation to vote for Speaker of the House William
B. Bankhead for vice president.

Governor Stark's antics in Chicago were awfully difficult to
explain in Missouri. His supporters tried hard. The St. Louis
Post-Dispatch tut-tutted, waffled in all directions, and finally gave
its senatorial candidate an editorial slap on the wrist: "The Governor has taken a gamble—and a not too dignified one."

Back to Missouri went the candidates, to slug it out for the rest
of the campaign. My father maintained his usual back-breaking
schedule, ignoring the heat, making ten and twelve speeches a
day up and down the state. Milligan and Stark continued to
denounce him as a tool of Pendergast, and the newspapers maintained the same silly chorus. All the time Dad had in his files a
letter from Stark which could have settled the campaign the moment he released it. It was an effusive thank you, which Stark
had written to my father for introducing him to Mr. Pendergast
and persuading Boss Tom to endorse Mr. Stark for governor. But
Dad's conscience would not permit him to release it. It was a personal letter between him and Lloyd Stark when they were friends,

and he believed that letters between friends were confidential, even after they became political enemies.

The best answer to the Pendergast smear was an endorsement from FDR, and as the campaign roared to a climax, Dad made one last try to get it. The chairman of the Brotherhood of Locomotive Engineers wired the White House on July 28, demanding a statement from the President. On July 30 he got the following reply from Steve Early: "The President asks me to explain to you personally that while Senator Truman is an old and trusted friend, the President's invariable practice has been not to take part in primary contests."

Thanks to his friends in the Senate, my father got the next best thing to a presidential endorsement—the presence of FDR's majority leader, Senator Alben Barkley, who came out to St. Louis to speak for him. Although Alben in the flesh no doubt impressed many voters, the meeting itself was a political disaster. The St. Louis Democratic organization was backing Stark, and only 300 people turned out to hear Senator Barkley and Carl Hatch of New Mexico. The meeting was held in the Municipal Auditorium Opera House and the 300 listeners looked pretty forlorn in an auditorium with a capacity of 3,500. The *Post-Dispatch* had great fun describing the "monster Truman rally."

It was the sort of news that could sink a campaign. There was now only one week left before primary day. But Lloyd Stark came to our rescue once more. He suddenly announced that the Truman campaign was operating with an immense slush fund supplied by Boss Tom Pendergast. This struck Truman headquarters, where deficit financing was now the vogue, as hilarious. My father promptly wired Senator Gillette, denying the charge and asking him to demand evidence from Mr. Stark. The senator from Iowa immediately telegraphed the governor, asking him for proof. None, of course, was forthcoming, and Gillette, on the very eve of primary day, issued a statement saying, "In fairness to Senator Truman and before the primary polls open, the public should know of the sending of this telegram and the Governor's failure to acknowledge it."

At the same time Bennett Clark made a dramatic entry into the race. Personally, Senator Clark leaned toward Maurice Milligan, but he was so far behind by now that it would have been political idiocy to endorse him. My father was the only man who could stop Mr. Stark from taking over the Democratic party in Missouri. But Senator Clark seesawed about coming out for Dad. First he said he would vote for Truman but would not campaign for him. Finally, several of Dad's Senate friends pointed out that Dad had campaigned for him in 1938, and it was gross ingratitude, among other things, for him to sit on his hands.

In the first days of August, Senator Clark leaped into the fray, lashing Lloyd Stark with sarcasm in his best style. He charged that the governor had "licked Pendergast's boots" to win his support for his 1936 governorship race and now was trying to use the Pendergast name as a smear to defeat Harry Truman. Rather hysterically, Governor Stark replied that the Truman campaign had collapsed and everyone in Missouri but Senator Clark and Senator Truman knew it.

Meanwhile, another behind-the-scenes drama was taking place in St. Louis. The nominal head of the St. Louis organization was Bernard Dickmann, the mayor. But a rising star in the city politic was a young Irish-American, Robert Hannegan. They had a candidate running for governor, Larry McDaniel. In the opening rally at Sedalia, Truman supporters had cheered vociferously for McDaniel every time his name was mentioned. They supported him and expected the St. Louis organization to return the compliment. As my father's campaign gathered momentum, the St. Louis leaders grew more and more jittery. They kept getting calls from numerous Truman supporters around the state, but particularly from southeast Missouri where Dad had a tremendous following, warning them that they were going to vote against McDaniel unless St. Louis came out for Truman. Mr. Hannegan, shrewdly sniffing the political wind, decided Dad looked like a winner and tried to persuade Mayor Dickmann to switch. But the mayor stubbornly stayed with Stark. Mr. Hannegan proceeded to pass the word among his own followers, who probably outnumbered Mr. Dickmann's, that Senator Truman was the man to back.

My father ended his campaign with a rally in Independence. Lloyd Stark issued one last plea to "save Missouri from Pendergastism." The newspapers continued to pour mud on the Truman name, right down to the final hour. The *Post-Dispatch* declared on August 5: "The nomination of Harry Truman . . . would be the triumph of Pendergastism and a sad defeat for the people of Missouri." The *Globe-Democrat* topped even this bit of hysteria by printing between the news articles throughout the paper "Save Missouri—Vote against Truman."

After taking this kind of abuse in St. Louis for a week, more than a few members of the Truman team were feeling rather glum on primary day. My father's confidence remained unshaken, but the early returns made many of his friends wonder if he was living in a dream world. All during the early evening of August 6, 1940, Stark maintained roughly a 10,000-vote lead. Dad had to admit that things did not look encouraging. But with that fantastic calm which he has always maintained in moments of crisis, he announced, "I'm going to bed." And he did.

Mother and I stayed up, glued to the radio. I remember answering the phone about 10:30. It was Tom Evans, calling from campaign headquarters. He was very discouraged—and astonished when I told him that my father was already asleep.

Mother and I finally went to bed around midnight, very weepy and depressed. Dad was still behind. I remember crying into my pillow and wondering how all those people out there could prefer a stinker like Lloyd Stark.

About 3:30 A.M. the telephone rang. Mother got up and answered it.

"This is Dave Berenstein in St. Louis," said a cheerful voice. "I'd like to congratulate the wife of the senator from Missouri."

"I don't think that's funny," snapped Mother and slammed down the phone.

As she stumbled back to bed, Mother suddenly remembered that Mr. Berenstein was our campaign manager in St. Louis. Then she realized what he had said. She rushed into my room, woke me up, and told me what she had just heard. Mr. Berenstein soon called back and explained why he was extending his congratulations. Dad had run very well in St. Louis and was now ahead of Governor Stark.

For the rest of the night and morning Dad's lead seesawed back and forth, drooping once to a thin 2,000, then soaring to 11,000, and finally settling to 7,396. By 11 A.M. Senator Truman was a certified winner. Just as in 1948, he was bouncing around after a good night's sleep, shaking hands and accepting congratulations, as refreshed and lively as a man just back from a long vacation. The rest of us were staggering in his wake, totally frazzled from lack of sleep and nervous exhaustion.

My father captured St. Louis by some 8,000 votes—just about the same as his margin of victory. But he also polled about 8,000 more votes out-state than he had done in 1934—running against two candidates who supposedly had strong out-state support. And he drubbed both Stark and Milligan in Jackson County as well. Obviously, the people who knew him best were least impressed by the gross attempts to link him with Tom Pendergast's downfall.

Maurice Milligan conceded his defeat, wired my father his congratulations, and assured him that he would support him in November. But from Governor Stark there was only silence. He never congratulated my father, and it was clear that he intended to sulk throughout the November election campaign. He wrote FDR a long, whining letter blaming his defeat, among other things, on a drought which prevented (for some reason) the farmers from going to the polls to vote. In reply FDR assured "Dear Lloyd" of his "personal feelings" for him and urged the governor to get behind the Democratic ticket.

Not even urging from the President himself, however, dissuaded Governor Stark from sulking in his mansion. My father considered his conduct unforgivable. During the November campaign Edward J. Flynn, the Democratic National Chairman, visited Missouri and told Dad that the party had scheduled speaking engagements for Governor Stark in Iowa, Nebraska, and Kansas. Dad got really angry and did a little table-pounding. The governor was obviously trying to build up some national prestige in order to land a federal appointment in Washington. By the time Mr. Flynn left Missouri, Mr. Stark's speaking dates had been canceled.

I have said earlier in this book that my father was a forgiving man. But there *are* some sins he considers unforgivable, and one of them is a refusal to close ranks after a primary fight and support the party ticket. He considers this principle fundamental to the success of the two-party system, and he believes that the two-party system is essential to the political structure of the nation. The contrast between his attitude toward Lloyd Stark and Maurice Milligan is a perfect illustration. In September Dad asked FDR to reappoint Milligan as federal attorney—he had resigned to enter the race, in accordance with the provisions of the Hatch Act which forbids federal employees from participating in politics. The following year President Roosevelt considered naming ex-Governor Stark to the National Labor Mediation Board. My father asked his friend former Senator Sherman Minton, recently made a federal judge, to write a strong letter to FDR, informing him that the appointment would be personally obnoxious to Dad. Ex-Governor Stark remained a private citizen.

The November campaign for the Senate was almost an anticlimax, after the primary battle. My father spent much of his time in Washington fighting for—and finally winning—passage of his transportation bill. But his opponent, Manvel Davis, copied his primary style and went into every county in Missouri, making an energetic fight out of it. On August 22 the Republicans connived with the presiding judge of the Jackson County Court to pull the kind of dirty trick that convinced me—at least at the time—that all the terrible things Mamma Truman said about Republicans were true. With farm income battered by the depression, my grandmother had been forced to refinance the various mortgages against her farm in 1938. She did so by borrowing $35,000 from Jackson County. The new presiding judge in 1940, elected on an anti-Pendergast slate, foreclosed on this mortgage before my father or Uncle Vivian knew what was happening. The process servers sold the farm at auction, and Dad was forced to move his mother and sister Mary into a small house in Grandview, where a few months later, coming down an unfamiliar staircase, Mamma Truman missed the bottom step, fell, and broke her hip.

It constantly amazes me that my father's faith in human nature and his ebullient optimism about life survived these experiences without even a tinge of bitterness.

In the final stages of the fall campaign the Republicans tried another maneuver that was aimed at the strong residue of Klan feeling in many rural parts of Missouri. They distributed thousands of imitation ballots in which my father's name was printed "Harry Solomon Truman." With these went a whispering campaign that Dad's grandfather, Solomon Young, was Jewish, not

[135]

German. I remember a friend handing me one of these ballots. I stared incomprehensibly at it and laughed. I had never heard an anti-Semitic word uttered in our house, so the accusation did not arouse an iota of concern in me. My father treated the whole thing as if it were ridiculous.

In numerous speeches Manvel Davis tried mightily to paint my father as a tool of "the Dickmann-Pendergast axis"—which was pretty silly, since everyone knew that Barney Dickmann had gone down clinging to Governor Stark. Mr. Davis also spent a lot of time calling Dad a rubber-stamp senator and begged the Jeffersonian Democrats—as distinguished from the New Deal Democrats—to desert Truman and repair to the Davis standard. Dad practically ignored him and devoted most of his campaign to defending FDR's third-term bid against the savage attacks of most of the state's papers. Mr. Davis's energetic campaign did make a fairly impressive impact, but my father won by 40,000 votes.

The St. Louis *Post-Dispatch,* obviously working on the assumption that its readers had no memories whatsoever, proceeded to eat its previous words and pretend that it had been behind Dad all the time: "Senator Truman has been on the whole a satisfactory Senator. Now seasoned by experience, he should make an even better record in his second term."

The day after the election my father flew back to Washington. Because of the world crisis Congress was still in session. When Dad walked into the Senate chamber, every senator in the place rose and applauded. These professional politicians knew what he had achieved out there in Missouri. No one could call him names anymore, or smear him with ugly guilt by association. He was the United States Senator from Missouri in his own right.

[CHAPTER]

Eight

EARLY IN SEPTEMBER, 1941, we became permanent Washington residents—more or less. Congress was obviously going to stay in session for the duration of the world crisis. It was a harrowing time. Hitler ruled supreme in western Europe, and the British had retreated to their island fortress, where they shuddered under a rain of German bombs. Churchill's voice, summoning his people to blood, sweat, and tears, thrilled us over the airwaves, and President Roosevelt pushed the U.S. defense program to full throttle.

Our transfer to Washington caused a minor crisis in my own life. Early in 1940 I had decided to change from the piano to vocal training and had begun taking singing lessons from Mrs. Thomas J. Strickler in Kansas City. A permanent move to Washington meant that I could only see Mrs. Strickler at random intervals, when we went home to Independence for holidays or during the summer months. But my mother and father decided it was more important for me to spend a full, uninterrupted year at Gunston Hall and get a diploma from that school. So we moved from Independence to Washington, taking Grandmother Wallace with us. We rented another apartment on Connecticut Avenue, and settled down to life as year-round political—that's the poor kind—capitalists.

My father, watching the mushroom growth of army camps, the multiplication of battleships and merchant ships, the retooling of thousands of factories for war work, became more and more worried about this vast national effort. He feared it would either collapse into chaos, or produce mass disillusion, when its inevitable corruption and mismanagement was revealed to a shocked public. He knew, from his memory of World War I days, that this was what had happened in the early 1920s. Congress had waited until after the war to start digging into the contracts between the government and businessmen, and the stench that emerged had played no small part in creating the cynical amoral mood of the twenties. Moreover, during the senatorial campaign, he had spoken out emphatically in support of a strong defense program, and numerous citizens, aware of his interest, warned him that from what they could see there was an alarming amount of waste and confusion in the construction of Fort Leonard Wood, right there in Missouri.

After he was sworn in for a second time on January 3, 1941, my father departed from Washington for a month-long, 30,000-mile personal inspection tour of the defense program. He roamed from Florida to Michigan. On February 10 he was back in Washington, and he rose to make a fateful speech in the Senate. I say fateful because it was to change the course of all our lives. I suppose that is true of almost every event I have described in this book. But earlier speeches or election victories, while they played vital roles in my father's political growth, could not really be said to have made him a national figure. This speech did. He told his fellow senators of staggering waste and mismanagement he had seen with his own eyes, in his personal inspection tour of the defense program. On the day he spoke, the House voted to raise the ceiling on the national debt to $65 billion. Obviously, this vast spending spree needed a watchdog. In Senate Resolution 71 Senator Truman recommended the creation of a committee of five senators who would shoulder this large responsibility.

The twists and turns of politics are both fascinating and amusing. When my father submitted his resolution and warned against the chaos threatening the defense program, Congressman Eugene Cox of Georgia had already made a similar speech, in the House of Representatives, calling for a similar investigation. The Roosevelt Administration shuddered at the thought of a Cox-led investigation—he hated FDR. Jimmy Byrnes, the senator from South Carolina, one of Roosevelt's chief spokesmen in the Senate, seized on Dad's suggestion as an ideal way to put Cox out of business. At the same time he demonstrated just how much the Roosevelt Administration really wanted anyone investigating its programs.

After persuading the Senate to pass my father's resolution, Senator Byrnes, as head of the Audit and Control Committee, voted him a grandiose $10,000 to conduct the investigation. Dad had asked for $25,000 and he finally got $15,000. He committed more than half of this to hiring the best lawyer he could find, big, heavy-set Hugh Fulton. My father got him by calling Attorney General Robert Jackson and asking him to suggest one of his best men. Mr. Fulton wanted $9,000 a year. Dad swallowed hard and gave it to him. Mr. Fulton had a distinguished record in the Justice Department. He had recently won several big cases against crooked tycoons. One of his big recommendations, as far as Dad was concerned, was his fondness for getting up early in the morning. They were soon meeting between 6:30 and 7 A.M. in Dad's office to outline future investigations and plan the day's work.

My father gave the same careful attention to selecting the other members of his committee. Majority Leader Alben Barkley and Vice President Henry Wallace did their utmost to pack the committee with Roosevelt yes-men. Dad dismissed more than a few of his fellow senators with remarks like, "He's an old fuddy-duddy" or "He's a stuffed shirt." They finally settled on Tom Connally of Texas, Carl Hatch of New Mexico, James Mead of New York, Mon Wallgren of Washington, and Republicans Joe Ball of Minnesota and Owen Brewster of Maine. Senators Hatch and Wallgren were close personal friends of Dad's and, like him, hard workers without an ounce of the grandstander in them. Senators Connally and Mead were Roosevelt men, but not in any slavish or dependent way. They were also tremendously influential in Washington, and they helped my father borrow investigators from government agencies so that the committee could operate on its meager budget. Among these key men were a future Supreme Court Justice, Tom Clark; a future Democratic national chairman, Bill Boyle of Kansas City; and a future White House appointments secretary, a shrewd, witty Irishman named Matt Connelly.

[139]

My father knew that his first and biggest problem was to convince his fellow senators—especially his fellow Democrats—that his committee could serve a positive purpose without doing a hatchet job on the Roosevelt Administration. At the same time he had to convince the Senate that there was something worth investigating out there. He chose as his first target the army camps. They were not controversial, and they dealt with fundamentals that anyone who ever owned a house might understand.

In standard Truman style, the committee went to nine typical camps and conducted hearings on the spot. What they found was almost incredible. At Indiantown Gap, Pennsylvania, the estimate for construction of the camp's utilities had been $125,000. The actual cost came to $1,725,000. At Camp Wallace, Texas, costs jumped from $480,000 to $2,539,000. At Camp Meade, Maryland, the commanding general had coolly ignored the advice of the architect-engineer and had chosen a site that was almost totally lacking in drainage, construction roads, and other necessities.

The prices that the government paid enabled one architect-engineer to earn 1,478 percent above his average annual profits. A contractor earned 1,669 percent. Unions were no less guilty of plundering. Time-and-a-half and double-time wage rates at Fort Meade cost the government $1,808,320. The army's attitude toward money almost gave Dad apoplexy. They claimed they had no way of knowing how much things should cost, because plans for expansion—five volumes, no less—had been drawn up in 1935 and then lost somewhere in the library of the Army War College. Often, instead of buying equipment, the army rented it and wound up paying twice as much as its original cost.

In August, 1941, my father documented $100 million of waste in the $1 billion camp-building program. The army immediately went to work at changing its procedures, and Lieutenant General Brehon B. Somervell, who later became chief of the Quartermaster Corps Construction Division, estimated that the army had saved a hundred million dollars by heeding the Truman Committee's criticisms.

My father asked the Senate for more money to continue his investigations. This time he got $85,000. The Truman Committee was off and running. I know that is a cliché, but it is also an accurate description of the pace Dad set for himself for the next three years. He was always on a plane or a train en route to hear testimony at a shipyard or an aircraft production plant, an army base or a munitions depot. I missed him intensely while he was gone, but during these years, by way of consolation, he began to write me my first letters. I was now seventeen, and he obviously felt I was too old to be included in his letters to Mother with a side remark or a closing "kiss Margie for me." Of course, this decision also involved a little self-improvement for me. It was understood that I had to write letters to him, too. Or else.

The first of these letters came from Springfield, Missouri, dated October 1, 1941:

My dear Margie,

Your very nice letter came yesterday to the Melbourne Hotel in St. Louis. I am glad you like your Spanish and the teacher of it. In days to come it will be a most useful asset. Keep it up and when we get to the point when we can take our South American tour you can act as guide and interpreter.

Ancient History is one of the most interesting of all studies. By it you find out why a lot of things happen today. But you must study it on the basis of the biographies of the men and women who lived it. For instance, if you were listening in on the Senate committee hearings of your dad, you would understand why old Diogenes carried a lantern in the daytime in his search for an honest man. Most everybody is fundamentally honest, but when men or women are entrusted with public funds or trust estates of other people they find it most difficult to honestly administer them. I can't understand or find out why that is so—but it is.

You will also find out that people did the same things, made the same mistakes, and followed the same trends as we do today. For instance, the Hebrews had a republic three or four thousand years ago that was almost ideal in its practical workings. Yet they tired of it and went to a monarchy or totalitarian state. So did Greece, Carthage, Rome. . . . I'm glad you like Ancient History—wish I could study it again with you. Buy this month's National Geographic and see how like us ancient Egypt was. Here is a dollar to buy it with. You can buy soda pop with the change.

Lots of love to you,
Dad

[141]

Four days later another, totally different letter came from Nashville, Tennessee:

Dear Margie,

I have a hotel radio in my room. The co-ed singing program is now on, and the charming young lady who is the "Charming Co-ed" hasn't half the voice of my baby.

You mustn't get agitated when your old dad calls you his baby, because he always will think of you as just that—no matter how old or how big you may get. When you'd cry at night with that awful pain, he'd walk you and wish he could have it for you. When that little pump of yours insisted on going 120 a minute when 70 would have been enough, he got a lot of grey hairs. And now—what a daughter he has! It is worth twice all the trouble and ten times the grey hairs.

Went to the Baptist Church in Caruthersville this morning and the good old Democratic preacher spread himself. He preached to me and at me and really settled the whole foreign situation—but it won't work. . . .

Last week I had dinner in Trenton and the Chinese Consul General at Chicago was on the program with me and he made a corking speech to the United States Senator present and not to the audience at all. It's awful what it means to some people to meet a Senator. You'd think I was Cicero or Cato. But I'm not. Just a country jake who works at the job. . . .

Lots of love,
Dad

A month later, he was down in Roanoke, Virginia, sending me another history lesson:

Dear Margie,

Yesterday I drove over the route that the last of the Confederate army followed before the surrender. I thought of the heartache of one of the world's great men on the occasion of that surrender. I am not sorry he did surrender, but I feel as your old country grandmother has expressed it—"What a pity a *white* man like Lee had to surrender to *old* Grant." She'd emphasize the white and the old. That "old" had all the epithets a soldier knows in it. But Grant wasn't so bad. When old Thad Stevens wanted to send Lee to jail, Grant told him he'd go too. If Grant had been satisfied like Gen. Pershing to rest on his military honors and hadn't gone into politics, he'd have been one of the country's great.

But Marse Robert *was* one of the *world's* great. He and
Stonewall rank with Alexander, Hannibal and Napoleon as
military leaders—and Lee was a good man along with it.

> Kiss Mamma and lots for you,
> Dad

A week later he was in a sentimental mood again:

My dear Margie,

I wanted to say my dear baby and then I thought what a
grand young lady I have for a daughter—and I didn't. You
made your papa very happy when you told him you couldn't
be bribed. You keep that point of view and I'll always be as
proud of you as I always want to be. Anybody who'll give up
a principle for a price is no better than John L. Lewis or any
other racketeer—and that's what John L. is. . . .

Your dad won the brass ring in the Washington Merry-Go-
Round day before yesterday. Why? Because the two liars who
write it said that publicity means not so much to him. It doesn't,
but they don't believe it.

I am hoping I still get the nice letter. There is one awful
three days ahead. I'm going to have to show up graft and mis-
use of govn't funds. It will hurt somebody—maybe the one who
doesn't deserve it. But your dad has gotten himself into a job
that has to be done and no matter who it hurts it will be . . .

> Lots of love,
> Dad

I'm sorry to report I can't remember why I refused to be
bribed. But I do remember all too vividly Dad's attitude toward
John L. Lewis, which was formed in the first days of the Truman
Committee. Mr. Lewis was playing his usual game of threatening
the nation with disaster by calling all his miners out on strike.
Dad's committee had been functioning less than a month, but he
already regarded himself as the voice of the Senate in regard to
the National Defense Program, and so he boldly inserted himself
into the brawl and summoned Mr. Lewis to a hearing. Forced to
negotiate in the glare of the spotlight my father was holding on
him, Mr. Lewis was unable to perform any of his backstage antics.
Then Dad turned the heat on the mine owners. When it became
obvious that the Southern branch of the coal mining establishment was blocking a settlement, my father warned them that he
was going to summon the real owners of the mines—Northern

[143]

capitalists and bankers—to the witness stand and force them to admit that their attempt to insist on lower wages for Southern workers was totally fraudulent. By nightfall the strike was settled.

My father's unflattering reference to the column, "The Washington Merry-Go-Round," was also in character. He detested most columnists—especially those who wrote about Washington politics. Like most of his harsh dislikes, it was based on facts, experience.

Toward the press as a whole, my father's attitude was more positive. He always recognized the importance of getting information to the people. He did his utmost to tell responsible reporters everything possible about the work of the Truman Committee. His releases came to be known as "Truman Hours" and were always timed to give both press and radio reporters a chance to meet their deadlines.

At the same time he fretted over the dangers of too much publicity. Early in 1942 he wrote to one close friend:

> My committee has had so much publicity in the last sixty days that its work is not nearly as efficient as it was before that time. We are in a situation where the slightest mistake will cause us serious difficulty. . . . One bad tactical error, political or otherwise, can ruin the whole structure much more easily than it could have done when we were first starting.

By the time he wrote these words the Truman Committee was no longer investigating the defense program—it was the war effort. On December 7, 1941, my father was in Columbia, Missouri, at a small hotel—the kind of place he retreated to at the end of the '48 election campaign. Already he had found that the only way he could get any rest was to hole up in an isolated spot on a Sunday. That historic day was gray and gloomy in Washington. Nursing a cold, I stayed in the house and listened to the New York Philharmonic, simultaneously telling myself I should be doing my homework. Suddenly there was a voice interrupting the lovely music, announcing that Japanese planes had attacked some obscure, distant place known as Pearl Harbor. Since the Japanese had been attacking China for over three years, and Pearl Harbor sounded Chinese to me, I couldn't see what all the fuss was about. Mother wandered by, and I remarked crossly that the network had a heck of a nerve, interrupting good music to talk about a foreign war.

"What was the name of the place you said they were attacking?"

"Pearl Harbor."

My mother gasped and rushed for the telephone. The next thing I heard was her voice excitedly talking to my father in Missouri, telling him that the Japanese were attacking Hawaii.

Out in the Pennant Hotel in Columbia, Missouri, Dad put on his clothes and raced across the road to a private airport, where he begged the owner to get him to St. Louis as fast as possible. They flew in a small plane, and he arrived just in time to catch a night flight to Washington. It was quite a trip. Every time the plane landed, another congressman or a senator got on. Ordinary citizens were ruthlessly ejected, and pretty soon the plane was a congressional special. They arrived in Washington around dawn. With no sleep, Dad rushed to the Capitol. I soon followed him, thanks to a neat trick I pulled on my mother. I was still running a fever, but I fooled Mother into thinking it was gone by holding my mouth open after she inserted the thermometer. I was not going to let a cold keep me away from seeing history made. Mother gave me her entrance ticket and I zoomed to the special session of Congress. By the time I got there the only seat left was in the photographers' gallery. This gave me the same view that the rest of the nation later saw in the movie theaters, as President Roosevelt announced the day of infamy and called for war. I then followed the senators back to the Senate, where I heard my father vote for a declaration of war.

Almost immediately, powerful voices in Washington, who wanted to run the war their own way, tried to dismantle the Truman Committee. Under Secretary of War Robert P. Patterson wrote to President Roosevelt: "It is in the public interest that the Committee should suspend for the time being. It will impair our activities if we have to take time out to supply the Truman Committee all the information it desires." But my father was no slouch at Washington infighting. Secretary Patterson wrote this letter on December 13, 1941. On December 10, Dad had written the President, assuring him that the committee would be "100 percent behind the Administration" and would scrupulously avoid interfering in military or naval strategy or tactics.

This statement was rooted not only in sound political instinct but in my father's deep knowledge of American history. Shortly before he formed the committee, he had borrowed from the

Library of Congress "Reports of the Joint Committee on the Conduct of the War," the hearings of the congressional committee that had played watchdog during the Civil War. This outfit had considered themselves great strategists, and were constantly interfering in strictly military affairs, sniffing treachery in every lost battle, hiring and firing generals and generally harassing President Lincoln to the point of near distraction. After Pearl Harbor, Senators Vandenberg, Brewster, and Taft came to my father and asked him to broaden his committee by appointing more Republicans and widen its jurisdiction to include all aspects of the war. My father did expand the committee to ten senators, but he absolutely refused to make it a Committee on the Conduct of the War. "Thank goodness I knew my history and wouldn't do it," he said later.

At the same time, when it came to watchdogging the war effort, Senator Truman was, if anything, tougher than he had been on the defense program. To one new committee investigator, early in 1942, he wrote:

> Go into the investigation . . . with all you've got. Don't let those fellows get any statement out of you that they are doing a good job. Don't compliment them. . . . If you do and it is later found they haven't done a good job, then they can say our committee agreed with what they did.

With this approach, Dad soon took on some of the biggest names in Washington.

One was Jesse Jones, who wore so many hats he sometimes sounded like a one-man government. As head of the Reconstruction Finance Corporation he had the power to lend hundreds of millions to various companies to enable them to do defense work. He was also Secretary of Commerce, and in this office he had access to very powerful business connections, aside from being a millionaire himself. An arrogant man, he was not used to having his decisions questioned. But my father discovered from Harold Ickes, among others, that Mr. Jones was largely responsible for a truly alarming aluminum shortage. Alcoa (The Aluminum Corporation of America) dominated the production of this metal, so vital for aircraft manufacturing, and they conned Jones into signing a plant expansion contract which gave them monopoly control of the market while the government put up all the money to build the plants.

The mere possibility of being summoned before a committee to answer for his actions aroused Jesse Jones's wrath, and he turned on every iota of influence he had in Washington to make Senator Truman back down. This only made Dad madder, and Mr. Jones soon appeared before the Truman Committee, where he weakly admitted the original contract was a flagrant violation of the government's interest and agreed to renegotiate it. At the hearing my father treated him courteously. He made it a point, no matter how mad he might be at a man in private, never to browbeat him when he was a witness before his committee. He detested congressional committees that abused their powers and turned their hearings into witch-hunts or circuses. At one point in the committee's tussle with John L. Lewis, one of the senators called the coal miners' leader a "charlatan." Dad instantly called his colleague to order with a sharp rebuke.

In the aluminum mess, my father found far more fault with Alcoa than he did with Jesse Jones. He was enraged and astounded by the way this supposedly great American company had disregarded the national interest in making interlocking agreements with I.G. Farben, the German corporate giant. In order to keep Farben out of Alcoa's American markets, Alcoa agreed to stay out of the magnesium production field, and even let Farben buy American magnesium, which Alcoa owned, at prices far below those charged American users of the metal. As a result, in 1941, Germany was producing 400 percent more magnesium—another vitally needed metal for war planes—than the United States. When my father released these findings in January, 1942, as part of his first annual report, they created a sensation. The *New Republic* and *The New York Times* joined in calling the revelations a decisive contribution to the prosecution of the war.

When it came to revealing shortages, my father played no favorites. Poet Archibald MacLeish, in charge of the Office of Facts and Figures, released a glowingly optimistic report to the nation, assuring everyone that we had more than enough rubber stockpiled to last for the duration. The Truman Committee grimly replied, a few weeks later, that there was in fact an alarming rubber shortage and published the figures to prove it.

[147]

My father was passionately committed to winning the war, and he absolutely refused to let anyone or anything stand in the way. Part of this passion was rooted, I think, in the frustration he felt because he was too old to get into the fight. It was not for want of trying. In 1940 he had gone over to the War Department and tackled General George Marshall. Dad was still a colonel in the army reserve, and he had kept up his study of field artillery.

"I would like very much to have a chance to work in this war as a field artillery colonel," he said.

General Marshall pulled down his spectacles, eyed my gray-haired father, and said, "Senator, how old are you?"

"Well," said Dad lamely, "I'm fifty-six."

"You're too damned old. You'd better stay home and work in the Senate."

Tartly, Dad replied, "You're three years older than I am."

"I know. But I'm already a general."

Some five years later General Marshall came to the White House to see the President of the United States, who happened to be the same reserve colonel he had so abruptly rejected. Matt Connelly, now serving as Dad's appointments secretary, was a great tease. "General," he said, "if the man in the other room"—meaning Dad—"were to ask the same question now that he did in 1940, what would you say?"

General Marshall declined to lose his magisterial calm. He thought for a moment and said, "Well, I would tell him the same thing, only I would be a little more diplomatic about it."

My father was crushed when Harry Vaughan, who was a lieutenant colonel, talked himself onto active duty and went winging off to Australia. Mr. Vaughan had replaced Vic Messall as Dad's chief administrative assistant. Dad arranged to tour some California defense plants to coincide with Mr. Vaughan's departure, and they went out on the train together. From Los Angeles he wrote me the following letter. The opening was to become a familiar refrain to his lazy, non-letter-writing daughter.

Friday, Mar. 13, 1942

Dear Margie:

Your old dad was sorely disappointed when he found no letter awaiting him at the St. Francis Hotel in San Francisco.

There was one from your mother and two from Aunt Mary—but *none* from Margie. You see the number averaged up all right. I'd expected three and I had three but not from three people.

You are now a young lady eighteen years young and you are responsible from now on for what Margie does. Your very excellent and efficient mother has done her duty for eighteen very short and very happy (to me) years. Your dad has looked on and has been satisfied with the result.

You have a good mind, a beautiful physique and a possible successful future outlook—but that now is up to you. You are the mistress of your future. All your mother and dad can do is to look on, advise when asked and hope and wish you a happy one. There'll be troubles and sorrow a plenty but there'll also be happy days and hard work.

From a financial standpoint your father has not been a shining success but he has tried to leave you something that (as Mr. Shakespeare says) cannot be stolen—an honorable reputation and a good name. You must continue that heritage and see that it is not spoiled. You're all we have and we both count on you.

I've had a pleasant and restful trip. Met a young Captain in San Francisco who told me his name is Truman Young. He's a great grandson of the famous Brigham. I delivered Mr. Vaughan at Ft. Mason and we hated to part. The General gave me his plane—I flew to L.A. Will see Sen. Hatch tomorrow and you on Monday. Kiss your Mamma for me & lots of 'em to you.

Dad

My father's interest in the Far East remained intense for several reasons. Mother had a cousin, a brigadier general who was with MacArthur and Wainwright on Corregidor, and Dad had another cousin, Lou Truman, who was an aide of the commanding general at Pearl Harbor. With Harry Vaughan and another good Missouri friend, Roy Harper, in Australia, my father was an avid reader and seeker of news from that part of the world. On June 30, 1942, Dad wrote to me from Washington—Mother and I were back in Independence—remarking that a visiting general from Australia was coming to see him: "I guess he can tell me all about Harry Vaughan and Roy Harper. I hope he'll tell me all about the war in the Far East and Down Under. . . ."

Dad soon became philosophic about being out of the fighting war. Even before he went to California with Harry Vaughan, he was consoling Eddie McKim, who had met with similar frustration when he tried to join up:

> Ed, somebody must do just what you are doing; create the wealth to make the wheels go around and help the guns to fire. The fact that you are sending a boy and have four more children to support is reason enough for you to stay on the job where you are. . . . Harry Vaughan would have been much more useful in the operation of the war as my Secretary than he will be as a Lieutenant Colonel of the Field Artillery teaching a lot of shave-tails the fundamentals, and that is what he is doing. . . . Keep on producing . . . to pay the bill, and I will keep on standing on the lid as hard as I can to keep the costs down.

More than anything else, my father's memories of his World War I days were the source of his determination to let no one stand in the way of winning the war as fast as possible. He reacted almost angrily when a friend on the Chicago *Times,* Herb Graffis, told him that he was building a reputation that would make him a good presidential candidate:

> Regarding the last paragraph of your letter, the ruination of more good legislative workers is brought about by that Presidential bee than any other one thing. I can name you a half a dozen fellows in the United States Senate who have been ruined by just having the bee fly close to them. I have no further political ambition, and the thing I am most interested in now is to win this war as quickly as possible. I think I told you I was on the Front in the last war firing at ten forty five on November Eleventh, and I am not so sure all my gang would have come back if I had moved forward. . . . I am not a candidate for anything but reelection to the United States Senate in 1946, and I am announcing that right now.

During these war years my father worked so hard and was away from home so much, I sometimes wondered if he might forget what Mother and I looked like. But this was a foolish fear. First, last, and always Dad was a family man. When we went back to Independence during the summer months and left him to his own devices in Washington, he often sounded as if we had abandoned him on a desert island. In 1942, after being alone for almost a month, he wrote:

> It has been a most dull and lonesome June for me. Get up at 5:30, drink tomato juice and milk, go to work, eat some toast and orange juice and work some more, maybe have a committee fight and a floor fight, go home, go to bed and start over.

During one of these abandoned periods he startled me by reporting that he had gone to "a picture show." I was one of the great movie addicts of the '30s and '40s, but Dad rarely if ever went and when he did go, he seldom enjoyed himself. This time was no exception. "I've forgotten what it was," he coolly informed me. "I know it was rather silly and I did not see it all." (The thought of seeing a movie from the middle and not waiting to see the first part made me gasp with horror.) However, the movie house threw in a "good old-fashioned vaudeville show," as Dad called it, and this inspired a flood of reminiscence, which gave me a short course in the history of the theater in Kansas City:

> I wish they'd never closed the old Orpheums. I saw many famous actors at ours in Kansas City when I was on West Ninth Street. I saw Sarah Bernhardt there and Chic Sale, Eva Tanguey, and John Drew. The Four Cohans and other famous musical shows used to come to the old Grand at 7th and Walnut when your dad worked at a bank and acted as an usher at night. I saw Pickford, *The Floradora Girls*, *The Bohemian Girl*, Williams and Walker, famous Negro actors, Jim Corbett and a lot of others you've read about.
>
> Your Mamma and I used to go to the Willis Wood at 11th and Baltimore to hear Vladimir de Pachmann play Mozart's Ninth Sonata, and see Henry Irving and Ellen Terry play *Julius Caesar* and *Othello*, Richard Mansfield play *Richard III* and *Dr. Jekyll and Mr. Hyde*—and then be afraid to go home.

In the Senate Dad continued to prove that he was afraid of nobody in Washington. He found that the powerful labor leader Sidney Hillman had deliberately ignored a Michigan company's low bid on a defense housing project, because he claimed that their labor practices would have led to a strike. Mr. Hillman had been designated by FDR as one of the two top men in the defense program, and was a White House intimate in the bargain. My father strode onto the Senate floor and declared:

> I cannot condemn Mr. Hillman's position too strongly. First the United States does not fear trouble from any source; and, if trouble is threatened, the United States is able to protect itself. If Mr. Hillman cannot or will not protect the interests of the United States, I am in favor of replacing him with someone who can and will.

The more my father studied the defense program, the more he became convinced that it was a two-headed monster, with the business representative, William S. Knudsen, and the labor representative, Mr. Hillman, pulling in opposite directions. The Truman Committee's first annual report recommended that the whole setup be junked, and the production side of the war effort be placed in the hands of a single man with authority to make all the major decisions. In line with his determination not to embarrass the President, Dad had let Mr. Roosevelt see the report well in advance of its publication. The day after the report appeared, the President announced the establishment of the War Production Board under the leadership of Missourian Donald M. Nelson. According to most historians of these days, he was Harry Hopkins's choice for the job—and Harry Hopkins was the Roosevelt man that Dad knew and liked best.

It is clear, from my father's own words, that he played no small part in the choice. He said to Mr. Nelson when he appeared before the committee:

> We have fought to get you this job. We are going to fight to support you now in carrying it out. If you meet any obstacles in the carrying out of this job where this committee can turn the light of publicity on the subject to call attention to legislation that should be enacted to give you the necessary means to carry the job out, we want to be informed, and we are at your service.

Obviously, the Truman Committee was doing a lot more than simply criticizing the war effort. It was playing a major role in giving it shape and direction.

The facts that prove this are a little dry, but I think they are important. Dad's support of Nelson was part of his fundamental conviction that the war effort had to be controlled by civilians. Everywhere he looked, he saw generals and admirals taking over the civilian economy, and issuing orders and making decisions as if they were on a military base. He became so alarmed that on November 26, 1942, he went on the "March of Time" news broadcast and told the nation that civilian control of the economy was "the most important question of the day."

"Any attempt on the part of these ambitious generals and admirals to take complete control of the nation's economy," he said, "would present a definite threat to our postwar political and economic structure."

On February 11, 1943, Dad made another speech on the subject in the Senate. He was particularly incensed at this time because his good friend Lou E. Holland, of Kansas City, whom Dad had helped name as chairman of the Smaller War Plants Corporation, had been ousted and replaced with an army colonel. "I believe uniforms should be reserved for the purposes for which they were adopted; namely to distinguish the combatants on the field of battle," Dad said. He insinuated rather strongly that these "so-called" officers were nothing more than big businessmen in disguise, and he pointed to facts he had already publicized in committee hearings, about the army's tendency to favor big business in their procurement programs.

The dangers my father saw in this growing military control were many and diverse. He did not really fear a military take-over of the government. But he did believe that the military were very insensitive to civilian needs and, if unchecked, were inclined to starve the civilian side of the economy to the point where severe morale problems might have developed. Also, when it came to signing contracts for war material or inspecting the finished products, a man in uniform can be ordered to do things, while a civilian, in Dad's words, "can tell the admirals and the generals where to head in."

In this capacity, Donald Nelson was a severe disappointment to my father. He frequently crumpled under military pressure and gave the brass hats more and more control. Grimly Dad went to work to prove the dangers with facts. He was in an ideal position to do so, because every day he received hundreds of letters, telegrams, and phone calls from people working in defense plants and in shipyards, telling him about corruption or mismanagement in their immediate area.

In January, 1943, army inspectors in an Ohio plant of the Wright Aeronautical Corporation, a subsidiary of Curtiss-Wright, told my father that defective engines were being delivered to our combat forces. These army men had turned to the Truman Committee in desperation, because their superior officers at the plant, and their superiors in Washington, had overruled and suppressed their reports and blithely collaborated with Curtiss-Wright executives to accept these defective engines and parts.

The story was so shocking that my father's first inclination was to conceal it from the public, because of the terrific impact it was certain to have on morale. But to his amazement and wrath, in secret hearings the army absolutely refused to admit there was anything to the charges. Dad and his fellow senators had to sit there and listen to generals and colonels lie in their teeth. Then the army announced it was making its own inspection and issued a complete whitewash. That was too much for Dad, and he ordered the committee to publish their facts. The same day the Department of Justice went to court and formally accused Curtiss-Wright of delivering defective material.

The army fought back with a ferocious publicity campaign. Under Secretary of War Robert Patterson flatly denied the validity of the Truman Committee's findings. Curtiss-Wright, which was second only to General Motors in the procurement of war contracts, filled newspapers and magazines with an advertising campaign that trumpeted its own excellence, and inspired innumerable articles and stories accusing the Truman Committee of serving "a half baked loaf" and damaging civilian and military morale out of a greedy hunger for political sensationalism. Even *The New York Times,* I regret to say, swallowed the story and called the committee's report "ill-advised."

Dad sent Hugh Fulton to New York to talk to the *Times* brass, and show them the facts. He then informed Under Secretary of War Patterson that he was going to call him before the committee. Patterson had declared that the army never received a single defective engine from Curtiss-Wright. Dad knew that the army, once the committee broke the story, had dismantled hundreds of engines and reinspected them. On this second go-around, a shocking percentage of the engines had been found to contain defective parts, and, worse, they failed critical tests. Once the Under Secretary of War was confronted with these facts, he was man enough to admit that he was wrong. He called on Dad in his office, apologized, and promised to stop the anti-Truman Committee publicity campaign.

Around this same time my father tangled with the admirals, with equally spectacular results. He caught them collaborating with a subsidiary of U.S. Steel, accepting steel plate for warships that had been produced with fake specifications and falsified records. When the committee broke the story, Charles E. Wilson, vice chairman of the War Production Board, publicly reprimanded the chairman of the Board of U.S. Steel for "poor management." Just as in the Curtiss-Wright fiasco, the admirals and the steel company's executives collaborated in a publicity campaign to deny the charges. Dad evened the score by attacking from the opposite flank.

In a committee report issued on April 22, 1943, my father stressed the need for new ship construction because of the enormous losses we had been taking from German submarines. The navy had been working hard to give the public the impression that the antisubmarine war was going well. Dad, acting on his conviction that "certainty is always better than rumor," gave the public the facts—during 1942 we had lost a million tons of shipping a month. Secretary of the Navy Frank Knox blandly dismissed the figures. "Senator Truman got his figure," he said, ". . . from some uninformed source, probably common gossip." This time Dad let one of his fellow senators do the fighting for him. Owen Brewster of Maine called on fellow Republican Knox and informed him that he was headed for an open committee session, where he was going to have to do some public word-eating. Lamely, the Secretary of the Navy issued a statement that Senator Truman's figures were correct.

Another point on which my father tangled with the generals was their manpower demands. Again and again he spoke out against their tendency to build an army too big for the country to support. These criticisms forced them to reduce the size of the army by several million, and to his satisfaction, this reduction did not have the slightest effect on their over-all strategic planning. In 1943 a bill was introduced in the Senate which would have empowered the government to draft workers and shift them around the country at will. Again Dad rose to severely criticize such a measure, which he insisted was unnecessary. Like the generals, the people running the War Manpower Commission tended to vastly exaggerate shortages in various parts of the country, and when all these imaginary shortages were added up, we had a manpower crisis.

To prove there was no crisis, my father did an investigation of Dallas, Texas, where the War Manpower Commission reported the North American Aviation plant was short 13,000 workers. But Dad had received a complaint from a source inside the plant, which stated that far from there being a worker shortage, the plant was actually overstaffed, and there was widespread loafing. Truman Committee investigators soon confirmed this complaint. A subsequent investigation of Dallas by the War Production Board under its executive vice chairman, Charles E. Wilson, confirmed Dad's conclusion that there was no critical shortage of manpower in the Dallas area. Even then, however, the War Manpower Commission refused to take Dallas off its critical list. Only when my father forced Paul McNutt, head of the WMC, to appear before the committee at a public hearing did he face up to the facts and agree to revise his list.

Another battle in which my father played a prominent part had to do with the structure of the postwar world. The internationalists in the Senate, of which Dad was emphatically one, wanted President Roosevelt and the Democratic party to come out strongly for an effective world security organization. The subject was frequently discussed at Truman Committee conclaves. Finally, three members of his committee, Republicans Joseph Ball of Minnesota and Harold Burton of Ohio, and Democrat Carl A. Hatch of New Mexico, joined with Senator Lister Hill of Alabama to introduce Senate Resolution 114, which soon became known as B^2H^2. It called on Congress and the President to begin making concrete plans for postwar international machinery with power adequate to maintain the peace.

The resolution received very little encouragement from the White House. FDR, remembering Wilson's experience with the

League of Nations, was extremely cautious about discussing his postwar plans with Congress. He feared that he might antagonize the powerful isolationist sentiment among both Republicans and Southern Democrats. My father was one of the most vigorous backers of B^2H^2. He spent endless hours buttonholing fellow senators, urging them to support it. "The bipartisan character of this proposal is the best thing that has happened in Congress in many years," he said in a public statement of support.

From March 20, 1943, when the resolution was introduced, until early November, the battle over B^2H^2 raged in Congress and the press. Finally, the head of the Senate Foreign Relations Committee, Senator Tom Connally of Texas (also on the Truman Committee), introduced a resolution calling for the "establishment and maintenance of international authority with power to prevent aggression and preserve the peace of the world." The Senate approved it overwhelmingly. To this day my father considers his work on behalf of B^2H^2 and its descendant, the Connally Resolution, one of the most important achievements of his senatorial career.

At the time I knew little of these behind-the-scenes dramas. I had enrolled in George Washington University in 1942 and was struggling to fight my way through horrendous required courses, such as botany, as well as staggering amounts of my major subject, history, which I loved. Dad was delighted when I decided to major in history. But his delight soon turned to chagrin, when he discovered that I was as contrary as the rest of the Trumans and was concentrating on English history, not American. However, his spirits rose in 1944, when I took a required course in American history. When we got to the Civil War, he envisioned himself somehow finding time to overwhelm me with his vast and complex knowledge of the various military campaigns. But our teacher was not interested in the military history of the country. He concentrated on social and political history and skipped over the whole military side of the Civil War in about twenty minutes. Dad's outrage was absolutely spectacular. Mother and I loved it. Battles —who needs them.

With all the pressure he was working under, my father seldom if ever said a cross word to me intentionally. I was still his baby. But the paths of father-daughter relationships don't always run smoothly, especially when daughter is emerging from her cocoon of shyness and coping with the problems of late adolescence. One night early in 1944 the Truman Committee gave a dinner for General George C. Marshall, the army's chief of staff. I was one of the supernumerary guests. I happened to be standing near the door when the General arrived, and Dad introduced me. Then someone called him away, leaving me and the General together. I fell in love instantly with this remarkable man. He asked me what I was studying in college. When I told him it was history, we got into a fascinating discussion. What impressed me—even staggered me—was his eagerness to know *my* opinion of my courses and the teaching techniques I was seeing. He was amazingly interested in education, and he discoursed for some time on his belief that film is one of the best ways to teach history. He urged me to suggest it to my professors.

Finally, after twenty or twenty-five minutes, Dad came over and said, "You can't monopolize the guest of honor and the General of the Armies, you know." My mouth fell open. I had forgotten I was talking to General Marshall. He was marvelous at making you forget his importance, while simultaneously making you feel that you and what you were saying were important to him.

When I got home that night, I was on Cloud 9. I floated around the apartment, rhapsodizing about the attention General Marshall had paid me. Finally, Dad could stand it no longer. He looked up from a report he was reading and brought me abruptly down to earth. "Why wouldn't General Marshall sit down and talk with the daughter of the head of the investigating committee of the war effort?" he snapped.

I was shattered. I could have taken this crack from Mother, because she is the cynic of the family. Again and again she had pointed out to me that I should be suspicious of people who were too nice to me, because Dad was a powerful senator. But somehow, Dad pointing it out made it almost unbearable. (Now, of course, he freely admits he was wrong—he didn't know General Marshall very well at the time.) I retired to my bedroom and cried for an hour. It was a perfect excuse not to study for a chemistry exam the next day, and I came within an eyelash of flunking it. Dad never knew that he upset me. But I learned the lesson of his growing importance.

I got another glimpse of this importance—albeit in a somewhat negative way—the day we christened the *Missouri,* in the Brooklyn Navy Yard. It was my first real visit to New York. John Snyder's daughter Drucie and another close friend, Jane Lingo, were invited along to be my maids of honor at the ceremony. The night before the launching we went to see *Oklahoma.* It was my first Broadway show. Drucie, Jane, and I were so excited we stayed up all night, we literally did not go to sleep for one second. By the time we arrived at the Navy Yard, we were glassy eyed. It was a gray January day, typical New York weather. We stood under the bow of the *Missouri,* which was as high as a fifteen-story building, while workmen knocked away the beams that were holding her on the ways. Everything was on a very tight schedule. The speech-making had to be finished just in time to give me a chance to swing my magnum of champagne, and then the last timber would be knocked aside and down the ways she would go.

What with no sleep and the excitement of the occasion, I missed what was really going on. The admirals on hand were busy revenging themselves on Dad for previous humiliations. Admirals and generals are a clannish bunch. Embarrass one and you've embarrassed them all—that tends to be their philosophy. Dad was supposed to give the main speech. One or two admirals were supposed to make brief remarks before him. Instead, they rambled on and on and on. When Dad finally got to the microphone, he had about three minutes to deliver a fifteen-minute speech. I never heard him talk so fast in my life.

Then came the signal. I gave a mighty bash with my magnum. Nothing happened to the *Missouri.* It seemed to have a mind of its own and was not in the mood for launching. Playfully I put my hand on the bow and gave her a shove. Meanwhile, I was getting a champagne shower. The christening platform was about a third of the way up the fifteen-story-high bow. Normally, once the bottle, which was in a sterling silver jacket, broke, it was hauled to the deck as the ship slid down the ways. The workmen above us were dutifully doing this job—but because the "Mighty Mo" refused to move, the champagne streamed out of the broken bottle right down on me and the commanding admiral. This was an accident—it was not part of the let's-torment-Truman program but it did not make Dad any happier. Finally, the "Mo" started to move, and just as it struck the water, the sun came out. It was the only time we saw the sun all day. All the navy men solemnly agreed that it was a good omen.

Two years later, when Dad was in the White House, he was still sending off sparks whenever he thought of the treatment he had received from the navy brass that day. On the eve of a trip to Florida he wrote:

> The darned navy have tried to give me an impossible schedule. As you know, every Admiral in nine hundred miles will want to be seen with the President. But they are going to be disappointed. I'll never forget what the same Admirals did to me and my sweet daughter at the launching of the Missouri.
> The same Admirals should read Josh Billings—should have read him before the launching. He said "Always be nice to your pore relations—they may suddenly become rich someday and it will be hard to explain."

At the time, however, his dizzy daughter and her equally dizzy friends restored his good humor with a stunt that is still remembered by old-timers at the Waldorf. We went to dinner in the hotel's Empire Room and just as crêpes suzette were being served for dessert, all three of us went to sleep, sitting up in our chairs. While waiters got hysterics, Mother politely suggested that we ought to go to bed. We nodded, abandoned our crêpes, went upstairs, and collapsed.

This incident may account for a mildly worried tone in the advice Dad gave me on my twentieth birthday:

> My dear daughter,
> On Thursday, the day after tomorrow, you'll be twenty years old. It doesn't seem possible but the facts of time make it so. I hope that you have a most happy birthday and that you'll have an unlimited number of them in the future. That, of course, will depend upon you and circumstances. You first and then what happens as old Father Time marches into the future. You must meet contingencies as they arise, and face them squarely. And I'm sure you will. You should have enough of your mother's will power and strength of character and your dad's affability to make out.

He wrote this letter from Jacksonville, Florida, where he had gone to make a Jackson Day dinner speech. On this trip he was not impressed either by Florida or by the crowd he drew:

> Florida, as represented by Jacksonville, is one heck of a place. The sun was shining brightly when I arrived Sunday, but it turned cold in the night and clouded up, then Monday it got warm and Monday night it stormed and rained and blew a gale, breaking windows and keeping the customers away from my speech. They wouldn't have come anyway, but they had an excuse. There were about two hundred and they were kind and enthusiastic. The optimistic national committee man and committee woman assured me there'd be two thousand—but zeros are easy to put on in politics.

More and more Senator Harry S. Truman was becoming a name and a voice that people wanted to hear (wind and weather permitting). The work of his committee appealed immensely to Americans everywhere. The idea that my father was "obscure" at this point in his political career is utter nonsense concocted by writers who specialize in overdramatizing politics. When fifty press gallery reporters were asked to list the ten Americans who had contributed the most to the war effort, Dad was the only member of Congress whom they named. His independence had won him a following, and the Democratic party simply had to acknowledge this as a fact. He even survived a distinct chill emanating from the White House—a temperature change that withered more than one promising political career during the Roosevelt era.

Part of this chill was caused by Dad's independence. He persisted in criticizing the manpower policies and many other aspects of the Roosevelt Administration's conduct of the war. But most of the temperature drop came from a literary double cross. In the fall of 1942 *American Magazine* hit the newsstands with an article, "We Can Lose the War in Washington," a wide-ranging, sensational critique of the whole war effort. The article had my father's name on it. Less than a week later the Democrats took quite a drubbing in the 1942 elections. It was the first—but, alas, not the last—time that Dad took a writer's word for what was in a document. Harassed and pressured as he was, he fell victim to one of the oldest dodges in the magazine business.

The magazine sent a girl down to Washington with a copy of

the final manuscript. She put on a marvelous act in Dad's office. She told him that the presses were ready to roll and begged him to stop everything he was doing and read the article. Then she implied it wasn't really necessary, because everything that was in it was exactly what Dad had told the writer.

My father had insisted in his original agreement that nothing could be printed unless he initialed each page of the manuscript. Now with the poor girl having fits, Dad's soft heart melted. "Well," he said, "you look like an honest girl." Without reading the manuscript he initialed each page, and she went racing gleefully back to New York. Later that day he did read the article, and his heart almost stopped beating. The piece read as if it had been written by a Roosevelt-hating Republican.

That very night my father sent committee lawyers hustling to New York and they went to court to block the circulation of the issue. But Sumner Blossom, the editor of *American Magazine*, smugly informed the court that the issue had already gone to press and Senator Truman had approved the article. After all, hadn't he initialed it? Legally Dad had no case, so he could only grind his teeth and accept the responsibility. The article, combined with the Democratic disaster on Election Day, made Dad's name anathema in the White House for months. Harley Kilgore of West Virginia, one of the stalwarts of the committee, finally explained what had happened to the President, and FDR agreed to forgive and try to forget.

In months to come my father had more pleasant experiences with other magazines. *Time* put him on its cover on March 8, 1943. The article was inaccurate in many minor ways, and the cover portrait made him look like Rip Van Winkle, but they called him "a billion dollar watchdog" and praised the work of the committee. The *Reader's Digest* also lavishly praised the committee as "the public's most accessible court of appeals." By this time more and more Democrats realized that the style and standards my father set for the Truman Committee had stolen all the thunder from Republican criticisms of the war—criticisms that would have been far more partisan, and aimed more directly at the President.

In his letter to me about his Jackson Day dinner speech in Florida, Dad, with his usual modesty, did not even bother to mention that the speech, under-attended though it was, contained one of his most important public statements. He urged the renomination and reelection of FDR for a fourth term to fight the war to a victorious conclusion. Dad explicitly identified the work of his committee with the administration, praising it for welcoming the criticisms he made (most of the time, anyway) and warning Republicans against playing politics with any of the committee's disclosures. He made similar speeches in Topeka, Kansas, and at state Democratic conventions in Missouri and Connecticut in the coming months. *The New York Times* was soon reporting that Dad's words "had the effect of giving a stamp of approval to the nation's war leaders and war program from a source which command's considerable respect." The *Times* concluded that the speeches were "an important boost for President Roosevelt's nomination and for his chances with the electorate next November."

After something happens, particularly an election or some other historical event, we tend to believe that it was inevitable. It is hard, often impossible, to recapture the frame of mind that prevailed before the event. Early in 1944 there was considerable alarm within the Democratic party about their prospects in the coming presidential election. Although the war was going reasonably well, there was as yet no sign of an imminent Axis collapse. D-Day had yet to come. The home front was seething with labor unrest. The civilian side of the war effort was wracked by personal feuds, and Congress was almost out of the President's control. Dad's support—entirely unsolicited by the White House—was not only welcome, but needed.

Privately, I might add here, my father was very critical of the way the Roosevelt Administration handled the politics of the home front. In a letter to his fellow Young Turk, Lewis B. Schwellenbach, who had become a federal district judge in Washington, he remarked in mid-1943:

> The political situation is bad everywhere. If an effort had been made to do things in the way that would make people against the Administration a better job along that line couldn't have been done. In Missouri nearly every man in charge of the Office of Price Administration have been people who thoroughly hated the Administration and everything it stands for, and naturally they do the harsh things that are necessary for the

enforcement of price control and production management in such a way as to put all the blame on the White House, and I have been informed that that same policy in appointments has been followed in most of the States.

Once more my father voiced his disapproval of this Roose-veltian approach to political opponents: "The President's mistaken notion he was getting co-operation by taking the enemy into the camp is something I never did believe in and I don't believe in that policy now."

Throughout the early months of 1944 my father was in the forefront of a vital, politically explosive home-front battle—the debate over reconversion to a peacetime economy. He called for a reconversion plan, now. The military and their big-business supporters did everything in their power to wreck Donald Nelson's inclination to follow Dad's lead in this direction. I stress this theme again, because I don't believe that people realize the lead-ership that Dad exerted on major policy decisions which shaped the entire war effort. Most of the American public, preoccupied by the war news that poured in every day from the far-flung battlefronts, ignored this aspect of things. But acute observers in Washington were very much aware of it. On March 5, 1944, Donald Nelson released to the press a letter he had written to Senator Francis Maloney of Connecticut in which he outlined his future policy on reconversion. Almost every detail was drawn from recommendations made by the Truman Committee. On March 11 the Kiplinger *Washington Letter* observed: "WPB [the War Production Board] especially is allied closely to Truman brand of thinking and WPB is already moving along the Truman lines."

In the last part of 1943 my father and Hugh Fulton prepared a paper outlining some of the problems of reconversion. The report pointed to the tremendous opportunities open to America if they developed programs to use resources and facilities devel-oped by the war. The report called on the War Production Board to begin giving "special attention" to this aspect of the war effort. But the military pressure inside the War Production Board was simply too strong; when Nelson made some tentative steps in the direction my father suggested, the battle that erupted cost him his job. As a result, the American economy went steaming into the abrupt end of World War II with practically no plans for reconversion. It seems especially ironic that the man who first suggested careful planning to make the transition from peace to war as smooth as possible was then in the White House, stuck with the gigantic headaches that developed.

My father was far more interested in the battle over reconversion than he was in the rumors and suggestions that were already beginning to float around, naming him as the Democratic candidate for vice president. On May 26, 1944, he went to Brooklyn and made one of his most significant wartime policy speeches, to the Chamber of Commerce there. Called "The War in Review," it blasted the military for their opposition to removing restrictions on civilian production. He was especially incensed at the army's suggestion that any workers who were idled by cutbacks and cancellations in the defense program should be held by government order in a manpower pool. That's their way, Dad said, "of referring to what I call unemployment."

Some of the letters Dad wrote me around this time are fascinating in retrospect. He seemed to sense, and simultaneously recoil a little from, the destiny that was facing him. On May 14, 1944, he wrote me from Hot Springs, Arkansas:

> Sometimes your dad wishes he'd gone on and been a music hall pianist or a bank vice president. You see Arthur Eisenhower started in the National Bank of Commerce after your pa did and is now its executive vice president—and he didn't know how to turn on a gas jet when he came to Kansas City—asked old Mrs. Trow our boarding housekeeper, for a coal oil lamp. But that's not to his discredit. It just shows how great is opportunity in good ole USA. And it is greater now than ever. If I didn't believe I'd lived in the greatest age in history, I'd wish to live in yours, but I'd want you and your mother to live with me.
>
> Your old dad would be very, very happy if his daughter would always have a letter waiting for him when he gets to a new place.
>
> You are all he has for the future and you, of course, cannot appreciate what you mean to him.

My father was inclined to ignore the vice-presidential rumors and suggestions that began coming his way in early 1944 because they were not new to him. As early as 1942 letters began arriving from friends in Missouri, urging him to run for the office. These mounted in frequency as the fame of the Truman Committee investigations grew. Again and again he gave them much the same answer he gave to Adelbert E. Weston, a friend from Neosho, Missouri, on April 25th, 1944:

> I have no intention of running for Vice President. I don't want the job and I've never solicited it and don't expect to. . . . I've been trying to do a job in the Senate, and would like to stay here and do it. It takes a lot of work and a lot of time to get started in the Senate, and then to throw it all away would just be something unheard of.

Earlier in the year he had written to another friend, Harry G. Waltner, director of the Unemployment Compensation Commission of Missouri. He had sent Dad a clipping from the Independence *Examiner,* in which the publisher, "Pop" Southern, had declared that Dad had no ambition to be vice president.

> The old man is right [Dad wrote]. I have worked nine years learning how to be a United States Senator and I see no reason in the world to throw it away. The Vice President simply presides over the Senate and sits around hoping for a funeral. It is a very high office which consists entirely of honor and I don't have any ambition to hold an office like that.

To another friend, Frank Schwartz of Detroit, he spelled out in more detail why he wanted to remain in the Senate. Writing on June 16, he said:

> It takes six or seven years for a man to get adjusted in the Senate so he can be of some use to his community. I am a member of three of the most important and three of the nosiest committees in the Senate—the Appropriations, Military Affairs, and the Interstate Commerce Committee, and in addition to that I have this Special Committee to Investigate the War Program, and I feel that the Committee has made some contribution to the war effort, and it is the only contribution I can possibly make.

These were all letters to personal friends, and in no way intended for publication at that time. Frank Schwartz was, in addition, a delegate to the coming Democratic Convention. They are, I think, a pretty good indication that Dad really did not want the job of vice president. They refute, once and for all, the assertions of a few who claimed to be close to him that he wanted it and in fact connived to get it. But the best proof of all, as far as I am concerned, is an answer he sent to me on July 9, 1944, in response to a question I asked him by mail from Missouri about the mounting furor:

My dear Sweet Child,

It was a very nice letter and I was so happy to get it in the first mail yesterday. Yes, they are plotting against your dad. Every columnist prognosticator is trying to make him VP against his will. It is funny how some people would give a fortune to be as close as I am to it and I don't want it.

Bill Boyle, Max Lowenthal, Mr. Biffle and a dozen others were on my trail yesterday with only that in view. Hope I can dodge it. 1600 Pennsylvania is a nice address but I'd rather not move in through the back door—or any other door at sixty.

[CHAPTER]

Nine

THE LETTER that closed the last chapter was written only ten days before the 1944 Democratic Convention opened. The pressure on my father to run for vice president was obviously growing intense. Most important, the comment about the back door of 1600 Pennsylvania Avenue made it very clear that Dad had been told what almost everyone in the White House circle—and not a few Democrats outside it—knew. Franklin D. Roosevelt was a sick man.

For someone with my father's knowledge of the past, this created a very unpleasant prospect. It was obviously on his mind when he remarked to a *Post-Dispatch* reporter: "Do you remember your American history well enough to recall what happened to most vice presidents who succeeded to the presidency? Usually, they were ridiculed in office, had their hearts broken, lost any vestige of respect they had had before. I don't want that to happen to me."

In his struggle to avoid the nomination, my father was hampered by some previous appointments of his own, and several unexpected twists of fate. The most important of the appointments was his choice of Robert Hannegan as national chairman of the Democratic party. President Roosevelt had offered the job to Dad, in 1943, but he had declined, preferring to continue as head of the Truman Committee. He had recommended Bob Hannegan, who, thanks largely to Dad's influence, had become Commissioner of Internal Revenue.

Mr. Hannegan did not want the job either. He even asked Dad how he could avoid it.

"Don't take it unless the President calls you personally," Dad said.

A few days later FDR phoned and made the request very personal. Mr. Hannegan called Dad. "What do I do now, coach?" he asked.

"You take it," Dad said.

Before many more months went by, Bob Hannegan was working almost full time to make my father vice president. It was not just sentiment. One of the shrewdest politicians, Bob—and many other leading Democrats—had become convinced that with Henry Wallace on the ticket, the Democrats were in serious danger of being beaten. As vice president, Wallace had been a calamitous failure. An aloof, intensely shy man, he had made no attempt to ingratiate himself with members of the Senate—the one important service a vice president can provide a President. His ultra liberal pronouncements alarmed conservatives and moderates alike and he made enemies by the score within the party by a much publicized political brawl with Jesse Jones. At this point the Democrats needed all the friends they could find. A Gallup poll in July showed Roosevelt beating Thomas E. Dewey, whom the Republicans had nominated in June, by only 51 percent to 49 percent of the popular vote.

My father's solution to this Democratic dilemma was a return to the kind of ticket that had helped the party sweep the country in 1932 and 1936—a Texan for vice president. His choice was Speaker Sam Rayburn. Toward the end of March, 1944, Dad was at a cocktail party in San Francisco with Mr. Sam, and he proposed a toast to him as the next vice president of the United States. He repeated the proposal during his speech at a Democratic party dinner, and he was delighted when he got an enthusiastic response. A week later he repeated the performance in St. Louis. But Mr. Sam's fellow Texans torpedoed him a few weeks later. Conservatives, already restive about the New Deal's support of Negro rights, turned the state convention into a donnybrook between pro- and anti-Roosevelt Democrats. The liberal wing of the party plumped for Mr. Sam but the so-called regulars would not even name him a delegate to the convention. When a man cannot deliver his own state, his potential as a candidate withers very fast. Regretfully—he really did want the nomination —Mr. Sam withdrew his name from contention.

Although my father stubbornly refused to recognize it, he had all the qualifications which he saw in Mr. Sam—and even a few more. Missouri and Texas were very similar when it came to both political and ideological geography. His achievements as head of the Truman Committee had given him a national reputation. But Dad continued to backpedal furiously from the job, while others, notably Jimmy Byrnes and Henry Wallace, were working mightily to obtain FDR's blessing.

Jimmy Byrnes was an interesting man, suave, decisive, and energetic. He had won FDR's admiration as his "assistant president" in charge of the war effort in the White House. Mr. Byrnes wanted to be vice president very badly, because he knew with far more certainty than Dad that it was going to lead to the presidency. Few men were in a better position to see President Roosevelt's weariness and declining vitality. Henry Wallace was equally eager for the nomination. At this point he saw himself as a savior figure, the man best qualified to keep the Democratic party faithful to the New Deal. In January, 1944, he had proclaimed: "The New Deal is not dead. If it were dead the Democratic party would be dead and well dead. . . ."

There would seem to be considerable evidence that President Roosevelt did not want either one of them. The story has long been told that FDR finally yielded to the hostility of the city bosses—notably Ed Kelly of Chicago and Frank Hague of Jersey City—who assured him that they could not deliver their heavily Catholic constituencies for Byrnes, because he had abandoned Catholicism in his youth and become a Protestant. James Farley recently told me that the true story is the exact reverse—it was the President who *ordered* the bosses to spread this story, to eliminate Mr. Byrnes. As for Vice President Wallace, FDR sent him off on a trip to China on May 20, which kept him out of the country for the vital two months before the convention.

President Roosevelt, ever the astute politician, did not want to alienate either one of these powerful men. He was also acutely conscious of the need to create the illusion, at least, of an open convention because the Republicans were trumpeting the charge of one-man rule, and many segments of the party, notably the South, were restive under his no longer vigorous leadership.

Vice President Wallace did not allow his absence from the country to damage his position. He had powerful supporters, notably Sidney Hillman and his associates in the CIO, who worked day and night to line up delegate support for him. Jimmy Byrnes, a shrewder and tougher man, took a more direct approach. First, he had his good friend, Bernard Baruch, sing his praises almost continuously, while the President was vacationing at Baruch's South Carolina estate, Hobcaw Barony. On June 13 the President told Bob Hannegan that he would prefer Byrnes above any other candidate, and Mr. Byrnes extracted from him something very close to an endorsement.

But over the next month Mr. Byrnes had several more conversations with the President which made it clear that he did not have FDR's unqualified support. The best he could get out of the weary Chief was a promise that he would not express a preference for anyone. Mr. Byrnes then demonstrated his shrewdness—perhaps duplicity is a better word—by phoning my father in Independence.

In 1949, when Mr. Byrnes had turned to the right and begun attacking the policies of the Truman Administration, Dad made the following memorandum about that phone call:

> As to the nomination in Chicago in 1944, Mr. Byrnes called me from Washington Friday morning at 8 A.M. before that Convention was to meet, after he heard that Mr. Roosevelt was about to ask me to go on the ticket with him, and told me (I was in Independence, Mo.) that Roosevelt wanted him for Vice President. Byrnes asked me to nominate him. I agreed to do it. . . . I was very fond of him . . . until I found out the facts about Chicago, which was only on Friday of last week!

From Mr. Byrnes's point of view, this was a very neat, though unethical, move. If the backstairs fighting had been limited to these maneuvers, the 1944 convention would have been a battle between Wallace and Byrnes. The "assistant president" had, on paper at least, eliminated Harry Truman from the race. But other men had been getting other things down on paper that would undo this devious plan. FDR had been talking to many people.

Sidney Hillman told him that he and other leaders of the labor movement were unalterably opposed to Byrnes. Ed Flynn, the Democratic boss of the Bronx and one of Mr. Roosevelt's closest friends, reported to the White House after a personal cross-country survey and told the President that Wallace was certain to cost the Democrats several large states. Sam Rosenman, architect of Roosevelt's New Deal speech and numerous other FDR talks, and Harold Ickes, both men with impeccable liberal credentials, also told him that Wallace had to go. The President and Flynn, huddling on July 6, decided that my father was by far the best candidate. Truman "just dropped into the slot," Ed Flynn wrote later.

Still dreading a convention fight—the President told Sam Rosenman that it would "kill our chances for election this fall"—FDR ordered Mr. Flynn to convene the party's top brass on July 11 and casually mention Dad as a candidate, to see what would happen. The brass included Bob Hannegan; Frank Walker, the postmaster general; Ed Pauley, the treasurer of the Democratic National Committee; Ed Kelly, Democratic boss of Chicago; and George Allen, the secretary of the Democratic National Committee. All were totally opposed to Wallace, and before the meeting was over, each of them was convinced that he had suggested Dad as the best man. Such was the magic of FDR's political expertise.

As the leaders were leaving, Frank Walker, knowing the President's penchant for changing his mind, suggested that Bob Hannegan get something in writing. Pretending that he had misplaced his coat, Mr. Hannegan returned to the White House second-floor study and asked him for a written endorsement. On the back of an envelope, the President scribbled: "Bob, I think Truman is the right man. FDR"

Earlier on this fateful day the President had had lunch with Henry Wallace. He showed Mr. Roosevelt a Gallup poll which gave him 65 percent of the rank and file Democratic vote for vice president and claimed that he had 290 first-ballot convention votes—almost half what he needed for nomination. The President could have solved the whole thing on the spot by telling Mr. Wallace that he was not the White House candidate. But, again, he preferred to avoid a confrontation. Instead he gave Mr. Wallace

[172]

a letter, addressed to Senator Samuel Jackson, the chairman of the convention. In it he said:

> . . . I have been associated with Henry Wallace during his past four years as Vice President, for eight years earlier while he was Secretary of Agriculture, and well before that. I like him and I respect him, and he is my personal friend. For these reasons I personally would vote for his renomination if I were a delegate to the convention.
>
> At the same time, I do not wish to appear in any way as dictating to the convention. Obviously the convention must do the deciding. And it should—and I am sure it will—give great consideration to the pros and cons of its choice.

This was another example of Mr. Roosevelt's magnificent political guile (I say magnificent because I admire politics and politicians, and appreciate the agonizing situation in which the President found himself that July). FDR reiterated his "personal feelings" for Lloyd Stark after my father had defeated him in Missouri. He was saying the same thing here, in a more oblique way.

Meanwhile, Bob Hannegan was collecting another letter from the President, which he wrote while his special car was on a siding in Chicago:

> July 19, 1944
>
> Dear Bob:
>
> You have written me about Harry, Truman and Bill Douglas. I should, of course, be very glad to run with either of them and believe that either one of them would bring real strength to the ticket.
>
> Always sincerely,
> Franklin Roosevelt

Other versions of the story have the President writing the letter in the White House on July 11, before he left for the West Coast via Chicago. Grace Tully in her memoir maintains that the President originally put Bill Douglas first and Bob Hannegan had her retype it, reversing the order of the names. There is no evidence for this in the files of the Roosevelt Library, and Bob Hannegan denied it in a conversation with Sam Rosenman only a few weeks before his death in 1949. The letter was dated July 19

[173]

so that Mr. Hannegan could make maximum use of it when the convention opened. Whether the President wrote it in Chicago or in Washington, it is very clear that he was reaffirming his decision to back my father for the vice presidency. The addition of William O. Douglas's name was designed to make it appear that he was not dictating anything to the convention. At this point Mr. Douglas had no organized support whatsoever, and the nomination was totally beyond his grasp.

Harry Hopkins confirmed this conclusion in conversations with several persons. "People seem to think," he told Jonathan Daniels, then a White House press aide, "Truman was just suddenly pulled out of a hat—but that wasn't true. The President had had his eye on him for a long time and . . . above all he was very popular in the Senate. That was the biggest consideration. The President wanted somebody that would help him when he went up there and asked them to ratify the peace." Hopkins later told Robert Sherwood, "I'm certain that the President made up his mind on Truman months before the convention."

Meanwhile, Dad, Mother, and I drove to Chicago totally oblivious to all this frantic backstage warfare. My father was convinced that he had finally and totally squelched the attempt to make him vice president, and if he hadn't, he intended to stamp out the last few flickers of it in Chicago. Just before we left Independence, he told my cousin Ethel Noland's mother: "Aunt Ella, I'm going up there to defeat myself."

My personal feelings were rather mournful. Vice President Wallace's daughter, Jean, was a personal friend of mine and I knew she must feel hurt, as I would have been, if my father was being jettisoned. But twenty-year-olds are not long on sympathy, and I must confess I was also looking forward eagerly to seeing a national convention, in which Dad would play a pretty big role. I had no idea—and neither did he—how big his role would become.

So Dad could do his politicking without depriving us of sleep, he had reserved a suite on the seventeenth floor of the Stevens Hotel. Mother and I were installed in the Morrison Hotel and told to enjoy ourselves in the standard female style when visiting a big city—shopping. I had a Washington girl friend with me, and we managed to inspect every department store in Chicago before the convention ended.

Over in the Stevens Hotel, Bob Hannegan was working on Senator Truman and getting nowhere. He kept insisting he was not a candidate for vice president. He was for Byrnes. Not even the scribbled note Mr. Hannegan had obtained from FDR convinced Dad. He noted that it had no date, and simply assumed that since it was written, Mr. Roosevelt had changed his mind and endorsed Jimmy Byrnes. At one point Mr. Hannegan gave up in despair and informed an astonished Ed Flynn, as he arrived on the scene, "It's all over, it's Byrnes." Mr. Flynn, who, more than anyone else, knew that FDR's choice was Truman, immediately put through a long-distance call to FDR, en route to California aboard his special train, while another conclave of party leaders gathered in the room. After listening to Mr. Flynn and Mr. Hillman tell him that Jimmy Byrnes would bring political disaster to the party, the President reiterated that Dad was his final choice.

My father, meanwhile, was making even more desperate efforts to avoid the inevitable. He summoned his friend Tom Evans from Kansas City to Chicago and told him to go around and inform delegates that Senator Truman was not a candidate. He already had Eddie McKim and John Snyder doing the same thing. But all three friends soon found they were fighting a very strong tide flowing in the opposite direction. Eddie McKim decided Dad needed some straight from the shoulder advice. Late Monday night Dad reiterated to him and several friends that no one could persuade him to be vice president. As Eddie recalled it, he, Roy Roberts of the Kansas City *Star,* and John Snyder began disagreeing with Dad. They described the political situation and pointed out to him the many reasons why he was valuable to the Democratic ticket.

Dad shook his head. "I'm still not going to do it."

"Senator," Eddie said, "I think you're going to do it."

"What makes you think I'm going to do it?" snapped Dad.

"Because there's a ninety-year-old mother down in Grandview, Missouri, that would like to see her son President of the United States."

Dad walked out of the room and refused to speak to Eddie for the next twenty-four hours. Late the following day, Eddie, irrepressible as ever, tackled him once more.

"I don't care whether you ever speak to me again or not," he said. "I only told you what I believed. I think you should take this nomination."

Dad just looked at him.

"Okay," said Eddie. "Let's call it quits right now."

"I apologize for my action," Dad said. "I was mad at you. But I'm still not going to do it."

The following morning, Dad had breakfast with Sidney Hillman. He told the powerful labor leader he wanted his support for Mr. Byrnes. Mr. Hillman shook his head. "Labor's first choice is Wallace. If it can't be Wallace, we have a second choice, but it isn't Byrnes."

"Who then?" Dad asked.

"I'm looking at him," said Mr. Hillman.

This was the man whom my father had abused rather vehemently on the floor of the Senate, for playing labor politics with war contracts. But Sidney Hillman was not the kind of man who held a personal grudge. His first concern was a man's position on labor's rights, and he knew that Dad was on the good side of that issue. My father got the same response from other labor leaders that day, particularly from his old Railroad Brotherhood supporters, A. F. Whitney and George Harrison. William Green, head of the American Federation of Labor, went even farther and told Dad bluntly, "The AFL's for you and will support no one else." By this time Dad must have felt like a man running backwards on a platform that was moving ahead at about sixty miles an hour. He didn't feel any better after he went before the Maryland delegation and asked them to support Jimmy Byrnes. Governor Herbert R. O'Conor of Maryland told him, "You're crazy as hell!"

The next day the various state delegations caucused to name vice presidential candidates. Dad was still backpedaling but the Missouri delegation simply refused to let him get away with it. A resolution was introduced endorsing him as their candidate. As the chairman of the delegation, Dad immediately ruled it out of order. Sam Wear, one of the faithful few who had supported him in the 1940 primary campaign, shouted, "There is no one out of order here but the chairman of this delegation." Another plotter asked Dad to come to the door, to rule on whether a non-delegate could be admitted to the room. While Dad was distracted with this minor bit of business, Sam Wear reintroduced the resolution, and it was voted unanimously.

That afternoon Bob Hannegan administered the coup de grâce. He summoned Dad to his hotel room and sat him down on the bed while he put through a call to President Roosevelt in San Diego. He wanted my father to speak to the President personally. Dad, whose Missouri dander was way up by now, refused. But he sat there, listening with astonishment while FDR's always formidable telephone voice came clearly into the room.

"Bob, have you got that fellow lined up yet?"

"No," said Mr. Hannegan. "He is the contrariest Missouri mule I've ever dealt with."

"Well, you tell him if he wants to break up the Democratic party in the middle of a war, that's his responsibility."

There was a click and the phone was dead. My father got up, walked back and forth for a moment, and then said, "Well, if that is the situation, I'll have to say yes. But why the hell didn't he tell me in the first place?"

It was the first, but by no means the last, indication of the radically different political styles of the two men. In politics, and in every other kind of relationship, Dad believed in dealing straight from the shoulder whenever possible. Mr. Roosevelt obviously enjoyed juggling friends and potential enemies, to keep them all within the charmed political circle on which he rested his power.

While this conversation was taking place, Henry Wallace's backers were making a major effort to win the nomination for him in the convention hall. They had adopted the daring strategy of attempting to stampede the convention. Wallace himself had made a brilliant, rousing speech, seconding FDR's nomination for the Iowa delegation. It was unprecedented for a candidate for either the presidency or vice presidency to address a convention before the voting began. But breaking precedents often pays off in politics, and the party leaders became very alarmed by Mr. Wallace's tactics. They told Dad that they wanted to nominate him that very night—Thursday, the twentieth—immediately after Mr. Roosevelt made his acceptance speech by radio from the West Coast.

Dad decided there was really only one man who should do the nominating job for him—his fellow senator from Missouri, Bennett Clark. While Bob Hannegan, Ed Pauley, and the others departed for the convention hall, Dad went searching for Senator Clark. He was not in the room assigned to him at his hotel, and it took several frantic hours of scurrying around to discover that he was hiding out, for some unknown reason, in another hotel. There my father found him fast asleep. He pounded desperately on the door, with absolutely no success. Then a valet arrived delivering a suit. Dad walked into the room behind him, awoke Senator Clark, and asked him to nominate him. Of course he said yes, but he was a little panicky at the thought of getting together a speech on about an hour's notice.

Meanwhile, Mother and I had been told what was happening— or more correctly, I had been told. Mother and Dad had discussed the topic of his nomination exhaustively, and she had helped him decide against it. I later found out that a large part of their reason was me. They dreaded the thought of what might happen to an already skittish and rather independent twenty-year-old suddenly catapulted into the dazzling glare of White House publicity. They had seen the unhappiness it had caused in President Roosevelt's children. I don't claim to have been the main reason for their reluctance, of course. But I was another negative factor, in the many other negatives that added up to their original no.

Soon after we arrived at the convention hall, it became obvious that my father was not going to be nominated that night. The Wallaceites were in charge. Ed Kelly, the boss of Chicago, was, I have since been told, playing his own shrewd political game. He had allowed the Wallace supporters to pour into the convention hall in staggering numbers, to create a stampede for their candidate. Mr. Kelly's secret hope was a deadlock between Wallace and Truman, which might have resulted in the choice of an alternate candidate. The one he had in mind was Senator Scott Lucas of Illinois. Isn't politics wonderful?

Even the convention hall organist capitulated to the Wallace crowd and played "Iowa, That's Where the Tall Corn Grows," the Iowa state song, so many times that it's a wonder his fingers didn't sprout kernels. Ed Pauley became so infuriated that he ordered Neale Roach, another Democratic party official, to chop the wires leading to the organ's amplifiers unless the keyboard virtuoso came up with another song immediately. Meanwhile, Bob Hannegan threw open the outer doors of the stadium and more people poured into the arena. It was already about 120 degrees on the floor of the hall. People began to collapse from lack of oxygen, and a panicky Ed Kelly, realizing he had helped to create a monster demonstration that was in danger of devouring him, screamed that there was a fire hazard. Chairman Jackson gaveled the convention into recess, and the Wallace stampede collapsed.

The rest of the night was devoted to intensive politicking. At least a dozen state delegations lined up behind favorite sons. There was a very real chance that Dad and Wallace might deadlock now. A number of prominent New Dealers were working for Wallace. Part of the New York delegation split away from Ed Flynn's control. When the convention reassembled on Friday, July 21, there was tension in the air. Mother, beside me, looked exhausted. She was probably the only person (from Missouri anyway) in the convention hall who wouldn't have been brokenhearted if Dad lost. Oblivious to the problems ahead, I had no such inclination. I wanted my father to win, and I writhed through the long afternoon.

Nothing seemed to go right at first. Bennett Clark gave a very brief, limp nominating speech, and response from the delegates was tepid. Then a delegate from Iowa was on his feet and California yielded to him. In an exciting speech Mr. Wallace was called the personification of Democratic vision. There were five seconding speeches, all equally ecstatic, and the galleries, well packed with CIO-led Wallace supporters, whooped and screamed after every one of them. Ten other candidates were nominated and seconded—a total of twenty speeches that consumed the better part of three hours. Ed Kelly put his man, Senator Scott Lucas, into contention and gave the Wallace-packed gallery a chance to shout him down.

"We want harmony at this convention," Mr. Kelly said.

"We want Wallace," screamed the galleries.

"We want a ticket," Mr. Kelly said.

"We want Wallace."

Until this point my father had been in Bob Hannegan's private Room H, under the speaker's stand, talking to delegates and state leaders. He had not had anything to eat all day. Since he is a very light breakfast man, he was hungry, and as the chairman intoned, "The clerk will call the roll of votes," Dad emerged from his underground headquarters and bought a hot dog, which proved he was starving, because he normally loathes hot dogs. He sat down with the Missouri delegation. I kept my eyes on him as the count began.

Alabama gave its 24 votes to its favorite son, Senator John Bankhead.

Arizona and Arkansas went for Truman.

California's delegation said it would like to wait.

Then, to everyone's amazement, 9 of Florida's 18 votes went to Wallace and all of Georgia's 26. The South was supposed to be solidly against the vice president. But Ellis Arnall of Georgia was not a typical Southern governor. In the Midwest Mr. Wallace did well, taking his home state of Iowa and also Kansas, likewise expected. Nobody from Kansas votes for anybody from Missouri if he can help it. Thanks to his labor backing, the vice president also swept Michigan and Minnesota. Suddenly, at the one-third mark, Mr. Wallace was 100 votes ahead.

Missouri remained faithful to Dad but other states began dividing in weird ways. New York couldn't even agree on who was voting for whom. Ohio went in six different directions. Pennsylvania gave 46½ to the vice president and only 23½ to Dad. The Wallace-weighted galleries were going wild. By the time the vice president had swept Washington, West Virginia, and Wisconsin, the clamor was close to the stampede proportions of the previous night.

At the end of the roll call two of the biggest states, California and New York, had not yet announced their totals. The Golden State came first, and my heart sank at the count: Wallace, 30; Truman, 22. The vice president was ahead, 406½ to 244. The galleries stamped and screamed.

Now New York with 92½ votes was the only state left. There was plenty of Wallace support in New York, we knew. A furious argument was raging inside the New York delegation. Someone challenged the figures that the chairman, Senator Jackson, was about to announce; he ordered the delegation to be polled. This took thirty-five minutes—but the final count stopped the slide to Wallace. It was 69½ for Truman, 23 for the vice president. Puerto Rico gave its 6 votes to Dad, and the final count, at the end of the first ballot, was: Wallace, 429½; Truman, 319½; Bankhead, 98; Lucas, 61; and Barkley 49½. Eleven other favorite sons also held handfuls of votes.

The chairman asked the required question: "Does any delegation wish to alter its vote?" There were no takers. Most of the favorite sons were still hoping for a deadlock. By now it was about six o'clock. The convention had been in session over six hours and several delegations were screaming that they were famished. I remember feeling a few pangs of hunger myself. I started to envy my father, who had found himself another hot dog, somewhere down on the convention floor, and was cheerfully munching it and chatting with his fellow Missourians.

Normally, the convention would have adjourned at this point and resumed balloting in the evening. But Bob Hannegan, with unerring tactical instinct, decided this would be a mistake. Aides had told him that there were huge crowds of Wallace supporters outside waiting eagerly to grab a majority of the seats for the evening session. Inevitably they would make another attempt at a stampede, in the style of the previous night. Ignoring the cries of the hungry delegates, Mr. Hannegan ordered Chairman Jackson to start a second ballot.

It was a terrific gamble. If this ballot ended with Dad still behind, chances of a Wallace victory or a deadlock and a bolt to a favorite son were very strong.

At first the vice president was ahead, but so many delegations were splitting and passing it was hard to tell what was happening for a while. The big disappointment among Dad's supporters was Alabama's refusal to switch from Senator Bankhead. That had been the original plan, but Senator Bankhead was sniffing the wind, and he thought it was starting to blow in his direction. Illinois and Kentucky also stayed with their favorite sons, Lucas and Barkley.

Then came the first switch. Maryland's Governor O'Conor, who had told Dad he was crazy on Monday, threw his 18 votes to Truman. Michigan and the CIO remained loyal to Wallace, but New York did not hesitate this time. They delivered 74½ for Truman and only 18 for Mr. Wallace. Dad was now ahead, 246 to 187.

Now came the swing vote, the one that started the Truman landslide. Governor Robert Kerr, on direct orders from Democratic party treasurer Ed Pauley, switched Oklahoma's 22 votes to Dad. Ed Pauley later recalled that Bob Kerr paled when he pointed his finger at him. Bob had been the keynote speaker of the convention and had given a magnificent talk. He would have made an ideal compromise candidate. But he was a good Democrat, and he sacrificed his personal ambitions without a moment's hesitation, when he got the signal.

But in the W's, Washington, West Virginia, Wisconsin, the

[181]

vice president rallied amazingly. He cut Dad's lead to a half vote, and then with 6 votes from Indiana and 16 from Kansas, both of whom had passed, Mr. Wallace edged ahead by 20½. But Massachusetts, Mississippi, and Montana came through for Dad, and the count finally stood at 477½ for Truman and 473 for Wallace.

There was a pause. Thousands of voices rose and fell, some murmuring, some shouting. The chairman asked the delegates if the count was to be made official. Before a motion could be made, Senator Bankhead rose and swung Alabama's 22 votes to Dad. South Carolina boosted him to 501. Then Indiana and Illinois announced that they were caucusing to change their votes. In a moment Indiana was declaring 22 votes for Truman, and Illinois, New York, and a dozen other states were screaming for recognition. I can't believe anybody really knows who voted what in the ensuing pandemonium. But when I heard Kansas swinging 16 votes to Truman, I knew it was all over. By the time the final tally was announced by the befuddled clerks, at least forty-four state delegations had changed their votes, and Truman was the winner, 1031 to 105.

A phalanx of policemen seized my father and fought their way through the roaring crowd to the platform. Bob Hannegan held up Dad's arm while the convention hall went insane. They seemed ready to scream all night, and Dad finally seized the chairman's gavel and banged for order. "Give me a chance, will you please?" he begged them. Then he delivered one of the shortest acceptance speeches on record.

> You don't know how very much I appreciate the very great honor which has come to the state of Missouri. It is also a great responsibility which I am perfectly willing to assume.
>
> Nine years and five months ago I came to the Senate. I expect to continue the efforts I have made there to help shorten the war and to win the peace under the great leader, Franklin D. Roosevelt.
>
> I don't know what else I can say except that I accept this great honor with all humility.
>
> I thank you.

Everyone yelled some more, and the chairman recessed the convention. My father fought his way off the platform and, aided by another phalanx of police, soon reached the box where we were sitting. There we were practically besieged by a horde of shouting sweating photographers, who begged us ad infinitum for "just one more" until Dad had to call a very firm halt and concentrate on getting us out of the stadium alive. The crowd was still frantic with excitement, and he was genuinely concerned for our safety.

It was a thoroughly justified concern. People in crowds do things which they would never dream of doing if they were alone with you. One woman who shall out of charity remain nameless—she was the wife of one of Dad's close friends—threw herself practically on top of me in a hysterical hug and I felt—I swear I even heard in that cauldron of sound—my neck crack. Everyone wanted to touch us. We were pushed and pounded and battered until I thought for a moment I would collapse with sheer fright. To this day, the sight of a large crowd terrifies me (except across the footlights).

Thank goodness, there were enough police to form a defensive ring around us. Otherwise I am sure one of us would have been seriously hurt. As we got to the street and the waiting car, Mother turned to Dad and said, "Are we going to have to go through this for all the rest of our lives?"

Dad wisely declined to answer her. I don't remember much else of what happened that night. It took hours for the fear I felt in the middle of that crowd to wear off.

The next morning, Saturday, July 22, Mother held a press conference and answered as patiently as she could all sorts of silly questions about Dad's eating habits, clothing styles, work routines, and the like. I stood beside her, hoping no one was going to ask me anything. Suddenly, into the room charged Dad, saying, "Where's my baby? I have a telegram for her." That was the beginning of my *real* antipathy for the word "baby."

Dad soothed my wrath by giving me as a souvenir a telegram from President Roosevelt:

> I SEND YOU MY HEARTIEST CONGRATULATIONS ON YOUR VICTORY. I AM OF COURSE VERY HAPPY TO HAVE YOU RUN WITH ME. LET ME KNOW YOUR PLANS. I SHALL SEE YOU SOON.
>
> FRANKLIN D. ROOSEVELT

That same day we started back to Independence and Dad stayed with us until August 1, primary day in Missouri. Roger Sermon, the mayor of Independence, was running for governor, and Bennett Clark was up for reelection. Dad did some politicking for them, but they both lost. Bennett Clark stubbornly refused to abandon his isolationist views, and by 1944 they were hopelessly out of date.

Dad went back to Washington immediately after the election, and from there he wrote me an interesting letter about a meeting with the Republican nominee and his forecast of the campaign.

> I was going into the Union Station (in St. Louis) to take the B&O as Dewey came out. There were not ten people there to meet him. More people came and spoke to your dad accidentally than came to meet Mr. Dewey on purpose. That can't be so good and I just now happened to think of its significance. . . . This is going to be a tough, dirty campaign and you've got to help your dad, protect your good mamma. Nothing can be said of me that isn't old and unproven—so this little "deestric attorney" will try to hit me by being nasty to my family. You must remember that I never wanted or went after the nomination—but now we have it, (to save the Democratic Party—so the Southerners and the AF of L and the RR Labor say) we must win and make 'em like it. Maybe your dad can make a job out of the fifth wheel office. . . .

On August 18 my father met President Roosevelt at the White House, and wrote me a letter about it later in the day. It tells the story in somewhat circular fashion, but I think it is best to print it exactly as he wrote it.

> Washington, D.C.
> Aug. 18, '44.
> My dear Margie — Today may be one in history. Your dad had a most informal luncheon with Mr. Roosevelt on the terrace behind the White House, under a tree set out by old Andy Jackson. Mrs. Boettiger [the President's daughter, Anna] was also present. She expected your mother to come with me. When I went to leave the Pres. gave me a rose out of the vase in the center of the small round table at which we ate for your mother and Mrs. B. gave me one for you. You should have seen your Pa walking down Connecticut Ave. to the Mayflower Hotel, where a date with Mr. Hannegan was in prospect with his hat blown up by the wind (so he looked like a college boy—gray hair and all) and two rose buds in his hand. He should have been arrested as a screwball but wasn't.
> I told the President how very grateful ? I was for his putting

the finger on me for V.P. and how I appreciated the honor ? etc., etc. ad. lib. and then we discussed "sealing wax and many things" to make the country run for the Democrats.

You should have been with me at the press conference in the front room of the White House Offices. Hope I made no hits, no runs, no errors—particularly no errors.

We had roast sardines (think they were Maine baby halibut) on toast, peas, beans, tomatoes, asparagus all mixed up in a salad—very nice when you left out the peas & carrots, and lots of good brown toast, then pickled clingstone peaches and a teaspoon full of coffee all served on beautiful White House china and with lovely silver and butlers etc. galore.

When we first sat down there were movie cameras set up all around. We were in our shirt sleeves. The Pres took his coat off and I had told him if I'd known that was what he intended to do I'd have put on a clean shirt and he said he had that very morning. Well so had I. Then the flash light newspaper picture boys had an inning equal almost to the box at Chicago. The President got tired or hungry and said "Now boys one more that's enough" and it ended.

You'll see it all in the movies and in the papers. Hope to see you Monday. Keep up those music lessons and I'm anxious to know what the surprise is. Chopin's A♭ Opus 42? Rigaudon? Polacca Brilliante? What?

Kiss mamma. Here's some expenses.

> Lots & lots of love,
> Dad

Mother and I were in Independence, but President Roosevelt was not aware of this fact and that is why he gave Dad the roses. The purpose of this letter was mainly to give me a thrill. My father did not set down here what he really thought after he left the luncheon with the President. Nor did he tell the whole truth to the reporters who were waiting for him outside the White House. "He's still the leader he's always been and don't let anybody kid you about it. He's keen as a briar," Dad said.

In private, he was appalled by Mr. Roosevelt's physical condition. The President had just returned from a Pacific inspection trip. It had been an exhausting ordeal for him, and he had suffered, we now know, at least one cardiac seizure during the journey. My father later told close friends how the President's hands shook so badly at the luncheon that he could not get the cream from the pitcher into his coffee. He spilled most of it into the saucer. He talked with difficulty. "It doesn't seem to be any mental lapse of any kind, but physically he's just going to pieces," Dad said. "I'm very much concerned about him." The President alluded only once, and then obliquely, to the seriousness of his condition. He asked Dad how he planned to campaign, and Dad said that he was thinking of using an airplane. The President vetoed the idea. "One of us has to stay alive," he said.

My father saw President Roosevelt only two more times between that August date and the inauguration. On September 6 he went to the White House with Governor Coke Stevenson of Texas to discuss the problem of keeping rebellious Texas Democrats in the party. After the election he attended a White House reception with Eddie McKim at which there were no chance to discuss politics or anything else with the President.

My father kicked off his campaign with a rally at his Missouri birthplace, Lamar. That was a day to remember—or forget—depending on your point of view. Missourians were enormously proud to have one of their own on the national ticket. There had only been two previous nominations, both for vice president away back in 1868 and 1872, and both had lost. Everyone who had a few spare gallons of gas for dozens of miles around poured into the little town. No less than nine U.S. senators escorted Dad to the rally. Estimates on the size of the crowd varied wildly, from a low of 12,000 to a high of 35,000. One thing was certain, it was too big for Lamar. Toilet facilities and the sewage system broke down. The parking field was turned into a huge mudhole by a heavy rainstorm the previous day. Poor Harry Easley, who was the chairman in charge of the day, almost went crazy. "All I can say," he muttered, summing it up, "is never have a big affair in a small town."

But everyone was goodnatured about the inconveniences, and Tom Connally gave one of his old-fashioned, oratorical-fireworks-style speeches that had everybody ready to parboil Republicans, or eat them raw if necessary, before it was over. Dad made no attempt to top that untoppable Texas flamboyance. He simply stated the basic issue of the campaign—Thomas E. Dewey was not qualified either to direct a global war or to win the peace.

As my father had predicted, the campaign was dirty, and a lot of the dirt was thrown at him. The Republicans knew they had no real issues. To attack President Roosevelt's conduct of the war sounded unpatriotic. So they concentrated on Dad and a few other people in the White House circle, especially poor Sidney Hillman. As one magazine writer noted, "The competence of Mr. Roosevelt's current running mate is the nearest thing the country has to a burning issue." Some of the stories were just plain silly. *Time* magazine described how Dad had supposedly broken down and wept, pleading his incompetence, when he was nominated for vice president. Other tales were more on the ugly side. The Republicans revived the 1940 canard that Dad was one fourth Jewish, and his middle initial stood for Solomon. "I'm not Jewish, but if I were I would not be ashamed of it," Dad said to the delight of his many Jewish friends. But one attack Dad did not dismiss lightly was the snide remarks that Clare Booth Luce made about Mother.

For the seven and three-quarters years that the Trumans were in the White House, Mrs. Luce was never invited to attend a single social function there. One day, about in the middle of that long freeze, her husband, Henry Luce, the publisher of *Time,* visited Dad and asked him for an explanation, obviously hoping to negotiate a truce. Dad pointed to the picture of Mother that he always keeps on his desk, and gave Mr. Luce a brief history of its travels to France and back with him during World War I. Mrs. Luce stayed uninvited.

In the closing hours of the campaign, the Hearst papers unleashed the biggest smear of them all: Harry S. Truman was an ex-member of the Ku Klux Klan. They based their stories on obvious lies told by a few of Dad's enemies in Jackson County— especially one whom he had helped to send to jail for embezzlement. This story was quickly refuted by on-the-spot testimony from other friends back home.

Dad received the following telegram from his brother Vivian on October 27, 1944, while he was staying at the Blackstone Hotel in Chicago. It shows how the smear artists were operating—and how Harry Truman's friends remained faithful to him:

STATEMENT OF O L CHRISMAN. MY NAME IS O L CHRISMAN. I AM 77 YEARS OLD AND HAVE LIVED IN JACKSON COUNTY MISSOURI SEVENTY FIVE YEARS. I HAVE KNOWN

SENATOR HARRY S TRUMAN SINCE HE WAS A BOY TWELVE
TO FIFTEEN YEARS OLD. . . . ON OR ABOUT OCTOBER
11TH 1944 BRUCE TRIMBLE CAME TO MY HOME
WITH ANOTHER MAN WHO HE INTRODUCED AS A
REPRESENTATIVE OF A NEW YORK NEWSPAPER.
MR TRIMBLE AND THE NEWSPAPER MAN INTERROGATED
ME AT GREAT LENGTH RELATIVE TO MY KNOWLEDGE
OF SENATOR TRUMANS RELATIONSHIP WITH THE KLAN
I TOLD THEM THAT I HAD SEEN HIM AT A MEETING
OF THE KLAN IN CRANDALLS PASTURE MORE THAN TWENTY
YEARS AGO. I TOLD THEM THAT THERE WERE
MORE THAN FIVE THOUSAND MEN AT THIS MEETING
AND THAT THERE WERE HUNDREDS OF THEM WHO WERE
NOT MEMBERS OF THE KLAN I TOLD THEM THAT
I DID NOT KNOW OF SENATOR TRUMAN EVER HAVING
BEEN A MEMBER AND THAT I NEVER KNEW OF ANYONE
THAT CLAIMED TO KNOW THAT HE HAD BEEN A MEMBER
OF THE KLAN. TRIMBLE AND THE NEWSPAPER MAN
TRIED REPEATEDLY TO GET ME TO SAY THAT I KNEW
THAT HARRY TRUMAN HAD BEEN A MEMBER. THESE MEN
CAME TO MY HOUSE AT SEVEN OCLOCK IN THE EVENING
JUST AS I WAS ABOUT TO GO OUT TO MILK MY COW.
AFTER TWO HOURS OF QUESTIONING I SIGNED A STATEMENT
TO THE EFFECT THAT I HAD SEEN HARRY S TRUMAN AT
A KLAN MEETING AS STATED ABOVE AND THAT IF
HE EVER BECAME A MEMBER OF THE KLAN I DID NOT
KNOW IT . . . THE NEWSPAPER MAN TRIED REPEATEDLY
TO GET ME TO SAY THAT TRUMAN HAD APPEARED
ON THE PLATFORM AND HAD MADE SPEECHES AT KLAN
MEETINGS. THIS WAS NOT TRUE AND I HAVE NEVER
HEARD OF HIM MAKING SPEECHES OR APPEARING ON
THE PLATFORM AT ANY KLAN MEETING=
    SIGNED O L CHRISMAN   SENT BY J V TRUMAN

My father did his campaigning aboard a special car, the *Henry
Stanley*. Mother stayed in Washington with me, because I had
a few dozen courses in college to pass. My first contact with the
campaign was a late October trip to New York with Mother to
hear Dad speak in Madison Square Garden. By accident we hap-

pened to be on the scene for the most dramatic episode of his campaign.

In a show of Democratic unity, Harry Truman and Henry Wallace were to occupy the same platform. New York had numerous Wallace sympathizers, and there was good reason for suspecting that they would make up a heavy percentage of the audience. My father and his entourage arrived, already worried about this problem. The crowd was large and restless. They waited several minutes and there was still no sign of Mr. Wallace. Several eager pro-Wallace Democrats urged Dad to go onstage and let Mr. Wallace arrive late. But George Allen, who was handling the political arrangements for Dad's tour, immediately saw what the Wallace men were planning to do. Dad would get the bare minimum of applause—or perhaps a few boos—when he appeared. Then, when Mr. Wallace came down the center aisle, they would tear the roof off the Garden, and the story would make headlines.

"Mr. Truman goes on when Mr. Wallace goes on," said George Allen grimly.

Meanwhile, desperate efforts were being made to locate Mr. Wallace. Word reached them that he had left his hotel, and then they were told that he had returned to his hotel because he forgot his glasses. Then he had left his hotel once more but was walking to the Garden, a strange performance if there ever was one. Eddie McKim, who was there with Dad, later said, "When Wallace came in and was shown back into the Garden offices [where Dad was waiting], he was mad as a wet hen. The only one he spoke to was Truman and he [Wallace] was in a very sour mood. Finally, they walked out through the entrance onto the platform arm in arm and smiling at each other, but I think they were about ready to cut each other's throats."

It was an ominous sign of things to come, but my father, who hates to think the worst of anyone, hesitated to pass judgment on the incident.

"Do you think that thing was planned, staged deliberately?" he asked Eddie McKim on the way back to the hotel.

"I think it was," Eddie said.

"Well," Dad said, "that's a funny deal, but it didn't work."

We joined Dad for the last leg of his tour. It was my introduction to whistle-stop campaigning, and I loved it. We paused for an exciting torchlight parade at Parkersburg, West Virginia. At Pittsburgh, we had a twenty-six-man motorcycle escort for a dash to nearby McKeesport for lunch. I was awed by the crowds, who were very well behaved, and even more impressed by meeting Orson Welles, who had dinner with us and spoke on the same platform with Dad that night.

In Missouri, instead of going home to Independence we took a suite at the Muehlebach Hotel in Kansas City. My father yielded to the pleas of his Battery D boys and other Missouri friends who journeyed to Kansas City to be on hand for the victory celebration. This was one election where he did not pull his early-to-bed routine. Instead, he stayed up with his friends and played the piano for them while they huddled around the radio, nervously listening to the returns, which gave the Republicans an early lead. Dewey did not concede until 3:45 A.M. By that time I was completely exhausted and much too excited to sleep. I was up for the rest of the night.

My father finally got rid of his friends and threw himself down on a bed in the suite where they had been celebrating. His old friend from southwest Missouri, Harry Easley, stayed with him. For the first time the full reality of what he was facing struck Dad. "He told me that the last time that he saw Mr. Roosevelt he had the pallor of death on his face and he knew that he would be President before the term was out," Mr. Easley recalled. "He said he was going to have to depend on his friends. He was talking about people like me, he said. We sat there and had quite a long deal."

Whenever I think of this moment in my father's life, I am always profoundly touched by it. There is something intensely American about it, this picture of a man close to assuming the most awesome responsibility in the world's history, talking it over with a man not unlike himself, from a small Missouri city, a friend who had stood loyally by him whenever he needed help. If there is a more lonesome feeling in the world than being President, it must be facing the near inevitability of getting the job in the worst possible way—coming in through the back door, as Dad put it. That night his mind was obviously filled with the history of the other men who had reached the White House that way.

Would he end as most of them had ended, beaten men, physically, spiritually, and politically?

While other Democrats—including his daughter—celebrated on that election night in 1944, Vice President-elect Harry S. Truman lay awake in Kansas City, worrying.

[CHAPTER]

Ten

ONE THING that especially worried my father was the image of him as a bumbling, ineffectual second-rater that many newspapers had striven to construct during the campaign. In one of his few really bitter public remarks about the press, he accused the newspapers of creating a "straw man." In those same remarks, he urged the papers to bury this straw man. My father was speaking, as he often did, with that amazing objectivity which enabled him to look upon himself as a public servant in a way that made listeners think he was talking about a separate person. I have never heard him express the least concern about the names he was called by other politicians or by newspaper editorialists. But at this point in his career, so close to assuming the enormous responsibilities of the presidency, he was concerned about the impact of his image—if I may use a word that was not in vogue at the time—on the nation.

One symptom of this derision and contempt was the failure of his Republican vice presidential opponent, Senator John Bricker of Ohio, to send Dad a telegram, conceding his defeat and offering his congratulations. In some ways my father found this more unforgivable than Lloyd Stark's failure to make a similar gesture, in the 1940 senatorial campaign. Mr. Stark at least had the excuse of bitter personal disappointment. Senator Bricker's discourtesy seemed studied and much more gross. Fortunately, Mother and I, the grudge bearers of the family, did not have much time to worry about it. We were much too busy coping with our first experience as national figures. The mail was overwhelming. Everyone I had ever met seemed to have seized a pen or rushed to a typewriter to congratulate me. Total strangers also joined the avalanche. It was an exhausting job to answer all of them, especially in longhand. We were totally devoid of secretarial help.

My father, meanwhile, relaxed from the rigors of the campaign for a few days in Florida. But he too found he was operating on a larger political stage. "It was impossible for me to dodge the publicity," he wrote to me. "Reporters were at the train at Memphis, Birmingham, Jacksonville, Tampa, and one was in the front yard when we arrived at the . . . house." Worse, his luck with Florida weather remained bad. A cold wave followed him in from Kansas City. But he assured me that he was nevertheless determined to "get three days rest, really and truly."

As I have said, we stayed in Kansas City for election eve and Election Day, and the victory produced some pretty wild celebrating. I was rather shocked by the way some of the local politicians handled their liquor. I mentioned this to Dad in the letter I wrote to him while he was in Florida and got an interesting comment in return:

> Your views on . . . the middle-aged soaks are exactly correct. I like people who can control their appetites and their mental balance. When that isn't done, I hope you'll always scratch them off your list.

After Christmas the only thing we thought about was the inauguration. Mother and I combed Kansas City for the better part of a week, trying to decide on a wardrobe. I finally settled for a simple gray-green woolen dress with a hat to match. For warmth, all I chose was a fur scarf, one of the worst mistakes I ever made in this department.

For my father the inauguration was a political nightmare. President Roosevelt decided, because it was wartime and also because he wanted to conserve his strength, to take the oath of office on the South Portico of the White House. Only 7,800 people were invited—which sounds like a lot, until you remember we are a very big country. Moreover, only a handful of people could get blue tickets, which gave them a place on the portico.

[193]

On January 13, 1945, Dad wrote to his mother and sister:

> . . . I'm glad you all decided not to come to this brawl we
> are having. I'm in trouble at every turn, but I guess I'll live
> through it. Can't get tickets enough to get everyone in. Some
> people have all the nerve. A banker in Nashville is having a
> reception and Sam Rayburn, the Speaker of the House, is hav-
> ing one. And Oscar Ewing, vice chairman of the National
> Committee, is having one, the Presidential Electors are having
> a dinner, and Hannegan and Pauley are having a reception.
> All these things run from the 18th to the 21st, and some of 'em
> are at the same time and blocks apart and I'm supposed to be
> at all of 'em and "grin and bear it."
>
> Maybe I can—in fact, I'll have to. When it's over I'll be very
> much pleased. I told FDR the other day he should have boarded
> his automobile and driven to the Supreme Court and been
> sworn in and I should have taken the oath at a regular Senate
> session and there'd have been no feelings hurt and no expense
> at all.

My problem was not "prima donnas and stuffed shirts," as Dad
called his tormentors, but examinations. Inauguration week coincided with my midterms and I had to somehow cram in a lot of
studying while simultaneously entertaining aunts and uncles,
friends and neighbors from Kansas City and Independence.
They swirled through our five-room apartment on Connecticut
Avenue at all hours of the day and night. To complicate my woes,
Inauguration Day was incredibly miserable—a cold rain mixed
with sleet came pouring out of a gloomy sky. Mother and I had
quite a set-to over my determination to brave the icy downpour
protected by nothing but my new fur scarf. I finally departed with
them for the religious ceremonies at St. John's Church across
Lafayette Square from the White House, wearing my school coat
and feeling very sorry for myself.

A few hours later I stood on the South Portico between Mrs.
Woodrow Wilson and Senator Harry Byrd of Virginia, shivering
in the cold, looking for two girl friends from Kansas City who
were standing in the slush on the White House lawn. I had a terrifying examination in the governments of Europe, one of my
major courses, on the following day, and my mind kept jumping
from the history in which I was participating to the history I

would have to write tomorrow. We were jammed on the portico, practically sardine style. The guest list for the portico was limited to 140, but a number of people who had been invited by the President to a religious service in the East Room—and who had *not* been invited to the inaugural ceremony—simply sashayed out on the portico, sans tickets, and joined—or more correctly, created—the crush.

My father took his oath of office first, administered in accordance with political tradition by the outgoing vice president, Henry Wallace. Meanwhile, just inside the French doors that led to the portico, President Roosevelt was arriving in a wheelchair, pushed by his son James in his marine uniform. The President looked haggard, his face pale, with dark circles under his eyes.

Out on the portico, James Roosevelt and a Secret Service man lifted the President to his feet and he grasped the edge of the speaker's lectern. He shook hands with my father, took his oath of office, and then gave one of the briefest inaugural addresses in history—less than five minutes in length. He stood coatless, the freezing wind whipping his hair. He looked so worn and spent, I suddenly found myself feeling depressed at the climax of a day that I had thought was going to be one of the high points of my life.

Immediately after the inauguration ceremony, there was a tremendous buffet lunch for 1,805 guests. President Roosevelt could not face the ordeal of shaking hands with this mob and retired to the family rooms of the White House almost immediately. Dad, Mother, and Mrs. Roosevelt gamely threw themselves into the breach, shaking hands with every one of these frozen VIPs, who had endured the ceremony out on the windswept, slushy lawn.

A heavy percentage of the guests were from Missouri. The Roosevelts, in line with their desire to play down the inauguration, had generously given us the lion's share of the guest list. Practically every politician above the precinct level had trekked to Washington to honor Missouri's first vice president. Before the reception there was a lot of kidding about the danger of light-fingered Missourians departing with most of the White House's silver. A few days later, when the White House staff finished its post inaugural silver count, only one spoon was missing. The honor of Missouri had survived temptation.

[195]

At the end of this first reception my father retreated to his Senate office to call Mamma Truman and I stumbled home to take a nap. Mother and Mrs. Roosevelt stayed on duty to shake 678 more hands at a tea for second-rank VIPs—undersecretaries, Democratic National Committee people, and family friends. It was Mother's first taste of White House receiving. Fortunately for her peace of mind, she had no idea she was practicing for seven and three-quarters years of these endurance contests.

This may sound strange, after what I have written about my father's acute awareness of President Roosevelt's failing health, at the nominating convention and on election night, but once the election was over, he simply stopped thinking about it. I cannot recall a single instance when he ever discussed the possibility of becoming President with Mother or me after he became vice president. This is perfectly understandable, if you think about it for a moment. Mr. Roosevelt was not *visibly* ill. He was failing, he looked alarmingly weary. But a good rest might easily restore him to health again—as far as Dad knew. In the first months of 1945 there was a distinct impression that the President's health had improved. Mother commented on it, with evident relief, in a letter to my cousin Ethel Noland. Another equally strong possibility was the end of the war. This would have lifted a tremendous burden from the President's shoulders. Still another reason was the tradition that the vice president does not make comments or inquiries about the President's health. The best way to avoid such a gaffe is by shutting the subject completely out of your mind. This is what my father tried to do.

Besides, he had very little time to think about the Big If. After two more hectic days of partying I collapsed with a beautiful case of the flu, and he plunged into the vice presidency with his previously stated determination to make it more than a fifth-wheel job. Only two days after he was inaugurated, President Roosevelt departed for Yalta and left my father with a task that was to give him more than a few frantic moments. In a style that totally lacked his usual political finesse, the President fired Jesse Jones as Secretary of Commerce and asked Dad to persuade the Senate to approve Henry Wallace in his place. Defeated in his attempt to become the Democratic party's heir apparent, Mr. Wallace was now trying to use his great personal influence with the President to land one of the most powerful—if not the most powerful—jobs in the administration. The Secretary of Commerce also controlled the Reconstruction Finance Corporation, which had already lent $18 billion to small and large businesses. There was still $8 billion left in the original war authorization.

Evidently President Roosevelt had hoped that the switch could be accomplished behind the scenes. But Jesse Jones refused to go in peace. Instead, he released the President's letter to him, in which FDR literally asked him to resign because Henry Wallace wanted his job. Mr. Jones also released his reply, a savagely sarcastic blast that practically called the President a hypocrite to his face. Mr. Jones also flatly declared that Henry Wallace was not qualified to handle the vast financial responsibilities of the RFC.

Immediately, Senate liberals began girding their loins to do battle for Mr. Wallace. Southerners, conservatives, and Republicans—just about everyone who had any reason to oppose President Roosevelt—grouped around "Uncle Jesse," as they called Mr. Jones. It looked for a while as if the Supreme Court packing donnybrook would be replayed, in wartime, with possibly disastrous consequences.

My father went to work. He dragged senator after senator down to his office to cajole him into going along with the President. But it soon became obvious that there was no hope of the Senate giving Mr. Wallace control of the RFC. So Dad, with the help of Senator Tom Connally, worked out a shrewd compromise. He divided the two jobs and persuaded Senator Walter George of Georgia to introduce a bill creating an independent Federal Loan Administration. Then he returned to pushing Mr. Wallace as Secretary of Commerce, urgently reminding reluctant senators— and there were still plenty of these—that the Senate rarely if ever declined to give the President his own way on the selection of his Cabinet officers.

In these delicate maneuvers Mr. Wallace was his usual uncooperative self. He went to New York to attend a rally on his behalf and made a truculent speech, insisting he had a right to both jobs. Only desperate efforts on the part of Dad and Senator Claude Pepper of Florida, Mr. Wallace's chief Senate supporter, held together a tremulous majority. But there were still some hair-raising moments ahead. My father worked out with Majority Leader

Alben Barkley a strategy which called for swift action on Senator Barkley's part. As soon as the Senate convened on February 1, he was supposed to introduce the George bill, which would eliminate the chief objection to Mr. Wallace as Secretary of Commerce. But the anti-Wallace senators called for an executive session, which would have forced an immediate vote on Mr. Wallace for both jobs. That dramatic roll call ended in a tie, 42 to 42, in effect a victory for the administration, and Senator Barkley rose to introduce the George bill. But Senator Robert Taft of Ohio, one of the Senate's shrewdest parliamentarians, leaped to his feet to ask Mr. Barkley if he would yield, so Senator Taft could change his vote from yea to nay.

My father, sitting on the rostrum, instantly saw what Mr. Taft had in mind. Under the Senate's rules this would have given Senator Taft the right to call for another roll-call vote. Only one Wallace-hating senator had to change his mind, and abandon the administration, to send Mr. Wallace to ignominious defeat. For a moment, Senator Barkley started to say he would yield, then he realized in mid-sentence what Senator Taft had in mind and said he would not do so. Senator Taft objected violently and asked Dad for a ruling. Coolly, my father ruled that Senator Taft might make his motion "at any later time" and let Mr. Barkley keep the floor. The George bill was immediately introduced and the senators demonstrated their opinion of Henry Wallace by voting 72 to 12 to take the RFC out of his hands. A few weeks later Mr. Wallace was confirmed as Secretary of Commerce.

Woodrow Wilson may have described the vice presidency as an office of "anomalous insignificance and curious uncertainty." But Dad also found it was hard work. In this letter to his mother and sister, he paints a good picture of his vice presidential routine:

> I used to get down here to the office at seven o'clock and always wrote you a letter promptly in reply to yours. But now I have to take Margaret to school every morning and I don't get here until 8:30. Reathel Odum is always here at that time and we wade through a stack of mail a foot high. By that time I have to see people—one at a time just as fast as they can go through the office without seeming to hurry them.
>
> Then I go over to the Capitol gold-plated office and see Senators and curiosity seekers for an hour and then the Senate meets

and it's my job to get 'em prayed for and goodness knows they need it, and then get the business to going by staying in the chair for an hour and then see more Senators and curiosity people who want to see what a V.P. looks like and if he walks and talks and has teeth.

Then I close the Senate and sign the mail and then maybe go home or to some meeting, usually some meeting, and then home and start over. . . . I am trying to make a job out of the Vice Presidency and it's quite a chore.

I owe all the boys in the family who are in the service a letter and have at least a hundred more to dictate. I've seen ten or fifteen people since I started this and answered the phone as often.

In another letter around this time, he wrote:

We are having about the usual merry-go-round here. I was so tired last night I could hardly walk. Went to bed at nine o'clock and slept right through to seven this morning.

Another reason for this exhaustion was the vice president's social schedule. According to protocol, a veep outranks everyone in Washington but the President. Hostesses like to have him at their parties, and it is assumed, since he supposedly has nothing to do, he will accept any and all invitations. John Garner had brusquely ignored this assumption and lived an intensely private life. But my father loved parties and people, and he cheerfully accepted more invitations than any other vice president in recent memory. For a while scarcely a night went by without him and Mother departing from our Connecticut Avenue apartment, looking tremendously regal in evening dress.

Sometimes I went along to luncheons. I can't say that I really enjoyed myself very often. Because of protocol, Dad and Mother would be sitting at the head of the table and I would be well below the salt, often surrounded by complete strangers. A fussy eater, I tended to turn up my nose at dishes such as cold poached salmon en gelee and often went home hungry.

One invitation my father regretted accepting was to a National Press Club party. Someone asked him to play the piano and he cheerfully obliged. Actress Lauren Bacall, also a guest, climbed onto the top of the upright and gave him one of her sultriest stares. Dad, sensing trouble, tried to look the other way, giving the impression that he was playing from sheet music that was somewhere off to his left. But he was trapped between his instinctive politeness, which made it impossible for him to hurt Miss Bacall's feelings, and his equally instinctive political awareness that he was flirting, not with Miss Bacall, but with trouble.

Miss Bacall was merely obeying her press agent, who had seen an excellent opportunity for a publicity-winning picture. The agent was right. The picture was splashed through newspapers and magazines for the next month. Mother did not care for it much. She thought it made Dad look undignified and much too carefree for the vice president of a nation at war.

Most of the time my father had a good time as vice president without getting into trouble. He continued to attend luncheon meetings of Lowell Mason's Chowder, Marching and Baseball Club. At one of these he pulled a typical gag on his protocol-conscious fellow politicians. When Dad arrived for lunch, he unobtrusively took a seat at the very bottom of the table, along with Billy Richardson, who was vice president of the Washington Senators. Sam Rayburn was sitting on Mr. Mason's right, and on his left was a very junior senator. After grace, Matt Connelly arose and issued a vehement protest about the seating order. "Mr. Chairman," Matt solemnly declared, "it seems to me that you know nothing whatever about protocol, because here you have the vice president sitting way down here at the bottom of the table, furthest from the salt, and you've got a very junior senator sitting on your left-hand side, and I think this is an affront to the vice president and I think you should correct this before we go ahead with our eating."

Burton K. Wheeler of Montana rose to agree emphatically, and several other solons added wordy senatorial style affirmations. It looked as if Chairman Mason might be impeached before the luncheon began.

With suitable solemnity, Mr. Mason yielded. "You're right and I apologize," he said. "Therefore, I shall ask the vice president to come up and sit here next to me."

Whereupon Billy Richardson arose, walked up the room, and sat down next to Mr. Mason. The vice president of the United States, who had cooked up the whole intricate joke, sat there laughing. It was Dad's way of saying that nothing had changed between him and his old friends.

To underscore this point, he declined to take over the swanky "gold plated" vice president's office in the Capitol and remained in his familiar four rooms in the Senate Office Building. He knew that nothing offended a politician more than the feeling that someone in a higher office was getting a swelled head or putting on the dog. But things beyond the world of personal relationships had changed and as the weeks passed Dad got several blunt reminders of this fact.

One day he was sitting in the small office the vice president has at his disposal in the Capitol. It is just off the Senate floor. My father noticed a young man sitting outside his office. He had been there most of the day. "Who is that young fellow who's been out there, does he want to see me?" Dad asked Harry Vaughan, who had recently returned from Australia.

"No, he doesn't want to see you," said General Vaughan.

"Who is he?"

"Secret Service."

"Well, what the hell is this?" Dad said. "When did this happen?"

"It started a day or two ago."

"Bring him in," Dad said. "I ought to meet him."

He shook hands with the young man, George Drescher, destined to be in charge of the White House Secret Service detail. "I don't see much sense in this but if you fellows are detailed to do it, I'll give you all the cooperation I can," he said.

Thereafter, a Secret Service man rode to work with him each day in the front seat of his official car.

The Secret Service guard, a very good idea, originated with General Vaughan. My father had made him his military aide— the first in the history of the vice presidency. Looking over Dad's security arrangements and knowing President Roosevelt's precarious health, General Vaughan was appalled. He went to Secretary of the Treasury Henry Morgenthau and said, "Mr. Secretary, it seems a little bit incongruous to me to have seventy-five or a hundred people guarding the President and absolutely no one guarding the vice president."

Mr. Morgenthau agreed and detailed three men. This was the

beginning of our long, often hectic, but never unfriendly relationship with the Secret Service, probably the finest, most dedicated group of men I have ever met.

Another more alarming reminder of his role in the government hit my father on February 20. A rumor swept the Capitol that President Roosevelt had died. He was en route home from Yalta aboard the USS *Quincy* at this time. Badly shaken, Dad called the White House and learned that there had indeed been a death in the presidential party—Major General Edwin M. "Pa" Watson, the President's appointments secretary, had died at sea. With a sigh of relief, Dad went back to being "a political eunuch," as he playfully called the vice presidency at times.

Occasionally we took a trip with Dad when he had a weekend speaking engagement. One of these expeditions brought us to New York, where he wrote a rather interesting letter to his mother and sister Mary on the stationery of the old Sherry Netherland Hotel.

> Dear Mamma & Mary:
> Well we got our business transacted yesterday, and went to a show last night—"The Barretts of Wimpole St." about the Brownings. It's just about as interesting and entertaining as is Browning's poetry. All the tall brows and so-called "intellectuals" do much "ohing" and "ahing" about it and Margaret wanted to see it. I'd rather have gone to an opera or *Oklahoma,* or even a prize fight would have been more entertaining to me. But I brought Marg and Bess up here to see what they wished to see and I had a good time seeing them enjoy the show and watching the antics of the rest of the crowd. The place was full and we sat in the second row. Naturally got pointed out as the visiting fireman and had a kind of reception between acts and afterwards. They send a couple of secret servicemen along with me nowadays to see I don't misbehave or do what I choose. But I guess it's necessary.

Another trip my father took around this time had a more melancholy purpose. On January 26 Tom Pendergast died in Kansas City. More than a few people wondered what Harry Truman would do. He was vice president of the United States now and Tom Pendergast was an ex-convict. Dad did not hesitate for even five seconds. He flew to the funeral. "He was always

[202]

my friend and I have always been his," Dad said. He was recalling those lines that he had written when he was county judge, asking himself who was closer to heaven, the Boss or the hypocrites who condemned him on Sunday and did business with him on Monday. The sad truth about Tom Pendergast, who many thought was still worth millions, was revealed when his estate was audited. After heavy debts were subtracted, there was barely $13,000 left to his heirs. Dad's presence at the funeral meant a great deal to Mr. Pendergast's family, and that is all Dad cared about.

Although my father tried not to think about President Roosevelt's health, there were times when he could not avoid the unpleasant truth that the President was continuing to decline. On his return from Yalta, he reported to the Congress on his historic meeting with Prime Minister Churchill and Marshal Stalin. The President spoke seated in his wheelchair in the well of the House of Representatives. He looked terribly weary and his speech was lifeless and rambling. Worse, he told Congress nothing about the Yalta agreements that they did not know already from reading the newspapers.

Not even my father could bring himself to comment favorably on the President's Yalta speech. He had to resort to sarcasm, when some friendly reporters caught him in the hall just after the joint session of Congress adjourned.

"What did you think of the speech, Senator?" they asked, using the title Dad still preferred.

"One of the greatest ever given," he replied and then joined the reporters in hearty laughter.

A few weeks later my father joined the President at the head table for the annual dinner of the White House Correspondents Association. Like everyone else, he was appalled by how bad Mr. Roosevelt looked and even more alarmed by his dazed, vacant manner.

After President Roosevelt's return from Yalta my father had a chance to see him only twice, on March 8 and March 19 at the White House. On neither visit did they discuss anything significant. The President continued to make no effort to bring Dad into the inner circle of the administration. This worried him deeply. But he was more concerned by the continued deterioration of the President's relations with Congress. The brawl over

Mr. Wallace had reawakened many old animosities, and the President's insistence on a "work or fight" bill—which would have empowered the government to draft workers—also outraged many senators on both sides of the aisle. A grim example of the Senate's hostility was the overwhelming rejection of liberal Democrat Aubrey Williams for the relatively minor post of Rural Electrification administrator. My father had done his best for Mr. Williams, but he, poor man, took the brunt of the pent-up resentment many senators still felt about being forced to vote for Henry Wallace as Secretary of Commerce.

In spite of denunciations by scores of senators, the administration still insisted on a compulsory manpower bill. Other senators seethed over the President's refusal to take them into his confidence about Yalta and his seeming lack of interest in the way the Russians were installing a Communist government in Poland. Arthur Vandenberg, leader of the internationalistic Republicans, fulminated against what was happening in Poland. But not a word was spoken from the White House to reassure him.

On March 30, 1945, the Senate was thrown into turmoil when one of those "other little things" the President had vaguely referred to in his speech on Yalta was suddenly revealed. Britain had been promised six votes in the forthcoming United Nations, and Russia and the United States were supposed to get three each. Numerous senators denounced the idea, among them Senator Vandenberg, who was the key to Republican cooperation on a peace treaty and the Senate approval of the United Nations. My father was horrified by the clumsy handling of such a delicate issue. He was convinced that America must not commit the blunder that wrecked the peace after World War I—a blunder that was in large part caused by President Wilson's poor relations with the Senate.

Around the same time the senators were equally aroused by the discovery that Marshal Stalin seemed to think so little of the already scheduled conference at San Francisco, to set up the United Nations, that he was not even sending his foreign minister, V. M. Molotov, to head the Russian delegation.

On April 3, 1945, the Senate voted 46 to 29 to reject the compulsory manpower bill, in spite of all the pleas and politicking by the White House, the army, the navy, and dozens of other high administration officials on its behalf. In succeeding days the Senate sounded like it might even reject a perfectly reasonable treaty with Mexico on water rights the two nations share on the Colorado and Rio Grande rivers. But perhaps the best proof of how low the Roosevelt Administration had sunk in the Senate's estimate was the vote on April 10 on an amendment to the Lend-Lease Act, proposed by Senator Taft of Ohio. It called for compulsory cancellation or drastic readjustment of lend-lease contracts, as soon as the war ended. It was nothing less than a direct slap in the President's face. The vote was 39 to 39 and my father was given his first and only chance to cast a tie-breaking vote as vice president. "On this amendment," he said, "the Yeas are 39 and the Nays are 39. The chair votes No. The amendment is not agreed to."

Thus he rescued President Roosevelt from humiliation. But the closeness of the vote was a humiliation in itself. Grimly, my father resolved to see the President as soon as possible and work out a program to revitalize his relationship with the Senate. By now this concern had pretty well obscured his worries about President Roosevelt's health. Perhaps, unconsciously, Dad preferred to worry about the political situation, because he could do something about that. There was nothing he could do about the other worry and he has a habit of dismissing ineffectual thoughts from his mind.

By this time President Roosevelt had departed for a projected three-weeks vacation at Warm Springs, Georgia. He had assured my father not long before he left that a good rest there would completely restore him to his old vigorous self. The President was deluding himself. We know now that no one—including President Roosevelt himself—was aware of how sick he was. George Elsey, who later became one of Dad's top aides and was at this time working in the White House map room, says that everyone in the White House was concerned about President Roosevelt's health for several years. But his doctor, Rear Admiral Ross T. McIntire, deliberately deceived the President about his true condition. This conviction was shared by William D. Hassett, who was FDR's correspondence secretary, and also served Dad in that capacity. Perhaps the most heartbreaking conversation in the history of this tragic time was the talk that Bill Hassett had with heart specialist

Dr. Howard Bruenn about the President's health, on March 30, 1945.

"He is slipping away from us and no earthly power can keep him here," Bill said.

"Why do you think so?" Dr. Bruenn asked contentiously.

"I know you don't want to make the admission and I have talked this way with no one else save one," Bill replied. "To all the staff, to the family, and with the Boss himself I have maintained the bluff; but I am convinced that there is no help for him."

On April 11 my father held a press conference for the Senate reporters. In the light of what was to happen the following day, his words were tinged with irony. Someone called him Mr. Vice President and he said, "Smile when you say that." He kidded with the reporters over recent publicity about Senate absenteeism. Senators were now elaborately asking the vice president's permission to attend committee meetings and make other necessary departures from the floor. "When they hold up two fingers and say they want to go to an appropriations committee, I tell them they can go," Dad said. "When they hold up one finger, I tell them they can sit there and suffer."

Then he grew serious. "It's wonderful, this Senate," he said. "It's the greatest place on earth. That takes in a lot of territory, but I say it and I mean it. The grandest bunch of fellows you could ever find anywhere. And there isn't one of 'em who couldn't do better in private business. I was sitting there today looking them over, and you know, there isn't a one but what could make three times what he does here if he worked for some private corporation. And there isn't one of us who would be anywhere else if he could."

"It's a good place for public service, isn't it, Senator?" somebody asked.

"It's the best place there is," Dad said. With a grin, he added, "I did what I could. I did my best. I was getting along fine until I stuck my neck out too far and got too famous—and then they made me V.P. and now I can't do anything."

The words obviously reminded him of the political worries that were nagging at his mind. "No, sir," he said, almost mournfully, "I can't do anything."

The events of the next fateful day have been told and retold in newspapers, magazines, and books. For us who lived it, the early hours were thoroughly routine. I rode to school with my father in his chauffeur-driven car, with the Secret Service man sitting beside the driver in the front seat. Dad spent most of the day in the Senate listening to more windy debate on the Mexican water treaty. He was so bored he began writing a letter to his mother, while he sat at his elevated desk, presiding. He was looking forward to a relaxed evening. Eddie McKim was in town, and at Dad's suggestion, he was busy organizing a poker game in his suite at the Statler Hotel.

I was also looking forward to a very pleasant evening. I had a date with a new boyfriend, and we were going to stop by a birthday party for my close friend and next door neighbor, Annette Davis, before going on to dinner and the theater. The Senate finally adjourned at 4:56 P.M., with absolutely nothing decided on the Mexican water treaty. Outside a misty rain was falling, typical April weather for Washington, D.C. This worried my father a little because he was planning to fly to Providence, Rhode Island, the following morning, to address the Rhode Island Democrats at their Jefferson Day dinner.

In no hurry, since he was not planning to eat dinner at home that night, my father sauntered into his "gold-plated" Capitol office. There he was told that Speaker of the House Sam Rayburn had called, asking if he would stop by his office for a few minutes to talk over some bills on which the House and Senate were in disagreement. Dad dutifully headed for Mr. Sam's office. He then planned to dash over to his Senate Office Building quarters, sign the day's mail, and depart for Eddie McKim's room at the Statler and an evening of friendly poker. He told General Vaughan to phone Eddie and tell him they would be a little late, but they would definitely get there.

Down the dark marble corridors my father strolled to Sam Rayburn's "Board of Education," as insiders called the Speaker's private office, where he maintained the tradition of his mentor, Cactus Jack Garner, of "striking a blow for liberty." Waiting for Dad, along with the Speaker, was Lew Deschler, the parliamentarian of the House of Representatives, and James M. Barnes, a White House legislative assistant. After the draggy afternoon Dad had spent in the Senate, he was more than ready to join Mr. Sam in a liquid blow for liberty. As the Speaker mixed the bourbon with the right amount of water, he casually told Dad that Steve Early, the White House press secretary, had left a message, asking my father to return the call immediately. He did so without a moment's hesitation.

In a strained voice, Steve Early said, "Please come right over as quickly and as quietly as you can."

Apologizing to Sam Rayburn, my father walked over to his Senate office by unfrequented underground corridors. There he seized his hat and told one of his secretaries that he was going to the White House. Although some people have found it hard to believe, he was still unaware of what had happened. Not even the urgency in Steve Early's voice was able to penetrate Dad's rigid resolve *not* to think about the President's health.

Four days later, when he wrote a long letter to his mother and sister Mary about these harrowing minutes, he said:

> I thought that the President had come to Washington to attend the funeral of the Episcopal Bishop Atwood, for whom he was an honorary pallbearer, and who was his good nd. I thought that maybe he wanted me to do some special piece of liaison work with the Congress and had sent for me to see him after the funeral and before he went back to Warm Springs.

My father's walk through the underground corridors to his Senate office had taken his Secret Service detail completely by surprise. They now had no idea where he was. With no time to look for them, he went downstairs and into the street, where he found his car and chauffeur waiting for him. "We got to the White House in almost nothing flat," Dad told his mother. It was 5:25 P.M. when his black limousine swung through the northwest gate and up the long semicircle to the front entrance of the White House. Two ushers were waiting for him, and they led him to an elevator which carried him up to Mrs. Roosevelt's second-floor study. Steve Early and Anna Roosevelt and her husband, Colonel John Boettiger, were there. Tragedy was visible in their stricken faces. Gently, sadly, Mrs. Roosevelt placed her hand on my father's shoulder and said, "Harry, the President is dead."

For over an hour, while he wrote his letter to his mother at his

Senate desk and strolled down to Sam Rayburn's office, my father had been the President, without knowing it. Mr. Roosevelt had died in Warm Springs at 4:35.

"Is there anything I can do for you?" Dad asked.

Mrs. Roosevelt shook her head. "Is there anything we can do for you?" she asked. "For you are the one in trouble now."

Dad's first reaction was a tremendous surge of sympathy and grief. My father had disagreed with some of President Roosevelt's policies, but the disagreements were minor. His admiration for the man as a political leader, as the creator of the modern Democratic party, was immense. No matter what office Dad held, he would have been grieved by the President's death. Now, in the presence of Mrs. Roosevelt's calm courage, and the awful knowledge of what the news meant to him personally, grief and awe and shock combined to create emotions of terrible intensity.

Yet, within minutes, my father began making decisions. Here, in a passage which he omitted from the April 16 letter to his mother, part of which he published in his memoirs, he tells the events of the next hour:

> Just at this time the Secretary of State came in and he and Early thought a Cabinet meeting should be called at once so I authorized the Sec. of State to notify all the members of the Cabinet to report to the Cabinet Room at 6:15. I told Mrs. Roosevelt and her daughter and son-in-law that anything necessary to be done for their help and convenience would be done. Mrs. R. said she wanted to fly to Warm Springs that evening and did I think it would be proper for her to use a government plane. I told her that as soon as I was sworn in I would order that all the facilities of the government should be at her command until the funeral was over. That wasn't necessary, but it made her feel that her using the plane was all right.
>
> I went to the Cabinet Room and was the first to arrive. They came in one at a time. Madm. Perkins [Frances Perkins, the Secretary of Labor] was the second or third to come in. She hadn't heard the news which had been released and broadcast two minutes after I left Mrs. Roosevelt.
>
> As soon as all the Cabinet members in town had arrived, I made a formal statement, asking them to remain in their respective offices.
>
> Mr. Biffle, the secretary of the Senate, came to the White

House right away and helped me get Bess and Margaret to the White House.

I sent for the Pres. Pro Tempore of the Senate, the Majority Leader, Mr. Barkley, the Minority Leader, Mr. White, the Chm. of the Foreign Relations Committee, Mr. Connally, the Speaker of the House, Mr. Rayburn, the Majority Leader of the House, Mr. McCormack, the Minority Leader of the House, Mr. Martin, Mr. Ramspeck, the House whip, and one or two others from each of the legislative branches.

I instructed the Attorney General, Mr. Biddle, to call the Chief Justice of the Supreme Court to come at once and administer the oath of office to me and if he could not get the Chief Justice to get Mr. Justice Jackson to come.

I think these crisp words convey, better than anything I could write, the image of a man who was, in spite of his grief, taking charge as a national leader.

My father personally called Mother and me from the President's office in the west wing of the White House. In a party mood, I started to tease him about not coming home to dinner, grandly informing him that *I* was going out. Miraculously, Dad did not lose his temper. He simply told me in a voice of steel to put Mother on the line.

I went back into my bedroom to finish dressing. I was vaguely aware that Mother had hung up rather abruptly. It wasn't like her and Dad to have such brief conversations. Suddenly Mother was standing in the door of my bedroom with tears streaming down her face. My Grandmother Wallace, who shared the bedroom with me, gasped, when Mother, in a choked voice, told us that President Roosevelt was dead.

The next two hours were lived in a kind of daze. Things were seen, thought, felt, and heard with a strange mixture of confusion and clarity. It was rather like going under or coming out of anesthesia, or recovering from a blow on the head. I felt totally dazed but certain things, sometimes important details, sometimes minor ones, leaped into focus with almost blinding clarity. I remember calling my boyfriend, Marvin Braverman, and telling him why I couldn't keep our date, and his voice echoing the news back to me over the wire: "Dead!" I remember our doorbell ringing. I answered it in my slip—I was changing from my party dress—and found myself talking to a woman reporter from the Associated Press. I slammed the door in her face. Minutes later, Secret Service men arrived to inform us that there was a big crowd gathering outside the apartment building. We went out the back door to avoid them, but some of the smart curiosity seekers were waiting for us there, along with numerous photographers. Flash bulbs exploded all around us, and for a moment I felt very angry. But Mother calmly ignored them. She steered me into the back seat of the car and we headed for the White House.

After visiting Mrs. Roosevelt to express our sympathy, Mother and I went to the Cabinet Room, where all the members of the Cabinet except Postmaster General Frank Walker were assembled, along with the political leaders of Congress whom my father had summoned. Only Alben Barkley was absent. He had elected to stay with Mrs. Roosevelt. The White House staff was searching frantically for a Bible. Dad would have preferred to use his family Bible, which was in his office bookcase. But there was no time to send someone to get it. Finally, in William Hassett's office, the searchers found a small, inexpensive Bible with red-edged pages, which had been sent to the correspondence secretary as a gift. William D. Simmons, the burly chief White House receptionist, apologized to my father for its rather garish style. But that was the least of Dad's worries at that moment. He assured Mr. Simmons that it was fine.

My father was now ready to take the oath. He was standing beneath the portrait of Woodrow Wilson, one of his presidential heroes. Chief Justice Harlan F. Stone stepped to the end of the long Cabinet table. My father picked up the Bible in his left hand. Beneath his thumb, he held a small piece of paper, on which the presidential oath of office was typed. After the ceremony he gave it to me. It is a very interesting historic souvenir.

Chief Justice Stone began, "I, Harry Shippe Truman—"

Dad raised his right hand and responded, "I, Harry S. Truman, do solemnly swear that I will faithfully execute the office of the President of the United States, and will, to the best of my ability, preserve, protect, and defend the Constitution of the United States."

"So help you God," added Chief Justice Stone, indicating his own deep emotion. These words are not part of the official oath but they were used spontaneously by George Washington when he took his first oath of office.

"So help me God," said Dad and solemnly raised the Bible to his lips.

This, too, was something George Washington had done. The time on the clock beneath Woodrow Wilson's picture was 7:09.

[CHAPTER]

Eleven

MOTHER AND I LEFT the White House immediately after my father took the oath. He stayed to conduct a brief meeting of the Cabinet. Dad sat down in the raised chair at the head of the table for the first time. Before he could speak, Steve Early, the press secretary, came in and said that the reporters wanted to know if the San Francisco Conference on the United Nations would begin as scheduled on April 25. Tom Connally, chairman of the Senate Foreign Relations Committee, had issued a wholly unnecessary statement predicting a postponement. Without hesitation my father told Mr. Early that he considered the conference crucial to winning the peace. The press secretary departed to give this message to the newsmen.

My father then spoke briefly and solemnly to the Cabinet members. He assured them that he intended to carry out President Roosevelt's foreign and domestic policies. But he also told them that he was going to be "President in my own right." He told them that he wanted their advice and that they should not hesitate to differ with him, whenever they felt it was necessary. But he was going to make the final decisions. Again, in this brief scene, there is the unmistakable note of a man taking charge, a man who knew what it meant to be President and was determined to do his utmost to live up to the responsibilities of the job that Dad still calls "the greatest in the world."

After the Cabinet meeting, Secretary of War Henry Stimson

stayed behind. In a low, tense voice he told my father that he had an extremely urgent matter to discuss with him. Briefly, with a minimum of details, he described a weapon of enormous explosive power on which the United States had been working for years. He did not use the term "atomic bomb," which left Dad more puzzled than informed. The main impact of the conversation was to add a lot more weight to the already enormous responsibility on Dad's shoulders.

For another few minutes my father discussed with Secretary of State Stettinius and White House press secretary Steve Early and Jonathan Daniels the need to reassure our Allies and the world that our support of the San Francisco Conference was unchanged. Dad directed Steve Early to issue a formal statement, making this clear. But he wisely declined to hold a press conference, although the White House correspondents were clamoring for one. Escorted by a small army of Secret Service men, he went out to his car and drove home to our apartment.

There Mother and I were still in a state of shock. If he had depended upon us for food and drink, he would have starved to death—and the poor man was starving. It was now almost 9:30 P.M. and he had had nothing to eat since noon. Fortunately, the parents of my friend Annette Davis, who was having the birthday party, had canceled their celebration. They fed Mother and me, and when Dad arrived home, we were sitting in their apartment talking. He joined us, and Mrs. Davis gave him a man-sized turkey and ham sandwich and a glass of milk.

With that astonishing equilibrium which he never loses in moments of crisis, my father ate this impromptu supper and then calmly announced he was going to bed. From his bedroom, he called his mother in Grandview. Mamma Truman had, of course, heard the news by now. With the help of Dad's brother Vivian, she had been fending off a cascade of phone calls from reporters. My father assured her that he was all right, but for the next several days he was going to be very busy. It would be a while before she had a letter from him. Actually, it would only be four days. Then, what is most phenomenal to an insomniac like me, Dad turned out the light, slipped under the covers and was asleep within five minutes.

The next morning, Friday, April 13, he began his first full day as President. Thank goodness he is not a superstitious man. He was up at 6:30, had his usual light breakfast, and then chatted for a half hour or so with Hugh Fulton, the former chief counsel of the Truman Committee. Poor Mr. Fulton was suffering from what Dad calls "Potomac fever." Basically, this very common Washington disease involves delusions of grandeur and an itch for power and publicity. The news that my father had become President had aroused the virus in Mr. Fulton, in its most acute form. Dad soon learned from friends that Mr. Fulton was telling everyone in Washington that he was going to be the acting President—the implication being that Harry S. Truman did not have the talent to do the job. Although they parted amicably enough that morning, Mr. Fulton was never offered an official post in the White House.

As my father got into his car, surrounded by the inevitable swarms of Secret Service men, he saw one of his old friends, Associated Press reporter Tony Vacarro, standing nearby. He invited him to hop in and they rode down to the White House together. He got there a little after 8:30 A.M. At nine sharp Eddie McKim and Matt Connelly arrived. Dad had called them the night before, from the White House, and told them to be there at this time.

My father apologized profusely for forgetting to invite Eddie to the ceremony the previous night. Eddie stood in front of Dad's desk, completely at a loss for words for the first time in his life.

"Well, Mr. President," he said, shifting from one foot to another, "it doesn't count what's gone before. What counts is what happens now." Then he just stood there, while Dad stared at him in astonishment.

"Do you have to stand there?" Dad asked.

"Well, Mr. President, I suddenly find myself in the presence of the President of the United States and I don't know how to act!"

It was Dad's first glimpse of the tremendous awe with which so many people regarded the presidency. "Come on over here and sit down," he said.

Eddie obeyed and Dad asked, "Do you have to go home?"

"Well—I was leaving this afternoon for Omaha."

"Well," Dad said, "I need you. Stick around a while. I need some help."

From the very first moment of the first day, my father understood the importance of having men around him who were personally loyal to him. He had no illusions that the deep devotion that Mr. Roosevelt's staff felt for him could be transferred to a new President. Dad had the same attitude toward the Cabinet, but there he knew it would be necessary to make the transition more gradually, because Cabinet appointments involved Congress and the President's political relationship to the nation.

Matt Connelly brought with him the letters my father never had gotten around to signing the previous day. One of them was a letter to Olive Truman, the wife of his cousin Ralph. After signing it, Dad scribbled the following postscript: "I've really had a blow since this was dictated. But I'll have to meet it. Hope it won't cause the family too much trouble."

That morning my father saw Secretary of State Stettinius and the Joint Chiefs of Staff, the Secretaries of War and the Navy, and Admiral William D. Leahy, who functioned as President Roosevelt's Chief of Staff in the White House. Dad immediately asked the Secretary of State for a thorough report on the major foreign policy problems of the United States, particularly in Europe. By that afternoon it was in his hands, and it made grim reading. Relations with Russia had deteriorated disastrously since the Yalta Conference. The Joint Chiefs of Staff expected the war with Germany to last another six months, and the war with Japan another eighteen months. Both predictions were, of course, wrong. In little more than four months, the President and the nation would be catapulted into the postwar era.

After the Joint Chiefs left, Admiral Leahy stayed behind to ask my father if he wanted him to remain on the job. The Admiral was as crusty an old sea dog as they come. He had graduated from Annapolis in 1897 and rounded Cape Horn in a sailing ship in 1898. He had no illusions about the saltiness of his own character and was not at all sure that Dad could take him, ungarnished, as it were. He was the first but by no means the last public official to misjudge President Harry S. Truman.

"Are you sure you want me, Mr. President? I always say what's on my mind."

"I want the truth," Dad told him. "I want the facts at all times. I want you to stay with me and always to tell me what's on your mind. You may not always agree with my decisions, but I know you will carry them out faithfully."

The Admiral was surprised—pleasantly surprised. "You have my pledge," he told Dad. "You can count on me."

At noon that day my father went up to the Capitol and lunched with thirteen key senators and four representatives. In some personal memoranda he made at the end of the day, he noted that by the time the luncheon was over and he went back to the White House he had seen "*all* the senators." He added that he was "most overcome" by the affection and encouragement they had showered on him.

At the time many people regarded this as simply a sentimental gesture. But my father knew exactly what he was doing. He was trying to bridge the chasm which had opened between the White House and the Senate. Later that day Senator Arthur Vandenberg of Michigan, the leading Republican internationalist and a key figure in the American delegation to the San Francisco UN Conference, wrote in his diary: "Truman came back to the Senate this noon for lunch with a few of us. It shattered all tradition. But it was both wise and smart. It means that the days of executive contempt for Congress are ended; that we are returning to a government in which Congress will take its rightful place." With obvious pleasure, Senator Vandenberg added that at Dad's request General Vaughan had sent him the last box of cigars they had in the old vice presidential office, with Dad's card. On the card General Vaughan had written, "Our swan song."

The main purpose of the luncheon, aside from healing political wounds, was to discuss with the Senate and House leaders my father's desire to address a joint session of Congress on the following Monday. Surprisingly, several of the senators thought that this was a bad idea. They seemed to feel that Dad should not expose himself so soon to a comparison with President Roosevelt's undoubtedly superior oratorical gifts. My father listened politely to these and other objections and then quietly informed them that he was coming, and they had better prepare themselves for his visit.

Later that afternoon my father conferred with Jimmy Byrnes. He had resigned as assistant president five days before Mr. Roosevelt's death and returned to South Carolina. James Forrestal, the Secretary of the Navy, had telephoned Mr. Byrnes from the White House on the night of President Roosevelt's death and sent a government plane to South Carolina to fly him to Washington—two rather startling gestures, wholly unauthorized by Dad.

Nevertheless, my father was glad to see Mr. Byrnes for several reasons. Perhaps most important, Mr. Byrnes had accompanied Mr. Roosevelt to Yalta and had taken extensive shorthand notes of the conference. Dad desperately needed to know, as soon as possible, all the agreements and the nuances of the agreements that Mr. Roosevelt had made at this crucial meeting. For more than a half hour, my father queried Mr. Byrnes intensively on Yalta, Teheran, and other conferences between Mr. Roosevelt, Mr. Churchill, and Marshal Stalin. As they talked, my father decided to make Mr. Byrnes his Secretary of State.

Dad's chief reason was his concern over presidential succession. According to the Constitution at that time, the Secretary of State was next in line to succeed the vice president. But my father was convinced that any successor to the President should be an elected official, not an appointed one. The fact that Edward Stettinius was Secretary of State made Dad's concern on this point even more acute. Mr. Stettinius had never even been a candidate for elective office. Mr. Byrnes had been a senator from South Carolina, had served briefly as a Supreme Court Justice, and then had gone to the White House as Mr. Roosevelt's chief assistant on the home front. He was eminently qualified to serve as President. Finally, my father felt that this appointment—the highest he had in his power to dispose—might mitigate the bitter disappointment Mr. Byrnes obviously felt over FDR's failure to back him for the vice presidency in Chicago.

Here my father made his first miscalculation as President. Although Mr. Byrnes, as Dad put it later, "practically jumped down my throat to accept" when he offered him the job, their relationship was flawed almost from the beginning by Mr. Byrnes's low opinion of Harry Truman and his extravagantly high opinion of himself.

My father spent the rest of the afternoon conferring with Secretary of State Stettinius and Charles E. Bohlen of the Department of State, who had acted as interpreter at the Yalta meetings with Stalin. The subject was Russia's gross violation of the Yalta agreements, particularly in Poland. The Russians were totally ignoring

[218]

the solemn agreement to create a representative Polish government and were installing their Communist lackeys, known as the Lublin government, in Warsaw. My father decided there was no time to waste, and he immediately cabled Prime Minister Churchill, who seemed inclined to denounce the Russians publicly for their conduct. Dad felt this might cause a major breach among the three Allied leaders at the worst possible moment, and he urged insead that we "have another go" at Stalin.

With some reluctance, the British prime minister agreed and a diplomatic crisis, which might have prolonged the war, was averted.

In this same afternoon meeting my father was able to use the melancholy fact of President Roosevelt's death to score a diplomatic breakthrough, with the help of our ambassador in Moscow, W. Averell Harriman. Mr. Harriman had been summoned to see Stalin when the news of Mr. Roosevelt's death arrived in the Russian capital. He immediately urged the Russian leader to make a gesture which might repair the strong impression that Russia was no longer interested in co-operating with the United States to create a peaceful postwar world. Stalin offered to send Mr. Molotov to the San Francisco Conference, if the new American President would back up Mr. Harriman's request for him. My father immediately cabled the American Embassy his strong approval of this request, and one of the major stumbling blocks in the path of the San Francisco meeting was removed.

So, with one crisis averted and what seemed like a major step toward repairing Soviet-American relations achieved, and with an equally urgent repair job begun on Capitol Hill, Dad wearily pondered a stack of memoranda on his desk. There was a request from the Secretary of State for instructions for the American delegation to the conference in San Francisco, and reports on our relationships with Russia, Germany, France, Great Britain, Italy, and a dozen other countries. There were copies of the cables exchanged between Stalin, Churchill, and Mr. Roosevelt. Somehow he would have to read as much as possible of this mass of words before going to bed. Dad piled it all into his briefcase and returned to Connecticut Avenue, where Mother and I were waiting for him.

My father was upset to find our apartment building practically under a state of siege. Secret Service men guarded every entrance, and no one could enter without producing complete identification. Dad had told Mrs. Roosevelt that he had no intention of moving into the White House until she was ready to leave. But it was obviously impossible for us to stay here much longer. Wisely, Mother had decided it would be best if I did not go to school that day, so we personally had suffered a minimum of inconvenience. But our neighbors, who had to come and go to earn a living, were by no means as fortunate.

The following morning my father arose at dawn to continue his reading of top-secret documents and departed for the White House at around 8:15. He found his desk already covered with telegrams and cables. His first visitor was his old friend John W. Snyder. He had been in Mexico City, at an inter-American banking conference, and had flown to Washington as soon as he heard of President Roosevelt's death. Mr. Snyder was in the process of leaving the government, after some ten years of service, to take a position as executive vice president of a leading St. Louis bank. It was the fulfillment of one of his life's ambitions, and he admits that he was very dismayed to hear Dad inform him that he wanted him to stay in Washington as Federal Loan Administrator.

"I told him that my boss at the bank would be extremely upset at this change in plans," Mr. Snyder recalls, "but he stopped me cold on that one by calling him long distance and getting his approval. I was still hemming and hawing, when Jimmy Byrnes walked into the office and said, 'Don't let him talk back to you, Harry, you're the President. Draft him.' I capitulated."

My father was delighted. Not only was he getting on his team one of his oldest, most trusted friends, but a man who was widely respected by business and banking interests. Mr. Snyder had been one of Jesse Jones's top assistants in the RFC. As head of the Defense Plant Corporation, he had lent $11 billion to private industry, to help create the American war effort.

As a courtesy, one or two days later, my father telephoned Jesse Jones and said, "Jesse, the President has just appointed John Snyder to be federal loan administrator."

"Did he make that appointment before he died?" asked Mr. Jones.

"No," Dad answered with a smile, "*he* made it just now."

[220]

Jones made an understandable mistake, Dad says. "Those first few days, even I occasionally found myself still thinking of Mr. Roosevelt as the President."

Meanwhile, around the nation newspapers and magazines were making a valiant effort to tell their readers about the new President. The man who made the greatest impact was probably Roy Roberts, the big, broad-beamed managing editor of the Kansas City *Star*. He and one of his reporters, "Duke" Shoop, had wangled an invitation to see my father for a few minutes the previous afternoon. In a widely syndicated article Mr. Roberts struck a chord which was, while true in one sense, wildly wrong in projecting any genuine appreciation of Dad's abilities. "The new President is the average man," Mr. Roberts wrote. He went on to add some really incredible nonsense about Dad "approaching forty and still looking at the rear of the horse as he plowed the corn rows." Then, stuck with his average-man thesis, Mr. Roberts tried to argue that this would be my father's "greatest asset as he undertakes these new overpowering responsibilities." From there his analysis became almost laughable, if it had not been so misleading. "He is really more southern in viewpoint than midwestern," Mr. Roberts wrote. ". . . If he develops a weakness, it will be in not always understanding the newly aroused mass consciousness of industrial labor."

Later in the week, *Time* magazine won my prize for the worst analysis and the murkiest crystal ball: "Harry Truman is a man of distinct limitations, especially in experience in high level politics. He knows his limitations. . . . In his administration there are likely to be few innovations and little experimentation."

At 10:30 that Saturday morning President Roosevelt's funeral train arrived in Washington from Warm Springs. My father made another gesture toward political unity and invited Henry Wallace and Jimmy Byrnes to go with him to the station and join the funeral procession. It was a hot, very humid day. The streets were packed with people, many of them weeping. There was very little conversation in the presidential limousine. Dad felt acutely that he was on display as President for the first time and did not feel it would be appropriate for him to chat in his normal manner, as if he was on his way to some routine ceremony. Mr. Wallace and Mr. Byrnes began, for some odd reason, to discuss President

Roosevelt's political mistakes. Among his worst, they agreed, was his attempt to purge Democrats who had not gone along with his 1937 court-packing plan.

At the train my father paid his respects to Mrs. Roosevelt and the other members of the family and then rode back to the White House in the funeral procession. It was heartbreaking to watch the tears streaming down the faces of the people on the streets. The flag-covered coffin was carried on a caisson drawn by six white horses. Ahead, the United States Marine Band and the United States Navy Band alternately played solemn funeral music. There was not a sound except the clop of the horses' feet, the drone of military planes overhead, the hum of car motors.

At the White House my father went directly to his west-wing office. He did not want the Roosevelt family to feel his presence was an intrusion. Moreover, he had work to do. At 11:30 Harry Hopkins, the tall, thin, cadaverous man who was closer to Roosevelt than anyone else in the government, appeared in the doorway. He had left the Mayo Clinic, where he was being treated for a serious digestive disorder, to fly to Washington for FDR's funeral. By great good luck, my father felt closer to him than to anyone else in the Roosevelt Administration. They had known each other since the early 1930s. They shared a similar style. Both were direct, practical men.

"How do you feel, Harry?" Dad asked.

"Terrible," Mr. Hopkins replied.

My father explained why he had asked him to leave the hospital. At Cairo, Casablanca, Teheran, and Yalta, Mr. Hopkins had sat beside Mr. Roosevelt while he conferred with Marshal Stalin and Mr. Churchill. Dad wanted to know everything Mr. Hopkins remembered, and in particular, because Dad valued his judgment so highly, he wanted Mr. Hopkins's personal assessment of the Russian leader and his associates.

After Mr. Hopkins left, Admiral Leahy arrived with two important messages from Mr. Churchill. He wanted to know if the President was ready to issue a joint statement hailing the junction of American and Russian armies in Europe, an event which was now only days, perhaps hours, away. The second message asked my father's opinion of a project created by the Chiefs of Staff. It called for launching pilotless old bombers, crammed with explosives, against German cities. Mr. Churchill feared the Nazis might retaliate in kind against London. He wondered if it was necessary, with the war going so well. Reluctantly he had given his approval to it. After talking with Admiral Leahy, Dad decided to postpone the project indefinitely and wired Mr. Churchill accordingly. His goal, from the moment he took office, was to end the war as quickly as possible, with a minimum of carnage.

That afternoon Mother and I joined Dad to attend the state funeral for President Roosevelt in the East Room of the White House. The walls were covered with flowers from the floor to the ceiling—a stupendous sight in that huge room. The heat was almost unbearable, and the thick scent of the flowers made it almost impossible to breathe. I came very close to an attack of claustrophobia. I fought it off by concentrating on Bishop Angus Dun who was conducting the service. A drop of perspiration kept balancing on the tip of his nose. It was easier to wonder when the drop would fall off than it was to think about the overpowering scene around me.

About ten o'clock that night Mother and Dad and I went to Union Station and boarded the funeral train for the trip to Hyde Park. It was a huge train—seventeen cars—and it was crammed with practically every official of the American government. In retrospect, it seems a terribly dangerous thing to have done in time of war. If sabotage or an accident had wrecked that train, the nation would have been crippled. Three times couplings broke as they tried to get us out of the station. Because of the enormous crowds along the right of way, and because it was a funeral procession, we moved very slowly. Flares glowed all along the track, illuminating thousands of grief-stricken faces. Sleep was practically impossible. When I did sleep I had nightmares about trying to open a window and escape from a small suffocating room. I don't think even Dad got more than a few hours' sleep that night. For one thing he was still working. He spent much of the night outlining his speech to Congress and discussing it with Jimmy Byrnes and others.

We arrived in Hyde Park about 9:30 on the morning of April 15. It was a clear, sunny day, mercifully cooler in the lovely Hudson River Valley than it had been in swampy Washington. To the dull beat of the West Point band's drummers we followed the coffin, carried by eight servicemen, into Hyde Park's rose garden. After the graveside service cadets from West Point fired a final salute, which practically sent poor little Fala, FDR's Scotty, into a fit. By noon we were on our way back to Washington.

Now the real politicking began. Every congressman and senator on the train was trying to get to see the President. He was working on the speech he had to give tomorrow, and it must have been maddening to be interrupted so often, but he smiled and shook hands with each of them and asked them to come see him in the White House.

The following day my father addressed the joint session of the Congress. Mother and I sat in the gallery, and for a moment, as he walked to the rostrum and stood there beside Sam Rayburn, he looked up and—he later told me—saw Mother and me. Dad was terribly nervous up there on the rostrum. He was always nervous before a speech, but this one, so enormously important, doubled his normal tension. He walked to the microphone and began to speak at once.

"Just a minute, Harry," Sam Rayburn whispered. "Let me introduce you."

The microphones were turned on, and everyone in the chamber —and in the country—heard him. Then the Speaker added: "The President of the United States."

It was a good speech, as far as I could tell. I especially liked Dad's conclusion:

> . . . I have in my heart a prayer. As I have assumed my heavy duties, I humbly pray Almighty God, in the words of King Solomon:
> "Give therefore thy servant an understanding heart to judge Thy people, that I may discern between good and bad: for who is able to judge this Thy so great a people?"

The Congress interrupted him again and again with tremendous applause and gave him a standing ovation when he finished.

The comment on his speech that my father liked most came from his mother: "Harry will get along. I knew Harry would be all right after I heard him give his speech this morning. I heard every word of it, but Mary, my daughter, is going to read it to me.

Everyone who heard him talk this morning will know he is sincere and will do his best."

That afternoon we moved into Blair House. My father had decided that it was impossible for us to stay in our Connecticut Avenue apartment, so Blair House was made ready for us.

This lovely old house was just across the street from the White House. I fell in love with the place the moment I walked into it. Every room, especially on the first floor, was a little masterpiece of architecture and decoration. Almost every piece of furniture was a rare antique from eighteenth-century America or from France. Crystal chandeliers gleamed above Aubusson rugs. Magnificent gilt-framed mirrors redoubled the beauty of the drawing rooms, and the wood-paneled dining room was utterly charming.

The silver service, the china, were exquisite. There was enough china to serve meals for two weeks without once repeating the pattern. Best of all, the food matched the surroundings. A few days after we moved in, we had a visit from a member of the Blair family. They had given the house to the government as a residence for the entertainment of foreign VIPs. The Blairs went back to Francis Preston Blair, a newspaperman and a member of President Andrew Jackson's "Kitchen Cabinet." In later years the family settled in St. Louis, Missouri, and sent several distinguished politicians to Washington. Mr. Blair was tremendously pleased that the first President to reside in Blair House was from Missouri. So was Dad, and he took time off from his reading of crisis-filled reports to talk American history with him.

The following day I went back to school—another ordeal. I was pursued by a horde of reporters and photographers everywhere I went. At a more discreet distance I was trailed by the Secret Service man assigned to me, John Dorsey. At first the photographers almost reduced me to tears, but after I had retreated to a private room and pulled myself together, my Truman common sense came to the fore, and I decided to let them take pictures until they wore themselves or their lenses out; then, I hoped, they would go away and stop bothering me and the rest of George Washington University. It worked beautifully. I remained calm and invited my sorority sisters and even my professors to say cheese and let the photographers click away. They were satisfied by the end of the day. I have followed the impromptu formula

I devised that day, ever since. There is really no point in trying to play Garbo and fight off the picture boys. If you try to beat them at their game, they will go out of their way to take bad pictures of you.

My father, meanwhile, had more important things to worry about. Like his first press conference.

The largest mob of reporters in White House history—348—showed up for it. On the whole, it was like most press conferences, a combination of the trivial and the important. My father impressed everyone by how swiftly and forthrightly he answered the reporters' questions. Mr. Roosevelt was fond of playing hide-and-seek with the press, tantalizing them with semi-answers and evasions. Dad's approach was drastically different. He either answered a question directly, or declined to answer it just as directly.

One reporter asked him whether the Negroes in America could look forward to his support for fair employment practices and the right to vote without being hampered by poll taxes. "I will give you some advice," Dad said. "All you need to do is read the Senate record of one Harry S. Truman." Someone else wanted to know if he was planning to lift the ban on horseracing. "I do not intend to lift the ban," Dad said. Another man asked his views on the disposal of synthetic rubber plants. "That is not a matter for discussion here. It will be discussed at the proper time," was the reply. Then there was the goofball who asked, "Mr. President, do you approve of the work of the Truman Committee?" A roar of laughter saved Dad the trouble of answering that one. Perhaps his most important statement—one that drew a rare burst of applause from the reporters—was his reply to the following question: "Do you expect to see Mr. Molotov before he goes across—"

"Yes, I do."

"Before he goes to San Francisco?"

"Yes. He is going to stop by and pay his respects to the President of the United States. He should."

As his press secretary, my father had decided to retain, on a temporary basis, Leonard Reinsch, a radio newsman from Ohio. But Dad knew that Mr. Reinsch, with his radio orientation, would never be acceptable to the fiercely clannish newspapermen of the White House press corps. On the morning of April 18 Dad asked the man he wanted to take the enormously important job of

White House press secretary to visit him. It was his old friend Charlie Ross, valedictorian of his high school graduating class and now a contributing editor of the St. Louis *Post-Dispatch*. At fifty-nine, Charlie felt reluctant to say yes. The brutal hours, the pressures of the job required a younger man. There was also the problem of salary. The *Post-Dispatch* was paying Charlie $35,000 a year. The White House could pay him only $10,000.

"Charlie," Dad said sadly, "I know that. But I also know you aren't the kind of man who can say no to the President of the United States."

If ever there was an example of my father's remarkable ability to judge men, this was it. He was selecting for one of the most sensitive and confidential jobs in his administration a man from a paper that had always attacked him with savage partisanship. But Dad, as usual, separated the trivial from the essential, the man from the issue. He knew that he and Charlie Ross shared a common heritage, believed in the same ideals, sought the same goals. Charlie knew it too, and he backed away from his first instinct, which was outright refusal. He asked for a little time to think it over.

That night Charlie Ross decided to say yes. "This man needs help," he told his wife.

An interesting observation, which suggests that even Charlie did not know my father very well at this time. He too subscribed to the average-man theory that Roy Roberts purveyed—although he did not think the word "average" was synonymous with mediocre. In an estimate of Dad written on the night FDR died, Charlie called him "better than average. . . . He may not have the makings of a great President but he certainly has the makings of a good President."

On the evening of April 19 Charlie visited my father at Blair House and told him he would take the job. Dad was, of course, delighted, and the two graduates of the class of 1901 began reminiscing about the years they had shared.

"Say," Charlie suddenly said, "won't this be news for Miss Tillie?"

Dad immediately decided to call Miss Tillie and tell her the news. "I think it's about time I got that kiss she never gave me on graduation night," Dad said.

Miss Tillie Brown was in her eighties, but very much with it. She was tremendously pleased and flattered by the call. "How about that kiss I never got?" Dad asked. "Have I done something worthwhile enough to rate it now?"

"You certainly have," Miss Tillie said.

Miss Tillie was so excited, she promptly called the Independence *Examiner* to tell them about her chat with the President. The *Examiner* in turn contacted the wire services, and within minutes agitated phone calls were pouring into the White House, demanding to know what the devil was going on. Since when did the President leak his most important appointments to country newspapers in Missouri, and ignore the titans of the AP, UP, and *The New York Times*? Dad had to call a special press conference the next morning to announce Charlie's appointment. Fortunately, Charlie's popularity among the press corps muted any resentment the White House reporters felt about being scooped by Miss Tillie. The Washington *Post* declared: "There is no more beloved nor highly regarded newspaper man in this city than Charlie Ross." *The New York Times* said: "It would be hard to single out a Washington writer who has been more highly regarded or better liked."

My father was learning the hard way that everything a President says and does is news. During one of these first hectic weeks he decided to stroll down to his bank. No one argued with him. People are not in the habit of arguing with the President about minor matters. Only when he was in midpassage did he realize that he was creating a public disturbance. An immense crowd swarmed around him. The Secret Service men were aghast and called for help. Sirens screamed as Washington police rushed to respond. A monumental traffic jam, plus a mob in which women and children might easily have been trampled, was the result of Dad's first—and last—stroll to the bank.

Even his hundred-yard trips from the White House to Blair House became a problem. The first day or two he was startled to discover that as he reached Pennsylvania Avenue, lights in all directions turned red—a little gambit that the Secret Service had worked out with the capital police. Traffic jammed and Dad felt guilty about it. So he ordered the practice to cease. "I'll wait for the light like any other pedestrian," he said. But the day he tried this, a big crowd immediately gathered around him, making the

Secret Service extremely nervous and slowing the traffic to a crawl. So he gave up and let the Secret Service guide him on a circuitous path from the rear door of the White House to a car that took him to an alley entrance behind Blair House.

My father worried a good deal about the problems he was creating for the rest of the family. "It is a terrible—and I mean terrible—nuisance to be kin to the President of the United States," he told his mother and sister. "Reporters have been haunting every relative and purported relative I ever heard of and they've probably made life miserable for my mother, brother, and sister. I am sorry for it, but it can't be helped."

If the Trumans were having their troubles with the press, the press was also having trouble with President Truman. One daily habit Dad absolutely declined to abandon was his preference for getting up early and taking a long walk. A. Merriman Smith, the UP White House correspondent, one of the wittiest and most delightful men in the press corps, described his own and his colleagues' reactions to this aspect of the Truman Administration:

> At first I thought there might be something of a farm boy pose in Mr. Truman's early rising. That was before I got up every morning at six o'clock for the next three weeks in order to record his two minute walk across Pennsylvania Avenue. Slowly and sleepily I began to realize that this man was in earnest. He *liked* to get up early. He wasn't doing it for the publicity or the pictures.

Smitty, as everyone called him, described Dad's walking speed as "a pace normally reserved for track stars." The combination of exercise and farmer's hours wreaked havoc on the White House scribes, who had a predilection for a playboy lifestyle and had been spoiled by Mr. Roosevelt's preference for starting the day late. "If I stayed up after nine thirty," Smitty mournfully reported, "I was a yawning wreck and by ten thirty in the morning I was ready for lunch." Glumly, Smitty concluded that getting to know the new President depended entirely upon one's "physique and endurance."

Privately, Dad enjoyed wearing the press boys down a little. Some months later he wrote his mother about a similar workout he gave the photographers:

> I took the White House photographers for a stroll yesterday

morning and most wore 'em out. I go every morning at 6:30 to 7:00 for a half hour's real walk usually doing two miles. I told them that I'd let them take pictures provided they walked the whole round with me. Most of 'em made it, some did not. I invited all of them to come again this morning without their cameras but none of 'em did.

From behind his desk my father was surprising a lot of other people who were inclined for one reason or another to underrate him. Our ambassador in Moscow, W. Averell Harriman, rushed to Washington, because, he said,

> I felt that I had to see President Truman as soon as possible in order to give him as accurate a picture as possible of our relations with the Soviet Union. I wanted to be sure that he understood that Stalin was already failing to keep his Yalta commitment. Much to my surprise, when I saw President Truman I found that he had already read all the telegrams between Washington and Moscow and had a clear understanding of the problems we faced. For the first time I learned how avid a reader President Truman was. This was one of the reasons he was able to take on so rapidly the immense problems he had to deal with at that time.

Joseph C. Grew, the Under Secretary of State who was appointed Acting Secretary while Mr. Stettinius was at the United Nations Conference, had been in the diplomatic service since 1904. He wrote to a friend:

> If I could talk to you about the new President you would hear nothing but the most favorable reaction. I have seen a good deal of him lately and I think he is going to measure up splendidly to the tremendous job which faces him. He is a man of few words but he seems to know the score all along the line and he generally has a perfectly clear conception of the right thing to do and how to do it. He is personally most affable and agreeable to deal with but he certainly won't stand for any pussyfooting in our foreign relations and policy, all of which of course warms my heart.

Perhaps the most interesting reaction to the new President came from a man who had worked intimately with President Roosevelt for a long time—Harold D. Smith, the director of the Bureau of the Budget. His hitherto unpublished diary is in the files of the Truman Library. Here are some excerpts from it describing his first meeting with Dad on Wednesday, April 18:

> When I entered the President's office, he was standing by the window looking out, but he quickly turned to come over and shake hands with me. This was a startling contrast to seeing President Roosevelt, who could not move from his chair. . . . I commented that our time was short and there were several matters that I would like to take up with him at this session. I started to say that the first one was pretty obvious, but the President interrupted me with "I know what's on your mind and I'm going to beat you to it. I want you to stay. You've done a good job as Director of the Budget, and we always thought well of you on the Hill. I have a tremendous responsibility and I want you to help me."
>
> When I mentioned the fact that he should be aware that the Director of the Budget was always bringing up problems, President Truman said that he liked problems so I need not worry on that score. I told him how I had once remarked to President Roosevelt that I would not blame him if he never saw me again, for I was in the unhappy position of constantly presenting difficulties. . . . President Truman laughed and said he understood the kind of role that I had to play . . . adding that he was used to dealing with facts and figures so I need not hesitate about presenting situations to him in some detail. . . . His whole attitude pleased me because it showed that he was anxious to plunge deeply into the business of Government.

One week later Mr. Smith returned for another forty-five-minute conference which ranged over a wide variety of problems, more money for the Tennessee Valley Authority, the problem of using Lend-Lease money for postwar rehabilitation, the G.I. Bill of Rights. Summing up back in his own office, Mr. Smith wrote:

> The whole conference was highly satisfactory from my point of view. . . . The President's reactions were positive and highly intelligent. While he agreed with nearly all of our propositions, I did not feel that I was selling him a bill of goods. Rather I felt that the propositions were sound because he agreed with them.

[CHAPTER]
Twelve

MY FATHER'S OVERRIDING CONCERN in these first weeks was our policy toward Russia. There is a school of historians in our universities that is attempting to rewrite the history of the postwar world according to the following scenario. Under the wise guidance of Franklin D. Roosevelt, American-Soviet relations were perfect. Then Harry S. Truman arrived in the White House and proceeded to provoke the eager-to-co-operate, disinterested, peace-loving Russian statesmen into the antagonism known as the cold war. To prove I'm not making this up, allow me to quote from a recent statement by Yale professor Gaddis Smith, described as a specialist in diplomatic history:

> The times demanded a philosopher, a humane skeptic. Instead the United States got a dedicated battler with the outlook of a company commander who never reasoned why.

Here is a so-called historian who ignores all the years of achievement and experience that filled Harry Truman's life between 1918 and 1945. He ignores his accomplishments as head of the Truman Committee, he ignores, above all, Dad's dedication to international peace, so clearly visible in his fight for civilian control of the war effort and for a Senate commitment to the United Nations. Finally, he ignores the truth about the historical situation which my father faced as President.

Relations between Great Britain, Russia, and America were

deteriorating months before Mr. Roosevelt died. As early as September 9, 1944, Ambassador W. Averell Harriman cabled the President from Moscow:

> Our relations with the Soviets now that the end of the war is in sight have taken a startling turn evident during the last two months. The Soviets have held up our requests with complete indifference to our interests and have shown an unwillingness even to discuss pressing problems. . . . I have evidence that they have misinterpreted our general attitude toward them as an acceptance of their policies and a sign of weakness. . . . This job of getting the Soviet Government to play a decent role in international affairs is . . . going to be more difficult than we had hoped.

The brawl over the number of votes Russia would have in the United Nations, Stalin's insistence on the right of the great powers to exercise a veto over decisions of the international organization, his insistence on a puppet government in Poland, the ruthless suppression of non-Communists in other countries of Eastern Europe which the Red Army controlled had been a series of shocks to President Roosevelt's hope for postwar co-operation. He went to Yalta, almost in desperation, risking his fragile health in a final effort to restore the tottering alliance.

But at Yalta FDR was negotiating not from strength but from weakness. He was hampered by the conviction—shared by the Joint Chiefs of Staff and almost every other member of his administration except Admiral Leahy—that Russian aid was essential to the final defeat of Japan. America had been crashing through the island defenses of the Japanese Empire and raining bombs on the home islands at a prodigious rate. But the main Japanese armies in China, Manchuria, and in Japan were relatively untouched, unconquered, and still imbued with fanatical determination to fight to the last man.

To extract from Stalin a promise to enter the Pacific war, Mr. Roosevelt made many concessions to the Russian dictator at Yalta. When Admiral Leahy protested giving the Russians control of Dairen, the Chinese port in Manchuria, Mr. Roosevelt shook his head in resignation and said, "Bill, I can't help it." Leahy was even more shocked by the agreement on Poland. "Mr.

President," he said, "this is so elastic that the Russians can stretch it all the way from Yalta to Washington without ever technically breaking it." The President replied, "I know, Bill, I know it. But it's the best I can do for Poland at this time."

Mr. Roosevelt had scarcely returned from Yalta when he began getting telegrams from Prime Minister Churchill about the Russian communization of Poland. On March 13 the prime minister cabled: "Poland has lost her frontier. Is she now to lose her freedom? I do not wish to reveal a divergence between the British and the United States government, but it would certainly be necessary for me to make it clear that we are in presence of a great failure and utter breakdown of what we settled at Yalta."

Anxiously Mr. Roosevelt cabled Stalin: "I must make it quite plain to you that any such solution which would result in a thinly disguised continuation of the present Warsaw [Communist] regime would be unacceptable and would cause the people of the United States to regard the Yalta agreement as having failed."

Stalin's reply was a series of scorching telegrams, bluntly accusing Roosevelt and Churchill of treacherously negotiating with the Germans to sign a separate peace on the western front so that they could continue to fight the Russians on the eastern front. The telegrams, sparked by American attempts to persuade the German army in Italy to surrender, were grossly insulting. "I cannot avoid a feeling of bitter resentment toward your informers, whoever they are," Mr. Roosevelt replied, "for such vile misrepresentations of my actions or those of my trusted subordinates."

On March 24, 1945, President Roosevelt received a cable from Mr. Harriman describing further difficulties with Stalin. A mutual friend, Anna Rosenberg Hoffman, who was with him at the time, described the President's reaction:

> He read it and became quite angry. He banged his fists on the arms of his wheelchair and said, "Averell is right; we can't do business with Stalin. He has broken every one of the promises he made at Yalta." He was very upset and continued in the same vein on the subject.
>
> These were his exact words. I remembered them and verified them with Mrs. Roosevelt not too long before her death.

As this book was being completed, another hitherto unknown

Roosevelt cable to Churchill was discovered in the files of the Roosevelt Library. Dated April 6th, it emphatically supported a cable which Churchill had sent the previous day, urging "a firm and blunt stand" against the Russians. "We must not permit anybody to entertain a false impression that we are afraid," FDR wrote. "Our Armies will in a very few days be in a position that will permit us to become 'tougher' than has been heretofore advantageous to the war effort."

In the evening hours during his first weeks in office my father read these cables between Prime Minister Churchill, President Roosevelt, Marshal Stalin, and Ambassador Harriman. He saw, as James MacGregor Burns, Mr. Roosevelt's biographer, has recently written, that "the edifice of trust and good will and neighborliness that Roosevelt had shaped so lovingly was crashing down around him" at his death.

Still Mr. Roosevelt refused to lose hope. On April 12, the day of his death, he sent two cables, one to Ambassador Harriman for Stalin saying that he wished to consider the "Berne misunderstanding"—Berne was the Swiss city where the negotiations for the surrender of German forces in Italy began—"a minor incident." The other cable went to Prime Minister Churchill: "I would minimize the general Soviet problem as much as possible because these problems in one form or another seem to arise every day and most of them straighten out in one form or another as in the case of the Berne meeting. We must be firm, however, and our course thus far is correct."

This was precisely the balance that my father attempted to achieve in his dealing with the Russians. He was determined to insist on Russia's fulfilling the Yalta agreements. At the same time he made every attempt to maintain—perhaps the more correct word would be revive—the high hopes of postwar co-operation with which America had joined Russia in the fight against naziism. His first attempt to achieve this difficult balance came less than two weeks after he took his oath of office. Foreign Minister Molotov arrived in Washington to pay his respects to the President, as Dad had made it clear he expected him to do. Before he arrived, my father had a series of top-secret conferences with his chief foreign policy advisers. He made it clear that he intended to be "firm but fair." He realized that we could not expect to get

100 percent of what we wanted in dealing with the Russians, but on important matters he felt we should be able to get 85 percent.

On Sunday, April 22, the Soviet foreign minister arrived in Washington. He called on my father at Blair House that evening after dinner. Dad told him that he "hoped that the relations which President Roosevelt had established between our two countries would be maintained." Mr. Molotov expressed a similar sentiment and said he thought that the Crimean decisions were "sufficiently clear" to overcome any difficulties which had arisen. He also wanted to know whether the agreements in regard to the "Far Eastern situation" still stood. Dad replied that he intended to carry out *all* of the agreements made by President Roosevelt.

After drinking a toast to the three heads of state, Mr. Molotov departed with Ambassador Harriman and Secretary of State Stettinius. At the State Department they were joined by Anthony Eden, the British foreign secretary, and they proceeded to get down to the hard facts about the future of Poland. The American and British spokesmen got nowhere with the stubborn Russian foreign minister. He absolutely refused to make any concessions to liberalize the Polish government. My father learned about this the next morning, and he immediately convened another top-secret meeting. For this crucial conference he called in Secretary of War Stimson, Secretary of the Navy Forrestal, Admiral Leahy, General Marshall, Admiral King, Assistant Secretary of State James Dunn, General John R. Deane, head of the military mission in Moscow, and Mr. Bohlen. Secretary of State Stettinius opened the meeting by reporting on his conversations with Mr. Molotov. He said it was "now clear that the Soviet government intended to try to enforce upon the United States and British governments" their puppet government in Poland and obtain its legal acceptance. Speaking very emphatically, Dad said that he felt that agreements with the Soviet Union so far had been a "one-way street" and that could not continue. If the Russians did not wish to co-operate "they could go to hell."

A great deal has been made about this statement. But we must remember that this was a remark my father made in private, surrounded by his top advisers. Some historians have a bad tendency to confuse presidential remarks made in private letters or conversations and the public policy of a President. For instance,

Thomas Jefferson once remarked in a private letter to James Madison that every society ought to have a revolution every nineteen or twenty years. Madison demolished this theory in his reply, and Jefferson never mentioned it again, in public or in private. When he was confronted with a real revolution, led by Aaron Burr, President Jefferson reacted with angry vigor to maintain the authority of the American government.

Similarly, although my father was privately angry with Mr. Molotov and determined to be firm, he never for a moment used intemperate or insulting language with him. He was blunt about telling him what he thought Russia should do. But this was precisely what he thought Mr. Roosevelt would have done in his place—and what all his top advisers, who had been Mr. Roosevelt's advisers, felt that he should do. His conversation with Mr. Molotov at 5:30 on April 24, 1945, makes this very clear.

Practically everything Mr. Molotov said was pure double-talk. He discoursed on the importance of finding a common language to settle "inevitable difficulties." He said his government stood by the "Crimean decisions," but whenever my father asked him to apply these decisions to Poland, Mr. Molotov began talking about Yugoslavia. Not once throughout this labyrinth of evasion did Dad lose his temper. He reiterated that he desired the friendship of the Soviet government, but it could only be on the basis of "mutual observation of agreements and *not* on the basis of a one-way street."

Huffily, Mr. Molotov said, "I have never been talked to like that in my life."

"Carry out your agreements and you won't get talked to like that," Dad replied.

At the end of the conference my father handed Mr. Molotov a carefully worded statement, which he proposed to release that evening, calling on the Russians to fulfill their agreement on Poland. He asked Mr. Molotov to transmit it to Marshal Stalin immediately.

I do not see how an objective observer can find anything but the right combination of firmness and frankness in Dad's side of this historic conversation. We must remember, too, that Mr. Molotov was no shrinking violet who might wither at a single harsh word. He was a tough, blunt, sarcastic character in his own right, a man who soon demonstrated at San Francisco his enormous capacity for being unpleasant in public. There may, in fact, be some grounds for blaming him for the early stages of the cold war. Many of the Americans who dealt with him remain convinced that he invariably gave Marshal Stalin the worst possible version of his negotiations with the United States and Britain.

While he stayed in Lee House, next door to us in Blair House, Mr. Molotov provided lots of material for light conversation as well as serious reflection. He and his associates had a habit of staying up most of the night, a way of life they had apparently acquired during the revolution. They constantly startled the Secret Service by wandering into the Blair House garden at three and four o'clock in the morning. Whenever one of his suits came back from the cleaners, Mr. Molotov's valet turned all the pockets inside out to make sure there were no concealed bombs. One of his bodyguards insisted on standing watch whenever the Blair House staff made the foreign minister's bed. Dad noticed that Mr. Molotov never sat with his back to a door or window. His eating habits also caused mild consternation among the Blair House staff. The first morning his breakfast consisted of salad and soup. This, we later learned, was not an unusual breakfast for a Russian. But it made Mr. Molotov seem even stranger to those of us who were seeing a representative of Russia at close range for the first time.

Two days after he saw Mr. Molotov, my father had an even more momentous conference with Secretary of War Stimson. He informed Dad in detail about the project to create the atomic bomb.

The brief discussion of the bomb that Mr. Stimson had with Dad, a half hour after he became President, covered little more than a general description of the weapon's power and its possible impact on the war. Major General Leslie Groves, who was in charge of the Manhattan Project, joined the meeting by entering the White House through the back door. This was typical of the super-secrecy with which the whole operation was shrouded. Mr. Stimson handed my father a memorandum which began, "Within four months we shall in all probability have completed the most terrible weapon ever known in human history, one bomb which could destroy a whole city." The report went on to discuss in very wary terms the possibility that other nations could produce the bomb, adding, "Probably the only nation that could enter into production in the next few years is Russia."

Mr. Stimson feared that, in the state of moral achievement which the world had reached, the bomb was simply too dangerous to handle. He was afraid that modern civilization might be "completely destroyed." He also felt that the new weapon was "a primary question of our foreign relations." In their ensuing conversation, after my father finished reading this thoughtful, wide-ranging memorandum, Secretary Stimson added that if the bomb worked it would "in all probability shorten the war." But that *if* was a very large word. When Vannevar Bush, head of the Office of Scientific Research and Development, gave my father a scientist's version of the bomb, Admiral Leahy was present, and he scoffingly declared, "That is the biggest fool thing we've ever done. The bomb will never go off, and I speak as an expert in explosives."

General Groves's report, twenty-four pages long and crammed with scientific data, stated that a test of the bomb would be made in the middle of July, if everything remained on schedule. If it succeeded, the explosion would yield an equivalent force of about 500 tons of TNT. A second bomb, which could be used against Japan, would be ready around the first of August and would be the equivalent of 1,000 to 1,200 tons of TNT. The correct figure turned out to be 20,000 tons—graphic evidence of how little even the top people knew about the awesome weapon they were creating.

In his memorandum Secretary of War Stimson recommended the creation of a distinguished committee to study the question of using the bomb against Japan. My father immediately agreed and ordered the formation of this group, which came to be known as the Interim Committee. The impression that some people have, that my father made a snap decision to use the bomb, could not be farther from the truth. Mr. Stimson, seventy-eight years old, one of the most respected Americans of his time, was the chairman of the Interim Committee. Mr. Byrnes was Dad's personal representative. The other members included Dr. Vannevar Bush; Dr. Karl T. Compton, president of the Massachusetts Institute of Technology; and James B. Conant, president of Harvard. Assisting the committee was a scientific panel, whose members were

Enrico Fermi, Ernest O. Lawrence, Robert Oppenheimer, and Arthur H. Compton. All of them had played major roles in the development of the bomb.

The same day that my father had this fateful conference with Secretary Stimson, the United Nations Conference opened in San Francisco. In Europe the war was hurtling toward a conclusion. German resistance was collapsing on all fronts. Ironically, Heinrich Himmler tried to negotiate a separate surrender to the Western Powers. Dad and Mr. Churchill agreed, in a telephone discussion, that they must immediately reject the offer and notify Marshal Stalin.

Here was an opportunity for the Americans and the British to commit the treachery which Stalin had accused Mr. Roosevelt of plotting. Having read these insulting telegrams, my father took not a little pleasure in informing Marshal Stalin that he had rejected the German offer: "In keeping with our agreement with the British and Soviet governments, it is the view of the United States government that the only acceptable terms of surrender are unconditional surrender on all fronts to the Soviet, Great Britain, and the United States."

Two days later word was flashed from Europe that American and Russian forces had finally met on the Elbe River. It meant the beginning of the end of the European war. From San Francisco, meanwhile, came word from Secretary of State Stettinius that Molotov was refusing to budge on the communization of Poland. The political problems of peace were already crowding into the White House. My father decided that it was absolutely vital for him to know exactly what Marshal Stalin and Prime Minister Churchill were thinking on a broad range of topics. Random discussions of specific problems, attempts to deal with doctrinaire, obnoxious underlings like Molotov, were getting nowhere. So he asked Harry Hopkins to undertake a personal mission to Moscow. He also requested Joseph E. Davies, former ambassador to Russia, to make a similar journey to London, to talk with Churchill as the President's personal representative. Both of these men were in poor health, and it bothered Dad's conscience to ask them to undertake these grueling trips under wartime conditions. But they accepted their assignments without a moment's hesitation, knowing what was at stake.

On May 1 my father found time to write his mother: "I have been as busy as usual trying to make the country run. . . . I am hoping we will be able to move into the White House next week and then I want you to come to see us. I'll make all the arrangements from here, so keep it dark until I tell you about it." By this time Mrs. Roosevelt had moved out of the White House, and Mother and I had gone over to inspect our future home. What we saw made me yearn to stay in Blair House. The White House looked splendid from the outside, and the public rooms which tourists visit were beautifully painted, decorated, and appointed. But the private quarters were anything but comfortable in those days. It was not unlike moving into a furnished apartment, where no new furniture or equipment had been purchased for twenty or thirty years. The furniture looked like it had come from a third-rate boarding house. Some of it was literally falling apart. Grubby was the over-all word that leaped into my mind. Even more unpleasant was a bit of information Mrs. Roosevelt left with us before she departed. Here is how Dad reported it to his mother and sister:

> Mrs. Roosevelt told Bess and me that it [the White House] is infested with rats! Said she was giving three high-hat women a luncheon on the south portico when a rat ran across the porch railing. She said each of them saw the rat but kept pretending that she didn't. But they all finally confessed that they'd seen it.

Mother, ever the good soldier, plunged into conferences with painters and White House staff people. She assured me that the old place would look a lot better once we got some fresh paint on the walls and she was right. I chose Wedgwood blue for my sitting room, which had a pretty marble fireplace. For my bedroom, with my own antique white furniture, I chose pink with deep pink draperies and white window curtains. Mother preferred blue for her bedroom and gray for her sitting room and cream for Dad's bedroom and off-white for his oval study. Getting my grand piano into my study proved to be quite an engineering challenge. They had to take the legs off and swing it through a second-floor window with a block and tackle. Dad decided he wanted a piano in his study, too.

[241]

We moved in on May 7 so that Dad could celebrate his birthday in the White House, the following day. We had no idea just how much celebrating we and the rest of the country would do on that day.

On May 6 and May 7 reports of the final collapse of German resistance poured into my father's office. Finally, on May 7, General Eisenhower cabled that the German generals had surrendered unconditionally to him at 2:40 that morning. The next day he expected to have Russian signatures on the agreement. That morning Dad got up and wrote a letter to his mother, telling her the story:

Dear Mamma & Mary:

I am sixty-one this morning and I slept in the President's room in the White House last night. They have finished the painting and have some of the furniture in place. I'm hoping it will all be ready for you by Friday. My expensive gold pen doesn't work as well as it should.

This will be an historical day. At 9:00 o'clock this morning I must make a broadcast to the country announcing the German surrender. The papers were signed yesterday morning and hostilities will cease on all fronts at midnight tonight. Isn't that some birthday present?

In that letter he commented on the trouble he had had with both Mr. Churchill and Mr. Stalin about the cease-fire date. A few days later he was far more explicit in a letter that he wrote to Mrs. Roosevelt, here published for the first time. My father told her how the Germans continued trying to surrender only to the Americans and British, and kept fighting the Russians, until General Eisenhower warned them that we would reopen full scale hostilities and "drive them into the Russians" (Dad's words). The Germans finally agreed to surrender unconditionally to be effective at 12:01 midnight of May 8–9.

Stalin and I had agreed on a simultaneous release [of the victory statement] at 9 A.M. Washington time, 3 P.M. London and 4 P.M. Moscow time. . . . The Germans kept fighting the Russians and Stalin informed me that he had grave doubts of the Germans carrying out the terms. There was fighting on the Eastern front right up to the last hour.

In the meantime Churchill was trying to force me to break

faith with the Russians and release on the 7th, noon Washington time, 6 P.M. London, 7 P.M. Moscow. I wired Stalin and he said the Germans were still firing. I refused Churchill's request and informed Stalin of conditions here and in England and that unless I heard from him to the contrary I would release at 9 A.M. May 8th. I didn't hear so the release was made, but fighting was still in progress against the Russians. The Germans were finally informed that if they didn't cease firing as agreed they would not be treated as fighting men but as traitors and would be hanged as caught. They then ceased firing and Stalin made his announcement the 9th.

He had sent me a message stating the situation at 1 A.M. May 8th and asking postponement until May 9th. I did not get the message until 10 A.M. May 8, too late, of course, to do anything.

I have been trying very carefully to keep all my engagements with the Russians because they are touchy and suspicious of us. The difficulties with Churchill are very nearly as exasperating as they are with the Russians. But patience I think must be our watchword if we are to have World Peace. To have it we must have the wholehearted support of Russia, Great Britain and the United States.

My father's first thought, after announcing the glorious news of the victory in Europe, was the war with Japan. In a letter to his mother, written the day before the Germans surrendered, he said: "We have another war to win and people must realize it. I hope they will, anyway." He ended his V-E Day statement with the words, "Our victory is only half over." He then added a plea to Japan's leaders to lay down their arms in unconditional surrender—the only terms which Mr. Roosevelt had said he would accept from either Germany or Japan.

Some people have criticized this approach, claiming that the modification of this demand would have persuaded Japan to surrender earlier and avoided the use of the atomic bomb. It is sad, how each generation's hindsight is based on a criticism of the preceding generation. Mr. Roosevelt and Mr. Churchill were attempting to avoid the error of World War I, which left Germany uninvaded, virtually intact. This permitted Hitler to propound the myth that Germany had not really lost the war and create a new military machine to launch World War II.

My father was very much aware that unconditional surrender was particularly unfortunate for dealing with Japan, where military fanaticism already made suicide preferable to surrender on the field of battle. On Okinawa thousands of Japanese soldiers destroyed themselves with hand grenades rather than give up, in spite of the obvious fact that the battle was lost. So, in this announcement, Dad did his utmost to soften the term unconditional surrender for Japan:

> Just what does the unconditional surrender of the armed forces of Japan mean for the Japanese people?
> It means the end of the war.
> It means the termination of the influence of the military leaders who brought Japan to the present brink of disaster.
> It means provision for the return of soldiers and sailors to their families, their farms, and their jobs.
> And it means not prolonging the present agony and suffering of the Japanese in the vain hope of victory.
> Unconditional surrender does not mean the extermination or enslavement of the Japanese people.

On May 11 the presidential plane, the *Sacred Cow,* touched down at Washington, and my father personally escorted his mother down the steps while an inevitable swarm of reporters and photographers recorded the event. Dad had hoped to fly out and pick her up, so she would have no uneasy moments on her first flight, but Germany's surrender killed that idea. Mamma Truman was her usual peppery self. She eyed the crowd of newsmen and snapped, "Oh, fiddlesticks, why didn't you tell me there was going to be all this fuss. If I'd known, I wouldn't have come."

True to the family tradition of teasing each other to distraction, on the way to the White House in our car, I told Mamma Truman that Dad was going to make her sleep in Lincoln's bed. Mamma replied that she was ready to sleep on the floor, before she made such a concession to her Southern principles. Dad finally had to shush me and calm her down by assuring her that she was going to sleep in the Rose Room, where visiting queens and other prominent female VIPs stayed. Mamma decided that the bed was much too high and too fancy for her taste and chose to sleep next door in a charming smaller bedroom. She left the grandeur of the Rose Room to my Aunt Mary.

Mamma Truman was her usual uninhibited self in the White House. She went exploring on her own and had lively comments to make on everything and everyone. One night during her stay Joseph Davies had dinner with us. Dad and he began discussing politics, and when the ambassador happened to mention a certain politician's name, Mamma Truman asked, "Isn't he a Yankee?"

"Yes, Mamma," Dad said, "but you know there are good Yankees as well as bad and good Rebels."

"Well, if there are any good Yankees, I haven't seen one yet," Mamma Truman replied.

Toward the end of her stay Mamma was coming down a small four-step stairway at the end of the hall in the east wing when she slipped and fell. She picked herself up and did not say a word about it. The only hint she gave of trouble was her refusal to go to church with us the next day. Not until she was back in Missouri did she tell her daughter Mary about the fall.

After Mamma Truman went home, we settled into White House living. It was not easy. My friends had to run a gauntlet of guards to see me. Mother was busy from dawn to dark, appearing at various lunches and teas. My biggest gripe was the White House food. There were simply too many cooks on the staff, working various shifts, to allow room for any personal touches. It was hotel kitchen food, adequate but uninspired. I discovered another hotel touch when I wandered down to the kitchen one night during our first few weeks in 1945 and found locks on all the iceboxes. I squawked to the President of the United States, but not even he could do anything about it. The locks were necessary, he was told. The staff was so large, it was impossible to keep track of everybody as they came and went and without locks it would have been ridiculously easy for people to start lugging home steaks, hams, and other goodies.

Fortunately, President Roosevelt had installed a small kitchen on the third floor which he often used when he was alone in the White House. Dad permitted his midnight-snack-loving daughter to stock its tiny icebox with Cokes, ice cream, and other fattening materials for after-hours dining.

During our first months in the White House we had to cope with Mrs. Nesbitt, the housekeeper we inherited from the Roosevelts. Her taste in food was atrocious, and her attitude toward the Trumans was openly condescending. One night when Mother was away, brussels sprouts were served at dinner. Dad made a face and pushed them aside. He hates brussels sprouts. I told this to Mrs. Nesbitt. The next night, we got brussels sprouts again. Tensely, I informed Mrs. Nesbitt that I did not want to see another brussels sprout in the White House, much less on our dinner table. The next night we got them again! I called Mother and told her that either Mrs. Nesbitt went, or I went. "Don't do or say anything until I get there," Mother told me.

I reluctantly obeyed, and Mother tried to cope with Mrs. Nesbitt by giving her detailed instructions on menus and other household matters. "Mrs. Roosevelt never did things that way," Mrs. Nesbitt grandly declared.

Mother just looked at her, and that night she had a talk with Dad about Mrs. Nesbitt. A few weeks later she retired.

Dad was never particularly happy being waited on by the numerous servants in the White House. It offended his ingrained Missouri sense of equality. The White House staff was astonished, for instance, when Dad introduced his brother Vivian to Alonzo Fields, the head butler, and they shook hands before Vivian sat down at the table. Dad and Mother made it a point to know each servant by name, and whenever a new man went on duty in the dining room, Fields introduced him. Dad would stand up, shake hands with him, and say, "Now don't be disturbed by me. You just do what Fields tells you and I know we will be glad to have you aboard."

Mother and I, on the other hand, not being particularly domestic, never fretted over being waited on. Mother, who is nothing if not frank, said to me only a few months ago when we were reminiscing about our White House days: "There's only one thing I miss. All that help." And she sighed. I agreed, and Dad could only shake his head and wonder where two people raised in Missouri could get such notions.

During the tumultuous middle months of 1945 my father had little time to worry about such things. The Russians continued to be impossible, even though Dad, faithful to the Yalta agreements, pulled our troops back to the stipulated zones of occupation, turning over most of eastern Europe to their control.

Meanwhile, General Charles de Gaulle began behaving like a spoiled boy. To my father's astonishment, he refused to withdraw French troops that had occupied the German city of Stuttgart. Then, in an even more outrageous move, he sent troops across the border into northwest Italy to seize part of the Aosta Valley. He also sent troops rampaging into Syria and Lebanon, intent on reclaiming French power there. General De Gaulle may have achieved a good deal with his policy of "grandeur" for France in the 1960s. I seriously doubt it. His headstrong nationalism was—and is—anachronistic. In the weeks after Germany's surrender he exasperated everyone. At one point there seemed to be a serious possibility that French and American troops might start shooting each other in the Aosta Valley.

What particularly angered my father was the General's contemptuous indifference to Russian reactions to his unilateral grandstanding. If we had let him get away with his grab for Italian and German territory, Stalin would have had a perfect example to excuse his seizure of Poland and the rest of eastern Europe. In the course of this argument, De Gaulle was almost as insulting to Dad as Marshal Stalin had been to President Roosevelt. Prime Minister Churchill wanted Dad to release the correspondence to the public—knowing that it would have finished De Gaulle politically in France. Admiral Leahy also favored such a move. My father decided against it. He sensed—quite accurately —that without De Gaulle, France would be politically unstable and easy prey for a Communist take-over.

My father made General De Gaulle behave by issuing a very simple order.

He asked Admiral Leahy: "The French are using our guns, are they not?"

"Yes, sir," replied Admiral Leahy.

"All right, we will at once stop shipping guns, ammunition, and equipment to De Gaulle."

Even tougher tactics had to be used to restrain Marshal Tito from grabbing Trieste and the surrounding countryside for Yugoslavia. In this test of wills, for a while it looked as if full-scale warfare might be necessary. Air units were alerted, five armored divisions were prepared for an advance through the Brenner Pass, and units of the Mediterranean fleet headed for the Adriatic.

Marshal Tito soon changed his mind about occupying Trieste.

On the home front my father also had to show a little steel in his relations with Congress. He vetoed a bill which would have extended the deferment of agricultural workers. As a farmer who went to war in World War I, Dad could see no reason for this measure. But he also displayed more than a little shrewdness in his congressional politics, born of his years on the Hill. One of Mr. Roosevelt's most cantankerous opponents had been Kenneth McKellar, the senior senator from Tennessee. He had been in the Senate since 1916 and was now president pro tem, which meant, with Dad transferred to the White House, he was the Senate's chief executive officer. Dad decided that in this capacity he should sit in on Cabinet meetings. Old "Mac" was very flattered by this attention from the Executive Branch and only much later did he realize that this new role made it very difficult for him to be an anti-Truman Democrat in the Senate.

The first test of this policy was my father's decision to reappoint David Lilienthal chairman of the Tennessee Valley Authority for another nine years. Senator McKellar had been feuding with Mr. Lilienthal ever since he took office, and the TVA chairman had almost no hope of being reconfirmed. In his diary, shortly after President Roosevelt died, Mr. Lilienthal noted:

> The Associated Press carries this story today: "Elevation of Vice President Truman to the Presidency puts Senator Kenneth McKellar of Tennessee in one of the most powerful positions any man ever held in the Senate" and so on.
> When I pick enemies, I make 'em good!

Ironically, Mr. Lilienthal, relatively unacquainted with the inside approach to Senate politics, was dismayed when he learned that Senator McKellar was sitting in on Cabinet meetings. On April 23 Mr. Lilienthal noted in his diary: "McKellar had a conference with the President the other day. He may already have a commitment that I shall not be named."

On May 1 when Mr. Lilienthal saw my father in his office, Dad told him that McKellar had already promised "the biggest explosion in the Senate in twenty years" if Dad renominated Mr. Lilienthal. "I guess we will have it," Dad said. Mr. Lilienthal was amazed by his unworried, matter-of-fact tone.

Then, solemnly, my father asked him if he would be prepared to do something to save face for Senator McKellar. Mr. Lilienthal was about to object, when Dad continued, "I want to know if you are ready to assure me that you will carry on the TVA for me in the same fine way that you did for my predecessor, and do your best to keep it out of political difficulties?"

Mr. Lilienthal grinned. "That's easy. I shall be honored to serve under you, and I will certainly try to carry on as well in the future as I have in the past twelve years. . . . As for keeping out of political difficulties, you know from your own public career that you can't please everyone."

My father nodded and said that he was very familiar with Senator McKellar. "I had to fight him many times on the Appropriations Committee and I know how arbitrary and mean he can be."

Almost in bewilderment, Mr. Lilienthal confided to his diary:

> And that was about all there was about McKellar. No talk about what a "rap" he as President was assuming in naming me in spite of the President of the Senate; no talk, such as Byrnes and President Roosevelt had given me, about what McKellar could do to disrupt the peace if his wishes concerning me were not respected—none of that—just, there it was.

On May 23 Mr. Lilienthal informed his journal:

> The shootin' is over. . . . When I compare what actually happened with what Justice Byrnes predicted to the late President would happen as recently as November, I rub my eyes. McKellar, his power increased, did go the limit, to wit, a "personally and politically objectionable issue" (in fact, he made me a triple-threat man: "objectionable, obnoxious, and offensive"), but they got absolutely nowhere with anyone, either in the committee or on the final go-round Monday afternoon, when the name was confirmed, with only McKay and Stewart recorded nay on a voice vote. . . . I am incredulous.

Each day callers streamed into my father's office. He tried to see as many of these "customers" as possible. After lunch—usually at one o'clock—he would take a half hour nap, and resume his appointments for the rest of the afternoon, working until six or six-thirty. Often he took a quick swim or a stroll around the grounds before returning to our side of the house for dinner at seven. Most previous Presidents reserved their afternoons for paper work. Dad was doing his paper work at night, and he very soon developed the habit of signing the innumerable documents the President must sign each day while he talked with his visitors.

During these first months, my father tried to make a brief memorandum on each visitor. He thought they might be helpful in compiling a history of his presidency. But after October, 1945, he abandoned the habit, partly because he was under too much pressure, but also because an amazing number of people who came to see the President did nothing but waste his time. Let me give you a sample of what I mean from Dad's early appointment schedules.

On Monday, May 14, at 9:30 Senator George Radcliffe of Maryland "came in to pay respects and to assure me he was still the same friend he had always been to me and if ever he could be helpful in any way he wanted me to understand he was available."

At 9:45 Major General William Donovan came in to "tell how important the Secret Service is and how much he could do to run the government on an even basis."

At 10:00 there was a policy meeting with the Secretary of State, the Secretary of War, and other high officials.

At 10:15 the Honorable Sergio Osmeña, president of the Philippines, came in and "signed the agreement to furnish the U.S. with all the military and naval bases it needed."

At 10:30 Mr. F. L. Altschuler, railroad man from Kansas City —"just came in to pay respects."

At 10:45 the representatives of the Gulf Ports Association "came in to tell importance of Gulf ports—in which I did not put much house. I did sympathize with them, however, and told them I knew a great deal about the Gulf Coast."

At 11:00 the Honorable Elmer Davis came in to thrash out the problem of the military government's attitude toward news in Germany.

At 11:15 came Mr. Herbert Rivers from Kansas City, "one of AFL pillars here in Washington and has always been a personal friend. Came in to talk labor with me."

At 11:30 Admiral Richard E. Byrd "came in to tell me how to

settle world peace—in his opinion Stalin was going to ruin peace proposal or program and was cause of veto [in the UN]—When I informed him Churchill was cause of veto, his whole thesis collapsed."

At 12:00 Mr. Myron Blaylock, national committeeman from Texas, came in to pay his respects "and to say Texas was for me."

At 12:15 the Honorable Donald Nelson, who was leaving government service, "came in to say goodbye."

At 12:30 the Secretary of the Interior, Harold Ickes, came in to discuss an appointment which Dad did not approve. But because President Roosevelt had named him, he was letting Ickes send his man up to the Senate.

At 12:45 Mrs. Charles B. Gilbert, president of the American Legion Auxiliary, presented the first poppy of the year to the President.

After lunch the procession resumed. At 2:00 Dr. T. V. Soong "came in to discuss financial situation in China and urged me to give China the balance of $200 million, which I did."

At 2:30, Anthony Eden, the British foreign secretary, and other members of the British delegation to the San Francisco Conference came in "to pay respects and to discuss the world situation."

At 2:45—

And so it went, this incredible combination of the trivial and the momentous, for the rest of the day, which ended at 8:15 with a War Bond show in the East Room of the White House, presided over by Bob Hope. I was thrilled to meet Mr. Hope and the other members of his troupe, which included Vera Vague and Jerry Colonna. Dad noted at the bottom of his daily schedule: "Had a good time at the show."

Some of these appointment schedule entries are important for the light they throw on various aspects of my father's thinking at this time. On May 18 at 2 P.M. he wrote:

> Held Cabinet meeting—explained to Cabinet members that in my opinion the Cabinet members were simply a Board of Directors appointed by the President, to help him carry out the policies of the government; in many instances the Cabinet could be of tremendous help to the President by offering advice whether he liked it or not. But when President made an order they should carry it out. I told them I expected to have a

Cabinet I could depend on and take in my confidence and if this confidence was not well placed I would get a Cabinet in which I could place confidence.

I told the Cabinet members the story about President Lincoln—when he was discussing the Proclamation—every member of his Cabinet opposed to him making Proclamation—he put the question up to the whole Cabinet and they voted no—that is very well, the President said, I vote yes—that is the way I intend to run this.

At 5 P.M. that same day "Honorable James F. Byrnes—came in to tell me I should not send Harry Hopkins to Russia. I told Jimmy I thought I would send him. No need for anyone else to get any credit but the President."

The next day at 9:45 A.M. my father made the following notes: "Discussed with Bob Hannegan advisability of making Cabinet changes and whether or not it was too soon to make them now—explaining to him and Steve Early, who was present most of the time, that I could not possibly outline a policy for my own administration unless I had a Cabinet who was in entire sympathy with what I wanted to do and unless I had a Cabinet with administrative ability. . . ."

At 11 A.M. that same day, Harry Hopkins arrived to discuss his trip to Moscow:

> I asked him to go to Stalin . . . and tell him just exactly what we intended to have in the way of carrying out the agreements, purported to have been made at Yalta—that I was anxious to have a fair understanding with the Russian government —that we never made commitments which we did not expect to carry out to the letter—we expected him to carry his agreements out to the letter and we intended to see that he did.
>
> I told Harry he could use diplomatic language or he could use a baseball bat if he thought that was the proper approach to Mr. Stalin.
>
> I also told Harry to tell Stalin I would be glad to see him—facts in the case are I thought it his turn to come to the U. S. as our President had been to Russia—he would be royally entertained. . . .

Two nights later my father made the following memorandum on his conference with Joseph Davies:

I told him I was having as much difficulty with Prime Minister Churchill as I was having with Stalin—that it was my opinion that each of them was trying to make me the paw of the cat that pulled the chestnuts out of the fire. . . .

I told him it seemed to me Churchill should be informed of situation, but I had no messenger I could send to him. I could not possibly send Hopkins to Churchill at the same time I was sending him to see Stalin. Further said I did not want to give impression I was acting for Great Britain in any capacity, although I wanted support of Great Britain in anything we do so far as peace is concerned. . . .

Behind the scenes, getting rid of Mr. Roosevelt's Cabinet was anything but the simple task that my father made it seem in public. Politically it was important for him to avoid public brawls with the Roosevelt men. Yet, as his memorandum on Cabinet changes makes clear, he had a very poor opinion of many members of Mr. Roosevelt's team. Dad's approach to the presidency was quite different from Mr. Roosevelt's. He believe in delegating much more authority than Mr. Roosevelt was inclined to give his Cabinet officers. Mr. Roosevelt really ran his administration as a one-man show, confident of his own enormous popularity and his ability to keep track of all the strings. Dad was convinced that the government was simply too large for such an approach and was determined to get men with more administrative ability—as well as more loyalty to him—in the Cabinet.

My father was startled to discover that many of Mr. Roosevelt's Cabinet did not take their pro forma resignations very seriously and in one or two cases almost refused to resign. Secretary of State Stettinius was enraged when Dad's emissary, George Allen, informed him in San Francisco that, when the conference was over, the President expected to replace him with Jimmy Byrnes. At first Mr. Stettinius haughtily rejected Dad's offer to appoint him as head of the American delegation to the UN. George Allen had to do quite a lot of soothing before Mr. Stettinius calmed down and accepted the UN job. It took him days to compose a satisfactory letter of resignation. Attorney General Francis Biddle was even more exercised when my father informed him that he was replacing him with Tom Clark. After the press conference at which Dad made this announcement, he made the following memorandum:

> Mr Biddle took a very unsatisfactory attitude towards his resignation—I told him I was going to accept it. I was very sure if he got an opportunity to get the "crackpots" worked up here they would jump on me. As it was he did not get an opportunity and they did not ask me any questions—apparently from viewpoint of unbiased spectators the [press] conference was a success.

Not all of the Cabinet was so difficult, of course. Mrs. Frances Perkins was eager to leave and remained a friend. Dad replaced her with his old friend Lewis Schwellenbach of Washington, one of the original thirteen Senate "Young Turks" of 1934. Claude Wickard gracefully yielded to Clinton Anderson of New Mexico as Secretary of Agriculture; Frank Walker, whose health was very poor, was happy to hand over the Post Office to Bob Hannegan. Forrest Donnell, the Republican who had replaced Dad as senator from Missouri, denounced Bob as a crooked politician for two hours in the Senate, but he was confirmed, 60 to 2. It is really amazing how little impact the fiercest invective makes in that Cave of Winds.

Only a few days after Germany surrendered, my father learned—the hard way—that there was a limit to the amount of authority he could delegate to his Cabinet officers. On the day of the surrender, Leo Crowley, the administrator of the Lend-Lease program, and Acting Secretary of State Grew came to Dad's office and asked him to sign an order which they assured him President Roosevelt had approved before he died. It authorized the Foreign Economic Administration (the official name for Lend-Lease) and the State Department to cut back on Lend-Lease as soon as Germany surrendered. This was a subject which had aroused angry debate in Congress. As you will recall, Dad had cast his only vice-presidential vote in the Senate to block a Republican attempt to eliminate all Lend-Lease aid the moment the war ended, no matter what the wartime contracts for its delivery stipulated.

My father signed the order without reading it, and Mr. Grew and Mr. Crowley immediately began executing it. It empowered them to cancel all Lend-Lease shipments to Russia and our other allies, immediately. Even ships that were at sea were ordered to return and unload their cargoes. Neither Mr. Crowley nor Mr. Grew gave Dad the slightest intimation that they were going to interpret the order so literally. The abrupt cutoff of supplies infuriated the Russians and alarmed the English. Protests and pleas poured into the White House, and Dad was forced to rescind the order. In his memoirs my father said the experience made him resolve never to sign any document until he had read it.

But the real lesson was one that he hesitated to state in his memoirs—the extreme hostility which certain men in the government, such as Mr. Crowley, felt toward Russia. It did not make my father's task any easier, to find a middle path between these men and the Henry Wallace types, who could not believe the Russians were capable of any wrongdoing. By and large the Wallace group was more numerous in 1945. Averell Harriman recalls being in San Francisco during the UN Conference and giving an off-the-record talk to the press on his view of Russian-American relations, based on his insider's knowledge as ambassador to Moscow. His tough-minded realism was greeted with dismay by his audience. Two reporters became so enraged by his criticism of Russia that they walked out of the room.

At San Francisco the Russians and the Americans fought the first of many verbal battles in the UN. A total deadlock developed over two major questions. Mr. Molotov and his delegation wanted to give the great powers on the Security Council a complete veto over any question raised in either the Security Council or the Assembly. We insisted that complaints could be brought to the Security Council by a member country and considered if seven out of the eleven members of the Council agreed, and we flatly refused to give the Security Council the right to veto the Assembly's freedom of discussion. The American delegation, with my father's firm backing, rejected this attempt to inflict totalitarianism on the United Nations. Dad knew that the Senate would never accept American participation in an organization in which the small states would enjoy the right of free speech only when the big states approved of what they were saying.

Fortunately, Harry Hopkins was in Moscow, and he was able to thrash out with Stalin personally the first of these difficulties, the blanket veto in the Security Council. The Russian dictator overruled Molotov's rigid all-or-nothing demands and, with this breakthrough, it was easier to persuade Stalin to make a similar concession on freedom of debate in the Assembly. The UN was rescued from potential disaster and the conference ended on a note of high optimism. Late in June my father flew to San Francisco to give a speech at the official signing. Mother and I had already gone home to Independence, so he made the trip without us.

Dad's reception in San Francisco was wild. He rode in an open car at the head of a seventy-five-car entourage while ticker tape and torn paper poured down and a million people jammed the sidewalks. Political pundits were astonished by the enthusiasm he generated, and even Dad was a little amazed. "That cheering," he said, "was not for the man, it was for the office. It was for the President of the United States." Later that evening Dad sat around his hotel suite with some old friends. Referring to the remark he made earlier in the day, he said, "As long as I remember that, I'll be all right. When a man forgets such things in public life, that is when the country begins to realize it does not want him anymore."

On the way home Dad made an unscheduled stop in Salt Lake City, Utah. There was a sentimental reason for it. In these first months of his presidency, he often seemed to act out of a desire to put himself in touch with men and places from his past. Salt Lake City was a place that had deep meaning for him, because it was associated intimately in his memory with Grandfather Young.

The next day Dad flew on to Kansas City to visit with us in Independence for a few days. He turned out the biggest crowd in the history of Jackson County when he landed. The following night he received a degree from the University of Kansas City. In an off-the-cuff talk he gave that day, he summed up his thinking at this point in his presidency, in very personal terms:

> The night before last, I arrived in Salt Lake City, Utah, at 10 P.M. from San Francisco, which I had left on the same time schedule at 8 P.M. I left Salt Lake City the next morning after breakfast . . . and arrived in Kansas City, Missouri, in exactly three hours and a half.
>
> My grandfather made that trip time and time again from 1846 to 1854, and again from 1864 to 1870, and when he made

that trip it took him exactly three months to go, and three months to come back.

That is the age in which we live. . . .

We must become adjusted to that situation. No farther from here to Salt Lake City, or Salt Lake City to San Francisco, than it was from here to Lonejack in eastern Jackson County, when we used to go to the picnics there on the sixteenth of August to celebrate the beginning of the Democratic campaign in the fall.

I am anxious to bring home to you that the world is no longer county-size, no longer state-size, no longer nation-size. It is one world, as Willkie said. It is a world in which we must all get along.

En route to this degree granting ceremony, Dad stopped at his old friend Eddie Jacobson's haberdashery store to get some white shirts, size 15½–33. To Eddie's embarrassment he did not have the size in stock. White shirts were one of the many items that were in short supply in those closing days of World War II. Naturally, the newsmen reported Eddie's shortage and within forty-eight hours Dad was practically buried in white shirts from all sections of the country.

Dad had a lot of fun on this visit home. He declared that henceforth Kansas City would be part of "Greater Independence." At a luncheon given him by the Jesters, a Masonic organization, he chatted with his old friends about how it felt to be President. "It seems everybody is anxious that I do the best I can and keep from going high hat or stuffed shirt. Well, the only thing I have to do is remember Luke 6:26 ('Woe unto you when all men shall speak well of you! For so did their fathers to the false prophets')." With a smile, he added: "When I hear the Republicans say I'm doing all right, then I know damn well I'm doing wrong."

After four hectic days in Missouri my father flew back to Washington and submitted the United Nations Charter to the Senate, with a strong recommendation that it be ratified. "The choice is not between this charter and something else. It is between this charter and no charter at all," he said. "It can be improved—and as the years go by it will be—just as our own Constitution has been improved. . . ." He was relaxed and personal with the senators he knew so well, remarking that it was a pleasure to get one more chance to give a speech to them. "You remember how I was tied down during the last three months I was here. I could not speak except to rule on parliamentary questions and two or three times I was ruled out of order because I tended to make a speech on such a question." In regard to the "comparatively few" points of disagreement at the UN Conference, he made an even more senatorially wise remark. "As you know, if you want to get a headline all you need to do is fall out with some of your friends, and you will always get it."

To everyone's amazement, all opposition to the UN practically melted away. Everyone had expected Senator Burton K. Wheeler to lead the assault on the Charter. He was the man who had killed the Supreme Court revision bill in 1937. He was the Senate's best parliamentarian—and an outspoken isolationist. Everyone waited anxiously for the anti-UN maneuvers they were sure he had up his sleeve. But they forgot that Burt Wheeler was also one of Harry Truman's closest friends. As Dad left the Senate chamber, he made a point of shaking hands with him.

There is no better example of my father's inside knowledge of the Senate at this point in his presidency than the amazingly accurate prediction he made to his mother of how the senators would vote on the UN Charter. On July 3, the day after he made his speech, he wrote:

> Went to the Senate yesterday and you should have seen the carrying on they did. I could hardly shut 'em up so I could speak. And they did the same thing after I finished. Some said the Senate never did carry on so over a President or anybody else. Well anyway, I believe we'll carry the Charter with all but two votes.

Scarcely a word of opposition was heard from Senator Wheeler and from more than a few other senators who were expected to rampage against the idea of America joining the UN. The charter, of course, profited from FDR's foresight in creating a genuinely bipartisan American delegation to the San Francisco Conference. From the Democratic side of the aisle Tom Connally voiced his support, and Arthur Vandenberg echoed him on the Republican side. After less than a month of debate, the Senate approved American membership in the UN by an astonishing 89 to 2— exactly as my father had predicted.

[CHAPTER]

Thirteen

WITH THE UN off his mind, my father was free to concentrate on three far more complex, intertwined problems—the atomic bomb, the invasion of Japan, and the Big Three Conference with Prime Minister Churchill and Marshal Stalin, scheduled to begin on July 15 in Germany.

For over a month Mr. Churchill had been pressing my father for an early conference between him and Marshal Stalin. On June 4, 1945, the prime minister sent Dad a telegram containing a phrase that would grow very familiar in years to come:

I AM SURE YOU UNDERSTAND THE REASON WHY I AM
ANXIOUS FOR AN EARLIER DATE (SAY THE 3RD OR 4TH OF
JULY). I VIEW WITH PROFOUND MISGIVINGS THE RETREAT OF
THE AMERICAN ARMY TO OUR LINE OF OCCUPATION IN THE
CENTRAL SECTOR, THUS BRINGING SOVIET POWER INTO
THE HEART OF WESTERN EUROPE AND THE DESCENT OF AN
IRON CURTAIN BETWEEN US AND EVERYTHING TO THE
EASTWARD. I HOPE THAT THIS RETREAT, IF IT HAS TO BE
MADE, WOULD BE ACCOMPLISHED BY THE SETTLEMENT OF
MANY GREAT THINGS WHICH WOULD BE THE TRUE
FOUNDATION OF WORLD PEACE. NOTHING REALLY IMPORTANT
HAS BEEN SETTLED YET, AND YOU AND I WILL HAVE TO BEAR
GREAT RESPONSIBILITY FOR THE FUTURE. I STILL HOPE
THEREFORE THAT THE DATE WILL BE ADVANCED.

My father had stalled on a date for the conference because he wanted to put it off until the atomic bomb was tested. If the bomb was a success, there would probably be no need for Russia to enter the war against Japan—and no need to make any more concessions to the Soviets in Europe for their promise to help in the Far East. Dad had been wrestling with the atom bomb and the plans to end the Japanese war almost continuously since his April conference with Secretary of War Stimson. On Sunday, June 17, he made the following memorandum:

> Went down the River today on the Potomac to discuss plans, issues and' *decisions.* Took Charlie Ross, straight thinker, honest man, who tells me the truth so I understand what he means; Matt Connelly, shrewd Irishman, who raises up the chips and shows me the bugs, honest, fair, "diplomatic" with me; Judge Fred Vinson, straight shooter, knows Congress and how they think, a man to trust; Judge Rosenman, one of the ablest in Washington, keen mind, a lucid pen, a loyal Roosevelt man and an equally loyal Truman man; Steve Early, a keen observer, political and otherwise, has acted as my hatchet man, absolutely loyal and trustworthy, same can be said about Rosenman.
>
> We discussed public relations in Germany, Italy, France, Holland, Belgium, England and Russia. Food, Fuel, Transportation and what to do about it. Japanese War and the relations with China, Russia, and Britain with regard to it; Supreme Commander and what to do with Mr. Prima Donna, Brass Hat, Five Star MacArthur. He's worse than the Cabots and the Lodges—they at least talked with one another before they told God what to do. Mac tells God right off. It is a very great pity we have to have stuffed shirts like that in key positions. I don't see why in Hell Roosevelt didn't order Wainwright home and let MacArthur be a martyr.
>
> Don't see how a country can produce such men as Robt. E. Lee, John J. Pershing, Eisenhower, ànd Bradley and at the same time produce Custers, Pattons and MacArthurs.
>
> I have to decide Japanese strategy—shall we invade Japan proper or shall we bomb and blockade? That is my hardest decision to date. But I'll make it and when I have all the facts. . . .

The only one of these advisers whom I have not mentioned is Fred Vinson. "Papa Vin," as I always called him, was a congressman from Kentucky for several terms, then a federal judge, and after that a wartime administrator for President Roosevelt. He was a very solid, thoroughly shrewd politician from Kentucky, and a very likeable man in the bargain. In the first twelve months of Dad's presidency, "Papa Vin" was one of his most important advisers. Then he was elevated to the Supreme Court and passed out of the inner circle.

The day after he wrote this memorandum, Dad had a climactic conference with the Joint Chiefs of Staff to decide the final strategy against Japan. They handed him plans for a November 1 assault on the Japanese home island of Kyushu with a total force of 766,700 men. Some of the chiefs predicted light casualties—but Admiral Leahy strongly disagreed. He pointed out that in the bloody Okinawa campaign just ending, American losses (41,700) had been 35 percent of the attacking force. The Japanese still had an estimated 5,000 planes ready for kamikaze assaults. There were an estimated 2,000,000 troops in the Japanese home islands. Facing the Americans on Kyushu would be seventeen well-equipped battle-ready divisions.

If the capture of Kyushu, the westernmost Japanese island, did not persuade Japan to surrender, in the spring of 1946 there were plans for a landing on Honshu, the main Japanese island, where a climactic battle would be fought on the Tokyo Plain. On both Kyushu and Honshu, Japan's soldiers would, if their performance on Okinawa was any indication, fight with total fanaticism to defend their sacred home soil. Based on this assumption, General George C. Marshall predicted total American dead on land and sea might reach 500,000 men.

Moreover—and this was a very big moreover—the entire American battle plan was based on the assumption that Russia would enter the war before the American invasion. This would pin down Japan's crack one-million-man Manchurian army, as well as the additional one million troops on the Asian mainland fighting the Chinese. If substantial portions of these troops could be shuttled back to Japan—by no means an impossibility, in spite of our air and sea superiority—American losses might be many times that already appalling figure. More than anything else, these facts explain Dad's policy toward the Russians during these crucial months.

The atomic bomb was not mentioned in this conference. It

[261]

continued to be a question mark. No one really knew whether it would work. At Los Alamos, during these same weeks, scientists were still trying to perfect a detonator that would be completely reliable for triggering the bomb. Later statements by some scientists connected with the project that they were 90 percent certain of success were certainly not reflected in the reports that reached the White House. Admiral Leahy still kept insisting that the bomb would be a dud. Jimmy Byrnes was more optimistic, but he still felt that we needed the Russians in the war to help us bring it to a speedy conclusion. Behind these problems loomed another specter, mentioned again and again in cables from Prime Minister Churchill: the possibility that with the Allies heavily involved in the Pacific, there would be nothing to prevent Russia from taking over most of war-ravaged, prostrate Europe.

Not until June 27, 1945, did new detonators arrive at Los Alamos from the Du Pont Company, reducing the chances of misfire from one in 300 to one in 30,000. On July 1, while my father was returning to Washington from his four-day stopover in Independence, the climactic test was set for July 16. The official estimate of the power of the bomb was 5,000 tons. Actually this was a guess. During the first week in July the top scientists at Los Alamos set up an informal betting pool, to see who would come closest to the actual explosive yield. These insiders' guesses ranged from 45,000 tons to zero, with the majority betting on very low figures. Robert Oppenheimer, for instance, bet the explosion would yield no more than 300 tons.

Meanwhile, the Interim Committee had handed my father a report on the use of the bomb—if it worked. This report, submitted on June 1, recommended that the bomb should be used against Japan as soon as possible. Even after this report was made, the scientific panel that was advising the Interim Committee continued to debate the possibility of other alternatives. What about demonstrating the weapon to representatives of the United Nations on a barren island, or in the desert? This was the recommendation of a team of scientists in Chicago who had developed the first controlled nuclear chain reaction in 1942. The scientific panel, pondering this suggestion, and balancing it against their conservative estimates of the bomb's power, rejected this idea as unlikely to convince the fanatical Japanese, who would naturally be inclined to be extremely suspicious of our claims to possess such a superweapon in the first place.

What about dropping the bomb on some relatively uninhabited area of Japan? There were large drawbacks to this idea. In the first place, we did not have very many bombs. The giant plants constructed in secrecy at Oak Ridge, Tennessee, had only created enough plutonium to build three bombs, and even this small number had been possible only with a day-and-night crash program. Dropping one bomb on an uninhabited area, where it would do relatively little damage, might not impress the Japanese. If we gave them forewarning of the area, they were very likely to move Allied prisoners into the locality and dare us to go ahead. Above all, such advance warning might destroy what my father and his advisers saw as the chief virtue of the bomb—its shock value.

If we wasted two out of the three bombs we possessed in ineffective demonstrations, and the third failed to bring the Japanese to terms, the invasion of Kyushu would probably begin as scheduled, Russia would come into the war on August 8—Stalin had already assured Harry Hopkins of this—thousands of Americans would die, and the Russians would demand a share in the occupation of Japan, with the same nightmarish results that were already beginning to haunt the Allies in Germany.

At the June 18 meeting my father also discussed with his chief advisers the possibility of blockading and bombarding Japan into defeat with conventional weapons. General Marshall, surely the most authoritative military figure in the meeting, dismissed this possibility. He pointed out that no nation had been bombed as intensively as Nazi Germany. But the Germans remained in the war until their home territory was invaded and occupied by Allied troops. The army air force spokesman at the meeting, General Ira Eaker, concurred. He pointed out that it would be more difficult to knock out Japan's scattered industry from the air than Germany's relatively more concentrated factories. Moreover, once the Japanese realized we were trying to knock them out by air power alone, they would intensify their air defenses, and we could expect very heavy losses among our attacking fliers. Admiral Leahy continued to insist that he preferred the blockade and bombardment solution, but no other military man in the room agreed with him. While accepting this expert advice, my father ordered redoubled efforts by the army and the navy to bring Japan to her knees with conventional weapons.

The stage was now set for the Big Three meeting. At Winston Churchill's suggestion, the code name for the conference became "Terminal." Mr. Churchill's code name was "Colonel Warden," Marshal Stalin's was "Uncle Joe," and Dad was "The Other Admiral." Coded cablese is a language all its own, and it is fascinating to read when you know the reality behind the curious nicknames.

One thing is evident from my talks with my father and from reading the memoranda and letters that he wrote at that time: he did not want to go to this conference. There were several reasons for this. High on the list was his political instinct that the American people did not like to see their Presidents cavorting abroad, at state dinners in royal palaces. The dreadful political consequences of President Wilson's journey to Europe in 1919 were never far from his mind. His close association with Congress also made him aware of how deeply they suspected and resented President Roosevelt's habit of making agreements at secret conferences, that were revealed to the Congress only piecemeal if at all.

Finally, there was the problem of how to tell the Russian dictator about the atomic bomb, if the July 16 test should prove successful. It would be almost insulting to Stalin not to tell him about it. This in turn raised the sticky question of what to do if he began asking questions. Prime Minister Churchill had a veto over any decision Dad might make, because in 1943 at Hyde Park, the prime minister and President Roosevelt had entered into a secret agreement which stated "the suggestion that the world should be informed about Tube Alloys [British code name for the bomb] with a view to international agreement regarding its control and use is not accepted. The matter should continue to be regarded as of the utmost secrecy; but when a bomb is finally available, it might perhaps, after mature consideration, be used against the Japanese who should be warned that the bombardment will be repeated until they surrender." The Interim Committee, incidentally, had no knowledge of this agreement when they discussed the problem of whether or not to use the bomb against

Japan. Once more we see the tremendous complexity of presidential decision making.

My father's reluctance was visible in a letter he wrote to his mother on July 3:

> I am getting ready to go see Stalin and Churchill and it is a chore. I have to take my tuxedo, tails, . . . high hat, top hat, and hard hat as well as sundry other things. I have a brief case all filled up with information on past conferences and suggestions on what I'm to do and say. Wish I didn't have to go but I do and it can't be stopped now.

On the eve of his departure he had to deal with another Cabinet crisis caused by the strange presumption of another of Mr. Roosevelt's appointees. Henry Morgenthau had been Secretary of the Treasury throughout almost all of Mr. Roosevelt's administrations. He was married to a close friend of Mrs. Roosevelt's and was used to having ready access to the White House. At the Quebec Conference between Mr. Roosevelt and Mr. Churchill, Mr. Morgenthau had proposed a plan to turn Germany into an agricultural nation by demolishing its vast industrial plants in the Ruhr and elsewhere. The so-called Morgenthau Plan was a fanciful scheme at best; it would have reduced 60,000,000 Germans to the status of beggars, and left a heritage of hatred that the Communists would have been happy to reap. To my father it was the politics of revenge which had failed so tragically after World War I. He had no intention of implementing the plan, and Mr. Morgenthau was not among the list of presidential advisers invited to journey to the Potsdam Conference. Mr. Morgenthau demanded an appointment with Dad and insisted that he join the conference. Dad told him he thought the Secretary of the Treasury was "badly needed" in the United States—which he was, as postwar inflation was already beginning to soar.

Mr. Morgenthau grandly declared that either he went to Potsdam, or he quit.

"All right," Dad replied, "if that is the way you feel, I'll accept your resignation right now."

In Mr. Morgenthau's place my father appointed Fred Vinson. He had planned to give the job to him eventually, but he very much regretted having to leave him behind on the trip to Potsdam. On Sunday, July 7, Dad left Norfolk aboard the cruiser *Augusta*. He would have preferred to fly, but with no vice president, and the whole question of presidential succession so muddled, it was too risky.

One can now see clearly the reasons why the high hopes so many held for this conference ended in disappointment and frustration. But it is important to remember how hard Dad tried, at that time, to create a peaceful postwar world. From this viewpoint, the judgment of some of the best newspapermen is worthwhile. Arthur Krock, writing in *The New York Times* on June 14, 1945, commented:

> The just criticism has often been made, especially of our government, that plenary conferences are called and entered upon without the preparation required for effective discussion and solution of the issues. But if the next Big Three meeting is unsuccessful, no such criticism can be made of President Truman. . . . If any chief of the Big Three states, when the meeting is held, encounters unexpected obstacles on unforeseeable issues, it will not be the fault of President Truman or his envoys.

My father had sent Mr. Davies and Mr. Hopkins to London and Moscow to lay the groundwork for the meeting. On the *Augusta* he took from his briefcase long memoranda prepared by the State Department on all of the problems we were facing in Europe and the Far East. He prepared an agenda for the conference, and carefully outlined his major goals. Even Jimmy Byrnes, whose later comments on my father are not especially kind, wrote that the American party arrived in Germany with "objectives thoroughly in mind . . . and the background papers in support of them fully prepared." Admiral Leahy said that the President "squeezed facts and opinions out of us all day long."

In between squeezings Dad managed to tour the *Augusta* from "the bridge to the bilges," to quote Admiral Leahy again. On one of these inspection tours he found a young man named Lawrence Truman from Owensboro, Kentucky, who was the great-grandson of Grandfather Truman's brother. "He's a nice boy and has green eyes just like Margaret's. Looks about her age," Dad told his mother and sister. As a good politician, he ate meals in each of the ship's messes—the officers', the warrant officers', the petty officers', and the crew's. He went down the chow line, aluminum tray in hand, with the crew.

Landing at Antwerp on July 15, Dad and his party flew to Gatow Airfield, ten miles from the Berlin suburb of Babelsberg, where he was to stay. The conference had long been called the "Berlin meeting," but too much of the German capital had been destroyed to permit any sizable gathering there. So the Russians selected Potsdam, about twenty-five miles from Berlin, as a less damaged site, and chose a number of palatial houses in nearby Babelsberg for residences. By nightfall Dad was settled in a three-story yellow stucco house, which formerly belonged to the head of the German movie industry. It was on a lake swarming with mosquitoes. Prime Minister Churchill had another large house only a few blocks away, and Stalin was also nearby.

Thanks to the hard work of the communications specialists who preceded him, Dad was able to pick up a telephone and call us in Independence. It was a "scrambler" phone, which automatically garbled what was being said for anyone who tried to tap the line. But for us on the receiving end, it was amazingly clear. Overseas phone calls in those days were usually pretty garbled, but Dad sounded as if he were calling from around the corner. He spoke to us almost every day while he was in Potsdam. He never mentioned affairs of state. It was just family chit-chat. Even when he was trying to settle the problems of the world, he kept in touch with his family world in Missouri.

The next morning my father learned that Stalin would be a day late—he had suffered a slight heart attack. Dad took advantage of this delay to spend several hours with Winston Churchill. This delighted the prime minister, who had wanted to meet Dad in London before they met Stalin. But my father had turned down this idea, because he felt it would only feed the Russian dictator's paranoia by giving him another chance to claim, as he had frequently done in his cables, that the British and the Americans were "ganging up" on him.

Friendship was instant between Mr. Churchill and Dad. Their talk ranged over a wide variety of topics, from the Pacific war to their tastes in music. They found themselves in hearty agreement on everything but music. Mr. Churchill loved martial music and just about nothing else in that department. He was startled to find Dad's taste running to Chopin, Liszt and Mozart.

Later the prime minister's physician, Lord Moran, asked Mr. Churchill: "Has he real ability?"

"I should think he has," replied Mr. Churchill. "At any rate, he is a man of immense determination."

The following day, after spending more time with Dad, the "P.M." told Lord Moran: "He seems a man of exceptional charm and ability. . . . He has direct methods of speech and a great deal of self confidence and resolution." Several days later Lord Moran noted in his diary: "Winston has fallen for the President."

That afternoon my father drove into Berlin and saw the desolation and tragedy Hitler's madness had wreaked on that once impressive city. When he returned, he found an extremely excited Secretary of War Stimson waiting for him. He handed Dad a message which read:

TOP SECRET
URGENT
WAR 32887
FOR COLONEL KYLES EYES ONLY. FROM HARRISON FOR
MR. STIMSON
OPERATED ON THIS MORNING. DIAGNOSIS NOT YET COMPLETE
BUT RESULTS SEEM SATISFACTORY AND ALREADY EXCEED
EXPECTATIONS. LOCAL PRESS RELEASE NECESSARY AS
INTEREST EXTENDS GREAT DISTANCE. DR. GROVES PLEASED.
HE RETURNS TOMORROW. I WILL KEEP YOU POSTED.

This was the first word received from General Leslie Groves's Washington office, reporting the successful test of the atomic bomb in New Mexico. It was flashed from Washington by George Harrison, who was acting as chairman of the Interim Committee while Mr. Stimson was in Germany. The local press release meant that the explosion had attracted enough attention to require a public statement by the army that an ammunition dump had accidentally exploded.

The following morning Premier Stalin visited my father at his residence, which was already being called the "little White House" although it was yellow (little or summer White Houses were seldom white). My father persuaded him to stay for lunch, and they talked "straight from the shoulder." Dad found he liked the way Stalin looked him in the eye when he spoke and the meeting ended with Dad in a very optimistic mood. Although he sized up Mr. Stalin as a very determined, forceful man, he found him personally quite likable in this first encounter.

That afternoon the Big Three met for the first time at ten minutes past five in the ornate, 300-year-old Cecilienhof Palace. Two huge wrought iron chandeliers hung above a big circular table, at which the leaders and their delegations took their places.

Marshal Stalin proposed that my father become the presiding officer. Although he thanked them for the "courtesy," he did not relish the task. In a hitherto unpublished letter he wrote the following day to his mother, he described some of his problems:

> Mr. Stalin made a motion at the conference that I act as chairman and Churchill seconded it. So I preside. It is hard as presiding over the Senate. Churchill talks all the time and Stalin just grunts but you know what he means.
>
> We are meeting in one of the Kaiser's palaces. I have a private suite in it that is very palatial. The conference room is 50 x 60 with a big round table in the center at which we sit. I have the Secretary of State, Mr. Davies, Admiral Leahy, and Mr. Bohlen, the interpreter, and each of the others have the same number. Then I have the Russian Ambassador of our country and a half dozen experts behind me.
>
> They all say I took 'em for a ride when I got down to presiding. It was a nerve-wracking experience but it had to be done. The worst is yet to come; but I'm hoping. I have several aces in the hole I hope which will help on results. . . .

The following morning Secretary of War Stimson received another flash from Washington, which he rushed to the "little White House" in Babelsberg.

TOP SECRET
PRIORITY
WAR 33556
TO SECRETARY OF WAR FROM HARRISON. DOCTOR HAS JUST RETURNED MOST ENTHUSIASTIC AND CONFIDENT THAT THE LITTLE BOY IS AS HUSKY AS HIS BIG BROTHER. THE LIGHT IN HIS EYES DISCERNIBLE FROM HERE TO HIGHHOLD AND I COULD HAVE HEARD HIS SCREAMS FROM HERE TO MY FARM.

Big Brother was the atom bomb that had been exploded at Alamogordo Air Base in New Mexico. The Little Boy was atom bomb number two, ready to be used against Japan. "From here to Highhold" meant from Washington to Secretary Stimson's estate, Highhold, on Long Island, 250 miles away. "From here to my farm" meant from Washington to George Harrison's farm at Upperville, Virginia, forty miles away. The medical terminology baffled the young officers who were manning the American communications center at Postdam. They thought that seventy-seven-year-old Mr. Stimson had just become a father.

While this was a sensational indication of the bomb's power, it was not factual enough for my father. He wanted a complete report from General Groves before he made any decision connected with the new weapon. While he waited for this report, he had to continue negotiating with Prime Minister Churchill and Marshal Stalin.

My father meant it when he said he wanted results at Potsdam. He had brought with him his Joint Chiefs of Staff and put them to work with their Russian counterparts on a coherent plan for ending the Japanese war. He wanted to settle the future of Germany, and he wanted to extract from Stalin a genuine commitment to make the Yalta Declaration on Liberated Europe a reality. On both these points he was more or less frustrated. Stalin was not really interested in making firm agreements on anything that involved surrendering control of nations or territories occupied by the Red Army. He was, on the other hand, eager to obtain concessions of every sort that contributed to the growth of Russia's power.

Stalin revealed his inner thinking in an offhand remark to Ambassador Averell Harriman. The ambassador congratulated him on the defeat of Germany and said that it must be very gratifying to see Russia's army in Berlin. Stalin shrugged and said, "Czar Alexander got to Paris." Faced with a prostrate Europe, the Russian leader saw no reason why he could not push communism to the English Channel. There was, as it turned out, no reason—but Harry S. Truman's determination not to let it happen.

At Potsdam Stalin coolly asked for a share in control of the Ruhr, Germany's industrial heartland, for control of one of Italy's

African colonies, and for a say in the destinies of Lebanon and Syria. Secretary of War Stimson worriedly wrote in his diary that the Russians "are throwing aside all their previous restraint as to being only a continental power and not interested in any further acquisitions and are now branching out."

My father remained unruffled by these demands. He assured the Secretary that they were largely "bluffs" to distract attention from the Russian seizure of eastern Europe. Though he knew exactly what was going on, Dad maintained a friendly face and struggled to reach agreement on important matters. He extracted from Stalin a promise to hold free elections in Poland. In return he agreed to give Russia the port of Koenigsberg to satisfy their need for a northern warm water harbor.

In these debates, Mr. Churchill was not always helpful. More often than not, he was concerned with maintaining the colonial influence and holdings of the British Empire. This badly weakened his position when, for instance, he argued for Russia's withdrawal from eastern Europe and Iran. He was also haunted by an agreement he had made with Stalin, in a private conversation, in October, 1944, that created "spheres of responsibility" in southeastern Europe. At that time he had agreed to assign Rumania and Bulgaria to the Soviet Union and Greece to Great Britain.

In the midst of this complicated wrangling came the detailed report on the atomic explosion at Alamogordo Air Base. It arrived on July 21, the fourth day of the conference, at 11:35 A.M. Major General Groves and his second-in-command, Brigadier General Thomas F. Farrell, had labored two consecutive days and nights to complete it. At 3:00 P.M. Secretary of War Stimson brought it to the little White House. At this suggestion my father had invited Secretary of State Byrnes to join them. Mr. Stimson began reading the report aloud but he was so excited, he frequently stumbled over words.

> 1. This is not a concise, formal military report but an attempt to recite what I would have told you if you had been here on my return from New Mexico.
> 2. At 0530, 16 July 1945, in a remote section of the Alamogordo Air Base, New Mexico, the first full scale test was made of the implosion type atomic fission bomb. For the first time in history there was a nuclear explosion. And what an explo-

sion! . . . The bomb was not dropped from an airplane but was exploded on a platform on top of a 100-foot high steel tower.

3. The test was successful beyond the most optimistic expectations of anyone. Based on the data which it has been possible to work up to date, I estimate the energy generated to be in excess of the equivalent of 15,000 to 20,000 tons of TNT; and this is a conservative estimate. Data based on measurements which we have not yet been able to reconcile would make the energy release several times the conservative figure. There were tremendous blast effects. For a brief period there was a lighting effect within a radius of 20 miles equal to several suns in midday; a huge ball of fire was formed which lasted for several seconds. This ball mushroomed and rose to a height of over 10,000 feet before it dimmed. The light from the explosion was seen clearly at Albuquerque, Santa Fe, Silver City, El Paso and other points generally to about 180 miles away. The sound was heard to the same distance in a few instances but generally to about 100 miles. Only a few windows were broken although one was some 125 miles away. . . .

The report went on for many more pages, describing in detail such things as the damage done to a steel tower seventy feet high, a half mile from the explosion. The data was supplemented by a personal statement from General Groves's deputy, Brigadier General Thomas F. Farrell, who had been at a control shelter only 10,000 yards from the explosion. He spoke of an "awesome roar which warned of doomsday."

Secretary of War Stimson noted in his diary that my father was "tremendously pepped up" by these details and said that it gave him "an entirely new feeling of confidence." Some historians have attempted to twist these words into an argument that Dad felt he could now make the Russians dance to his tune, or threaten them with complete destruction. Nothing could be further from the truth. My father never considered using the atomic bomb against Russia, and there is not an iota of evidence that he ever made a threat to do so, even by implication. His feelings of elation and relief were connected with the problem of getting Russian cooperation in the final assault on Japan. Every time he was confronted across the conference table by Stalin's double-talk and intransigence, he had been forced to mute his objections lest the Russians renege on this crucial military commitment. The lives of hundreds of thousands of American soldiers were at stake and this primary consideration came before achieving ideal governments in Bulgaria, Rumania, Hungary, and Poland. Now, it was obvious that we no longer needed Russia to end the Pacific war. This freed my father to negotiate with far more boldness and bluntness.

Winston Churchill, in his comments on Potsdam, reflects precisely this shift in attitude. He told his foreign secretary, Anthony Eden, after news of the bomb arrived: "It is quite clear that the United States do not at the present time desire Russian participation in the war against Japan."

The following day my father convened a conference of his chief advisers in the little White House at Babelsberg to make the final decision about the use of the bomb. More than two months of thought by the best available minds was at his fingertips. Once more he polled the men in the room. Only one man had changed his mind. Commander of the Army Air Force General Hap Arnold now thought Japan could be bombed into submission with conventional weapons. He pointed out that, in a single raid, B-29 bombers had obliterated sixteen square miles of Tokyo. One city after another had been devastated with awesome results, once the B-29s began dropping incendiary bombs rather than high explosives. But none of the other military men—especially General Marshall—concurred with General Arnold. Anyway, my father saw that conventional bombing, even if it worked—and no one doubted that it might take months, even a year—would cause more Japanese deaths than the use of one or two atomic bombs. The fire raid on Tokyo, by the Japanese government's estimate, had killed 78,650 people. My father's decision—and this I think has been largely forgotten—was aimed at saving *Japanese* as well as American lives. His later comments on his decision make this clear: "It was not an easy decision to make. I did not like the weapon. But I had no qualms if in the long run *millions of lives* could be saved."

Note I have italicized the word "millions." He was not talking about Allied casualties in the invasion of Japan, which even the darkest pessimist never estimated at more than 750,000 men.

Mr. Churchill joined my father and his advisers at the end of their conference. He emphatically agreed that the bomb should be used, if Japan refused to surrender. His recollections stress, even more vividly than Dad's words, how its use would save Japanese lives:

> I thought immediately myself of how the Japanese people, whose courage I had always admired, might find in the apparition of this almost supernatural weapon an excuse which would save their honor and release them from their obligation of being killed to the last fighting man.
> . . . To avoid a vast, indefinite butchery, to bring the war to an end, to give peace to the world, to lay healing hands upon its tortured peoples by a manifestation of overwhelming power at the cost of a few explosions, seemed, after all our toils and perils, a miracle of deliverance.

After this meeting my father formally authorized the United States Army's Strategic Air Forces to drop the atomic bomb. He had discussed a list of targets with Secretary of War Stimson, and selected four, Hiroshima, Kokura, Niigata, and Nagasaki. The bomb was to be dropped on one of these cities as soon after August 3 as the weather permitted visual bombing. All met the specifications that he had laid down. They had not been bombed before and were major war production centers.

George Elsey, who was working in the map room at Potsdam, was the man to whom my father gave the order. "I recall it vividly because he wrote it down in longhand and handed it to me for transmission," Mr. Elsey says. "He gave authority for the first bomb to be dropped, at the discretion of the military commanders on the scene because weather and other factors had to be taken into account. But in no circumstances did he want the bomb to be dropped until *after* he left Potsdam. He wanted to be away from the Russians [and their prying questions] and on his way home before the actual dropping of the first bomb."

The time had now come to issue the final warning to Japan. My father had refused the advice of Acting Secretary of State Grew to issue the warning early in June. He felt that it would be more effective if it came at the Potsdam Conference. Although Russia, not being at war with Japan, could not sign the Potsdam Declaration, their presence at the conference would underscore to the Japanese the overwhelming superiority of force that now encircled them.

Mr. Grew had also pressed my father to specify that the Americans would permit the Japanese to retain the Emperor after their defeat. Now a major decision had to be made on this point. Should it be included in the Potsdam Declaration?

This raised complex political questions. A great many members of Congress were bitterly hostile to the Emperor. So was a large section of the American public. Throughout the war the Emperor had been associated with Japanese fanaticism. His use by the military clique had made him a loathsome figure. When Mr. Grew had been confirmed by Congress as Under Secretary of State, he had been grilled severely on his opinions about the Emperor and had been forced to say publicly that he did not particularly favor his retention. My father and Secretary of State Byrnes, when they faced the final decision on the question at Potsdam, were keenly aware of this domestic political problem. But they looked a step beyond it, to another equally important point.

By announcing in their call for surrender that the Japanese could keep the Emperor, they were in effect *imposing* him on the Japanese people. How did they know, after the cataclysm that had engulfed Japan under the Emperor's leadership, that the Japanese people would want him to remain? He might, as many American experts, such as Assistant Secretary of State Dean Acheson, believed, be too heavily identified with the military to be tolerated, even as a figurehead. Moreover, Chiang Kai-shek, leader of China and a major ally in our war against Japan, had to approve the declaration and he would never accept a formula that specified the Emperor could remain in power. So the final clause read as follows: "The occupying forces of the Allies shall be withdrawn from Japan as soon as these objectives have been accomplished and there has been established in accordance with the freely expressed will of the Japanese people a peacefully inclined and responsible government."

With this decided, my father now tackled the sticky question of how and what to tell Stalin about the atomic bomb. He decided to tell him as soon as possible, but to confine his remark to a very general description. At the end of the plenary session on July 24,

[275]

Dad strolled over to the Russian leader and told him that the United States had created a new weapon "of unusual destructive force." Prime Minister Churchill and Secretary of State Byrnes stood only a few yards away, studying Stalin's reaction. He was remarkably cool. He simply said that he hoped the Americans would "make good use of it against the Japanese." My father, Mr. Churchill, and Mr. Byrnes concluded that Stalin had failed to grasp the significance of the statement. It did not occur to them, at that time, with so many other immense problems on their minds, that Stalin, thanks to his very efficient spies at Los Alamos, knew almost as much about the bomb as they did.

Two days later my father released the Potsdam Declaration. Signed by China, Great Britain, and America, it spelled out for the Japanese exactly what terms they could expect if they surrendered: the end of their militaristic government, temporary occupation of the Japanese home islands, disarmament and return home of their soldiers, establishment of a democratic government and basic human freedoms, as well as the guarantee that Japan could rebuild her industries and have access to the world's raw materials. The declaration pointed to the devastation that had been visited on Germany and called on Japan to surrender or face "complete and utter destruction." This last phrase was as far as my father was prepared to go in revealing the atomic bomb. At the core of his thinking, he remained convinced that the shock value of the bomb was its most potent power.

On this same July 26 the cruiser *Indianapolis* reached Tinian in the Pacific and delivered to the 509th Composite Air Group the uranium-235 portion of the atomic bomb. The plutonium charge was en route to the same destination by air. By 6 A.M. Tokyo time, July 27, the Japanese had the full text of the Potsdam Declaration. The same day thousands of leaflets were dropped from American planes, urging the Japanese people to accept the surrender terms. The militarists debated with the civilians in the Cabinet about what to do. Finally, their prime minister said he would regard the declaration with *mokusatsu*. Later some Japanese —and those peculiar historians who are determined to indict America for moral obloquy—claimed that this word had several shades of meaning ranging from "treat with silent contempt" to "no comment." They claimed that we seized on the first meaning and ignored the second possibility. They ignore the fact that on the following day, after the word *mokusatsu* had been widely published in the Japanese newspapers, the prime minister collapsed under the pressure of the militarists in his cabinet, and at 4 P.M. issued a clarification: "I consider the joint proclamation of the three powers to be a rehash of the Cairo Declaration. The government does not regard it as a thing of great value; the government will just ignore (*mokusatsu*) it. We will press forward resolutely to carry the war to a successful conclusion."

The stage was now set for some very hard bargaining at Potsdam. Freed from the need for Russia in the Pacific war, my father was ready to move toward a tougher approach to Stalin. But before Dad could begin, the conference was disrupted by very unexpected news. Prime Minister Churchill had stood for reelection on July 5. On July 26 he went home to learn the results. It had taken three weeks to count the votes from British soldiers around the world. To everyone's amazement—including Marshal Stalin's —Mr. Churchill and his Conservative party were overwhelmingly defeated.

Clement Attlee, leader of the Labour party, became prime minister. Since he had served with Mr. Churchill in the coalition War Cabinet and had been at Potsdam, there was no obvious break in British policy.

But many people sensed a serious change in the conference's mood and tone. Admiral Leahy recorded his impression in his journal: "There was a notable coolness in their [the Russians'] attitude after Attlee took over."

Previous writers on Potsdam have explained this change by concentrating on Mr. Churchill's familiarity with Marshal Stalin, and the fact that the Russian leader was now faced with two men whom he did not know well. I think there is another, more realistic explanation.

Stalin was used to Mr. Churchill's opposition, and was also used to ignoring it. He knew that Britain no longer had the strength to enforce its wishes. The Americans were the ones he wanted to cajole into giving him what he wanted—because they alone had the power to stop him. He was sorely disappointed when he discovered that Dad was equally tough in his own quiet way, without Mr. Churchill around. It was when Stalin realized that he could

[277]

not get very far with the new American President that the Russian coolness noted by Admiral Leahy became evident.

On a personal level my father felt sorry for Mr. Churchill, but he was not sorry to see him leave Potsdam. This is clear from a comment that Dad made in a letter to his mother and sister on July 28: "It is too bad about Churchill but it may turn out to be all right for the world." Obviously, Dad thought he would have a better chance of reaching an agreement with Stalin without Mr. Churchill in the way. Dad was wrong, but it shows how eager he was to agree.

To demonstrate his new approach, my father offered Stalin a package proposal. He would agree to the new Polish border with Germany on a provisional basis, with the understanding that a final decision on it would be made at a peace conference. In turn, he wanted Stalin to agree to the American desire to readmit Italy to the family of nations as swiftly as possible. As for German reparations, he proposed that Russia accept 10 to 15 percent of the capital equipment in Germany's western zones of occupation in return for raw materials from the eastern zone, and that Russia drop its unrealistic demand for $10 billion in cash.

The package approach took Stalin by surprise. He wanted to deal with each item separately, where his native stubbornness was his greatest asset. But he could think of no reason to object to my father's approach, and so he reluctantly agreed to these proposals. Thanks to Dad's skill as a negotiator, Potsdam ended on a note of unity. It was, he knew, a very superficial unity—but it was better than public hostility.

In the final meeting at Potsdam Stalin revealed his displeasure with my father in a most insulting way. Twice Dad had tried to open a discussion which he believed was vital for the future peace of Europe and the world—the internationalization of all inland waterways, including the Danube and Rhine rivers, the Kiel Canal, and the straits of the Bosporus, as well as the Panama and Suez canals. Dad's study of history had convinced him that all major wars of the previous two centuries had originated in the area from the Black Sea to the Baltic and from the eastern frontier of France to the western frontier of Russia. He envisioned a world in which all nations would have the right to free passage of goods and vessels along these waterways to all the seas of the world. The British supported this idea, but Stalin was clearly uninterested. "We have many more urgent problems before us. This one can be put off," he snapped.

At my father's request, Secretary of State Byrnes tried to set up a special committee to consider the subject. But the Americans and British could not even get the Soviet representative to submit a statement. When Dad brought it up again at the July 31 plenary session, Stalin dodged the subject once more. On August 1, when they began considering the final communiqué on the meeting to be released to the public, my father expressed his regret that no agreement had been reached on the subject of waterways. He asked, however, that the final communiqué include it as a subject that was discussed. Stalin objected. He said the communiqué was already too long.

Earnestly, my father looked across the table at Stalin and spoke to him in a very personal way. "Marshal Stalin, I have accepted a number of compromises during this conference to conform with your views, and I make a personal request now that you yield on this point. My request is that the communiqué mention the fact that the waterways proposal has been referred to the Council of Foreign Ministers which we have established to prepare for peace settlements." He explained this would give him an opportunity to discuss the subject with the American Congress. However, before the Russian interpreter could finish repeating Dad's words, Stalin broke in. "Nyet!" he snapped. To make sure Dad knew what he was saying, he added in English, "No. I say no!"

Dad's face flushed with anger. He turned to the American delegation and exclaimed, "I cannot understand that man!"

"Jimmy," he said to Mr. Byrnes in a low voice, "do you realize that we have been here seventeen whole days? Why, in seventeen days you can decide anything!"

For my father, Potsdam was exhausting as well as exasperating. Prime Minister Churchill and Marshal Stalin preferred late hours, and each of the heads of state were required to give lavish dinners which lasted until almost midnight. There was also a need to entertain lesser dignitaries at small lunches and dinners. In his letter to his mother and sister on July 23, Dad gave a good description of Russia's hospitality:

> Stalin gave his state dinner night before last and it was a wow. Started with caviar and vodka and wound up with water-

melon and champagne, with smoked fish, fresh fish, venison, chicken, duck, and all sorts of vegetables in between. There was a toast every five minutes until at least twenty-five had been drunk. I ate very little and drank less, but it was a colorful and enjoyable occasion.

When I had Stalin and Churchill here for dinner, I think I told you that a young sergeant named Eugene List, from Philadelphia, played the piano, and a boy from the Metropolitan Orchestra played the violin. They are the best we have, and they are very good. Stalin sent to Moscow and brought on his two best pianists and two feminine violinists. They were excellent. Played Chopin, Liszt, Tschaikovsky. I congratulated him and them on their ability. They had dirty faces though and the gals were rather fat. Anyway it was a nice dinner. . . .

At Dad's dinner Eugene List played Chopin, and Dad stood by the piano and turned the pages for him personally. They had had to scour Europe to find a copy of the score, which Mr. List did not have the time to memorize. Mr. Churchill was bored by all this classical music, and he retaliated at his dinner by having the Royal Air Force Band play a series of ear-shattering military marches.

At one of these dinners Dad's already sinking opinion of Marshal Stalin slipped even lower. They began discussing Poland, and Dad asked him what happened to the thousands of Polish officers who the Germans said were slaughtered by the Russians in Katyn Forest after they had surrendered to the Russian army in 1940. Marshal Stalin shrugged. "They just went away," he said, and dropped the subject.

In spite of his disillusionment, my father did not lose his sharp eye for details, or his sense of humor, at Potsdam. At one of the dinners he was amazed to see Stalin join in toast after toast, drinking a clear liquid which Dad assumed was vodka. Finally, he asked the Russian dictator how he did it. Stalin smiled and replied that he was really drinking French table wine.

In his entourage that accompanied him to Potsdam, Dad had included an old Missouri follower, Fred Canfil. Fred had been a county courthouse employee when Dad was elected county judge, and he attached himself to Harry Truman with total devotion and loyalty. He was not terribly bright, but he was built like a bull, and he had a voice which could shatter glass at a hundred paces. One day, as the plenary session was breaking up, Dad called Fred over and introduced him to Marshal Stalin. "Marshal Stalin, I want you to meet Marshal Canfil."

Dad did not bother to explain that Fred was a federal marshal in the state of Missouri—thanks to a recent presidential appointment. In Russia, a marshal is a formidable character, and after that, the Russian delegation treated Fred with enormous respect.

Dad also found time to entertain his nephew and namesake, Sergeant Harry Truman. Harry was stepping on a troopship to go home when a presidential order whisked him to Potsdam for several days of high-style relaxation. Dad also drove fifty miles to visit with Colonel Louis Truman, son of his cousin Ralph, and in the course of these travels, found himself a doctor. He heard that Wallace Graham, son of his old family doctor of the same name, was stationed near Potsdam, and invited him over for a visit. He liked him so much, he asked him to become the White House physician. An intensely idealistic young surgeon, Dr. Graham politely told the President that he would rather not take the job.

"I want to take care of as many people as possible, not just one man," he said.

"Even if that one man is the President of your country?" Dad asked.

"I've got a hospital full of men who've shed their blood for their country," Dr. Graham said. "I can't leave them."

"Do you realize who you're talking to?" Dad asked.

"Yes, sir, I'll obey orders, sir," Dr. Graham said. But he insisted on staying with his hospital until all his wounded men were discharged or moved home. Only then did he report for duty at the White House. There he wangled an agreement from Dad that he could continue his practice of surgery at the army's Walter Reed Hospital.

While Dad was in Potsdam, he had been importuned by numerous heads of state to visit their countries. At first he had agreed to very brief, informal visits, but the long stay at Potsdam and the imminent use of the atomic bomb changed his mind. He canceled all his prearranged visits, leaving a distraught Charlie Ross to explain it to the press, and headed for home. He paused

[281]

only long enough to have lunch with King George VI aboard the British battle cruiser *Renown*. "I'd rather fly," he told his mother. "I could be home a week sooner. But they all yell their heads off when I talk of flying."

By five o'clock on the afternoon of August 3, the *Augusta* was at sea. On August 6, the fourth day at sea, Dad and Secretary of State Byrnes were having lunch with the crew. They sat at separate tables in different sections of the large mess. Dad was chatting with sailors from Connecticut, New York, California, New Jersey, and Minnesota when Captain Frank H. Graham, a map room officer, handed him a message. Here is what he read:

> HIROSHIMA BOMBED VISUALLY WITH ONLY ONE TENTH
> COVER AT 052315A [7:15 P.M. Washington time August 5].
> THERE WAS NO FIGHTER OPPOSITION AND NO FLAK.
> PARSONS REPORTS 15 MINUTES AFTER DROP AS FOLLOWS:
> "RESULTS CLEAR-CUT SUCCESSFUL IN ALL RESPECTS.
> VISIBLE EFFECTS GREATER THAN IN ANY TEST. CONDITION
> NORMAL IN AIRPLANE FOLLOWING DELIVERY."

"Captain," Dad said, "this is the greatest thing in history. Show it to the Secretary of State."

A few minutes later the map room delivered another message, this one from Secretary Stimson:

> BIG BOMB WAS DROPPED ON HIROSHIMA AUGUST 5 AT
> 7:15 P.M. WASHINGTON TIME. FIRST REPORTS INDICATE
> COMPLETE SUCCESS WHICH WAS EVEN MORE CONSPICUOUS
> THAN EARLIER TEST.

My father jumped up and called to Secretary Byrnes, "It's time for us to get on home." Then he turned to the crew. "Please keep your seats and listen for a moment. I have an announcement to make. We have just dropped a new bomb on Japan which has more power than 20,000 tons of TNT. It has been an overwhelming success."

My father and Mr. Byrnes were so excited that they abandoned their food and rushed to the officers' wardroom, where he repeated the announcement. There was tremendous cheering and excitement in both places.

Thanks to the excellent histories of World War II from the

1. A portrait of Dad, taken around 1900.

2. This is my great-grandfather Solomon Young. He was very important in Dad's early life.

3. In this picture, left to right, are my aunt Mary Jane Truman, Dad, two cousins Laura Everhart and Myra Colgan Hornbuckle, my uncle Vivian, and our cousin Nellie Noland. It was probably taken on the Truman farm.

4. Dad and his aunt, Mrs. Margaret Ellen Noland (called Aunt Ella), and her daughter, Cousin Ethel Noland. Cousin Ethel became the family historian.

5. This is one of my favorite pictures of Dad. It was taken during World War I, somewhere in France.

6. This picture was taken in the summer of 1934, when Dad was running for the Senate.

7. Mamma Truman and Dad, on the Truman farm, during his Senate years.
She followed his career closely and never hesitated to give him advice.

8. Independence gave Dad a farewell dinner before he left for Washington to take his Senate seat. I was photographed in profile because I could not stand any more flashbulbs in my eyes.

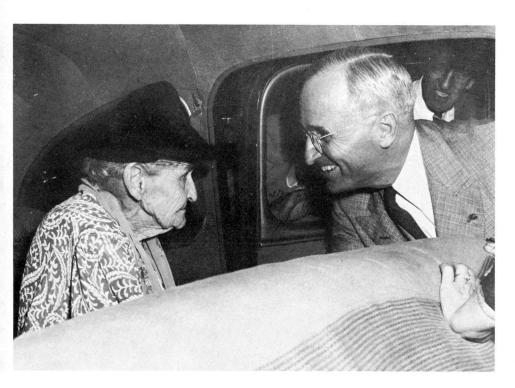

9. A typical Mamma Truman look. Behave yourself or else. Dad was launching his campaign for vice president the day this picture was taken.

10. Cold, wet, dark, and crowded, the historic 1944 inauguration—not on the steps of the Capitol but on the South Portico of the White House.

11. Dad being sworn in as President, April 12, 1945.

12. Dad's first full day in the White House, April 13, 1945.

13. The opening of the Potsdam Conference. A few days later, this group changed. Winston Churchill was replaced by Clement Attlee, second from the right in the background.

14. On his way home from Potsdam, Dad visited King
George VI aboard the British cruiser HMS *Renown*.

15. Two of my favorite men, Dean Acheson and George Marshall, talking
with Dad.

16. One of the few pictures of all three of us aboard the *Ferdinand Magellan*, with not a handshaker in sight, during the 1948 campaign.

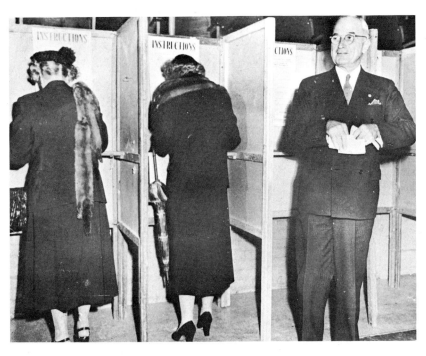

17. Mother is on the left, and I am in the center, casting my first vote for a President of the United States in 1948. Look at those awful hemlines!

18. The Distinguished Contributor to the Federal Register joins the White House press corps for a briefing at Key West. These were hard-working vacations, but everybody had a good time, too.

19. The usual airport wind blows me apart and does not bother Dad as we get off the *Sacred Cow* in Kansas City.

20. Mother, the baseball fan of the family, was delighted that this opening game was not called on account of rain. How I got trapped into going I'll never know.

21. Dad and his oldest and closest friend during his White House years, Press Secretary Charlie Ross.

22. My favorite picture of Dad and the
"Former Naval Person," taken, appropriately,
on board the *Williamsburg*.

23. Dad says good-bye to General Eisenhower on his way to organize
NATO in 1951.

24. Dad greets Princess Elizabeth and Prince Philip when they visited in 1951. This was fairly typical of the way important visitors from overseas were met.

25. Dad adds to General MacArthur's medals a Wake Island.

26. This one picture tells the whole story of 1952. Mr. Stevenson did not really want the nomination. Dad persuaded him to take it.

27. As you can see, January 20, 1953, was a great day for the Trumans. Dad is plain Mr. Truman at last.

28. Dad enjoying himself at Uncle Vivian's farm. He was a good horseman. He taught me how to ride.

29. My entry for the most dramatic photograph ever taken of Dad. By *The New York Times,* of course!

30. Showing a great lady around the Truman Library.

31. Dad is up to his ears in Texans here. On his right is Lyndon Johnson, and on his left John Nance Garner (celebrating his ninetieth birthday) and Sam Rayburn.

32. Dad getting an honorary degree at Oxford. How do you like *that* hat?

33. Four Presidents at the funeral of House Speaker Sam Rayburn.

34. President Johnson signs the Medicare Bill at the Truman Library on July 7, 1965. It was the realization of the struggle for a national health policy that Dad began during his Presidency.

35. Escorting some distinguished visitors from the house in Independence.

36. The Harry S. Truman Library in Independence, Missouri.

37. Taking a morning stroll in Independence, the place he loved most.

Japanese point of view which have been written in the last few years, we now know that even after the first atomic bomb, Japan was not ready to surrender. By prearrangement, my father issued a statement immediately after the news of Hiroshima demanding that they give up. More millions of leaflets were dropped over Japan, urging the Japanese people to force their government to stop the war. But the grip of the militarists was still so strong that no one dared to come forward as a peace negotiator. It became evident that a second bomb would have to be dropped. Three days later this bomb smashed Nagasaki. Some people have wondered why this second bomb was dropped so soon. This was in accordance with my father's original order, which he signed on July 24.

The second paragraph said: "Additional bombs will be delivered on the above targets as soon as made ready by the Project's staff." From the very beginning, Dad's advisers, particularly Major General Leslie Groves, had been convinced that it would take two bombs to convince the Japanese to surrender. The double blow left no doubt that the first holocaust in Hiroshima was not some kind of fluke or accident. The Japanese reacted precisely as my father and his advisers had predicted they would. The grim reality that we could produce many of these terrible weapons—although we actually had only one more in reserve at the time—made Emperor Hirohito decide to surrender. The Emperor asked only one guarantee—"that the Potsdam Declaration does not compromise any demand which prejudices the prerogatives of His Majesty as a sovereign ruler." My father agreed, but in a way that did not compromise *his* position that the people of Japan must remain free to choose their own form of government. His reply stated:

> From the moment of surrender, the authority of the Emperor and the Japanese government to rule the state shall be subject to the Supreme Commander of the Allied Powers who will take such steps as he deems proper to effectuate the surrender terms. . . . The ultimate form of government of Japan shall, in accordance with the Potsdam Declaration, be established by the freely expressed will of the people.

By this time the Russians were in the war, rampaging through

Manchuria. Japan's cause was obviously hopeless. The Emperor summoned the senior military commanders in Japan and asked them to make sure the armed forces obeyed his decision to surrender. In spite of these precautions, there was a last-ditch attempt by military fanatics to stage a coup—this after two atomic bombs.

On August 12, in the midst of these frantic days, Dad wrote this interesting letter to his mother:

> Since I wrote to you last Tuesday there hasn't been a minute. The speech, the Russian entry into the war, the Japs' surrender offer and the usual business of the President's office have kept me busy night and day. It seems that things are going all right. Nearly every crisis seems to be the worst one but after it's over it isn't so bad.

The final testimony for the rightness of Dad's decision on the atomic bomb comes from the Japanese themselves. Cabinet Secretary Sakomizu said the atomic bomb "provided an excuse to surrender." Hirohito's chief civilian adviser, Marquis Kido, said, "The presence of the atomic bomb made it easier for us, the politicians, to negotiate peace."

So the great moment came. After an all-day wait on August 14, the message was flashed from our embassy in Berne, Switzerland, where the surrender was negotiated, informing Dad that the Emperor had accepted his terms. Dad immediately summoned White House correspondents and all the available members of his Cabinet to his office. In a typically thoughtful gesture, he also invited Cordell Hull, the former Secretary of State, who had been seriously ill. Standing behind his desk, Dad announced that Japan had surrendered unconditionally. A huge crowd soon assembled outside the White House, as the news was flashed throughout the city of Washington and the nation. Dad and Mother went out to the fountain on the north lawn, and he greeted them with a V-for-victory sign. Then he went back in the house and called his mother. Three days later, he finally found time to write her a letter:

> I have been trying to write you every day for three or four days but things have been in such a dizzy whirl here I couldn't do anything but get in the center and try to stop it. Japan

finally quit and then I had to issue orders so fast that several mistakes were made and then other orders had to be issued. Everybody has been going at a terrific gait but I believe we are up with the parade now.

From now on, however, it is going to be political maneuvers that I have to watch. . . .

Already he was confronting the problems of peace.

[CHAPTER]

Fourteen

EVEN BEFORE HE GOT HOME from Potsdam, my father began thinking about the tremendous domestic problems that confronted him and the nation. He summoned John Snyder to meet him at the dock, and all the way up on the train from Norfolk to Washington they discussed domestic problems. In Potsdam Dad had realized that the Russians were basing their aggressive plans on the assumption that the United States would plunge into another economic depression as soon as the war was over. Dad was determined not to let this happen. "He had seen how much depended on keeping America strong," Mr. Snyder says.

Aboard the *Augusta* Dad had begun work on a domestic policy statement. On September 6, 1945, only four days after the official V-J Day, Congress reconvened at his request and received a special message from him that—temporarily—took their legislative breaths away. It was 16,000 words long, the longest message any President had sent Congress since Theodore Roosevelt. Its twenty-one points ranged from a comprehensive unemployment compensation program to a full employment law which would assert the right to work for everyone able and willing to work and the responsibility of the government to assure that right, to a permanent Fair Employment Practices Committee to eliminate job bias of every sort. It included a call for more regional river valley developments like the TVA, a wide-ranging veterans program, generous aid to small business, and a housing program that aimed at 1,500,000 homes a year for the next ten years.

For my father, this sweeping twenty-one-point message symbolized "the assumption of the office of President in my own right. . . . It was my opportunity as President to advocate the political principles and economic philosophy which I had expressed in the Senate and which I had followed all my political life."

It is amusing, in the light of later claims that my father sabotaged Mr. Roosevelt's New Deal, to recall the squawks of rage this program evoked. Republican House Minority Leader Joseph Martin of Massachusetts said, "Not even President Roosevelt ever asked for as much in one sitting. The scenery is new and there is a little better decoration and he [Mr. Truman] does dish it out a little easier. But it is just a plain case of out New Dealing the New Deal." Representative Charles Halleck of Indiana moaned that it was a call for "more billions and more bureaus." Others took a more cynical view. They thought Truman didn't mean it. The magazine *Nation's Business* assured its readers that "progressive democracy, liberalism and one-worldism" were on the loose in the "oratorical sense" but there was really nothing to worry about since "not in twenty-five years has understanding and cooperation between the White House and Capitol Hill been so cordial, so informal." Behind these smooth words lay the smug assurance that the President was a captive of a conservative Congress.

Before many more weeks passed, a lot of people—particularly members of Congress—learned that my father meant every word of that twenty-one-point message and he had no intention of allowing Congress to smother or ignore it. He did try to restore some of the balance between the President and the Congress, which had swung heavily to the White House side during the war, by refraining from sending completely drafted bills to implement these twenty-one points. President Roosevelt had been in the habit of doing this for legislation he wanted. My father felt strongly that Congress as the legislative branch should write the laws. But he was equally convinced that the President was responsible for seeing that they got written. When the Senate passed a very unsatisfactory unemployment compensation bill and the House Ways and Means Committee, thanks to the usual coalition of Southern conservatives and Republican reactionaries, refused even to bring it to the floor, much less repair it, Dad summoned the Democratic members of the committee to the White House. On his appointment sheet beside their names on September 27, he wrote: "The works and twenty-five dollars. I told 'em either I am the leader of the Dem. Party or I'm not. That the Senate had let me down. They had no right to follow the Senate."

In a letter to his mother and Mary on September 19, Dad made it clear that this was no isolated incident. "I've been raising hell since Monday," he wrote. "From now on that will have to happen, I guess. I hate to do it. But it's my job."

He did not spend all his time raising hell with recalcitrant congressmen. He also tried to approach them as a friend and fellow Democrat, without the prerogatives of his office. On September 22, 1945, he wrote to his mother, "I'm going down to Jefferson Island today to spend the weekend, and talk to a lot of Congressmen and Senators. It won't be a very pleasant time but it may be helpful."

Jefferson Island was in Chesapeake Bay. Dad spent an exhausting Saturday and Sunday there pitching horseshoes, playing cards, eating raw oysters, and trying to do some politicking with the 200 Democratic congressmen who attended the annual affair.

Simultaneously, Dad tried to build up support for his program by making public appearances in various parts of the country. He still could not resign himself to being a prisoner in the White House. But his experience on these brief junkets soon convinced him that moving the President was like "moving a circus" and such trips, if the President was going to survive, had better be made sparingly. On September 15 he flew home to Independence to spend a weekend with his mother, and bring me back to George Washington University. His attempt to be "just plain Harry Truman" in his home town soon threatened Independence and Kansas City with chaos. He dropped into the barber shop of his old friend Frank Spina, who had been a member of his battery. "None of that fancy stuff, I don't want anything that smells," he reminded him as Frank started to cut his hair. The rest of the story Dad tells in a letter to his mother:

> I . . . hadn't been in the chair five minutes until Tenth Street was blocked and the crowd was so thick trying to look into the front window that the police and Secret Service had to push them back. The hall by the elevator was jammed full

of starers also. But Frank finally got the job done. The police made a path for me to the car and we went on to the office. At the Federal Bldg. the steps out in front were full and so was the hallway. It took all the Secret Service men and police to get me to the elevator.

Early in October he flew to Caruthersville, Missouri, to appear at their annual fair. He spent two days there, shaking hands with thousands of people, breakfasting with the ladies of the Baptist Church and lunching with the ladies of the Presbyterian Church, riding a "40 & 8" mock locomotive with a crowd of Legionnaires, presenting a silver loving cup to the winning jockey of the President Truman Derby. One newsman, exhausted from trying to keep up with him, remarked that he had done everything but have himself shot from a cannon. Dad was not enjoying himself very much either, as is evident from this comment to his mother and sister:

> We had a nice time at the Fair if you can call it a nice time to be followed around by thirty newsmen and photographers everywhere and to be mobbed every time an appearance is made . . . I had to ride in an open car and give 'em a Cheshire Cat grin and almost freeze stiff but the onlookers seemed to enjoy it.

From the fair Dad drove to Reelfoot Lake in Tennessee for a day of rest. In a letter written from the White House, he told his mother what happened:

> We were lodged in a beautiful house—but I may as well have been in the center of Chicago so far as rest was concerned. They brought in school children from every school in forty miles, the Legion, the State Police force, and all the state and county officials for ten counties around to see whether a President walked and talked and ate and slept as other folks do—but it was a change of scenery anyway. They were all good people.

Another reason Dad decided against leaving the White House was the crisis atmosphere which prevailed in the country, as America struggled to adjust to the abrupt arrival of peace. On October 13, he wrote his mother, "The pressure here is becoming so great I can hardly get my meals in, let alone do what I want to do." In another letter he summed up part of the problem: "Everybody wants something at the expense of everybody else and nobody thinks much of the other fellow." He also ruefully admitted that he was having trouble with his staff:

> It's funny but I have almost as many prima donnas around me as Roosevelt had, but they are still new at it.
> They don't get humored as much by me as they did by him. I fire one occasionally and it has a salutary effect.

By now my father had enough experience to take a pretty dim view of many of the ultra liberals who had tended to cluster around President Roosevelt. After attending a meeting of the Roosevelt National Memorial Committee in the East Room, he wrote on his appointment sheet: "Same bunch of Prima Donnas who helped drive the Boss to his grave are still riding his ghost."

One of the Truman prima donnas who eventually got the ax was Jake Vardaman. A former St. Louis banker who had served in the army in World War I, he had done some work for Dad in his Senate campaigns, and gone into the navy in World War II. Dad made him his naval aide, and Mr. Vardaman immediately acquired an acute case of Potomac fever. Aboard the presidential yacht he became the sailor par excellence, hurling nautical terms right and left. Before lunch one day he announced that he was going to "break out the silver." This aroused guffaws and hoots from ex-army artillerymen Truman, Vaughan, and Snyder. In the White House Mr. Vardaman proceeded to stick his nose into almost every office and tell them how it should be run. Then he made the blunder of all blunders. He descended upon Mother's side of the White House and started telling *them* how to do the job. That was the end of Mr. Vardaman as naval aide. Dad elevated him to the Federal Reserve Board, and he repaid him for this kindness by voting against every Truman policy for the next seven years. He also went around Washington spreading the nasty story that he was kicked out of the White House because he did not drink or play cards.

A Roosevelt prima donna who was also on his way out at this time was Harold Ickes. A complex man with many good qualities—my father admired him because he had administered the Interior Department with great integrity and complete disregard for special interest pressures—Mr. Ickes had an exaggerated opinion of his own importance. He had brawled repeatedly with President Roosevelt, and at one point had been barred from the White House for six months. He loved a quarrel—the more spectacular the better—which put him and Dad at opposite poles. Worse, Mr. Ickes also loved to gossip. It did not take Dad long to notice that almost everything that was discussed at a Cabinet meeting was paraphrased, after having been dipped in acid, by Drew Pearson on the following day. Dad suspected Mr. Ickes and finally proved it. At Eddie McKim's suggestion, the staff planted a story on "Honest Harold" that they told to no one else. Dad recalls with a grim smile that it too showed up in Mr. Pearson's column. Thereafter, Mr. Ickes's days in the Truman Administration were numbered.

Early in 1946 Mr. Ickes practically handed my father the reason for his resignation. Dad had appointed Ed Pauley Under Secretary of the Navy. He was very impressed by the firmness and negotiating skill Mr. Pauley had displayed in dealing with the Russians on the tricky matter of reparations. James Forrestal, Secretary of the Navy, was already saying he wanted to resign, and Dad thought Mr. Pauley would make an excellent successor—and eventually a very good Secretary of Defense in the unification of the armed forces which was another Truman Administration goal. Ickes, summoned to testify before the Senate committee considering Mr. Pauley, proceeded to accuse him of playing politics with offshore oil reserves. He made this accusation without a shred of evidence to support him, and without even a hint of warning to Dad that he was opposed to Pauley.

Very angry but controlling it, my father said grimly at his next press conference that he backed Pauley, no matter what Mr. Ickes said. Honest Harold immediately sent Dad his resignation, claiming that Dad had publicly displayed his lack of confidence in him—which was the truth. The letter, as my father put it later, was "the sort of resignation a man sent in, knowing it would not be accepted. Honest Harold was more than a little astonished when he got a phone call from the White House informing him that his letter was accepted—immediately. He asked permission to stay on the job another six weeks. Dad gave him two days to clean out his desk.

In spite of all my father's efforts, things did not improve in the country, or in Washington, D.C. A wave of strikes threatened to cripple the economy. Management lobbied fiercely for the removal of wartime price controls. Mournfully, Dad informed his mother and sister that he had canceled plans to come to Kansas City on November 15 and fly on to Oklahoma for another personal appearance on the 18th:

> I am going to have to cancel all my dates for every place until I get things going here. The Congress are balking, labor has gone crazy, and management isn't far from insane in selfishness. My Cabinet, that is some of them, have Potomac fever. There are more Prima Donnas per square foot in public life here in Washington than in all the opera companies ever to exist.

On the international scene my father had to cope with imminent signs of famine in Europe. Reserves of food in the United States had to be rushed across the Atlantic to avert this catastrophe, forcing him to maintain wartime food rationing controls here. Along with the epidemic of labor-management conflicts, Dad had to struggle with increasing pressure to demobilize America's armed forces as quickly as possible. With an aggressive Russia pressing its claims from the Kurile Islands to Iran to Berlin, Dad knew that such a step was not in the best interests of the nation. So did most of his military commanders, and all except one loyally supported him.

My father and his military planners in Washington were operating on figures given them by General Douglas MacArthur that he would need 500,000 men to occupy Japan. On September 18 General MacArthur blithely made a unilateral statement that he would need only 200,000 regular army troops. The White House was forced to issue a special statement on demobilization, promising that no one would be held in the service a day longer than necessary. Dad authorized Acting Secretary of State Dean Acheson —Secretary of State Byrnes was in London for a foreign ministers conference—to make a statement that included the rather harsh words: "The occupation forces are the instruments of policy and not the determinants of policy . . . and whatever it takes to carry this out will be used to carry it out."

Already General MacArthur was arousing my father's political suspicions. Twice in the months after the war ended, Dad invited him to return to Washington, as General Eisenhower had done after the end of the war in Europe, to receive the tribute of a grateful nation. Both times MacArthur refused, pleading the urgency of his duties as commander of the Allied Occupation in Japan. My father suspected that he preferred to await a political summons from the Republican party, so he could combine a triumphal return with a nomination for the presidency.

My father was particularly irked because the demobilization problem was linked with his hopes for one of his most important programs—universal military training. He sent a request for this program up to Congress, and followed it with a speech before a joint session on October 23, 1945. Carefully he pointed out:

> . . . Universal military training is not conscription. The opponents of training have labeled it conscription and by so doing have confused the minds of some of our citizens. Conscription is compulsory service in the army or navy in time of peace or war. Trainees under this proposed legislation, however, would not be enrolled in any of the armed services. They would be civilians in training. They could be no closer to membership in the armed forces than if they had no training. Special rules and regulations would have to be adopted for their organization, discipline, and welfare.

Dad's plan called for a year of training for every young man in the nation, whether physically qualified for actual combat service or not:

> There should be a place into which every young American can fit in the service of our country. But some would be trained for combat, others would be trained for whatever war service they are physically and mentally qualified to perform.

No program that he presented to Congress aroused deeper feelings in Dad than this one. You can sense his anxiety in the words he wrote to his mother a few hours after he made the speech:

> It is 10:40 and I have been listening to a rebroadcast of my address to Congress on military training. When I listen I don't know why they applauded—except maybe because I am the President of the United States and they probably wanted to

be respectful. But in spite of that we need the program which the President urged them to adopt.

Congress refused to agree with him. Dad was terribly frustrated by his failure to get UMT across and he remains frustrated to this day. He is convinced that if we had had universal military training, there would have been no war in Korea, and possibly no war in Vietnam. The Communists would not have dared to challenge us because we would have been ready to respond with maximum strength and maximum speed.

Another of Dad's major frustrations at this time was his inability to create a Missouri Valley Authority, similar to the TVA. This was a dream he had nurtured from his earliest days in the Senate, but it was an enormously complex problem. He began talking about it with David Lilienthal as early as September 18, 1945. In his journal Mr. Lilienthal gives a very realistic description of Dad in action—discussing the problem:

> "In the Missouri Valley—" He took off his glasses and rubbed his eyes. "—that's the hard one . . ." He explained the conflicts between the downstream people and those upriver, how dams below Sioux City wouldn't do, would fill up with silt in a year; there wasn't any power in that part of the river. Flood control dams would have to be built on the little streams and kept empty—and so on, with a loquacity and excited interest that reminded me of his predecessor on such a subject. He went down the list of Senators in each of the nine states—all against MVA except two. "We'll have to figure out something . . . We have got to figure out something that they will accept."

Mr. Lilienthal said he hoped Dad meant that it would be a regional authority that could deal with the people on the spot. He dreaded the possibility that Dad might propose a National River Basin Board, one of the pet ideas of Secretary of the Interior Ickes.

Dad shook his head. "I'm against it. If these things are going to be just part of the bureaus here in Washington we might as well leave them in the hands of Congress."

A relieved Mr. Lilienthal agreed. He said that one of the things about working in a decentralized agency that he liked was that people "can get at you and you feel you are part of their life."

Dad nodded. "Do you know why I go back home every once in a while? So people can kick me around."

Another problem that required a vast amount of my father's time and attention during these first postwar months was atomic energy. His talks with David Lilienthal convinced Dad that this was the perfect man to head the Atomic Energy Commission. He had both the administrative ability and the breadth of vision Dad wanted for this enormously important job. Behind the scenes there was a terrific battle going on between Congress, the White House, and the army about the final control of atomic energy. General Leslie Groves was busily deciding what facts could or could not be disclosed to members of Congress. He was also negotiating agreements with foreign governments to give us access to more uranium, without bothering to tell the State Department.

On October 3, 1945, my father sent a message to Congress, calling for the creation of an Atomic Energy Commission for the development of peaceful domestic uses of the atom, as well as an international atomic policy, which he proceeded to hammer out in conferences with Prime Minister Attlee and Canadian Prime Minister MacKenzie King. After a tremendous amount of wrangling between Congress, the military, and the scientists, some of whom favored military control, Dad settled the dispute by emphatically calling for an AEC composed "exclusively of civilians."

Our atomic energy policy was intimately connected with our relationship to Russia. Some remarks that my father made on this subject in a press conference around this time show how hard he was trying to reach an understanding with Moscow. One reporter asked: "Mr. President, I have read that one of the causes for the lack of accord between this country and Russia grows out of the fact that we have the atomic bomb and Russia doesn't."

"It isn't true. It isn't true at all," Dad said. "The difficulty, I think, is a matter of understanding between us and Russia. That has always been a difficulty, principally because we don't speak the same language. It is a most difficult matter to translate the meaning of what I am saying right now into Russian, so it will mean the same thing in Russian as it means in English. The same thing is true when you translate Russian into English. When I was at the conference with Stalin at Berlin, he had an interpreter and I had one, and it took the four of us to be sure that we each understood the meaning of the other."

Later in the same talk Dad said that he would love to go to Russia. "I think Russia has been badly misrepresented in this country as we have been badly misrepresented in Russia. If there is complete understanding, there wouldn't be very many difficulties between us, because Russia's interests and ours do not clash and never have. We have always been friends and I hope we always will be."

Secretary of State Byrnes found Mr. Molotov totally hostile and disagreeable at the foreign ministers meeting in London. Still my father persisted in hoping for the best, and continued making friendly statements about Russia. At a press conference on October 8 he insisted that the London meeting was not a failure but only one step in arriving at eventual peace settlements. He was not a bit alarmed, he said. He had no doubt that the world situation would work out just as he believed the domestic situation would eventually settle down. He foresaw a new era of international friendliness and understanding.

These words concealed Dad's mounting concern about Russia's intentions and our ability to live in peace with our erstwhile ally. They were consolidating their grip on the countries of eastern Europe and fomenting guerrilla warfare in Greece. Yugoslavia was still insisting on its right to Trieste. The Russian army was showing no sign whatsoever of moving out of Iran, and Stalin was repeating his demands for control of the straits of the Bosporus, which would mean the virtual occupation of Turkey. He wanted to replace our Occupation regime in Japan with a "Control Council," which would have meant the kind of partition that gave him a third of Germany.

To make the situation even more difficult for my father, Secretary of State James F. Byrnes was beginning to act as if he was a totally independent operator. Shortly before he left for another foreign ministers conference—this one in Moscow—he conferred with a group of senators from the Special Committee on Atomic Energy and the Committee on Foreign Relations without bothering to tell the President. Two days later the members of this special committee arrived at the White House in a flap, to inform Dad that his Secretary of State seemed ready to give away vital atomic secrets in Moscow. Dad reported this complaint to Secretary Byrnes but assured him that he was confident the senators were wrong. He wanted the Secretary to have the widest possible latitude to receive any proposals the Russians might make on sharing atomic energy and defusing the atomic arms race.

From December 12 to Christmas Day, when my father left the White House for Independence, Mr. Byrnes was negotiating in Moscow. Dad had expected the teletype in the White House map room to hum with messages detailing Russian proposals, not only on atomic energy, but on the other major problems that Mr. Byrnes was supposed to discuss: the Balkan nations, China, the Japanese Occupation, and—an item which Dad had specifically ordered on the agenda—Russia's refusal to get out of Iran. Instead, there was almost total silence from Moscow. Mr. Byrnes obviously did not feel any need to seek the President's advice.

Mother and I had returned to Independence for a family Christmas. My father stayed in the White House alone, worrying over the silence from Moscow. Writing to his mother on December 24, he explained why he was not coming home until Christmas Day: "It'll take sixteen Secret Service men and about that many newsmen to get me to Kansas City and back. The reason I didn't come sooner was to let all of 'em have Christmas Eve anyway at home."

That same night my father received a very brief message from Secretary Byrnes, giving only an optimistic summary of what had been discussed at Moscow. The next day Dad flew home to Independence and was resting there on December 27 when Charlie Ross called to tell him that Secretary Byrnes wanted the White House to arrange for him to make an all-network speech to the American people on the results of the Moscow conference. Several hours later the State Department's communiqué on the conference was handed to Dad—an hour after it had been released in Washington.

Thoroughly incensed, my father flew back to Washington the next day, to find Senator Vandenberg threatening to resign as Republican spokesman of our bipartisan foreign policy. He thought that Secretary Byrnes had agreed to give the Russians atomic secrets without hammering out inspection safeguards. It took hours to calm him down and issue a statement clarifying the cloudy wording of Secretary Byrnes's communiqué. Later that day

Dad boarded the presidential yacht *Williamsburg* with a number of advisers to work on a major speech he was preparing for January 3. They were anchored off Quantico, Virginia, when Secretary of State Byrnes called from Washington to ask about his all-network broadcast.

Charlie Ross took the call. My father was sitting next to him and told him what to say in reply. "The President asks me to tell you that you had better come down here post haste and make your report to the President before you do anything else."

At 5 P.M. that afternoon the Secretary of State boarded the *Williamsburg* and got a lecture which made it very clear to him that he was not the President of the United States. Harry S. Truman was President and he expected to be the man who made the final decisions on all aspects of our foreign policy. A few days later, after studying the documents Mr. Byrnes brought home from Moscow, Dad summoned him to the White House and read him a long handwritten letter which spelled out in detail his disappointment with Mr. Byrnes's accomplishments at Moscow. He felt we had made concessions—particularly on the matter of recognizing the puppet governments in Rumania and Bulgaria and Poland—in return for very little from the Russians beyond an agreement to continue talking. Dad summed up his position in the last line of his letter: "I'm tired of babying the Soviets."

Two other problems that bother us today began troubling my father in these first postwar months. The first was Palestine. From the moment Dad took office American Jews began pressuring him to support the idea of a Jewish state in Palestine. On April 20, 1945, Rabbi Stephen S. Wise, chairman of the American Zionist Emergency Council, conferred with Dad at the White House, and left declaring that Dad supported Mr. Roosevelt's policy of unrestricted immigration to Palestine.

What Dr. Wise did not know was that President Roosevelt had conferred with King Ibn Saud of Saudi Arabia on the way home from Yalta, and promised this monarch that the United States would confer with Palestine's Arab neighbors before supporting Jewish immigration to that part of the world. The British, who controlled Palestine, were restricting immigration to 1,500 Jews a month—all that the Arabs would tolerate. My father wanted them to admit 100,000 Jews—all of them displaced persons in

[298]

Europe—and behind the scenes he worked very hard to obtain British assent to this plan. He felt that with 600,000 Jews and over 2,000,000 Arabs in Palestine, another 100,000 would not unbalance the population, and at the same time it would be a significant gesture which would stabilize the situation, quiet extremists among the Jews, and give the big powers time to work out a long-term solution. The British refused to budge, and the Arabs made it clear that the 100,000 displaced persons plan was unacceptable to them, too.

While deep in this backstage diplomacy, my father had to fend off pressures from American Jews that he found personally very irritating. They simply refused to face the fact that America had to consider its relations to the Arab nations as well as to a Jewish state that was for the moment only a possibility. Early in September Dad received a letter from his mother, enclosing a request from a Jewish friend of a friend to have the Palestine problem put on the agenda of the London conference. My father came very close to blowing up at this attempt to involve his mother in international politics.

> There isn't a possibility of my intervening in the matter [Dad wrote his mother]. These people are the usual European conspirators and they try to approach the President from every angle. The London conference is for a specific and agreed purpose and if the little country referred to was in any way involved it will have its day in court, but the call will come from the State Department and through regular channels. Don't ever let anybody talk to you about foreign affairs. It is a most touchy subject and especially in that part of the world.

On September 27, 1945, Nathan Straus, president of radio station WMCA in New York City, spent fifteen minutes urging Dad to propose the immediate creation of a Jewish state. On September 29 Dr. Stephen Wise returned for another call, bringing with him Dr. Abba H. Silver, another member of the American Zionist Emergency Council. They warned my father that he was in danger of losing Jewish votes, if he did not act promptly on behalf of Israel. On the same day Joseph Proskauer, president of the American Jewish Committee, a non-Zionist group, and Jacob Blaustein, chairman of the Executive Committee, called to tell

Dad that not all Jews supported the Zionist program, or wanted to see the creation of a separate Jewish state.

In dealing with this confusing, deeply emotional problem, my father insisted on maintaining a realistic view of Middle East politics and the interests of the United States. He felt sorry for the Jewish people, particularly those pathetic survivors of Hitler's concentration camps who were now homeless refugees in Europe. But no President can permit his emotions to interfere with his duty to the American nation. As Dad said in a letter to his mother: "Wish I could accommodate every friend I have in every way they'd like—but I'm in such a position now that I can't do as I please myself! They'll have to bear with me."

When Prime Minister Attlee came to Washington in November to discuss a common policy on atomic energy, he and my father also conferred on Palestine and agreed to set up a joint British-American committee to consider Palestine and recommend a wide-ranging solution early in 1946.

The other problem, at least as tangled as Palestine, was China. Russia showed no sign of leaving Manchuria, which she had occupied at the close of the war with Japan. She was stripping the factories of heavy equipment there and shipping it to Russia and turning over tons of captured Japanese arms to the Chinese Communists. At Yalta and at Potsdam, Stalin had promised to back Chiang Kai-shek as the ruler of China. He had piously declared that he wanted a unified China, free of all foreign influence. It soon became apparent that he meant free of all foreign influence—except Russian.

There were over 1,000,000 Japanese troops in China, and 50,000 American marines, sent there to help keep order and assist the Nationalist Chinese in disarming their ex-enemies. The ambassador to China, Major General Patrick J. Hurley, was an excitable, unstable man, given to wild statements and accusations of disloyalty. He came home from China accusing State Department officials in the American mission there of sabotaging his attempts to create a coherent policy. He had brought the Communist leader, Mao Tse-tung, to Chungking to discuss a coalition government with Chiang Kai-shek's Nationalists. General Hurley thought he had achieved an agreement, but by the time he arrived in Washington, the two parties were no longer speaking to each other and our Embassy in Chungking was reporting that civil war was imminent.

Ambassador Hurley met with my father and discussed the situation. They parted at 11:30 A.M., agreeing that he would return to China as soon as possible to see if he could restore a spirit of co-operation. Less than two hours later Dad received a phone call from a White House reporter informing him that his ambassador had delivered a scorching speech at lunch to newspapermen, attacking "professional diplomats" at the lower levels of the State Department and asserting that the United States had no clear-cut policy toward China.

My father acted swiftly. He knew how much was at stake in China and he reached out for the best possible man to tackle the immense job of bringing order out of the chaos that was threatening there. He called George C. Marshall at his home in Leesburg. The General had just retired from the army and was in fact in the process of carrying his things into the house where he hoped to spend a tranquil old age. "General," Dad said, "I want you to go to China for me."

"Yes, Mr. President," General Marshall said.

That was all there was to it. Not a moment's hesitation, not a breath of complaint about abandoning plans he had made for years. On December 15 General Marshall departed for Chungking. Dad hoped that his prestige could persuade the Chinese to create a unified government—or if worst came to worst and war did break out, he could from his vast military experience give Chiang Kai-shek the advice he needed to win.

It is fascinating to look back on the year 1945 and see the emergence of all the major national and international problems with which my father was to grapple for the next seven years: our relations with Russia, the status of Palestine, the tangle in China, and, on the home front, the struggle between a President who was determined to represent all the people and a Congress inclined to serve special interests. All these gigantic headaches demanded attention, simultaneously. It was easy to see why the President worked an eighteen-hour day.

[CHAPTER]
Fifteen

MY FATHER STARTED THE NEW YEAR—1946—off with a real bang. On January 3 he made a speech to the nation scorching congressional hides for failing to act on his program, and calling on the greatest pressure group in the world—the American people—to put the heat on their lawmakers to get some action. There were growls, howls, and snarls from Congress, of course. On January 7 Dad wrote his mother and sister:

> The Thursday speech seems to have stirred up a terrible row and that was to be expected. Anyway I wouldn't take a word of it back. We do things or we do not and I can't sit still and not tell why nothing is done.

To my father's delight, since he was trying to force the Southern Democrats to vote with their party and stop acting like Republicans, the man who answered his speech with the hottest words was Senator Taft. Gleefully he wrote his sister:

> If I had picked a man to answer the speech, so it would do the most good, I would have picked Taft to do it. He only added fuel to the fire I had already started.

In this letter he added a touching personal note.

> Jim Pendergast, his wife and two daughters, were here with me for dinner last night. They are as nice as they can be and the terrible shadow which old Tom left them always haunts

them. But Jim is a good man and his family are all right. They were my friends when I needed them and I am theirs.

Also on the personal side was another statement: "Margaret is working very hard on her school studies and I hope will come out all right with them." Truer words were seldom written, even by a President. I was finally in the home stretch at George Washington University, but the combination of trying to major in history and be a White House belle at the same time was not easy. In some ways I was finding it as difficult as Dad to face up to the fact that we were living in a goldfish bowl. Everything he said and did was news, everything I said and did was gossip. I couldn't even go to a concert at Constitution Hall and get carried away by the beauty of Lauritz Melchior's voice without getting my name in the paper. I was sitting in the presidential box with four of my friends from George Washington and we applauded Mr. Melchior until our hands ached. The next day I found myself described as leading a "clapping marathon."

"Judging from Margaret's expression leaving the Hall, she enjoyed the concert as much as, well—'The Rugged Path,'" wrote the gossip columnist. "Margaret is still talking about Spencer Tracy in that play." From there the story discussed my possible future career as a singer, my passion for collecting shoes, and my preference in perfume. Dad enjoyed seeing my name in print instead of his own for a change and sent a clipping of the story to his mother. I hated it.

Mother disliked publicity even more than I did. She hates people to fuss over her and, unlike her daughter, dislikes performing in public. Around this time I was her maid of honor at the christening of an army bomber. The air corps was not as efficient as the navy had been for me at the christening of the *Missouri,* and they forgot to score one of the champagne bottles, so that it would break. Mother slammed it against the side of the airplane six times while I smiled fiendishly and said: "If Mother can't break that bottle, nobody can."

"Be quiet," Mother warned me. But I was too old to shush.

"Fine thing for a tennis champion," I told her.

If there was one thing Dad dreaded, it was the thought of someone in his family getting involved in politics. He felt deeply that the Roosevelts had made a serious mistake in this area. He also knew how angry he would get if one of us started to receive the kind of abuse which Mrs. Roosevelt had to endure. All of this feeling rushed into a letter he wrote to his sister Mary on January 16, when she asked his advice about going to an Oklahoma political meeting:

> For goodness sake, refuse it. They are only using you to advertise themselves. You remember what awful places the Roosevelt relatives were in the habit of getting him tied up with. It won't help me a bit for you to go to Oklahoma to a political meeting and it will give these columnists like Pearson and the rest of the gossips a chance to say that my family, particularly the women of my family, are courting the limelight. So please don't go.
>
> Now I don't want to appear to be in the role of a tyrant—but I know politics and political repercussions better than anyone in the family.
>
> I want you and Mamma to have everything I can possibly give you and I want to see you enjoy as many things as you desire but political appearances are not in the category of the enjoyments I anticipate for you.
>
> I have kept Bess and Margaret out of the political picture as much as I can and I am still trying to keep them from being talked about.
>
> This sort of appearance would give all the mudslingers a chance. I have a lot of pleasant things in mind for you if I can ever get this place to run as it should. . . .

Before the month of January was over, the country was in turmoil. Everybody seemed to be out on strike. First General Motors, then the steel workers, then the threat of John L. Lewis and his coal miners. My father was seriously disturbed by the shortsightedness of the nation's labor leaders. He knew they were simply giving ammunition to the reactionaries in Congress and cementing the Southern Conservative–Republican coalition. On January 23, 1946, he wrote a letter to his mother and sister which gave a very clear picture of his thinking:

> Things seem to be going the wrong way here in labor matters but I am hopeful of an ultimate settlement. The steel strike is the worst. We can handle most of the others. People are some-

what befuddled and want to take time out to get a nerve rest. Some want a life guarantee of rest at government expense and some I'm sorry to say just want to raise hell and hamper the return to peacetime production hoping to obtain some political advantage.

The steel people and General Motors I am sure would like to break the unions and the unions would like to break them, so they probably will fight a while and then settle so both will lose and in the long run only the man in the street will pay the bill.

Big money has too much power and so have the unions—both are riding to a fall because I like neither. . . .

My father's paramount goal on the home front was a stabilization of the economy to end forever the boom and bust cycle that had brought the nation to the brink of chaos in the Great Depression. From the beginning, he insisted that this could only be achieved if both labor and management exercised social responsibility. He did everything in his power to persuade both sides to do so. In November, 1945, he had convened a labor-management conference to work out machinery for dealing with major labor disputes. On December 3, 1945, in a special message to Congress, he outlined a fact-finding program which would have established by impartial investigation how much money workers deserved to get, based on their productivity and how much money the company could afford to pay, based on its profits. Dad specified that it was a program that should only be used "sparingly and only when the national public interest requires it." The company would be required to open its books to the fact-finding board, and for thirty days, while the board investigated, it would be unlawful to call a strike or a lockout.

For this attempt to achieve an honest compromise, my father was abused savagely by both labor and management. Philip Murray, the head of the CIO, denounced the Truman Administration for its "abject cowardice." George Meany, secretary-treasurer of the AFL, declared that his union would never accept legislation which "compels workers to work even for a minute against their will." The General Motors Corporation haughtily withdrew from the jurisdiction of a special fact-finding board, appointed by the White House, when the board attempted to consider its ability to pay. With their treasuries full from five years of wartime wages, the unions were almost eager to take on management in a test of strength. The corporations refused to yield unless all controls were lifted from prices—something Dad refused to do.

Never was there a sadder illustration of the limits of a President's power. Dad once defined leadership as the art of persuading people to do what they should have done in the first place. If they bullheadedly refuse to take this advice, there is not much that the leader can do, in a free society. So, by the end of January, 1946, there were 1,000,000 workers out on strike. Before the end of the year, the public would have to endure no less than 5,000 strikes. Dad was not quite as concerned about battles between employers and employees of the Bestwear Button Factory or the Dandy Hat Company. What deeply concerned him were strikes in the basic industries—coal, oil, steel, the railroads—strikes that imperiled the whole American nation. In these disputes he felt that the President must act as the guardian of the people's welfare.

The most painful of these conflicts for my father personally was the railroad strike of May, 1946. As we have seen, he had publicly demonstrated his deep sympathy for railroad workers more than once while he was a senator. They in turn had supported him in 1940, his hour of greatest need. But a railroad strike, coming on the heels of a coal strike, threatened to force a shutdown of thousands of industries and throw the country into chaos. Twenty railroad unions had been negotiating with management for months. A fact-finding board offered a settlement which management accepted and the unions rejected. At Dad's urging, however, eighteen of the rail brotherhoods agreed to continue negotiating. But the Brotherhood of Locomotive Engineers, headed by Alvanley Johnston, and the Brotherhood of Railroad Trainmen, headed by A. F. Whitney, both old friends of Dad, refused to go along. They scheduled a strike for May 18.

My father put his personal labor representative, John R. Steelman, former chief of the Conciliation Service, to work. Three days before the strike deadline Mr. Steelman reported that the eighteen brotherhoods that had agreed to negotiate were ready to accept the original arbitration terms, but Mr. Whitney and Mr. Johnston remained immovable. Dad called them into his office and said: "If you think I'm going to sit here and let you tie up this whole country, you're crazy as hell."

"We've got to go through with it, Mr. President," Mr. Whitney said, "our men are demanding it."

"All right," Dad said. "I'm going to give you the gun. You've got just forty-eight hours—until Thursday at this time—to reach a settlement. If you don't I'm going to take over the railroads in the name of the government."

On Thursday Mr. Whitney and Mr. Johnston still talked strike. My father went before Congress and asked for a law that would enable him to draft strikers against the public interest. He denounced Whitney and Johnston as men who placed their private interests above the welfare of the nation. While he spoke, John Steelman continued to negotiate with the two union leaders. Midway through his speech, Les Biffle, the secretary of the Senate, handed Dad a message. He read it and smiled grimly. "Gentlemen," he said, "the strike has been settled, on terms proposed by the President." Congress exploded with cheers and applause.

An embittered Whitney declared that his union would use $47 million in its treasury to defeat Harry Truman for reelection in 1948. The next day he revised his estimate somewhat, and said they would spend $2,500,000. (In 1948 he changed his mind again and supported Harry Truman for reelection.) CIO spokesmen called Dad the No. 1 strike-breaker of the American bankers and railroads.

These pro-labor critics were baffled when, a few weeks later, my father vetoed the harshly anti-labor Case bill. In their agitation they did not notice that in his railroad strike speech Dad had cautioned Congress against taking vengeance on labor "for the unpatriotic acts of two men." Dad consistently baffled extremists of every stripe throughout his presidency. They did not realize he actually believed the quotation from Mark Twain which he kept on his White House desk: "Always do right. This will gratify some of the people and astonish the rest."

My father had no illusions about the uproar this attitude toward the presidency was likely to cause. On February 9, 1946, he wrote to his sister:

> The Republicans and crackpot Democrats have started out on an organized campaign to discredit me for their own selfish ends. You must not let it worry you and I hope it won't cause you any unhappiness. . . .

On February 20, he elaborated on this subject at more length.

> I suppose the Republicans are happy [he was referring to the
> turbulent labor situation] but it won't be for long. This situa-
> tion had to develop and the sooner the better. You see Hearst
> and McCormick and the bitter-end Republicans had a notion
> they could cajole me into being something besides a forward-
> looking Democrat. I was elected on the Democratic platform
> too—and they seemed to forget that.

Late in February the fire that my father had been trying to
build under Congress produced its first payoff—the Employment
Act of 1946. It was not precisely what he had asked for—it did not
give him enough money to move forcefully on behalf of a full
employment policy. But the act created a Council of Economic
Advisers to give the President the expertise he needed to keep
employment at or near capacity. It marked a major step forward,
beyond the Roosevelt Administration's policy, and Dad made this
clear in his letter to John McCormack, the House majority leader,
urging passage of the bill: "It is time that the people be reassured
by the Congress that the government stands for full employment,
full production, and prosperity, not unemployment and relief."
Once more my father was using his keen sense of the past to
create a policy for the future. He was determined to avoid the
terrible unemployment which shook the nation after World War
I, and to a large extent, he was successful. On March 3 he wrote
his sister:

> Things are looking up, I think. Congress is still balky, but
> maybe we'll have a few good and well deserved funerals—politi-
> cal and real which may help that situation. But we can only
> hope for the best.

While he was conducting these domestic battles, my father was
by no means ignoring the rest of the world. News from Russia
was, as usual, in the forefront of his thoughts. All of it was dismaying in the light of his continuing hope that he could work
out a settlement with Stalin. On February 9, 1946, the Russian
dictator had made a speech in Moscow on the eve of a so-called
election. It was a brutal, blunt rejection of any hope of peace with
the West. Stalin blamed World War II on capitalism, and declared

that as long as capitalists controlled any part of the world, there was no hope of peace. The Soviet Union must rearm, and forget all about producing consumer goods. He called for trebling Russian production of iron, steel, and coal and doubling all production to "guarantee our country against any eventuality."

A few days later a long dispatch from George F. Kennan, the chargé d'affaires in Moscow, arrived in the State Department. An expert on Russia, who had been studying that country for over thirty years, Mr. Kennan analyzed the Russian approach to the world, not from the viewpoint of communism but from the far more profound viewpoint of Russian history. "At the bottom of the Kremlin's neurotic view of world affairs is the traditional and instinctive sense of insecurity," Mr. Kennan wrote—an insecurity based on the feeling which Russia's Communist rulers shared with the czars that "their rule was relatively archaic in form, fragile and artificial in psychological foundations, unable to stand comparison or contact with political systems of Western countries." Stripped of their Marxist justifications, Kennan said that the Soviet leaders would "stand before history, at best, as only the last of that long succession of cruel and wasteful Russian rulers who have relentlessly forced the country on to ever new heights of military power in order to guarantee the external security of their internally weak regimes."

This report, eventually published as "The Sources of Soviet Conduct" in the July 1947 issue of the magazine *Foreign Affairs,* signed by "X," has been considered one of the primary documents of the cold war, and the assumption seems to have been made by numerous historians that it profoundly shaped the thinking of the Truman Administration. I can say without qualification that such an assertion is nonsense. George Elsey, who had by this time emerged from the obscurity of the map room to become one of Dad's administrative assistants, confirms my impression that the Kennan Report did not strike anyone in the White House as particularly surprising. "Essentially it didn't tell us anything we didn't already know," Mr. Elsey says. Whatever shock value the report achieved was on those wishful thinkers who bought the gospel preached by Henry Wallace and Senator Claude Pepper of Florida, that the trouble with Russia was all America's fault. It was terribly tempting to believe that peace could be achieved, if only we were more agreeable. At this point in 1946, Mr. Wallace and his imitators had a very large following.

My father attempted to defuse Mr. Wallace politically by bringing into his Cabinet a man whom he was told would be a moderate liberal voice—Justice William O. Douglas. He sent James Forrestal, his Secretary of the Navy, to ask Mr. Douglas to become Secretary of the Interior. Mr. Forrestal, who himself had no doubts about Russia's aggressive intentions, noted in his diary that Mr. Douglas called Stalin's speech "the declaration of World War III." But he could not persuade the Justice to accept the President's invitation.

While the professional liberals were creating the illusion of easy compromise, my father was getting reports of continuing Russian pressure, all over the world. Lieutenant General John R. Hodge, commanding the American forces in Korea, warned that the Communists showed absolutely no interest in reuniting the country, except on their own terms. They had launched a brilliant propaganda campaign, selling themselves as saviors of the 30,000,000 Korean people. On May 3, 1946, Dad received a query from General Joseph T. McNarney, commander of the United States forces in Europe, asking for instructions if—it seemed very likely at the time—the Communists should attempt a coup d'état in France. In Iran they were playing the same game, fomenting civil strife through a Communist front organization. My father authorized Secretary of State Byrnes to begin making speeches telling the American people the truth about Russia. But he himself did not feel ready to commit the immense prestige of the presidency behind an anti-Russian position. He wanted peace in the world too deeply to give up hope, even though hope was ebbing fast.

In the midst of this mounting tension, Dad had to take a trip to Missouri with his good friend Winston Churchill. To understand how this happened, I have to backtrack a little. Not long after Dad returned from Potsdam, the president of Westminster College, in Fulton, Missouri, paid a visit to General Vaughan in the White House. The president's name was Frank McCluer, and he and General Vaughan had been classmates there. Dr. McCluer, who was known as "Bullet" because he was only five feet tall and shaped, so General Vaughan says, like a projectile, wanted to invite Winston Churchill to speak at the college. General Vaughan brought Dr. McCluer in to see Dad. He read the letter Dr.

McCluer was sending to Mr. Churchill and scribbled on the bottom of it: "Dear Winnie, This is a fine old school out in my state. If you come and make a speech there, I'll take you out and introduce you."

So, on March 3, at 3 P.M., Dad, General Vaughan, Mr. Churchill, and the usual entourage of Secret Service men and aides boarded the B&O at the Silver Spring, Maryland, station. They had a delightful time on the way out. Dad assigned General Vaughan to keep Mr. Churchill liberally supplied with his favorite liquid refreshment. When the General delivered the first drink, Mr. Churchill held it up to the light, and said, "When I was a young subaltern in the South African war, the water was not fit to drink. To make it palatable we had to add whiskey. By diligent effort I learned to like it."

Dad proposed to teach Mr. Churchill the intricacies of poker, about which he claimed to know nothing. He soon had the poker-playing Missourians doubled up with comments such as, "I think I'll risk a few shillings on a pair of knaves." But their laughter dwindled as he displayed a startling knowledge of the game, plus some sly remarks that he had played something like it during the Boer War.

In Fulton, Missouri, Mr. Churchill's desire for liquid refreshment became something of a problem. Fulton was a dry town. Dad ordered General Vaughan to spare no effort or expense to find their speaker a drink. After some frantic scouting, the General produced the wherewithal and arrived in Mr. Churchill's room, liquor and ice water in hand. "Well, General, I am glad to see you," said the guest of honor. "I didn't know whether I was in Fulton, Missouri, or Fulton, Sahara."

Less than an hour later my father introduced Mr. Churchill. From the hindsight of the furor Mr. Churchill's speech caused, Dad's introductory words are worth repeating.

> I had never met Mr. Churchill personally until a conference we had with Mr. Stalin. I became very fond of both of them. They are men and they are leaders in this world today when we need leadership. . . . I understand that Mr. Churchill is going to talk about the sinews of peace. I know he will have something constructive to say to the world. . . .

Mr. Churchill proceeded to denounce Russian aggression in magnificently chosen words. The most memorable of these became part of the vocabulary of our era.

> From Stettin in the Baltic to Trieste in the Adriatic, an iron curtain has descended across the continent. From what I have seen of our Russian friends and allies during the war, I am convinced that there is nothing they admire so much as strength and there is nothing for which they have less respect than for military weakness.

Mr. Churchill urged an Anglo-American "fraternal association" to stop Russia's persistent aggression.

Up and down the United States and around the world the speech created headlines. It was the first bold denunciation of Russia's tactics by a man of Mr. Churchill's stature. Bert Andrews of the New York *Herald Tribune* echoed most of the press when he wrote that on the evidence of my father's applause at one point in Mr. Churchill's speech and the fact that he had read the speech before delivery, "Mr. Truman went along largely with what Mr. Churchill had to say, if not entirely."

The truth is the precise opposite, and I have before me as I write the best possible evidence—my father's comment on the speech, in his letter of March 11 to his mother and sister. "I'm glad you enjoyed Fulton," he wrote. "So did I. And I think it did some good, *although I am not yet ready to endorse Mr. Churchill's speech.*" (The italics are mine.) Dad did not have the slightest idea what Mr. Churchill was going to say at Fulton until they met in the White House before boarding the train to Missouri. He approved of *Mr. Churchill* saying it, because he was not a head of state. In fact the ex-prime minister made a point of reminding his listeners that he represented no one but himself. My father in no sense considered the speech a break with Russia, nor did he want one. In fact, he later invited Marshal Stalin to come to Missouri and deliver a speech, stating Russia's point of view on the various disputes that were imperiling the peace.

There is also the report of General Walter Bedell Smith, our new ambassador to Russia, of his interview with Stalin on April 5, 1946. General Smith began the interview with a question which my father had instructed him to ask. "What does the

Soviet Union want and how far is Russia going to go?" He went on to assure Stalin that America deeply sympathized with the suffering that the Soviet people had endured during the war and understood Russia's desire for security and a share of the world's raw materials. But they could not tolerate Russia's methods in seeking these objectives. At the same time General Smith insisted that we had no aggressive plans. He pointed out how swiftly we were demobilizing our armed forces and insisted we asked nothing of Russia but the support of the principles of the United Nations Charter.

Stalin replied with grim evidence of his paranoia. He accused the United States of allying itself with Great Britain to "thwart Russia." He declared that Churchill's speech at Fulton was an unfriendly act. "Such a speech if directed against the United States would never have been permitted in Russia." Never was there more tragic evidence of the Russian dictator's complete inability to understand a free society.

General Smith could only reiterate that we had no intention of allying ourselves with Great Britain. He said the Iron Curtain speech reflected no more than "an apprehension which seems to be common to both the United States and Britain." Finally, he asked Stalin once more, "How far is Russia going to go?"

Coolly, Stalin replied, "We're not going much further." That, it seems to me, is an admission that he had already gone pretty far and knew it.

Stalin ended the interview by reaffirming his desire for peace and refusing my father's invitation to visit the United States. "Age has taken its toll. My doctors tell me I must not travel, and I am kept on a strict diet," he said. "I will write to the President, thank him and explain the reasons why I cannot now accept."

On the same day that General Smith was having this confrontation with Stalin, Senator Claude Pepper of Florida was denouncing Winston Churchill's Fulton speech and warning the United States against becoming "a guarantor of British imperialism." He urged a foreign policy based on a climactic Big Three conference that would settle everything. But before the conference began, we should "destroy every atomic bomb which we have" and dismantle our atomic factories.

People like Senator Pepper made it immensely difficult for my father to conduct a sane, coherent foreign policy. In the Cabinet meeting of April 19, Secretary of State Byrnes complained mightily of the damage they were doing. For months we had been negotiating with Iceland to continue the use of the immense air base we had built there during World War II. There was an active Communist party in Iceland, and the island's premier was anxious to negotiate an agreement quietly. But Senator Pepper and Secretary Wallace suddenly rose up and denounced the idea of a base in Iceland as hostile to Russia. Immediately Iceland's Communists raised a terrific uproar, making an agreement with us politically impossible for the premier.

My father knew that he could not tolerate this kind of sabotage —the word he used to describe the activities of Wallace and his followers—indefinitely. But to smack him down at the wrong moment might endanger our relations with Russia. Also there was the political value of keeping his supporters in the Democratic party. So, as with the Russians, Dad tried to be patient and hope for the best.

But Henry Wallace, like Jimmy Byrnes, thought he should have been President. This lent an inevitable arrogance to his actions. I don't deny, at the same time, that he meant well. The situation was complicated by the fact that Dad liked him personally and admired his soaring idealism. But Mr. Wallace lacked what the French call *mesure* and what Missourians call common sense.

In March, before Walter Bedell Smith left for Moscow, Mr. Wallace usurped the role of both the President and the Secretary of State by advising the new ambassador on how to launch a "new approach" to Moscow. He followed this up with a letter to Dad, outlining his ideas. Dad ignored him—the politest way he could think of telling Mr. Wallace that he was not the Secretary of State.

On July 23 Mr. Wallace wrote another letter—twelve pages of single-spaced typing—which accused the United States of threatening Russia and paying only lip service to peace at the conference table. He accused us of trying "to build up a preponderance of force to intimidate the rest of mankind," and heaped scorn on my father's attempt to create a step-by-step program to internationalize atomic energy. He also accused the administration of encouraging military men who favored a "preventive war" with Russia.

Secretary of State Byrnes was about to depart for the Paris Peace Conference, where many issues raised at Potsdam a year earlier were coming to a boil. Once more Mr. Wallace was trying to alter U.S. foreign policy. This time my father wrote him a polite note, thanking him for his advice and sending a copy of the letter to Secretary Byrnes. Firmness had been Mr. Byrnes's byword since Dad stiffened his backbone after the Moscow conference, and Dad made it clear that he was still behind this policy by joining some 3,000 Washingtonians—including members of Congress, the Chief Justice of the United States, members of the Cabinet, and assorted friends—who saw Secretary Byrnes off at the National Airport. "The country is behind Mr. Byrnes in his effort to get a just peace for the world, a peace founded on the Atlantic Charter and the Charter of the United Nations on which this country squarely stands, now—and from this time forward," Dad said.

On September 10 Mr. Wallace came to the White House for a fifteen-minute appointment with my father, to discuss Department of Commerce affairs. He brought with him a copy of a speech which he told Dad he planned to deliver in New York on September 12. Would he like to look at it? Dad thumbed through it rapidly, while Mr. Wallace pointed to pertinent remarks that he thought my father would like. The most important of these was the sentence, "I am neither anti-British nor pro-British—neither anti-Russian nor pro-Russian." At numerous points in the speech Mr. Wallace sharply criticized Russian policies and attitudes. Dad got the distinct impression that Mr. Wallace was moving much closer to the Truman point of view on Russia, and he told him he was delighted to hear him saying these things, and even more pleased to see him taking to the hustings in an election year. The 1946 congressional elections were only two months away, and the Democrats needed all the help they could get.

On the morning of September 12 my father had a press conference. Mr. Wallace had released the text of his speech the night before. Reporters asked Dad about a sentence which Mr. Wallace had inserted in the speech, after he left the White House. It followed the sentence about being neither pro-British nor anti-Russian. "When President Truman read these words, he said they represented the policy of this administration."

"That is correct," Dad said.

This was nothing but the simple truth. But the trouble began when the same reporter asked, "My question is, does that apply just to that paragraph or to the whole speech?"

"I approved the whole speech," Dad said.

Once more my father had made the mistake of trusting someone. Like the seemingly sweet and honest girl from *American Magazine,* who hoodwinked him into endorsing an attack on the Roosevelt Administration, Henry Wallace had cajoled him into this generous but inaccurate remark.

I am trying to be objective when I say this, and perhaps I am being too hard on my father. When I discussed this bit of history with Matt Connelly recently, Matt said bluntly: "It was nothing but a double cross. Wallace showed the President one speech and made a different one."

There is some truth to those words. Listeners that night heard Mr. Wallace make a bitter attack on the foreign policy of the Truman Administration. At least four times he departed from his text to add three or four wildly pro-Russian sentences which brought roars of approval from the crowd. He also dropped most of his qualifying criticisms of the Soviet Union. He did not have the courage to make them before his vociferously pro-Soviet audience, which had been whipped to a frenzy by the extravagant remarks of the speaker who preceded him, Senator Claude Pepper.

A global uproar exploded. Senator Robert A. Taft declared that "the Democratic party is so divided between Communism and Americanism, that its foreign policy can only be futile and contradictory and make the United States the laughingstock of the world." Senator Arthur H. Vandenberg, in Paris with Secretary of State Byrnes, angrily declared that "the Republican party could only co-operate with one Secretary of State at a time." The Republican National Committee charged that the President had "betrayed Mr. Byrnes and was bidding for the support of the CIO Political Action Committee which favored appeasing the Russians abroad and promoting Communism at home." Representative Eugene Cox of Georgia telegraphed Dad that the speech was "the worst thing that could have happened to the country."

Two days later, September 14, my father tried to repair the damage. He issued a statement explaining that he only approved the right of the Secretary of Commerce to deliver the speech:

> I did not intend to indicate that I approved the speech as constituting a statement of the foreign policy of this country.

There has been no change in the established foreign policy of our government. There will be no significant change in that policy without discussion and conference among the President, the Secretary of State and Congressional leaders.

But Henry Wallace refused to shut up. Obviously enjoying the furor, he announced that he planned to make more foreign policy speeches and leaked to Drew Pearson the text of his July 23 letter to Dad. Charlie Ross, in one of his few mistakes of judgment, decided to release the letter to all the reporters, a decision my father angrily countermanded. He did not want to show even the slightest sign of approving the letter's contents. The release of this confidential letter infuriated Dad. On September 18 he summoned Mr. Wallace to the White House for a long conference. In a letter Dad wrote to his mother and sister, before the meeting, he remarked:

> I'm still having Wallace trouble [he then wrote over Wallace in tiny print "Henry," to make sure his mother wouldn't think he was feuding with his in-laws] and it grows worse as we go along. I think he'll quit today and I won't shed any tears. Never was there such a mess and it is partly my making. But when I make a mistake it is a good one.

After two and a half hours of discussion, Mr. Wallace declined to quit. Dad summed up what he had heard in a memorandum the following day:

> Mr. Wallace spent two and one half hours talking to me yesterday. I am not sure he is as fundamentally sound intellectually as I had thought. He advised me that I should be far to the "left" when Congress was not in session and that I should move right when Congress is on hand and in session. He said that FDR did that and that FD never let his "right" hand know what his "left" hand did.
>
> He is a pacifist one hundred percent. He wants us to disband our armed forces, give Russia our atomic secrets and trust a bunch of adventurers in the Kremlin Politburo. I do not understand a "dreamer" like that. The German-American Bund under Fritz Kuhn was not half so dangerous. The Reds, phonies and the "parlor pinks" seem to be banded together and are becoming a national danger.
>
> I am afraid that they are a sabotage front for Uncle Joe

Stalin. They can see no wrong in Russia's four and one half million armed forces, in Russia's loot of Poland, Austria, Hungary, Rumania, Manchuria. They can see no wrong in Russia's living off the occupied countries to support the military occupation.

But when we help our friends in China who fought on our side it is terrible. When Russia loots the industrial plant of those same friends it is all right. When Russia occupies Persia for oil that is heavenly although Persia was Russia's ally in the terrible German war. We sent all our supplies which went to Russia by the Southern Route through Persia—sent them with Persia's help.

The most my father could extract from Mr. Wallace was a promise to keep quiet as long as the Paris Peace Conference lasted. This agreement lasted only for the time it took Mr. Wallace to reach the reporters who were waiting for him in the White House lounge. There he proceeded to start quoting Dad again. "I found the President is confident that we can keep peace with Russia," he intoned. He added that he would not make any more campaign speeches for the Democratic party. If he could not talk about foreign policy, he could not talk about anything.

In a letter to his mother, written the following day, my father explained what happened in terms that I think are much too charitable for what Mr. Wallace did:

> Henry is the most peculiar fellow I ever came in contact with. I spent two hours and a half with him . . . arguing with him to make no speeches on foreign policy—or to agree to the policy for which I am responsible—but he wouldn't. So I asked him to make no more speeches until Byrnes came home. He agreed to that, and he and Charlie Ross and I came to what we thought was a firm commitment that he say nothing beyond the one-sentence statement we agreed he should make. Well, he answered questions and told his gang over at the Commerce all that had taken place in our interview. It was all in the afternoon Washington News yesterday, and I was never so exasperated since Chicago.

This is what finished Wallace with my father. The following day Secretary of State Byrnes sent a memorandum to Dad warning him that he could not function as Secretary of State if Wallace continued his criticism of our foreign policy. Since Dad was already holding Mr. Byrnes's resignation in his desk drawer—they had agreed to part the previous April and Mr. Byrnes was staying only long enough to complete the German peace negotiations—this was not exactly the terrifying threat that Mr. Byrnes made it seem in his memoirs. It was what Mr. Wallace had already said, and his friends were now embellishing, that decided my father. The New York *Herald Tribune* ran a story quoting friends who explained that Mr. Wallace meant it literally when he told reporters the previous day that he could not campaign for the Democratic party "because I am an honest man."

The following day my father telephoned Mr. Wallace and asked for his resignation. Two hours later Dad called a press conference and told reporters:

> The foreign policy of this country is the most important question confronting us today. Our responsibility for obtaining a just and lasting peace extends not only to the people of this country but to the nations of the world.
>
> The people of the United States may disagree freely and publicly on any question, including that of foreign policy, but the government of the United States must stand as a unit in its relations with the rest of the world.
>
> I have today asked Mr. Wallace to resign from the Cabinet. It had become clear that between his views on foreign policy and those of the administration—the latter being shared, I am confident, by the great body of our citizens—there was a fundamental conflict.
>
> We could not permit this conflict to jeopardize our position in relation to other countries.

A week later Dad told his mother and sister:

> The Wallace affair seems to have straightened out and I am very glad he is gone. He simply could not be a part of the team and it had to come some time.
>
> Coming before an election, no one could say he'd been mistreated after it. Anyway, the country's foreign policy is of more importance than the election.

Those were brave words, and Dad meant them. At the same time he could not conceal from himself or from those around him his deep concern about the impact of the Wallace blow-up on the congressional elections. On September 18, in the midst of the turmoil, he wrote a letter to me in which he said:

> To be a good President I fear a man can't be his own mentor. He can't live the Sermon on the Mount. He must be a Machiavelli, Louis XI of France, Caesar, Borgia, Napoleon's chief minister whose name has escaped me [above this clause he later wrote Talleyrand], a liar, double-crosser and an unctuous religio (Richelieu), a hero and a what-not to be successful. So I probably won't be, thanks be to God. But I'm having a lot of fun trying the opposite approach. Maybe it will win.

Alas, the Democrats did not win the 1946 elections. Probably nothing my father could have said or done would have changed the results. But Dad added to his woes by making one of the few serious political mistakes of his life. He accepted the advice of Bob Hannegan, the party's national chairman and the man who had hitherto displayed good political judgment, that it would be better if the President did not campaign. Polls showed that the combination of the Henry Wallace incident and the continuing drumfire of press criticism had sent Dad's popularity plummeting. Mr. Hannegan seemed to think that the less the voters saw of the President, the better it would be for the party. Dad would never have accepted this approach if he had thought that real trouble was brewing. But Mr. Hannegan combined this advice with a curious (in retrospect) optimism. At a Cabinet meeting on October 18 he reported that everything looked rosy, although he admitted to worries about Missouri, Kentucky, and Pennsylvania.

Bereft of national leadership, Democratic congressmen tried to run on their own, or in some cases on Franklin D. Roosevelt's ghost. A few congressmen actually played recordings of FDR's voice. My father maintained his silent act, even when he returned home to Independence to vote. We went by special train, but he did not make a single whistle-stop speech. Even in Missouri, where the train stopped three times, he only came out on the rear platform and shook hands with local politicians. At Jefferson City school children were let out of classes for an hour to meet the train. The kids begged him to make a two-hour speech. But Dad only wagged his finger at them, and clamped his hand across his mouth. Sam Rayburn, who rode out to St. Louis with us en route home to Texas, predicted that Dad would tear the Republicans apart at the traditional Democratic rally in Independence on November 1. But Dad turned thumbs down on this idea, as well as on the pleas of some Democrats to make an election-eve radio speech.

Mamma Truman, a keen political observer in her own right, may have been expressing her concern, as well as her tart sense of humor, when General Vaughan asked her on election morning if she had voted on the way down to see her son in Independence.

"I certainly did," she replied, "and I am thinking of voting again on my way home."

Perhaps Mr. Hannegan's political strategy might have worked—although I personally doubt it—if John L. Lewis had not decided he was bigger than the President of the United States and smarter than any other politician in the country. In the spring of 1946, while my father was struggling to keep the railroads going, he had settled a nationwide coal strike called by Mr. Lewis by taking over the mines and forcing the mine owners to give Mr. Lewis's miners what the UMW leader had called at the time the best contract he ever signed. In September and October Mr. Lewis began quarreling with the government administrator who was supervising the mines. The disagreements, Dad said, "were nothing of vital importance—purely details of interpretation of the contract that could have been settled easily by a half-hour discussion."

On November 1, with the cold winter weather just beginning across the nation, Mr. Lewis announced that he considered the contract null and void and was taking his miners out on strike. Apparently Mr. Lewis was gambling on two possibilities—that he could embarrass the President of the United States into more humiliating concessions on election eve or that he could browbeat the electorate into sending a pro-labor Congress to Washington—possibly both. Mr. Lewis was an arrogant man whose ambitions were almost boundless.

This time Mr. Lewis lost both his gambles. The President of the United States refused to make a single concession to settle the illegal strike. The American voters were enraged by Mr. Lewis's arrogant flouting of the law and obvious assumption that he was a privileged character. They voted pro-labor Democrats into oblivion by the dozen and sent to Congress a thoroughly reactionary majority.

On Wednesday, November 6, my father awoke aboard his special train, en route to Washington, and discovered that he had a bad cold and a Republican Congress. He immediately decided he needed a new national chairman for the Democratic party and a new strategy to deal with what promised to be a thoroughly hostile Congress and a dispirited Democratic party. Only 34,000,000 people had voted in the election—which meant that millions of Democrats had stayed home.

Defeatism was rampant. On November 7 Senator J. William Fulbright of Arkansas made the brilliant suggestion that my father appoint Senator Arthur Vandenberg as Secretary of State and then resign, making Senator Vandenberg President, so the Republicans could control both the executive and the legislative branches of the government. Dad ignored this bit of idiocy. Believe it or not, some reporters took it seriously, and Charlie Ross, in response to questions, had to issue a formal denial that the President planned to resign. Dad also quietly rejected less pretentious advice offered him by James Forrestal, his Secretary of the Navy. Mr. Forrestal urged him to try to work out a nonpartisan approach with Congress in crucial areas, such as labor legislation, foreign affairs, Palestine, and national defense. "He agreed to the principle," Mr. Forrestal noted in his diary, "but I am a little depressed by the fact that he seems to feel that not much will come of such an attempt, that political maneuvering is inevitable, politics in our government being what they are."

My father knew what was coming from the Republican Congress and he moved swiftly and decisively to seize the political initiative. On November 11, 1946, he issued a statement pledging his co-operation with Congress and calling for the exercise of wisdom and restraint and the "constant determination to place the interest of our country above all other interests."

That same day he wrote one of his interesting letters to his mother and sister. It is a good glimpse of the constant mixture of domestic and international politics in Dad's mind.

Dear Mamma & Mary:
Well I had a press conference this morning and I think I took all the fire out of the Republican victory. Then I went

out to the Arlington Memorial to the tomb of the Unknown Soldier, laid a wreath and made a speech to the National Guard of the United States. The Secretary of War and the Secretary of the Navy were with me at Arlington.

It is an impressive ceremony. I have been officially present three times. In 1944 I was there as V.P. elect while Mrs. Roosevelt laid the flowers—and was not so cordial to me as she would have been to Henry Wallace under the same circumstances. But she has reformed I think. Because I had a very cordial letter from her on the election, in which she said she was sure I would have no more—and maybe not as much trouble with the Congress coming up than I had with the supposedly Democratic Congress I had had for the last two years. She may be right. Anyway Henry Wallace and Claude Pepper will be in the minority and that is helpful.

Last year Mr. Attlee, the British Prime Minister and Mr. MacKenzie King, the Canadian Prime Minister were present with me when I laid the wreath. Mr. King was here last week and we had a most pleasant visit. He is an honest man. I can always get along with an honest man.

Mr. Molotov was here a couple of days ago and I smiled at him and had the usual pictures taken. But—I'm sure Mr. Molotov is not so honest! He represents a totalitarian state—a police government. Really there is no difference between the government which Mr. Molotov represents and the one the Czar represented—or the one Hitler spoke for. I'm told that there are more than fifteen millions of people in concentration camps and at slave labor in Russia today; and I'm inclined to believe it. They are kidnapping Germans, they have Japanese, Lithuanians, Estonians, Latvians, Poles, Finns, they are making to work against their wills. How can I deal with such terrible conditions? I don't want to go to war with them. I hope we don't have to go to war again for six hundred years. Maybe we won't have to!

Meanwhile, Dad's cold persisted and he developed a most annoying cough. Dr. Graham began to worry about him and decreed that a vacation was in order. Where does a President vacation? It was no small task to find a place that could accommodate twenty or thirty reporters, a staff of sixteen, and another fifteen or sixteen Secret Service men. After some investigation Dad made a choice which he never regretted—the submarine base at Key

West, Florida. On November 18 he wrote his mother and sister from there, obviously delighted with the place:

> Dear Mamma & Mary:— It was nice to talk with you even if they did cut us off at the end. I hope you are both in health and that you are having nice weather as we are here.
>
> I left Washington yesterday morning in a rain and a fog with the temperature at 40°. Arrived here at 3 P.M. in sunshine and 80°. They put me up in a southern built house with "galleries" all around, upstairs and down. It is the commandant's house—and at present there is no commandant—so I did not "rank" anyone out of his house.
>
> I have arranged a schedule so that I get up at 7:30 (two hours later than I usually do), go over and have a swim, have breakfast at nine and then go to a nice sand beach a half mile away and get sun and sea water. Come back at noon, have lunch at one and then a nap and sit around and talk until dinner at seven, go to bed when I get ready and then do it over. I've just returned from the beach after trying out the schedule and my cough and cold are nearly gone already.
>
> I am seeing no outsiders. From now on I'm going to do as I please and let 'em all go to hell. At least for two years they can do nothing to me and after that it doesn't matter.

Refreshed by five days of sun and thoroughly imbued with the determination expressed in the last line of this letter, my father flew home to do battle with John L. Lewis. He had kept in close touch with the efforts to head off the strike, which Mr. Lewis had set for November 20. In a memorandum he wrote on December 11, Dad described the strategy which he had outlined:

> I discussed the situation with the secretaries in the White House at the morning meeting after the strike call, and informed them it was a fight to the finish. At the Cabinet meeting on Friday, before the election, the Attorney General was instructed to take such legal steps as would protect the government. Discussions were held with the Cabinet and special meetings were called. . . . The instructions were fight to the finish.

My father knew exactly what Mr. Lewis had in mind. The Secretary of the Interior, Julius Krug, told him that Lewis was boasting he would "get Krug first . . . and then he would wait until 1948 to get the President." In a meeting at Key West, Dad and his aides hammered out the final strategy. Two days before Mr. Lewis's strike call date, Attorney General Tom Clark served an injunction on Mr. Lewis, issued by Federal District Judge T. Allen Goldsborough. Mr. Lewis defied it, and his miners struck. The government's lawyers argued that it was a strike against the government, and hence the injunction was legal. The court found in favor of this argument, and Mr. Lewis was ordered to stand trial for contempt. On December 4, 1946, he was fined $10,000 personally, and the union was fined $3,500,000.

"Bushy-browed John L.," as Dad called him in one of his letters around this time, announced he would appeal to the Supreme Court. Charlie Ross announced that the President was going on the air that night to make a direct appeal to the miners to go back to work. Faced with the threat of annihilation of his prestige and authority as a union leader, Mr. Lewis capitulated. On December 7 he ordered his miners back to work "immediately, under the wages and conditions of employment in existence on and before November 20, 1946." Two days later Dad wrote to his mother and sister:

> Well, John L. had to fold up. He couldn't take the gaff. No bully can. Now I have the auto workers, steel workers and RR men to look forward to. They'll get the same treatment if they act the same way.

From now on there would be no doubt in anyone's mind about who was in charge of the White House.

Sixteen

Dear Daddy,
   Please sign your John Hancock on these 11 dollar bills for Rosalind. Thank you. (Don't you have a single pen that works?)
                                                                    Sistie
   You didn't try all of them.
                                                                    Dad

As you can see from the preceding exchange, the Trumans did not let John L. Lewis, Stalin, Molotov, Henry Wallace, et al., ruin their high spirits. When we were together as a family, we acted pretty much as we always did, constantly teasing each other and playing jokes at every opportunity. Dad's favorite sport was selecting the most outrageous tie he could find—I sometimes think he sent General Vaughan or one of his other pals out on special expeditions to find some of his worst horrors—and wearing it to breakfast. He would sit there with great aplomb, ignoring insults re color blindness and bad taste from me and Mother.

One night, early in our White House sojourn, I invited two friends to spend the night with me in Lincoln's bed. Dad heard about it and conjured up a fiendish plan to scare the life out of us. Mayes, one of the White House butlers, was a tall, rather cadaverous man who resembled Old Abe. Dad decided to put his presidential high hat on Mayes's head and pop him in the doorway of our room at the stroke of midnight. Mr. President rushed downstairs in search of his accomplice and discovered to his chagrin that Mayes was not on duty. Mayes later confided to me that he had no desire whatsoever to play an apparition, and was very glad that he was not working that night.

Although he treated the subject lightly, Dad sometimes liked to think that the White House was haunted. Early in September, 1946, he sent Mother a letter describing how he woke up in the middle of the night, distinctly hearing a knock on the door of his bedroom. He listened and the sound was repeated. He got up and went to the door, opened it and nothing was there. But he heard the sound of footsteps moving down the hall. In a letter to me, written around the same time, he said:

> I told your mother a "hant" story which you'd better have her read to you. This old place cracks and pops all night long and you can very well imagine that old Jackson or Andy Johnson or some other ghost is walking. Why they'd want to come back here I could never understand. It's a nice prison but a prison nevertheless. No man in his right mind would want to come here of his own accord.

A few days later, he commented again about visiting spirits:

> Now about those ghosts. I'm sure they're here and I'm not half so alarmed at meeting up with any of them as I am at having to meet the live nuts I have to see every day. I am sure old Andy could give me some good advice and probably teach me some good swear words to use on Molotov and de Gaulle. And I am sure old Grover Cleveland could tell me some choice remarks to make to some political leaders . . . I know. So I won't lock my doors or bar them either if any of the old coots in the pictures out in the hall want to come out of their frames for a friendly chat.

One night early in 1946, as we were getting ready for a big reception at the White House, Dad remarked that Senator Bricker was among the invited guests. This led to some rather acid comments about the senator's failure to send him a congratulatory telegram after the 1944 elections.

Only a day or two earlier King Ibn Saud of Arabia had sent Dad a magnificent gold scimitar with a priceless diamond in the handle surrounded by emeralds and rubies. "If you trip old

Bricker when he comes down the receiving line," Dad said to Mother, "I'll give you the diamond out of old Saud's sword."

"Why don't you ask me?" I said. I had already spent several hours mentally wearing that diamond.

"I wouldn't ask you. You'd do it," Dad said.

"I'll do it even for one of the smaller stones in the setting."

At this point Mother ordered both of us to behave. But I kept right on offering to do the dirty deed. By the time Senator Bricker appeared for his ceremonial handshake, Dad was thoroughly unnerved and kept eying me as he and Mother shook hands with the guests. He really thought I was going to upend the old reactionary.

When Dad is in a sarcastic mood, he can be deliciously wry. His mother was upset by a local newspaper attack on him. He told her: "They can't do me any harm now. As Ed McKim says, there's no promotion in this job." Early in June 1946, Mother and I made our annual retreat to Independence. In one of his first letters to us, he described some emergency repairs on the White House:

> They are fixing the hole in the middle of the hallway, opposite my study door. All the rugs are rolled back and a great scaffold has been constructed under the hole. Looks like they intend to hang a murderer in the White House hallway. There are some gentlemen in Congress—and out of it—who would take great pleasure in hoisting your Dad on that scaffold! But they'll have to catch him first. I hope to dry some of their political hides on a frame before I'm through.

He then discussed some of our touchy relatives, and said:

> I don't know what the Trumans and the Wallaces and the Campbells and the Gates and the others of the clan will do for a clearing house when your Dad's gone. I don't suppose you'd take over? It's a lot of fun making prima donnas happy— male and female. . . . Look at the Supreme Court—and my Cabinet. .

In the middle of July, 1946, Dad enjoyed his first break in his crisis-filled schedule. For the better part of two weeks nothing really worth mentioning happened. In an ironic mood, he told his mother:

The foreign affairs and even domestic affairs have been so quiet and as they should be that I have had to start a political fight to give me a chance to do something. Had the tamest Cabinet Meeting today I've had since April 12, 1945. The Secretary of Labor said he hadn't had a major strike to deal with since June 10th and that it looked as if he and Dr. Steelman would have to stir up some trouble so that they would have something to do. The Secretary of State opined that foreign affairs were in such a state that there were no waves not even in Trieste or Nanking. I've had the stomachache because things are so quiet. Haven't had a crisis for two weeks. Looks like the country is going to hell or Republican.

The political fight Dad mentioned was a battle between him and Congressman Roger C. Slaughter of the 5th Missouri Congressional District. Dad had always had a very strong personal interest in this district. It was the one he had helped to create in the early 1930s by lobbying in the Missouri State House—and then had taken away from him by Tom Pendergast. Mr. Slaughter had cast one of the key votes in the House Rules Committee that blocked the creation of the Fair Employment Practices Committee. At his news conference on July 18 Dad said that Mr. Slaughter should not be renominated because he had opposed every bit of legislation the President of his own party had sent to Congress. "If Mr. Slaughter is right, I am wrong."

To his mother, Dad wrote:

> I gave Mr. Smart Alec Slaughter a kick in the pants yesterday and maybe I can find some more entertainment of the same kind. Suppose the K.C. Star and Indp. Examiner had a nice fit over it. Now we must beat him.

Mr. Slaughter was defeated in the primary, but to Dad's chagrin, a Republican beat the Democratic candidate in the fall election, and the 5th Missouri was in the hands of the enemy. This was mortifying. Privately, Dad told his mother that he had been given very misleading advice about the strength of the local Democratic organization. The American presidency may be the most powerful office in the world, but it is not infinitely powerful, not in our rough and tumble American democracy.

Lest you think that the presidency is nothing but frustration piled on frustration, this might be the place to let Dad tell the story of one of his most satisfying appointments—Fred Vinson as Chief Justice of the Supreme Court.

I was on the Williamsburg when Chief Justice Stone died. We were in the lower Chesapeake Bay. I ordered an immediate return to Washington and began a study of the office of Chief Justice.

There had been only twelve appointments up to that time. Mine would be No. 13. So I began to canvas the background and records of the members of the high court. No conclusion was reached.

One day I had an inspiration and called the retired former Chief Justice, Charles Evans Hughes. I told him I would like to come out to see him on a matter of business. He told me that I could not do that but that he would come to see me immediately.

He arrived at the Presidential office in a short time and I told him I wanted to discuss with him eligibles for Chief Justice.

He told me that he suspected that was what I wanted and he pulled a piece of old fashioned yellow foolscap from his pocket with names of the Justices of the Supreme Court and Judges of the various Courts of Appeals and State Courts on it.

We discussed them one by one, or he did. Finally when we came to the end of the list he told me that the Chief Justice of the United States should not only know the law but that he should understand politics and government. Then he said, "You have a Secretary of the Treasury who has been a Congressman, a Judge of the Court of Appeals, and an executive officer in President Roosevelt's and your cabinets." He thought that Fred Vinson was fully qualified for Chief Justice.

I called Justice Owen Roberts in Philadelphia and asked him to come and see me. I told him what I wanted to talk about.

He came and when we were seated he came forth with the same sort of yellow foolscap with a red line down the left hand side that Mr. Hughes had used. We went over very nearly the same list that Mr. Hughes and I had used and Justice Roberts came up with exactly the same recommendation as Justice Hughes had made.

The President-elect of Colombia was at the White House

for a luncheon a short time after that and I talked with Secretary of the Treasury Vinson about the Supreme Court and asked him if he'd accept an appointment as Chief Justice if it were offered to him. I told him that I was not offering the appointment but that I'd like to know his attitude.

He said that any man who had been in the law would jump at such an offer and of course he'd take it if he had the chance. No further conversation took place.

I went back to the Presidential office and at 4 o'clock at the press conference announced the appointment of Fred M. Vinson as Chief Justice of the United States and John W. Snyder as Secretary of the Treasury. Mr. Snyder had not been told what would happen and Sec. Vinson had only received a feeler. Both were agreeably and very much surprised.

Among the minor pleasures of Dad's off hours was reading letters from crackpots—what we all called nut mail. "There are immense numbers of nuts in the USA," Dad remarked to his mother, after she had shipped him a batch of screwball letters. One day in the summer of 1946, while Dad was aboard the *Williamsburg* off Bermuda, he heard Dr. Graham say that he always answered every letter he got, no matter how nutty it was. "I asked him to let me see some of them," Dad told his mother in a letter a few days later. "He brought me about two dozen and I gave them one tear across the middle and threw them in the ocean. He almost wept because he thought I'd lose some prospective votes by his not answering their letters. He's the most conscientious boy I ever saw. Just like his Dad."

Earlier in 1946 an oddball broke into the National Gallery and cut a hole in Dad's portrait. His comment on it, in a letter to me, was a little more serious:

> Somebody went to the National Gallery and cut a hole in my picture last night. It is one the young Virginia painter made and a very good one. He evidently thought well of it because he was insuring it for $10,000. Somebody had gotten left out on meat [these were rationing days] or something like that. It is funny how human beings react. They always want more from their leaders than they can give them and they always like to put mud on their Presidents. That's bad for the Presidents!

[331]

Dad was even able to joke about serious things. One of his proudest accomplishments as President was the creation of the Central Intelligence Agency. Before it was established, intelligence was gathered by a half dozen agencies, and very little of it reached the President. One day he sent the following memorandum to Admiral Leahy and Rear Admiral Sidney W. Souers, the first CIA chief:

> To My Brethren and Fellow Doghouse Denizens:
> By virtue of the authority vested in me as Top Dog I require and charge that Front Admiral William D. Leahy and Rear Admiral Sidney W. Souers, receive and accept the vestments and appurtenances of their respective positions, namely as personal snooper and as director of centralized snooping. . . . I charge that each of you not only seek to better our foreign relations through more intensive snooping but also keep me informed constantly of the movements and actions of the other, for without such coordination there can be no order and no aura of mutual trust.
>
> H.S.T.

This refusal to let the seriousness of his work make him solemn was typical not only of Dad but of the men around him. Matt Connelly was one of the great all-time teasers. He loved to hang ridiculous nicknames on people and would solemnly introduce "Corporal" Vaughan and "Field Marshall" Canfil to befuddled visitors. Bill Hassett was known as the "Bishop" because he was a solemn, scholarly Catholic.

In a letter to his mother in September, 1946, Dad gives a good picture of the way the boys relaxed by tormenting each other:

> Some Hearst columnist by the name of Tucker had called Harry Vaughan a fat, lazy major general who ought to be a corporal and they really made Vaughan believe that Tucker was right. I really felt sorry for both Vaughan and Graham [who was kidded for answering nut mail] before the raggers let up on them.

Dad played a delightful joke on Dr. Graham early in September, 1946. Here is how he described it to his mother:

> Made Doc Graham a brigadier general yesterday and nearly embarrassed him to death. I told him to come to the morning

Secretaries Conference at nine o'clock. I had something I wanted to discuss with him. He came and I asked Vaughan if he had anything from the War Department and he said that General Ike wanted to promote one of the Missouri gang. I read the document and everybody objected. We had a lot of fun and I pinned the stars on him. He's been walking on air ever since.

Down at Key West the atmosphere was even more relaxed. Dad handed out cards to visitors that read: DON'T GO AWAY MAD . . . JUST GO AWAY. Ice water got poured on those who were unwary enough to lie on the beach with their eyes closed. Announcing a fishing expedition with Admiral Leahy, Dad said he was going along as the Admiral's aide. "You know how these admirals are," he said, "they get so they can't do anything without an aide, even bait a hook."

Dad never liked to fish. Mother was the fisherman in the family. He went along just to be companionable. He was not a good fisherman, and he seldom caught more than one fish. Often he caught none. But one day off Bermuda he had a moment of glory. The President and his aides were using several thousand dollars' worth of equipment supplied to them by friends on the island. They were catching nothing with their high-powered reels and poles. Dad became impatient and announced he was going to show everyone how they caught fish in Missouri. He baited a hook at the end of a line that he was holding in his hand and dropped it over the side. Like Babe Ruth when he pointed to the fence, he made good. In less than a minute he had landed the biggest fish of the day.

At the White House Dad superintended a running battle between Alonzo Fields, the head butler, and John Pye, who used to prepare lunches for some of the staff in the executive wing. Charlie Ross, Bill Hassett, Matt Connelly, General Vaughan, and others dined there, largely because it was convenient and quick. Pye never ceased trying to persuade Dad to join them, and when he yielded, Pye strutted around the White House, about ten feet tall. Fields, of course, would be preparing to serve lunch in the main house, so Dad would have Matt Connelly call and ask if it was all right if the President ate in Pye's dining room. The conversation would then go something like this:

"Is Dr. Graham nearby?"

"Oh yes, he's right here on duty."

"Then I guess it would be safe for the President to take a chance. But if he wants good food—and safety—he ought to come over here."

Pye, of course, would be vastly indignant and swear by all the angels in heaven that his food was untainted and just as good as the food Fields was serving. Sometimes Reathel Odum, Mother's secretary, and I would join the staff in Pye's dining room and then Fields would grow indignant and condemn Pye as an interloper who was taking his customers away. One day my low resistance to germs supplied Fields with unique ammunition. Pye baked a cake for me, and it was a very good cake. I ate a lot of it. A few hours later I came down with the flu and was flat on my back for several days. Fields told everyone he met that Pye had poisoned me. Actually he and Pye were good friends and the barrage of insults that they exchanged was part of the usual kidding atmosphere around the Truman White House.

The modern presidency is such a demanding, enervating job that it is absolutely necessary for the President to have periods, however brief, for complete escape from the pressures of the office. Along with Key West, Dad and Mother sometimes used a retreat which President Roosevelt had created on the site of a former Civilian Conservation Corps camp in the Catoctin Mountains about sixty-five miles from Washington, near Thurmont, Maryland. FDR had called the camp Shangri-la, and Dad let the name stand. Later, President Eisenhower changed it to Camp David.

The main building was a nine-room, one-story lodge, paneled inside in natural oak. There was a floor-to-ceiling stone fireplace in the living room, and each of the four bedrooms had smaller fireplaces. The extra warmth was badly needed. Deep in the woods, Shangri-la was damp and cold most of the time. I thought it was a terrible place and went there as little as possible.

Earlier in 1946, before he found Key West, Dad had tried to arrange a cruise aboard the *Williamsburg* along the Maine coast. On August 22, 1946, he told his mother why he gave it up:

> The Maine coast cruise ended in a blowup. Everybody and his brother whom I didn't want to see tried by every hook or crook to rope me into letting him come aboard or having me be seen with him. So I just cancelled the trip.

Dad had solved the problem, then, by sailing to Woodrow Wilson's favorite retreat, Bermuda. Dad had a pleasant time—he called the island a paradise—but he decided he did not like to be so far away from the White House, without adequate communications. He told his mother:

> We'll be here for a week and then go back to the White House and *stay* there from now until the end of the term. It is the only place I should be. It took me a long time to find it out. But it is the fact.

Another reason why he decided the *Williamsburg* was not the answer to his vacation problems was described in the following letter to his mother:

> Off the Va. Capes, 9/2/46
>
> Dear Mamma & Mary:— We are just coming to Hampton Roads on a beautiful calm, cool sunny Sunday morning after a rather stormy passage from Bermuda. We left there Friday morning early. It was sunny and the sea was calm. But by dinner time we'd run into rain squalls and a rough sea. The Williamsburg being a pleasure craft did all sorts of antics in the heavy seas. I became seasick at the dinner table and rushed to my quarters and to bed. Stayed there most of yesterday. Ate no breakfast or lunch but did manage a cup of tea and two sandwiches about eight o'clock last night.
>
> Saturday morning it was so rough that furniture, paper, ink bottles, magazines, clothing and pillows got completely mixed on my floor. . . .
>
> It looked as if the place never would look the same again, but it does and you'd never know anything had happened.

After that experience on the high seas, Dad used the *Williamsburg* only for weekend get-aways, on the calmer waters of the Potomac or Chesapeake Bay. Dad followed a policy of working a seventeen or eighteen-hour day in the White House for five or six days, and then taking a complete break and sleeping most of the time. He was particularly fond of doing this aboard the *Williamsburg,* and his letters to me and to his mother and sister are studded with remarks about the yacht which ended with "I expect to do nothing but sleep," or "I hope I can get some sleep." While I have said that Dad's health was good, it was not perfect. Moreover, he had a tendency to ignore his illnesses until they either went away or floored him. For instance, on July 16, 1946, he wrote to his mother:

> Early last week after our trip to Shangri-la I cultivated a sore throat and an infected ear but both are all right now. That's the first time I ever had a bad ear. But couldn't let up. Things had to go on as usual or they'd have said I was physically incompetent. No one ever knew the difference.

From this point of view, Dr. Graham was the perfect physician for Dad. He had a lot of common sense and was not an alarmist. But he could also be very firm about taking a vacation or doing something about a cold or sore throat. Firmness helps when you are dealing with someone as stubborn as Harry S. Truman. Dad had always admired and respected Dr. Graham's father and this personal link added a certain indefinable something to his son's authority.

Dad's thirst for good music sometimes drew him out of the White House in the evening. In the summer he often drove down to Watergate to listen to the outdoor concerts there. He would arrive late, and sit in his car on a road above the amphitheater, and then send me the concert program with comments on the performances.

Occasionally, he was not above using his presidential power to get the music he wanted. One night he went to an indoor concert to hear Oscar Straus and his orchestra. Pictures were taken before the concert started. At intermission, Dad sent Secret Service man Jim Rowley around with a request for the "Blue Danube" waltz. Mr. Straus, who was a crotchety old character, told Jim he couldn't play it because the orchestra hadn't rehearsed it.

"I told Jim to tell him all right, but we'd have the pictures we'd made before his appearance torn up," Dad told us in a letter. "He played the waltz and needed no rehearsal!"

In the fall of 1946, Dad revived the regular White House social program. In one sense he hated to do it. It put additional strain on him, and he already had too much to do. It also put a tremendous strain on Mother, since she had to superintend the preparations. She had plenty of help, of course, but she still felt responsible. Moreover, with sixty-two heads of diplomatic missions and their wives, it was necessary to divide the traditional diplomatic dinner in two. Here is the schedule for our first full winter in Washington.

November 26, Tuesday, Diplomatic Dinner, 8 P.M.
December 3, Tuesday, Diplomatic Dinner, 8 P.M.
December 10, Tuesday, Judicial Reception, 9 P.M.
December 17, Tuesday, Cabinet Dinner, 8 P.M.
January 7, Tuesday, Diplomatic Reception, 9 P.M.
January 14, Tuesday, Dinner to the Chief Justice and the Supreme Court, 8 P.M.
January 21, Tuesday, Reception to the Officials of the Treasury, Post Office, Interior, Agriculture, Commerce and Labor Departments and Federal Agencies, 9 P.M.
January 28, Tuesday, Dinner to the President Pro Tempore of the Senate, 8 P.M.
February 4, Tuesday, Army and Navy Reception, 9 P.M.
February 11, Tuesday, Speaker's Dinner, 8 P.M.
February 18, Tuesday, Congressional Reception, 9 P.M.

From another point of view, Dad liked these dinners, because the traditional ceremony was a dramatic statement of the power and prestige of the presidency. With his enormous respect for the great office, he was always eager to enhance it, no matter how much of a drain the effort made on his energies. The big moment at these affairs was the "Little Procession." It is a really splendid ceremony. The members of the Cabinet and their wives would meet in Dad's study. At 8:45, four husky young men, one sailor, one soldier, one airman, and one marine, commanded by an officer, would arrive and request permission to take the colors. Dad would grant the permission, and the color guard in precise military formation would pick up the American flag and the President's flag and march to the head of the stairs, practically banging their feet through the old White House floorboards.

Meanwhile, downstairs, the diplomats were arriving, their full evening dress ablaze with decorations. The two color bearers would station themselves at the door to the Blue Room. Precisely on the stroke of nine, Dad and Mother would lead the Cabinet members and their wives in order of precedence down the stairs and into the Blue Room where they received the diplomats beneath the big chandelier. The Cabinet members received the guests in the Red Room. Then everyone went to the State Dining

Room where tea, coffee, sandwiches, and cake were served. You may be surprised to learn that liquor was never served at diplomatic receptions in the White House. Meanwhile, in the East Room, the Marine Band would begin playing and would continue to make music for dancing until midnight. Usually a noted singer would also be on hand to perform. Commenting on the Cabinet dinner to his mother, Dad wrote, "It was a beautiful affair. It looked like the pictures in the books about the White House. . . . Everybody seemed to enjoy it and we got upstairs (a most important item) at 10:40."

The signal that the reception was officially over was the departure of the color guard. When they carried the two flags back to Dad's office, Mother and he usually beat a hasty retreat to the elevator and upstairs.

Because President Roosevelt had been confined to a wheelchair, the Little Procession had been abandoned during his three administrations. Old Washington hands were enormously pleased to see Dad restore it. Edith Helm, the social secretary, wrote in her memoirs: "The receptions, especially, of the Truman period marked the very peak of official entertaining in the old White House—and spectacular events they were." That is the voice of authority and experience speaking. Mrs. Helm's White House memories went back to Woodrow Wilson's day.

Eventually, toward the end of the reception season, the down-to-earth Missouri side of Dad's nature overcame his love of presidential panoply. In a letter to his mother on February 13, he wrote:

> This is the first time I've been glad to have Lent come. I'm sick and tired of smirking at people I don't like. So a rest will come in handy.

Mother felt pretty much the same way. Toward the close of the social season, she wrote to me:

> These two weeks are really going to be a handshaking two weeks—conservative estimate forty-one hundred—I'll be plenty glad when February 19th arrives!

Those words remind me of a lesson I learned in this, my first social season in the White House. No rings. At one of my first receptions I stood in line shaking hand after hand and suddenly felt a vague pain. I looked down and saw that my ring had been pressed into my flesh.

Even though he was surrounded by aides, servants, and Secret Service men, Dad went into his usual decline when Mother and I left him to spend the summer in Independence. I scarcely reached home when he was writing: "Your Pop has missed you and your Mamma very much." When I failed to write regularly, as usual, I got queries such as, "Is your arm paralyzed?" The next time around, he would try to lure me to the writing table with sentiment. For example:

> Dear Sistie: I am lonesome this morning—thought maybe I might get a letter from my little girl. But I suppose she's busy with breathing exercises, vocal gymnastics and young gentlemen and so hasn't had the time.

As these words indicate, I had definitely made up my mind to become a professional singer and was spending the summer (of 1946) working on my technique. My decision to pursue my singing career was not made without a lot of soul-searching. I knew I was exposing myself to some malicious criticism. I knew political hatchetmen would make my ambition the target for sneak attacks on the White House. These headaches and heartaches, which Dad calmly pointed out to me, only aroused the Truman determination in my blood. I could see no reason why my father becoming President meant I should be denied the chance to become an individual capable of standing on my merit, to experience the satisfaction of achievement. Dad wholeheartedly concurred. But that did not stop him from worrying about me.

> I am glad you are working hard at your music. If you love it enough to give it all you have, nothing can stop you [he wrote to me on August 23, 1946]. There is only one thing I ask—please don't become a temperamental case. It is hard to keep from it I know—and no one knows better than I. But it is not necessary nor does it help in your public relations. It makes no friends and to succeed at anything you must have friends on whom you can rely. That is just as true of a musical career as it is of a political one or a business career.

Along with affairs of state and the danger of me becoming a

prima donna, Dad fretted over picking out a stage name for me. At this point I was determined to use one of these artificial monikers because I was determined to succeed on my own merits as a singer, with no help from the name Truman. I later abandoned this idea as totally unrealistic. Waitresses from Keokuk can change their names and identities and make it big on the stage or screen, but it is a vain hope for a President's daughter. I am sure Dad knew this from the start, but he went along with my inclination, and managed to have a lot of fun suggesting alternatives. "There are a lot of good names in the family on both sides. For instance, Mary Jane Holmes, your great-grandmother, Harriet Louisa Gregg, another great-grandmother, Matilda Middleton, a great-aunt, Peggy Seton, another great-aunt. Susan Shippe, a great-grandmother . . . Mary Margaret Gates would look good in headlines, and Peggy Gates would probably catch 'em.

"I also have some partiality for Mary Margaret Truman. Mr. Dooley in his column some years ago said safe crackers and stage stars were the only great professions which required assumed names. He may have something there."

A few days later, he sent me the following letter on the same topic.

> Here is a telegram from a nut over in Connecticut who admits it! The only reason I'm sending it to you is because it is signed by a very euphonious name. . . . What a stage name that would make—and you might see visions too! And you have to see visions to get real headlines. Look at Henry Wallace, Pepper, Huey Long, Bilbo, Talmadge of Georgia—and remember Joe Stalin, Hitler, Mussolini, Franco, Porfirio Díaz and a dozen others.
>
> But you are not interested in them. You are thinking of Adelina Patti, Alice Nielsen, Melba, Tetrazzini, Sembrich and a dozen others of the great opera.

You may think that living in the White House guarantees the best available technology. But when I sent Dad a record I had made in Missouri, he and Mother discovered that the victrola was as decrepit as the rest of the place. They ordered a new Capehart, but meanwhile sat around listening to me on "this wretched machine," as Mother called it. "Your voice shows you've been working hard. It seems to have more volume and a beautiful tone," Dad said.

I was debating whether to stay in Missouri or go to New York to continue my studies there. For the moment I opted for Missouri, to Dad's vast relief. "I'm glad you decided to stay at home and study rather than go to the wilds of that terrible town at the mouth of the Hudson," he wrote. Even though he was pleased by this decision, Dad simply could not resign himself to the fact that I was twenty-two years old, a college graduate, and determined to go my own way. He kept trying to lure me back to the White House. On October 1, 1946, he pulled out all the stops to describe his visit to West Point for an Army football game. "Twenty-one hundred bosoms were all aflutter when I arrived hoping to see my daughter. So just to get even I had to stand them up and make 'em quake in the knees for me!" He then added a long list of interesting people he had met at the commandant's house and concluded, "You see what you've missed besides all those fluttering hearts." Then he turned sarcastic and added, "By the way, I wish you'd send me a late news photo so I won't forget how you look."

Two weeks later he was still teasing me on the same subject.

> Dear Margie:— Was glad to read your good letter which your Ma was kind enough to let me see. I think you'd better send me a picture—a late one so I'll be sure and recognize you when I come home. I was afraid the four or five pictures I have on my desks will not be a good likeness now—particularly one on a tricycle in coat and panties.
>
> If you are really turning into the prima donna you want to be you may by this time weigh some two hundred ten and be as buxom as Melba or Lillian Russell by all the rules. I want to be sure.
>
> This place without you is very dreary. I don't know what your mamma and I will do when you go on tour. I guess I'll have to go to an orphan's home and get me a substitute. How would that do? It might work.

An interview was arranged with Metropolitan Opera star Frederick Jagel in New York. He was encouraging and constructive. I reported what he said to Dad. Although he was deep in his struggle with John L. Lewis, Dad somehow found time to take my career seriously, too:

> I am happy that he thinks you have a good chance to sing successfully. Of course if that is what you want—that is what I want you to have. It seems to me you have gone about your career in the right way.
>
> You have finished your college education. You have worked long hard hours to get your voice in condition for the final trials. You are willing to take the necessary advice from honest people about what to do to make your preliminary trials. Your Daddy will support you to the end on whatever it takes to make these trials. But daughter, don't fool yourself. You know what it takes.
>
> Your Dad doesn't want you to fail publicly. Not that he wouldn't be for you win, lose or draw—but because of conditions a failure would be unbearable for you. You *won't* fail! You have your Dad's tenacity and your Ma's contrariness—and together they should make you.
>
> Now you'd better tell me what the expenses are to date. We must not be charity patients of anybody.

Seventeen

ONE OF THE MOST IMPORTANT LETTERS my father ever wrote me came from Key West, Florida, on March 13, 1947:

Dear Margie:— We had a very pleasant flight from Washington.

Your old Dad slept for 750 or 800 miles—three hours, and we were making from 250 to 300 miles an hour. No one, not even me (your mother would say I) knew how very tired and worn to a frazzle the Chief Executive had become. This terrible decision I had to make had been over my head for about six weeks. Although I knew at Potsdam that there is no difference in totalitarian or police states, call them what you will, Nazi, Fascist, Communist or Argentine Republics. You know there was but one idealistic example of Communism. That is described in the Acts of the Apostles.

The attempt of Lenin, Trotsky, Stalin, et al., to fool the world and the American Crackpots Association, represented by Jos. Davies, Henry Wallace, Claude Pepper and the actors and artists in immoral Greenwich Village, is just like Hitler's and Mussolini's so-called socialist states.

Your Pop had to tell the world just that in polite language.

I hope the historians who picture Dad as plunging recklessly and even enthusiastically into the cold war read this letter. The day before it was written he addressed a joint session of Congress, to call for a historic departure in American foreign policy, now known as the Truman Doctrine. Dad asked Congress to back his declaration that

> it must be the policy of the United States to support free peoples who are resisting attempted subjugation by armed minorities or by outside pressures. . . . This is no more than a frank recognition that totalitarian regimes imposed on free peoples, by direct or indirect aggression, undermine the foundations of international peace and hence the security of the United States.

To back up these words, my father asked for $400 million in aid to Greece and Turkey, the two countries most immediately menaced by Russia's imperial ambitions. But nowhere in the speech did Dad mention Russia. There were two reasons for this omission. By placing the emphasis on the fight between totalitarianism and freedom, Dad was attempting to rally the same emotional commitment that had fired America in the war against Hitler. Second, he was still hoping to avoid a complete break with Russia.

But he knew, at the same time, that Stalin would regard his step as decisive. It was the real beginning of the cold war, on our side of the Iron Curtain, the moment when the leader of the free world said, "No more" to the men from Moscow. That is why Dad called it "this terrible decision." That explains the anguish and exhaustion he talks about in his letter. That is why he pondered and analyzed and discussed it for so many weeks.

The crisis in both Greece and Turkey had been simmering since the end of World War II. Russia had made outrageous territorial demands on the Turks, including the right to set up air and naval bases on Turkish territory at the mouth of the Dardanelles. In Greece, Stalin was supplying guns and ammunition to a 20,000-man guerrilla army that had the legitimate government tottering. The Turks, forced to support a 600,000-man army in the face of Russia's threats, were on the brink of financial collapse.

My father had been in close touch with the situation in both countries. But he and the entire nation were catapulted into a crisis when the British government handed our State Department a note informing them that Britain could no longer afford to support the 40,000 troops it was maintaining in Greece or supply further aid to the Greek government. It was the first intimation of the appalling bankruptcy of the British Empire, in spite of a fifty-year loan of three billion seven hundred and fifty million dollars which we had made to them in August, 1946. But the stunning—one might even say outrageous—part of the British note was its deadline. Mr. Attlee and his government were pulling their troops out on March 31—less than six weeks away. If Greece fell— and this was almost a certainty if we did nothing—Turkey, isolated in the eastern Mediterranean, would inevitably succumb in short order. Under Secretary of State Dean Acheson, who received the British note, immediately telephoned my father and his new Secretary of State, General Marshall, who had replaced James Byrnes on January 7, 1947.

Three weeks of incredibly intense effort followed. My father knew that extending such aid in peace time was without parallel in American history. He also knew he was faced with a hostile Republican majority in Congress. All the legislative skills he had honed in his ten senatorial years were thrown into the effort. Republican senators, led by Senator Vandenberg, were invited to the White House to hear the grim facts about these two threatened countries. They were also told that the peoples of Italy, Germany, and France, their economies wrecked by the war, as well as a host of small, fragile states in the Middle East, were waiting to see whether the United States was prepared to resist the onward march of communism. Simultaneously, Dad had to fend off foolish advice from his own party. The Democratic Congressional Conference called a meeting—supposedly secret but very well reported, like so many secret meetings in Washington—and voted to warn Dad against supporting "British policies" in the Mediterranean. Thank goodness, the Constitution and long tradition have made the foreign policy of the United States the responsibility of the President.

Even with all my father's expert cajoling, Congress took two weary months to make up their minds about giving aid to Turkey and Greece. Meanwhile, he had to supply what emergency funds he could scrape together from other aid programs. In a burst of impatience, he told his mother:

> When the Congress gets all snarled up it is necessary for them
> to find someone to blame—so they always pick on me. But they

are not fooling anyone. The people, I'm sure, are not to be fooled by a lot of hooey put out by ignorant demagogues. Woodrow Wilson said that most members of Congress just had a knot on their shoulders to keep their bodies from unraveling.

I don't go that far, but I sometimes think that if Congressmen talked less and worked more for the public interest they would come out much better and so would the country.

My father understood, from almost his first day in the White House, that a President cannot be passive, the obedient servant of Congress or the blind follower of polls. This is especially true when the nation is confronted, as it was in the 1940s, with crisis after crisis around the world, where swift action was essential. As George Elsey put it succinctly:

> You can't sit around and wait for public opinion to tell you what to do. In the first place there isn't any public opinion. The public doesn't know anything about it; they haven't heard about it. The President must decide what he is going to do and do it, and attempt to educate the public to the reasons for his action.

Mr. Elsey also has some harsh words for the hindsight specialists who spend a year or two writing a book about decisions such as aid to Greece and Turkey, ignoring the fact that they were hammered out under tremendous pressure. "You don't sit down and take time to think through and debate ad nauseum all the points," he says. "You don't have time. Later somebody can sit around for days and weeks and figure out how things might have been done differently. This is all very well and very interesting but quite irrelevant."

When the Greek-Turkish crisis exploded, however, my father had at his disposal a resource which was typical of the foresighted planning he brought to the presidency. After a year in the White House, he saw that the President himself, bombarded as he was day and night by people with information, problems, proposals, and schemes, could never find time to make a comprehensive study of a particular subject, such as Russian-American relations. Analyses by foreign service officers, such as the "containment" theory proposed by Mr. Kennan, were helpful, but Dad wanted even more comprehensive reports, written from the White House point of view. So, in the summer of 1946, he asked Clark Clifford, his former naval aide, whom he had made his special counsel, to prepare a "position paper" on Russian-American relations.

Mr. Clifford passed the task along to his assistant, George Elsey, and Mr. Elsey spent most of the summer of 1946 writing it. He went to every major agency of the government—the State Department, the War and Navy Departments, the new Central Intelligence Agency. Mr. Elsey, who is now president of the American Red Cross, produced an immensely perceptive, enormously detailed document—a hundred pages in length—which was handed to my father over Clark Clifford's signature in September, 1946. It analyzed Soviet foreign policy in terms of its publicly stated goals and activities throughout the world. It summarized Soviet-American agreements from 1942 to 1946 and the violations of these agreements by Russia. It analyzed Soviet activities affecting American security, pointing to the construction of air bases in northeastern Siberia from which the United States could be attacked, and the construction of large numbers of submarines for commerce raiding if war did break out. It detailed Russian attempts to weaken America's position abroad, particularly in China, and reported on Russian subversive movements and espionage within the United States. Finally, it made recommendations for American policy toward the Soviet Union, based on this realistic assessment of the present and recent past. There was, of course, no obligation for the President to accept these recommendations, but they gave him and the men around him a background in depth against which they could judge future Russian moves and formulate an American response to them.

Clark Clifford handed this report to my father one evening around five o'clock. He stayed up most of the night reading it, and early the next morning he called Mr. Clifford at his home. "How many copies of this report do you have?" he asked.

"Ten," Mr. Clifford said.

"I want the other nine," Dad said. "Get them right in here."

Mr. Clifford put the other nine on his desk within the hour. "This has got to be put under lock and key," Dad said. "This is so hot, if this should come out now it could have an exceedingly unfortunate impact on our efforts to try to develop some relationship with the Soviet Union."

Once more we see that my father, in the face of facts that could have justified massive pessimism or even angry aggression, still hoped to resolve the conflict between Russia and America peacefully. In fact, he agreed wholeheartedly with the last sentence of the report, which in many ways was the policy he adopted:

> Even though Soviet leaders profess to believe that the conflict between capitalism and communism is irreconcilable, and must eventually be resolved by the triumph of the latter, it is our hope that they will change their mind and work out with us a fair and equitable settlement when they realize that we are too strong to be beaten and too determined to be frightened.

One of the amusing byplays of this drama was my father's absolute refusal to consult Bernard Baruch before announcing the Truman Doctrine. Dad never had a very high opinion of Mr. Baruch. Presidents get more advice than they can possibly use and anyone who made a career of being an unsolicited, unrequested presidential adviser had to be a phony. But Mr. Baruch had great prestige in Congress and several members of the Cabinet urged my father to see him first and get him on his side. Dad replied:

> I'm just *not* going to do it. I'm not going to spend hours and hours on that old goat, come what may. If you take his advice, then you have him on your hands for hours and hours, and it is *his* policy. I'm just not going to do it. We have a decision to make and we'll make it.

In May Congress finally passed the Greek-Turkish aid bill, with very little help from Mr. Baruch. Meanwhile, the Republican majority in Congress was doing its utmost to make things difficult for Dad on the domestic front. Partisan politics is, I know, inevitable in a democracy. But I do not think I am being too Democratic when I say that the Republicans in this Congress carried partisanship to horrendous extremes. On atomic energy, for instance, my father took the position, that politics and the atom simply did not mix. He appointed four Republicans and one independent—David Lilienthal—to the newly formed Atomic Energy Commission. Senator Taft and his fellow believers in yesterday immediately launched a vicious, sustained attack on Mr. Lilienthal and indirectly on the TVA. Dad was thoroughly disgusted by this performance. He recognized it for what it was— another attempt by Congress to encroach on the powers of the presidency. He sent Clark Clifford to Mr. Lilienthal to ask him if he was ready to fight to the finish. Mr. Lilienthal said he was ready. Dad said he would "stick with him if it took a hundred and fifty years."

Many of the charges against Mr. Lilienthal revolved around supposed Communists in the TVA. The battle was actually the first round in the ugly disloyalty issue that was to loom larger and uglier in later years. For two months witness after witness, from Dr. Conant of Harvard to Dean Acheson, backed the appointment of Mr. Lilienthal. Finally, on April 3, 1947, Senator Bricker of Ohio moved to recommit the AEC nominations. It was a crucial moment. In his diary, Mr. Lilienthal tells how he waited with Dad in his office, "a grim gray look" on Dad's face, from 5 P.M. until exactly 5:12, when Charlie Ross stuck his head in the door and said, "The Senate voted to reject the Bricker motion."

It meant the nominations were all but confirmed. My father shook hands with the slightly dazed nominees and said to Mr. Lilienthal, "You have the most important thing there is. You must make a blessing of it or"—he pointed to the large globe in the corner of his office—"we'll blow that all to smithereens."

Two days later my father wrote his mother and sister, telling them what he thought of the Republicans and Senator Taft in particular:

> The Atomic Energy Commission fight finally came to a test vote. Mr. Taft has succeeded in making a real fool of himself as have several so-called leading Republicans. I am of the opinion that the country has had enough of their pinhead antics.

Unfortunately, the Republicans were by no means convinced of this fact. Although the wave of strikes which had plagued the nation during 1946 had largely subsided, John L. Lewis and some other labor leaders were still talking in very belligerent language. This gave the reactionaries in Congress an opportunity to put together and pass that masterpiece of negative legislation known as the Taft-Hartley Act. Once more, Congress was directly challenging the President. In his 1947 State of the Union Message, my father had specifically warned Congress not to adopt "punitive legislation." He insisted that "industrial peace cannot be achieved merely by laws directed against labor unions." At the same time he was aware that the labor-management situation needed government leadership. He called for the creation of a joint commission to study the problem, a sweeping extension of the Labor Department's abilities and powers to assist in collective bargaining, and the elimination of certain unjustifiable labor union practices, such as strikes by minority unions and some kinds of secondary boycotts.

The Taft-Hartley bill was passed by overwhelming majorities in both the House and Senate early in June 1947. The House voted 320 to 79, with 103 Democrats joining 217 Republicans, and the Senate voted 54 to 17, with 17 Democrats joining 37 Republicans. The vote reflected the strong anti-labor sentiment of the country. Most people didn't really know what was in the bill. They just felt that labor unions needed to be cut down to size.

There were many moments in my father's administration which would qualify him as a subject for a profile in courage. But Taft-Hartley is among my favorites, because it was one of his loneliest as well as his most courageous moments. His Cabinet, reflecting the mood of the country, urged him almost unanimously to sign the bill. Only two Cabinet members, Secretary of Labor Schwellenbach and Postmaster General Hannegan, urged a veto. His closest friend in the Cabinet, Secretary of the Treasury Snyder, strongly favored signing it. This was one of those times when a President has to look himself in the mirror, remember what the presidency means, and let his conscience—and nothing but his conscience—be his guide. Dad decided to veto it.

He did not arrive at this decision overnight, by any means. He spent two full weeks studying the bill. He had it analyzed by his Secretary of Labor and his Attorney General, the Secretary of Commerce, and the Secretary of the Interior. The National Labor Relations Board chairman made a study of the enormous administrative problems posed by the bill. Presidential counsel Clark Clifford prepared an exhaustive study of the bill's legislative history and worked with Dad's chief labor adviser on condensing hundreds of sheets of memoranda into concise reports for each provision of the bill. Dad carefully sifted through this evidence as it reached his desk, and thus made his decision to veto on the widest possible view of the facts.

While he was responding to his presidential conscience, my father did not by any means stop being a politician. The two are by no means incompatible. Dad was convinced that he was right on the Taft-Hartley bill and he was determined to convince the American people. He sent his veto back to Congress with a 5,500-word message that used such terms as "startling," "dangerous," "far-reaching," "unprecedented," "unworkable," "unique," "complex," "burdensome," "arbitrary," "unnecessary," "impossible," "clumsy," "drastic," and "unwarranted." He followed this up with a radio message to the nation, denouncing the bill as "a shocking piece of legislation . . . bad for labor, bad for management, and bad for the country." Senator Taft came blazing back in a radio rebuttal, and in both the Senate and the House proceeded to muster more than the required two-thirds majority to override Dad's veto.

On June 28, 1947, four days after the vote to override, Dad wrote to his mother:

> The situation here is very bad. I am afraid the Taft-Hartley Law will not work. But I'll be charged with the responsibility whether it does or does not work. I've come to the conclusion that Taft is no good and Hartley is worse. . . . Isn't it too bad that public men can't always be public servants?

Sharp as the exchanges between Congress and the President were over the Taft-Hartley Act, my father never stopped working for good relations between the President and the legislative branch. He remained in close touch with Les Biffle, the secretary of the Senate, and on July 23, 1947, he went up to the Capitol for a luncheon with senators of both parties. At the end of the meal one of the senators asked him if he would dare to break a precedent, and walk onto the Senate floor, and take his old seat. Dad said he had broken so many precedents already, he could see no harm in breaking one more. So he strolled into the Senate chamber and took his seat. There was applause from both sides of the aisle, and the Senate's presiding officer, Arthur Vandenberg, remarked:

> There are few situations in the life of a Senator for which there is not some available precedent. The present happens to be one, however, for which no precedent is known. The chair is very happy to welcome the former Senator from Missouri to his

old seat in the Senate. . . . The ex-Senator from Missouri is recognized for five minutes.

Dad rose and gave a brief off-the-cuff speech, affirming that the best ten years of his life were spent in the Senate.

Les Biffle had carefully planned the entire incident in advance, a necessity because Dad would never have risked a rebuff to the dignity of the presidency. Though his appearance was only a gesture, it did help soothe senatorial feelings and take much of the bitterness out of the Taft-Hartley controversy.

My father wanted to close the breach between him and the Republican Congress, not merely for his own political good but for the survival of the free world. Even while he was pushing the Greek-Turkish aid bill through Congress, he was receiving more and more alarming reports about the condition of the other nations of Western Europe. The worst winter in the history of Europe, months of freezing weather, snow and sleet storms, followed by floods in the spring, had all but wiped out the modest postwar recovery that France, Italy, England, and the other free nations of the West had begun. Most shocking was the British situation. On August 1 my father received a report from the Secretary of State, which informed him that the British had drawn two and three-quarters billion of the loan we had given them the previous summer, leaving less than one billion in their account. This meant that in another six months the British would be bankrupt. Lewis Douglas, ambassador to England, wrote: "We run the serious risk of losing most of Western Europe if the crisis here develops as it now seems almost certain to develop." Writing to his sister in August, Dad expressed his deep concern:

> It looks as if my work never ends. When one crisis is over we have another one. The British have turned out to be our problem children now. With Palestine on one side and Ruhr coal on the other, they've decided to go bankrupt and if they do that, it will end our prosperity and probably all the world's too. Then Uncle Joe Stalin can have his way. Looks like he may get it anyway.

Fortunately, once more my father was forewarned and ready to act. Early in the spring he had begun the job of selling the American people their biggest peacetime challenge—a commitment to aid the free world on a scale that made the Greek-Turkish aid bill seem like petty cash. He sent Dean Acheson to keep a date he had made to speak on foreign policy in the small town of Cleveland, Mississippi, on May 8. Mr. Acheson gave a speech which sounded the alarm bell Dad wanted the nation to hear. Europe was nearly bankrupt and exhausted. They could not buy our exports—and they needed them desperately. It was time to work out a program of aid that would enable them to become self-supporting as soon as possible.

A month later, speaking at the Harvard graduation in Cambridge, Secretary of State Marshall spelled out the details of the great program that bears his name—the Marshall Plan. He emphasized the core of my father's idea—that it was not a program of relief but of revival, not an offer of perpetual support but of temporary co-operation. To prove it, General Marshall declared that the initiative and the responsibility for the plan must be a joint effort. We wanted Europe's best thinking on how the money should be spent. Finally, Dad insisted on leaving the door open for the co-operation of Russia and her satellites:

> Our policy is directed not against any country or doctrine but against hunger, poverty, desperation, and chaos [General Marshall said]. Its purpose should be the revival of a working economy in the world so as to permit the emergence of political and social conditions in which free institutions can exist.

Many people say that my father is one of the best politicians who ever lived in the White House. They may be right. I'd also like to point out that he consistently used his political expertise to further the best interests of America. It fascinates me to see how often his innate modesty and sound policy coincided. During the summer of 1947, while sixteen European nations were meeting in Paris to compose a comprehensive statement of their needs, Dad and his aides were discussing in the White House what the program should be called. Clark Clifford suggested "the Truman Plan." He pointed out that Dad had supplied most of the ideas and all of the leadership.

"Are you crazy?" Dad said. "If we sent it up to that Republican Congress with my name on it, they'd tear it apart. We're going to call it the Marshall Plan."

"He was right, of course," Clark Clifford told me when we discussed his years with Dad recently. "But I still think it deserved to be called the Truman Plan."

On September 22 the European nations delivered their report. By this time the Russians had walked out, denouncing the Marshall Plan as a "vicious American scheme" and forbidding any of their satellites to have anything to do with it. Unfortunately, Congress had adjourned without enacting any additional foreign aid. But my father had been working hard on softening them up, and in the final days of the session, he persuaded the Republican majority in the House to send an eighteen-man fact-finding committee to Europe to see for themselves if General Marshall was telling the truth. Many of these congressmen, such as Everett McKinley Dirksen of Illinois, were isolationists when they sailed aboard the *Queen Mary* and internationalists—or at least backers of the Marshall Plan—when they returned. But Senator Taft and the Republican leaders of the Senate, excepting Arthur Vandenberg, of course, were fiercely critical of the whole idea and not in the least inclined to do anything about it until the new session of Congress began in January, 1948.

On October 1, Dad wrote to me:

> I've had the most terrible and terrific ten days since April 12, 1945. I've worked from sun-up to sun-down and a couple of hours before and five after every day. . . . Every Republican is trying to put your pa in the hole and every Wallaceite is making a contribution in that direction—as is Old Bill Southern, Roy Roberts, Frank Kent, Bertie McCormick and his kinfolk Cissy Patterson. . . .

Almost as soon as he received the report from the Paris conference, my father instructed one of his newest aides, Charles S. Murphy, who had just moved to the White House after more than a decade as legal adviser to the Senate, to draw up a report for him on the advisability of summoning a special session of Congress to enact the Marshall Plan without further delay.

On October 17, 1947, Mr. Murphy submitted his report, recommending that a special session be summoned. Europe could not survive another winter without aid. The question, Mr. Murphy wrote, "took precedence over all other questions and the consequences of failure are too grave to permit the President to stop anywhere short of the full use of his constitutional powers in his efforts to meet the requirements of the situation." The report admitted that the leaders of Congress were certain to be resentful and critical of such a decision. But quiet, soft-spoken Charlie Murphy was a man who agreed with Dad's thinking on politics and responsibility. He pointed out that Congress had the habit of postponing questions "no matter how tragic the consequences" so the sooner the issue was brought before them the better.

On November 17, 1947, Congress met in response to my father's summons. In a series of special messages he told the astonished lawmakers—and the American people—that the Marshall Plan called for a total outlay of $17 billion, with an appropriation of $6,800,000,000 needed by April 1, 1948, to enable Europe to survive the following fifteen months. Between October 17 and December 19 Dad and the members of his White House team, and other toilers in the State Department, the Treasury, and almost every other executive department of the government, had spent incredible numbers of hours working out a rational balance between how much Europe needed and how much the American economy could afford to give. Three special committees—one headed by Averell Harriman, the Secretary of Commerce; the second by Julius Krug, Secretary of the Interior; and the third by Dr. Edwin Nourse, chairman of the Council of Economic Advisers—synthesized massive amounts of factual information on which my father based his proposal to the Congress:

> We must now make a grave and significant decision relating to our further efforts to create the conditions of peace. We must decide whether or not we will complete the job of helping the free nations of Europe recover from the devastation of war. Our decision will determine in large part the future of the people of that continent. It will also determine in large part whether the free nations of the world can look forward with hope to a peaceful and prosperous future as independent states. . . .
>
> I recommend this program . . . in full confidence of its wisdom and necessity as a major step in our nation's quest for a just and lasting peace.

The tremendous pressure Dad was under at this time can be seen in this letter he wrote to his sister:

Dear Mary:— I've been trying to write you all week but have been covered up with work and am so tired when night comes, I just fall into bed and go to sleep. Went to bed at 8:30 last night and I'm still tired after sleeping at least eight hours.

Have been trying to get the message ready for the special session and it is a job. The Republicans and Republicats, their helpers in the Democratic party are of course doing what they can to put me in a hole.

But I've got to face the situation from a national and an international standpoint and not from a partisan political one. It is more important to save the world from totalitarianism than to be President another four years. Anyway a man in his right mind would never want to be President if he knew what it entails. Aside from the impossible administrative burden, he has to take all sorts of abuse from liars and demagogues. . . .

The people can never understand why the President does not use his supposedly great power to make 'em behave. Well all the President is, is a glorified public relations man who spends his time flattering, kissing and kicking people to get them to do what they are supposed to do anyway.

Then the family have to suffer too. No one of the name dares do what he'd ordinarily be at liberty to do because of the gossips. They say I'm my daughter's greatest handicap! Isn't that something? Oh well take care of yourself and some day the nightmare will be over and maybe we can all go back to normal living.

Love to you
Harry

The device of calling a special session captured the initiative from Mr. Taft and his fellow negative thinkers. Internationalist Republicans, such as Arthur Vandenberg in the Senate and Charles Eaton in the House, rallied to Dad's support. His leadership won almost unbelievable unanimity from the nation's press. The sheer courage of his performance inspired his old friend Charlie Ross to write one of the most wonderful letters that my father ever received. Remember that Charlie had come to work at Dad's request, with a certain feeling of pity for the accidental President. On Christmas Day, 1947, Charlie told Dad what thirty months with Harry S. Truman had taught him:

Dear Mr. President:

There is nothing in life, I think, more satisfying than friendship, and to have yours is a rare satisfaction indeed.

Two and a half years ago you "put my feet to the fire," as you said. I am happy that you did. They have been the most rewarding years of my life. Your faith in me, the generous manifestations of your friendship, the association with the fine people around you—your good "team"—all these have been an inspiration.

But the greatest inspiration, Mr. President, has been the character of you—you as President, you as a human being. Perhaps I can best say what is in my heart by telling you that my admiration for you, and my deep affection, have grown steadily since the day you honored me with your trust.

May this Christmas, and all your Christmases, be bright!

Sincerely yours,
Charles G. Ross

The Russian reaction to the Marshall Plan was savage. Throughout Europe, Stalin sent orders to his Communist leaders to redouble their efforts to seize power before the plan could begin its restorative work. The possibility of civil war in Italy and France was discussed in my father's office. B-29s had to be rushed to Greece to support the central government. The Italian government, grappling with a severe food shortage, appealed desperately for immediate shipment of all available supplies. Then in February, 1948, while Congress was still debating the Marshall Plan, the government of Czechoslovakia was toppled by a Communist coup. Leaders who looked to the West, such as Jan Masaryk, were murdered or imprisoned.

In London in December, 1947, Secretary of State Marshall had tried one last time to reach agreement on Germany. The Russians sang their old song about reparations, dredging up the $10 billion figure that my father had absolutely ruled out at the Potsdam Conference. They followed this up with a barrage of charges, accusing America, France, and Britain of every sort of treachery in Germany. General Marshall calmly informed Mr. Molotov that he considered further discussion useless and began meeting with Britain and France to plan the merger of their zones in Germany and the creation of the West German federal government. Ominously, early in March, the Russian-controlled press in Eastern Germany began warning West Germans not to cooperate with the Americans because the "unavoidable withdrawal of the Allies which will come about very suddenly in the near future" would leave them in a very exposed position. From Berlin General Lucius Clay flashed a warning that war "may come with dramatic suddenness."

At the center of things, my father, of course, was grimly aware of what seemed to be coming. From Key West, on March 3, 1948, he wrote me one of his most extraordinary letters:

Dear Margie,
I'm going to give you a record for yourself regarding these times. It will be a terrible bore. But some time in the future you may want to know the facts.

He then recounted his career from the 1940 election to his election as vice president, emphasizing the seeming inevitability of it all, how he won in 1940 against all odds, and was forced to take the vice presidency against his will:

As you know I was Vice President from January 20th, to April 12th, 1945. I was at cabinet meetings and saw Roosevelt once or twice in those months. But he never did talk to me confidentially about the war, or about foreign affairs or what he had in mind for the peace after the war.

I had been instrumental in starting the campaign in the Senate and had spent the summer of 1943 in trying to sell the country on the famous B^2H^2 resolution which endorsed the United Nations. I'll tell you someday how B^2H^2 originated. B^2H^2 stands for Ball, Benton, Hatch, Hill, all Senators at that time and [the first] three of them on my committee!

Well the catastrophe we all dreaded came on April 12th at 4:35 P.M. At 7:09 I was the President and my first decision was to go ahead with the San Francisco Conference to set up the UN.

Then I had to start in reading memorandums, briefs and volumes of correspondence on the World situation. Too bad I hadn't been on the Foreign Affairs Committee or that FDR hadn't informed me on the situation. I had to find out about the Atlantic Charter—which by the way does not exist on paper—the Casablanca meeting, the Montreal meeting, Teheran meeting, Yalta, Hull trip to Moscow, Bretton Woods and . . . other things too numerous to mention. Then Germany folded up. You remember that celebration which took place on May 8th, 1945—my 61st birthday.

Then came Potsdam. Byrnes, Adm. Leahy, Bohlen, interpreter now counsel to State Dept., the present ambassador to Russia, Ross and one or two others from the White House went along. I told Byrnes and Leahy to prepare an agenda to present to the conference. We worked on it and had one ready when we arrived at Potsdam. . . .

Stalin was one day late, Churchill was on hand when I arrived. I found the Poles in Eastern Germany without authority and Russia in possession of East Prussia, Latvia, Estonia and Lithuania, as well as Rumania and Bulgaria. Churchill had urged me to send our troops to the eastern border of Germany and keep them there.

We were about 150 miles east of the border of the occupation zone line agreed to at Yalta. I felt that agreements made in the war to keep Russia fighting should be kept and I kept them to the letter. Perhaps they should not have been adhered to so quickly because later I found force the only way to make Russia keep agreements. I did not know that then. Perhaps if we had been slower moving back we could have forced the Russians, Poles, Bulgars, Yugos, etc., to behave. But all of us wanted Russia in the Japanese war. Had we known what the atomic bomb would do we'd never have wanted the Bear in the picture. You must remember no tests had been made until several days after I arrived in Berlin. . . .

Well many agreements were made at Potsdam . . . agreements for the government of Germany—not one of which has Russia kept. We made agreements on China, Korea and other places, none of which has Russia kept. So that now we are faced with exactly the same situation with which Britain and France were faced in 1938–9 with Hitler. A totalitarian state is no different whether you call it Nazi, Fascist, Communist or Franco Spain.

Things look black. We've offered control and disarmament through the U.N., giving up our most powerful weapon for the world to control. The Soviets won't agree. They're upsetting things in Korea, China, in Persia [Iran] and in the Near East.

A decision will have to be made. I am going to make it. I am sorry to have bored you with this. But you've studied foreign affairs to some extent and I just wanted you to know your Dad as President asked for no territory, no reparations, no slave laborers—only peace in the world. We may have to fight for it. The oligarchy in Russia is no different from the Czars, Louis XIV, Napoleon, Charles I and Cromwell. It is a Frankenstein dictatorship worse than any of the others, Hitler included.

I hope it will end in peace. Be a nice girl and don't worry about your Dad's worries—but you'll hear all sorts of lies about the things I have told you—these are the facts.

I went to Potsdam with the kindliest feelings toward Russia —in a year and a half they cured me of it.

Lots of love,
Dad

War was obviously very close. On March 17, 1948, my father went before Congress with another special message. This time he did not mince words or hesitate to name names. He bluntly said: "The Soviet Union and its agents have destroyed the independence and democratic character of a whole series of nations in Eastern and Central Europe." He condemned "this ruthless course of action" and deplored "the tragic death of the Republic of Czechoslovakia." He called for the immediate passage of the Marshall Plan, the adoption of universal training, and the temporary revival of the draft. Although he did not state the dreadful statistics, he told Congress the ominous truth when he said, "Our armed forces lack the necessary men to maintain their authorized strength." Later the same day he flew to New York and addressed the Friendly Sons of Saint Patrick. There he spelled out for the nation what he had told me in his letter on March 3:

> We must not be confused about the issue which confronts the world today.
> The issue is as old as recorded history.
> It is tyranny against freedom. . . .
> We will have to take risks during the coming year—risks perhaps greater than any this country has been called upon to assume. But they are not risks of our own making, and we cannot make the danger vanish by pretending that it does not exist. We must be prepared to meet that danger with sober self-restraint and calm and judicious action if we are to be successful in our leadership for peace.

This was the spirit in which my father stood firm at Berlin, the spirit that created the Berlin airlift and sustained two million people who had chosen in free elections to overwhelmingly reject communism. A man of peace who had seen war, Dad was ready to go to the limit of his strength and patience in pursuit of peace. But he was not prepared to pay the price the Communists were asking—surrender. He made that clear to the Russians—and he made it equally clear to those Americans who were clustering around Henry Wallace, denouncing the Marshall Plan, and Harry S. Truman. I think his words still have relevance today:

> We must not fall victim to the insidious propaganda that peace can be obtained solely by wanting peace. This theory is advanced in the hope that it will deceive our people and that we will then permit our strength to dwindle because of the false belief that all is well in the world.

[CHAPTER]

Eighteen

WHILE COPING with these literally world-shaking problems, Dad had to bear the burden of two more personal worries, one very serious, and the other definitely unserious, to almost everybody but him, Mother, and me. On February 14, 1947, Mamma Truman broke her hip. On March 15 I launched my career as a singer. The two events are intertwined, and that is why I shall try to tell both stories simultaneously.

Dad constantly worried and fretted about his daughter, the would-be singer, in New York. When he wasn't doing that, he lamented my absence at the White House. "Margie will probably go up to New York sometime next week to continue her voice lessons and we'll be lonesome again," he wrote to his mother and sister on January 17, 1947.

> But she wants to do it and she wants to do it without exploiting the White House. And I'll have to agree to it I suppose, although I'd rather she'd stay at home. But I don't want her to be a Washington socialite and she doesn't want to be.

Those were among the truest words Dad has ever written. Actually, he was pleased that I wanted to have a career. It was largely the complications of being the President's daughter that disturbed him. On January 30 he wrote more philosophically to his mother and sister:

> Margaret went to New York yesterday and it leaves a blank

place here. But I guess the parting time has to come to every-body and if she wants to be a warbler and has the talent and will do the hard work necessary to accomplish her purpose, I don't suppose I should kick.

Most everyone who has heard her sing seems to think she has the voice. All she needs is training and practice.

He urged me to get plenty of both. "I hope your work is getting results," he wrote on February 6:

It takes work, work and more work to get satisfactory results as your pop can testify. Don't go off the deep end on contracts until you know for sure what you are getting—and what *you* have to offer.

I am only interested in your welfare and happy future and I stand ready to do anything to contribute to that end. But re-member that good name and honor are worth more than all the gold and jewels ever mined. Remember what old Shakespeare said, "Who steals my purse steals trash, but who filches my good name takes that which enriches not himself and makes me poor indeed." A good name and good advice is all your dad can give you.

I am counting the days until you come home.

When Mamma Truman fell in her bedroom and broke her hip, Dad immediately rushed his personal physician, Dr. Wallace Graham, to her side, and the following day flew to Grandview himself in the *Sacred Cow*. But Mamma Truman was by no means at death's door, as he feared. She was as alert and spunky as ever. General Vaughan, who was with Dad, made the mistake of scolding her: "You're giving us more trouble than all the Republicans," he said.

"I have no time for any smart remarks from you," she snapped. "I saw that picture of you last week—wasting time putting wreaths on the Lincoln Memorial."

Dad was so encouraged by this and other evidence of his moth-er's strength that he returned to Washington the following day. I came down to celebrate my twenty-third birthday with him on February 17, and he took me to see *Pinafore*. At the end of the show, thanks to some careful planning on the part of the White House, the whole cast burst into "Happy Birthday." Dad beamed. To be able to spring these nice surprises on people was one of the few compensations he received for his ordeal in the White House.

Back to New York I went, to my labors in the musical salt mines. I was starting to feel very discouraged about my future. The world of concert music seemed as impenetrable as ever. Then, on February 26, I got my first break. Carl Krueger, conductor of the Detroit Symphony Orchestra, invited me to sing over a nationwide radio hookup on Sunday, March 9. I accepted and went to work at a frantic pace, practicing in Town Hall and Carnegie Hall to accustom my voice to large areas.

On March 2, two days before I was to leave for Detroit, I came down with my favorite disease—a sore throat. I decided to ignore it. The following day I wrote in my diary, "I am going on that train tomorrow if it kills me or I have double pneumonia." By the time I checked into the Book-Cadillac Hotel in Detroit, after a seemingly endless ride in an unheated train, my throat was practically closed. Dr. Krueger, if he had been more interested in me and less in the publicity that I could generate, would have sent me home. My top tones had vanished. But he assured me that my voice was fine. The next day I had to spend hours posing with Dr. Krueger for photographers and sit through an interminable dinner at the Detroit Club. I began to have very strange sensations in my chest. The following morning I could hardly breathe.

Dad was in Mexico during these three harrowing days—I had turned down his pleas to make the trip with him to accept Dr. Krueger's invitation—but Mother was in the White House, and someone—perhaps my voice coach, Mrs. Strickler—told her about my alarming decline. A few hours later I was confronted by Dr. Graham, who took my pulse and temperature and told me I was not going to sing on Sunday. "You have bronchial pneumonia," he informed me.

I tried to protest, but by now I could barely talk. I felt miserable, both physically and mentally. I was sure that everyone would say that I had panicked and collapsed before my big test. That night Dad arrived back from Mexico, and the *Sacred Cow* landed in Detroit the following morning to take the patient back to the White House.

There I spent four days inhaling Benzoin and imbibing penicillin. On the fourth day I rose and on the fifth announced my determination to return to Detroit. Everyone begged me to stay in bed another week, but my Truman contrariness was at high tide, and on Saturday, March 15, I arrived in Detroit accompanied by Dr. Graham and Reathel Odum, Mother's secretary.

On March 13, in the same letter that he told me about the announcement of the Truman Doctrine, Dad included a pep talk for me:

> Now in addition to that terrible (and it is terrible) decision, your good old 94-year-old grandmother of the 1860 generation was unlucky and broke her leg—you, the "apple of my eye"— my sweet baby also had bad luck with your first appearance. Well, daughter, the dice roll—sometimes they are for you— sometimes they are not. I earnestly believe they were for you this time. I am just as sure as I can be that Sunday night at 8 P.M. another great soprano will go on the air. So don't worry about anything—just go on and sing as you sang that "Home, Sweet Home" record for your Dad—and nothing can stop you— even the handicap of being the Daughter of President Truman! . . .
>
> More love than you can realize now,
Dad

The entire Truman Administration was glued to the radio, at 8:28 Eastern Standard Time, on March 16, 1947. By now, numerous other things had gone wrong. Dr. Graham had ordered sunlamp treatments for me at the White House and the Medical Corps attendant left me under the lamp too long. I got a very bad sunburn, which did nothing to help me relax. The zipper of my dress, a long tailed blue chiffon with a many-layered billowing skirt, broke while I was putting it on and Reathel had to sew me into it. I was singing in an empty auditorium, with only the orchestra for company. Unknown to me. Dr. Krueger had arranged for two dozen reporters and critics to sit in the back row, ignoring the fact that I was singing into a radio microphone and the empty hall created acoustical problems that would make it very difficult for them to judge my voice. The announcer who introduced me yakked about who I was for several unnecessary minutes. Finally came the moment of truth. I sang "Cielito Lindo," a Spanish folk song, "Charmante Oiseau," an aria from Felician David's "La Perle du Brasil," and "The Last Rose of Summer."

As soon as my performance was over, Dr. Krueger unleashed the photographers on me again, and I staggered back to the Book-Cadillac in Detroit, exhausted. Dad telephoned to tell me that he thought I had been wonderful. But of course, I knew he would have said that if I had croaked like a frog. I was more anxious to hear what the critics said. On the whole they were very kind. Most of them found my voice quite acceptable and foresaw a promising future for me, with more training and experience. I was thrilled by praise from other singers, such as Robert Merrill, and by an offer from Hollywood to appear in a film named "Las Vegas," for a fee of $10,000. I was wise enough to decline that one, however, without even bothering to ask Dad. I knew what he would say.

Best of all, the public seemed to like me. I received thousands of letters, which had me writing thank you notes and signing mail for the next several weeks.

On March 22 Dad wrote to his mother, giving her a good description of his feelings about my debut:

> It was a great relief to have it over with. Don't think I ever spent such a miserable day and when that "bird" just kept talking just before she came on I wanted to shoot him.
> Mrs. Vinson, the wife of the Chief Justice, called up Bess and said that he walked the floor and cussed the roof off while he was making that announcement. I felt like doing the same thing, but all the gang who were with me at Key West and all the help in the house were seated around listening in at the same time so I had to sit still and bear it.

With me out of the way, Dad devoted most of his worries to his mother. She was not recovering as well as he wished or hoped from her fall. At ninety-four, bones heal very slowly, if at all. "I hope you'll get someone to help you and that you'll take good care of yourself," Dad wrote to his sister. "I worry about both of you a lot—but what makes me more worried I can't seem to do anything about it."

I went ·back to New York, to launch a concert career, which now seemed a very real possibility. Mother joined me to consult on clothes. On May 5 I signed contracts for appearances in Pittsburgh and Cleveland. I spent a week of intensive practice with my accompanist, Mrs. Carlton Shaw, and another week working on publicity pictures and press releases. Dad, of course, was following all this very carefully. In between worrying about the Russians and the Eightieth Congress, he worried about whether I would survive my travels around the country without another case of pneumonia, and if I managed this and became a success, whether I might develop into a prima donna. On May 14 he wrote me:

> The best of luck, your dad's praying for you. Wish I could go along and smooth all the rough spots—but I can't and in a career you must learn to overcome the obstacles without blowing up. Always be nice to all the people who can't talk back to you. I can't stand a man or woman who bawls out underlings to satisfy an ego.

I was packing for my appearance in Pittsburgh when Mother telephoned me with shattering news. Mamma Truman was on the point of death. Dad had flown to Independence. He did not want me to change my plans, because it might be a false alarm. In Pittsburgh, on the morning of May 19, came another phone call, telling me that Mamma Truman was not expected to live through the day. That made singing out of the question. I canceled my appearance and took a plane for Kansas City. My concert manager was absolutely wonderful about this decision and told me not to worry about all the defunct tickets I had just created. I spent five days with Dad, while he spent every available moment at Mamma Truman's bedside. She was terribly weak, but her mind was still amazingly clear. She brightened when she saw me, and that made the tangle of canceled concerts I had left behind me worthwhile.

Dad signed the Greek-Turkish Aid Act in his Muehlebach Hotel office on May 22, after it had finally cleared the Senate. The doctors had given Mamma Truman up two days before this date, but she declined to co-operate. On the twenty-fourth she awoke early in the morning and asked for a slice of watermelon. Dr. Graham said she could have anything she wanted. Half the Democrats in Missouri were soon looking for watermelon, which was out of season. One was found and rushed to Grandview. Mamma Truman ate most of it, and the following day she was talking politics, while the doctors watched and listened, dumbfounded.

"Is Taft going to be nominated next year?" she asked Dad.

"He might be," Dad said.

Mamma Truman thought about this for a few moments. Senator Taft was her most unfavorite Republican, and that is saying a lot. "Harry, are you going to run?" she asked.

"I don't know, Mamma."

Mamma Truman frowned at the mere thought that her son might pass up an opportunity to thrash Senator Taft. "Don't you think it's about time you made up your mind?" she asked him.

On May 29 Mamma Truman was so improved that Dad and Mother and I flew back to Washington. Early in June we took a trip to Canada, but Dad kept in close touch with Grandview by mail and telephone. "Tell Mamma to 'behave' herself," he wrote on July 10. A few days later his sister Mary sent him very disappointing news. Mamma Truman's broken bone was not healing, and the doctors were now saying that she would probably never get out of bed again. On July 25 Dad wrote to Aunt Mary:

> It is certainly too bad after all the effort and work you put forth for her that Mamma can't get up. But it has been a great fight and we almost won it. Anyway we know that everything possible was done.

By this time Mother and I had gone home to Missouri. I was practicing hard, getting ready for a reconstructed concert tour. There was no trace of worry, only the usual complaints about loneliness in the letters Dad sent me in mid-July.

> It is very lonesome around here even if I do work from daylight until dark [he wrote on July 16]. It is much nicer when someone is around making a "noise." Then the "ghosts" continue to walk up and down the hall and around the study. . . .
>
> I hope your lessons are working out to advantage. I sure want that postponed concert tour to be a grand success. . . .
>
> Don't eat too much chocolate ice cream, be nice to your aunts and go see your country grandma once in a while. . . .

On July 19, he was teasing me.

> Do you need anything—money, marbles or chalk? You may have anything I have. You should see the most beautiful and ancient ring the latest Arab visitor gave me. It is a peculiar stone carved evidently in ancient Egypt. The ring itself was made before Christ. I can't get it on.

Early in the morning of July 26 his sister Mary called Dad at the White House to tell him that Mamma Truman had pneumonia and was close to death. Dad had to stay in the White House long enough to sign the armed forces unification bill, one of the great achievements of his administration, but he was airborne before noon. He was dozing in his cabin when his mother's face suddenly appeared before him with amazing clarity. Dad sat up, terribly shaken. A few minutes later Dr. Graham handed him a report which the pilot of the plane had just received. Mamma Truman was dead. "I knew she was gone when I saw her in that dream," Dad said. "She was saying goodbye to me."

We met Dad at the airport at 3:30 P.M. He was calm, but very sad. Mamma Truman had been part of his life for so long, he found it hard to realize she was gone. In spite of his grief, he immediately took charge. He appointed me his deputy, charged with making sure "none of the family gets pushed around during the funeral.'"

The next two days were hectic. Dad spent most of his time in Grandview, talking to people who came to pay their respects. The following day, July 28, I summed up in my diary as follows:

> Monday, July 28th, 1947
>
> The funeral was at home in Grandview. It was brief, as Mamma Truman wished. The house was covered with flowers and even the floor was carpeted with floral tributes. The Cabinet sent a huge wreath of red roses and President Alemán of Mexico a huge wreath. One of the gardenias came from Cuba and one of the glads from the Senate. Mother got an enormous spray of red roses, Mamma Truman's favorite, for the casket. All the other flowers were sent to hospitals. We all drove to Forest Hill Cemetery for the services and they were short too. She is beside Grandfather Truman now.

On August 1 Dad was still feeling his loss.

> Someday you'll be an orphan just as your dad is now [he wrote to me]. I am going up to Shangri-la today and will meet your ma at Silver Spring on Monday as I return to town. Wish you were coming back with her. This place is a tomb without you and your mother.
>
> I have been looking over the thousands of letters, cards & telegrams about your old grandmother. They come from every

state and every country and are very kind. Have heard from the Pope, King George, Chiang Kai-shek, the Queen of Holland and every President in the Western Hemisphere.

But the ones I appreciate most come from home. Heard from men & women your mother and I went to school with—some I hadn't heard from in forty years. Got one from the colored man who always waits on me at the Kansas City Club and one signed Fields [head White House butler], Pye [another butler] and Prettyman [his valet], one signed by all the sergeants who guard my plane. I like them more than all the topnotchers. Your dad just can't appreciate a formal stuffed-shirt approach. Had letters, cards and wires from all Senators, House members and governors, even Dewey and Taft.

I picked up my singing career again with an appearance in Los Angeles. I sang in the Hollywood Bowl on August 26, 1947, with Eugene Ormandy conducting the orchestra. On October 17 I relaunched my concert tour in Pittsburgh. Mother, Mr. and Mrs. John Snyder, Mrs. Fred Vinson, Pearl Mesta, and several other Washington supporters flew in to boost my morale. Dad would have given anything to come, but he absolutely vetoed the idea, in spite of strong pleas from the mayor of the city and Senator Myers of Pennsylvania. "I'm afraid I'd upset the apple cart if I went," he wrote to me a few days before the event. I understood exactly what he meant. He wanted me to get the publicity, and it is impossible for anyone, even the President's daughter, to manage this when the Chief Executive and his traveling circus arrive on the scene.

The concert was a success and I took off on a swing through the south and southwest, singing every second or third night at places like Amarillo, Forth Worth, Oklahoma City, Little Rock, Memphis, and Shreveport. Dad kept very good track of me as you can see from this letter he wrote on December 3, 1947:

My dear daughter:— I called you last night because I was not sure you were comfortably and properly situated in Des Moines.

You should call your mamma and dad *every time* you arrive in a town. . . . Someday maybe (?) you'll understand what torture it is to be worried about the only person in the world that counts. You should know by now that your dad has only three such persons. Your ma, you and your Aunt Mary. And your

Aunt Mary is running around just as you are. [Aunt Mary was very active in the Order of the Eastern Star.] So—you see beside all the world and the United States I have a couple of other worries.

On December 21 I ended my tour with a concert in Constitution Hall in Washington, D.C. It was one of the most wonderful nights of my life. Dad could join the audience here without turning the city inside out. Every seat was filled. The Cabinet sent me a great basket of red roses and I received eleven bouquets over the footlights. I sang better than I had sung anywhere else throughout the tour. Dad was immensely pleased. I really think in some ways he enjoyed the evening more than I did.

It was a perfect prelude to our first White House Christmas. The thought of Christmas at home without Mamma Truman was too painful for Dad. So he invited the whole family to join us at 1600 Pennsylvania Avenue. Here is how he summed it up in a memorandum he wrote on his calendar that day:

> We have a most happy and pleasant Christmas, with all the brothers of Bess present. Frank, George & Fred with their wives Natalie, May & Christine with two children of Fred—David & Marion. . . .
>
> My sister, Mary Jane came on the 22nd and I am sure spent an enjoyable time. My brother could not come—in fact I didn't ask him because he told me he intended to have his family at the farm. He has four boys all married but one and a lovely daughter. I called him and he said 22 sat down to dinner at his house. I am sure they had a grand dinner—a much happier one than a formal butler served one, although ours was nice enough.
>
> But family dinner cooked by the family, mother, daughters, granddaughters, served by them is not equalled by White House, Delmonico's . . . or any other formal one.

[CHAPTER]

Nineteen

ALONG WITH international crises and personal grief and singing debuts, 1947 was the year of the Truman Traveling Troupe. This was the nickname I conjured up for the inevitable "circus" that Dad took with him on his trips to Mexico, Canada, and Brazil. These trips were not vacations—they did not have the slightest resemblance to the trip Dad took to Bermuda in 1946. They were serious political expeditions, aimed at building solidarity between the United States and our sister nations in the Western Hemisphere. With Russia threatening aggression in Europe and Asia, Dad felt it was vital to build friendship on our borders.

I did not go with Dad to Mexico in early March. I was preparing for my concert debut. He tried everything to entice me to join him, but I am just as stubborn as he is, when I make up my mind to do something. So he flew off without me.

Tremendous crowds greeted him in Mexico City. Relations between Mexico and the United States had frequently been strained and at times downright hostile in the past. We fought one war with them, and almost went to war a second time in 1914 and again in 1916. My father was anxious to sweep away the legacy of suspicion of the United States that these confrontations had created. So he made the first state visit ever undertaken by an American President to Mexico.

He was delighted by the enormous crowds. In response he broke away from his Mexican and American Secret Service escorts and mingled with the people. In an address to the Mexican legislature, he pledged that the United States would continue to observe the nonintervention clause of the Good Neighbor Policy. But he insisted that nonintervention did not mean indifference. Dad also managed to exhaust Secret Service men and reporters by climbing up and down pyramids and temples outside Mexico City, unbothered by the thin air—the altitude is over 7,000 feet—that later gave several Olympic athletes all sorts of trouble.

The following day my father drew upon his knowledge of history for a gesture that aroused the deepest emotions in the Mexican people. He suddenly announced he wanted to visit Chapultepec. The State Department types in the American Embassy were aghast. Almost exactly one hundred years ago, the American army had stormed this fortress in its successful assault on Mexico City. Among the Mexican garrison had been several hundred young cadets who fought to the last man, with incredible bravery. A handful of them—six, I believe—were trapped on the roof and committed suicide by leaping over the walls rather than surrender. A shrine to *Los Niños Héroes* had been erected by the Mexican people in Chapultepec.

After touring the fortress my father went straight to this shrine and placed a wreath before it. Then he stood with bowed head, paying silent tribute to the memory of these young men who had died so heroically for their country. A contingent of contemporary cadets was drawn up in precise military formation, and when they saw the President of the United States make this almost unbelievable (to them) gesture, tears streamed down their cheeks. "Brave men do not belong to any one country," Dad said. "I respect bravery wherever I see it." At a luncheon in the U.S. Embassy later that day, President Alemán of Mexico conferred on Dad the title of Champion of Inter-American Solidarity.

I joined the Traveling Troupe for our next trip, to Canada, on June 9, 1947. We spent a really delightful three days there. The prime minister, MacKenzie King, was one of the most charming statesmen I have ever met, with a delicious sense of humor. We loved the old world charm of Ottawa. It was like a trip to London with only one tenth the trouble. Even that quintessential Missouri Democrat, Harry S. Truman, admitted that he liked the "royal" touches that were a standard part of our greeting. We walked up miles of red carpet and regularly received three cheers and a tiger. Dad spoke to a joint session of Parliament. He hailed the Canadian-American tradition of friendship and reiterated the Truman Doctrine. In a press conference he told reporters that the United States wanted only peace in the world and friendship with every nation. He told them to underline "every." There was the usual whirl of receptions, lunches, and dinners, plus a stop at Niagara Falls to get the view from the Canadian side, which they solemnly assured us was the best.

Canada and Mexico were only warm-ups for the main event of the Truman Traveling Troupe—our September visit to Brazil. General Marshall had been representing the United States at the Inter-American Conference for the Maintenance of Continental Peace and Security. The conference was a diplomatic triumph for the United States. The twenty American nations represented there agreed to sign a pact which forbade any one of them from committing aggression against another nation in our hemisphere, and also bound them to act in concert against an aggressor. Dad was so pleased with this dramatic affirmation of inter-American unity that he decided he would fly there and join in signing the treaty, and at the same time join Brazil in celebrating the one hundred twenty-fifth anniversary of her independence, on September 7. We flew out of Washington aboard the *Independence,* the lovely DC-6 that had replaced the *Sacred Cow,* on Sunday, August 31.

A stopover in Trinidad for rest and refueling turned into a wild combination of comedy and adventure. In order to reach Rio in time for a scheduled reception, we had to take off from Trinidad at the ungodly hour of 3 A.M. It was raining as it can only come down in the tropics, in thick, drenching torrents. To complicate matters, we all had to dress in formal clothes. Mother and I in our best dresses and hats and Dad and his entourage in striped trousers and morning coats. We looked like a bunch of broken-down actors leaving town one jump ahead of the sheriff. But we finally got aboard the plane, buckled ourselves into our seats, and were watching the propellors begin to spin when somebody said, "Where's Charlie?"

Charlie Ross was still asleep, back in the commandant's house where we had spent the night—or more exactly half the night.

Correspondence secretary Bill Hassett volunteered to go get him. By the time Bill had finished sloshing through several miles of jungle in the downpour, both he and Charlie were not exactly visions of sartorial splendor. In fact, their striped pants looked like they had spent the previous year at the bottom of a laundry bag. We finally decided to put them in the middle of the procession and hope for the best. A tailor with a hot iron was not included on the staff of the Truman Traveling Troupe.

After a fascinating flight across the Brazilian jungle and the Amazon, we arrived at Galiao, across the bay from Rio de Janeiro, where Secretary Marshall and Mrs. Marshall, and Ambassador and Mrs. William D. Pawley met us. A letter Dad wrote to his sister Mary tells the rest of the story from his point of view.

> We were met at the dock by the President, First Lady and Cabinet members of Brazil. We landed on an island in the bay [Galiao], and came ashore in launches. We paraded through the main streets of the town. There must have been over a million people out and I never saw a more enthusiastic crowd.
>
> We went to the Embassy and had dinner with General and Mrs. Marshall and Ambassador Pawley and his wife. Then next morning—Tuesday—drove up to Petropolis where I closed the conference. . . .
>
> We spent a quiet Wednesday at the Embassy. The President's three daughters took Margie to the opera, Tosca. I slipped in for the second act and then left after they caught me and gave me a standing ovation. . . .

I had only one complaint about our reception. As we crossed the harbor, our battleship *Missouri* and the Brazilian battleship *Minas Gerais* thundered out 21-gun salutes. As an old artilleryman, Dad was totally unbothered by the boom of cannon. In fact, he liked it. My sensitive ears found it intolerable. So many salutes were fired in the following days, Admiral Leahy finally got tired of watching me standing there with my hands over my ears and presented me with a roll of absorbent cotton. It didn't do much good.

On September 3, Dad again eluded his Secret Service men —even more totally than he had in Mexico City. He and Dr. Graham climbed a thousand feet up nearby Mount Corcovado and brought back a half-dozen orchids. This soon got into the news, and every orchid grower in the United States, so it seemed, sent samples from his garden or greenhouse to us in Washington.

On Friday evening came the climax of our visit, a state dinner given by the foreign minister at Itamarati Palace. Here is Dad's description of it in a letter to his sister Mary:

> We went to Itamarati Palace (and palace it is) to a state dinner . . . after which some beautiful dancers were put on. We sat at one end of a beautiful pool of water lighted all the way around by candles and on which four swans swam and at the other end was a stage. The pool was flanked by royal palms at least 150 feet high.
>
> After the concert and dance we walked around and met people. That good-for-nothing King Carol of Rumania came and sat by me. I turned my back on him and he got up and left me alone. The President of Brazil said he had crashed the party.
>
> Last night we had our state dinner for the President at the Embassy. It was a nice affair. Today we review the parade (the Independence parade), go aboard the Mo and start home and will I be glad!

Dad neglected to add in this letter the marvelous bit of dialogue he exchanged with King Carol of Rumania. Dad had met Carol's son, King Michael, who had given him a vivid history of how his father had wrecked Rumania with his erratic combination of greed for power and pursuit of his illicit love, Madame Lupescu. So Dad had no use for Carol on five or six counts. When Carol introduced himself, Dad said, "I met your very fine young son in Washington. I think he is greatly to be commended for his courage in staying on the job." With that he turned back to Brazil's first lady, Mrs. Dutra, who was on his left, and resumed conversing with her.

Carol was hard to discourage, however. "Mr. President, do you speak French?" he asked.

Dad looked over his shoulder at him and said, "No French— and very little English."

This time Carol got the message. He stood up, bowed stiffly, and departed.

During the parade we stood at attention in the reviewing stand while what seemed like the entire Brazilian army marched by for four and a half hours. It was a beautiful, even a spectacular show, and the military music was magnificent. But my poor feet almost collapsed. I never felt more relieved in my life when Matt Connelly whispered to me that there was a camp stool at the back of the reviewing stand, and I could sit down on it for exactly two minutes. Matt actually timed me—and everyone else—with a stopwatch, so that no one got more than the allotted break.

At the end of the parade, we boarded my ship, the *Missouri*, while every gun in the Brazilian navy and in their shore batteries blasted salutes to us. We relaxed on the fantail of the *Missouri*, enjoying the magnificent view of Rio from the harbor, and then staggered off to bed. We were looking forward to twelve days of beautiful, restful isolation aboard the big ship.

For the first few days we seemed to be getting it. Dad wandered around wearing a yachting cap given to him by a Washington club. He called it his "six-star hat," which meant that he outranked five-star Admiral Leahy. He ate with the officers, the chief petty officers, and the crew. He chatted with sailors and marines on and off duty, and watched the *Missouri* refuel our two escorting destroyers. Best of all, as far as he was concerned—and worst of all, as far as I was concerned—was artillery practice which included firing at drone planes with the 40-millimeter and five-inch guns. The five-inchers make the most agonizing imaginable bang.

On our third day out of Rio, odd things suddenly began happening aboard the Mighty Mo. Sailors started wearing the weirdest uniforms—their pants on backwards, their leggings worn above bare feet. Other sailors swung long canvas billies at their posteriors. In the officers mess, some of the ensigns and lieutenants sat at the table with their chairs turned backwards, and another group sang ridiculous songs throughout the meal. We were approaching the equator, and the traditional initiation ceremonies practiced by sailors for several hundred years when they crossed the line were about to begin.

I thought it was all pretty ridiculous. I've never been fond of initiations or secret ceremonies, but Dad loved every minute of it. He chuckled with delight while the shellbacks—those who have already crossed the line—laid out tables full of leg irons, saws, knives, whips, and other instruments of torture.

As night fell, a barrage of rockets and flares went up, informing us that Davy Jones had arrived aboard the ship. The band began playing, "Sailing, Sailing Over the Bounding Main," and the bugler sounded five ruffles—one more than Dad himself got when he came aboard. We all assembled on the superstructure deck to greet Davy. Dad was wearing a sport shirt and a baker's hat, Mother was similarly attired, and I had been forced to don a raincoat, boots, and a sou'wester hat.

Davy Jones handed a communication from Neptunus Rex to Captain Dennison, the commander of the *Missouri*. The captain dutifully read it aloud:

> Greetings! Hear ye! As you enter my royal domain, in latitude 0 degrees, 0 minutes longitude, 36 degrees 30 minutes west, you will have your ship and crew in readiness for a rigid inspection by me and my court. This you will communicate to all infections of the land under your command, to wit: all tadpoles, pollywogs, sand crabs, sea lawyers, deck massagers, and plow deserters.
>
> Hear ye again! You will change course and speed so as to enter my aqueous domain early tomorrow morning.

"I have heard on good authority you have on board the No. 1 pollywog of your country, Captain," Davy solemnly said after this announcement was read.

"That's correct," Captain Dennison said and introduced Dad.

"How do you do, Mr. Jones," Dad said.

Davy, who was really a chief petty officer, was so awestruck by finding himself face to face with the President that he blew his lines. Captain Dennison rescued him by introducing the No. 1 shellback of the United States Navy, Admiral Leahy.

"I remember you very well," Davy said. "I first met you in 1898 when you crossed the line in the battleship *Oregon* while en route around Cape Horn to take part in the battle of Santiago."

Davy then said goodnight, and everybody went to bed.

I wrote in my diary that night: "Grown men have to act like boys now and then, I suppose. I haven't seen anything like it since I was in junior high school and even then we weren't so silly."

At eight bells the next morning, we were summoned to fall in on deck. We were at latitude 0 degrees, 0 minutes. Ten minutes later the *Missouri*'s loudspeaker blared: "King Neptune and his royal party standing towards the ship."

Neptune wore a long white beard and a green robe. His queen wore a similar costume, and was smoking a long black cigar. The royal family were accompanied by a staff of sixty, which made them more formidable than the Truman Traveling Troupe. The band played six ruffles, and a one-gun salute was fired. Then—an incredible sight—the Jolly Roger—the old pirate skull and crossed bones—went soaring up the *Missouri*'s mast. King Neptune was in command. After inspecting the ship, he took his seat with his queen on a throne set up on the fantail. Admiral Leahy, the senior shellback, sat on His Majesty's left. Above the throne a banner announced the royal policy, "Expect no justice."

The royal prosecutor then summoned the No. 1 pollywog to stand trial. Dad advanced to the foot of the throne, and the royal prosecutor accused him of having insulted King Neptune by using "a despicable and unnatural means of travel, namely by air" on his trip south.

Dad pleaded guilty, but said that a No. 1 pollywog had to do this sort of thing occasionally. The royal prosecutor, in one of his few displays of benevolence that day, decided to recommend a light sentence. "In recognition of the fact that you have finally delivered this large number of pollywogs for judgment before his royal court, His Majesty is disposed to exercise some leniency in your case. You are commanded to furnish each member of his royal court a card bearing your autograph, and you will further be prepared to continue to furnish a bountiful supply of Corona Corona cheroots for the shellback members of the President's mess during the remainder of this cruise and forever after."

Dad agreed to "cop this plea" and was proclaimed a trusty shellback.

Mother was the next victim. She too was charged with flying by air, and she was also blamed for showing "typical feminine disregard of our royal whim" by having "so cozened and comforted our No. 1 pollywog and otherwise made home so delightful for him that you have delayed for many years this long-sought audience with Harry S. Truman."

Mother pleaded guilty and things looked grim for her, for a moment. But the royal prosecutor decided that he would indulge in his "royal prerogative and pleasure to grant an occasional amnesty every few centuries." So he proclaimed Mother a trusty shellback and first lady of Neptune's domain.

I was next. I was accused of living in a fish bowl (the White House) without getting permission from His Royal Highness. To

[379]

escape worse punishment I had to bow down before the King and then lead six pollywog ensigns in "Anchors Aweigh."

The rest of the Truman Traveling Troupe did not fare so well. Most of them got clamped to the royal operating table and had some royal medicine—a dreadful mixture of alum, mustard, quinine, and epsom salts—poured down their throats. They were then jabbed with electrically charged pitchforks until they reached the domain of the royal barber who anointed them with grease. Finally the royal undertaker flipped them backwards from a teetering chair into the royal tank. They crawled out of there, shivering and covered with grease, and had to negotiate a sixty-foot double line of shellbacks who powdered their rear ends with heavy ropes. Everyone got the business, including the reporters, and then the shellbacks went to work on the crew. I wrote in my diary: "I didn't much like this horseplay." But Dad thought it was so much fun that two months later he held a black tie dinner in the White House for the shellback members of the Truman Troupe.

I had more fun playing deck tennis on the *Missouri*. Stanley Woodward, the chief of protocol, and I made quite a team.' We beat almost everybody who came up against us. Sometimes the deck would be wet from spray and that made the going even trickier. There is a hilarious picture of me swinging at a high lob while Stanley is kicking his foot excitedly in my direction. The two-dimensional photograph makes it look like he is boosting me off the deck on the end of his toe.

We were at sea for twelve happy days. Don't get the impression, however, that Dad was out of touch with what was happening. The communications center on the *Missouri* averaged 52,000 words of messages from the White House each day, and he made numerous presidential decisions on board. Because of the world situation, he ordered Secretary of Defense Forrestal to be sworn in ahead of schedule. When a hurricane devastated Florida and churned up the ocean around us, he authorized special federal aid for the state.

On Sunday, September 21, I was back home in Independence, and Dad had already spent a full day of work in the White House. It was a wonderful trip, rich in unforgettable memories. But I summed up a typical Truman reaction to an exotic three weeks with the following line in my diary: "We all had family dinner together. My own bed feels so good!"

[CHAPTER]

Twenty

BEFORE THE 1948 CAMPAIGN picked up the kind of steam I have
described in the opening pages of this book, my father had to deal
with one more large international problem which had intensely
emotional domestic roots—Palestine—and an equally pressing national problem—civil rights.

In some ways Palestine was the most difficult dilemma of his
entire administration. He did his best to solve it, and even today
he admits his best was probably not good enough. Perhaps the
situation was impossible, from the start. I have already mentioned
the intense pressure which numerous American Jews put on Dad
from the moment he entered the White House—and his increasing
resentment of this pressure.

But my father never allowed his emotions to influence the
creation of a sound policy. Nor did he allow a minor personal
annoyance to interfere with his deep sympathy for the tragic
remnants of Europe's Jews, who were huddling, miserable and
demoralized, in refugee camps. By now Dad and the rest of
America knew the full dimensions of Hitler's terrible "final solution," and his heart went out to these pathetic survivors. At the
same time he had to face the unrelenting stand of the Arabs
against further Jewish immigration to Palestine. Russia stood in
the wings, ready to take advantage of any miscalculation.

Both the Republican and Democratic platforms in 1944 had
backed unrestricted Jewish immigration to Palestine. This was
another strong factor in Dad's position. He had campaigned and

[381]

won on the Democratic platform and felt committed to it. President Roosevelt had authorized Rabbi Stephen Wise to tell newsmen that he gave "full backing" to the Palestine plank. But he had also assured King Ibn Saud that no decisions would be made on Palestine without full consultation with the Arabs, and he confirmed this promise in a letter a week before his death. Once more FDR was relying on the magic of his personal diplomacy to reconcile two peoples, who were in many ways more hostile than the Russians and the Americans.

The election of the Labour government in Great Britain added fuel to the smoldering situation. For eleven annual Labour party conferences, and as recently as May, 1945, a few weeks before the election, Labour had declared that it was "in favor of building Palestine as the Jewish national home." The impending shift in British policy aroused Arab leaders and they sent a stream of vehement letters to the White House.

Dad, the man in the middle, tried to work out a compromise that he thought was both just and merciful. As early as the Potsdam Conference, he discussed with the British the immediate admission of 100,000 Jewish refugees from war-torn Europe to Palestine. If the British, who controlled the country under a League of Nations mandate, had accepted this idea, the explosive elements in the situation might have been defused.

But Labour Prime Minister Attlee and his foreign secretary, Ernest Bevin, did a dismaying about-face when they came into power in London. They took the advice of the senior officials in the British Colonial Office and turned their backs on the Labour party's repeated calls for a Jewish national home. They announced that no more than 1,500 immigration certificates a month would be issued. For the next two years Dad continued to press his 100,000-refugee compromise on Mr. Bevin and Mr. Attlee. Meanwhile, the situation in Palestine drifted into the hands of the extremists. The Haganah, the illegal Jewish armed force which had been formed to defend Jewish settlements against roving Arab bands, began attacking and destroying radar installations, police stations, railway bridges, in a campaign to weaken British control. This provoked Mr. Bevin into angry outbursts against the Jews for wanting "to get too much to the head of the queue." The American State Department career men were equally convinced that Jewish desires had to be balanced against the danger of driving the Arabs into the arms of the Soviet Union.

With Dad's support, Britain and America created a Committee of Inquiry, six Americans and six Englishmen, to study the situation thoroughly and make a report to both governments. The committee held hearings in Washington and London and traveled throughout Western Europe and the Near East. Their report was a strong endorsement that Palestine become a national home for the Jewish people. It refuted the notion that the idea had been nurtured by wealthy foreign Jews. Many Jews of Western Europe, especially the refugees, believed in it so thoroughly they were prepared to give their lives for it. Finally, the committee accepted Dad's idea that 100,000 immigration certificates—approximately the number of Jews then in refugee camps in Germany and Austria —be issued immediately. Dad hailed this report. Ernest Bevin, the British foreign secretary, who had previously said he would back any unanimous conclusions—and the 100,000-certificates recommendation was unanimous—rejected it, and called on the United States to share all the problems of Palestine with Great Britain, including the cost of maintaining some 90,000 troops in the country.

At this point the full dimensions of Britain's financial collapse were not yet evident, and Dad was assuming that they were prepared to share at least some of the burdens of maintaining the peace and standing firm against Russian aggression. He rejected Bevin's proposal but demonstrated amazing patience with the foreign secretary, who continued to make indiscreet public comments on Palestine. On June 12, 1946, at a Labour party conference, Bevin sneered that Truman wanted 100,000 Jews admitted to Palestine because the Americans did not want any more Jews in New York City. Later, at the height of the Greek-Turkish crisis, he made a similar remark on Palestine which aroused violent anti-British hostility in the United States and threatened Dad's whole program of resistance to Russian aggression.

The effort Dad was making to untangle the mess in Palestine can be seen in a comment he made to his mother on July 31, 1946:

Had the most awful day I've ever had Tuesday—saw somebody every 15 minutes on a different subject, and held a Cabinet luncheon and spent two solid hours discussing Palestine and got nowhere.

In the autumn of 1946 Mr. Bevin announced that Great Britain was washing its hands of Palestine and handed the entire dispute to the United Nations. There the Russians leaped eagerly into the troubled waters, lashing out at the British and declaring themselves thoroughly in favor of the Jewish aspiration for a national home. In the light of later developments in the Middle East, it is indeed ironic to recall this bit of history. It was, of course, the most cynical of political gambits. Stalin himself was anti-Semitic and anti-Zionist, but Russia was looking for any opportunity to establish a foothold on the shores of the Mediterranean.

The UN, after months of wrangling, voted in favor of partitioning Palestine into two states, one Jewish and one Arab. Dad did his utmost to remain neutral during this vote. He was deeply disturbed by the pressure which some Zionist leaders put on him to browbeat South American countries and other nations where we might have influence into supporting partition. "I have never approved of the practice of the strong imposing their will on the weak, whether among men or nations," Dad said. When I speak of pressure, perhaps a bit of statistics will help. In 1947, 1948, and 1949 the White House received 86,500 letters, 841,903 postcards, and 51,400 telegrams on the subject of Palestine.

In spite of the UN vote, the British and the Arabs remained irreconcilable to partition and it soon became apparent that the solution could be imposed only by force. But the UN had no army, and the demobilized American armed forces were practically impotent, even if Dad had been willing to consider committing them. In April, 1948, in the midst of the grave crisis with Russia, which Dad felt was drawing us close to war, he asked the Joint Chiefs how many troops we would need if we took over the trusteeship of Palestine. The answer was 104,000, as a minimum, and the United States could not send more than a division—about 15,000—anywhere without "partial mobilization."

A passage from a letter which Dad wrote to Mrs. Roosevelt around this time sheds more light on the problems he was facing.

August 23, 1947
The action of some of our United States Zionists will eventually prejudice everyone against what they are trying to get done.

[384]

I fear very much that the Jews are like all underdogs. When they get on top they are just as intolerant and as cruel as the people were to them when they were underneath. I regret this situation very much because my sympathy has always been on their side.

After the partition vote, he sounded a similar note in a letter to Henry Morgenthau, Jr.:

December 2, 1947

Dear Henry,

I appreciated very much your telegram of November twenty-ninth but I wish you would caution all your friends who are interested in the welfare of the Jews in Palestine that now is the time for restraint and caution and an approach to the situation in the future that will allow a peaceful settlement.

The vote in the United Nations is only the beginning and the Jews must now display tolerance and consideration for the other people in Palestine with whom they will necessarily have to be neighbors.

A few months later, it was the British who were being criticized in another letter to Mrs. Roosevelt.

February 2, 1948

General Marshall and I are attempting to work out a plan for the enforcement of the mandate of the United Nations. I discussed the matter with Franklin, Jr. the other day and I sincerely hope that we can arrive at the right solution.

Your statements on Great Britain are as correct as they can be. Britain's role in the Near East and Britain's policy with regard to Russia has not changed in a hundred years. Disraeli might just as well be Prime Minister these days.

I understand all that and I am trying to meet it as best I can.

By no means all the leaders of the American Jewish community attacked Dad's policy. When the Anglo-American Committee of Inquiry's report was made public, Supreme Court Justice Felix Frankfurter, probably the most prominent supporter of Palestine in public life, told Dave Niles, the White House specialist on minority groups, that he had only one regret, "that Justice Brandeis did not live to see this report—he would have called it a miracle." Frankfurter then launched into a tirade against those

Jewish spokesmen who, he said, "preferred a Jewish state on paper rather than doing something real for human beings."

More than once, the Palestine question was put to Dad in terms of American politics. At a Cabinet luncheon on October 6, 1947, Bob Hannegan almost made a speech, pointing out how many Jews were major contributors to the Democratic party's campaign fund and were expecting the United States to support the Zionists' position on Palestine. My father observed that if they would only keep quiet, the situation might yet be rescued without war. He refused to go beyond the report of the United Nations Special Committee on Palestine, which had recommended partition.

Many Zionists were vigorously protesting the boundaries allotted the Jewish state, which excluded the southern section of Palestine, the Negev. On November 19, Chaim Weizmann, the future president of Israel, visited Dad and described, with the eye of the imaginative scientist that he was, what Israel could do with the Negev, if it was given to them. His vivid description ignited the enthusiasm of the ex-senator who had toiled for years to create regional development and flood controls in the Missouri Valley, and Dad immediately telephoned our representative at the UN and told him to support the inclusion of the Negev in the Jewish state. But the UN refused to agree.

My father was blamed for this failure, and attacks on him by Jewish spokesmen, and would-be spokesmen, multiplied. On March 11, 1948, Dad was forced to open his press conference with one of the angriest statements he ever made:

> I want to pay attention to a vicious statement that was made by a columnist in a New York gossip paper, in which he said I had made the statement to the editor of a New York paper here that the Jews in New York were disloyal. I had thought I wouldn't have to add another liar's star to that fellow's crown, but I will have to do it. That is just a lie out of the whole cloth. That is as emphatic as I can put it.

By now, the British had announced that they were withdrawing from Palestine on May 15, and they made it clear that they could not care less what happened after that. The Arabs and the Jews seemed to be preparing for war. Remember that we were bracing for war with Russia at the same time and this was absorbing most of Dad's waking hours. Partition now seemed out of the question, if war was to be avoided. The State Department, which had never favored partition, advanced an alternate plan for a temporary UN trusteeship that would replace the British mandate and maintain a status quo. My father never formally committed himself to this plan. It was conceived by career officers in the State Department who were convinced that our support of partition would cost us the friendship of the Arab states and the loss of their vast oil resources. Meanwhile, the Jews announced that the moment the British withdrew they intended to declare the creation of the State of Israel.

At this point in the mounting tension, Eddie Jacobson, Dad's old partner in his Kansas City men's clothing store, called at the White House. He begged my father to issue a statement supporting the idea of this Jewish state. A great deal of myth and emotional exaggeration has been wrapped around this meeting. I have been told by very intelligent people, and have read in the memoirs of men whom I admire, such as Dean Acheson, that Eddie Jacobson was responsible for Dad's entire stand on Israel. There is even a myth that Eddie saw Dad secretly innumerable times during his White House years, using his friendship to bring Dad over to a pro-Jewish point of view. The whole thing is absurd. Eddie Jacobson was one of the hundreds of army friends my father made during World War I. After the clothing store folded, Dad saw comparatively little of him. I don't believe they ever discussed politics, except in the most offhand fashion.

Far from welcoming his White House visit on March 13, 1948, my father was intensely angered by it. He resented the attempt to use the emotions of friendship to influence the policy of the United States as vehemently as he resented other people who attempted to influence him through his mother, his sister, or other members of the family. He was angry, and he made it very clear to Mr. Jacobson that he knew he had not made the trip spontaneously—he had been persuaded by Zionists who were determined to put every conceivable pressure on the President.

At the same time I want to make it clear that Eddie Jacobson was, first and foremost, a loyal American. He made it clear to Dad, as he wrote in a memoir of his meeting, which is on deposit in the

Weizmann Archives in Rehovoth, Israel, that "I never wanted him to do anything for the oppressed Jewish people abroad if doing so would result in the slightest damage to the best interests of my country. On this subject, my friend and I could never have any disagreement."

Eddie was soon reduced to asking my father if he would agree to see Chaim Weizmann. Again Dad refused. But when Eddie compared Dad's hero worship of Andrew Jackson to his feelings for Weizmann, Dad agreed to see him, privately. He did so, the day following his dramatic message to Congress explicitly condemning Russian aggression, and the two men talked for three-quarters of an hour. Once more Dr. Weizmann begged Dad to support the inclusion of the Negev in any Jewish state. My father assured him that this idea had his full support. He also made it clear that the United States still backed the idea of partition and wished to see it achieved as soon as possible. In fact, he told Dr. Weizmann that Warren Austin, the head of our UN delegation, would make an important statement to this effect the following day.

Warren Austin did make an important statement in the UN the following day. But it was not the statement Dad expected him to make, in support of partition. Instead Ambassador Austin announced that the United States was *abandoning* partition and now supported a UN trusteeship to replace the British mandate. Headlines and Zionists exploded across the country and the world. My father was called a traitor, a liar, and a lot of other unjustified names. Dr. Weizmann was one of the few Jewish spokesmen who remained silent. He knew that Dad had been double-crossed.

Bitterly, on his calendar for March 19, 1948, Dad wrote:

> The State Dept. pulled the rug from under me today. I didn't expect that would happen. In Key West or enroute there from St. Croix I approved the speech and statement of policy by Senator Austin to U.N. meeting. This morning I find that the State Dept. has reversed my Palestine policy. The first I know about it is what I see in the papers! Isn't that hell? I am now in the position of a liar and a double-crosser. I've never felt so in my life.
>
> There are people on the third and fourth levels of the State Dept. who have always wanted to cut my throat. They've succeeded in doing it. [Secretary of State] Marshall's in California and [Under Secretary of State] Lovett's in Florida.

The following day he wrote: "I spend the day trying to right what has happened. No luck . . ."

Lamely, my father tried to explain that the trusteeship idea did not rule out American support of partition but merely postponed it. Mrs. Roosevelt tried to resign as a member of the American delegation and withdrew her letter only on Dad's personal plea. It was one of the worst messes of my father's career, and he could do nothing about it but suffer. To tell the truth about what had happened would have made him and the entire American government look ridiculous. Not even in his memoirs did he feel free to tell the whole story, although he hinted at it. Now I think it is time for it to be told. Perhaps the truth will give future Presidents the power to deal with such insubordination among the career officials in the government.

In a letter to his sister on March 21, 1948, Dad went even further, describing the really shocking arrogance of the State Department career men.

> I had to appear before Congress on Wednesday and state the Russian case. I had been thinking and working on it for six months or more. I had discussed it with all the members of the Cabinet and many others. As usual the State Department balked. They tried by every means at their command to upset my plans. I had thought when General Marshall went over there he'd set them right but he has had too much to do and the third & fourth levels over there are the same striped pants conspirators. Someday I hope I'll get a chance to clean them out.
>
> Not only did they try to stop my Russian speech but they have completely balled up the Palestine situation. It was not necessary either. But it may work out anyway in spite of them.

On May 14 Israel declared itself a state. Eleven minutes later Charlie Ross issued a statement announcing a de facto recognition of Israel by the government of the United States. This was a decision made by Dad alone, in spite of the opposition of the State Department conspirators who for a time even had Secretary of State Marshall convinced that recognition should be withheld.

As the *American Jewish Historical Quarterly* pointed out in a long review of Dad's policy published in December, 1968, this de facto recognition of Israel was not an act taken to gain Jewish votes. It was an action taken with the conviction that recognition was in America's national interest. Moreover, de facto recognition was simply the recognition of a reality. It was a minimum step, which Dad absolutely refused to go beyond until after the 1948 elections were over. When it was clear that Israel's government was permanent, de *jure* recognition was extended on January 31, 1949. The United States was, in fact, the only country in the United Nations, other than South Africa, to withhold this de jure recognition of Israel so long. In spite of the large political advantages to be gained from taking the opposite course, Dad simply refused to do so because he did not think it was right.

In September, 1948, when the United Nations released the report of Count Folke Bernadotte, the mediator who had been assassinated, General Marshall supported it in the United Nations Assembly, although it drastically reduced Israel's size. Once more, Zionists screamed that America's policy of "betrayal" was anti-Israel, anti-Semitic. Democratic National Chairman Howard McGrath pleaded desperately with Dad to issue a statement supporting Israel on Rosh Hashanah. It would, in the words of one adviser, make "rich material for the holiday sermons. Praise and thanksgiving would be echoed from every Jewish home and no Jewish leader could fail to sing the President's praise." My father turned him down. He was concerned about Israel's treatment of their Arab citizens, and he felt that withholding this recognition was a way of guaranteeing their good behavior.

Late in October a New York delegation called on Dad and warned him that unless he offered Israel de jure recognition, raised the arms embargo, and supported the widest possible boundaries for Israel, he would inevitably lose New York State. Dad looked them in the eye and said: "You have come to me as a pressure group. If you believe for one second that I will bargain my convictions for the votes you imply would be mine, you are pathetically mistaken. Good morning."

Other Zionists urged Eddie Jacobson to attempt another assault on my father. But Eddie, a wiser man by now, told them rather peremptorily that Chaim Weizmann and Dad remained close friends, and Dr. Weizmann had himself told Eddie there was "nothing to worry about concerning Israel." Only after Thomas E. Dewey issued a strong, very biased statement accusing Dad of betraying United States pledges to Israel did Dad make a statement. In his Madison Square Garden speech of October 24, 1948, he simply reiterated his support for the Democratic platform plank which accepted the wider boundaries of the original partition resolution.

The *American Jewish Historical Quarterly*, at the end of its sixty-seven-page analysis of Dad's policy toward Israel, concluded:

> President Truman's policy and action between May and November, 1948, do not suggest a course based on political expediency. They reflect more, as had all of Truman's decisions on this matter, the tremendous uncertainty and complexity of the Palestinian affair, and his belief that foreign policy was no place for political maneuvers.

On the first anniversary of the passage of the United Nations Partition Resolution, Dad wrote to Chaim Weizmann, one of the few Jewish leaders who had never lost faith in him:

> As I read your letter I was struck by the common experience you and I have recently shared. We have both been abandoned by the so-called realistic experts to our supposedly forlorn lost causes. Yet we both kept pressing for what we were sure was right—and we were both proven to be right.

In spite of the extremists who harassed him on all sides and the intransigence of his own State Department, my father achieved a compromise in Palestine that blended justice and realism. We managed to retain Britain's friendship, and we did not lose our access to Arab oil or, during Dad's administration, the friendship of most of the Arab states. To his deep regret, he was never able to persuade either side to agree to the internationalization of Jerusalem, which was a key point in his policy. Nor could he persuade the Arabs to join Israel in accepting U.S. aid for an ambitious program of development for the entire Middle East.

During the same harrowing early months of 1948, when he was trying to cope with both Palestine and Russia, Dad also prepared and submitted to Congress the most ambitious civil rights program ever proposed by an American President.

Based on the report of a committee of fifteen distinguished Americans whom Dad had appointed, it called on state, city, and the federal governments to make a united effort to close "a serious gap between our ideals and some of our practices." It was a gap, Dad said, that "must be closed." He called for establishing a commission on civil rights, a joint congressional committee on civil rights, and a civil rights division in the Department of Justice. He asked for a Fair Employment Practice Commission and stronger protections of the right to vote and a federal anti-lynch law. Dad knew that the Southern wing of the Democratic party would rise in fury against him, as they did, almost immediately. But he did not waver for a moment. One reason was the answer he gave to a reporter who asked him for a background comment on the message. He obviously was hoping to involve Dad in a complex ideological discussion. "The Constitution, containing the Bill of Rights, was the only document considered in the writing of that message," Dad said.

An even deeper and more personal view of my father's approach to civil rights is in a letter he wrote to his sister only a few weeks before his mother's death:

> I've got to make a speech to the Society for the Advancement of Colored People tomorrow and I wish I didn't have to make it. Mrs. R. and Walter White, Wayne Morse, Senator from Oregon, & your brother are the speakers. . . . Mamma won't like what I have to say because I wind up by quoting Old Abe. But I believe what I say and I am hopeful we may implement it.

Some people thought that my father could be persuaded to change his mind on civil rights. Shortly before the 1948 nominating convention, a group of compromisers, who shall be nameless here, practically pledged the support of the Dixiecrats if Dad would only "soften" his views on civil rights. Dad replied:

> My forebears were Confederates. I come from a part of the country where Jim Crowism is as prevalent as it is in New York or Washington. Every factor and influence in my background— and in my wife's for that matter—would foster the personal belief that you are right.
>
> But my very stomach turned over when I learned that Negro soldiers, just back from overseas, were being dumped out of army trucks in Mississippi and beaten.
>
> Whatever my inclinations as a native of Missouri might have been, as President I know this is bad. I shall fight to end evils like this.

My father's beliefs on civil rights were radical in the best sense of that word. They went to the root, the source. From the same profound understanding of the Constitution and the Bill of Rights came Abraham Lincoln's vision of America, which Dad quoted to the NAACP in his speech at the Lincoln Memorial:

> If it shall please the Divine Being who determines the destinies of nations, we shall remain a united people, and we will, humbly seeking the Divine guidance, make their prolonged national existence a source of new benefits to themselves and their successors, and to all classes and conditions of mankind.

[CHAPTER]

Twenty-One

On NOVEMBER 11, 1948, Dad wrote to his sister Mary from Key West, "I didn't know I was so tired until I sat down."

This was the only time, as far as I know, that he admitted how much effort he had put into the 1948 campaign.

November 11 was always a historic day for him. "I am on my way to the beach to take a swim," he told Mary. "Just thirty years ago I was firing a final barrage at the Heinies at a little town called Hermaville northeast of Verdun. Some change of position I'd say."

Although Dad strictly forbade us to gloat in public—"Now we've got 'em licked let's be generous and make 'em like it," he cautioned Mary—he could not restrain a few private expressions of delight over his victory.

"The White House sent me a big scrapbook of editorials from all the papers over the country—and my, how they've banqueted on crow."

Winston Churchill, still out of office, underscored the importance of Dad's reelection in his letter of congratulations:

> My dear Harry,
> I sent you a cable of my hearty congratulations on your gallant fight and tremendous victory. I felt keenly the way you were treated by some of your party and in particular Wallace who seemed to us over here to be a greater danger than he proved. But all this has now become only the background of

your personal triumph. Of course it is my business as a foreigner or half a foreigner to keep out of American politics, but I am sure I can now say what a relief it has been to me and most of us here to feel that the long continued comradeship between us and also with the Democratic Party in peace and war will not be interrupted. This is most necessary and gives the best chance of preserving peace.

I wish you the utmost success in your Administration during this most critical and baffling period in world affairs. If I should be able to come over I shall not hesitate to pay my respects to you.

    With kind regards,
      Believe me

Your friend,
Winston S. Churchill

Mrs. Churchill predicted your success. Sends her compliments and good wishes to your wife. . . .

Dad's reply is also rather interesting:

November 23, 1948

Dear Winston:

I can't tell you how very much I appreciated your cable and your good letter of November eighth.

I had a terrific fight and had to carry it to the people almost lone handed but when they knew the facts they went along with me. It seemed to have been a terrific political upset when you read the papers here in this country. Really it was not—it was merely a continuation of the policies which had been in effect for the last sixteen years and the policies that the people wanted.

I hope everything is going well with you and that sometime or other we will have a chance for another meeting.

Please remember me to Mrs. Churchill and tell her I appreciate the fact that she was a good prophet. . . .

Sincerely yours,
Harry S. Truman

Mother and I joined Dad in Key West for his vacation. We needed a rest almost as much as he did. Mother, in fact, had come down with a terrible cold and sore throat, and for two nights before we left the White House, Dad got up at ungodly hours like three in the morning to make sure that she took her medicine.

The highlight of our stay in Key West, at least in my memory, was the impromptu victory parade staged by the White House reporters and aides. Everybody wore the wackiest costumes you have ever seen in your life. Charlie Ross had on a pair of bathing trunks and an old-fashioned, Abraham Lincoln style stovepipe hat. The whole thing was a surprise, and someone snapped a picture of me and Mother laughing like a couple of lunatics. It *was* funny, and wholly in the spirit of that triumphant vacation.

It was on this visit, if my memory is functioning correctly, that the final installment in the saga of Dad's unloseable eyeglasses was enacted. He was swimming and I was sitting on the sea wall watching. The ocean was a little rough and waves were breaking on the wall. He swam over to urge me to join him. I declined, reminding him that the last time he had persuaded me to get wet, he told me the water was warm, and I came out feeling like a human icicle. Just then a wave broke on the sea wall, and Dad went under. One of the Secret Service men standing nearby jumped in sunglasses and all. This was unnecessary heroics. Dad was perfectly all right. But the unexpected ducking had knocked off his glasses and they vanished into the swirling depths. The loss was no special crisis. He had several reserve pairs of glasses in his quarters. But the Secret Service men thought they could find them, and several agents in bathing suits began to search the bottom. They had no luck. Later Dad was sitting on the sea wall and happened to glance at the beach. He noticed something glinting in the sunlight on the shore. He pointed to it and the astonished Secret Service men trotted around to examine it. There, believe it or not, were the glasses, washed up by the tide.

We flew back to Washington and Dad spent most of Thanksgiving Day signing thank you letters in response to the thousands of congratulations he had received.

> At Key West I must have signed five thousand [he told his sister Mary], and since I came back here it has been terrific. . . . I went to the office at 9 o'clock and stayed until 2 P.M. and cleaned up a batch of so many I couldn't count them—but I can sign from 500 to 1000 an hour.

Two weeks later Dad attended a kind of postscript to the campaign—the Gridiron Dinner. This traditional Washington shindig is run by the capital newsmen. It requires politicians of all stripes and types to laugh and be laughed at. Dad described the evening in rather pungent terms to his sister:

> The Gridiron Dinner was quite a trial to me because I couldn't say what I wanted to say. If I'd been beaten it would have been much easier to speak. They ribbed Dewey unmercifully. Had a lunatic engineer act, that was a scream. They took Jake Arvey, Hague, Flynn of N.Y., and old Crump for a long hard ride. But they were exceedingly nice to me.
>
> Dewey made a speech in which he tried hard to be funny. It was funny in the beginning but he became very sneering and sarcastic in the last half.
>
> Of course when I came to speak—the last thing on the program—I couldn't be the least bit elated, triumphant or overbearing. I told them I'd not seen most of them for three months, supposed they'd been on a vacation from the White House. Told them they'd ridden in the wrong boat, and then made a very solemn and serious speech on the grave responsibility we are facing and told them that the country is theirs, not mine, but they'd have to help me run it. Complimented Dewey on being a good sport and sat down.
>
> You never saw such an ovation. Had to get up three times. Some of those old hardboiled Republican newsmen openly cried. . . .

Although Dad wrote this letter on White House stationery, we were no longer living in the Great White Jail. Just in time, Dad discovered that the White House was literally falling down. For more than a year he had been prodding the Commission of Grounds and Buildings to take a good look at the place. He had begun to worry about it one night in 1947 at an official reception, when the guard of honor came in to take the colors away. As the husky young color bearers stamped across the floor in precise military unison, Dad looked up and saw the big chandelier above his head—and the heads of all his guests—swaying. A few weeks later, when the butler brought him breakfast in his study, he felt the whole floor sway, as if it was floating in space. Several weeks after he reported these alarming observations to the commission, he learned his fears were well founded.

The time and place in which he learned it makes an almost

incredible story. The news arrived in the middle of the last official reception of the '46–'47 winter. Dad was listening to Eugene List, the young pianist he had discovered at Potsdam, play for "the customers," as he called the guests in a letter to his mother.

> I was somewhat nervous through the entertainment because Mr. Crim the usher and Jim Rowley came and told me that the engineers had found that the chain holding the center chandelier was stretching. Well, the survey had been made three or four weeks ago and it was a nice time to tell me. I let the show go on and ordered the thing down the next day. If it had fallen, I'd been in a real fix. But it didn't.

Early in 1948 Dad told his sister what the engineers had finally concluded.

> I've had the second floor where we live examined—and it is about to fall down! The engineer said that the ceiling in the state dining room only stayed up from force of habit! I'm having it shored up and hoping to have a concrete and steel floor put in before I leave here. The roof fell in on Coolidge and they put a concrete and steel third floor on to take its place and suggested that the second floor be done the same way. But Old Cal wouldn't do it. He wanted it to fall like the roof did I guess.

The shoring up was quite an operation. For months we had to live with a forest of pipes running up through our private rooms. They were particularly thick in Dad's study, my sitting room, and Mother's bedroom. You had to walk around them to get out the doors. It was not what I called gracious living. Meanwhile, Dad appointed a committee of experts to examine the entire house from roof to foundations and tell him what needed to be done. Their report made hair-raising reading. The foundation was sinking into the swampy ground beneath it. There was no visible support for the ceiling in the Green Room but a few very rusty nails.

In the summer of 1948 the old house just started to fall apart. One of the two pianos in my sitting room—a spinet—broke through the floor one day. My sitting room, I should add, was just above the family dining room. Dad jotted on his diary-calendar: "How very lucky we are that the thing did not break when Margie and Annette Wright were playing two-piano duets." A few days later he told his sister:

The White House is still about to fall in. Margaret's sitting room floor broke in two but didn't fall through the family dining room ceiling. They propped it up and fixed it. Now my bathroom is about to fall into the red parlor. They won't let me sleep in my bedroom or use the bath. I'm using Old Abe's bed and it is very comfortable.

On November 7, 1948, when we returned from Missouri, the White House engineer and architect refused to let us into the place. Dad told his sister that he

found the White House in one terrible shape. There are scaffolds in the East Room, props in the study, my bedroom, Bess's sitting room and the Rose Room. . . . We've had to call off all functions and will move out as soon as I come back from Key West.

At that time he thought it would "take at least ten months to tear the old second floor out and put it back." By the time we came back from Key West, the experts had taken a harder look at the situation, and. decided that there was nothing that could be saved but the outside walls. The entire house would have to be gutted and rebuilt.

This meant that we had to move across the street to Blair House. There were no complaints on my part, except the usual moans during the packing and unpacking days. As I've explained earlier, I much preferred Blair House to the White House. But Blair House created serious entertainment problems for Dad and Mother. As he told his sister Mary, "It is a nice place but only half as large—so we have no place to put guests." This applied not only to overnight guests but the standard official visitors at White House receptions. Instead of being able to entertain 1,200 or 1,500 at a single reception, everything had to be scaled down to half size and this meant that poor Mother was in perpetual motion as a hostess. But Mother, good soldier that she is, "met the situation" Truman-Wallace style. There was, Dad pointed out in a letter he wrote toward the end of 1948, one consolation: "It's a shame the old White House had to fall down. But it's a godsend it didn't when we had 1,500 people in it."

Between moving out of the White House, getting settled in Blair House, and answering the tens of thousands of letters that poured in congratulating Dad on his victory, we found Inaugural

Day on top of us before we realized it. Of course, numerous aides and a committee had been working to make the day a smash, even before the election. They had plenty of money to spend, because the Republican Congress, expecting a Dewey victory, had abandoned its public parsimony and voted a whopping sum for the event.

The weather on January 20 was perfect, very cold, but with bright winter sunlight pouring down from a clear blue sky. Dad started the day at 7 A.M. by eating breakfast with 98 members of Battery D and their wives. Mother and I came along and watched while he was presented with a gold-headed cane and a leather book in which each man had signed his name. Mother remarked that the cane would obviously last long enough for Dad to give it to his grandson. Dad promised to use it faithfully on his morning walks and then issued his marching orders for the parade. They were to be the guard of honor around his car on the ride from the Capitol down Pennsylvania Avenue to the White House reviewing stand. He wanted them to maintain their old World War I cadence—120 thirty-inch steps per minute. "I'm sure you can still do it for a mile and a quarter," he told them.

Although most of the boys were ten to fifteen years younger than Dad, there was a groan at the thought. They had been up until 3 A.M. the previous morning at the inaugural gala in the National Guard armory, enjoying the show put on by musicians, actors, dancers, and other show-biz politicians.

After we attended services at St. John's Episcopal Church, Dad drove to the Capitol to take the oath of office. His inaugural speech was memorable to me for many reasons. Although he served almost two full terms, it was the only Inaugural Address he ever gave. More important, he enunciated what I still think is the best definition of the difference between communism and democracy.

> Communism is based on the belief that man is so weak and inadequate that he is unable to govern himself, and therefore requires the rule of strong masters.
> Democracy is based on the conviction that man has the moral and intellectual capacity, as well as the inalienable right, to govern himself with reason and justice.

[400]

He then spelled out four cardinal points of American foreign policy, which the United States followed for the next twenty-five years. First was unfaltering support of the United Nations; second, the achievement of Europe's recovery through the Marshall Plan; third, military assistance to strengthen freedom-loving nations against the dangers of aggression. Fourth came the policy that caught everyone by surprise. Dad called for "a bold new program for making the benefits of our scientific advances and industrial progress available for the improvement and growth" of the under-developed parts of the world.

Point Four, as the proposal was immediately dubbed by the press, fired the imagination of the globe. Excited farmers in the Middle East sent letters to the local American Embassy, addressed to "The Master of the Fourth Spot." Arnold Toynbee predicted that Dad's call for the wealthy nations to come to the aid of the world's poor "will be remembered as the signal achievement of the age." Before the program was killed by unimaginative Republicans in the middle 1950s, more than 2,000 Americans from Boston, St. Louis, and Seattle and a hundred other towns and cities taught people in Indonesia, Iran, and Brazil better ways to grow their food, purify their water, educate their children. When the Democrats returned to office in 1960, Point Four became John F. Kennedy's Peace Corps.

The Point Four Program was suggested by Benjamin Hardy of the State Department, who first aroused White House aide George Elsey's enthusiasm for it. But the President's enthusiasm was the decisive factor. It was a feeling that came naturally to an ex-senator who knew and admired the achievements of the TVA in bringing prosperity to the underdeveloped valleys of Tennessee and an ex-farmer who had seen the miraculous rise in productivity wrought by the scientific and educational programs of the U.S. Department of Agriculture.

In spite of his enthusiasm for the idea, Dad's modesty almost persuaded him to omit it from his Inaugural Address. In fact, his desire not to seem to crow over his victory inclined him to make the Inaugural Address as simple and matter-of-fact as possible. In his mind, he at first bracketed it with the State of the Union address which he made to Congress a few days before the inauguration. He was inclined to limit the Inaugural Address to domestic affairs and concentrate on international matters in the State of the Union.

George Elsey, who was assigned the job of drafting both speeches, became more and more unhappy with this approach. He stayed behind in the White House, working, while Dad and other aides were relaxing in Key West. "I finally wrote a long memorandum in which I argued as persuasively, and as forcefully as I could," George says, "that the President had one and only one inaugural opportunity and that he had other state of the union messages and would have still future state of the union messages." In the inaugural, George argued, Dad was addressing the world and ought to make a speech that suited the occasion. After thinking it over, Dad agreed. With this background, it is even easier to see why Point Four was greeted with enthusiasm in the White House. Benjamin Hardy had had no success whatsover selling his idea within the Department of State. At this point, with the memory of the Palestine double cross still fresh, Dad and his aides took special pleasure in finding so much genuine merit in an idea that the striped pants boys had pooh-poohed.

After a quick lunch in Les Biffle's Senate office, Dad led the inaugural parade from the Capitol down Pennsylvania Avenue to the reviewing stand in front of the White House. The boys of Battery D strutted proudly beside his car in two long lines. Before they got started, Dad had to settle an argument which almost ended in a brawl. No one could remember—or at least agree—on who had carried the guidon in France and "Captain Harry" had to issue a ruling to settle the dispute. The aging artillerymen made it to the reviewing stand without a man falling out, but I heard later that they were not very lively at the inaugural ball that night. One man told his wife as he limped to the table, "The Germans never came so near killing off Battery D as their captain did today!"

The inaugural parade was great fun. Drucie Snyder and I salaamed like a couple of happy screwballs when the George Washington University float went by. When Strom Thurmond, the defeated Dixiecrat candidate, rode past as part of the South Carolina delegation, Dad turned aside and became deeply involved in conversation with others on the reviewing stand. Tallulah Bankhead acted out what politicians wanted to do, but didn't—she gave Mr. Thurmond a long, lusty boo. Among the many things that Mr. Thurmond undoubtedly disliked about this Inaugural Day was its completely integrated character. On direct orders from Dad, for the first time in history black Americans were admitted to all official and unofficial functions. Walter White, head of the NAACP, praised Dad for "recognizing the new place of all ordinary Americans."

After three and a half hours of West Point cadets, Annapolis midshipmen, Missouri Mules, and bare-legged girl drum majorettes, we dashed to the National Gallery of Art for a reception, arriving an hour late. Dad and Vice President Barkley each made two speeches and shook hands with about a thousand VIP's. Then we raced back to Blair House to dress for the inaugural ball.

For the inauguration I had worn a scarlet suit and hat. Now I donned a tulle and brocade gown, called "Margaret pink"—a phrase which did not catch on like Alice blue, but you'll never hear me complaining about it. Who needs a color named for her? The inaugural ball was so jammed, real dancing was impossible. People simply got out on the floor and swayed to the music of Xavier Cugat, Benny Goodman, and Guy Lombardo. I had my own box, and Drucie Snyder and two other girl friends joined me, all of us escorted by White House aides. (The aide who danced with me, Bill Zimmerman, was decorated for heroism in Korea. Years later, he ruefully told me people remembered him more for the picture someone snapped of him dancing with me at the inaugural than for his feats of courage under fire.) That night Bill and the other White House military aides were ablaze in gold braid, gold lace epaulets, and decorations. But no amount of artificial splendor could outshine the smile on Dad's face. I am sure that if he had to pick the happiest day of his political life, this would have been it.

The celebrating tapered off with a few more parties and receptions in the next few days, and then the Truman cousins trekked back to Missouri, and the Washington Trumans settled into Blair House and went to work. Dad had a Democratic Congress, but there was still the old tendency of Southern and Western conservatives to vote Republican on a dismaying number of issues. The world was still seething volcanically in various places and there were several major changes to be made in the Cabinet. The

[403]

most important was the retirement of Secretary of State General George C. Marshall, after a serious kidney operation, and his replacement by Dean Acheson.

I was very sorry to see General Marshall leave our official family. I shared Dad's enormous admiration for him. Among my fondest memories are the Sunday visits that we made to the General and Mrs. Marshall, in their lovely house in Leesburg, Virginia. I usually did the driving. Dad was inclined to drive with his mind on affairs of state. When there were problems to discuss, the President and the General would retire to his study, while I visited with Mrs. Marshall. Sometimes, however, the visit was purely social.

The General's farm was on the site of the battle of Ball's Bluff, one of the first serious engagements between the North and South in the Civil War. One day Dad and General Marshall roamed the rather rough terrain discussing the battle, in which Senator Edward Baker of Oregon, a close friend of Abraham Lincoln, was killed leading the Union forces. They found a little cemetery, about 40 by 20, with twenty-one unknown dead buried in it. Rambling further into the woods, they found a little stone marker which said, "Colonel Edward Dickenson Baker was killed here." Both Dad and General Marshall were so intrigued, they persuaded Wayne Morse of Oregon to find out where Senator Baker was buried. Was it on the battlefield? No, he turned out to be interred in San Francisco, in a cemetery which he owned, and had promoted into a handsome fortune. The oddities of history are almost endless.

Dean Acheson, the new Secretary of State, was tall and aristocratic, the quintessence of the so-called Eastern Establishment. Yet he shared with George Marshall and Harry Truman an uncompromising honesty and a total dedication to the goals and best interests of the United States of America. When you think of how different these two Secretaries were, it becomes one more tribute to Dad's ability to work harmoniously with men of almost opposite temperaments and background. I responded to these two men in very different ways. With General Marshall, my affection was tinged with awe. With Mr. Acheson, a very definite attraction had just a touch of acid in it, for reasons we shall soon see.

[404]

It was Mr. Acheson who assumed the greatest and most important legacy of Secretary of State Marshall's tenure, that logical but crucial—and angrily debated—step beyond the Marshall Plan, known as the North Atlantic Treaty Organization (NATO). The historic pact—America's first peacetime military alliance—was signed on April 4, 1949, by the foreign ministers of twelve nations. But my father had been working on the problem of winning Senate approval for this major innovation in American foreign policy for over a year. On March 17, 1948, Great Britain, France, Belgium, the Netherlands, and Luxemburg had signed a fifty-year political, economic, and military alliance in Brussels. In his address to Congress on the same day, urging the swift passage of the Marshall Plan, Dad had praised this significant step toward European unity, and declared that "the determination of the free countries of Europe to protect themselves will be matched by an equal determination on our part to help them to protect themselves."

Throughout the spring of 1948, Dad and Under Secretary of State Robert M. Lovett spent long hours working with Senator Arthur Vandenberg on the problem of persuading Congress. It was formidable. There was a deep prejudice, buttressed by the warning in Washington's Farewell Address against "entangling alliances." But Dad had labored since he took office to persuade Americans that this prejudice no longer made sense, because the world had simply grown too small for any country, even one as protected by ocean barriers as America, to remain isolated. So, slowly and carefully, a resolution took shape, which Dad wanted Senator Vandenberg to propose to the Senate.

Arthur Vandenberg was a great senator, and a great American. But he was something of a prima donna, who required very special handling. Dad understood this, of course. He had an amazing ability to read the character of almost every man in the Senate. Bob Lovett, another outstanding American who made a great contribution wherever he served, from Under Secretary of State to Secretary of Defense, had won the senator's friendship and confidence. With extraordinary patience he worked through draft after draft of what eventually became the Vandenberg Resolution. Introduced as Senate Resolution 239 on June 11, 1948, it declared the "sense of the Senate" supported "regional and other collective arrangements for individual and collective self-defense" and the "association of the United States by constitutional process" with these regional defense organizations. It was, in essence, the application of the concept developed by Dad and General Marshall for the Americas—the treaty we went to Brazil to sign—to the rest of the world. Equally important to Dad, the resolution carefully pointed out that the right of individual or collective self-defense was affirmed under Article 51 of the United Nations Charter. The Vandenberg Resolution was approved by a resounding 64-to-4 vote. Thus the Senate—a Republican Senate at that—was on record as supporting the general principles on which NATO was based.

But even with the support of the Vandenberg Resolution, NATO did not sail smoothly through the Senate. It was violently attacked by Robert Taft, because he was opposed to the idea of giving military assistance to our allies. Other senators, notably Forrest Donnell of Missouri, denounced it because it might involve us in a war we did not want. As if we ever wanted one! Dean Acheson did a magnificent job of defending the treaty against these and other attacks. He was well supported by Senator Vandenberg, who rightly called the treaty "the most important step in American foreign policy since the promulgation of the Monroe Doctrine."

Equally crucial was the support that came from Dad. He sent the Secretary of State a telegram from Key West, lavishly praising his testimony before the Senate Foreign Relations Committee, and authorized him to publish it. When the treaty was signed, Dad insisted that Mr. Acheson was the one who should do it. Dad and Vice President Barkley stood on either side of him, but my father wanted the man who had done the most work to have his name on the historic document.

The impact of the treaty in Europe was what counted. The Senate's advice and consent to it by an 82 to 13 vote made it clear to our friends and our enemies that we were determined to defend the free nations of Western Europe against the kind of aggression that had swallowed Czechoslovakia.

At the Paris foreign ministers conference in June, 1949, the Russians were on the defensive for the first time. Andrei Vishinsky, their chief spokesman, was an almost pathetic figure, afraid to agree even on a statement about the weather without discussing it with an angry, sullen Stalin in Moscow.

Today, a revived and powerful Western Europe is a fact of life that we tend to accept as a matter of course. Occasionally, we should stop and think about how the history of the world in the last twenty-five years would have changed, if Western Europe, with its enormous industrial and scientific potential, had become part of the Communist empire.

But NATO was more than a dam to hold back the threatening Communist flood. In Dad's view it was another step toward achieving the necessary economic and military strength to negotiate with the Russians as equals. Experience had taught him that force—equality or superiority of force—was the only thing the Russians understood. Even before he was reelected, he had begun the fight to restore our depleted military strength. On May 7, 1948, for instance, he made the following memorandum:

> Had a most important conference with Marshall, Forrestal, Snyder, Jim Webb of Budget and Forrestal's budget man.
>
> We are faced with a defense problem. I have wanted a universal training program, a balanced regular setup, ground, air, water, and a reserve to back up the regular skeleton training force.
>
> The Congress can't bring itself to do the right thing—because of votes. The air boys are for glamour and the navy as always is the greatest of propaganda machines.
>
> I want a balanced sensible defense for which the country can pay. If the glamour boys win we'll have another 1920 or another 1941. God keep us from that! And it is so sensible and easy to keep from it—but—
>
> Marshall is a tower of strength and common sense. So is Snyder and Webb. Forrestal can't take it. He wants to compromise with the opposition!

My father's critical comment on Mr. Forrestal should not be construed as his final judgment on the man. He was a dedicated American who literally wore himself out in the service of his country. He had done a tremendous job in the struggle to unify the armed services, and Dad had made him the first Secretary of Defense. Mr. Forrestal was equally dedicated to Dad. In a letter to a fellow Cabinet member, he called him "the best boss I have ever known." After the armed services unification bill was fought through Congress, he wrote him the following letter:

28 July 1947

My dear Mr. President:

The fact that we have a bill, which, as you have expressed it, gives us the beginnings of a national military policy for the first time since 1798, is due first and last to your own patience, tact and knowledge of legislative procedures. With the exception of Clark Clifford, I know probably more than anyone else, how much restraint you had to exercise under trying and sometimes provoking circumstances. I believe the result will justify your forbearance.

As I told you Saturday, I will do my best to live up to the confidence you have reposed in me. If I fail, I know it will not be because of lack of support from you.

Respectfully yours,
James Forrestal

The indecision which Mr. Forrestal displayed on rearming and in the Berlin crisis may well have been the first symptoms of the tragic mental breakdown he suffered after he left the Cabinet early in 1949—a breakdown that culminated in his suicide in May of that year.

Trying to persuade Congress to give the country the balanced defense force he wanted was a terribly frustrating job, as Dad's memo makes clear. The services themselves were unco-operative, each lobbying fiercely for the biggest possible slice of the pie. Complicating the struggle was the problem of rearming Western Europe—the next logical step beyond the NATO treaty. The Soviet Union had thirty divisions in Eastern Europe, all armed with the latest weapons. We had three and a half, plus two and a half British divisions. The French and other nations could field perhaps a dozen divisions, but they were equipped with antiquated guns, obsolete tanks, and inferior air support. To give you an idea of how weak we were at this time, for a reserve force we had in the United States only a pitiful two and one-third divisions. The logical and obvious step was to rearm our friends in Europe as swiftly as possible. So, on July 25, 1949, Dad sent to Congress a request for $1,400,000,000 for this purpose.

The reaction of the Congress was almost unbelievable. You

would think that they had never even heard of the North Atlantic Treaty. Senator Vandenberg deserted his bipartisan role to make a wild attack on the bill, and he was joined by Walter George, Henry Cabot Lodge, and William Fulbright. In the House of Representatives, desperate pleas by Speaker Sam Rayburn were ignored, and there was a reckless vote to cut the appropriation in half. My father had to pull out all the stops in a speech to the Golden Jubilee Convention of the Veterans of Foreign Wars, on August 22, 1949, to turn the situation around:

> The cost of such a program is considerable, but it represents an investment in security that will be worth many times its cost. It is part of the price of peace. Which is better, to make expenditures to save the peace, or to risk all our resources and assets in another war?

There was a reason for the collapse of bipartisan support in the Congress for Dad's foreign policy—a reason that had nothing to do with the Russian threat in Europe or the wisdom of helping free nations resist it. In the spring of 1949 the Nationalist Chinese government of Chiang Kai-shek began to fall apart and the Generalissimo prepared to flee to Formosa with the remnant of his followers and China's monetary reserves. Communist Chinese armies soon controlled all parts of the vast country. Almost immediately Republicans in Congress began preaching the doctrine that Harry S. Truman's foreign policy had "lost" China. Most of these critics were the same people who savagely attacked the Marshall Plan and voted against aid to Greece and Turkey. They were the roadblocks to all the creative foreign policy innovations which my father and his administration struggled to extract from a reluctant Congress. Can you imagine what they would have said, if the Democratic President had simultaneously proposed a massive program to rescue Chiang Kai-shek? Not only would the cost have been in the billions—the rescue would have necessarily required a two- or three-million-man American army. This from a nation that had only two and one-third divisions in reserve.

No American President can make decisions in foreign policy, involving the lives and fortunes of millions of Americans, without the support of Congress and the people. Sometimes, as in the case of Korea, these decisions must be made in an excruciatingly short space of time, and the President must use all the political expertise he possesses to sell his foreign policy to the Congress and the American people. When he fails in this crucial task, the country suffers the kind of instability we have experienced since 1965. I think it is evident by now that Harry S. Truman was a master of this aspect of the presidency. It is also evident that Dad was a skillful politician, who kept in contact with the American people. My father knew that neither he nor any other man could have sold the American people the idea that their sons, barely returned from the greatest war in history, should abandon their careers and their educations once more, to fight for Chiang Kai-shek.

Thoughtful Republicans knew the truth about China. Senator Arthur Vandenberg wrote in his diary: "If we made ourselves responsible for the army of the Nationalist government, we would be in the China war for keeps and the responsibility would be ours instead of hers. I am sure that this would jeopardize our own national security beyond any possibility of justification." Mr. Vandenberg wrote to Senator William F. Knowland of California: "The vital importance of saving China cannot be exaggerated. But there are limits to our resources and boundaries to our miracles. . . ."

The shortest answer to the accusation that we "lost China" is to point out that we never owned or possessed it. At the same time, any fair-minded examination of our attempts to save Chiang Kai-shek from losing it will show a President doing everything in his power to prevent this catastrophe. As we have already seen, my father sent the Generalissimo the greatest American soldier of the era, George C. Marshall. When General Marshall saw some of the appalling deficiencies of the Chinese Nationalist army (described in vivid detail in *Stilwell and the American Experience in China* by Barbara Tuchman), it convinced him that the Nationalist government's only hope was a truce and a coalition government with the Communists, who controlled much of North China. This solution might have given Chiang time to pull his spiritless, undisciplined army together, so that he might have survived a test of strength with the Communists at some later date. If he chose to fight, General Marshall advised him to concentrate his forces—a primary military doctrine—and achieve genuine control of southern China before he ventured into North China and Manchuria.

But Chiang arrogantly declined to take any advice from the man whose military genius had helped win World War II. Instead, Chiang launched an ambitious, aggressive attempt to smash the Communists and simultaneously seize control of all China. As a result, he spread his armies disastrously thin, and they lost control of the countryside. Meanwhile, we continued to supply his government with both military and economic aid, to the tune of $2 billion.

My father remained in close touch with the situation, even after General Marshall came home in January, 1947, to become Secretary of State. In July of that year, Dad sent Lieutenant General Albert C. Wedemeyer to the troubled nation for another personal report. General Wedemeyer, who had commanded American forces in China, saw practically no chance of rescuing the situation. He placed his finger on the central problem of Chiang's government: "To gain and maintain the confidence of the people, the Central Government will have to effect immediately drastic, far-reaching political and economic reforms. Promises will no longer suffice. Performance is absolutely necessary. It should be accepted that military force in itself will not eliminate Communism."

By the fall of 1948 the situation was almost beyond hope. Chiang was not only losing the support of the people, he was losing control of his soldiers, too. Whole divisions, with all their American equipment, went over to the Communists. On November 9, 1948, Chiang sent my father a frantic appeal for help.

Around the same time General David Barr, who was the commanding officer of the U.S. Military Advisory Group in China, sent the following report to the White House: "I am convinced that the military situation has deteriorated to the point where only the active participation of United States troops could effect a remedy. No battle has been lost since my arrival for lack of ammunition or equipment. Their military debacles, in my opinion, can all be attributed to the world's worst leadership and many other morale destroying factors that led to a complete loss of will to fight."

A letter to Arthur Vandenberg, written the following year, shows that Dad's thinking on China is clearly rooted in disenchantment with the Nationalist government:

[411]

The Far Eastern situation has been a peculiar one, as is often the case in a horse race—we picked a bad horse. That was the development of the situation in China. It turned out that the Nationalist Chinese Government was one of the most corrupt and inefficient that ever made an attempt to govern a country and when I found that out, we stopped furnishing them with materiel. Most of the Communists' materiel was materiel which was surrendered by the Chinese Nationalist Government for a consideration. If Chiang Kai-shek had been willing to listen to General Marshall, General Wedemeyer and General Dean he never would have found himself in the condition he is in now. After the surrender of Peiping where ammunition, trucks, and artillery materiel we had furnished was turned over to the Communists I cut off everything to the Chinese Government. It had to be done gradually, however, because Nationalists were still holding the line of the Yangtze River and I didn't want to pull the rug from under Chiang Kai-shek at that time.

In the next paragraph my father added a shrewd prophecy, which has already come partly true, and may yet come completely true. "I think you will find . . . that the Russians will turn out to be the 'foreign devils' in China and that situation will help establish a Chinese Government that we can recognize and support."

On the day after Dad took his oath of office for the second term, Chiang Kai-shek resigned and handed what was left of his government over to General Li Tsung-jen. He was powerless to prevent the onrushing Communists from crossing the Yangtze and seizing south China. On May 5 Dad received a letter from him which, I think, says more about what really happened in China than any other document I have seen on the subject:

> General George C. Marshall, under the instructions from your good self, took up the difficult task of mediation in our conflict with the Chinese Communists, to which he devoted painstaking effort. All this work was unfortunately rendered fruitless by the lack of sincerity on the part of both the then government and the Chinese Communists.
>
> In spite of this, your country continued to extend its aid to our government. It is regrettable that, owing to the failure of our then government to make judicious use of this aid and to

[412]

bring about appropriate political, economic and military reforms, your assistance has not produced the desired effect. To
this failure is attributable the present predicament in which our
country finds itself.

In late 1948 the State Department professionals had urged Dad
to issue a statement to the American people explaining the gross
inadequacies and corruption of the Nationalist government. They
were hoping to defend themselves and Dad from the wild accusations about China that were already being flung around by the
"China First" politicians in Congress. From the point of view of
domestic politics, it was shrewd advice. By taking the offensive on
the subject, Dad might easily have saved himself a lot of abuse.
As usual, however, he preferred to risk his domestic political
reputation for the best interests of the United States abroad. He
turned down the idea because it would have administered the coup
de grâce to Chiang's government.

In the summer of 1949, with the Communists in complete control of China, this was no longer a consideration, and my father
felt it was only just to himself and to Secretary of State Acheson
to make a thorough explanation of what had happened in China
to the American people. On August 5 Secretary of State Acheson
issued the China White Paper, a massive document, which, with
appendices, ran to over a thousand pages. It detailed overwhelmingly reasons for the Communist victory which I have summarized here.

The facts made the China-First Republican politicians look
silly, and they responded with rage and a new determination to
repeat their big lie until it became an article of Republican faith.
Not love of China but hatred of Dad and his policies, and above
all hatred of his stunning victory in 1948, was their motivation.
They also stooped to mythmaking and invented a devil: Communists in the government. Here they received a priceless boost
from the trial of Alger Hiss. The former State Department official,
friend of Dean Acheson, adviser to President Roosevelt at Yalta,
a man with impeccable credentials—Harvard law degree, clerk to
Justice Oliver Wendell Holmes—was tried for allegedly perjuring
himself before the House Un-American Activities Committee by
denying that he had given state secrets to journalist Whittaker

Chambers who was at that time a member of a Communist espionage ring.

When the subject was first brought to my father's attention, during the summer of 1948, he bluntly condemned the investigation as "a red herring." He had long detested the methods of the House Un-American Activities Committee, and he had no hesitation about blasting their claim that there was a Communist spy ring operating in the capital. He said that the evidence for such a ring existed largely in the head of Congressman Karl Mundt, then acting chairman of the committee. All the evidence that their investigation had produced was submitted to a grand jury, and no indictments had been forthcoming. In the interim Whittaker Chambers had produced his astonishing hoard of secret documents on microfilm, hidden in a hollowed-out pumpkin on his Maryland farm. Dad, with his dislike of the Un-American Activities Committee still foremost in his mind, had the following discussion with a reporter, in a post-election news conference.

"Mr. President, do you still feel, as you did during the late summer, that this Congressional investigation has the aspects of a 'red herring'?"

"I do," Dad said stubbornly.

Another reporter asked, "Mr. President, are you at all interested in this charge, of Mr. Nixon's [Congressman Richard M. Nixon], that the Department of Justice proposes to indict only Chambers—or first Chambers, and thus destroy his usefulness?"

"The Department of Justice will follow the law," Dad said.

Which, of course, is precisely what the Department did. Mr. Hiss was prosecuted for perjury, and he was found guilty, on January 25, 1950, after two of the longest, most bizarre trials in American history. Among those who had appeared as a character witness for him was Dean Acheson. Mr. Hiss's brother, Donald, had been a partner in Mr. Acheson's law firm. When reporters asked the Secretary of State what he thought of Hiss now, he replied: "I do not intend to turn my back on Alger Hiss," and explained that he was acting in accord with the 25th chapter of the Gospel according to St. Matthew, beginning with verse 34. ("I was hungry and you gave me food . . . a prisoner and you came to me.") He immediately drove to the White House and told Dad what he had said. Dad calmly reminded him that he was talking to an ex-vice president who had flown to the funeral of a friendless old man who had just been released from the penitentiary. He understood—and approved.

But we are getting ahead of our story. The real villain, the specialist in gutter tactics, Senator Joe McCarthy of Wisconsin, did not come onstage until February, 1950. You will recall we were trying to understand why bipartisanship had collapsed— or at least sagged badly—and both the Senate and the House were acting as if they might renege on the solemnly signed and consented-to North Atlantic Treaty. It is difficult, even frightening, to predict what might have happened if grim news had not arrived from Europe. First came an economic shock—Great Britain, for two centuries the world's keystone of financial stability, was devaluing the pound. Then a military shock. The Russians had exploded an atomic bomb.

On September 3, 1949, an air force WB-29 weather reconnaissance plane on a patrol from Japan to Alaska was routinely exposing filter paper at 18,000 feet over the North Pacific east of the Kamchatka Peninsula. The crew suddenly noticed that the paper, which was sensitive to radioactivity, was telling them that there was an unusual amount of it in the air around them. A second filter paper, hastily exposed, produced an even higher radioactive count. Within hours, other planes were checking the air in different parts of the Pacific and reporting radioactivity as high as twenty times above normal. Within four days the filter papers had been studied in our atomic laboratories and fission isotopes—proof of an atomic test—were found in them. My father was immediately informed.

The news caused a kind of panic in the Pentagon and the Atomic Energy Commission. They rushed to the White House and urged my father to issue an immediate statement, announcing that the Russians had the bomb. J. Robert Oppenheimer was one of the most vehement in this pressure group. Seldom in his two terms as President did Dad's basic inner calm show to better advantage. He simply refused to be stampeded into making a statement. The UN was meeting in New York, and the Russians were showing signs of being more co-operative than they had been in years. The world was still reeling from the British devaluation of the pound. Even though there was a strong possibility of a leak, he decided to take his time and think over exactly what kind of statement he should make. Not even a visit from David Lilienthal, who was flown down from his vacation house on Martha's Vineyard, changed Dad's mind. He thought about it for another two weeks and then issued the following careful statement:

> We have evidence that within recent weeks an atomic explosion occurred in the USSR.
>
> Ever since atomic energy was first released by man, the eventual development of this new force by other nations was to be expected. This probability has always been taken into account by us.
>
> Nearly four years ago I pointed out that "scientific opinion appears to be practically unanimous that the essential theoretical knowledge upon which the discovery is based is already widely known. There is also substantial agreement that foreign research can come abreast of our present theoretical knowledge in time." . . .
>
> This recent development emphasizes once again, if indeed such emphasis were needed, the necessity for that truly effective, enforceable international control of atomic energy which this government and the large majority of the members of the United Nations support.

The leadership my father displayed in this announcement—plus the grim import of the news—had a dramatic impact on Congress. The billion-dollar military assistance to our NATO allies was swiftly passed. But Dad, with the responsibility for the future security of the nation on his shoulders, was forced to look beyond this victory to one of his most difficult decisions. The speed with which Russia had become an atomic power meant that they were in possession of much more information and nuclear expertise than our scientists had thought possible. The year 1952 was the date that most of them had set for Russia's first atomic explosion. Some had predicted 1955.

This raised the grim possibility that the Russians were perfectly capable of developing a new, more terrible weapon, which at this time was only being discussed in the laboratories—the H-bomb. The power of the hydrogen atom would be a hundred to a thousand times more destructive than the uranium atom. The debate over whether to create such a weapon split the Atomic

Energy Commission and its leading scientists. The chairman, David Lilienthal, a man whom Dad liked, was opposed. So was J. Robert Oppenheimer, the father of the A-bomb.

My father appointed Secretary of State Dean Acheson, Secretary of Defense Louis Johnson, and Mr. Lilienthal to a special committee to study "Campbell," the code name for the superweapon. Dad thought about this hard choice throughout the fall and early winter of 1949. At one point David Lilienthal warned him that the Joint Atomic Energy Committee of Congress, led by Senator Brien McMahon, were working themselves into a frenzy over the problem and preparing to descend on the White House to blitz Dad into saying yes.

"I don't blitz easily," Dad said with a hard smile.

The Joint Committee on Atomic Energy was a constant problem to my father. He did his utmost to work with them as he would and did work with any other congressional committee. But they were dealing with the most sensitive, highly confidential subject in the government, and it was extremely difficult to decide how much they should be told because of the constant danger of security leaks. There is nothing a senator or a congressman loves more than a headline, and some of them tend to put headlines ahead of the best interests of their country. Early in November, 1949, while my father was still thinking about the H-bomb and waiting for his special committee to report to him, Senator Edwin Johnson of Colorado blabbed the information about the H-bomb debate on a television show. Dad was furious, and called in Chairman McMahon to give him an angry lecture. Senator Johnson replied by accusing David Lilienthal of trying to give away the secret of the H-bomb to Canada and Great Britain. Politics is really a lovely sport.

Senator Johnson's blunder added the glare of publicity to the other agonizing aspects of the decision on the H-bomb. Then came confidential news from England that made everyone in the White House wince. The British had discovered that Dr. Klaus Fuchs was part of a Communist spy ring that had been operating at Los Alamos during the creation of the atom bomb. The German-born Fuchs, who was a naturalized British citizen, had given the Communists crucial information which undoubtedly enabled Russia to achieve an atomic explosion three years ahead of schedule. It was the most dismaying possible development. Klaus Fuchs had stolen most of his information during the war years. But he had returned to the United States as recently as 1947 as part of a British team that attended a conference that discussed declassifying hitherto secret scientific documents on atomic research. My father and his aides could only shudder at the impact this news would have on the Communists-in-government crowd in Congress.

On January 31 Secretary of State Acheson, Secretary of Defense Johnson, and Atomic Energy Commission Chairman Lilienthal met with my father in his office at 12:35. They informed him that, after long and careful deliberation, they had agreed that we should launch a program to investigate the possibility of building an H-bomb. At the same time they recommended a searching reexamination of our foreign policy and our strategic plans. Mr. Lilienthal, who had signed the agreement with reservations, made his doubts about the decision clear in a brief statement. He pointed out that we could no longer rely on atomic weapons for the defense of the country. As a weapon the H-bomb really made no sense, because it could achieve nothing but the annihilation of an enemy—not a reasonable or tolerable goal for any nation, but especially intolerable for a democracy.

My father agreed with what Mr. Lilienthal was saying. "I've always believed that we should never use these weapons," he said. "I don't believe we ever will have to use them, but we have to go on making them because of the way the Russians are behaving. We have no other course." Then, in a grimmer tone, he added that if Senator Johnson had kept his mouth shut, it might have been possible to examine the whole issue quietly, but now, so many people were in a furor about the possibility of Russia achieving such a weapon, he had no alternative but to go ahead.

My father sat down and signed the already prepared statement for the press, announcing in the simplest possible terms the decision to pursue the superweapon. "It is part of my responsibility as Commander in Chief of the Armed Forces to see to it that our country is able to defend itself against any possible aggressor," he said. As he signed the statement, he remarked: "I remember when I made the decision on Greece. Everybody on the National Security Council predicted the world would come to an end if we went ahead. But we did go ahead and the world didn't come to an end. I think the same thing will happen here."

Two days later the British Embassy reported that Klaus Fuchs would be arraigned on February 3. My father looked grimly at the man who brought him the news, Admiral Sidney Souers, his chief of intelligence, and said: "Tie on your hat."

[CHAPTER]

Twenty-Two

ON FEBRUARY 9, 1950, six days after the news of Klaus Fuchs's treachery stunned the Western world and nineteen days after Alger Hiss was found guilty, Senator Joseph McCarthy of Wisconsin addressed the Republican Women's Club of Wheeling, West Virginia. He held up a piece of paper on which he said was a list of 205 names of Communist party members in the State Department. The list had been given to the Secretary of State, declared the senator, yet these men were still in the State Department, "shaping policy." From Wheeling the senator flew to Salt Lake City, where he made a similar speech, and then to Reno, where he repeated his charges and wired the White House, demanding action. Ten days later he talked until nearly midnight on the floor of the Senate, denouncing "eighty-one known Communist agents in the State Department," one of whom was "now a speech writer in the White House."

This was absolute nonsense, of course, and my father did not take it seriously. The first time Senator McCarthy's name was mentioned in a press conference, Dad curtly dismissed him. His reckless accusations seemed, at that time, simply one more attempt by the reactionaries in Congress to sabotage the Truman program.

In his letter to Dr. Chaim Weizmann in late 1948, my father remarked, "It does not take long for bitter and resourceful opponents to regroup their forces after they have been shattered. You in Israel have already been confronted with that situation; and I expect to be all too soon."

The prediction came true, a few weeks after his second administration began. The reactionaries, an unimaginative lot, first tried the most obvious trick in the political book—smearing the President by finding corruption in his administration. Their target was Major General Harry Vaughan.

We have met General Vaughan briefly at various other points in this book. He had a unique ability to make Dad laugh. He has one of the quickest wits I have ever known, and a fine eye for the more absurd aspects of life. Mother sometimes took a dim view of his humor; it was irrepressible, and nothing and no one was sacred. One day she wore a flowered hat to a luncheon with Senate wives, who were all similarly attired. General Vaughan remarked that they all looked like a "collection of well-tended graves."

Dad valued Harry Vaughan, not only for his humor but because he knew that he was absolutely loyal to Harry S. Truman. He was also a very efficient, very intelligent liaison man with a unique ability for putting people at ease. He handled many non-military chores, somewhat in the style of "Pa" Watson, President Roosevelt's military aide. But Dad never gave General Vaughan the authority that Pa Watson possessed.

When my father appointed General Eisenhower the chief of staff in 1946, he called in Harry Vaughan and said: "Harry, I called you in here because I wanted you and the General to have an absolutely clear understanding about how I wanted this to work. Whenever I want anything brought particularly to General Eisenhower's attention, I will give it to you and you will give it to the General and call it to his attention."

Then my father turned to Ike and said: "General, whenever you want anything to come to my attention quickly without any loss of time, you send it to Harry and he will bring it in and give it safe hand to me."

Then he turned to General Vaughan with a twinkle in his eye and said: "And at all other times you will mind your own damned business."

Ike was very pleased by this arrangement. As he left the White House, he told General Vaughan that Pa Watson, Mr. Roosevelt's military aide, had been given far more authority. FDR told the Secretary of War, "Whenever Pa Watson tells you anything it's an order from me. Even if I never heard of it, it's an order from me."

Ike shook his head. "You can imagine how Pa Watson ran the Army."

The opening round of the get-Truman attack on General Vaughan was led by Drew Pearson, who had made a fool of himself, as we have seen, by filing an election eve column discussing Mr. Dewey's cabinet choices. Mr. Pearson was not a reactionary, but he was more than ready to co-operate with them to serve his own dubious purposes.

Dad's opinion of Drew Pearson was summed up very succinctly in a letter he wrote to Bob Hannegan on September 10, 1946. Bob had written Dad a rather unnecessary note denying a Pearson broadcast which implied that he would not be a Truman supporter in 1948. Dad replied:

> I appreciated your note of the ninth, but you didn't have to write it.
> Whenever I get my information from Pearson, I hope somebody will have my head examined—I'll need it.
> Articles like that are merely an attempt to upset the "apple cart" and Pearson and your friend Winchell are the "sphere heads" for that purpose. If either one of them ever tell the truth, it is by accident and not intentional.

General Vaughan first ran afoul of Mr. Pearson in 1946, when one of Pearson's assistants talked himself onto a government aid mission to Greece. The Greek government informed the White House, through General Vaughan, that the man, a Greek-American, was persona non grata because of his previous political activities. He was promptly bumped from the mission. Mr. Pearson warned General Vaughan that he would "get him" if his man was not promptly restored to the official list. General Vaughan, with Dad's complete approval, told Mr. Pearson to get lost.

For the next two years Mr. Pearson sniped continually at General Vaughan in his column. At one point he formally accused him of taking a huge bribe to fix a tax case. Again with Dad's knowledge and approval, the FBI investigated this claim for several years, questioning people in Kansas City, Washington, and New Orleans. They found nothing. But meanwhile, Mr. Pearson was able to scream that a man on the President's staff was "under investigation."

[422]

In February, 1949, Mr. Pearson made the horrifying announcement that General Vaughan had accepted a medal from the "fascistic" government of Argentina, which at that time was ruled by the dictator Juan Peron. Dad was told to fire General Vaughan immediately. There is in the Constitution a prohibition against an American officer accepting a decoration from a foreign government. For decades the practice had been to accept such medals and turn them over to the State Department until permission to keep them was granted by Congress. Diplomatic experience had shown that many nations did not understand this constitutional prohibition and were very offended when our military men or civil servants refused the proffered medal.

General Vaughan had duly informed Stanley Woodward, chief of protocol for the State Department, of the Argentine ambassador's desire to confer the Grand Cross of the Order of the Liberator San Martin on him. He was told to accept it politely and turn it over to Protocol. The same decoration had been received without comment on August 31, 1948, by General Omar Bradley, chief of staff, and World War II Generals Devers, Hodges, Wedemeyer, Collins, and several others. Earlier, General Eisenhower and Admiral Chester Nimitz had been among the recipients.

Mr. Pearson let it be known throughout Washington and the nation that anyone who attended the party at the Argentine Embassy when General Vaughan accepted his decoration would be persona non grata henceforth in Pearsonville—a decree which did not cause any shivers of fear in the White House. Mr. Pearson was not among those invited to the Embassy for the ceremony. But he stood outside glaring ominously at all those who dared to brave his wrath. They included senators, congressmen, and most of the ranking officers of the Pentagon. Mr. Pearson ran up and down peering into cars like something out of a Marx Brothers movie. The climax came when General Hoyt Vandenberg, commander of the air force, arrived. Pearson was busy peering into another car so General Vandenberg strolled up to him, tapped him on the shoulder, and gave him his card. "I want to make sure you don't miss me," he said. The next day Pearson wrote in his column that the General had sneaked into the Embassy through a rear entrance.

After fifteen years in Washington, my father was used to ignoring Drew Pearson. But he was galled to see a supposedly responsible paper, the Washington *Post*, taking up the Argentine accusation on their editorial page. A few days later Dad attended a dinner given by the Reserve Officers Association in honor of General Vaughan. They were enormously proud of the fact that a reserve officer was the President's aide—a fact which, incidentally, raised hackles among the regular army brass in Washington. Kiddingly, Dad began an off-the-cuff speech by saying, "I don't know if I'm supposed to tell all I know on Vaughan or not." But as he reviewed General Vaughan's career and their long friendship, his temperature rose, and he ended by saying, "If any S.O.B. thinks he can get me to discharge any member of my staff or Cabinet by some smart-aleck statement over the air, he's mistaken."

This got into the papers, and General Vaughan soon became a target for headline hunters in Congress. In August, 1949, a subcommittee headed by Senator Clyde R. Hoey of North Carolina began an investigation into so-called "five percenters," who supposedly peddled their influence to government agencies for five percent of the government contract. The star witness was a character named John Maragon, a Greek-American, who, it turned out, was drawing a thousand dollars a month from an importer while he worked for the Allied mission to Greece. Because General Vaughan had helped to get him the job, he was pilloried as hopelessly corrupt. Pearson went almost berserk, picturing Maragon's enormous influence in the Truman Administration. He claimed that Maragon had stood beside my father when he reviewed the Atlantic fleet, accompanied Dad to Potsdam, and cajoled him into giving away half of Europe to Stalin. The truth is, Maragon was a passenger agent for the B&O Railroad, and General Vaughan had recommended him as a suitable person to handle travel accommodations and the transfer of baggage for the American commission visiting Greece. Pearson magnified this into Maragon as a State Department adviser and architect of the Truman Doctrine.

Maragon was one of those little men who loved to be on the fringes of big-time politics. They are tireless in attempting to do favors for anyone who will let them, and when they are out of earshot, they will loudly proclaim their important contacts in the White House, or Congress, or the State Department, alleging to their friends, or anyone who will listen to them, that the inner

[424]

wheels of the government cannot turn without their advice and consent. General Vaughan, who was relatively inexperienced in the duplicities of the Washington scene, took several years to realize that Maragon was misrepresenting his relationship with him. Only during Maragon's trial for perjury (committed before the Hoey Committee) did the General learn that Maragon had a habit of claiming to speak for him on various occasions, thus gaining access to various official and unofficial Washington functions.

General Vaughan appeared before the Hoey Committee for two days, testifying about his relationship with Maragon and another reputed five percenter, Colonel James V. Hunt. The General had accepted the gift of a factory reject deepfreeze from one of Colonel Hunt's clients—again totally unaware that his name was being used to peddle influence.

With great reluctance, Senator Hoey was forced to admit that there was no evidence of corruption on the General's part. But that did not prevent headlines and editorials about deepfreezes and influence peddling, which gave the impression that the Truman Administration was riddled with corruption. General Vaughan, dismayed and horrified, went to Dad and said that he felt he should resign as his military aide.

"Harry," snapped Dad, "don't even mention such a thing to me again. We came in here together and we're going out of here together. Those so-and-so's are trying to get me, through you. I understand exactly what's going on."

When you read the headlines the investigation created with practically no evidence of guilt by anyone, it is frightening to think of what might have happened if some of the behind-the-scenes plotting had succeeded. A loyal Louisiana congressman informed Dad that Pearson legmen were scouring New Orlean and its environs for Democrats willing to take a bribe and swear that Harry Vaughan had helped them fix an income tax case. General Vaughan has in his files affidavits from some of the men who were approached. Fortunately, these smear tactics got nowhere. A few others who regarded the General as fair game found out he could take care of himself rather handily. In the files of the Truman Library there are the papers of a libel suit General Vaughan instituted against the *Saturday Evening Post* for calling him a crook. It took him until 1960 to win it. He collected $ 10,000.

Senator Hoey was from North Carolina and conservative to his high-buttoned shoes and wing collar. Sulking in South Carolina was retired Secretary of State Jimmy Byrnes. He suddenly decided that the believers in yesterday were the men of tomorrow, and began harshly attacking the Truman Administration's Fair Deal, making it sound as if the world was going to come to an end if we gave the federal government enough power to improve the health and guarantee the civil rights of all the people. Speaking at Washington and Lee University late in June, 1949, Mr. Byrnes predicted that "the individual—whether farmer, worker, manufacturer, lawyer or doctor—will soon be an economic slave pulling an oar in the galley of the state."

Dad dashed off a letter to Mr. Byrnes, in which he wrote, "I now know how Caesar felt when he said, *Et tu, Brutus.*"

Mr. Byrnes, a tough man to beat in a verbal exchange, flashed back, "I am no Brutus, I hope you are not going to think of yourself as Caesar, because you are no Caesar."

At the same time Bernard Baruch, who spent most of his time in South Carolina, slashed at Dad with a wholly untrue statement that an industrial mobilization plan for the possibility of war had been rejected by the White House. A reporter asked Dad: "Do you think there is any connection between Mr. Byrnes's attack and Mr. Baruch's?"

"Draw your own conclusions," Dad replied.

Dad discussed Bernard Baruch with David Lilienthal around this time. "He's the same old Bernie. Gave five thousand to Dewey, then the day after election tried to give Bill Boyle money for us Democrats. He's behind Byrnes, financing him. He's just a disappointed man. When he had FDR down to his place in South Carolina, he had news photographers take pictures of the bedroom where FDR slept, with Bernie's picture big over it all. Next day after this appeared FDR went straight home."

Two years later, when Dad was preparing the book *Mr. President,* the memory of his nasty little exchange with Mr. Byrnes prompted him to include in it a verbatim copy of the handwritten letter he read to him early in 1946, telling him to stop "babying the Soviets." He thought people would be interested to see that this great neo-conservative had a gift for being on several sides of the issues, depending on where he thought his political advantage lay. Mr. Byrnes, maneuvered into a very embarrassing corner, took the easy way out. He denied ever seeing or hearing of such a letter.

The reactionary attack of 1949 darkened Dad's already dim view of the objectivity of our free press. Looking back on his experience after he left office, Dad said:

> After I sent my message on domestic policy to the Congress on September 6th, 1945, a campaign of vilification and misrepresentation in editing the news by the special interest controlled press began. It is difficult for the average citizen of this great republic to understand how a "free press" can be used to distort facts as a means of character assassination. I do not mean to condemn the whole press and charge all of the newspapers and magazines with this campaign, but the vast majority was guilty. This systematic attack was not confined solely to matters of policy and administration. Individuals were singled out and made the victims of character assassination in the hope of destroying public confidence in my administration.

Dad exempted most of the reporters from this accusation. During his two hundredth press conference early in October, 1949, one newsman asked him, "Do you become a little annoyed with us at times?"

"I never get annoyed with you," Dad replied. "I get annoyed with your bosses sometimes. I think most of you try your best to be entirely fair. I've never had any reason to quarrel with you."

He exempted columnists from this testimonial, however. Mingling fact and opinion as they invariably do, and frequently descending to personalities, they were among the chief distorters of the truth, in Dad's opinion. At one point he wrote an ironic memo to himself on the subject.

> I have appointed a secretary of columnists. His duties are to listen to all radio commentators, read all columnists in the newspapers from ivory tower to lowest gossip, coordinate them and give me the results so I can run the United States and the world as it should be. I have several men in reserve beside the present holder of the job, because I think in a week or two the present secretary for columnists will need the services of a psychiatrist and will in all probability end up in St. Elizabeth's [the mental hospital in Washington].

[427]

With the pounding he was already taking from the China First Republicans, the Southern conservatives and the "Sabotage Press" as my father called the really reactionary papers, it is understandable, I think, that he did not see anything particularly new or menacing in Senator Joe McCarthy's emergence. The Wisconsin senator persisted, of course, in hurling about figures and names which, to the day of his death, never produced the conviction or even the exposure of a single Communist. The next time he was mentioned in a press conference, Dad took him a little more seriously. "If people really were in earnest and had the welfare of the country at heart, and they really thought that somebody in the government was not loyal or did not do his job right, the proper person with whom to take that up is the President of the United States."

My father went on to point out that he had created a comprehensive federal loyalty program in 1947, which was in the process of screening every employee in the government. This loyalty program was worked out, Dad said, "with civil liberties in view." He referred the reporters to a speech which he had recently made to the nation's district attorneys and law enforcement officers, in which he stressed the vital importance of upholding the Bill of Rights, *"the* most important part of the Constitution of the United States."

Unfortunately, the Truman loyalty program satisfied neither the right-wing extremists, who were ready to sacrifice the Bill of Rights in their hunt for an infinitesimal minority of disloyal government employees, nor the super-liberals, who are still writing books condemning the mere fact that he instituted a loyalty program. With his long experience in Washington, my father was no stranger to reckless charges about communism and disloyalty. He had seen Martin Dies, first chairman of the House Un-American Activities Committee, in action and had been appalled when Vice President Garner told him, "The Dies Committee is going to have more influence on the future of American politics than any other committee of Congress." Dad did not agree with him, but in the next fifteen years, Mr. Garner's prophecy came dismayingly true.

My father's creation of a loyalty program, once the cold war became a fact of life, was simply a continuation of President

Roosevelt's Executive Order 9300 which set up a Committee of Five to consider charges of subversive activity made against government employees. When Dad issued Executive Order 9835, creating his loyalty program, he put Seth Richardson, a prominent conservative Republican, in charge of it, to prove to everyone in the nation that he had no interest in playing politics with the problem.

Along with careful provisions for review and appeal of findings, my father laid down one fundamental principle which explained not a little of the hostility which right-wing congressmen displayed toward his program. Under no circumstances was any committee of Congress to be given access to the confidential files of any government employee. These files contained large amounts of raw, unevaluated data collected by the FBI, which an unscrupulous congressman could use to wreck an honest man's reputation. At the same time Dad never wavered from his conviction that a loyalty review board was necessary in the current climate of world politics. The super-liberals who sneeringly point out that only .002 percent of the government employees examined were dismissed from their jobs or denied employment are incredibly naïve. Espionage rings are not large operations. It only took a half-dozen disloyal scientists and couriers to steal the secret of the atomic bomb.

What dismayed my father about the McCarthy phenomenon, more than anything else, was the eagerness with which supposedly respectable senators such as Styles Bridges of New Hampshire and Robert Taft of Ohio boarded the Wisconsin senator's sleazy bandwagon. Senator Taft said that Senator McCarthy "should keep talking and if one case doesn't work out, he should proceed with another." To his everlasting credit, my father did not run away from the fight. In his March 30, 1950, press conference, he bluntly told the assembled reporters, "I think the greatest asset that the Kremlin has is Senator McCarthy." While the reporters gasped, Dad coolly analyzed Republican party policy.

> The Republicans have been trying vainly to find an issue on which to make a bid for the control of the Congress for next year. They tried statism. They tried welfare state. They tried socialism. And there are a certain number of members of the Republican Party who are trying to dig up that old malodorous

dead horse called isolationism. And in order to do that, they are perfectly willing to sabotage the bipartisan foreign policy of the United States. And this fiasco which has been going on in the Senate is the very best asset that the Kremlin could have in the operation of the cold war.

Behind the scenes my father tried to combat Senator McCarthy by arming his Cabinet with knowledge. He had a very illuminating 5,000-word paper written under his direction, entitled, "A Study of Witch Hunting and Hysteria in the United States." It covered periods of public madness from the actual witchcraft craze in Salem, the Alien and Sedition Acts of 1798–1800, the anti-Masonry agitation of 1826–1840, the Know-Nothing anti-immigrant movement of 1840–1856, the Ku Klux Klan operation in the Reconstruction Era, and the post-World War I anti-Communist hysteria which coincided with a resurgence of the KKK. Reading it, you can't help but wonder if there is a permanent lunatic fringe in this country (and probably in other countries) which becomes swept up in these insane mass movements that thrive on hate and fear.

Ironically, while the know-nothings in Congress ranted and raved and made some people think that the government was about to collapse from internal subversion, my father was calmly directing a sweeping reappraisal of America's relationship to the Communist world. It flowed directly from the H-bomb decision, which had called for such a study. This could have been a perfunctory performance, if the President had chosen to rely on weapons of terror. But Dad meant it when he said that he hoped no nation would ever use atomic weapons again. Moreover, he was dissatisfied with a foreign policy which limited itself merely to checking Communist ambitions. This was much too negative and ultimately defeatist for a man who thought as positively as Harry S. Truman.

Although few of his biographers have noted it, he specifically rejected the policy of containment. "Our purpose was much broader," he said. "We were working for a united, free and prosperous world." The Berlin airlift, the Russian retreat from Iran, their diplomatic collapse in the face of the Marshall Plan and NATO had confirmed the wisdom of Dad's fundamental policy, to negotiate with the Russians from positions of strength. This insight was at the heart of Paper No. 68 of the National Security

Council, NSC-68, for short, the policy review which he had ordered in January.

Charles Murphy remembers vividly the genesis of NSC-68. "The President quietly set up a task force of State Department and Defense Department people to reexamine the strategic defense position of the United States and they came up with a memorandum toward the end of 1949. The President gave me a copy of this memorandum. I didn't get to read it during the day—I was busy working on something else—and I took it home with me that night. What I read scared me so much that the next day I didn't go to the office at all. I sat at home and read this memorandum over and over, wondering what in the world to do about it. The gist of it was that we were in pretty bad shape and we damn well better do something about it. So I recommended to the President that he put this into the machinery of the National Security Council where it had not been before. That is how it became the paper that got so well known as NSC-68."

In alarming detail, NSC-68 described the relative military weakness of the Western world, vis-à-vis the Communists. We were vastly outnumbered in terms of standing armies and our equipment, still World-War-II vintage, was rapidly becoming obsolete in the face of Russian advances in weaponry, planes and tanks. Since the Communists were obviously determined to continue to build their military capability, while we maintained a status quo approach, the long-range project of Communist versus non-Communist strength was grim. By 1954 Russia would achieve a stalemate in nuclear weapons. This meant that the Russians and the Chinese would have the power to deploy their vastly superior conventional forces and use them at will. The United States was therefore faced with three alternatives.

One, it could withdraw behind the shield of "fortress America" and let the rest of the world slide inexorably into the Communist orbit.

Two, it could attempt a quick preventive war, a combined atomic-conventional assault on Russia to eliminate the seat of Communist power.

Three, it could begin a massive program of rebuilding the defensive potential of the free world. This program envisioned the United States as the dynamic center of a free world community, sharing its wealth and its military and scientific knowledge to guarantee the long-range survival of free societies everywhere. This, of course, was the alternative which the NSC-68's authors recommended as the only reasonable policy for our nation.

We have been following that policy for so long, it is hard for us to realize that it was based on some drastic revisions of fundamental assumptions. Until NSC-68, for instance, it was assumed that we could not spend much more than twelve or thirteen billion dollars a year on defense without bankrupting the nation. The NSC's planners reported that we could devote as much as 20 percent of our gross national product to security without harming our economy. A military budget of fifty billion was recommended to implement the new goal of negotiation from strength. At the same time NSC-68 placed on the President a new burden—the need to view the security of the free world as synonymous with America's security. This required the most astute judgment to determine where a crisis situation in some distant part of the world threatened our security and where it did not threaten it.

In implementing this policy, my father was faced with some very difficult choices, particularly in Asia. Japan was only beginning its economic revival; its government was wholly dependent on U.S. support. The other great power in that region, China, was now in the hands of the Communists. Elsewhere local governments were weak or nonexistent, because for decades, and in some cases for centuries, the nations had been colonies. Korea, for instance, had been occupied by Japan since 1895. Divided in half by Stalin and Churchill at Yalta, it swiftly became a part of the cold war. The Democratic People's Republic of Korea was created in the northern half of the country, and a large army was trained and equipped by the Russians. We in turn encouraged the people of South Korea to proclaim a republic, and when we withdrew our troops on June 29, 1949, we left 500 officers and men behind to help train a South Korean defense force of 65,000 men.

On January 26, 1950, we negotiated a defense agreement with South Korea, committing us to continue military and economic assistance. My father signed the agreement with some reluctance, because he had no great admiration for President Syngman Rhee, who tended to be ultraconservative in his views and rather dictatorial in his methods. But his people were wholeheartedly anti-

Communist. Millions had fled into South Korea to escape the harsh Communist rule in the north.

A similar, even more complex situation existed in Indochina. There, Peking and Moscow had recognized the Democratic Republic of Vietnam, headed by Ho Chi Minh. On February 7 the United States extended recognition to the Emperor Bao Dai after finally persuading the French to grant Vietnam independence within the French Union. The complicating factor in Indochina was French colonialism. My father had rebuffed General de Gaulle's attempt to reestablish French control of Lebanon and Syria immediately after the end of World War II. He was no happier about France's attempts to regain control of Indochina, which began a civil war between the French and French-oriented Vietnamese and the followers of Ho Chi Minh.

In the files of the Truman Library there are two telegrams which Ho Chi Minh sent to my father, on October 17 and October 20, 1945, asking for an opportunity to participate in the recently established British-American-Russian-Chinese Advisory Commission for the Far East, and declaring that the people of Vietnam were "determined never to let the French return to Indochina and will fight them under any circumstances."

Ho Chi Minh was a known Communist, and the cold war was already getting colder. Dad was certainly not inclined to deal with him, if he could find a non-Communist alternative. He did not reply to this or subsequent telegrams from Ho Chi Minh. From the rigid, authoritarian Communist regime which Ho eventually imposed on North Vietnam, it is evident that there would have been little point in Dad's doing so.

What my father was trying to do in both Korea and Indochina was buy time in the hope that the seeds of independence and democracy could be planted and nurtured there. He did everything in his power to pressure the French into setting Vietnam on the path to freedom, as we had done with the Philippines. He had exerted similar pressure on the Dutch to free Indonesia. But it was a terribly delicate business to persuade allies that were badly needed in the defense of Europe to change centuries-old colonialist attitudes.

The most important part of NSC-68 was its clear call for a strong, rearmed America. This is why Dad sometimes called it "my five-year plan for peace." He was convinced that if he could persuade Congress to implement it swiftly, the Communists would never dare to launch an armed attack on a free world nation. Simultaneously, he saw a beautiful opportunity to turn the tables on the Communist witch-hunters in Congress. All right, he planned to say to them, you want to fight communism, you want to stop its onward march, at home and abroad? Then join me in making America and its allies so strong, we can frustrate communism's dream of world conquest—and guarantee a century of peace in the bargain.

With this in mind, in the spring of 1950, my father coolly announced that he was planning a little train trip. He was going out to the state of Washington to dedicate Grand Coulee Dam on May 11. The news gave the Republicans a severe case of the jitters. The one man who could answer McCarthy, Taft & Company was going to take his case to the people and they dreaded the prospect. On April 22 Dad wrote me lightheartedly, "I think you, your mother and I will have a grand trip next month. . . . The opposition seems to be scared stiff over what your dad will do on that trip and I'm going to fool 'em as usual. It will be a dignified, really nonpolitical performance for the benefit of our foreign program."

On May 7 we headed west aboard the *Ferdinand Magellan*. By now the planners had added two other dam inspections to our route.

Again and again Dad told people that he was not "politicking." Instead he was "reporting to the nation on its condition, on what it needs, and what I hope I can give it for its welfare and benefit, and on what I hope to contribute to world peace and what I hope to obtain for the welfare of all mankind." At the same time, Dad could not resist getting in a few licks at what he called "the calamity howlers," who kept saying that the country was being ruined by the Democratic party's program.

At Missoula, Montana, at 7:22 A.M. I listened half-awake while he came up with one of his best metaphors. He said that the local congressman, who happened to be Mike Mansfield, was a man who could see into the future, who planned for the future, who thought about the welfare of the whole country. He was the sort of man who could look at an acorn and see a giant oak tree with its great limbs spreading upward and outward in the years to come. But there were some people in Washington, D.C., who "take a look at an acorn and all they can see is just an acorn. . . . Even give them a magnifying glass, or even a pair of spyglasses, or even a telescope, they just shake their heads and all they can say is 'I'm sorry I can't see anything but an acorn there.' " He urged the citizens of Missoula to do something about politicians who specialized in this kind of "acorn thinking."

At Gonzaga University in Spokane Dad gave one of his most philosophic talks. This is a Jesuit university, and Dad was stirred by the religious atmosphere to speak in a deeply moving way about the goals and ideals of America.

> The same moral principles that underlie our national life govern our relations with all other nations and peoples of the world.
>
> We have built our own nation not by trying to wipe out differences in religion, or in tradition, or in customs among us, not by attempting to conceal our political and economic conflicts, but instead by holding to a belief which rises above all differences and conflicts.
>
> That belief is that all men are equal before God.
>
> With this belief in our hearts, we can achieve unity without eliminating differences—we can advance the common welfare without harming the dissenting minority.
>
> Just as that belief has enabled us to build a great nation, so it can serve as the foundation of world peace.

It was a delightful trip. There was none of the tension of 1948. Dad celebrated his birthday along the right of way, and got no less than eighteen birthday cakes. At small towns and in large cities, he was his usual forthright, hard-hitting self. *The New York Times* was impressed by the way he reduced the complex issues of world policy to "town size." Carl W. McCardle of the Philadelphia *Evening Bulletin* marveled at the "easy kinship between the President and the plain people of America." He said that there was little doubt that Dad had succeeded in doing two things. "First, he has laughed off the cry of socialism that the Republicans raised against his Fair Deal." Second, he has "tilled the soil and fixed things up generally for local Democratic Congressional candidates." Another reporter praised the "smooth working Presi-

[435]

dential staff, which makes it a business to know the interests of every community before it is reached, has a speech ready and keyed to local interest."

By the time Dad returned to the White House he had talked to 525,000 people, and the Democratic National Committee was practically dancing on the ceiling. Everyone agreed that the Republicans were in disarray, clinging to their phony Communists-in-government issue, without a shred of a positive program to oppose the economic opportunity at home and freedom's strength abroad that Dad was offering the people. Joe McCarthy was flailing away with his empty accusations before a subcommittee of the Senate Foreign Relations Committee, wounding more reputations, but also sounding and looking more hollow. A smashing Democratic victory in the fall elections would convince fundamentally sane Republicans, such as Senator Taft, that McCarthyism was politically bankrupt, and they would drop him.

So the scenario went in the late spring of 1950. It was a beautiful dream, and it might have come true, if the cold-eyed men in the Kremlin and their allies in Peking had not decided there was a prize ripe for picking in the Far East—a peninsula that thrust itself from the land mass of Asia like a weapon at the heart of Japan—Korea.

[CHAPTER]

Twenty-Three

BEFORE THIS TRAGEDY STRUCK, there are some happy moments to remember. As usual, the Trumans did not let the crackpots in Congress or elsewhere spoil their love of a good laugh. One of our favorites was the day in 1949 when Mother went up to the Capitol for lunch with the Senate ladies Red Cross unit. As she entered the building, who came wandering in the door as an ordinary tourist but the Duke of Windsor. One reporter got so excited he raced into the Senate press room yelling: "The Duke and Duchess of Truman are here!" Les Biffle promptly organized a lunch in honor of the Duke, and Mother went on to her Senate ladies.

Down at Key West the hijinks were funnier than ever. On December 8, 1949, the White House correspondents assembled in the press room of the bachelor officers quarters for a press conference. They had been relaxing in their usual style rather late the previous evening, and several were somewhat the worse for wear. But they woke up fast, when the President of the United States arrived flourishing his cane, and wearing his white pith helmet and one of his wilder tropical shirts. Instead of taking his usual stance in front of the mob, he strolled into their midst and sat down in a chair. Only then did they notice that he was armed with a pencil and a sheet of Western Union message stationery. Charlie Ross took the presidential position at the head of the group and solemnly announced: "Gentlemen, we have with us today as our guest a distinguished contributor to the Federal Register."

While Dad industriously took notes, Charlie proceeded to describe what the President had done so far today. It consisted largely of having breakfast and going down to the dock to see off two boatloads of fishermen.

The distinguished contributor to the Federal Register then turned on the reporters and began asking *them* questions. One by one, he asked when they went to bed the previous night. There were hoots of laughter as they struggled to sound respectable, muttering replies such as "one o'clock, roughly." Joe Fox of the Washington *Star* decided an outrageous lie was preferable to the truth, and solemnly answered, "Nine thirty, Mr. President." Bill Hassett, Dad's correspondence secretary, who was watching the show, said, "I'm glad they're not under oath."

"How many of you have had breakfast this morning?" Dad demanded.

A majority put up their hands. "Good. Good," he said. "Just a small percentage have not had breakfast. How many have written to their wives at least once a week since you've been down here?"

There was another show of hands, and Dad looked dubious. "Tony," he said to Anthony Leviero of *The New York Times,* "you had better check up, because I have had several telegrams wanting to know what these fellows were doing."

After finding out where he could cash a check—the question every reporter asks the moment he arrives in a new locale—the contributor to the Federal Register departed.

We also had a good time aboard the yacht *Williamsburg.* We spent the 1949 Fourth of July weekend aboard the old boat. Dad, Mother, a couple of my girl friends, and I arrived early, on Saturday, July 2. The next day Clark Clifford, Oscar Ewing, George Allen, Stuart Symington, and other VIPs were scheduled to come aboard. We decided to burlesque an official reception, and we really did a job of it. From somewhere in the bowels of the ship we fished up a weary, tattered red carpet. Then we persuaded the commander of the *Williamsburg* to run up every single flag in his locker. The Filipino mess boys doubled as a Hawaiian band, for background music. As the guests came up the ladder, they were pelted with confetti, and ruffles and flourishes blasted from drums and bugles. They didn't know what was happening. When they arrived at their staterooms, they found all sorts of ridiculous signs on their doors. George Allen had one saying, "Sucker." I summed it all up in my diary: "We laughed ourselves silly."

I joined Dad and Mother for that vacation at Key West. But most of the time, during the second term, I was a working girl. I went to New York, not long after the inauguration in 1949, and tried to pick up the pieces of my singing career which I had all but abandoned during 1948 for the great campaign. I had found a new manager in the course of the year—Jim Davidson, a top-flight professional who handled only a small number of first-rate singers. He offered to take me on, if I would agree to devote nine months of concentrated effort to getting my voice in shape for concert singing. I quickly accepted, and on the last day of January I moved to New York, taking along Reathel Odum, Mother's secretary—and previous to that Dad's Senate secretary—as a friend and companion. I did my best to meet Mr. Davidson's strict, very demanding standards. At the same time I continued to be a part-time White House belle. Each weekend I returned to Washington and performed various chores, such as christening new airliners for Pan American Airways. It was a rather schizophrenic existence—also rather exhausting.

One Washington event I made sure I didn't miss was the March visit of Mr. and Mrs. Churchill. Dad gave a dinner for them in the dining room of Lee House, which is the twin next-door neighbor of Blair House. Mr. Churchill was in marvelous spirits. The Labour government was steadily losing popularity in England, and he told Dad that he was planning to stand for reelection as prime minister and was sure he would win.

The small size of Blair House, as I have said, made entertaining doubly difficult. Large dinners had to be given at the Carlton Hotel. At official small dinners we usually had cocktails in Blair House, then crossed to Lee House for dinner. When I gave a dinner, the White House workmen stripped Blair House of carpets, moved all the furniture, and polished the floor for dancing, while we dined in Lee House. At dawn the next day Blair House was put together again.

When my friend Jane Watson, the daughter of Thomas J. Watson of IBM, became engaged and asked me to be a bridesmaid, I gave a small dinner at Blair House for her. We got talking about the problem of people stealing spoons and knives from the White House. Tom Watson, Jr., thought this was absolutely terrible, and he held forth for several minutes on the subject with surprising vehemence. Later that night while Tom and I were dancing, I slipped a spoon into his pocket. It was fiendish of me but great fun for the rest of us. Poor Tom was mortified when he discovered the stolen goods the next day. Only when I confessed that I was the practical joker did he calm down.

Throughout 1949 I had to cope with a rash of engagement rumors. They amused Dad, but most of the time they annoyed me. I felt sorry for the various male friends with whom I was being linked—always without a shred of truth. Moreover, it cut down on my available escort supply. Once someone was touted as my intended, he got very leery about taking me out thereafter.

My double life and my ferocious practice schedule wore me down, and a heavy cold, which I tried to ignore, developed into bronchitis. Dad put me to bed at Blair House and kept me there until I got in a very rebellious mood and decided to change my hair style. I cut my hair off until it was almost a shingle. Dad was horrified by the result, but I liked it. The poor man didn't know what to do. It wasn't like his awful bow ties, which we could torment him into changing. Every time he looked at me for days, he had a funereal expression on his face, as if I had contracted a fatal illness, or something.

He got a little revenge by suggesting that I arise at dawn and take a morning walk with him. I was away so much, he protested, he hadn't really talked with me for months. What better place for a father-daughter chat than a brisk dawn stroll? I had my doubts, but I was feeling a little guilty about being away, and I acquiesced. The scenario on the following morning went something like this.

The President sets out from White House at his usual 120 strides a minute. He pauses at the corner to find out why daughter is thirty feet behind him. "Come on, Margie," he says, "what's holding you up?"

"Where's the fire?" asks his gasping daughter.

Two more blocks at 120 paces per minute and the President pauses again. His daughter is now sixty feet behind him. "What's the matter with you, anyway?" he asks impatiently.

"I'm wearing high heels," explains daughter weakly.

"Why don't you buy some sensible shoes?"

End of father-daughter chats on morning walks.

I escaped from Dad's frowns by returning to the musical salt mines in New York. By the end of the summer my voice coach pronounced me ready to tackle the concert circuit again. Reathel and I took off on October 2, and I sang my way across a lot of the United States. Atlanta, Georgia; Raleigh, North Carolina; St. Louis, Missouri, with Vice President Barkley in the audience; Columbus, Ohio; and Battle Creek, Michigan. I ended my tour on November 26 at Constitution Hall. Dad and my voice coach sat side by side in the presidential box. He turned to her and said, "Don't be upset if I start tearing up programs during the concert. I always do that when I'm nervous."

"I do the same thing," my coach said.

Between them they tore up at least four programs, but the concert was a great success. I sang three encores, and Dad looked so pleased you'd almost think he had been reelected all over again.

Along the concert trail, and in nationally syndicated columns, there had been an inevitable number of nasty comments about me exploiting my role as the President's daughter to make money on my supposedly mediocre voice. I never claimed that I was one of the great singers of all time. But I did feel that I had achieved professional competence. I was pleased when the *Saturday Evening Post* asked me to write an article telling my side of the story. I pointed out, among other things, that I had gone to New York early in 1944, before there was even a hint of Dad becoming vice president, and submitted my voice to the judgment of professional coaches to see if I had the necessary potential. They assured me that I had the vocal equipment, if I was willing to put in the hours of practice it would take to reach professional competence.

The *Post* article was called "Why Shouldn't I Sing?" and when Dad read it, he was impressed by the amount of down-to-earth Truman-style facts I had managed to get into a magazine that he regarded (with good reason) as hostile to him. He was so pleased he read the article twice and wrote me the following letter:

April 22, 1950

Dear Margie:— I have just finished another reading of the article in today's Saturday Evening Post. It is a very good statement of the facts—made in such a way as to offend no one—not even your very touchy family on both sides! I really don't see how you ever succeeded in getting the terrible anti-Truman Post to publish the facts as they are. . . .

While I was out singing for my supper—and dreadful suppers they usually were on the great American road—my best friend Drucie Snyder, daughter of Dad's Secretary of the Treasury, was doing something a lot more important: falling in love. She became engaged to Major John Ernest Horton, one of the White House aides, late in 1949, with the wedding scheduled for January 26 in the National Cathedral. This was one of the major events of the Washington season and there was a whirl of parties connected with it. I think that Dru's marriage gave Dad something of a shock. We had always been so close that we were practically sisters in his eyes, and it made him realize that we had *really* grown up. On January 15, 1950, Dad and Mother went to a party for Drucie and in a philosophic mood, he penned the following note on his calendar:

Bess and I go to a "brunch"—whatever that is—at the Smith's place out in Va. They have a lovely place out on the road to Leesburg—about a mile south of the road and seven or eight miles west of Falls Church.

The party was for the daughter of the Sec. of the Treasury—one of my oldest and very best friends. I remember—as all men over sixty do—when Drucie was born. She has grown up along with Margie and Jane Lingo and now she is getting married to a nice boy John Horton of Kansas City.

When I came into the Blair House from the party above mentioned a call from my Air Aide, Gen. Landry, was awaiting me. He told me that Gen. H. H. (Happy) Arnold had died. The first of the Big Five to go. A grand man, a great commander and one of the original U.S. Air Force. He was a good friend of mine—a great loss.

They come, they get married, they pass. It is life—but sometimes hard to bear.

[442]

Four days later Dad wrote an interesting combination of an obituary and reminiscence for General Arnold. In the light of coming events, notice the last sentence.

> General of the Air Force Henry H. Arnold was buried in Arlington today. He was a great man. I knew him when he was a Major in the Signal Corps. He was at Ft. Riley, Kansas, in 1921 or 1922 when I was there.
>
> On another occasion at Ft. Riley I attended a party given by the Commandant for Lt. Col. Patton, afterwards "Blood & Guts" on the occasion of his promotion from Major. The Commandant was Lt. Col. Wainwright, known as "Skinny," who long afterwards held the bag for General of the Army MacArthur in the Philippines. Patton and Wainwright were tops in my book. I am not acquainted with MacArthur.

Dad's knowledge of military history frequently amazed many people. Joe Feeney, the genial ex-navy captain who became the White House congressional liaison man in 1949, had majored in history in college, and he loved to draw Dad into conversations on their mutually favorite subject. Two others who invariably joined the conversation—I should add that most of this talking was done at Key West, there simply wasn't time in the White House—were Charlie Ross and Bill Hassett, both very well-read gentlemen.

One night at Key West the four of them began discussing the great military battles of history. Charlie and Bill began disagreeing quite vehemently on who did what and why. "There's only one way to settle this," Dad said, and called for four settings of silverware. He placed them on the table and proceeded to give a step-by-step narration of the fourteen major battles of world history, starting with Hannibal's victory at Cannae. As they were going to bed that night, Joe Feeney said, "Mr. President, I never enjoyed anything so much. My father-in-law was a newspaper editor, but he was a great disciple of religious history. One night I listened to him for a couple of hours while he went over the thirty-six forms of religion, who the founders were, that sort of thing."

Dad's eyes brightened. "You know I've been doing some studying on religious history," he said. "Tomorrow morning down at the beach we'll talk about it."

As he promised, the next morning Dad took Joe with him for the five or six block walk to the private beach where he swam at Key West. They sat on the sea wall, and for two hours he discussed religious history with the same kind of detail that he had lavished on the fourteen great battles.

"Mr. Truman was so far ahead of the professors I had in history," Joe says, "that there was simply no comparison."

George Elsey made a similar comment to me. "When I first became an aide, I must confess I was a little condescending about the President's supposed expertise in history. After all, I had majored in history at Princeton and Harvard." George smiled ruefully and shook his head. "I soon found out that he was one of the most thoroughly informed men, historically, that I have ever met. When I made a historical reference or comparison, he not only agreed with me, but his comments very quickly made it clear that he was familiar with all the details."

Although I have been repeatedly exposed to Dad's prowess in history, there are still times when even I am a little staggered by the depth of his knowledge. For instance, I was going through his letter file for the year 1948 and came across a note he dashed off to a New Yorker, commenting on a newspaper editorial which had compared Henry Wallace to the Greek demagogue, Alcibiades. Dad disagreed. "Aeschines is the person Henry most resembles. Of course, when Alcibiades went over to the enemy, that is Sparta, he followed a line that Henry is now following. It is a most difficult thing these days to find reporters and editors who know anything about Ancient History."

Aeschines was a Greek politician who argued that it was hopeless for democratic Athens to oppose the power of militaristic Macedonia, and recommended surrender to them.

Dad's expertise in history was something that he brought to the presidency. In his seven and three-quarters years in the White House, he became an expert on many other matters as well. A good example of this aspect of his presidency was the debate over interest rates between the Federal Reserve Board and the Treasury Department. John Snyder favored one approach, and he made a forthright presentation of his case. But as usual Dad insisted on hearing every conceivable point of view on the subject. He sent for every top monetary man in the country to come to Washington to talk with him. Among them was that quintessential Republican, Winthrop Aldrich, chairman of the Chase National Bank. Joe Feeney made a special trip to New York to persuade Mr. Aldrich to come to Washington. He very grumpily agreed, after warning Joe in advance that he was on the side of the Federal Reserve Board.

Mr. Aldrich came in about ten o'clock one night for a fifteen-minute talk. Joe Feeney and four or five other aides were so intrigued by the potential clash of personalities between him and Dad that they lingered in the outer office, waiting to see what would happen. Fifteen minutes passed and no Mr. Aldrich. Thirty minutes, and still no Mr. Aldrich. An hour and a half elapsed before he finally emerged, looking a little dazed. "You know, gentlemen," he said to Joe Feeney and the other aides, "it's no wonder that he's the President. He's a better banker than I am."

For six weeks Dad talked this way to bankers and tax experts and economic advisers from as far away as California. Finally, he ruled in favor of the Federal Reserve Board. Joe Feeney cannot help sounding a little bitter when he looks back on the press reaction to the decision. "Every newspaper in the country said it was made in a twenty-minute discussion, and that John Snyder would probably resign that day, which was ridiculous."

Dad was always willing to experiment with new approaches to old problems. But unlike Presidents who have succeeded him, he found little use for the so-called political intellectuals from our universities, who have since become such a force—not a very positive one, in my opinion—on the Washington scene. George Elsey tells an amusing story about one attempt to use these theoretical gentlemen early in 1950. A social psychologist with a great professional reputation had known George in his student days at Princeton, and he took advantage of this acquaintance to make numerous suggestions about Dad's speeches, aimed at increasing their persuasive powers. George finally got tired of corresponding with him and invited him to come down to Washington and participate in the actual writing of a presidential speech.

The invitation was eagerly accepted, and the theorist was soon in the White House, talking about inductive reasoning and similar jargon of his trade. "I introduced him to my fellow speech writers Dave Bell and Dave Lloyd, both of whom knew of him by reputation," George says. "The speech was not a particularly sensitive one and there were no questions of security or other matters to bother us. So we invited the professor to have dinner with us that evening and work with us on the speech."

At 4:30 A.M. the professor walked out of the White House and returned to Princeton. He was never heard from again.

Even though his senatorial years were growing distant by 1949, my father still remained in close touch with the personalities and prejudices of most leading senators and congressmen. He continued to put up with their prima donna complexes, their idiosyncrasies, and their prejudices. (If you think I am exaggerating, let me reveal to you that when the Big Four—the Speaker of the House, the majority leader of the House, the president pro tem of the Senate, the majority leader of the Senate—came to Dad's office for their weekly meeting, they frequently got into an argument over who should go in first.) Most important, Dad maintained his friendship with senators on both sides of the aisle. Along with Senator Vandenberg of Michigan, he was friendly with Senator Styles Bridges of New Hampshire and Senator William Langer of North Dakota, both outspoken Republicans. While he used Joe Feeney for day-to-day liaison, Dad did a great deal of cajoling and arm twisting himself. "He could pick up a phone and talk to ninety percent of the people in the Senate any time of the day or night," Joe Feeney says. "Even some of his worst enemies—as far as the newspapers were concerned. When we were trying to push a bill through, we got suggestions from everyone, but it was hard to beat the President. He was really a fine professor in human chemistry. He generally knew where to go; if he couldn't go direct, he generally knew how to get there."

Even Joe Feeney, with his daily contacts on the Hill, was seldom ahead of Dad in judging how a senator would vote. One of the big battles of the second term was over the displaced persons bill. It aroused the forces of bigotry and reaction almost as viciously as the Communists-in-government agitation. Dad was fighting to get into the United States people who were languishing in refugee camps, five years after the war was over. Their own countries refused to take them back, or they could not return to their homelands because the Communists would kill them. In the course of this battle Joe Feeney came to Dad and told him excitedly that he had just persuaded a particular Eastern Democratic senator to switch his vote to the administration's side. Dad shook his head and said, "You'd better go back and talk with him again."

Joe did so, and returned to tell Dad flatly that he was wrong. The senator had promised once more to vote in favor of the bill.

"Joe," Dad said, "you and I had better go over and have a dip in the pool."

They went for a swim, and Dad gave him a very quiet lecture which began: "Now I want to tell you something. Politics is a very unusual game. You have to know the background of each senator and you have to know the reason why he's in the Senate."

The following day the vote was taken, and I regret to say we lost. Joe glumly called in the results and Dad said, "I'll make a bet with you, your friend wasn't with us."

"You're sure right," Joe said mournfully.

Dad also kept in close touch with public spokesmen outside of Congress. One of these was Walter White, the head of the NAACP. Another was Samuel Cardinal Stritch of Chicago. He rarely went to Chicago without having a private meeting with him. Another churchman with whom he was close was Richard Cardinal Cushing of Boston. Dad not only liked him but enjoyed him as a character of the first order. One time, when Dad was in Boston, he called Cardinal Cushing and told him he would like to come for a visit. He assumed it would be private and off the record as usual. When he arrived at the Cardinal's residence, escorted by Matt Connelly and Joe Feeney, there was a brass band out front and a brigade of Knights of Columbus with plumed hats. Dad got out of the car and said, "You know, this is the quietest reception I have ever had."

During these early months of the second term, Myron C. Taylor, the President's personal representative to the Vatican, resigned and Dad was faced with the problem of finding a replacement for this politically sensitive post. Monsignor Tiernan, Dad's old regimental chaplain, was retiring from the army after long service and was having a checkup at Walter Reed Hospital. Dad went over to see him and propositioned him, Baptist style. "Padre," he said, "I need someone to get at the Pope through the back door and I think you are the one to do it."

"I don't want that job," said Monsignor Tiernan. "I'm through working."

Another man with whom Dad conferred at the opening of the second term was Herbert Hoover. He had drawn him out of retirement to do an exhaustive study of the government, and recommend a sweeping reorganization to improve the efficiency of the executive branch. Mr. Hoover was deeply touched by this recognition, and he and Dad soon became close friends. One day, in a rush of emotion, he said, "Mr. President, I think you have added ten years to my life by giving me this job."

On August 10, 1949, Dad sent the former President the following telegram:

> THIS SHOULD BE AMONG YOUR HAPPIEST BIRTHDAYS.
> THE YEAR IMMEDIATELY BEHIND YOU HAS BEEN MARKED
> BY THE COMPLETION OF A NOTABLE REPORT
> WHICH WILL ALWAYS BEAR YOUR NAME. THAT REPORT
> REFLECTS THE RIPE JUDGMENT AND WISDOM WHICH YOU
> BROUGHT TO THE WORK OF THE HOOVER COMMISSION
> OUT OF YEARS OF STUDY AND EXPERIENCE IN
> GOVERNMENT SERVICE. I TRUST THAT MANY BIRTHDAYS
> AND MANY FRUITFUL YEARS LIE AHEAD ALL MADE
> HAPPY BY CONTINUED SERVICE IN THE CAUSE OF
> EFFICIENCY IN GOVERNMENT AND THE RESPECT AND
> AFFECTION OF YOUR FELLOW COUNTRYMEN.

During the summer of 1949 I had a delightful opportunity to even a score with Dad—a little bit, anyway. After all those years of being lectured and accused about my non-letterwriting, I was relaxing in Independence when I got a non-letter from him—a mere postcard. I promptly went out and bought a local postcard, a glossy full-color photograph of our house. The caption read: "Independence, Missouri—Summer White House." It went on to tell how this spacious mid-Victorian home was built about eighty years ago by Mrs. Truman's grandfather, George Porterfield Gates. "The house has fourteen rooms and has been completely remodeled and redecorated to meet the requirements of the President and his family." Beside that bit of baloney I wrote: "And I know who did it! Me!" (This was a tribute to a recent outburst of energy on my part which involved painting the kitchen.) Beneath this bravado I wrote: "Passed through here on my way from Kansas City to Grandview and stopped by this historic spot. . . . The X marks the room of its most famous resident. You send me cards, all you get is a card."

Guess whose room I marked with an X?

The chief reason why Dad's optimism soared in these first eighteen months of his second term was the smooth operation of the White House and the various agencies he had created to assist the President in policy forming and decision making. The Joint Chiefs of Staff, the National Security Council, the Central Intelligence Agency, the Council of Economic Advisers—all of these things did not exist when my father became President. Along with all his other problems, he had to tackle the job of organizing the White House to enable the United States to assume the leadership of the free world.

Best of all, the White House staff was operating with efficiency and loyalty and a minimum of palace guard tactics. There was one man who was most responsible for this phenomenon, in the opinion of almost every ex-aide with whom I have talked while preparing this book. He was Charles S. Murphy, the steady, genial lawyer from North Carolina. Everything began to mesh beautifully from the day that Charlie arrived on the scene, early in 1947. He shared Dad's calm, persistent approach to problems, and his awareness that they could not be solved by a slogan. Not only was his advice invaluable, thanks to his years as counsel to the Senate, but he was also a speech writer of extraordinary talent.

Charlie, who is a very modest man, insists that the President deserves most of the credit for the way the White House was run. The key to making the gears mesh was the morning staff meeting which usually took place at 9:30 A.M. It lasted thirty minutes and was attended by some ten or twelve staff members. On his desk Dad had a file with slots marked with the name of each man. He would look through this and hand the various men papers from their respective slots. Then each man was given a chance to speak. Current problems were discussed, appointments were arranged, and by the time the meeting was over, thirty minutes later, everyone knew what was going on in everybody else's bailiwick. "There was always time for some humor in these meetings," Charlie says. "And notwithstanding the fact that we all felt somewhat as if we were living in the eye of a hurricane, these staff meetings were usually relaxed. In fact, as I look back, I think they may have been the most relaxed periods that most of us enjoyed during the day."

The liveliest staff meetings took place before a press conference. At that time the aides would discuss the most likely questions to be asked, and Dad would discuss possible answers with them. Charlie Ross, as the working newspaperman of the group, developed a technique which was really startling. He would set aside three or four nasty questions in his mind, and in the midst of discussing another issue he would suddenly lash out with one of these toughies, in a harsh, almost insulting way. More than once, Dad almost lost his temper—which was exactly what Charlie was trying to prevent in the press conference. It was a rugged approach to preparation, but Dad and Charlie Ross both felt it was worth it. I doubt very much if any other President ever had a press secretary toughen him up this way. It was only possible because Dad and Charlie were such old and close friends.

There was a tremendous frankness between Dad and his staff. On neither side was anyone ever afraid to say exactly what they thought. There were times when Dad became discouraged about the way things were going. That was when his humility almost got out of control, and he would begin talking about the possibility that there were other people in the country who could do the job of President a lot better than he was doing it.

One of the staff would clear his throat, in the midst of one of these monologues, and say, "What did the cook say to the admiral, Mr. President?"

Dad would grin, shake his head, and remember a story that Admiral Nimitz had told him. It seems that there was once an admiral who had a birthday party aboard his flagship. The cook baked him a cake, and the admiral, very pleased by all the attention he was getting, laid on the praise with a trowel. "Cook," he said, "this is a fine cake. It's one of the best cakes I ever ate. I never ate a cake as light as this." On and on he babbled, praising the cake's color, its icing, its filling, its color, its size, its taste on the tongue and in the stomach.

[450]

Finally, the cook, a big black man, couldn't stand it any longer. "Admiral," he said, "you sure do talk silly."

Dad took great pains to have his staff organized with just the right balance between definite continuing responsibilities and flexibility to meet special problems. He knew there was an inevitable human temptation to build empires, especially for men so close to the seat of power. The staff reported directly to him at all times. But he also insisted that the Director of the Budget, Cabinet members, the Council of Economic Advisers, and other executive office units also have access to him directly. "Incidentally," Charlie says, "the President was quite an ego deflater in a gentle way."

Dad used to call the staff his "crew." Looking back, he is proudest of the fact that "not one of them went out and wrote a book on me." This perhaps is the best evidence of the loyalty and deep affection that Dad generated. There was a definite family feeling between him and all the men around him. When one of them was ill, or one of their relatives was ill, Dad was like a worried father, visiting them in the hospital, sending presents and get-well notes. An example of this feeling is a letter which his correspondence secretary, Bill Hassett, wrote to Dad in the summer of 1950.

Dad had written "the Bishop" a warm note the previous day telling him how much he appreciated him staying on the job, in spite of his obvious desire to retire. He had been working those outrageous White House hours for so many years. (He had also been Mr. Roosevelt's correspondence secretary.) Bill was a great asset to Dad. Not only did he have a delightful sense of humor and an unlimited vocabulary, as well as a fund of good stories and jokes, but he could write the friendliest letter with the most words saying absolutely nothing, turning down a request or soothing an irate voter. We used to call them "Hassett Valentines."

Bill responded to Dad's praise with words that sum up the feelings that Dad inspired in his "crew."

> Dear Mr. President:
> What can I say in acknowledgment of your letter of August 4th which you just handed to me—a letter so generous in its terms that it arouses sentiments not only of heartfelt appreciation but of deep humility as well? Few men could merit such

[451]

trust and confidence. To you I owe a debt of gratitude difficult to estimate and beyond all power of mine to repay.

As men we repress sentiment. We do our best to conceal our affection for one another; and yet I am sure you know the happiness that has been mine in your service and the inmost promptings of my heart. So worthy or unworthy, on to the un-discovered end, I am yours to command, Mr. President.

Affectionately,
Bill

[CHAPTER]

Twenty-Four

EARLY IN THE MORNING on June 24, 1950, Dad dashed off the following carefree letter to Stanley Woodward, the former head of protocol for the State Department, whom he had recently appointed ambassador to Canada.

> Dear Stanley:
>   . . . I am leaving for Baltimore shortly to dedicate an airport —why I don't know. I guess because the Governor of Maryland, the two Senators from that great state, all the Congressmen and the Mayor of Baltimore highpressured me into doing it.
>   What I started out to do was to tell, ask, invite or order you to Key West this coming winter. I've been looking over the report of our last visit. Don't get the idea that just because you are now Mr. Ambassador that the guy in the White House can't still harass you.
>   Seriously, Stanley, if we go south again I hope you will be able to come for a visit.
>   My best to Mrs. Ambassador.
>   Sincerely,
>   Harry S. Truman

I'm going home from Baltimore to see Bess, Margie and my brother and sister—oversee some fence building—not political, order a new roof on the farmhouse and tell some politicians to go to hell. A grand visit—I hope?

Obviously my father had no sense of impending trouble. Later in the morning he dedicated Friendship International Airport in Baltimore. He talked about the need for federal, state, and local co-operation in the development of airports and similar transportation projects, sounding one of his favorite themes—the importance of planning for the future, in spite of the croakers of doom who saw every change as a potential disaster.

> If we had listened to the old mossbacks . . . we would never have given up the stagecoach. Some of these old stagecoach mossbacks are still with us—still in Congress, if you please. But thank God they are not in the majority. . . .
>
> This airport exemplifies the spirit of growth and confidence with which our country faces the future. We would not build so elaborate a facility for our air commerce if we did not have faith in a peaceful future. This airport embodies our determination to develop the marvels of science and invention for peaceful purposes. It strengthens our economy to do its part in maintaining a peaceful world.

There were strong echoes of Dad's five-year plan for peace in these words, of his determination to achieve a position in the world where we could negotiate from strength with communism.

As soon as my father finished this speech, he boarded the *Independence* and headed for Kansas City. Mother and I were already there, and he was looking forward to spending a pleasant weekend with us, and as he told Stanley Woodward, paying a visit to his brother Vivian in Grandview, where they planned to discuss family and farm matters. Personally I was feeling rather pleased with life. I had just made my first national TV appearance on Ed Sullivan's "Toast of the Town." There were no clouds on my personal horizon, and no serious storm warnings on the Truman political horizon. Joe McCarthy was locked in combat with the Senate Foreign Relations Subcommittee headed by Senator Tydings of Maryland, and he seemed to be losing.

Mother and I were feeling so relaxed and lazy, we did not drive to Kansas City to meet Dad's plane. He landed at two o'clock and was greeted by his sister Mary and several old Kansas City friends. We had a very pleasant family dinner around six o'clock and then migrated to our small book-crammed library for Truman-style small talk. About nine o'clock the telephone rang. It was Secretary of State Acheson.

"Mr. President," he said, "I have very serious news. The North Koreans have invaded South Korea."

My father asked Mr. Acheson whether he should return to Washington immediately. After considerable discussion, they decided against it, for two reasons. First, they did not know the real extent of the North Korean invasion. During the previous year the North Koreans had made numerous raids across the frontier, sometimes involving as many as 1,500 men. Second, a night flight to Washington by the President of the United States was not only physically dangerous—it might panic the nation and the world.

None of us got much sleep that night. My father made it clear, from the moment he heard the news, that he feared this was the opening round in World War III. Large Bulgarian and Rumanian armies were massed on the border of Yugoslavia, which had broken with Stalin the previous year and asked for our support. There was a huge Russian garrison in East Germany. Iran and Turkey were, we knew, equally threatened by powerful Russian forces just across the border.

The next morning, my father issued orders, Commander-in-Chief style. We were to act as normal and as unconcerned as possible and do all the things we usually did on a Sunday morning. Mother and I went to church, and Dad drove out to the family farm to see his brother Vivian. He looked over new equipment Uncle Vivian had installed, such as an electric milking machine, and then drove back to Grandview. He told no one about his conversations with Secretary Acheson, not even his brother Vivian, who was quite disappointed when Dad explained that he could not stay for the family dinner that they had planned to have around noon.

Back home in Independence, my father was handed the cable which our ambassador to South Korea, John Muccio, had sent to the State Department the previous evening. It read:

ACCORDING KOREAN ARMY REPORTS WHICH PARTLY
CONFIRMED BY KMAG [Korean Military Advisory Group]
FIELD ADVISER REPORTS NORTH KOREAN FORCES INVADED ROK
[Republic of Korea] TERRITORY AT SEVERAL POINTS THIS
MORNING. ACTION WAS INITIATED ABOUT FOUR A.M. ONGJIN

BLASTED BY NORTH KOREAN ARTILLERY FIRE. ABOUT
SIX A.M. NORTH KOREAN INFANTRY COMMENCED CROSSING
PARALLEL IN ONGJIN AREA, KAESONG AREA, CHUN CHON AREA
AND AMPHIBIOUS LANDING WAS REPORTEDLY MADE SOUTH
OF KANGNUNG ON EAST COAST. . . . IT WOULD APPEAR
FROM NATURE OF ATTACK AND MANNER IN WHICH IT WAS
LAUNCHED THAT IT CONSTITUTES AN ALL-OUT OFFENSIVE
AGAINST ROK.

MUCCIO

In spite of this grim news, my father still hoped to remain in
Independence until the next day and return to Washington according to his already announced schedule. Foremost in his mind
was the need to prevent panic and thus confine the conflagration.
From the moment he heard the news he was thinking of ways to
prevent this act of aggression from becoming World War III.

For Mother and me, these were the most anxious hours we
had spent with Dad since the night of April 12, 1945. I went
about the motions of living, going to church, kneeling, standing, singing hymns, coming home, having Sunday dinner, feeling
but not feeling, trying to realize what was happening—and failing.

In Washington, the teletype machines were chattering. At 8 A.M.
General Douglas MacArthur sent a personal message to the Defense Department giving details of the North Korean invasion
and commenting: "Enemy effort serious in strength and strategic
intent and is undisguised act of war subject to United Nations
censure." The General added that he was placing all ammunition
available in his command at the disposal of the South Korean
armed forces.

At 12:35 P.M., Independence time, Secretary of State Acheson
called Dad. Mother and I had gotten back from church only minutes before the call came. The news was growing rather grim. The
North Korean attack was spearheaded by over a hundred modern
tanks, and amphibious landings had been made at seven points
along the east coast of South Korea. Tank-led columns were already threatening the South Korean capital of Seoul and vital
Kimpo Airport. The Secretary of State recommended an immediate call for a UN Security Council meeting to adopt a resolution
asking all the members of the UN to take action under the "last

[456]

resort" clause of the UN Charter—"Threats to the peace, breaches of the peace, and acts of aggression." Dad agreed completely and authorized him to issue the call immediately.

At the same time my father decided on an immediate return to Washington. He told Mr. Acheson that he wanted all the available top people from the State and Defense Departments to join him for dinner and a conference at Blair House that evening. Calmly, he sat down at the dining room table and ate lunch, and told us the bad news. Meanwhile, assistant press secretary Eben Ayers and Secret Service man Jim Rowley were phoning aides and the crew of the *Independence*. At 1:20, only forty minutes after he made the decision, we left Independence for Kansas City Municipal Airport. There was no time to tell the reporters what was happening so they could get an airplane ready and follow him. At exactly 2:13 the *Independence* roared down the runway and was airborne. Although I have no recollection of actually praying, there is a picture of me with my hands clasped together under my chin. It was a gesture that accurately expressed what I was feeling at that moment.

My father landed in St. Louis to pick up John Snyder and then flew east. From the air he wired Charles Claunch, the White House usher, to warn him that a Very Important Dinner should be ready at Blair House by 8:30. Mr. Acheson would give him the guest list. Claunch called Alonzo Fields, the head butler at the White House, who recruited two cooks and made up a menu en route to Blair House in a taxi.

Aboard the *Independence* Dad was thinking about the past. He remembered how the democracies had allowed dictatorships to swallow Manchuria, Ethiopia, Austria without acting—and in the end were forced to fight for their very survival in World War II. At least as important was the status of the United Nations. In two days the world organization was to celebrate its fifth birthday. Dad had no doubt that Secretary of State Acheson's prompt action in calling a Security Council meeting would result in a condemnation of North Korea's aggression. This swift move had caught the Russians flatfooted. They had been boycotting the UN over the Security Council's refusal to seat Communist China and expel Nationalist China. Thus they were unable to exercise their veto, which would have left the UN helpless to speak until the Assembly was convened—a process that would have taken weeks and perhaps months.

By 6 P.M., almost two hours before he landed, my father knew that our UN resolution denouncing North Korea's "unprovoked act of aggression" had been adopted by the Security Council, nine to nothing. But this now meant that the prestige of the United Nations was on the line. If North Korea succeeded in its conquest of South Korea, the UN would become ridiculous in the eyes of the world. The fate of the League of Nations, after its impotent denunciations of Fascist aggression in the 1930s, was something that Dad remembered all too well.

Finally, there was our own commitment as a nation to the countries of Western Europe, whom we had joined in the North Atlantic Treaty. More than a few of the politicians in these NATO nations were not entirely convinced that we would stand beside them in a crunch with the Russians. The test of our will to resist, the integrity of our declarations in the Truman Doctrine that we were prepared to meet Communist aggression against free nations, was at stake.

My father landed in Washington at 7:15 P.M. Sunday. Secretary of State Acheson, Secretary of Defense Johnson, and Correspondence Secretary Bill Hassett met the plane. They drove to Blair House, and Dad called us at 7:45 Washington time, 5:45 our time, to tell us that he had landed safely. No matter what was on his mind, he never failed to perform this ritual, for Mother's sake. She hated to fly, and worried every moment that he was in the air.

At 8:00 my father went downstairs to meet his assembled advisers. They included the Secretaries of State, Treasury, and Defense, Under Secretary of State James Webb, Secretary of the Army Frank Pace, Secretary of the Navy Francis Matthews, Secretary of the Air Force Thomas Finletter, and Generals Bradley, Collins, and Vandenberg, Admiral Sherman, Ambassador at Large Philip Jessup, and Assistant Secretaries of State Dean Rusk and John D. Hickerson. While they were waiting on the patio for dinner to be announced, Secretary of Defense Louis Johnson suddenly asked General Bradley to read a memorandum from General MacArthur on the importance of Formosa. My father cut him short by announcing that he wanted nothing discussed until dinner was over and the servants had withdrawn. Mr. Johnson's

[458]

attempt to seize the floor annoyed him, not only because it was indiscreet. It was another sign of the feud that Mr. Johnson had been conducting with Secretary of State Acheson because he was jealous of what he considered to be Mr. Acheson's and the State Department's greater influence with the President.

After dinner the conference got down to business. Secretary of State Acheson read "White III," the copy of Ambassador Muccio's telegram, and added what few details had filtered into Washington from Korea since that had been received. The situation was in a state of total confusion. But there were some hopeful reports. One enemy column had been stopped in the mountains northeast of Seoul. Mr. Acheson then read a six-page memorandum entitled, "Points Requiring Presidential Decision," which ranged over a wide variety of alternatives.

After considerable discussion around the table, my father decided to do three things.

1. Order General MacArthur to supply the South Korean army with all available weapons and ammunition.

2. Evacuate the dependents of the 500-man American military mission—the only soldiers we had in Korea. Ships and planes should be used to do this, and the air force was ordered to use all the planes it had at its disposal in the Far East to keep open Kimpo and other airports. However, the planes were strictly ordered to stay south of the 38th parallel.

3. The Seventh Fleet was ordered into the Formosa Straits and a statement was prepared declaring that the fleet would not permit the Chinese Communists to attack Formosa—nor permit Chiang Kai-shek's army to attack the mainland. At the same time Dad ordered a maximum effort to gather intelligence on possible Communist attacks elsewhere in the world. He also asked the Joint Chiefs of Staff to make an immediate study of our ability to attack Russian bases in the Far East, if they joined the fighting on the North Korean side.

My father insisted that every man in the meeting state his opinion of what should be done. Looking back on it, after he left office, Dad said that there was "complete, almost unspoken acceptance on the part of everyone that whatever had to be done to meet this aggression had to be done. There was no suggestion from anyone that either the United Nations or the United States should back

[459]

away from it. This was the test of all the talk of the last five years of collective security."

One crucial question that was debated, but not decided, that fateful night was whether we would have to commit American ground troops to save South Korea. General Hoyt Vandenberg, speaking for the air force, and Admiral Forrest Sherman, speaking for the navy, thought that air and naval aid would be enough. But General Omar Bradley and General Lawton Collins were much more pessimistic. They felt that the news received this far pointed towards a complete collapse of the South Korean army. They were all too aware of the balance of power in favor of the Communists. We had equipped the South Koreans only with enough light weapons to maintain order within their own country. They had no heavy artillery, no tanks, and no air force.

My father decided the only way to settle that momentous question was the usual Truman approach—get the facts. He told General Collins to order General MacArthur to send a survey party to South Korea immediately. He also ordered them to prepare orders for the 80,000 men we had on duty in Japan, so that they could move to Korea swiftly, if the grim decision had to be made.

As the meeting broke up, Secretary of State Acheson showed Dad a telegram they had received in the State Department from John Foster Dulles, who had just returned to Tokyo after addressing the South Korean Assembly.

IT IS POSSIBLE THAT SOUTH KOREANS MAY THEMSELVES
CONTAIN AND REPULSE ATTACK AND, IF SO, THIS IS
BEST WAY. IF HOWEVER IT APPEARS THEY CANNOT
DO SO THEN WE BELIEVE THAT U.S. FORCE SHOULD BE
USED EVEN THOUGH THIS RISKS RUSSIAN COUNTER MOVES.
TO SIT BY WHILE KOREA IS OVERRUN BY UNPROVOKED
ARMED ATTACK WOULD START DISASTROUS CHAIN
OF EVENTS LEADING MOST PROBABLY TO WORLD WAR.

At 11:55 P.M. my father's orders went chattering out over the Defense Department wire. General MacArthur received them personally in Tokyo. "Do you need any further instructions at this time?" the message concluded.

"No," was the reply.

Less than thirty hours had passed since we had first heard that

[460]

Korea was under attack, little more than twelve hours since we had heard that the attack was serious aggression. Seldom has any government reacted so swiftly to a crisis six thousand miles away.

The following morning, Monday, my father was in his White House office by 8 A.M. Because he had not been expected to arrive in Washington until that afternoon, he had no set appointments. The impromptu schedule set up by Matt Connelly listed, at 8 A.M., the following entry: "War in Korea." Beside it Dad wrote a series of question marks. At 10 A.M. he met with Charlie Ross, Charlie Murphy, and George Elsey to discuss a statement to the nation. They worked over a draft sent up from the State Department, until it satisfied all of them. It was calm and carefully restrained. It stressed our support of the United Nations resolution. As Charlie Ross took the statement off for mimeographing and Charlie Murphy hurried away on another errand, George Elsey, the youngest of the three aides, stayed behind to discuss the significance of what was happening. Not knowing the decision to send the Seventh Fleet to the Formosa Straits, he asked about the possibility of the Chinese Communists seizing the Nationalist-held island.

My father walked over to the globe in front of the fireplace and gave it a spin. "I'm more worried about other parts of the world," he said. "The Middle East, for instance." He put his finger on Iran, and said, "Here is where they will start trouble if we aren't careful."

"Korea," he said, "is the Greece of the Far East. If we are tough enough now, if we stand up to them like we did in Greece three years ago, they won't take any next steps. But if we just stand by, they'll move into Iran and they'll take over the whole Middle East. There's no telling what they'll do, if we don't put up a fight now."

Throughout the day, the news from Korea continued to grow more and more discouraging. At 3:50 P.M. the South Korean ambassador, Dr. John Myun Chang, visited the White House, escorted by Mr. Acheson. Very depressed, the ambassador said that President Syngman Rhee had telephoned to say that the South Korean forces lacked artillery, tanks, and aircraft. My father did his best to cheer up Mr. Chang. He assured him that help was on the way and pointed out that the fight was only forty-eight hours old. Between them, the President and the Secretary of State managed to calm him down, but he was still gloomy when he met with reporters outside the White House. "The hour is late," he said.

That night at 7:20 Secretary of State Acheson called and suggested another conference of top advisers at Blair House. Dad immediately agreed and scheduled it for 9 P.M. At 7:55 he called Independence and talked with Mother and me. He was calm and quiet. Already he could see the steps that lay ahead, the decisions he must soon make that might send young Americans into combat.

At 9 P.M. almost the same group of advisers, with one or two exceptions, assembled again in Blair House. They pondered the latest communication from General MacArthur, which said in part: "South Korean units unable to resist determined Northern offensive. Contributory factor exclusive enemy possession of tanks and fighter planes. . . . Our estimate is that a complete collapse is imminent." Enemy tanks were in the suburbs of Seoul. What to do? Our air force was already fighting over Korea. In the past twenty-four hours they had shot down three Yak Russian-built fighter planes that had attempted to strafe a Danish ship evacuating American dependents from Inchon. We suspected that Russians were flying these planes. The following morning my father told George Elsey that he had directed the air force "to protect the Korean army from the Soviet air force." Both the air force and the navy were ordered to provide full tactical support to the South Korean army. Orders to the Seventh Fleet in regard to Formosa were reaffirmed. The conference was over in forty minutes, and the orders were flashed to General MacArthur at 10:17 P.M. Eastern Daylight Time.

My father was still hoping to avoid the use of American infantry in Korea. He hoped that air and naval support might boost the morale of the South Korean army and stall the North Korean advance long enough to give the South Koreans time to regroup. After his advisers left, Dad ordered George Elsey and Charlie Murphy to go to work on the telephone, to round up a meeting of congressional leaders for the following morning. For a President, conferring with advisers, weighing and making crucial decisions, was only the first step. He also had to persuade Congress to support him.

The following morning, Tuesday, Dad made another decision. At 7:13 A.M., he asked the White House operator to get Averell Harriman, who was in Paris working on the Marshall Plan, to return to Washington immediately. Actually, Dad had been thinking of bringing Averell home for some time. Meanwhile, in Washington and around the world, diplomats, politicians and average citizens were holding their breaths, waiting to see what the United States was going to do about Korea. Skepticism was the order of the day. One Washington ambassador cabled his government: "The time has come when Uncle Sam must put up or shut up and my guess is he will do neither."

At 11:30 A.M., Tuesday, fifteen congressional leaders assembled in the Cabinet Room. When my father came in, he went around the table and shook hands with each of them. Then he took his seat at the head of the table and Dean Acheson, sitting beside him, told the congressmen what was happening and what we had decided to do. Some of the points that Mr. Acheson made were historically significant. It was vital for the United States to adopt a firm stand because the Korean forces appeared to be weakening fast and their leadership was feeble and indecisive. Moreover, the governments of many Western European nations appeared to be in a state of near panic as they watched to see whether the United States would act or not.

Whether it was the tension of the situation, or the exhausting pace at which he had been working, for some reason Mr. Acheson forgot to mention our role in the United Nations. Dad did not. He immediately noted this as the most important element in the situation. He then read the statement which he was going to release to the press after the meeting, announcing our intention to support the South Korean government. Then he added some very significant remarks. The act of aggression was obviously inspired by the Soviet Union, he said. If we let Korea down, the Soviets would swallow one piece of Asia after another. We had to make a stand somewhere or let all of Asia go by the board. If Asia went, the Near East would collapse and Europe would inevitably follow. Therefore, he had ordered our forces to support Korea as long as we could—as long as the Koreans put up a fight and gave us something we *could* support.

The congressional leaders asked a number of worried questions.

Did MacArthur have enough military power to support the South Koreans effectively? Would the nations of Western Europe back us in the Security Council, where we were submitting another resolution, calling on them and other free nations to assist us in resisting the North Koreans? Over Secretary of Defense Johnson's objections, my father permitted General Hoyt Vandenberg to give the congressional leaders secret details about our air strength in the Far East. Secretary of State Acheson said he had cablegrams from most of the countries of Western Europe, assuring him of support in the UN. He also said he did not think the Russians would return to the UN Security Council and exercise their veto. Even if they did, they could not veto the resolution which had been passed on Sunday, thanks to the Secretary of State's swift action. Senator Tom Connally summed up congressional opinion when he said that it was quite apparent that this was "the clearest test case that the United Nations has ever faced. If the United Nations is ever going to do anything, this is the time, and if the United Nations cannot bring the crisis in Korea to an end, then we might just as well wash up the United Nations and forget it."

My father nodded. He vowed that he was going to make absolutely certain that everything we did in Korea would be in support of and in conformity with the decision by the Security Council of the United Nations.

Secretary of State Acheson then turned to a discussion of the Soviet Union in regard to Korea. He pointed out that the President's statement simply referred to communism. The government was doing its best to leave the door wide open for the Soviet Union to back down without losing too much prestige. In connection with this policy, the Secretary of State begged the members of Congress not to condemn the Russians specifically for the Korean crisis. He held out the hope that if we left the door open the Soviet government might take this opportunity to withdraw.

Dad's statement, released at 12:30 P.M. on Tuesday, June 27, went through Washington and the other capitals of the free world like an electric shock. Joseph C. Harsch of the *Christian Science Monitor,* looking back on twenty years in Washington, said, "Never before in that time have I felt such a sense of relief and unity pass through this city." Both the Senate and the House

rose and cheered when the statement was read to them. Newspapers around the nation echoed Mr. Harsch. James Reston of
The New York Times said it had produced "a transformation in
the spirit of the United States government." The New York
Herald Tribune ran an editorial on the front page calling it "a
basic contribution to a genuine peace in our disturbed and distracted world." At 10:45 that night, the UN Security Council,
with the Russians still absent, passed another resolution, calling
on member nations to "render such assistance to the Republic of
Korea as may be necessary to repel the armed attack and restore
international peace and security to the area."

Wednesday was a day for good news. Dad was reassured about
the rightness of his decision by Averell Harriman, just back from
Europe. Averell described to my father from firsthand knowledge
the feeling of relief which had swept through Europe's capitals
when they learned that America was standing fast. Encouraging
news even came from Ambassador Muccio in Seoul. At 10 A.M.
he sent the following telegram:

> SITUATION HAD DETERIORATED SO RAPIDLY HAD NOT
> PRESIDENT'S DECISION PLUS ARRIVAL GENERAL CHURCH
> PARTY [heading the survey team my father had ordered]
> BECOME KNOWN HERE IT IS DOUBTFUL ANY ORGANIZED
> KOREAN RESISTANCE WOULD HAVE CONTINUED THROUGH
> NIGHT. COMBAT AID DECISION PLUS CHURCH'S ORDER
> HAVE HAD GREAT MORALE EFFECT. FORTHCOMING AIR
> STRIKES HOPED DEMORALIZE ENEMY, MAKE POSSIBLE
> REFORM KOREAN ARMY SOUTH BANK HAN RIVER.

My father was heartened by other telegrams which flooded into
the White House from citizens all over the country. Among them
was one from Thomas E. Dewey which read: "I wholeheartedly
agree with and support the difficult decision you have made."
The only sour note—and even that was not completely sour—came
from Senator Taft, who rose in Congress to accuse the Truman
Administration of inviting the North Korean attack by permitting
Korea to remain divided. Everything that was wrong in the Far
East, according to Senator Taft, was explained by the administration's "sympathetic acceptance of communism." The senator singled out for special criticism a speech that Secretary of State

Acheson had made earlier in 1950, in which he said that Korea lay outside the U.S.'s "defensive perimeter" in the Pacific. He called for the resignation of Secretary of State Acheson forthwith, and wondered if Dad had violated the Constitution by committing America to a "de facto war." Then he finally got around to saying that he approved of the "general policies outlined in the President's statement." Charlie Ross, when he heard the news of Mr. Republican's speech, gasped: "By God! Bob Taft has joined the U.N. and the U.S." Dad felt pretty much the same way.

On Thursday the news from Korea was almost all bad. At 7 A.M., our time, another teleconference was held between MacArthur's headquarters and the Pentagon. South Korean forces had suffered 50 percent casualties and had very little hope of forming a line at the Han River south of Seoul, their capital. Then came a telegram from our ambassador in Moscow, Alan G. Kirk. On June 27 my father had ordered the ambassador to ask the government of the USSR to "use its influence with the North Korean authorities to withdraw their invading forces immediately."

Foreign Secretary Andrei Gromyko now read the Russian reply to this request. The atmosphere was "calm and without constraint," Ambassador Kirk said, but the words were chilling:

> 1. In accordance with facts verified by the Soviet Government, the events taking place in Korea were provoked by an attack of forces of the South Korean authorities on border regions of North Korea. Therefore the responsibility for these events rests upon the South Korean authorities and upon those who stand behind their back.
>
> 2. As is known, the Soviet Government withdrew its troops from Korea earlier than the Government of the United States and thereby confirmed its traditional principle of noninterference in the internal affairs of other states. And now as well the Soviet Government adheres to the principle of the impermissibility of interference by foreign powers in the internal affairs of Korea.

John Foster Dulles, back from Tokyo, gave my father a very alarming report on the conduct of General MacArthur. When the North Korean attack began, Dulles rushed to MacArthur's headquarters. MacArthur was not there, and no one was aware of what was happening or had the slightest conception of what to do. Incredulously, Mr. Dulles asked if they weren't going to notify their commander. But not one of the General's aides had the nerve to call him when he was in seclusion. Dulles finally telephoned him personally and got him into action.

Dulles urged Dad to recall MacArthur immediately, and send a younger, more vigorous man to Japan to replace him. But my father pointed out that this was almost certain to cause a tremendous blowup among MacArthur's supporters in Congress—something he did not want to risk at this delicate moment, when he had Congress so totally on his side that they had just passed a one-year extension of the draft unanimously. Mr. Dulles was forced to agree.

At 4 P.M. that day my father held a press conference. Naturally the reporters were full of questions about Korea.

"Mr. President, everybody is asking in this country, are we or are we not at war."

"We are not at war," my father said.

"Mr. President, another question that is being asked is, are we going to use ground troops in Korea?"

"No comment on that."

"Mr. President, in that connection it has been asked whether there might be any possibility of having to use the atomic bomb?"

"No comment."

Another reporter asked him to elaborate on his view of the war.

"The members of the United Nations are going to the relief of the Korean Republic to suppress a bandit raid on the Republic of Korea."

"Mr. President, would it be correct against your explanation, to call this a police action under the United Nations?"

"Yes, that is exactly what it amounts to."

Note that this term, police action, was not my father's creation. He accepted it, as a very rough estimate of what was being done in Korea, with no idea of how it would be misused by his critics in the months to come.

At 5:00 P.M. Dad summoned another meeting of his Blair House team. He decided, after more intense discussion, to authorize the bombing of airfields and other military targets in North Korea and to order American ground troops to seize and protect the port

[467]

of Pusan, at the southernmost end of Korea—at that moment far from the combat zone.

At the very end of the day came one bit of news that seemed to brighten the gloom a bit, as far as Dad was concerned. Generalissimo Chiang Kai-shek had offered to send 33,000 troops to Korea if we would arm them with modern weapons and supply them. It raised Dad's hope of avoiding a massive commitment of American ground troops. Secretary of State Acheson feared it might give the Chinese Communists a chance to intervene. Dad decided to discuss it more fully with all his advisers the following day.

This same day, Thursday, June 29, General MacArthur landed in Korea to make a personal inspection of the situation. What he saw was not encouraging. The South Korean army had blown up the bridges across the Han River in a moment of panic, trapping three of their best divisions in Seoul. The roads were clogged with fleeing refugees and shattered remnants of South Korean army units. The North Korean army was massing on the other side of the Han, and there seemed to be nothing between them and the tip of the Korean peninsula to stop them. General MacArthur climbed back into his plane and returned to Tokyo. At 3 A.M., Washington time, the General's recommendations were received in the Pentagon: "The only assurance for holding the present line and the ability to regain later the lost ground is through the introduction of United States combat forces into the Korean battle area."

General MacArthur told his fellow generals that it would be a waste of time, money, and equipment to try to stop the North Korean invasion with the American air force and navy. He asked for permission to commit a regimental combat team immediately and urged a rapid buildup of our troops in Japan "for an early counteroffensive." Even an all-out effort by the "army-navy-air team," the General warned, "might be doomed to failure."

General Collins discussed the situation in detail with General MacArthur. The North Korean army had burst across the Han River by now and was rolling south. General Collins told MacArthur that it was his impression that "the President would wish carefully to consider with his top advisers before authorizing introduction of American combat forces into battle area."

[468]

MacArthur replied: "Time is of the essence and a clear-cut decision without delay is imperative."

At 4:30 A.M. Friday, June 30, General Collins called Frank Pace, the Secretary of the Army, and reported his conversation with General MacArthur. At 4:57 A.M. Mr. Pace called my father. He listened to the grim news and made the most difficult decision of the week without a moment's hesitation. He had known it was coming and had been bracing himself for it.

Aware of its enormous importance, Dad sat down later that morning and made the following notes:

> Frank Pace called at 5 A.M. E.D.T. I was already up and shaved. Said MacArthur wanted two divisions of ground troops. Authorized a regiment to be used in addition to the authorizations of yesterday, to be used at Mac's discretion.
>
> Was briefed . . . at seven o'clock. Called Pace and Louis Johnson and told them to consider giving MacArthur the two divisions he asked for and also to consider the advisability of accepting the two divisions offered by the Chinese Nationalist Government. That Gov't is still recognized as the 5th permanent member of the Security Council U.N. Since Britain, Australia, Canada and the Netherlands have come in with ships and planes we probably should use the Chinese ground forces.
>
> What will that do to Mao Tse-tung we don't know. Must be careful not to cause a general Asiatic war. Russia is figuring on an attack in the Black Sea and toward the Persian Gulf. . .

At 8:30 Friday morning my father convened another meeting of his Blair House team. When he brought up the subject of Chiang's troops, he found very little enthusiasm. Secretary of State Acheson renewed his fears of Chinese Communist intervention. The Joint Chiefs of Staff pointed to the time that would be lost transporting Chiang's men into Korea and reequipping them. They might even have to be retrained to use modern weapons. Instead, they recommended the commitment of the two U.S. divisions which General MacArthur had under his command in Japan. Reluctantly, my father decided to refuse Chiang's offer and approved the commitment of our two American divisions.

Step by step, in six fateful days, searching for alternatives before he made each move, my father found himself fighting his third war. At 11:00 A.M. on Friday, he convened a meeting of the

[469]

Cabinet, to which he invited eighteen leading members of Congress from both sides of the aisle. He told them that he was sending troops to Korea, but he did not make it clear that they were going into action immediately. Republican Kenneth Wherry arose and addressed Dad as though he were on the Senate floor. He wanted to know if the Congress would be advised before "our boys" began actual combat.

My father replied that ground troops had already been ordered into combat. Tensely, Senator Wherry said he thought Congress ought to be consulted before the President made moves like this. My father told him that it had been an emergency. It was no time for lots of talk. "I just had to act as commander in chief, and I did. I told MacArthur to go to the relief of the Koreans and to carry out the instructions of the United Nations Security Council."

Senator Wherry ignored him. Echoing Senator Taft's party line, he leaped to his feet again and reiterated that the President should consult Congress before taking drastic steps.

"If there is any necessity for congressional action," Dad said, "I will come to you. But I hope we can get those bandits in Korea suppressed without that."

Mr. Dewey Short, the Republican congressman from Missouri, cut Wherry down by asking for the floor and stepping up to the Cabinet table to say that he thought he was expressing the opinion of practically everyone in the Congress in saying that the Congress owed the President thanks for the quality of his leadership. Mr. Short said that he personally was very grateful to the President for his frankness in telling them what had been going on and having General Bradley give them a résumé of the military situation. Nothing more was heard from Senator Wherry for the rest of the meeting.

Several other senators declaimed at length upon the importance of getting soldiers from other countries into the fighting. Patiently, General Omar Bradley explained that this was not as easy as it sounded. They were equipped with different weapons, used different food from American troops. They had different military procedures. It would take six or eight months to train them to the point where they could be used in combat.

Vice President Barkley complained about the statement Dad was releasing, saying that "General MacArthur had been authorized to use certain supporting ground units." Mr. Barkley felt that the President was in control of the troops and was issuing orders to them. Dad had to explain that from a legal point of view MacArthur was working for the United Nations. "This is all very delicate. I don't want it stated any place that I am telling MacArthur what to do. He is not an American general now, he is acting for the United Nations. It would spoil everything if we said he was just doing what we tell him to do."

My father was feeling his way in a totally new situation—the first war against aggression fought under the auspices of a world organization of nations. It had to be fought successfully on both the military and the diplomatic fronts, and time was very short.

At the end of this terrible week Dad did something that was utterly typical of him. He thought of what other men around him had accomplished and somehow found the time to give them credit. He sent Dean Acheson the following handwritten note:

> Memo to Dean Acheson
> Regarding June 24 and 25
> Your initiative in immediately calling the Security Council of the U.N. on Saturday night and notifying me was the key to what followed afterwards. If you had not acted promptly in that direction we would have had to go into Korea alone.
> The meeting Sunday night at Blair House was the result of your actions Saturday night and the results afterward show that you are a great Secretary of State and a diplomat.
> Your handling of the situation since has been superb.
> I'm sending you this for your record.
>
> Harry S. Truman

[CHAPTER]

Twenty-Five

ONE LETTER of support which my father received around this time especially pleased him. It was from Henry Wallace. He enclosed a statement that he had issued defending the decision to resist aggression in South Korea. "When my country is at war and the U.N. sanctions that war, I am on the side of my country and the U.N.," he wrote. ". . . I cannot agree with those who want to start a propaganda drive to pull United Nations troops out of Korea."

Dad replied:

> Dear Henry:
> I certainly appreciated yours of the eighteenth, and the enclosed personal statement. We are faced with a very serious situation. I hope it will work out on a peaceful basis.

Among the most serious aspects of the situation was the President's relationship to Congress. In the course of the June 30 meeting, described near the end of the previous chapter, not only Senator Wherry, but Senator H. Alexander Smith of New Jersey, a moderate Republican, brought up the question of obtaining approval from Congress before Dad committed American ground troops on a large scale. My father, who had already achieved so much by working closely with Congress to create a genuinely bipartisan foreign policy, assured them that he would seek congressional support for any decisions he made. But he never said he would seek congressional *approval* because he believed then and believes now that the powers of the presidency were at stake in this issue, and these powers were in turn related to the very survival of the United States of America. A President without the power to make the swift decision he had made in Korea could not protect the United States in a world of jet aircraft and surprise attacks.

On July 3, at the President's request, the State Department prepared a memorandum, which listed eighty-seven instances in the previous century when the President as Commander in Chief had taken similar action. At this time, moreover, there was little need for my father to seek congressional support. He already had it, in overwhelming amounts. Letters and statements poured into the White House from all but a small group of diehard right-wing Republicans. Around the country and the world, the same air of euphoria prevailed.

But our hopes of swiftly repelling the North Korean "bandit raid" were not realized. The American troops flung into battle from Japan were not much better equipped than the South Koreans. Few of them had combat experience and they were cruelly mauled by the tank-led North Koreans. Americans gasped with shock as reports poured in from the battlefronts about the superiority of North Korea's weapons and the combat readiness of their well-trained troops. American soldiers finally established a perimeter around the port of Pusan at the heel of the Korean peninsula, and for the rest of the summer maintained a tenuous grip on this beachhead, beating off ferocious North Korean attacks.

The desperate fighting, the heartbreaking casualties were only part of my father's woes during this summer of 1950. He had to get congressional permission to shift the economy from a peace to a war basis. Six hundred thousand men had to be added to the armed forces in the shortest possible time. Four National Guard divisions were activated, the draft was expanded, and a massive recruiting program launched. By raising taxes and restricting consumer credit, my father tried to avoid the painful imposition of price controls, which had been the most unpopular government measure of World War II.

The lengthening struggle in Korea inevitably complicated my

father's relationship with Congress. The reactionaries began ranting sarcastically about Truman's "police action." Rumors about Communists in the government ballooned, upsetting moderate congressmen in both parties. The emotional situation led to one of the most distressing political defeats my father ever suffered in his warfare with the reactionaries. If there was one of these negative thinkers whom he disliked both personally and politically, it was Senator Pat McCarran of Nevada, chairman of the powerful Senate Judiciary Committee, which controlled 40 percent of the Senate's business. My father first tangled with him over the displaced persons bill, which he had hoped to see passed early in his second term. Dad wanted to admit 339,000 refugees, who were still languishing in camps in Europe, five years after the war had ended. Senator McCarran refused to have anything to do with the administration's bill. Instead, he introduced his own which was worse than the one that had been passed by the Eightieth Congress. Only after a tremendous thirteen-hour debate did the Senate finally reject McCarran's ideas and vote for the Truman bill, sponsored by Harley Kilgore of West Virginia.

This victory, on April 5, 1950, left Senator McCarran thirsting for revenge, and he got it when the Korean War aroused the nation to anti-Communist frenzy. My father was trying to prevent the government's loyalty program from turning into a witch-hunt. For over a year Senator McCarran had introduced into appropriations bills numerous riders giving government department heads the power to fire any employee on security grounds without the right of appeal. My father asked for legislation to give every accused person a fair hearing. In response, Senator McCarran introduced an internal security bill which set up a government within the government, the Subversive Activities Control Board, with sweeping powers to hunt down suspected Communists everywhere. My father promptly vetoed the bill, because, he said, it gave the government "thought control" powers that the framers of the Constitution never intended it to have. "There is no more fundamental axiom of American freedom than the familiar statement: In a free country, we punish men for the crimes they commit, but never for the opinions they have," Dad wrote.

Within twenty-four hours, in spite of heroic efforts by a forlorn little band of senators led by Hubert Humphrey, Congress overrode the veto by crushing majorities. Even Scott Lucas, the Democratic majority leader in the Senate, voted to override, because he was worried about his reelection in November.

Congress was by no means the only legislative body with which Dad had to cope during this agonizing summer of 1950. The United Nations was also restive and frightened by the large-scale fighting. The British and the Indian governments suggested peace plans which involved large concessions, such as the immediate seating of Communist China and the trading of Formosa for a withdrawal from Korea. They were politely informed that this was unacceptable to the United States. My father also had to fend off critics such as Bernard Baruch, who demanded immediate and all-out national mobilization, which would include price, wage, and rent controls as well as rationing. Lengthy reports were made to Congress and the American people in mid-July, explaining why such drastic measures were unnecessary. Although the term was not yet in use, my father was already formulating the concept of a limited war. Any lunge toward the posture of an all-out war might inspire a Russian attack and launch World War III.

Simultaneously, Dad had to keep the more headstrong members of the armed forces under control. Early in July he learned that the air force was planning high-level photo reconnaissance missions over Dairen, Port Arthur, Vladivostok, and other Russian Far Eastern bases, to see if Stalin was planning to move into Korea. My father immediately ordered the cancellation of these missions. It was the first appearance of a problem that was to vex him throughout the war in Korea—the clash between the global view of our security and interests which Dad maintained in the White House and the needs and desires of local commanders in the war zone.

To my father's dismay, the focus of this clash soon became the man in supreme command of the UN army, General Douglas MacArthur. Dad was not an admirer of the MacArthur style of generalship. MacArthur's fondness for personal publicity, his rhetoric to describe his own accomplishments, his petulant conduct during World War II, when he constantly badgered Washington for more support for his theater of war—all these things were against the code of Harry S. Truman, who put humility, giving credit to others, and team work at the head of his list of personal values. But my father recognized these differences between him and General MacArthur for precisely what they were—essentially differences in style. Such personal opinions had no place and no influence in the relationship between *President* Harry S. Truman and *General* Douglas MacArthur. In fact, as a student of military history, Dad was an admirer of General MacArthur's strategy in the South Pacific during World War II.

At the same time, my father was very much aware that General MacArthur had political ambitions. He had allowed himself to be put forward as a candidate in the Wisconsin presidential primary in the 1948 election. He took a drubbing and that was the end of his candidacy.

Even before the Korean War began, some rather strange things had happened in Tokyo which made my father suspect that General MacArthur was still working rather closely with the right-wing Republicans who had backed him in Wisconsin. When Chiang retreated to Formosa, it looked at first as if the Communists would follow him and swiftly capture the island. We had no plans —or desire—to defend Chiang, and with White House approval, the State Department sent instructions to MacArthur's headquarters, advising him how to deal with the press on the subject, so that he would say nothing that contradicted his superior in Washington. The memorandum was leaked, and was soon raising a hue and cry in the anti-Truman press and among the "animals," as Dad called the right-wingers in Congress.

On the other hand, my father was encouraged by General MacArthur's praise of his decision to resist aggression in Korea. When Dad appointed him United Nations Commander, the General sent the following radio message:

> I have received your announcement of your appointment of me as United Nations Commander—I can only repeat the pledge of my complete personal loyalty to you as well as an absolute devotion to your monumental struggle for peace and goodwill throughout the world. I hope I will not fail you.

But before the month of July was over, my father and General MacArthur had clashed again over Formosa. On July 19 Dad had carefully spelled out his policy toward Chiang Kai-shek:

> The present military neutralization of Formosa is without prejudice to political questions affecting that island. Our desire

is that Formosa not become embroiled in hostilities disturbing to the peace of the Pacific and that all questions affecting Formosa are to be settled by peaceful means as envisaged in the Charter of the United Nations. With peace reestablished, even the most complex political questions are susceptible of solution. In the presence of brutal and unprovoked aggression, however, some of these questions may have to be held in abeyance in the interest of the essential security of all.

On July 27, at a National Security Council meeting, my father decided to send a survey team to Formosa to estimate Chiang's military needs. This decision was not caused by any change of heart or mind on Dad's part toward Chiang. Intelligence reports indicated that the Communist Chinese were concentrating a large army along the coast opposite Formosa, and my father was determined to resist another apparently imminent act of aggression. The plan was to send Chiang the military aid he needed, quietly, with a minimum of mention in the press. You can imagine Dad's wrath when he picked up the newspaper on August 1 and discovered that the previous day General MacArthur had made an unauthorized trip to Formosa to do his own survey of Chiang's needs and explain why we could not use his troops in Korea. The glare of publicity which followed MacArthur everywhere made it look as if we were negotiating a mutual defense treaty with Chiang. The Generalissimo, no slouch himself in undercutting American policy, had urged in a public statement a few weeks before the General's visit that "no difficulties . . . will arise if United States relationships are placed in the hands of Douglas MacArthur."

Soon after MacArthur returned to Tokyo, Chiang announced "the foundation for Sino-American military cooperation has been laid." There was no doubt, he declared, of "final victory in our struggle against Communism."

My father was appalled, and immediately dispatched Averell Harriman to Tokyo to explain in detail our policy toward Chiang and Formosa as well as the entire Korean involvement. Dad also wanted to get from one of his most reliable associates a wide-ranging report on MacArthur's view of the war. When Mr. Harriman explained our Formosa policy, General MacArthur demonstrated an alarming ability to talk out of both sides of his mouth. He agreed that Chiang personally was a liability and at one point in the conversation, suggested letting him land with his army on the

[477]

Chinese coast, where he would be swiftly annihilated. Much troubled, Ambassador Harriman reported, "He did not seem to consider the liability that our support of Chiang on such a move would be to us in the East." Ambassador Harriman came away with the worried feeling that he and General MacArthur had not come "to a full agreement on the way we believed things should be handled on Formosa with the Generalissimo." At the same time General MacArthur had assured Mr. Harriman that he would "as a soldier obey any orders that he received from the President."

On August 26 Charlie Ross laid on Dad's desk a copy of the statement which General MacArthur had sent to the commander in chief of the Veterans of Foreign Wars, who were holding their annual convention. It was to be read to the convention on August 28, but a news magazine was already on the stands with the full text. The message was a lofty criticism of the American government's policy, with special emphasis on Formosa. He compared the island to "an unsinkable aircraft carrier and submarine tender" which threatened our bases in Okinawa and the Philippines. "Nothing could be more fallacious than the threadbare argument by those who advocate appeasement and defeatism in the Pacific that if we defend Formosa we alienate continental Asia," the General declared. "Those who speak thus do not understand the Orient."

Only the day before, my father had ordered our ambassador to the UN, Warren Austin, to assure Secretary General Trygve Lie that we had no desire to incorporate Formosa within the American defense perimeter and were prepared to have the United Nations investigate our actions on that island. MacArthur's statement created consternation in the UN and in the capitals of our allies around the world.

My father immediately met with the Joint Chiefs of Staff and Secretaries of State, Treasury, and Defense. Grimly, in a manner that was totally foreign to his usual style of conducting these meetings, he asked each man if he knew anything about MacArthur's message before it was released to the press. All of them said they were as surprised as the President. Dad ordered Louis Johnson to order MacArthur to withdraw the message. To my father's amazement, the Secretary of Defense hesitated to obey this direct order. Instead, he suggested issuing a statement that would have been little more than a light tap on General MacArthur's wrist—an explanation that his message to the VFW was "only one man's opinion."

When my father heard about this timidity—a shocking example of the awe with which General MacArthur was regarded by the Department of Defense—he called Mr. Johnson and dictated the following message: "The President of the United States directs that you withdraw your message to the National Encampment of Veterans of Foreign Wars, because various features with respect to Formosa are in conflict with the policy of the United States and its position in the United Nations." Dad followed this up with a long letter once more carefully explaining our policy, and enclosing Ambassador Austin's letter to Trygve Lie.

This episode was close to the last straw in my father's efforts to be patient with Louis Johnson. The Secretary of Defense had become an obstructionist force in the government. He had used the outbreak of the Korean War to sharpen and widen his feud with Secretary of State Acheson. He went around Washington making sneering remarks about disloyalty in the State Department and intimating that the Department of Defense was the only reliable force for a constructive foreign policy in the government. He had even discussed with opposition senators the possibility of his supporting a move to oust the Secretary of State. On September 11, at 4:00 P.M., Mr. Johnson came to the White House for an off-the-record meeting. "Lou came in full of pep and energy," Dad says. "He didn't know anything was wrong. I told him to sit down and I said, 'Lou, I've got to ask you to quit.'

"He just folded up and wilted. He leaned over in his chair and I thought he was going to faint. He said, 'Mr. President, I can't talk.' "

In Congress, the right-wing Republicans were attacking Johnson, as the man responsible for the poor showing of our army in the first months of fighting in Korea. Dad told Johnson that Democratic members of Congress had come to him and sworn that Mr. Johnson's continuance in the Cabinet would beat them in the November elections. This was a polite lie which, Dad knew, made him look timid. He did this to make it as easy as possible for Mr. Johnson to leave.

Frantically, for a few moments, Mr. Johnson tried to argue with

[479]

Dad. He cut him short. "I have made up my mind, Lou, and it has to be this way."

Minutes after Mr. Johnson left, my father walked into Charlie's office and said, "This is the toughest job I have ever had to do."

A few days later Dad told George Elsey:

> I had one hell of a time with Lou Johnson. I've never had anyone let me down as badly as he did. I've known for months —ever since May—that I would have to fire him, but I just couldn't bring myself to do it. You know that I would rather cut my own throat than hurt anyone. I've known Lou for thirty years and I hated to have to do this to him, but the worst part about this job I have is that I can't consider my personal feelings. I have to do what is right and I just couldn't leave Johnson there any longer. The terrible thing about all this is that Johnson doesn't realize he has done anything wrong. He just doesn't seem to realize what he's been doing to the whole government. I couldn't let it go on any longer.

Mr. Johnson proceeded to prolong the agony by handing Dad his letter of resignation the following day, unsigned and expressing the hope that he would not be asked to sign it. Dad's jaw tightened, and he said, "I'm afraid it has to be signed, Lou."

The Secretary of Defense signed and left the White House. My father immediately telephoned General George Marshall at Leesburg, Virginia, and asked him to become Secretary of Defense. Once more, this great man and soldier instantly obeyed his Commander in Chief.

My father also considered relieving General MacArthur, when he issued his flagrantly insubordinate statement about Formosa. But he decided against this move, because he had already approved the daring plan General MacArthur had conceived to break out of our Pusan beachhead and seize the offensive in Korea. It called for an end run by sea around the North Korean army and a lightning amphibious landing at Inchon, on the west coast of Korea. The Joint Chiefs of Staff were deeply worried by the dangers involved in the plan. MacArthur's landing force at Inchon was small—only two divisions—and the harbor was extremely tricky, with huge tides that rose and fell as much as twenty feet leaving miles of mud flats to be negotiated by our amphibious troops, if our timing went awry. But my father called it "a bold plan worthy of a master strategist," and backed MacArthur to the hilt. To make the plan possible, he had withdrawn troops from Puerto Rico, Hawaii, the Mediterranean, and handed them over to General MacArthur. Dad knew from his long study of military history that relieving a commander on the eve of battle inevitably damaged an army's morale. He believed in General MacArthur's ability to win the tremendous gamble at Inchon.

Win he did. On September 15, while everyone in the White House and the Pentagon sweated and prayed, the 1st Marine Division and the army's 7th Infantry Division stormed ashore, achieving complete tactical surprise. Simultaneously, our troops inside the Pusan bridgehead took the offensive. By September 29 Seoul had been recaptured. Dad sent General MacArthur a telegram that communicated not only his congratulations but the close and knowledgeable attention he had paid to his tactics and strategy.

> I know that I speak for the entire American people when I send you my warmest congratulations on the victory which has been achieved under your leadership in Korea. Few operations in military history can match either the delaying action, the way you traded space for time in which to build up your forces, or the brilliant maneuver which has now resulted in the liberation of Seoul.

The disintegration of the North Korean army was swift, as a result of General MacArthur's smashing blow. All opposition below the 38th parallel evaporated. Unfortunately, many of their men succeeded in fleeing across the border into North Korea, although they had to abandon most of their weapons while doing so.

A major decision now had to be made. Should we cross the 38th parallel in hot pursuit of the enemy's disorganized but by no means destroyed army? Was it possible that, by destroying this army, we could unite North and South Korea and create a free independent nation? The United Nations declared that this was their goal, and on October 7 they voted resoundingly for a resolution calling for "a unified, independent and democratic government" of Korea.

This goal was in harmony with traditional military doctrine, that the destruction of the enemy's armed forces was the only way to end a war. The Joint Chiefs of Staff, therefore, recommended that MacArthur be authorized to operate in North Korea. But he was warned that this permission depended upon one enormously vital fact—that "there has been no entry into North Korea by major Soviet or Chinese Communist forces, no announcement of intended entry, nor a threat to counter our operations militarily in Korea." At the same time General MacArthur was requested to submit a plan of operations—a request which, he made it clear, he resented. He was also explicitly told by the Pentagon: "No non-Korean ground forces will be used in the northeast provinces bordering the Soviet Union or in the area along the Manchurian border."

General MacArthur finally presented a plan of operations that was in entire harmony with these directives. He proposed to attack north until he had established a line about fifty miles above the enemy capital of Pyongyang. From there, if the situation warranted it, he would commit South Korean troops to occupy the remaining sixty miles of Korea between that point and the Yalu River.

Meanwhile, in Washington, ominous warnings filtered into the State Department from nations who were in contact with China. They all reported that the Communist government in Peking had declared that they would send troops into Korea if American troops crossed the 38th parallel. My father immediately sent this warning to General MacArthur. The Chinese repeated the warning over their official government radio a few days later. General MacArthur, and his intelligence chief, Major General Charles A. Willoughby, dismissed it as political blackmail, designed to frighten the United Nations and prevent them from voting overwhelmingly in support of the resolution for a free unified Korea.

The more my father thought about the complex situation, and General MacArthur's difficult personality and strong political opinions, the more he became convinced that the President should have a personal talk with his Far East commander. He wanted to find out exactly what MacArthur planned to do in Korea. Above all, he wanted to give the General a realistic appraisal of what he and his administration were thinking about the whole world. He worried about the tendency of the General and his staff to think too exclusively of the Far East. They had been away from home too long.

At first Dad thought of flying to Korea to visit the troops. But he decided this would take him away from Washington for a dangerously long period of time. He did not want to bring General MacArthur to Washington, because that would separate him from his troops for an equally dangerous period. So the decision was made to meet at Wake Island, in the Pacific. It was a decision that gave General MacArthur only 1,900 miles to travel, and Dad 4,700.

Before he left, my father discussed with his aides the possibility of bringing along something that General MacArthur might not be able to buy in Japan—some small present that would please him. Charlie Murphy found a young man in the Pentagon who had been MacArthur's personal aide. He advised Charlie to take some Blum's candy for Mrs. MacArthur. She was very fond of it and could not get it out there. Charlie bought five one-pound boxes and took them along on the plane. In Honolulu, Averell Harriman decided a five-pound box was better and bought one. So Dad's party arrived bearing ten pounds of Blum's goodwill candy.

Coming in to land at deserted, dusty Wake Island, they wondered for a moment if they had wasted their time. Dad, knowing General MacArthur's imperial tendencies, thought that the President should be the greeted, not the greeter. He had flown twice as far, and according to every standard of rank and protocol, General MacArthur, as the Far Eastern commander, should be on hand to welcome his Commander in Chief. Dad told the pilot of the *Independence* to check with ground control and find out if General MacArthur had already arrived. When this was affirmed, my father issued orders to land.

The plane taxied to the operations building, and everyone waited to see what would happen next. For a moment their suspicions seemed to be realized. There was no sign of General MacArthur. Then he strolled out, wearing his famous battered hat and fatigues, the shirt open at the collar. He and Dad shook hands and drove to the office of the airline manager where they talked for an hour, alone.

My father summed up their conference in this memorandum which he dictated to his secretary, Rose Conway:

> We arrived at dawn. General MacArthur was at the Airport with his shirt unbuttoned, wearing a greasy ham and eggs cap that evidently had been in use for twenty years.
>
> He greeted the President cordially and after the photographers had finished their usual picture orgy the President and the General boarded an old two door sedan and drove to the quarters of the Airline Manager on the island.
>
> For more than an hour they discussed the Japanese and Korean situation.
>
> The General assured the President that the victory was won in Korea, that Japan was ready for a peace treaty and that the Chinese Communists would not attack.
>
> A general discussion was carried on about Formosa. The General brought up his statement to the Veterans of Foreign Wars, which had been ordered withdrawn by the President. The General said that he was sorry for any embarrassment he'd caused, that he was not in politics at the time and that the politicians had made a "chump" (his word) of him in 1948 and that it would not happen again. He assured the President that he had no political ambitions.
>
> He again said the Chinese Commies would not attack, that we had won the war and that we could send a Division to Europe in January 1951.

My father now brought the General over to meet his advisers, who included Secretary of the Army Frank Pace, General Omar Bradley, Philip Jessup and Dean Rusk from the State Department, and Averell Harriman. There General MacArthur repeated much of what he had told Dad in private about Korea. By happy coincidence, we know exactly what he said in this much-debated meeting. Miss Vernice Anderson, Ambassador Jessup's secretary, had been brought along to help in the drafting and final typing of a communiqué Dad planned to issue at the end of the meeting. Miss Anderson was waiting in the next room for this assignment, and the door was partially open. She could hear everything that was being said and took shorthand notes. Not because anyone ordered her to, but because she thought it would not hurt to have a record of the meeting.

"What are the chances for Chinese or Soviet interference?" my father asked.

[484]

"Very little," General MacArthur said. "Had they interfered in the first or second months it would have been decisive. We are no longer fearful of their intervention. We no longer stand hat in hand. The Chinese have 300,000 men in Manchuria. Of these probably not more than 100–125,000 are distributed along the Yalu River. Only 50–60,000 could be gotten across the Yalu River. They have no air force. Now that we have bases for our air force in Korea, if the Chinese try to get down to Pyongyang there would be the greatest slaughter. . . . The Russians have no ground troops available for North Korea. The only possible combination would be Russian air support of Chinese ground troops. . . . I believe Russian air would bomb the Chinese as often as they would bomb us. . . . I believe it just wouldn't work."

General Bradley asked: "Could the 2nd or 3rd Division be made available to be sent over to Europe by January?"

"Yes," General MacArthur said. ". . . I hope to get the Eighth Army back by Christmas."

General MacArthur oozed optimism and goodwill. He urged Dad to proclaim a Truman Doctrine for the Far East, and told reporters, "No commander in the history of war has had more complete and admirable support from the agencies in Washington than I have during the Korean operation."

My father gave the General the Blum's candy for Mrs. MacArthur, they shook hands, and both climbed aboard their planes and headed back to work. In San Francisco the following day, Dad called the conference "very satisfactory." In a speech at the San Francisco Opera House, he said that he talked to General MacArthur to make it

> perfectly clear . . . that there is complete unity in the aims and conduct of our foreign policy. . . . I want Wake Island to be a symbol of our unity of purpose for world peace. I want to see world peace from Wake Island west all the way around and back again. The only victory we seek is the victory of peace.

He called on the Soviet Union and its satellites to join in the search for peace by living up to the principles of the United Nations Charter.

Meanwhile, in Korea, alarming things began to happen. On October 26 a Chinese prisoner was captured. On October 30 sixteen Chinese were captured near Hamhung and they told an

[485]

interpreter that they had crossed the Yalu River on a train on October 16—the day after the Wake Island conference where General MacArthur had dismissed the possibility of Chinese intervention. On November 1 the 8th Cavalry Regiment was attacked by masses of Chinese after receiving fire from mortars and Russian Katusha rockets. Fighting continued all night; the following day, when the regiment tried to retreat, they found more Chinese blocking the road. The regiment all but disintegrated in the chaotic fighting that ensued. Men fled into the hills and found their way south in small units. One battalion was trapped and almost completely annihilated. General Walton Walker, commander of the Eighth Army, sent a telegram to Tokyo describing "An ambush and surprise attack by fresh well-organized and well-trained units, some of which were Chinese Communist forces."

The only response from Tokyo was an order to resume advancing.

Absorbed by the drama in Korea—and deeply concerned by the appearance of Chinese soldiers—my father paid little attention to newspaper stories reporting trouble in Puerto Rico. On October 29, fighting and shooting broke out in San Juan. The troublemakers were the tiny Independence party which numbered approximately 1,500. They had attempted to seize the government by armed force, but the insurrection—if it even deserved that word—was swiftly suppressed. It never occurred to Dad or to anyone around him that this outburst of violence would soon reach all the way to Washington.

For one thing, Harry S. Truman was very popular in Puerto Rico. On October 16, 1945, he had told Congress, "It is now time, in my opinion, to ascertain from the people of Puerto Rico their wishes as to the ultimate status which they prefer and within such limits as may be determined by Congress to grant to them the kind of government they desire." Dad did not exclude the possibility of complete independence. On February 20, 1948, during a visit to San Juan, he said: "The Puerto Rican people should have the right to determine for themselves Puerto Rico's political relationship to the United States." Thanks to his urging, Congress passed laws which permitted Puerto Ricans to elect their own governor and other executive officers and create a constitution which gave the people of Puerto Rico control over their local affairs.

This did not satisfy fanatics of the Independence party. Overwhelmed at the polls by Muñoz Marin's Popular Democratic party which favored the commonwealth status for the island, and the Statehood party which wanted Puerto Rico to become the forty-ninth state, the *Indepentistas* preached hatred of the *Yanquis* and called for violent revolution.

On October 31 two members of this party, Oscar Collazo and Girsel Torresola, came to Washington, D.C. The following morning they took a tour of the city and learned, apparently for the first time, that my father was not in the White House but in Blair House. Both were armed. After lunch they went back to their hotel, and Torresola gave Collazo a lesson in how to use a gun. Dad, meanwhile, had returned from a busy morning at the White House to lunch at Blair House with Mother and Grandmother Wallace. He then went upstairs to take his usual afternoon nap.

Ever since we had moved into Blair House, the Secret Service had worried about its exposed position. Fronting right on the street, it created nightmarish security problems. They did their best with a bad situation, stationing guards in booths at the west and east ends of the house. Secret Service men were stationed inside the house, and a White House policeman was always on the steps leading up to the front door.

At about two o'clock on the afternoon of November 1, Torresola and Collazo approached Blair House from opposite directions, Torresola from the west, Collazo from the east. They planned to meet at the house steps and charge inside together. When Collazo was about eight feet from the steps, he whipped out his gun and began firing at Private Donald T. Birdzell, who was stationed on the steps. The pistol misfired on the first shot, but the second pull of the trigger hit Private Birdzell in the right leg. He staggered into the street, drawing his gun. Collazo bolted for the front door, which was wide open. Only a screen door with a light latch on it was between him and the interior of the house. But the guards in the east booth were, thank God, on the alert, and their shots cut Collazo down on the second step. From the west booth Private Leslie Coffelt fired another shot as Collazo tried to rise and he toppled face down on the sidewalk.

A moment before he fired, Private Coffelt was struck in the chest and abdomen by two bullets from Torresola's gun. Crouched in the hedge in front of Blair House, Torresola began blazing away at everyone. Another shot struck Private Birdzell in the left knee, toppling him to the street. Private Coffelt, in spite of his mortal wounds, managed to fire one more shot. The bullet struck Torresola in the head, killing him on the spot.

In three minutes, twenty-seven shots were fired. Upstairs in the front bedrooms, Dad and Mother were dressing to attend the dedication of a statue of Field Marshal Sir John Dill, the British member of the World War II Combined Chiefs of Staff. Mother, hearing the noise, strolled to the window and saw Private Birdzell lying in the street, blood streaming from his shattered leg. "Harry," she gasped, "someone's shooting our policemen." My father rushed to the window while gunfire was still being exchanged with Torresola. A Secret Service agent looked up, saw him, and shouted: "Get back! Get back!"

Dad obeyed with alacrity.

Washington was swept by panicky rumors that the President and seven Secret Service men were dead. Dad remained perfectly calm, and departed on schedule for the dedication of Field Marshal Dill's statue in Arlington Cemetery. "A President has to expect these things," he said.

Those words may be true enough, but a President's daughter does not expect such things. I was scheduled to sing that night in Portland, Oregon. One firm rule that I always followed on tour was complete seclusion on the day that I sang. This was not my invention. Every concert singer shuts out all distractions and uses his or her voice as little as possible for ten or twelve hours before facing an audience. I spent that day following this routine, going over my program with my accompanist, having a light lunch of soup and toast and lying down after it, mentally rehearsing the phrasing of my selections. I spent the rest of the afternoon reading a book. I avoided the radio because I did not want to be distracted by music other than what I was planning to sing—or by more bad news from Korea. Toward the end of the afternoon. I got a phone call from Mother. She had decided it would be better if I didn't hear about the assassination attempt, before I sang that night. "I just wanted you to know that everyone is all right," she said.

"Why shouldn't everyone be all right?" I asked, immediately alarmed. "Is there anything wrong with Dad?"

"He's fine. He's perfectly fine," Mother said.

I hung up with an uneasy feeling that *something* was wrong. I don't blame Mother for trying to keep the news from me. Fortunately, Reathel Odum and my manager talked it over and decided it would be a mistake to let me go to the concert hall without knowing the truth. If a local reporter started questioning me, minutes before I stepped on the stage, the shock would inevitably have a devastating effect on my singing. Not without some trepidation, they told me the news and showed me the afternoon papers. As soon as I found out that Dad was all right, I was quite calm. But the thought of someone trying to kill him made me uneasy for days. It still does.

I learned in the course of my research for this book that there had been other attempts on Dad's life, which he never mentioned to me. One of the most serious—at least it was so regarded by the Secret Service—was a warning they received from the mayor of a large city. His police had received a tip that someone would try to kill Dad with a high-powered rifle as he crossed the field at the Army-Navy football game. It is customary, you will recall, for the President to sit on the Army side of the field during one half and on the Navy side of the field during the other half. The Secret Service watches the White House mail closely, and they can often relate such a warning to other crank threats which have not been carried out and can, therefore, to some extent at least, be disregarded. But this one was obviously from a lone wolf—the most dangerous kind. Dad insisted that he was going to walk across the field, come what may. So the Secret Service men could only double their usual precautions. They had men stationed at every conceivable point throughout the stadium where a rifleman might position himself. Dad strode across the field, smiling and waving to the crowd, completely unbothered by the incident. But you can be sure that the Secret Service men held their breaths until he was safely seated on the other side of the field.

In the summer of 1947, the so-called Stern gang of Palestine terrorists tried to assassinate Dad by mail. A number of cream-colored envelopes, about eight by six inches, arrived in the White House, addressed to the President and various members of the staff. Inside them was a smaller envelope marked "Private and Confidential." Inside that second envelope was powdered gelignite, a pencil battery and a detonator rigged to explode the gelignite when the envelope was opened. Fortunately, the White House mail room was alert to the possibility that such letters might arrive. The previous June at least eight were sent to British government officials, including Foreign Secretary Ernest Bevin and former Foreign Secretary Anthony Eden. The British police exploded one of these experimentally and said it could kill, or at the very least maim, anyone unlucky enough to open it. The mail room turned the letters over to the Secret Service and they were defused by their bomb experts. The Secret Service still screens all our mail.

Let us return to that equally painful subject, the war in Korea. Throughout the last days of October and the first days of November, the situation continued to slide toward disaster. Other American units began reporting contact with the Chinese. There were obviously large numbers of them already in action. On November 6, the day before the 1950 elections, General MacArthur issued a demand to bomb the Yalu River bridges. Men and material were pouring across them and he said, "This movement not only jeopardizes but threatens the ultimate destruction of the forces under my command." With great reluctance, Dad gave him permission to destroy the Korean end of the bridges. But General Bradley pointed out to my father that within fifteen to twenty days the Yalu would be frozen, and the bombardment, so frantically insisted upon by General MacArthur, was hardly worth the risk of bombs dropping in Chinese or Soviet territory. The following day General MacArthur reported that enemy planes were engaging in hit-and-run raids across the Yalu and demanded the right to pursue them into their "sanctuary." Panic reigned in the UN until my father categorically rejected this request, which could only have widened the war. General MacArthur did not seem to realize that our planes were flying from privileged sanctuaries in Japan which could have been attacked by Russian or Chinese aircraft if we gave them the pretext by bombing targets in Manchuria.

The Election Day timing of these remarks, and General MacArthur's subsequent actions, made Dad and many members of his staff wonder if their intention was not largely political. They cost the Democrats votes in the election—a lot of votes. The Senate majority leader, Scott Lucas, lost in Illinois. Senator Francis

Myers, the Democratic whip, lost in Pennsylvania, and Millard Tydings lost in Maryland in one of the most scurrilous campaigns in American history. The really evil genius in that election was Joe McCarthy and his aides, who circulated faked pictures purporting to show Senator Tydings conversing with Earl Browder, head of the Communist party. It was a triumph of hatred and of fear.

After sounding the alarm about Chinese intervention in the gravest possible terms, General MacArthur now did a complete flip-flop. He decided that he could resume his advance to the Yalu. The Joint Chiefs of Staff nervously asked him to remember that he was under orders to use only Republic of Korea troops in these northern provinces. General MacArthur replied that he was using Americans for the advance but would withdraw them as soon as he had cleared the area. This was a definite act of disobedience. But the Joint Chiefs were far more worried about MacArthur's appalling strategy. He had divided his army into two parts, sending one up the eastern side of Korea, the other up the west, separated by a massive mountain barrier that made liaison impossible. He called it "a general offensive" to "win the war" and predicted that the troops "will eat Christmas dinner at home." In one communiqué he described his advance as "a massive compression envelopment." In another report he called it "the giant U.N. pincer."

During these fateful weeks, my father did not receive the kind of support and advice he deserved, either from the Joint Chiefs or from the Secretary of State and the Secretary of Defense. Dean Acheson admits as much in his memoirs. General Matthew Ridgway revealed, a few years ago, the kind of atmosphere that prevailed in the Pentagon. He told of sitting through hours-long discussions in the Joint Chiefs War Room reviewing the alarming situation in Korea. Everyone feared that MacArthur was plunging toward disaster, but no one had the courage to speak out. Finally, General Ridgway, who was not a member of the Joint Chiefs and therefore without a vote, asked for permission to speak. He declared that they owed it "to the men in the field and to the God to whom we must answer for those men's lives to stop talking and to act." The only answer he received was silence.

Later, General Ridgway buttonholed General Hoyt Vandenberg, commander of the air force. "Why don't the Joint Chiefs send orders to MacArthur and *tell* him what to do?"

Vandenberg shook his head. "What good would that do? He wouldn't obey the orders. What can we do?"

"You can relieve any commander who won't obey orders, can't you?" General Ridgway exclaimed.

General Vandenberg gave General Ridgway a look that was, Ridgway says, "both puzzled and amazed." Then he walked away without saying a word.

Early on November 28 General Bradley called to give my father bad news from Korea. The Chinese had struck the UN army with masses of troops. Thus began one of the grimmest days Dad spent as President. Fortunately for history, one of America's best reporters, John Hersey, was in the White House doing a series of articles on the President and he preserved an accurate record of my father's reaction to this crisis.

He remained calm. The staff met for their usual morning meeting and Dad discussed a number of routine problems with them. Then in a quiet voice, he told them what was happening. "We've got a terrific situation on our hands. General Bradley told me that a terrible message had come from General MacArthur. MacArthur said there were 260,000 Chinese troops against him out there. He says he's stymied. He says he has to go over to the defensive. It's no longer a question of a few so-called volunteers. The Chinese have come in with both feet."

Everyone sat there, stunned into silence.

"I'm going to meet with the Cabinet this afternoon," Dad said. "General Bradley will be there to discuss the situation. General Marshall is going to meet with the State and Treasury people. Acheson is informing the congressional committees. It may be necessary to deliver a special message in a few days declaring a national emergency. I want to have that meeting with the congressional leaders you were talking about, Murphy. Let's not wait until Monday; let's arrange it for Friday."

It was clear to everyone what a great disappointment this news was to my father. Then in the same quiet voice he went on: "This is the worst situation we have had yet. We'll just have to meet it as we've met all the rest. I've talked already this morning with

Bradley, Marshall, Acheson, Harriman and Snyder, and they all agree with me that we're capable of meeting this thing. I know you fellows will work with us on it, and that we'll meet it."

Crisply, Dad asked his staff to begin preparing the declaration of emergency, an appropriations message, and a speech to the people. Then he began signing documents while he continued to talk. "The liars have accomplished their purpose. The whole campaign of lies we have been seeing in this country has brought about its result. I'm talking about the crowd of vilifiers who have been trying to tear us apart in this country. *Pravda* had an article just the other day crowing about how the American government is divided, and how our people are divided, in hatred. Don't worry, *they* keep a close eye on our dissensions. . . ."

He finished signing the documents, and handed them back to Bill Hopkins, his executive clerk. "We have got to meet this thing just as we've met everything else," he said, "and we will. We will! Let's go ahead now and do our jobs as best we can."

During these awful days, my father remained loyal to his Far Eastern commander. On November 30 he wrote on his calendar:

> This has been a hectic month. General Mac, as usual has been shooting off his mouth. He made a preelection statement that cost us votes and he made a postelection statement that has him in hot water in Europe and at home. I must defend him and save his face even if he has tried on various and numerous occasions to cut mine off. But I must stand by my subordinates. . . .

By now the terrible truth about massive Chinese intervention in Korea was visible to everyone, including General MacArthur. Only the prudent generalship of his subordinate commanders, especially Walton Walker, leader of the Eighth Army, prevented the Chinese ambush from becoming a gigantic trap that could easily have destroyed the whole United Nations army. Both he and the commanders of the Xth Corps, operating on the western side of Korea, suspected a Chinese ambush and advanced with far more caution and with careful attention to lines of retreat than the supreme commander in Tokyo considered necessary. General Walker was, in fact, showered with rather abusive messages from Tokyo, asking him why he wasn't advancing faster.

[493]

When the Chinese struck in force, General MacArthur again plunged from optimism to panic. "We face an entirely new war," he reported on November 28, adding, "this command . . . is now faced with conditions beyond its control and strength." On December 3 he declared, "This small command is facing the entire Chinese nation in undeclared war. Unless some positive and immediate action is taken, hope for success cannot be justified, and steady attrition leading to final destruction can reasonably be contemplated." He called for "political decisions and strategic plans and implementation thereof adequate fully to meet the realities involved." Again he was demanding the right to attack Chinese bases and supply lines in Manchuria.

We now know that this panic was unnecessary. Thanks to the skill of his field commanders, the Eighth Army and the Xth Corps executed fighting retreats that enabled them to escape the Chinese trap relatively undamaged. When the Xth Corps evacuated the North Korean port of Hungnam, they took out 105,000 troops, 91,000 Korean refugees, more than 17,000 vehicles, and several hundred thousand tons of cargo. The Eighth Army fell back toward the 38th parallel with the 2nd Division fighting a ferocious rear guard action. We suffered a defeat that cost us about 13,000 killed and wounded—less than 5 percent of the UN army.

My father did not lose faith in General MacArthur because of this defeat. He was the last man in the world to give up on a subordinate because he was in trouble. What dismayed him was the General's frantic attempts to protect his public image by dumping the blame for the defeat on others—notably the President of the United States. Between November 28 and December 3, MacArthur gave at least seven interviews to various journalists explaining away—or trying to explain away—what was happening in Korea. All these statements only rephrased the story he gave to *U.S. News and World Report.* His inability to bomb Manchuria was "an enormous handicap without precedent in military history."

"I should have fired MacArthur then and there," my father has said. But he had too much respect for the General's long service to his country and his outstanding military record. He did not want to fire him in the aftermath of a defeat. Instead, Dad ordered the Joint Chiefs to send General MacArthur a new directive, which was applicable to all military officers overseas.

It instructed him that "no speech, press release or public statement" about the policy of the United States should be issued without first clearing it with Washington.

In his November 30 press conference my father defended the General vigorously. Edward T. Folliard of the Washington *Post* asked Dad what he thought of the criticism of General MacArthur in the European press.

"They are always for a man when he is winning, but when he is in a little trouble, they all jump on him with what ought to be done, which they didn't tell him before. He has done a good job, and is continuing to do a good job."

"The particular criticism," Mr. Folliard added, "is that he exceeded his authority and went beyond the point he was supposed to go."

"He did nothing of the kind," my father said.

At this same press conference, Tony Leviero asked Dad if attacks in Manchuria would depend on action in the United Nations.

"Yes, entirely," Dad said.

"In other words," Leviero continued, "if the United Nations resolution should authorize General MacArthur to go further than he has, he will—"

"We will take whatever steps are necessary to meet the military situation, just as we always have."

"Will that include the atomic bomb?" Jack Dougherty of the New York *Daily News* asked.

"That includes every weapon that we have," my father said.

Paul R. Leach of the Chicago *Daily News* asked: "Mr. President, you said every weapon that we have. Does that mean that there is active consideration of the use of the atomic bomb?"

"There has always been active consideration of its use. I don't want to see it used," my father said. "It is a terrible weapon and it should not be used on innocent men, women and children who have nothing whatever to do with this military aggression."

The press conference wandered off to other matters, and then Merriman Smith of the United Press asked: "Mr. President, I wonder if we could retrace that reference to the atom bomb? Did we understand you clearly that the use of the bomb is under active consideration?"

[495]

"Always has been," Dad said. "It is one of our weapons."

The truth, of course, as Dad had indicated in his previous comment, was that the atomic bomb would be used only as a last desperate resource. But he hoped that the threat of using it would force the Chinese to move more cautiously.

Now the reporters, sniffing a story, really went to work on him. "Does that mean, Mr. President, use against military objectives or civilian?" Robert G. Nixon of International News Service asked. Note the neat way that question penned my father into a corner. He tried to extricate himself by saying that was "a matter that the military people have to decide. I'm not a military authority that passes on those things."

My father was thinking of the way targets were selected for the atomic bombs dropped on Japan. He had ordered his military advisers to select authentic military targets, and they had done so. He was trying to avoid the implication that he or anyone else would willingly drop a bomb on a purely civilian target. He was trying to do this in a nice way, without cutting down Bob Nixon.

"Mr. President," said Frank Bourgholtzer, "you said this depends on United Nations action. Does that mean that we wouldn't use the atomic bomb except under United Nations authorization?"

This question tried to pin Dad into another corner. Numerous congressmen, mostly Republicans, were extremely touchy about the agreements which President Roosevelt had made with the British, giving them a say in the use of the atom bomb. When those agreements expired in 1946, Congress had absolutely refused to renew them. In fact, their intransigence had forced Dad to break off all direct relations with British research in atomic energy. Struggling to avoid giving his home-front critics political ammunition, Dad replied: "No, it doesn't mean that at all. The action against Communist China depends on the action of the United Nations. The military commander in the field will have charge of the use of weapons, as he always has."

Here my father was trying to say that even a UN army had permission to use all the weapons in its arsenal, if its survival was at stake.

None of the reporters tried to pursue these questions beyond the single answer my father gave them. There was no indication that the subject was considered the main theme of the press conference. They again went on to other things and the conference ended with a plea from Dad for the reporters and the nation to understand that "we have exerted every effort possible to prevent a third World War. Every maneuver that has been made since June 25 has had in mind not to create a situation which would cause another terrible war. We are still trying to prevent that war from happening."

The reporters departed and within minutes, the UP began carrying the following bulletin: "PRESIDENT TRUMAN SAID TODAY THE UNITED STATES HAS UNDER CONSIDERATION USE OF THE ATOMIC BOMB IN CONNECTION WITH THE WAR IN KOREA."

The AP was just as bad: "PRESIDENT TRUMAN SAID TODAY ACTIVE CONSIDERATION IS BEING GIVEN TO USE OF THE ATOMIC BOMB AGAINST THE CHINESE COMMUNISTS IF THAT STEP IS NECESSARY."

Only much later in the message did the AP explain the context of Dad's remarks on the atomic bomb and make it clear that they were *not* in the prepared statement which he had made on Chinese intervention, at the beginning of the conference. Charlie Ross hastily summoned reporters to his office and sternly told them that the story's implication—that new consideration of the atomic bomb was in the works, because of the Chinese intervention—was simply not true.

Meanwhile, the AP ticker kept piling distortion on distortion: "HE SAID . . . THE DECISION OF WHETHER TO DROP ATOMIC BOMBS WAS ONE FOR THE COMMANDER IN THE FIELD."

From New York the AP sent orders to its Washington Bureau to jump this to the top of the story. It now read as follows:

> FIRST LEAD TRUMAN KOREA
>
> WASHINGTON, NOVEMBER 30TH—(AP) PRESIDENT TRUMAN SAID TODAY USE OF THE ATOMIC BOMB IN KOREA HAS ALWAYS BEEN UNDER CONSIDERATION—AND WHETHER IT IS USED IS UP TO AMERICAN MILITARY LEADERS IN THE FIELD. . . .

An appalled Charlie Ross hastily put together a clarifying statement—but the damage had been done. The afternoon papers carried huge headlines making it sound as if my father were shipping A-bombs to MacArthur with a carte blanche to use them —the last thing in the world he would have done at such a moment. In Europe the story created an even bigger sensation. Italian papers declared that bombers loaded with atom weapons were ready to take off from Japanese airfields. The *Times of India* ran an editorial under the heading, "NO, NO, NO." London went into the biggest flap. The House of Commons had been debating foreign policy for two days, and Mr. Churchill and other Conservative leaders had been urging Prime Minister Attlee to go to America and confer with my father on Britain's numerous problems. When the news of the atom bomb story reached the House, the left wing of the Labour party immediately circulated a petition, which collected a hundred signatures, declaring that if Attlee supported Dad's supposed atomic intentions, they would bolt the party and bring down the government. A panicked Attlee announced that he would fly to Washington immediately.

It was all ridiculous, and very disheartening. Douglas Cater in his book, *The Fourth Branch of the Government,* about the relationship between the free press and the government, called the handling of this story a journalistic lapse that bordered on "complete irresponsibility."

Naturally, the person on whom this atomic flap took the most terrible toll was Charlie Ross. Inevitably, he felt responsible for his fellow newsmen's lapse. He thought he should have anticipated the question or asked Dad to clarify his remarks before the press conference ended. Charlie had been press secretary for more than five grueling years. "This job is like a prison," he wrote a friend on May 2, 1950. But he added, "The work remains, of course, extraordinarily interesting."

Charlie suffered from severe arthritis, and he also had a bad heart. He was at the top of Dr. Graham's worry list. After he wrote that letter, Charlie and the rest of the White House staff were plunged into the multiple crises of the Korean War. Then came the exhausting trip to Wake Island and the shock of the attempted assassination. Finally, on Monday, December 4, Prime Minister Attlee came hurtling into Washington for a summit conference which only increased the already impossible pressure— especially on Charlie.

The first day of my father's talks with the prime minister made it clear that Mr. Attlee's trip had been unnecessary. There were no real disagreements on any of the world problems they were facing together. But a very garbled account of the first day's meeting was published in a London paper. Several reporters asked Charlie to give them a more factual briefing on what was really being said. The following day Charlie discussed this problem with Dad and got permission to tell the reporters everything that did not endanger our security. After lunch that day aboard the yacht *Williamsburg* with leaders of Congress, Dad and Mr. Attlee spent the afternoon discussing the problem of maintaining the Allied coalition in the United Nations, in the face of the new Chinese aggression. Charlie arrived back at the White House in the early evening and gave forty reporters a detailed account of the day's discussions. He did his usual masterful job. Then he was button-holed by TV newsmen and asked to repeat some of the things he had said for their cameras. Charlie wearily agreed and sat down at his desk, while they set up a microphone on it. His secretary, Myrtle Bergheim, started kidding him, in the usual style of the Truman White House. "Don't mumble," she said.

"You know I always speak very distinctly," Charlie replied.

Suddenly, the cigarette he had just lit fell from his lips. He slumped back in his chair. Miss Bergheim immediately dialed Dr. Graham's number and he sprinted from his office in the main part of the White House. In less than a minute he was giving Charlie oxygen and administering a heart stimulant. But it was too late. "He was gone," Dr. Graham said, "before I got there."

Dad was shattered by the news. It seemed at the time like the last possible thing that could go wrong. He knew better than anyone how totally and unstintingly Charlie had given of himself in his job. Sadly, Dad sat down at his desk and wrote out in longhand a statement which is, I think, one of the most moving things he ever put down on paper.

> The friend of my youth, who became a tower of strength when the responsibilities of high office so unexpectedly fell to me, is gone. To collect one's thoughts to pay tribute to Charles Ross in the face of this tragic dispensation is not easy. I knew him as a boy and as a man. In our high school years together he gave promise of these superb intellectual powers which he attained in after life. Teachers and students alike acclaimed him as the best all-around scholar our school had produced.
>
> His years of preparation were followed by an early maturity of usefulness. In the many roles of life he played his part with

[499]

exalted honor and an honesty of purpose from which he never deviated. To him as a newspaperman truth was ever mighty as he pursued his work from Washington to the capitals of Europe to the far continents.

Here at the White House the scope of his influence extended far beyond his varied and complex and always exacting duties as secretary to the President. He was in charge of press and radio, a field which steadily broadened in recent years with continuous advance in the technique of communications. It was characteristic of Charlie Ross that he was holding a press conference when the summons came. We all knew that he was working far beyond his strength. But he would have it so. He fell at his post, a casualty of his fidelity to duty and his determination that our people should know the truth, and all the truth, in these critical times.

His exacting duties did not end with his work as press secretary. More and more, all of us came to depend on the counsel on questions of high public policy which he could give out of the wealth of his learning, his wisdom and his far-flung experience. Patriotism and integrity, honor and honesty, lofty ideals and nobility of intent were his guides and ordered his life from boyhood onward. He saw life steady and saw it whole. We shall miss him as a public servant and mourn him as a friend.

After the statement was typed, Dad walked down the short corridor to the lounge where the reporters were waiting. They formed a semicircle around him and he began to read the words, "The friend of my youth, who became a tower of—"

He could not go on. "Ah, hell," he said, and threw the typed words down on the table in front of the reporters. "I can't read this thing. You fellows know how I feel anyway."

His head bowed, Dad walked out of the room.

[CHAPTER]

Twenty-Six

I WANDERED into this vortex of grief and crisis. Five hours after Charlie Ross died, I gave the final concert of my 1950 tour at Constitution Hall. Although I was on a warm, first-name basis with all of Dad's aides, I was closest to Charlie. I treated him like an uncle and he treated me like a fresh niece. We were always exchanging wisecracks and friendly insults. From the perspective of his own grief, Dad had decided that I must not be told what had happened until the concert was over. This was easy enough to achieve. When the President of the United States gives an order, there are dozens of people ready to carry it out. It was far different from keeping the news of the attempted assassination from me. Then I was in a distant city, with only a handful of people to protect me from reporters. Dad's order was faithfully obeyed. I went onstage knowing nothing about Charlie's death.

But Dad could not control the reaction of the audience. Charlie Ross was one of the most popular men in Washington. News of his death had spread throughout the city. I was the only one in Constitution Hall who did not know about it. Coming on top of the bad news from Korea and the phony atomic bomb scare, Charlie's death may have made many people in the audience feel it was bad taste for me to be singing at all. At any rate, I soon sensed there was something wrong with their reaction. At the time I blamed it on Korea. I was sure it had nothing to do with the music. In fact, I thought it was one of my better performances.

At intermission, the music critic for the *Times-Herald* came back-stage and congratulated me.

The next day Dad arose at 5 A.M. to grapple once more with the crisis in Korea. He picked up the Washington *Post,* and read a savage review of my performance by the paper's music critic, Paul Hume. "She is flat a good deal of the time," he wrote. "She cannot sing with anything approaching professional finish. . . . She communicates almost nothing of the music she presents."

Dad saw red. For him, *this* was the last straw. His best friend had just died, the world situation was going from bad to awful, and now a critic was attacking his daughter with what seemed to be more malice than judgment. Dad sat down and wrote Mr. Hume a very angry, longhand note. He told him that he sounded like "a frustrated man that never made a success, an eight-ulcer man on a four-ulcer job and all four ulcers working."

Mr. Hume published the note and the uproar was vast. Dad never felt the slightest remorse about sending it. He always insisted that he had a right to be two persons—the President of the United States and Harry S. Truman, father of Margaret, husband of Bess Wallace. "It was Harry S. Truman, the human being, who wrote that note," he said.

A few days later he summed up his stand on his calendar-diary. Notice that he rested his case more on his judgment of my accompanist's performance on the piano. Dad would be the first to admit that he was somewhat prejudiced in my favor. But when it came to a performance on the piano, he was confident that his judgment was as good as any music critic's in the country.

> December 9, 1950
>
> Margie held a concert here in D.C. on December 5th. It was a good one. She was well accompanied by a young pianist named Allison, whose father is a preacher in Augusta, Georgia. Young Allison played two pieces after the intermission, one of which was the great A Flat Chopin Waltz, Opus 42. He did it as well as it could be done and I've heard Paderewski, Moritz Rosenthal and Josef Lhevinne play it.
>
> A frustrated critic on the Washington Post wrote a lousy review. The only thing, General Marshall said, he didn't criticize was the varnish on the piano. He put my baby as low as he could and he made the young accompanist look like a dub.
>
> It upset me and I wrote him what I thought of him. I told

him he was lower than Mr. X and that was intended to be an insult worse than the reflection on his ancestry. I would never reflect on a man's mother, because mothers are not to be attacked, although mine was.

I've been accused of putting my baby, who is the apple of my eye, in a bad position. I don't think that is so. She doesn't either —thank the Almighty.

Dad discussed the letter with his aides and was annoyed to find that they all thought it was a mistake. They felt that it damaged his image as President and would only add to his political difficulties. "Wait till the mail comes in," Dad said, "I'll make you a bet that eighty percent of it is on my side of the argument."

A week later, after a staff meeting, Dad ordered everybody to follow him, and they marched to the mail room. The clerks had stacked the thousands of "Hume" letters received in piles and made up a chart showing the percentages for and against the President. Slightly over 80 percent favored Dad's defense of me. Most of the letter writers were mothers who said they understood exactly how Dad felt and would have expected their husbands to defend their daughters the same way. "The trouble with you guys is," Dad said to the staff as he strode back to work, "you just don't understand human nature."

Meanwhile, Dad was meeting the crisis in Korea with that quiet courage he had displayed in the staff meeting on November 28. First, he coped with the defeatism of Prime Minister Attlee and his aides. They urged an immediate attempt to negotiate with the Chinese Communists. Dad absolutely refused to make such a move when we were in a weak position. Among the things the Communists were likely to demand were Formosa, including Chiang Kai-shek, complete control of Korea, and the right to participate in the Japanese peace treaty. Dad took this stand, even though his Joint Chiefs of Staff had joined MacArthur in massive pessimism, and told Mr. Attlee that they did not think a line could be held in Korea if the Chinese attacked in force. "We did not get into this fight," Dad said, "with the idea of getting licked. We will fight to the finish to stop this aggression. I don't intend to take over military command of the situation in Korea—I leave that up to the generals—but I want to make it perfectly plain that we cannot desert our friends when the going gets rough."

Dad and Secretary of State Acheson also gave Mr. Attlee a lesson in political consistency. They pointed out that the fate of Europe was intimately connected with Korea. We could not follow a policy of appeasement and surrender in Asia, and a policy of resistance and negotiation from strength in Europe. My father also disagreed with the British desire to seat Communist China in the United Nations at this time. It would be rewarding the Chinese for their aggressive, lawless actions in Korea. At that very moment there was a Chinese Communist negotiator at the UN, heaping abuse on the United States for their "aggression" in Korea and Formosa. Dad also rejected a rather unsubtle attempt by Mr. Attlee to win some control over General MacArthur's command. General MacArthur was the theater commander, and he had full charge—including full responsibility—for the conduct of war in his theater within the limitations which the President and the Joint Chiefs of Staff had clearly spelled out to him. Wars could not be run by a committee.

Mr. Attlee went home pledging full support to Dad's determination to stay in Korea—something he had come to Washington without the slightest desire to do. Meanwhile, our UN allies were crumpling in the face of the Chinese Communist propaganda assault. They refused to go along with a resolution condemning Chinese aggression in Korea, and, instead, created an agenda for the General Assembly in which the problem of Formosa took precedence over the problem of Korea. In Congress hysteria was the order of the day. Twenty-four Republican senators joined in a resolution offered by Senator James P. Kem, of Missouri, demanding to be informed about any "secret commitments" my father made to Attlee—a really laughable idea, in the light of the way Dad quietly strong-armed the prime minister into supporting his policy. A majority of the Republicans in the House of Representatives passed a resolution calling for the dismissal of Dean Acheson. General MacArthur was totally exonerated for the disaster that was threatening us in Korea. It was all Mr. Acheson's fault because he was "soft on communism."

Nor was the hysteria confined to Congress. On December 12 Joseph P. Kennedy, known at the time only as the former ambassador to London, issued a call for immediate withdrawal from Korea, Berlin, and Europe. He called American policy "suicidal" and "politically and morally bankrupt." Mr. Kennedy had been prominent among those Democrats advising appeasement of Hitler before World War II. He could be safely ignored, but it was harder for Dad to ignore Herbert Hoover, who issued a long, carefully thought out statement, calling for a new policy to "preserve this Western Hemisphere Gibraltar of Western civilization." In 1944 my father cabled President Roosevelt on the night of their victory, "Isolationism is dead." He was wrong. It had only been lying dormant, waiting for the moment when defeatism and panic gave it a new opportunity to strike at those who were trying to hold the nation steady on its course as leader of the free world.

In his next press conference my father blasted back at the attacks on his Secretary of State.

> How our position in the world would be improved by the retirement of Dean Acheson from public life is beyond me. Mr. Acheson has helped shape and carry out our policy of resistance to Communist imperialism. From the time of our sharing of arms with Greece and Turkey nearly four years ago, and coming down to the recent moment when he advised me to resist the Communist invasion of South Korea, no official in our government has been more alive to communism's threat to freedom or more forceful in resisting it.
>
> At this moment, he is in Brussels representing the United States in setting up a mutual defense against aggression. This has made it possible for me to designate General Eisenhower as Supreme Allied Commander in Europe.
>
> If communism were to prevail in the world—as it shall not prevail—Dean Acheson would be one of the first, if not the first, to be shot by the enemies of liberty. . . .

The comment about General Eisenhower was another, equally dramatic example of Dad's refusal to alter his fundamental policy, in spite of the trouble in Asia. The creation of an integrated European army had been patiently negotiated by Mr. Acheson and his assistants during the previous year. It was the climax to the decision to resist Stalin's aggression in Europe in 1947—a decision that gave Dad those six weeks of worry that he described to me in his letter. He was showing Stalin that, in their duel for world leadership, the United States did not intend to allow a temporary defeat to rattle them. Those last two weeks in December were the days when my father demonstrated the essential strength and potential greatness of the American presidency. The strength of the office lies in its simplicity—the fact that its enormous power is in the hands of a single man. Legislative bodies are notoriously incapable of dealing with periods of crisis. They tend to succumb to the panicky counsels of the timid. The President, as my father has often pointed out, can be as courageous and as great as he and he alone dares to be.

To deal with the panic in Congress, Dad met with congressional leaders of both parties in the Cabinet Room at 10 A.M. on December 13. He brought with him to the meeting the Secretary of State, the Secretary of the Treasury, the Secretary of Defense, and several other members of his Cabinet and White House staff. Carefully and calmly, he read to them top secret CIA reports on probable Russian moves around the world. They were, for instance, fiercely attacking our aid to Greece, Turkey, and Yugoslavia. They had also announced they "would not tolerate" the rearmament of Germany, which had become an essential part of our NATO strategy. The emphasis was on the global view of our security, not the battle in Korea. Only after the congressmen had heard these very sobering facts did Dad ask General Marshall to brief them on the situation in Korea. Speaking with the authority that only he possessed, the Secretary of Defense assured the congressmen that the situation was improving every day. Our army had retreated with very minor losses and was now regrouping with a very good chance of making a firm stand. My father then called on each of the congressional leaders, and all of them agreed that we had to increase our military strength immediately. Most of them favored declaring a national emergency—which was precisely what Dad was considering as his next step.

First, however, he decided to explain the situation to the American people. He went on radio and television at 10:30 P.M. on December 15 and called on everyone to join in a national effort to meet this crisis. "All of us will have to pay more taxes and do without things we like. Think of this, not as a sacrifice, but as an opportunity, an opportunity to defend the best kind of life that men have ever devised on this earth."

He did not flinch from the truth about the Chinese offensive. "As I speak to you tonight, aggression has won a military advantage in Korea. We should not try to hide or explain away that fact."

He called on the American people to shoulder a responsibility greater than any nation has ever borne in the history of the world. The goal was peace, a goal that could only be achieved by cooperating with other free nations and "with the men and women who love freedom everywhere. . . ."

During these harrowing days, my father deeply missed the presence of Arthur Vandenberg in the Senate. Senator Vandenberg may have been a bit difficult at times, but he was a man of vision, a politician who realized that the nation's interests had to be placed before politics. After several operations for cancer he was forced to retire to his home in Grand Rapids, never to return. Dad wrote him a number of touching letters lamenting his absence.

> You just don't realize [he wrote in the spring of 1950] what a vacuum there has been in the Senate and in the operation of our foreign policy since you left. That has always been one of the difficulties in the continuation of policy in our government. . . .
>
> I mentioned you yesterday in a press conference as one of those who could appreciate exactly what the country needs in its foreign relations.
>
> Personally, I am not confining that need to foreign relations alone. It is very seldom that men really become statesmen while they are yet alive, in the minds of the people and their associates. As you well know, I have always held you in that category. Take good care of yourself, and if there is anything I can do to contribute to your welfare and recovery, all you need do is name it.

Meanwhile in Korea, Walton Walker, the commanding general of the Eighth Army, was killed in a jeep accident and General Matthew Ridgway was named to replace him. He arrived in Tokyo on December 25 and within forty-eight hours was in Korea, taking charge. Seldom in American history has there been a more dramatic example of what gifted leadership can accomplish. One of the great combat leaders of his generation, Matthew Ridgway took an army whose confidence had been shaken by retreat and confusion of purpose and within a month restored its fighting spirit. General MacArthur, isolated in his Tokyo headquarters, was unaware of what was happening in the field. He continued to shower Washington with demands for the right to widen the war by bombarding Manchuria and unleashing Chiang.

Early in January, these opinions had to be taken seriously because General Ridgway, under fierce Chinese pressure, was forced to abandon Seoul, the South Korean capital. But he exacted a fearful toll from the Chinese as he fell back, and by mid-January the Chinese "Third Phase Offensive," which was supposed to knock the UN command out of the war, was an obvious failure.

In the midst of this Chinese offensive, and in fact just as it was petering out, the UN went into another political collapse. The General Assembly passed a new peace plan on January 13, 1951, offering Red China admission to the UN and handing over Formosa to her if she would agree to a Korean settlement. We had done everything we could to forestall this vote, but that meant little to the political opposition in Congress. Senator Taft called the offer "the most complete surrender to which the United States has ever agreed." To Dad's immense relief, Red China overplayed her hand. Arrogantly, she demanded immediate admission to the UN and the convening of a peace conference—with the right to continue the fighting. When the Third Phase offensive sputtered out, and the Eighth Army went over to the offensive on January 25, miraculously rigid spines suddenly began appearing in the General Assembly. On February 1 a large majority formally branded Communist China as an aggressor in Korea.

My father, with his knowledge of military history, had foreseen what now began to happen. We had the Chinese at the end of a leaky supply line running 260 miles back to the Yalu. Every foot of this line was being pounded by our airplanes. The Chinese army soon ran short of food, medicine, and ammunition. Typhus, spurred by the brutal Korean winter, seared their ranks. By the end of March, Seoul was recaptured, and the UN army was back on the 38th parallel once more. Behind them lay hundreds of thousands of Chinese corpses. Mao Tse-tung was being taught a very harsh lesson about the rewards of aggression.

Instead of expressing praise and pleasure for General Ridgway's achievements, General MacArthur became more and more contemptuous of the way we were fighting in Korea. He called it "an accordion war," sneering that all we could do was advance until our supply lines became overextended, and then we would be forced to fall back, while the enemy took the offensive until his supply lines were overextended. This was nonsense, and a soldier as experienced as MacArthur must have known it. Our supply lines were hardly vulnerable to the savage assault from the air that we were pouring on the roads and railroads of North Korea.

On January 13 my father wrote General MacArthur a long letter, explaining in the most intimate detail the thinking behind his policy to confine the war to Korea. Seldom has a President taken a theater commander so deeply into his confidence. He pointed out how much we would gain from a successful resistance in Korea. We would deflate—as indeed we did—the political and military prestige of Communist China. We would make possible a far more satisfactory peace settlement for Japan. We would lend urgency to the rapid expansion of the defenses of the Western world. Above all, he explained our need for "great prudence" pending the buildup of our national strength. "Steps which might in themselves be fully justified and which might lend some assistance to the campaign in Korea would not be beneficial if they thereby involved Japan or Western Europe in large-scale hostilities." Dad sent General Collins and General Vandenberg, commanders of the army and air force respectively, to Tokyo to elaborate on this explanation.

On March 15 General MacArthur specifically disobeyed his President's order to refrain from making unauthorized statements on policy to the press. He gave an extensive interview to Hugh Baillie, president of the United Press. He expressed to Baillie the utmost contempt for the decision to stop the Eighth Army's advance at the 38th parallel. "Our mission," he intoned, was "the unification of Korea." Legally, this statement was correct. The UN army was still operating under the UN resolution of October 7, calling for a united Korea. But realistically and diplomatically, the entrance of the Chinese had totally altered the situation, and it was foolish of him to speak out in this way without an iota of concern for the new policy that his President was struggling to form, to meet the new situation.

During these same months my father had many other things on his mind besides General MacArthur. He was engaged in a struggle to persuade Congress to take the final step in his program for the revitalization of Europe's defense. He wanted authorization to add four more American divisions to General Eisenhower's NATO army. This "great debate," as the newspapers called it, soon evolved into a Republican attack on the powers of the presidency. Senator Wherry introduced a resolution requiring prior congressional approval before the President could send troops anywhere. Dad replied that as Commander in Chief he could send the troops without congressional assent, but he was willing and even eager to consult with Congress on the matter.

From his sickbed, Arthur Vandenberg staunchly supported Dad's stand. He pointed out that to transfer any portion of the President's power as Commander in Chief of the Armed Forces would subordinate military decision to the political judgments of Congress. "We partially tried that system in the Civil War when the Committee on the Conduct of the War set a tragic precedent against any such bitter mistake." On January 15 he wrote to Dad:

> Nothing matters in this crisis except the welfare of our country. It calls for the greatest possible meeting of minds in behalf of invincible unity against an aggression which is clearly aimed at us. . . . You may be sure that you have all my prayers in the midst of the indescribably heavy burdens which you are carrying.

On March 6 Dad sent his last message to the senior senator from Michigan, whose health was failing rapidly:

> All of your friends are disturbed by reports that you have not been getting on so well lately. This is just a line to let you know that I am thinking of you and hope you will be back in your old place soon. The country needs you.

For the first time, Senator Vandenberg replied by addressing Dad on a first-name basis:

> My dear Harry: I am deeply touched by your telegram of March 6th. I know it is inspired by longtime personal friendship which you and I enjoyed. It moves me to greet you in this personal way. . . . I have abiding faith in the future of our good old U.S.A. . . .

A month later he was dead of cancer.

Dad won the great debate by skillfully maneuvering his spokesmen within and outside of Congress. Senator Taft and Senator Wherry, the chief exponents of a tie-the-President's-hands point of view, found themselves cut off and enveloped by arguments from Generals Marshall and Bradley, Secretary of State Acheson, and NATO Commander Eisenhower. The final Senate resolution left the President in full possession of all his powers, gave him the four divisions he wanted, but threw the Republicans a bone by agreeing that "no more could be sent, without further Congressional approval."

In Korea, meanwhile, the military situation continued to improve. But General MacArthur continued to deteriorate. He was obsessed, as he makes clear in his memoirs, with the idea of winning the global battle against communism then and there. "It was my belief," he wrote, "that if allowed to use my full military might, without artificial restrictions, I could not only save Korea, but also inflict such a destructive blow upon Red China's capacity to wage aggressive war that it would remove her as a further threat to peace in Asia for generations to come." How he hoped to accomplish this, short of massive atomic attack, he never explained. But this was the background for the thinking which led him step by step to insubordination and finally to outright sabotage of his President's policy.

With the United Nations army firmly entrenched on the 38th parallel and the Chinese Communist army battered to the brink of collapse—in the final stages of the UN offensive they surrendered by the thousands—my father decided it was time to move toward an armistice. He was anxious to end the fighting as swiftly as possible, and he thought the Chinese might feel the same way, now. So, he ordered the State Department to draft a carefully worded proposal. On March 20 General MacArthur was informed of this plan, as he was informed of all other major policy moves, well in advance of their implementation. The message to General MacArthur said in part:

> State Department planning a Presidential announcement shortly that, with clearing of bulk of South Korea of aggressors, United Nations now preparing to discuss conditions of settlement in Korea. United Nations feeling exists that further diplomatic efforts toward settlement should be made without any advance with major forces north of 38th parallel. Time will be

required to determine diplomatic reactions and permit new negotiations that may develop. . . .

My father and State Department officials met for long hours, drafting a statement which would enable the Chinese to negotiate an armistice with a minimum loss of face. They were well aware of the importance of face in the Orient. In the draft of Dad's statement he called on all those involved in Korea to give the Korean people the peace they deserved. He held out the possibility of negotiating on Formosa in another paragraph, which stated that "a prompt settlement of the Korean problem would greatly reduce international tension in the Far East and would open the way for the consideration of other problems in that area by the processes of peaceful settlement envisioned in the Charter of the United Nations."

General MacArthur, as a self-advertised expert on the Oriental mind, certainly knew the importance of face. He also knew the situation of the battered Chinese Communist army. I strongly suspect that he thought Dad's offer would be accepted by the Chinese, after some inevitable huffing and puffing. This prospect did not tie in with the MacArthur presidential program. If there was any negotiating to be done, he wanted to be the man who obtained the concessions from the enemy. At any rate, on March 24 the General issued a statement which made a cease-fire impossible. It opened with a paragraph that scoffed at Red China's vaunted military power and boastfully declared South Korea cleared of organized Communist forces. Communist weakness, he said, was being "brilliantly exploited by our ground forces" and the enemy was "showing less stamina than our own troops under the rigors of climate, terrain and battle."

Then came the crusher, the sentence that destroyed my father's peace negotiations before they even began: "The enemy, therefore, must by now be painfully aware that a decision of the United Nations to depart from its tolerant effort to contain the war to the area of Korea, through an expansion of our military operations to its coastal areas and interior bases, would doom Red China to the risk of imminent military collapse."

Even a nation that cared nothing about face would find it hard to swallow these overbearing remarks. Moreover, they implied our ability to impose humiliation on Red China—something we simply lacked the military strength to do at that time. The hollowness of the General's rhetoric immediately convinced the Chinese that we were insincere about wanting peace. They scornfully rejected MacArthur's ultimatum.

When this statement arrived in Washington, no one could quite believe it. White-lipped, my father summoned Secretary of State Acheson and several other advisers to the White House. First, he dictated a blunt statement to MacArthur, referring to his directive forbidding policy statements. But he was no longer trying to straighten out the General's apocalyptic thinking. As far as Dad was concerned, General MacArthur was dismissed. The only question left for discussion was the matter of timing.

Recalling the situation in later years, Dad said: "Dean Acheson and General Marshall and I decided we should send an ultimatum to the head of the Chinese government for a cease-fire in Korea. We sent the meat paragraphs to MacArthur for approval. Then he sent his own ultimatum to the Chinese. That is what he got fired for. I couldn't send a message to the Chinese after that. He prevented a cease-fire proposition right there. I was ready to kick him into the North China Sea at that time. I was never so put out in my life. It's the lousiest trick a Commander in Chief can have done to him by an underling. MacArthur thought he was the proconsul for the government of the United States and could do as he damned pleased."

As a politician, my father had to consider his programs in Congress. To fire MacArthur immediately would have endangered appropriations for the Marshall Plan and NATO. While Dad bided his time, the General and his political admirers in Congress collaborated on a new and more flagrant act of insubordination. On March 20 the General responded to a letter from Joseph Martin, the Republican minority leader of the House, sending him a speech which was a savage attack on Dad's foreign policy. Congressman Martin had asked for MacArthur's comments, and he got them. After a few sentences which implied that his views on Korea had been ignored by Washington, MacArthur wrote:

> Your view with respect to the utilization of the Chinese forces on Formosa is in conflict with neither logic nor . . . tradition.

[513]

It seems strangely difficult for some to realize that here in Asia is where the Communist conspirators have elected to make their play for global conquest, and that we have joined the issue thus raised on the battlefield; that here we fight Europe's war with arms while the diplomats there still fight it with words; that if we lose the war to Communism in Asia, the fall of Europe is inevitable; win it and Europe most probably would avoid war and yet preserve freedom. As you point out, we must win. There is no substitute for victory.

Congressman Martin read this letter to the House of Representatives on April 5. Headlines blossomed, and my father decided that it was time to act. On his calendar he made the following memorandum:

> MacArthur shoots another political bomb through Joe Martin, leader of the Republican minority in the House.
> This looks like the last straw.
> Rank insubordination. Last summer he sent a long statement to the Vets of Foreign Wars—not through the high command back home, but directly!
> I was furnished a copy from the press room in the White House which had been accidentally sent there.
> I ordered the release suppressed and then sent him a very carefully prepared Directive dated Dec. 5, 1950, setting out Far Eastern policy after I'd flown 4,404 miles to Wake Island to see him and reach an understanding face to face.
> I call in Gen. Marshall, Dean Acheson, Averell Harriman and General Bradley and they come to the conclusion that our Big General in the Far East must be recalled. I don't express any opinion or make known my decision.
> Direct the four to meet again Friday afternoon and go over all phases of the situation.

The following day Dad continued his terse narration:

> We met again this morning—Gen. Marshall, Dean Acheson, Mr. Harriman and Gen. Bradley.
> It is the unanimous opinion of all that MacArthur be relieved. All four so advise.
> I direct that orders be issued, press statement prepared and suggest meeting Monday before the Cabinet meets.

General Marshall's opinion was expressed in pungent terms.

[514]

He had spent the night reading the Defense Department's Mac-Arthur file. "The S.O.B. should have been fired two years ago," he said. On Sunday Dad discussed the situation with Chief Justice Vinson, Sam Rayburn, and Vice President Barkley. He did not, however, tell them that he was thinking of firing General Mac-Arthur.

On April 9 my father resumed his narration:

> Meet the Big Four, Barkley, Rayburn, McFarland, McCormack and explain far eastern situation. Receive comments suggesting certain actions.
>
> Meet with Acheson, Marshall, Bradley and Harriman. Go over recall orders to MacArthur and suggested public statement. Approve both and decide to send the orders to Frank Pace, Sec. of the Army, for delivery to MacArthur and Ridgway. Send message to Korean Ambassador. Message to be sent tomorrow at 8 P.M. our time. It will arrive at 10 A.M. Wednesday in Korea.
>
> Gen. Bradley called about 9 P.M. Said there had been a leak. He, Dean Rusk, Mr. Harriman came to see me. Mr. Murphy was also present.
>
> Discussed the situation and I ordered messages sent at once and directly to MacArthur.

On April 10 he summed up the results in amazingly matter-of-fact terms:

> Quite an explosion. Was expected but I had to act.
> Telegrams and letters of abuse by the dozens.

As a courtesy to General MacArthur, Dad had ordered Secretary of the Army Frank Pace, who was on an inspection tour of Korea, to go to Tokyo and personally hand MacArthur the orders relieving him of his command. But this message failed to reach Secretary Pace, because he was at the front with General Ridgway. The unfortunate leak created quite an emergency in the White House. It was, ironically, not a leak at all. Joe Short, who had taken Charlie Ross's job as press secretary, panicked when a Chicago *Tribune* reporter began asking him bluntly if MacArthur was fired. The panic spread to the rest of the staff and to Dad's top advisers. General Bradley told my father that MacArthur would almost certainly try to outmaneuver him politically by resigning if he heard the news before he was officially notified.

[515]

"He's going to be fired," Dad grimly replied, and he ordered everyone to go to work on a crash program to notify MacArthur immediately. Joe Short, meanwhile, was frantically mimeographing Dad's statement and the background documents. He made a second mistake and refused to call a press conference until these documents were ready, so it was not until 1 A.M. that the groggy White House reporters gathered to hear Dad's official statement which began:

> With deep regret, I have concluded that the General of the Army Douglas MacArthur is unable to give his wholehearted support to the policies of the United States government and of the United Nations in matters pertaining to his official duties. In view of the specific responsibilities imposed upon me by the Constitution of the United States and the added responsibility which has been entrusted to me by the United Nations, I have decided that I must make a change of command in the Far East. I have, therefore, relieved General MacArthur of his commands and have designated Lt. General Matthew B. Ridgway as his successor.

Many of my father's decisions had made headlines before. But nothing compared to the uproar which now ensued. Joe McCarthy sneered that Truman "decided to remove MacArthur when drunk." Richard Nixon demanded the General's immediate reinstatement. Senator William E. Jenner of Indiana roared, "I charge that this country today is in the hands of a secret inner coterie which is directed by agents of the Soviet Union. Our only choice is to impeach President Truman." Dad and Dean Acheson were burned in effigy in numerous towns, and even on a few college campuses. Something very close to mass hysteria gripped the nation. A · Gallup poll reported public opinion in favor of the General over the President, 69 to 29. Joe Martin called General MacArthur, long distance, and invited him to return immediately to Washington to address a joint session of Congress.

General MacArthur, of course, accepted. He enjoyed a triumphant welcome, first in San Francisco, and then in Washington, D.C., where he addressed the Congress. After condemning the Truman Administration's supposed appeasement of communism in Korea, he assured them that he was now going to close his military career and "just fade away, an old soldier who tried to do his duty as God gave him the light to see that duty." A distinguished senator told newspaperman William S. White, not long after the General spoke to Congress, "I honestly felt back there that if the General's speech had gone on, there might have been a march on the White House."

My father foresaw this public reaction. But he also knew from his study of American history that nothing dissipates faster than popular emotion, especially when it is based on lies or lack of information. General MacArthur began to fade away as a political issue soon after a special Senate committee, under the chairmanship of Richard Russell of Georgia, launched a careful investigation of his dismissal.

The General had claimed that the Joint Chiefs of Staff agreed with his policy and implied that only the President's threat of dismissal and disgrace kept them muzzled. But what the senators heard in their committee room was the Joint Chiefs condemning, without the slightest sign of a muzzle, almost every aspect of MacArthur's strategy. General Bradley said that MacArthur's ideas on widening the conflict "would involve us in the wrong war, at the wrong place, at the wrong time and with the wrong enemy." General Vandenberg, chief of the air force, said bombing Manchuria would be no more than "pecking at the periphery" and the losses we would take in planes and men would cripple the air force for years to come. General Collins said that he thought General MacArthur had violated almost every basic rule of military strategy in deploying his troops for the final drive to the Yalu, knowing that the threat of Chinese intervention was very real. Admiral Sherman heaped scorn on MacArthur's proposal of a naval blockade of China, unless the fleets of our allies joined us. Which was not very likely, when one of the ports that would have to be closed was the British crown colony of Hong Kong.

General MacArthur was fond of saying that he had a policy, and President Truman had no policy. But when he testified before Senator Russell's committee, it became quite clear that the shoe was on the other foot. One senator asked him, "Assume we embrace your program, and suppose the Chinese were chased back across the Yalu River, and suppose they then refused to sign a treaty, and to enter into an agreement on what their future course

[517]

will be, what course would you recommend at that stage?" General MacArthur had nothing to recommend. "I don't think they could remain in a state of belligerency," he replied grandly. He had no solution to the problem of maintaining an army across 420 miles of northern Korea, compared to the 110 miles of front we were required to defend along the 38th parallel. He admitted it would be madness to invade Manchuria and begin an all-out war with China's 400 million people. Where did this leave the General's much quoted phrase, "There is no substitute for victory"?

It was Harry S. Truman who had a policy. General MacArthur had nothing more than a collection of disorganized ideas.

Perhaps the man who best summed up the real source of the clash between Dad and General MacArthur was Secretary of Defense George Marshall. It arose, he told the senators,

> from the inherent difference between the position of a commander whose mission is limited to a particular area and a particular antagonist, and the position of the Joint Chiefs of Staff, the Secretary of Defense and the President, who are responsible for the total security of the United States. . . . There is nothing new in this divergence in our military history. What is new and what brought about the necessity for General MacArthur's removal is the wholly unprecedented situation of a local theater commander publicly expressing his displeasure at, and his disagreement with, the foreign policy of the United States.

In his memoirs, General Ridgway concluded:

> It was a boon to the country that the issue did arise and that it was decisively met by the elected head of the government, within the ample dimensions of his own high moral courage and without any pressure from political or military quarters. President Truman's decision should act as a powerful safeguard against the time, in some great future crisis, when perhaps others may be similarly tempted to challenge the right of the President and his advisers to exercise the powers the Constitution grants to them in the formulation of foreign policy.

The controversy over General MacArthur gave the worst elements in the Republican party their chance to confuse the democratic process. Joe McCarthy spewed lies and innuendoes on dozens

[518]

of reputations. He reached a kind of climax on June 14, 1951, when he delivered a 60,000-word speech in the Senate that attacked General George Marshall as a Communist conspirator. For Dad this was the most loathsome of the senator's many slanders. That a man who had devoted his entire life to the service of his country could be smeared as a traitor in the Senate of the United States was almost unbelievable to Dad. In his press conference a few days later, he treated the accusation with a contemptuous "No comment." When it was echoed by other congressmen and some local politicians, Dad called it "one of the silliest things I ever heard. I don't think that it helps the welfare of this nation to have people who are supposed to be responsible for its welfare making silly statements like that."

Although bipartisan foreign policy was dead on the Republican side of the aisle in Congress, it was not dead in the White House. One of my father's first thoughts, when the crisis over General MacArthur's removal confronted him, was the Japanese peace treaty. Even today, with all the grief and turmoil we have endured because of our involvement with Asia, it is evident that Japan, not China, was the real prize in the Far East. Its immense industrial capacity has already returned it to the status of a world power —on our side—while China still lumbers along in the ranks of the semideveloped nations. On the night that General MacArthur was fired, Secretary of State Acheson, on Dad's orders, called John Foster Dulles at 11 P.M. and asked him to come to Mr. Acheson's Georgetown home immediately. Mr. Dulles was told that MacArthur was being fired and the President wanted him to leave immediately for Japan to reassure Japanese leaders that the relief of MacArthur meant no fundamental change in American policy toward Japan.

Some Republican senators advised Mr. Dulles to quit and leave Dad in a hole. But Mr. Dulles had already invested several months in helping to negotiate the Japanese peace treaty and was intelligent enough to see its vital importance to the future security of the free world. To make sure that he did not lose his Republican franchise, he wrote Dad a rather tart memorandum, declaring that he would not be "a fall guy" for the Democrats, and demanding an assurance from the administration that there really was no major change in our Far Eastern policy. Once my father gave him this assurance, he was on his way to Japan. After the treaty was signed, Mr. Dulles was a key witness at the Senate hearings, even persuading such Republican irreconcilables as China Firster William Knowland to vote for it.

Only nine days after Senator McCarthy flung his slander at General Marshall, the first fruits of Dad's Korean policy became visible. Jacob Malik, the Soviet representative to the UN, announced that peace could be negotiated in Korea. Three days later the Chinese government said the same thing. After cautiously considering various alternatives and sounding the seriousness of the Soviet offer through our Embassy in Moscow, my father ordered General Ridgway to broadcast to the Chinese high command a statement that the United Nations would be willing to send representatives to discuss an armistice. The Communists accepted, and truce teams from both sides began negotiating.

My father knew this was only a first step. He had been negotiating with the Communists for almost six years now, and he was well aware that attrition was one of their favorite tactics. They were prepared to lie and bluster and talk endlessly about nothing, hoping in the end that the other side would grow weary and make concessions. It was terribly difficult to communicate this to the American people, who were inclined to think that a negotiation was a prelude to an early peace. When the truce talks droned on, and the fighting continued, the war became more and more divisive.

McCarthyism spread like a virus through the nation. The Sons of the American Revolution, at their annual convention, passed a resolution condemning the UN as a "thoroughly un-American and sinister organization" and called upon the United States to withdraw from it. One past president said: "Joe Stalin could ask for nothing better than the United Nations for taking over our country." Bill Hassett laid a clipping from the Kansas City *Star*, telling the story, on Dad's desk, on July 14, 1951. He replied: "The *Star* clipping which you handed me regarding the Sons of the American Revolution is really an eye-opener. These so-called investigators of un-American activities usually succeed in being more un-American than the people they want investigated."

My father asked Bill Hassett to prepare a letter to the SAR and he did it with alacrity. The draft read as follows:

Sometime back, without my approval or permission, I was voted a member of the Sons of the American Revolution.

I note that your organization desires the withdrawal of the United States from the United Nations. It seems to me that patriots usually are unpatriotic themselves when they make resolutions such as this.

I'll appreciate it most highly if you will strike my name from the rolls because I do not propose to be affiliated with an organization that is doing everything possible to bring on a third world war.

Dad decided this missive would only add to the general uproar, and never sent it.

Henry Wallace was one of those thoughtful Americans who were outraged by the McCarthyist attacks on Dad's foreign policy. On September, 19, 1951, Mr. Wallace wrote Dad a very strong letter, offering to speak out on what really happened at Yalta, and set the record straight. Dad replied in the following letter:

Dear Henry:

I can't tell you how very much I appreciated your good letter of the nineteenth. . . .

Your recollection of the situation in China and the supporting documents prove out the facts as set out in the China White Paper. It is a pity that the Republicans have nothing better to do than try to unearth what they consider to be mistakes of the past. I think the situation was handled as well as it could possibly be under the circumstances and with the facts available.

Thanks a lot for your thoughtfulness in writing me as you did.

My father tried to be philosophical about the abuse he was taking. Earlier in the year, he wrote an interesting letter to Max Lowenthal, his old aide on the Senate Interstate Commerce Committee. Max had drawn an interesting parallel between the eighteenth-century British Parliament's reluctance to support Dutch troops fighting in Belgium against the French with the Senate's inability to understand that our security was now a global problem. Dad replied:

Dear Max:

I certainly did appreciate yours of the fifteenth and I am familiar with that historical incident to which you refer from

[521]

Macaulay, in his History of England. Every effort was made to hamper the Duke of Marlborough and Prince Eugene in their attempt to hold Louis XIV out of the low countries—not only by Louis himself but by Britishers in the Parliament. The pattern is the same today in the Far East.

I received a cartoon the other day from the London Punch which showed a Senator making a speech—"What! Let Hannibal use the elephant on his own initiative?" It is this attitude that kept Hannibal from winning the second Punic War. There are innumerable instances parallel to the one taking place in the Senate.

Jefferson's decision to wipe out Barbary Pirates caused almost as much denunciation as my decision to implement the Atlantic Treaty—so conditions do not change but when all is said and done and history is written people never remember the men who tried to obstruct what was necessary to be done. I don't think anybody ever remembers the names of men who attacked Washington on account of the Jay Treaty, nor do they remember the attackers who vilified Jefferson for making the Louisiana Purchase. They almost brought impeachment against him. The same thing is true of Jackson and his efforts to maintain the Union.

There never was a man as completely vilified as Lincoln when he took the reins in his own hands and called for 75,000 volunteers to meet the secession of the Southern States. The same thing is true of Grover Cleveland in his ultimatum to England over the Venezuela boundary.

You will remember, and I know you can remember all the editorial writers jumping on Wilson for his sending Funston into Vera Cruz and Pershing into northern Mexico. I don't think anybody remembers the attackers any more than they will remember those of the present day.

It is the business of the President to meet situations as they arise and to meet them in the public interest. There are at least 176 instances parallel to what we face today.

I certainly did appreciate your good letter.

Along with his global worries and the war in Korea, my father also fretted about a traveling daughter during the spring and early summer of 1951. I went abroad for six weeks visiting England, France, Holland, Luxembourg, and Italy. I had an absolutely marvelous time, lunching with British and Dutch royalty, spending twenty minutes in private with Pope Pius XII, and, in between, trudging like a typical tourist through cathedrals and palaces. Even the St. Louis newspapers said I did a useful job as a "good will salesman." That really amazed and delighted Dad. Seldom did St. Louis papers say anything good about a Truman.

The high point of my visit was lunch with Winston Churchill at Chartwell, his lovely country home. Mr. Churchill wore an outfit which only he could have carried off with aplomb—one of his wartime siren suits and an American cowboy's ten-gallon hat. He took me on a tour of his gardens and fish ponds, discussing fish, shrubs, and other living things with so much affection and knowledge you almost thought they were people. At the fish pond he sat down on a stool, took some bread crumbs out of his pocket, and said something that sounded like "Hike. Hike. Hike." The fish immediately swam to him and took the crumbs he had thrown in the pond.

At the end of our lunch Mr. Churchill announced that he had a painting which he wanted me to take back to Mother and Dad, as a present. "I'll be glad to," I said, "if you put my name on it so that eventually it will be mine."

The great man was caught off guard. He harrumphed and wondered if I ought to talk to my father before he did a thing like that. "Just put my name on it," I said. "I can handle him."

Mr. Churchill's two daughters, Sarah, who was my friend, and Mary and her husband, Christopher Soames, were part of the luncheon party. They watched open-mouthed while he capitulated and put my name on the painting, which was a lovely view of his favorite North African landscape, around Marrakech.

Only later did Sarah tell me that I was the first person who had accomplished the feat of extracting one of his paintings from him. Not even the members of the family had been able to manage it.

In Holland I had to practice a little polite diplomacy. Queen Juliana remarked that they were looking forward to a visit to the United States, which seemed, in her mind, to be imminent. I had to think very fast and assure her that we would be delighted to see her in the new White House—which was not yet finished.

On June 19 Dad wrote me the following letter, expressing his pleasure with this response, as well as other aspects of my trip:

> Your postscript from The Hague came yesterday in the pouch but the letter to which it is a postscript has not arrived! I guess

the letter will come today. You handled the conversation with the Queen of Holland about the proposed visit of herself and the Prince Consort perfectly. I'm hoping they'll wait until we are settled in the rehabilitated White House before they come.

I sent you a copy of this week's Life by Mr. Harriman. Mr. Luce seems to have given you a fair shake—but wait it won't last. Your press over here has been excellent. You are making a great ambassador of good will. . . .

The President of Ecuador comes to town tomorrow for the usual round, tea at 4:00 P.M., dinner at 8 at the Carlton and his dinner at the Statler on Friday. Then he'll tell me what he wants, go to N.Y. and then back home. I hope we can get him home safely. I'm always worried when these heads of States come to town until they are safely at home again.

Congress is acting up terribly. No appropriations to date. Democrats acting perfect demagogues. Republicans acting as usual. They are about to sabotage my whole five year peace plan but I guess we'll survive it.

Toward the end of 1951 the picture in Korea began to brighten dramatically. The Communists had finally realized we were not going to be pushovers at the conference table. General Ridgway and his field commander, General James A. Van Fleet, had carved out a solid line across the peninsula, including a sizable hunk of North Korea which made the 38th parallel militarily defensible for the first time. We gave away a small hunk of South Korea, at the other end of the line. We made it clear to the Communists that we were not interested in withdrawing to the literal 38th parallel, thereby surrendering all the crucial high ground from which South Korea could repel an invader. After much screaming, the Communists yielded to our insistence on this point. A supervisory truce team composed of neutral nations was finally worked out. Only one point remained to be decided, the exchange of prisoners.

We had 132,000 Chinese and North Korean prisoners. Under strict instructions from Dad, our negotiators proposed that all prisoners of war who wished to be returned should be exchanged. He was keenly aware that two million people had fled from North Korea into South Korea when the Communists took power there. Grimly, my father declared: "We will not buy an armistice by turning over human beings for slaughter or slavery." For the

[524]

Communists, propaganda victories were as important as military victories. When they found out that 60,000 of the 132,000 did not want to return to Communist territory, they became enraged and refused to sign the truce agreement. If Dad had given way on this point, he could have ended the Korean War well before the 1952 elections. But I think by now it must be clear to you that Harry Truman never surrendered a principle to gain a political advantage. Although it grieved him that the fighting continued and American soldiers were still dying on Korea's barren hills, he would not waver from his stand, all through the year 1952.

Personally, the most trying part of the Korean War for Dad was the numerous ceremonies for Medal of Honor winners, or their survivors. He frequently told the men who won them, "I would rather wear this medal than be President of the United States."

He scolded himself for this weakness early in 1951. Typically, it was on a day when he should have been enormously proud of himself.

> Received the Woodrow Wilson Award today. A wonderful medal with a great citation on the back. Mrs. McAdoo, Mr. Sayre, and other highest of the high hats present. It was quite a ceremony. Did not deserve it but that is the case in most awards. But not in those Congressional Medals of Honor I awarded yesterday to the survivors of five Korean heroes. Hope I will not have to do that again. I am a damned sentimentalist and I could hardly hold my voice steady when I gave a medal to a widow or a father for heroism in action. It was similar to giving citations to the men who were shot protecting me at the Blair House— and I choked up just as I did then. What an old fool I am!

[CHAPTER]

Twenty-Seven

ONLY A FEW DAYS AFTER my father began his second term, General Vaughan asked him: "Are you going to run for reelection in 1952?"

Dad looked up at him in complete astonishment. "Have you lost your mind?" he asked.

The next twelve months did not change his thinking. On April 16, 1950, he wrote himself one of his most important memoranda:

> I am not a candidate for nomination by the Democratic Convention.
>
> My first election to public office took place in November, 1922. I served two years in the armed forces in World War I, ten years in the Senate, two months and twenty days as Vice President and President of the Senate. I have been in public office well over thirty years, having been President of the United States almost two complete terms.
>
> Washington, Jefferson, Monroe, Madison, Andrew Jackson and Woodrow Wilson, as well as Calvin Coolidge, stood by the precedent of two terms. Only Grant, Theodore Roosevelt and FDR made the attempt to break that precedent. FDR succeeded.
>
> In my opinion, eight years as President is enough and sometimes too much for any man to serve in that capacity.
>
> There is a lure in power. It can get into a man's blood just as gambling and lust for money have been known to do.
>
> This is a republic. The greatest in the history of the world. I want this country to continue as a republic. Cincinnatus and

Washington pointed the way. When Rome forgot Cincinnatus, its downfall began. When we forget the examples of such men as Washington, Jefferson, and Andrew Jackson, all of whom could have had a continuation in the office, then will we start down the road to dictatorship and ruin. I know I could be elected again and continue to break the old precedent as it was broken by FDR. It should not be done. That precedent should continue not by a constitutional amendment, but by custom based on the honor of the man in the office.

Therefore, to reestablish that custom, although by a quibble I could say I've only had one term, I am not a candidate and will not accept the nomination for another term.

On November 19, 1951, while Dad was vacationing at Key West, he took this memorandum out and read it to his staff. He wanted to let them know his decision, he said, so they would have plenty of time to plan ahead on their careers. However, he made it clear that he had no intention of making the announcement public for some time. It was a tremendous tribute to the loyalty Dad's staff felt for him, that the secret, one of the hottest in the history of the presidency, was kept for almost six months. Bill Hassett said it was "one of the most amazing things I recall from all my years in Washington."

That night at Key West the conversation immediately turned to the problem of selecting a Democratic nominee for 1952. Just before Dad made his announcement, Adlai Stevenson's name had come up in the conversation. Dad proceeded to express himself very bluntly on him as a candidate. He said that he hoped the Democratic party "would be smart enough to select someone who could win. And by that I *don't* mean the Stevenson type of candidate. I don't believe the people of the United States are ready for an Ivy Leaguer."

The talk then veered to the man who my father had always hoped would succeed him—Chief Justice Fred Vinson. But Dad had recently had a long talk with "Papa Vin" and had been unable to persuade him to run. He had two very good reasons. He hesitated to embroil the Supreme Court in politics. Neither he nor his wife felt his health was strong enough to enable him to sustain a grueling presidential campaign.

Beyond Chief Justice Vinson, my father and his aides faced the rather grim fact that there weren't very many prospective Democratic candidates. Alben Barkley wanted to be President, but he was too old. Estes Kefauver, the junior senator from Tennessee, had a virulent case of White House fever, but Dad considered him a lightweight. He had also alienated most of the big city Democratic leaders with his traveling television circus in 1950, which seemed to specialize in exposing crime and corruption in cities where Democrats were in the majority. Averell Harriman was capable of doing the job, and he wanted it, but he had never campaigned for political office. He could muster only nominal support from Democrats in his home state of New York.

Then, on January 6, 1952, came a shock from abroad. General of the Armies Dwight Eisenhower announced from his NATO headquarters that he was ready to accept a call to "duty" higher than his present responsibilities.

My father had sensed for some time that Ike was thinking of running for office. When he made one of his periodic visits to Washington early in November, 1951, to report on NATO, he had aroused intense political discussion. Ike commented wryly on the hubbub as another "great debate," and Dad replied, "I'm not interested in that. You can see anybody you want to and do anything you want to while you are here."

This remark should *not* be interpreted as endorsing Ike for President. At no time did my father ever look favorably on this idea. One version of the story that Dad offered to endorse Ike has him doing it in 1945, in Germany. Neither Dad nor anyone who was with him at that time recalls such a statement. However, General Harry Vaughan does remember a 1946 luncheon at the Pentagon at which Ike entertained Dad, Charlie Ross, Clark Clifford, himself, and a few other aides. There was a good deal of lighthearted banter around the table about army politics and civilian politics. In the course of it, Dad jokingly said to Ike: "General, if you ever decide you want to get into politics, you come to me and I'll sure endorse you."

No one took it very seriously. Certainly my father did not take it seriously. In fact, he came to regard references to Ike as a savior figure with considerable amusement. One day in August, 1950, the White House received a telegram which read: "May I urge you to suggest to President Truman that he name General Dwight

[528]

Eisenhower as assistant commander in chief of our armed forces."
Harry Vaughan put it on Dad's desk, and Dad scribbled on it,
"In a terrible quandary over this!"

Even if my father had known that Ike was planning to become
a candidate, he would still have chosen him for supreme commander in Europe. He was the right man for the job. Also, Ike
was humble to the point of obsequiousness in admitting how
strongly he approved of Dad's foreign policy. In the November,
1951, meeting at the White House, he told Dad and ten or twelve
other members of the Cabinet and staff that when he went to
Europe in February, 1951, he thought the idea of a European
defense force was "as cockeyed an idea as a dope fiend could have
figured out. I went over completely hostile to it," he said. "But
now," he went on, "I've shifted."

Even before that remark, Ike had made a habit of flattering
my father. After the 1948 election, he wrote a letter which was
almost too thick for Dad's taste. "You don't have to reaffirm your
loyalty to me," Dad wrote back. "I always know exactly where
you stand."

In July, 1949, Ike wrote another letter, in which he commented
on some stamps which the Post Office was designing for him. He
remarked that Dad no doubt would be around to make the final
decision on them. Dad replied:

> I certainly do appreciate your belief that I'll be able to decide
> on the postage stamps for 1954. As you know, that is two years
> beyond the end of this term, and, of course, I haven't made up
> my mind yet whether to quit or go ahead and be sure these
> stamps are gotten out for you. I rather think this is going a little
> bit far in the future though, and, in all probability, it would be
> better to take the matter up with the then Postmaster General
> a few months before the 1954 budget goes into effect.

Even after the General all but announced his candidacy in
January, my father still felt that Ike was on his side in the area
that mattered most, foreign policy. On January 31, 1952, he wrote
the following letter to him:

> Dear Ike:
> I certainly appreciated your good letter of the twenty-third.
> You can rest assured that no matter what the professional liars

[529]

and the pathological columnists may have to say, you and I understand each other.

I certainly hope that Lisbon meeting [of NATO] will turn out all right. . . . I think we are approaching a condition in world affairs where we can become powerful enough to ward off a third world war, if we continue the Foreign Policy which we have been pursuing. I think you understand it as thoroughly and completely as I do.

I hope everything is going well with you and that it will continue to go just that way. Please remember me to Mrs. Eisenhower.

As long as Senator Robert Taft had seemed to be the probable Republican candidate, my father thought any Democrat with a decent record could win. The emergence of Ike made Dad feel urgent about finding a Democratic candidate, early in 1952. The more he thought about it, the more he became convinced—somewhat reluctantly—that Adlai Stevenson of Illinois was the man. One of the White House aides, Dave Lloyd, had worked with Stevenson in the State Department and was constantly singing his praises. My father finally told Charlie Murphy to call Governor Stevenson and ask him to come to Washington for a talk.

Charlie and Dave Lloyd met Mr. Stevenson at George Ball's office, late in the afternoon of the day he arrived in Washington. They told him why the President wanted to see him, and Stevenson voiced great reluctance about running. Charlie Murphy went directly to the White House and told Dad what Governor Stevenson had said. A President never likes to be confronted by the unexpected, if he can avoid it.

About eight o'clock that night, Governor Stevenson came to Blair House and talked with my father for over an hour. In a memorandum he made later about their conversation, Dad wrote:

I told him what I thought the Presidency is, how it has grown into the most powerful and the greatest office in the history of the world. I asked him to take it and I told him if he would agree he could be nominated. I told him that a President in the White House always controlled the National Convention.

Mr. Stevenson talked all around the subject in his charming, intellectual way. By the time they parted, he had created total confusion, not only in his own mind, but in Dad's mind. The next

[530]

morning, when Charlie Murphy asked my father what Governor Stevenson's answer had been, Dad replied: "Well, he was a little reluctant, but he finally said yes." Only a few days later Mr. Murphy was astonished to learn that Mr. Stevenson was telling all his friends, including at least one prominent Washington newspaperman, that he had said no.

"This," Charlie Murphy says with masterful understatement, "was not a situation that you could live with." He arranged to meet Governor Stevenson for dinner at George Ball's house. They argued with Stevenson all evening but could not persuade him to say yes. "We left without any answer," Charlie says, "but at least we had gotten to the point that he understood now he hadn't said no."

Some weeks later Governor Stevenson wrote Mr. Murphy a very long letter, explaining why he did not feel he could be the candidate. The sad truth is that Mr. Stevenson was rather favorably inclined toward General Eisenhower and, like many liberals, even felt that perhaps it was time for a change of parties. My father, with his far greater knowledge of national politics, feared with good reason that the General would be totally unable to cope with the reactionaries in the Republican party and would become the captive of Senator Taft and his friends.

Another reason for Mr. Stevenson's reluctance became apparent later in the year. He did not want to be Harry S. Truman's hand-picked candidate. Mr. Stevenson had apparently been disheartened by an outbreak of corruption on the lower levels of Dad's administration. He seemed to feel that the President had been tainted with the weakness displayed by Internal Revenue collectors and a few wheeler-dealers in the Reconstruction Finance Corporation. He was unimpressed by the fact that many of the Internal Revenue collectors had been caught and fired before the Republicans in Congress ever began screaming about them, or by the complete overhaul of the RFC my father ordered as soon as signs of corruption were detected there. An assistant attorney general, T. LaMar Caudle, who was more naïve than corrupt, was fired the moment his dubious dealings with tax fixers came to light. When Howard McGrath, the Attorney General, attempted to defend Caudle, he too was fired. No sensible person can expect a President to do more than act swiftly and forthrightly when he finds this kind of unpleasantness in his administration.

To my father, who had passed through the corruption of the Pendergast machine without a single taint of it adhering to him personally, Governor Stevenson's attitude was simply incredible. Fortunately, at this time he was not aware that Mr. Stevenson held this opinion. Early in March, when the governor was in Washington again, he came to the White House and told my father that he had decided not to run because he was committed to a second term in the Illinois State House. "He did not think he could go back on that commitment honorably," Dad said.

By playing reluctant hero and attempting to maneuver the party into drafting him, Mr. Stevenson forfeited a crucial dimension of his candidacy. My father had planned to throw behind him all the resources of the Democratic party and the presidency, to build him into a national figure well before the election.

Meanwhile, Dad was left without a candidate. For a few weeks he reconsidered his decision not to run again. First, he had a small dinner at Blair House, with only a few of his closest advisers, such as Fred Vinson and Charlie Murphy. Later, he convened a larger meeting, which included the whole White House staff as well as several congressional leaders. At this meeting he polled the entire room—a dozen or more—and asked each man what he thought. Although they gave varying reasons, not one of them thought he should run again.

Mother felt the same way. So did I. Mother's opinion carried a lot more weight than mine, of course. Dad decided that the verdict seemed to be unanimous.

On March 29, 1952, my father was the chief speaker at the Jefferson-Jackson Day dinner in the Washington Armory. It was one of the biggest dinners in the history of the Democratic party— 5,300 people contributed a hundred dollars each, to raise over half a million dollars for the Democratic National Committee treasury. Dad gave one of his best speeches. He ridiculed the "dinosaur school of Republican strategy" which wanted to go back to "prehistoric times." Entwined in this sarcasm was a serious plea for a bipartisan foreign policy:

> Some Republicans seem to think it would be popular to pull out of Korea, and to abandon Europe, and to let the United

Nations go smash. They read it this way: "The American people aren't very bright. Let's tell them they don't have to build up defenses, serve in the army, or strengthen our allies overseas. If they fall for that, then we Republicans will be in—and that's all that matters."

Dad warned the Democrats that the Republican campaign would not be fought on the issues. They were going to wage a campaign of "phony propaganda" with Senator McCarthy as their real spokesman. "They are going to try what we might call the 'white is black' and the 'black is white' strategy." Another branch of this strategy, Dad said, was their smear that the government was full of grafters and thieves and all kinds of assorted crooks:

> Now I want to say something very important to you about this issue of morality in government. I stand for honest government. I have worked for it. I have probably done more for it than any other President. I have done more than any other President to reorganize the government on an efficient basis, and to extend the Civil Service merit system. I hate corruption not only because it is bad in itself, but also because it is the deadly enemy of all the things the Democratic Party has been doing all these years. I hate corruption everywhere, but I hate it most of all in a Democratic officeholder, because that is a betrayal of all that the Democratic Party stands for.

My father then summed up the Democratic party's record of service to the farmer, the worker, and world peace. Finally came the fateful words:

> Whoever the Democrats nominate for President this year, he will have this record to run upon. I shall not be a candidate for reelection. I have served my country long, and I think efficiently and honestly. I shall not accept a renomination. I do not feel that it is my duty to spend another four years in the White House.

Everyone not in on the secret was utterly astonished. There were cries of "no, no" from the audience. Photographers rushed from one end of the head table, where Dad was speaking, to the other end, where Adlai Stevenson was sitting. Even then, in spite of his non-candidacy, he was the front runner.

Meanwhile, my father continued to run the government of the

[533]

United States. In the months immediately following his announcement, he made two of his most controversial decisions.

Late in March it became clear to the President and the rest of the country that a steel strike was threatening to cripple our economy in the middle of a war. The Wage Stabilization Board had recommended giving the Steelworkers Union a boost of 26.4 cents an hour. The companies had arrogantly refused to bargain with the union, and they now insisted, with even more arrogance, that they would not grant the increase unless they were permitted to add $12 a ton to the price of steel. My father considered this nothing less than profiteering and refused to go along, even when his Director of Defense Mobilization, Charles E. Wilson, resigned over his stand. On April 7 the unions announced they were going out on strike. The lives of our men in Korea were threatened, and our NATO buildup in Europe would be fatally undermined by a long strike. Dad acted promptly out of his conviction that the nation was faced with an immense emergency. He issued Executive Order 10340 to seize the steel mills.

The following day he asked Congress for legislation which would give him the power he needed to operate the mills. Congress refused to act, and the steel companies took the government to court. Federal Judge David Pines ruled that Order 10340 was unconstitutional. Although the judge received a lot of publicity for supposedly defying the President, the man he really slapped down was the government attorney who handled the case. He was lamentably inept. "Our position is that there is no power in the courts to restrain the President," he declared. This was practically an open invitation for the judiciary to assert its power as the third—and coequal—branch of the government.

Within another week the Supreme Court announced it would hear the case. On June 2, 1952, the Court ruled, six to three, that the President had exceeded his constitutional powers. It was one of the strangest decisions in the Court's history. Each of the majority judges wrote separate opinions, since they could not agree on any fundamental reason why the seizure of the mills was unconstitutional. The arguments of the government's witnesses, Secretary of Defense Robert Lovett, Secretary of Interior Oscar Chapman, and others, that a national emergency existed, were ignored. Chief Justice Vinson dissented vigorously from the majority, and expressed grave dissatisfaction with "the complete disregard of the uncontroverted fact showing the gravity of the emergency and the temporary nature" of the seizure.

The most painful part of this episode was the attacks made on my father by some members of the press, and by the public relations men of the steel companies. He was accused of plotting to seize the nation's newspapers and radio stations, and set up a dictatorship. The steel companies filled newspapers and magazines with ads picturing the battle as the test of whether our free enterprise system will survive. For someone who had spent much of his time in public office attempting to prevent the greedy members of the business community from destroying free enterprise, this was hard to take. Even more galling was the talk of dictatorship to a man who revered the office of the presidency and the Constitution of the United States as deeply as Dad has revered them, from boyhood.

My father's second decision concerned the disposition of the offshore oil resources of the nation. Senator Pat McCarran of Nevada had introduced a resolution which attempted to convey to three states the rights to $100 billion worth of oil. Even before the bill reached Dad's desk, he announced, "I intend to stand up and fight to protect the people's interest in this matter." On May 29, 1952, he vetoed the bill. In his message he pointed out that during his first months as President, he had issued an Executive Order claiming federal jurisdiction over all the mineral resources of the continental shelf, which extends 150 miles or more off the coast of our country.

Even the traditional three-mile limit could not be claimed by the states, Dad noted, because the rights to these lands were obtained by the federal government through a letter which Secretary of State Thomas Jefferson had written in 1793. Scathingly, Dad condemned this "free gift of immensely valuable resources which belong to the entire nation, to the states which happen to be located nearest to them." The political repercussions, in Texas particularly, were grim. Many leading Democrats openly bolted the party. But my father never wavered from his conviction that he had acted rightly on behalf of all the people by refusing to kowtow to a minority of oil barons.

By now, the political campaign was really heating up. General Eisenhower asked permission to resign from NATO and become a candidate. My father brought him home immediately. I will not be so naïve as to claim that Harry S. Truman, the quintessential Democrat, did not begin to regard Ike with a slightly jaundiced eye, from the moment he announced he was a Republican. Nevertheless, I think a conversation, on which Dad made notes several weeks after Ike had come to the White House to give the President his last report on NATO, is worthy of some historical interest.

They got into a discussion of Point Four, and Ike made it clear that he thought very little of the program. What did he think was the answer to the world's economic problems? Dad asked.

"Birth control," Ike said.

"Do me a favor," Dad said.

"I'll be glad to, if I can," Ike said.

"Go make a speech on birth control in Boston, Brooklyn, Detroit and Chicago."

These were, of course, strongholds of the Catholic Church, and in 1952 any politician who made such a speech in any one of these places would be committing instant suicide.

Ike did not get the point at all. "He is not as intelligent as I thought," Dad wrote. "Evidently his staff has furnished the intelligence."

As they parted, Ike expressed considerable resentment over some rather nasty comments which certain segments of the press had already begun making about his candidacy. The General had thought that he was going to get the Republican nomination on a platter. But Senator Taft had other ideas, and Ike found himself in the middle of a dogfight for delegates. Senator Taft had plenty of newspaper support, and Ike suddenly had become the target of numerous uncomplimentary remarks. Dad grinned. "Ike," he said, "I suggest you go right down to the office of the Republican National Committee and ask them to equip you with an elephant hide about an inch thick. You're going to need it."

Meanwhile, the President's wandering daughter took off again. With my best friend Drucie Snyder Horton for company, I headed for Europe aboard the S.S. *United States* on her maiden voyage. My trip during the previous summer was "official"—which meant that I had to stay at embassies and consulates. This time I insisted on making it as unofficial as a President's daughter can manage it. I still had Secret Service men on my trail and there would, I knew, be receptions and welcomes wherever we went. But otherwise we would be relatively free agents.

Dad was just a little worried about having me and Drucie on the loose in Europe. Even now, we tend to get a little giddy when we are together, and we were much more adept at being silly when we were in our twenties. To make sure everything went well, I was ordered to report to the State Department to pick up my passport from no less than Dean Acheson. He had obviously been told to give me a little lecture on how to behave, lest the dignity of the United States be impaired. "Now remember, don't upset any apple carts," he said, pointing those formidable eyebrows at me.

In the same spirit I told him that I would behave myself according to *my* understanding of the word. "If that's not good enough for you, that's too bad," I said.

This did not exactly reassure the Secretary of State. Our session down at Foggy Bottom that day explains the touch of acid humor in our relationship which persisted until his death.

While I was in London, I got an amusing letter from Mother. She was very put out by a silly newspaper story that her grandfather's relatives were waiting to greet me in Ireland. The story claimed that Grandfather Wallace had been born there.

> The White House,
> July 4, 1952
> (It seems like Sunday
> with Dad at home)

Dear Marg—

Fred Vinson and Dad and I are going to the baseball game this afternoon. Double header! I haven't seen one in years. "Mama" Vinson said she wouldn't sit on a hard seat that long.

The thing about your grandfather Wallace being born in Ireland is popping up again and I want it settled, once and for all. You will probably have an excellent opportunity to do it in Dublin at a press conference. His name was David Willock Wallace and he was born in *Independence, Mo.* His father was Benjamin Franklin Wallace and *he* was born in Green County, Ky. There has never been a "Robert" (as quoted in the papers) in the entire family history. The current story is that I am the daughter of "Robert" and that he still lives somewhere in Ireland. I'm sick and tired of it. . . .

> Mother

Note that Mother is writing from the White House. We finally moved back into the Great White Jail in the spring of 1952. Dad was in the middle of coping with the steel strike and had very little time to enjoy the round of parties and receptions which began immediately after we moved in. As a housekeeper, Mother thoroughly enjoyed her new surroundings. The place was painted and papered and decorated down to the most minute details. Personally, I found it more hotel-like than ever.

The first part of the European trip was a delight. We had lunch with Queen Elizabeth and the Duke of Edinburgh in Buckingham Palace, toured Ireland and Scotland, oohed at a Dior showing in Paris, aahed up the Grindelwald in Switzerland, heard *The Marriage of Figaro* in Salzburg, and penetrated the Iron Curtain to tour Berlin. I wanted to see Potsdam, but I was sadly informed that it was out of the question. It was in Communist territory, and the cold war was very frigid at that point.

We left Berlin at night on the so-called HiCog (for High Commissioner of Germany) train. I noticed that our official escort, Sam Rieber, the deputy high commissioner for Germany, was very nervous. He was smoking cigarettes by the pack. At 2 A.M. Drucie and I were still sitting up, talking, when the train came to a grinding halt. Suddenly it was surrounded by Russian soldiers. Sam Rieber turned pale. He later admitted that he worried a year off his life that night. But the Russians turned out to have no interest in anything as spectacular as kidnapping the President's daughter. They were just playing their old game of harassment on the Berlin railroad. Unwittingly, they did us a favor. They had stopped the train in the suburbs of Potsdam, and from our windows we could see the moonlit walls and roof of the Cecilienhof Palace where my father had met with Marshal Stalin and Mr. Churchill.

Everything about our trip was idyllic, until we arrived in Sweden. There I discovered that all the angry things that Dad said about the hostile American press were mere understatements compared to the fabrications which the Swedish press began to concoct. First, there was a rumor that I was in love with Governor Adlai Stevenson. I denied this emphatically. Next the Swedish reporters went from imaginary gossip to fabrication of a nonexistent incident. I returned from a tour of City Hall to discover that three of the most important papers in Stockholm were carrying a vivid tale of how my Secret Service agents had "roughed up" newsmen and photographers who wanted to take a picture of me. The story was replete with sneering remarks, such as "Miss Truman is in no danger of her life here—if she does not plan to sing!"

All this was intensely irritating, but what really infuriated me was the reaction of our ambassador, W. Walton Butterworth, and his fellow diplomats in the American Embassy. Instead of categorically denying the story, they proceeded to attempt to back up the Swedish accusation and practically draw up an indictment of my Secret Service men.

I waited ten days to write a letter to Dad, hoping I would calm down a little. But the one I wrote was still a scorcher. I told him how Mr. Butterworth began apologizing to the Swedish Foreign Office and anyone else who would listen, without even bothering to ask me about the so-called incident.

> He had the chance to stop the editorial in the first place, but when the editor realized Butterworth was so dense, he saw a chance to embarrass the United States and the man running for reelection as Prime Minister. It's funny because the P.M. is not particularly pro-Russian and the two things don't go together. The press man at the embassy was also totally inadequate. Fortunately, the Secret Service boys kept their heads or it would have been much worse. Butterworth wanted them to apologize, which would have been ridiculous. . . . I hate to bother you with this but I have never seen firsthand before a man in high position try to put the blame on the little man who couldn't fight back, namely the Secret Service boys.

To my amazement, when I returned home I discovered that Secretary of State Acheson and everyone else in the State Department staunchly defended Ambassador Butterworth's behavior. For the first time I got a look at how closely they stick together down in Foggy Bottom. It made me understand why my father never stopped wishing that someone would shake up the State Department.

One mission I did accomplish successfully for Dad was to bring home from England a bottle of Truman's beer. Dad often teased Cousin Ethel, our family historian, about the fact that Truman's Beer and Ale is one of the biggest and best-known breweries in England. Cousin Ethel always winced every time she heard the family name associated with the liquor business. The next time

Dad went home to Independence, he strolled over to the Noland house and gave Cousin Ethel this sample of the handiwork of the English Trumans. Obviously Dad never forgot one of Mamma Truman's favorite sayings, "Being too good is apt to be uninter-esting."

I ended my letter from Sweden with some advice Dad didn't need. "Give it to 'em on September 1st and show everybody who's still on top and in control of the situation."

By this time the presidential campaign was on its way. The Republicans did exactly what Dad predicted they would do in his Jefferson-Jackson Day speech. They abandoned bipartisanship in foreign policy completely and conjured up the black-is-white story that "Korea was born at Yalta." General MacArthur gave the key-note address at their convention, predictably blaming the Democrats for everything in sight. Herbert Hoover cried out against "our bewildered statesmanship" and John Foster Dulles declared, in the foreign policy plank of the Republican platform, that the Democrats had "lost the peace." Dad was blamed for allowing Russia to absorb Latvia, Lithuania, Estonia, Poland, Czechoslovakia, and China. For a final whopper, Mr. Dulles, the negotiator of the Japanese treaty and a constant companion of Democratic officials in the State Department declared, "In the main, the Republican party has been ignored and its participation not even invited." Arthur Vandenberg must have spun in his grave on that one.

Dad was not in the least surprised by Mr. Dulles's political tactics. At one point during 1948, Mr. Dulles returned home from a conference with the Russians in Paris and did not even bother to pay a courtesy call at the White House. Instead he went directly to Albany to report to the man he thought was going to be the next President—Thomas E. Dewey. Not a few of Dad's aides were outraged by this snub and urged him to fire Mr. Dulles forthwith. But Dad felt that his foreign policy was more important than his personal pride, and he passed over the insult in silence.

He got a modicum of revenge in 1949, when Mr. Dulles ran against Herbert Lehman in an off-year election for the seat of the late Senator Robert Wagner. Mr. Dulles paid a call on Dad before the campaign began, and they got into a friendly discussion of who was going to win the election. Dad told him that he thought Senator Lehman would win because he knew how to talk to the average man in New York. "You'll get off on a high international plane," Dad said joshingly. "You've been making millions for the big fellows so long you don't know what people really think or what they're like." (Mr. Dulles had been a very successful Wall Street lawyer.)

He declined to take Dad's advice and campaigned precisely as Dad had predicted he would—making large oracular statements à la his mentor, Mr. Dewey. Mr. Lehman trounced him easily. The following day, Dad got a telegram that read: "YOU WIN. JOHN FOSTER DULLES."

Among the Republican campaign promises in 1952 were even bigger whoppers than the speechmakers told at their convention. They said they would repudiate the Yalta agreements and secure the "genuine independence" of peoples who had become Communist captives. How silly these claims look in the light of twenty years of history.

One of the stars of the Republican convention was Senator Joe McCarthy, who was introduced as "Wisconsin's fighting Marine." Ike should have seen the trouble that was coming his way when Joe called Douglas MacArthur "the greatest American that was ever born." He also said my father had started the Korean War for "publicity purposes" and urged everyone to study his "documents" in the Exhibition Hall which proved that the government was still infested by Communists. They proved nothing, of course. They were just his usual gobbledygook.

These tactics aroused my father's deep concern and made him all the more uneasy, because, right up to the eve of the Democratic Convention, Adlai Stevenson was still playing Hamlet. He even begged the Illinois delegation not to put his name in nomination.

On July 24, three days after the convention opened, my father, who had stayed in Washington worrying about Korea and other problems, got a phone call from Mr. Stevenson. He asked if it would embarrass him if he allowed his name to be placed in nomination. Dad hit the ceiling. He told Mr. Stevenson in very blunt terms what he thought about his indecision. "I have been trying since January to get you to say that. Why would it embarrass me?"

Mr. Stevenson did not realize how close my father had come to not supporting him. About two weeks before the convention, Alben Barkley asked Dad if he would support him for the presidency. Although he still felt the "Veep" was too old for the job, my father said yes, largely because none of the other candidates aroused any enthusiasm in him. But when Mr. Barkley went to Chicago to line up delegates, he found the influential labor leaders at the convention unanimously opposed to him. On the day the convention opened, he called Dad and dejectedly informed him that he was going to withdraw, and this freed my father from his obligation—which he would have regarded as irrevocable—to support the vice president. Mr. Barkley was so painfully disappointed that Dad telephoned the Democratic Chairman, Frank McKinney, and urged him to give the Veep the consolation of a farewell speech. He did so, and on the morning of July 23, Mr. Barkley gave one of his greatest talks, full of that wonderful humor and ridicule of Republicans and their pompous ways that by now had become his trademark.

Meanwhile, the convention was plunging toward chaos. Senator Kefauver, Senator Richard Russell of Georgia, Mr. Harriman, and Governor Stevenson all had blocs of supporters and none seemed capable of building up a majority. Visions of earlier Democratic Conventions, where discord had torn the party apart, began haunting my father. He decided to intervene powerfully on Mr. Stevenson's behalf. He telephoned the man who was sitting in for him on the Missouri delegation, Tom Gavin, and told him to spread the word that the President was behind Stevenson. But the governor of Illinois was still having trouble mustering majority support when Dad's plane landed at Midway Airport in Chicago on July 25.

My father had a political ace which he was now prepared to play. When Averell Harriman discussed making the race, Dad had told him that his candidacy had his approval—but not his backing —quite a different thing in party politics. He also wanted him to agree to one thing. If the convention was deadlocked, he would help him nominate the strongest candidate. My father made it clear that in his opinion this was Adlai Stevenson. Averell, a good party man, had agreed.

Now Dad told Charlie Murphy to find Mr. Harriman and order him to withdraw in Stevenson's favor. Mr. Harriman, knowing my father was in town and foreseeing the request, withdrew even before Charlie reached him. The addition of Mr. Harriman's 121 delegates sent Stevenson stock soaring, and he was elected on the next ballot. Dad took him out on the platform and introduced him, declaring: "You have nominated a winner, and I am going to take off my coat and do everything I can to help him win."

This is exactly what he did. But the campaign was doomed almost from the start by Mr. Stevenson's poor political judgment. No one liked Mr. Stevenson personally more than the Trumans. Even after he lost, my father regarded him as a great spokesman for the Democratic party. But the governor lacked the will and the force to win a presidential campaign. Among his many mistakes, the greatest one he made was his attempt to run as a new species of independent Democrat, with very little interest in defending the record of the Democratic administration he was hoping to succeed. He even let Richard Nixon, Joe McCarthy, and the other purveyors of the Communists-in-government big lie put him on the defensive. Equally galling to Dad was Mr. Stevenson's admission that there was "a mess in Washington" that he would clean up. Thus he capitulated to two of the worst Republican smears. From an organizational point of view, the campaign was an even worse fiasco. Mr. Stevenson set up his own headquarters in Springfield and there was very little liaison between his people and the White House.

My father did his utmost to co-operate with Mr. Stevenson, in spite of these problems. In a letter he wrote to him on August 16, 1952, he could not have been more forthright about his motives:

> Again, I want to say to you that I am at your disposal to help win the election and I also want you to understand that there is nothing further that can add to my career as a public servant. As I told you when you were here . . . I think there comes a time when every politician whether he be in a County, State or Federal office, should retire. Most of them find it impossible to do that—they either have to be carried out feet first or kicked out. I made up my mind in 1949 that that would not happen to me if I could get the national picture on a basis that would prevent world war three and maintain a domestic program that would give all sections of the population fair treatment.

Most of the time Mr. Stevenson's mistakes made my father more sad than mad. It was General Eisenhower who really aroused his wrath. Mr. Eisenhower tried, for a while, to confine himself to glittering generalities and stay above the battle. But one of his biggest supporters, the Scripps-Howard newspapers, warned him that his campaign "was running like a dry creek." Then Senator

Taft had a famous conference with the General, in which he extracted from him a promise to attack the Democratic party's foreign and domestic policies. When Ike started accusing the Democrats of betraying the United States at Yalta and failing to foresee the menace of Russian aggression thereafter, Dad boiled. He promptly quoted Ike's words before a committee of Congress in 1945. "There is no one thing," Ike said, "that guides the policy of Russia more today than to keep friendship with the United States."

> When I was going to school [Dad said], we had an old professor who was interested in teaching us how to make up our minds and make decisions. The lesson was on the history of battles of the War between the States and the discussion was on the battle of Gettysburg. And some kid in class got up and said what Lee should have done and what Meade should have done and this old professor said, "Now, young man, that's all very fine, but any schoolboy's hindsight is worth a great deal more than all General Lee's and General Meade's foresight."
>
> I can say the same thing about Ike. His hindsight may be extra good, but his foresight isn't any better than anybody else's.

This was one of my father's strongest convictions. More than once, he said to reporters and others who criticized his administration, "Any schoolboy's hindsight is worth a President's foresight."

What troubled my father was the fact that Ike was attacking policies he had helped to formulate and carry out. This seemed to Dad the worst kind of hypocrisy. But what really drove the Truman temperature right off the thermometer was Ike's endorsement of Senators William Jenner and Joe McCarthy, men who spent hours in the Senate vilifying Ike's old commander, George Marshall. Without General Marshall's help, Ike would have remained an obscure colonel, at most a brigadier or major general, perhaps commanding a division before the war ended. When Ike appeared on the same platform with William Jenner, and deleted a personal tribute to General Marshall from a speech he planned to make in Milwaukee because Senator McCarthy would have been offended by it, my father just about gave up on Candidate Eisenhower.

In late September we launched a whistle-stop tour to Hungry Horse, Montana, to dedicate a new dam there. After almost eight years as President, Dad was as tireless as ever, making six and eight speeches a day and wearing out everyone else on the train, including yours truly.

In the *Public Papers of Harry S. Truman, 1952,* the following entry appears on page 648:

> HUNGRY HORSE, MONTANA (Rear platform, 9:45 A.M.)
>
> Thank you very much for this souvenir of the horse. That makes a pair of them.
>
> I appreciate the privilege of being here. It has been a fine morning—had a good look at the project down here, and I am going to tell you something about it when I get "downtown."
>
> Where's Margaret?

Margaret had committed the unpardonable sin of not getting up that morning. I was teased unmercifully all the way across the rest of the country. But I got even with him in Ohio, later in the campaign. There, Mike Disalle, who was running for the Senate, introduced Dad as "Margaret Truman's father."

As always, Dad could take it as well as dish it out. "I'm a back number already," he said, ruefully.

There were times during the campaign when I think Dad's humor came close to matching Adlai Stevenson's—but of course I am a prejudiced witness. Defending the governor's use of humor in his speeches, Dad said: "They have been poking fun at our candidate, Governor Stevenson, because he likes to put his audiences in a good humor. I found a quotation, I think, that will cover that. It is an admonition in Matthew 6. It says, 'Be not as the hypocrites, of a sad countenance.' "

In Troy, Montana, he told his listeners that the GOP stood for "the General's Own Party," or to put it another way, "the Party of the Generals."

"There's a lot of truth in that," Dad said. "The Republicans have General Motors and General Electric and General Foods and General MacArthur and General Martin and General Wedemeyer. And then they have their own five-star General who is running for President. . . . I want to say to you that every general I know is on this list except general welfare, and general welfare is in with the corporals and the privates in the Democratic Party."

When Ike tried to argue that our World War II decision not to advance to Berlin and the 1947 decision to withdraw our troops from Korea were "political" mistakes which forced later military action, my father really let him have it. "He was personally involved in our decisions about Berlin and Korea," he told his listeners in a speech in Oakland. "He knows what happened in those cases and so do I." Dad went on to point out that the Joint Chiefs of Staff recommended withdrawing our troops from Korea in 1947. "The Chief of Staff of the Army, a man who joined in this recommendation, is the man who is now the Republican candidate for President."

As for Berlin, my father revealed that he had ordered Ike to work out with the Russians unrestricted access to Berlin as a condition to withdrawing our troops to the Occupation Zone lines. Ike delegated this job to General Lucius Clay. All Clay got from the Russians was an oral assurance, instead of a precise agreement in writing.

> Our troops were withdrawn, our bargaining position was lost and our right of access was never firmly established. General Clay, in his book, admits that this was a mistake. He is honest about it. He doesn't blame the civilian side of the government— which had nothing whatever to do with it. He doesn't even blame the commanding officer. But his commanding officer should, I think, step up and share some of the blame. The responsibility to arrange free access to Berlin lay squarely on that commanding officer, for I put it there.

As for Ike's statement that our plan of global resistance to communism was "a program of bits and pieces . . . an endless game of makeshift and make believe," my father said he never thought he would hear words like those from the lips of the man who was now the Republican candidate.

> He is a man who knows the toil and cost of building defenses, cementing alliances, and inspiring a common purpose in the hearts and minds of free peoples. He is aware of how easy and how dangerous it is to destroy the common faith and purpose on which the whole structure of our security is built, and yet he does not seem to hesitate now to utter the reckless words that can bring that structure down to ruin.

Ike's problem, Dad declared, was that he had fallen into the hands of the "Republican snollygosters." Dad fell in love with this wonderful word during this campaign. For those who don't know the political slang of the early 1900s, a snollygoster is a politician who is all words and very little action.

Dad had a lot of fun making Ike squirm over things that he had said in earlier years. One of his favorite quotes, which Dad repeated at numerous whistle-stops, was Ike's 1945 statement withdrawing himself from the presidential race: "Nothing in the international or domestic situation especially qualifies for the most important office in the world a man whose adult years have been spent in the country's military forces. At least, this is true in my case."

Dad would add with a grin: "It was true then. It is true now."

Dad had even more fun with another Eisenhower gaffe. Ike was fond of calling his campaign a crusade, and at one point he declared that his model was Oliver Cromwell and his Roundheads. Dad quickly pointed out, "Oliver Cromwell may have had his points, but his crusade, as I recall it, was one that started out as a matter of principle and finished up by destroying parliamentary government and butchering women and children. God save us from a crusade like that."

But when my father talked about Ike and General Marshall, his tone grew harsh. "If there is any one man to whom the Republican candidate owes a great debt of loyalty and gratitude, that man is George Catlett Marshall." He would then condemn without reservation Ike's support of Joe McCarthy and William Jenner. "Don't let anybody tell you that every Presidential candidate has to do that—that it is just part of politics. Franklin Roosevelt did not endorse every Democrat, and neither did Harry Truman. Governor Dewey in 1948 did not endorse Republicans who had disgraced the Republican label. But the Republican candidate this year did, with the same betrayal of principle he has shown throughout his campaign."

During most of the campaign, Dad had very little to say about General Eisenhower's running mate, Senator Richard M. Nixon of California. He made no comment on Mr. Nixon's "Checkers" speech, where he discussed the virtues of his cocker spaniel to exonerate himself from implications of corruption arising from some $18,000 given him by a "millionaire's club" of wealthy Republicans. Several times Dad refused to say whether he thought this fund was ethical or not. He took the position that this was something the public could decide for themselves. Following the Biblical injunction to "judge not," Dad always hesitated to take ethical stands on the actions of his fellow politicians. Privately, however, Dad made it clear that the fund confirmed his long-standing opinion of Mr. Nixon—that he was a spokesman for special interests.

For a while the election looked close. At the very least, Candidate Eisenhower knew he was in the fight of his life. Along with the smears and lies Dad was continually rebutting, the Republicans threw in a few dirty tricks aimed specifically at our campaign train. A "Truth Squad" followed us around the country, issuing statements that supposedly countered Dad's speeches. In Buffalo they hired a horde of school children who tried to drown out Dad with screams and catcalls, anticipating by twenty years the Students for a Democratic Society. It just proves that extremists from either end of the political spectrum have more in common than they think.

Finally, Candidate Eisenhower let one of his speech writers put into his mouth words that completely, totally infuriated my father. In a speech in Detroit, Ike announced he would "go to Korea in person if elected and put an end to the fighting." As politics, it was a master stroke. It was exactly what millions of Americans, unhappy and worried about the deadlock in Korea, wanted to hear. As a realistic policy it was a blatant lie. Equally fatuous was his promise that he would overnight arrange things so that the South Koreans would do all the fighting, and our troops could come home. "While he is on the back platform of his train, holding out this glowing hope," my father said angrily, "his staff are in the press car pointing out to reporters that he has not said *when* he would be able to do this. And he knows very well he can't do it, without surrendering Korea—until the present Korean conflict is at an end."

If Ike had a solution to the war, my father wanted to know why Ike had not given it to him when he was serving the President as one of his top military advisers. Mockingly, he asked Ike to give it to him now. "Let's save a lot of lives and not wait—not do a lot of demagoguery and say that he can do it after he's elected. If he can do it after he is elected, we can do it now."

Alas, it was all in vain. On Election Day General Ike went rampaging to a tremendous personal victory. Dad took some consolation in noting that the Democrats had actually won more congressional votes—although their distribution enabled the Republicans to capture control of Congress by a very narrow margin, one seat in the Senate and twelve in the House. "The people were voting for their great military hero," Dad concluded in a letter to Winston Churchill.

My father sent the President-elect a telegram of congratulations, in which he made a point of saying, "The *Independence* will be at your disposal if you still desire to go to Korea." Ike made the trip, which of course accomplished nothing.

Except for that one partisan jab, my father stopped playing politics the moment the election was over. His chief concern became the orderly transfer of power. He was determined that Dwight Eisenhower would not have to undergo the ordeal Harry S. Truman experienced when he was catapulted into the presidency. He remembered from his reading and observation of earlier administrations how outgoing and incoming Presidents, particularly when they were of different parties, tended to have as little as possible to do with each other. In a world on the edge of total violence, this was unthinkable. My father boldly changed the pattern, setting an historic precedent.

In his congratulatory telegram, he made his first overture toward co-operation:

THE 1954 BUDGET MUST BE PRESENTED TO THE CONGRESS
BEFORE JANUARY 15TH. ALL PRELIMINARY FIGURES
HAVE BEEN MADE UP. YOU SHOULD HAVE A REPRESENTATIVE
MEET WITH THE DIRECTOR OF THE BUDGET IMMEDIATELY.

When Ike accepted this offer, my father sent him a second message:

I KNOW YOU WILL AGREE WITH ME THAT THERE
OUGHT TO BE AN ORDERLY TRANSFER OF THE BUSINESS
OF THE EXECUTIVE BRANCH OF THE GOVERNMENT
TO THE NEW ADMINISTRATION, PARTICULARLY IN VIEW
OF THE INTERNATIONAL DANGERS AND PROBLEMS

[549]

THAT CONFRONT THIS COUNTRY AND THE WHOLE FREE
WORLD. I INVITE YOU, THEREFORE, TO MEET WITH
ME IN THE WHITE HOUSE AT YOUR EARLY CONVENIENCE
TO DISCUSS THE PROBLEM OF THIS TRANSITION, SO
THAT IT MAY BE CLEAR TO ALL THE WORLD THAT THIS
NATION IS UNITED IN ITS STRUGGLE FOR FREEDOM
AND PEACE.

Again Mr. Eisenhower accepted the offer and a meeting was set for November 18. Ike arrived at 2 P.M. with Henry Cabot Lodge, Jr., and Joseph M. Dodge, as his aides. First, Ike went into Dad's office and they had a private conversation. Here is the unadorned, rather blunt memorandum which my father made on their talk, two days later:

The President Elect came to see me day before yesterday, Nov. 18, 1952. When he came into the President's office he had a chip on his shoulder. . . .

I told him when he came into the Presidential office that all I had in mind is an orderly turnover to him. . . . I offered to leave the pictures of Hidalgo, the Mexican Liberator, given to me for the Presidential office, San Martin given to me by the Argentine Government and Bolivar, given to me by the Venezuelan Government, in the President's office. I was informed very curtly, that I'd do well to take them with me—that the Governments of these countries would, no doubt, give the new President the same pictures! Then I gave him the world globe that he used in World War II which he had given me at Frankfort when I went to Potsdam. He accepted that—not very graciously.

I told him that I wanted to turn the Administrative Branch of the Government over to him as a going concern and that I had instructed my White House Staff and all Cabinet Officers to co-operate in this undertaking.

Ike asked me if I had a Chief of Staff in the White House. I told him that there is an Assistant to the President, Dr. John Steelman, who coordinates the differences between Cabinet Officers and between the President's Secretaries, but that any member of the Cabinet and any Secretary or Administrative Assistant is at liberty to see the President at any time on any subject.

I advised him that his Appointment Secretary would be his

personal contact with the public. I told him that this man must be a real diplomat, able to say "No" nine-tenths of the time and make no one angry. I told him that his Press Secretary must be able to keep press and radio-television in line. He must be familiar with reporters' problems and be able to stand between the President and the press and radio. I advised him to obtain a correspondence secretary who could suggest answers to 75% of the mail, keep track of birthdays, special days, proclamations and be able to write letters he could sign after reading the first paragraph.

I told him he must have Assistants who could talk to State, Treasury, Commerce and Labor, that he must have one to act as personnel officer to head off job hunters and to investigate and make recommendations for all positions filled by Presidential appointments. I informed him that he should have a "minority group" assistant to hear complaints and assuage the hurt feelings of Negroes, Mexicans, Puerto Ricans, Indians and any other groups including Poles, Lithuanians, Irish and what have you.

I think all this went into one ear and out the other.

After this private talk, Ike, my father, and their advisers gathered for a seminar on the world problems the nation was facing. Mr. Acheson did most of the lecturing. He noted alarming weaknesses in our UN allies in regard to the principle of no forced repatriation of prisoners of war in Korea, and discussed NATO, Southeast Asia, U.S. commercial policy abroad, and other pressing matters. The Republicans just took notes and made no comment, except for one point in the statement which was issued at the end of the meeting. Henry Cabot Lodge refused to allow Ike to agree to oppose forced repatriation of the Korean War prisoners. Since this was the main reason why Dad wanted the meeting, he was very disappointed. A proposal by the Indian representative at the UN, which compromised on this vital issue through a smoke screen of double-talk, was in danger of passing. The Democrats were left to fight—and win—that battle on their own. When Ike departed, Dad had the feeling that he "had not grasped the immense job ahead of him."

Mr. Eisenhower obviously thought he could run the White House the way he ran the army. "He'll sit right here," Dad said, "and he'll say do this, do that!! And nothing will happen. Poor

[551]

Ike—it won't be a bit like the Army. He'll find it very frustrating."

On that score, I think the history of the Eisenhower Administration made Dad a good prophet.

As the time grew near for our departure from the White House, Dad became more and more philosophic about politics. Perhaps he also had a little more time to write memoranda to himself. Here is one of my favorites:

Had a memo from Mr. Lovett on plane production, prepared by the Sec. for Air and a Munitions Report which were most encouraging. Bob gave me a definition of a statistician—"A man who draws a straight line from an unwarranted assumption to a foregone conclusion." I gave him one for a consultant Washington style—"An ordinary citizen away from home."

Came over to the House after a long session with a new chairman of the Dem. Committee.

Bess and I talk to Margie at 6:30 on a three way hookup. We go down to the south porch at seven for dinner—a good dinner too—tenderloin of some kind, really tender, asparagus, and a cooked stuffed tomato, then a large piece of thick, light yellow cake with caramel sauce.

One of our squirrels comes up to the table and asks for a bite to eat. Turns up his nose at a crumb of bread soaked in cooked tomato juice. We send for some crackers and he accepts pieces of cracker and goes under a chair each time, sits up and eats. Bess hands him the pieces one at a time until he has eaten three whole crackers. Then without a bow or a thank you he walks down the steps and disappears. But he'll be back tomorrow night as usual for more to eat.

Mr. Hopkins, the chief clerk, informed me when I signed the documents and letters this afternoon that the mail had fallen below 5000 letters today for the first time since I've been President. I asked him a foolish question—why? The diplomatic chief clerk informed me that the mail always decreased in volume at the end of an Administration, particularly when the White House occupant was not coming back. Well, it is "The King is dead—Long live the king."

It is fortunate that I've never taken an attitude that the kudos and kow-tows are made to me as an individual. I knew always that the greatest office in the history of the world was getting them, and Harry S. Truman as an individual was not. I hope I'm still the country man from Missouri.

Even though the Democrats had lost the election, Dad and the members of his Cabinet continued to work toward many Democratic goals, right up to the final hours of his administration. On December 2 Attorney General James McGranery submitted an amicus curiae (friend of the court) brief in support of five cases filed by Negro plaintiffs challenging segregation in the field of education. Quoting Secretary of State Dean Acheson, Attorney General McGranery argued that racial discrimination had to be viewed in the context of "the present world struggle between freedom and tyranny." He said that segregation furnished grist for Communist propaganda mills and raised doubts even among friendly nations as to the intensity of our devotion to the democratic way of life.

Dad had, of course, already achieved a landmark breakthrough in the fight against segregation with his Executive Order 8802, abolishing segregation in the armed forces. On May 22, 1950, a presidential committee gave him a report, "Freedom to Serve," which spelled out in detail why the Pentagon was now convinced that equality of opportunity would produce "a better army, navy and air force." Later, Dad issued Executive Order 10210 banning discrimination against any person on the ground of race, creed or color in the companies of all contractors and subcontractors working for the federal government.

In these final White House days Dad also displayed one of his greatest gifts, his ability to laugh at himself.

> We had dinner at seven as usual, discussed ghosts, hosts and who'd died in the White House, and then dressed up and went across Lafayette Square to celebrate the anniversary of the new U.S.O. in the old Belasco Theater building. Mrs. T. had and has been interested in U.S.O. work so they wanted her to cut the birthday cake. Well, we all, Mrs. T., Margie and the President, dressed up and went over to the U.S.O. The Boss cut the birthday cake, they drew a number out of a box for the one to get the first slice that the First Lady cut, and a Marine won! The President made some asinine remarks, and we came back to the White House.

In that same memorandum Dad recorded a pretty good joke which the White House played on us. You will recall his conviction that the old place was really haunted. It was also drafty.

[553]

When the wind was northwest, it came whistling down the fireplace in the corner of my bedroom. To protect myself from this chilly blast, I had a bridge table leaning against the fireplace. I'll let Dad tell the rest of the story:

> It was agreed we'd go to bed at once because Margie and I had to board the train for Philadelphia at 8:15 tomorrow to go to the Army-Navy football game—our last appearance officially at this function. Mrs. T. can't go because of her mother's condition.
>
> Well, I went to bed and read a hair-raiser in Adventure. Just as I arrived at a bloody incident, the Madam bursts into my bedroom through the hall door and shouted, "Did you hear that awful noise?"
>
> I hadn't and said so—not a popular statement. So I put on my bathrobe and made an investigation.
>
> What do you think I found after looking all around? Why that Margie's bridge table had fallen from in front of the fireplace in her bedroom and knocked over the fireguard!
>
> It must have made a grand ghost sound where Margie and her mamma were sitting in Mrs. T.'s sitting room!
>
> I didn't hear it. What a relief when the cause of the noise was discovered by me. I left two very happy ladies and went back to bed.

Our last days at the White House were a mingling of joy and sadness. On December 4 we had a formal dinner for all the members of the Cabinet and their wives, as well as the regular White House aides. Dad made the following note on it:

> It was a grand affair. I told those present how I appreciated the advice, help and assistance I'd received from all of them and that if I'd had any success as the President of the United States, the greatest office in the history of the world, they had made it possible. The Chief Justice responded in a wonderful tribute to me.

The following day Grandmother Wallace died at 12:37 P.M. She had been ill for several weeks, and had been in a coma for the last few days of her life. It was a little awesome, to think of the way the world had changed in the ninety years she had lived. It redoubled my feeling of things coming to a close, of history changing direction.

After the New Year, Prime Minister Churchill arrived for another visit and enlivened our spirits immensely, as he always did. In the course of his stay my father gave him a small stag dinner to which he invited Robert Lovett, Averell Harriman, General Omar Bradley, and Secretary of State Dean Acheson. Everyone was in an ebullient mood, especially Dad. Without warning, Mr. Churchill turned to him and said, "Mr. President, I hope you have your answer ready for that hour when you and I stand before Saint Peter and he says, 'I understand you two are responsible for putting off those atomic bombs. What have you got to say for yourselves?'"

This could have been a rather unpleasant subject. But Bob Lovett, who is as witty as he is brilliant, came to the rescue. "Are you sure, Prime Minister, that you are going to be in the same place as the President for that interrogation?"

Mr. Churchill sipped his champagne and then intoned, "Lovett, my vast respect for the creator of this universe and countless others gives me assurance that he would not condemn a man without a hearing."

"True," said Mr. Lovett, "but your hearing would not be likely to start in the Supreme Court, or, necessarily, in the same court as the President's. It could be in another court far away."

"I don't know about that," rumbled Mr. Churchill, "but wherever it is, it will be in accordance with the principles of the English Common Law."

"Is it altogether consistent with your respect for the creator of this and other universes," Dean Acheson asked, "to limit his imagination and judicial procedure to the accomplishment of a minute island, in a tiny world, in one of the smaller of the universes?"

Mr. Churchill was somewhat taken aback by this observation. "Well," he said, "there will be a trial by a jury of my peers, that's certain."

Now the conversation was really soaring. "Oyez! Oyez!" cried our Secretary of State. "In the matter of the immigration of Winston Spencer Churchill. Mr. Bailiff, will you empanel a jury?"

Everyone eagerly accepted historic roles. General Bradley decided he was Alexander the Great. Others played Julius Caesar, Socrates, and Aristotle. The prime minister declined to permit

Voltaire on his jury—he was an atheist—or Oliver Cromwell, because he did not believe in the rule of law. Then Mr. Acheson summoned George Washington. That was too much for Mr. Churchill. He saw that things were being stacked against him. "I waive a jury," he announced, "but not habeas corpus."

They ignored him and completed the selection of the jury. Dad was appointed judge. The case was tried and the prime minister was acquitted.

Later in the evening he served as judge in an argument which compared Dad's merits as a statesman to his demerits as a pianist. The prime minister sat as judge and declared in favor of the President's statesmanship.

During this visit Mr. Churchill confessed to Dad that he had been very pessimistic when Harry Truman succeeded Franklin Roosevelt. "I misjudged you badly," the prime minister said. "Since that time, you, more than any other man, have saved Western civilization."

Finally came January 20, 1953, our farewell day. We had finished packing, and I put on my dress for the last time in the White House. Outside the atmosphere was chilly, both politically and meteorologically. Part of it, I will freely admit, was Dad's fault. In the middle of December he had become very riled when General Douglas MacArthur announced that he wanted to talk to President-elect Eisenhower, because he had a solution to the war in Korea. Ike immediately rushed to confer with the deposed Far Eastern General. Angrily, Dad told reporters that if General MacArthur had a solution to the war, he should come to Washington and inform the Defense Department immediately. Then he tore into Ike's trip to Korea, which he made immediately after conferring with MacArthur. Reporters noted that Ike had said that he had no "trick solution" for Korea. Dad wryly replied, "He was quoting me. I made the statement quite some time ago in the campaign." Then he called the trip "a piece of demagoguery."

Ike resented these remarks, but it seems to me that he should have realized Inauguration Day was hardly the time to display his pique. It was traditional for the outgoing President to have the incoming President to a pre-inaugural lunch at the White House. The Eisenhowers coldly rejected our invitation. Then Ike tried to force Dad to pick him up at the Statler Hotel en route to the inauguration ceremonies. Dad, *very* conscious of the fact that he was still President, replied, "If Ike doesn't pick me up, then we'll go in separate cars."

The President-elect capitulated, but when he arrived at the White House to pick Dad up, he refused to get out and greet us inside the house, in the traditional manner. Rather than hold up the inauguration, Dad came out and got in the car.

There was very little conversation during their one-mile ride to the Capitol. Ike remarked that he had not come to the 1948 inauguration because he did not want to attract attention from the President.

"You were not here in 1948 because I did not send for you," Dad said. "But if I had sent for you, you would have come."

When they reached the Capitol, they went to the sergeant-at-arms' office to wait for the summons to the platform. Ike suddenly turned to Dad and said: "I wonder who is responsible for my son John being ordered to Washington from Korea? I wonder who is trying to embarrass me?"

"The President of the United States ordered your son to attend your inauguration," Dad said. "If you think somebody was trying to embarrass you by this order, then the President assumes full responsibility."

My father had ordered John Eisenhower home from Korea as a gesture of thoughtfulness. He was not serving in the front lines, or in any particularly vital role in the army, so there was no reason to accuse either his father or Dad of favoritism, or of endangering the public interest. It astonished Dad that Ike resented this gesture. It still astonishes me.

On the way to the inaugural platform, I walked in the procession, several dignitaries behind Dad and Mother. Suddenly a man stepped from the crowd and kissed me on the cheek. I turned and found myself being embraced by General Marshall. That was the first and only time I felt a little sad at the 1952 inauguration. We were saying good-bye to so many wonderful people.

After the ceremony we piled into a White House limousine and headed for a luncheon at Secretary Acheson's house. As we rolled through the crowded streets, I was suddenly struck by a wild thought. I turned—I was sitting on the jump seat—and looking straight at Dad said, "Hello, *Mr.* Truman."

He got the joke immediately, and loved it. It was the first time since I was born—give or take one year when I was too young to know what was going on—when he was not sporting an official title.

A crowd of about 500 people was waiting for us outside the Acheson house. They startled us with a round of cheers. You might have thought we had just been reelected. The luncheon was attended by all the Cabinet members and ex-Cabinet members and White House aides. It was an absolutely wonderful affair, full of jokes and laughter and a few tears. Especially when Dad made a little speech, reiterating how grateful he was for all they had done to help him. Then we were back in the limousine, and on our way to Union Station, where the presidential car was waiting to take Dad and Mother to Independence. I was going to stay in Washington overnight and return to New York.

If we were startled by the crowd around the Acheson house at the end of P Street, we were amazed by the mob scene in Union Station. At least 5,000 people were in the concourse, shouting and cheering. It was like the 1944 and 1948 conventions. The police had to form a flying wedge to get us to the *Ferdinand Magellan*. Inside, the party started all over again. Newspaper men and women who had spent eight years tearing Dad apart came in to mumble apologies and swear they never meant a word of it. Half the executive branch of the government seemed to be trying to shake his hand, or, in the case of the ladies, give him a kiss. He soon had lipstick all over his face. We finally had to call a halt to it, so the train could get out of the station on something approximating its schedule. Dad went out to the old familiar rear platform and gave them a farewell salute:

> May I say to you that I appreciate this more than any meeting I have ever attended as President or Vice President or Senator. This is the greatest demonstration that any man could have, because I'm just Mr. Truman, private citizen now.
>
> This is the first time you have ever sent me home in a blaze of glory. I can't adequately express my appreciation for what you are doing. I'll never forget it if I live to be a hundred.
>
> And that's just what I expect to do!

I got off the train and stood beside Mrs. Fred Vinson as it pulled out. Everybody in the station started singing "Auld Lang Syne." It was absolutely thunderous. Beside me, Mommy Vinson was weeping. But I didn't feel in the least weepy now. This tremendous outpouring of affection for Dad was too wonderful. It made all those years in the Great White Jail almost worthwhile.

[CHAPTER]

Twenty-Eight

SHORTLY BEFORE WE LEFT Washington, a reporter asked my father if he planned to take down the substantial iron fence which had been put around our house in Independence after he became President.

"No, you can't," Dad said. "When Herbert Hoover went back to his home in California after 1932, the souvenir hunters almost tore his house down, and he had to put a fence around it. We are going to leave that fence there, not because we like it, but it's just the American way to take souvenirs. It was said in the first World War that the French fought for their country, the British fought for freedom of the seas, and the Americans fought for souvenirs."

The fence, kept on Herbert Hoover's advice, turned out to be our salvation. At the that time the nation was quite indifferent to the fate of its ex-Presidents. At Union Station Dad's Secret Service escort shook hands with him and said good-bye. He went home to Independence and began living at 219 North Delaware Street without any protection whatsoever. The local government of Independence did their best to help us, but they could not permanently station at the house a detail of police from their small force.

We were badly in need of some sort of protection. The house was already a tourist attraction. They had been selling picture postcards of it as the summer White House for years. In the first months thousands of people came by to gawk. You will notice by my choice of words that I take a somewhat negative view of the American people's attitude that Presidents and ex-Presidents are objects of curiosity. Dad often tried to explain patiently to me that it was a waste of time to get mad about it, that it was a tradition that went all the way back to Thomas Jefferson, who was plagued by hordes of curiosity seeks when he retired to Monticello. I still kept getting mad. The people who regarded our house as public property were the ones who annoyed me most. Often they would drive down the long alley on the right of our house, into the backyard where our garages are. When I was there, I would march right out and say to them, "Get off here. You're on private property and you're trespassing."

"Don't yell at them," Mother would tell me.

"I will yell at people who do things like that," I would tell her. "It's disgraceful."

Then there was a man who walked up to the front gate and insisted he had to see the President. One look and it was clear to us that he was a nut. We called the police, and they responded promptly. At the station house they discovered that he had recently been discharged from a mental institution in Pennsylvania. He had written Dad several threatening letters and had a loaded .45 revolver in his pocket.

By way of consolation for these problems, there was the continued demonstration of tremendous affection from ordinary people. I should add that probably most of the curiosity seekers who came by our house—even those who drove into our backyard—were also moved by affection for Dad. But I found it hard to reciprocate when they made life miserable for us.

The mail Dad received in his first months out of office was unbelievable. In the first two weeks, more than 70,000 letters poured in. Almost all of them were favorable, but, of course, they had to be answered. Dad soon found himself running a sizable office in Kansas City. Even without the mail he had two projects which were full-time jobs. The first was putting his papers in order, so he could begin to write his memoirs. The second was planning his presidential library.

Dad took his papers with him from the White House as have all Presidents since George Washington. The papers he regarded as confidential—only a small fraction of which have been used in

[561]

this book—fill several dozen filing cabinets. Then there are the public papers, some 3,500,000 documents, which fill several thousand cabinets and boxes. Archivists working with these have already published eight thick volumes, each almost a thousand pages long.

Lately, some historians have criticized Dad because he has refused to open his confidential files. But Dad is not acting out of selfish motives. From the day he left office he was conscious that he still had heavy responsibilities as an ex-President. During his White House years a President gets advice from hundreds of people. He wants it to be good advice. He wants men to say exactly what they think, to tell exactly what they know about a situation or a subject. A President can only get this kind of honesty if the man who is giving the advice knows that what he says is absolutely confidential, and will not be published for a reasonable number of years after the President leaves the White House.

The library was in some ways an even bigger job than putting his papers in order and writing his memoirs. Millions of dollars had to be raised, a site selected, an agreement reached with the government. At first Dad hoped to establish the library on his family's farm. He even had thoughts about rebuilding the farmhouse and living there in close proximity to the history of his presidential years. But the onward march of suburbia made this financially impossible. A builder offered to buy a large part of the farm for a shopping center, which has since become known as Truman Corners. Uncle Vivian was ready to retire from farming, and the sale of the land guaranteed him and Dad's sister Mary financial security for the rest of their lives. The problem of a site was solved by the city of Independence, which offered Dad a handsome piece of land in the city's public park, only about a mile from our house. Dad was so pleased, he went out on a speaking schedule to raise the final million dollars. The pace he set absolutely terrified me. It would have killed a man half his age.

The library, which was dedicated in 1957, is one of the great joys of Dad's old age. He worked on the planning of every detail, down to the art work on the walls. He even persuaded Thomas Hart Benton, the great Missouri painter, to contribute a striking mural. One room is an exact replica of Dad's White House office as it was decorated during his presidency. Another room is dedicated to the World War I phase of Dad's career, with many personal mementoes of Battery D. There is a wonderful collection of political cartoons of the two Truman Administrations. But the heart of the library is in the rooms Dad laid out, to teach young people (and a few of their elders) the six functions of the presidency. Walking through them is a real learning experience. There are exhibits which tell the story of the President as Chief Executive, as ceremonial Chief of State, as a legislative planner, as a political party leader, as director of the nation's foreign policy, and as Commander in Chief of the Armed Forces. For scholars almost every book published thus far on the Truman era is on the shelves, and on microfilm are the papers of all the other Presidents.

On October 21, 1953, President Eisenhower visited Kansas City. He telephoned Dad, Dad telephoned him, but there was no meeting. Dad had no desire for one. He resented intensely the effort which the Eisenhower Administration was making to "get him" and other members of the Truman Administration. The Republicans combed the government files attempting to dredge up charges against everyone and anyone in Dad's administration. They found nothing to justify their "mess in Washington" cry. Even worse was the attempt to implicate Dad in the Communists-in-government canard. The climax to this program came in the investigation of Harry Dexter White, a former government monetary expert who had been accused of Communist leanings. The House Un-American Activities Committee actually sent Dad a subpoena, summoning him to testify on the case. He rejected the summons with the scorn it deserved. "I have been accused, in effect," he said on television, "of knowingly betraying the security of the United States. This charge is, of course, a falsehood." For once, most of the newspapers were on Dad's side.

In 1954 Dad had his first serious illness. It was a gall bladder attack, and it hit him while he was attending an open air production of *Call Me Madam*. Mother rushed him to the hospital, and they operated promptly. He survived the operation beautifully, but he was almost killed by a bad reaction to some antibiotics they gave him. He had what he called "hives inside and out" and could keep no food down. Then, in a marvelous replay of his mother's reaction to illness, he woke up one morning and asked the nurse if he could have a soft-boiled egg in a white cup.

[563]

"Why do you want it in a white cup?"

"So that I'll know it's clean," Dad said.

He ate the egg and kept it down. That was the beginning of his recovery. The doctors said it would take him at least a year to return to his normal routine. But within two months he was back working six days a week, plus a few extra hours on Sunday. "I've never known hard work to hurt anybody," Dad says. "It's lack of work that kills people."

A year or two after his gall bladder adventure, Dad departed from the house for his morning walk, without noticing that the streets were a sheet of ice. Not far from the house, he slipped and cracked three or four ribs. He went home and called Dr. Graham, who put him in a harness. I came home for a visit three days later and our conversation went like this:

"How do you feel?"

"It hurts."

"What do you expect when you crack your ribs? Have you got that harness on Dr. Graham gave you?"

"No. I got tired of wearing that."

"You mean you're just sitting there letting the ribs heal by themselves with no help?"

"That's right."

Only one thing changed in Dad's routine as a result of this misadventure. Mother issued an edict, forbidding him to go out for his morning walk when there was snow or ice on the ground. For once, he obeyed.

On another front, Dad drew on his political skills—and his knowledge of Mother—to win an argument. For days Mother badgered him to cut the grass, which she insisted was disgracefully high. Dad kept insisting it looked perfectly all right to him. Finally, one Sunday morning, he got out the lawn mower and went to work. Numerous neighbors passed on the way to church and he greeted them cheerfully. Within the hour, it was obvious to half of Independence that ex-President Truman was skipping church that morning.

Finally, Mother came out, en route to church.

"What do you think you are doing?" she asked, horrified.

"I'm doing what you asked me to do," said Dad, with his most disarming smile.

The following day Mother hired a man to mow the lawn.

Most of the time, if the truth is to be told—and that is what I am trying to do in this book—Mother won those kinds of arguments. In the mid-1950s, when they visited California, Mother announced that she wanted to visit Disneyland. The ex-President issued a fifteen-minute statement criticizing this idea. Disneyland was for children. No one was going to catch him riding roller coasters, etc., etc. Mother remained perfectly calm. She asked Charlie Murphy, who was accompanying them, if *he* would take her. Charlie, being a perfect Southern gentleman, of course said yes. The next morning he presented himself at their hotel, ready to do his duty. There was Dad, dressed to the nines, obviously ready to go somewhere. "What are you planning for the day, Mr. President?" Charlie asked.

"What do you think I'm planning?" snapped Dad. "I'm going to Disneyland!"

He went, and enjoyed himself thoroughly.

What pleased Dad most about his retirement was the warm reception he got from his fellow citizens in Independence and Kansas City. He wasn't sure just how people would take living with an ex-President. Moreover, he was keenly aware that the local papers had wasted a good deal of ink tearing him apart while he was in the White House. But his worries on this score proved utterly groundless. When he and Mother arrived in Independence on their trip home from Washington, there were at least 10,000 people waiting for them in the railroad station. The road that runs by our house was renamed Truman Road, and dozens of businesses adopted Dad's first or last name. Dad did his best to put a stop to this trend, however. He has very strong convictions that no living politician should have anything named after him. This includes retired politicians. Only recently has he relented just a little on this rule and agreed to permit the new sports stadium being built in Kansas City to carry his name. I think Mother, the baseball fan of the family, had something to do with this decision.

Other aspects of Dad's routine in the first year or so out of the White House gave him some problems. For instance, where does an ex-President eat lunch? He tried going to various restaurants in Kansas City with old friends, but a mob scene of autograph hunters invariably developed. Eating became an ordeal, and he began to wonder if he was going to spend the rest of his life lunching alone in his office. Then a friend recommended the Kansas City Club. Dad hesitated over this idea, because the club was 95 percent Republican. He was an honorary member, along with President Eisenhower, General of the Armies Bradley, and a noted Kansas City judge. Dad finally decided to take the plunge and entered the reactionary sanctum. The results amazed him. Half the Kansas City Establishment stopped by to shake his hand. "There is no conversation so sweet as that of former political enemies," Dad decided.

Traveling beyond his Kansas City–Independence stamping grounds was, Dad found, just as complicated. In the summer of 1953 he proposed a trip to Washington. He had bought a new car and he wanted to give it "a real tryout." Mother had doubts about driving with him, but he assured her that he would obey the speed limits and convinced her they would have no difficulty traveling incognito.

They weren't on the road more than an hour, when Mother asked, "What does the speedometer say?"

"Fifty-five."

"Do you think I'm losing my eyesight? Slow down."

They slowed down. Other cars began passing them. Soon they heard people shouting, "Hi, Harry—Hey, wasn't that Harry Truman? Where are you going, Harry?"

"Well," Dad said, "there goes our incognito—and I don't mean a part of the car."

Everywhere they stopped along their route, Dad was instantly recognized by motel owners or filling station attendants. Local reporters were notified, and police chiefs rushed to escort or guard them. The trip became almost as well publicized as a whistle-stop campaign.

As you may have noticed by now, Dad likes to take trips. During their first liberated years he and Mother did quite a bit of traveling. I joined them for a wonderful month-long vacation in Hawaii, in March of 1953. In 1956 they went to England and had a delightful time. They visited Winston Churchill, and Dad received a degree from Oxford. For this ceremony he wore a red coat and a Henry VIII type hat, which made him laugh every time he looked in the mirror.

My father could have made a great deal of money in the years immediately after he left the White House. An astonishing number of jobs were offered to him. A clothing store chain, a sewing machine company, a motion picture company offered him executive titles with six-figure salaries. One offer guaranteed him a half million dollars if he signed an eight-year contract that would have required only an hour's work. But he saw through these proposals instantly: "They were not interested in hiring Harry Truman the person. It was the former President of the United States they wanted. I could never lend myself to any transaction, however respectable, that would commercialize on the prestige and dignity of the office of the Presidency." So he contented himself with the modest sums he earned from his memoirs and from writing comments on the political scene for the North American Newspaper Alliance.

Among Dad's favorite part-time occupations has been lecturing at universities. He has immensely enjoyed meeting young men and women of another generation and sharing his wisdom and experience with them.

Invariably, in these discussions, someone would ask Dad if he ever had any second thoughts about dropping the atomic bomb. Dad replied in words similar to this answer which he gave during a lecture in 1965:

> It was a question of saving hundreds of thousands of American lives. I don't mind telling you that you don't feel normal when you have to plan hundreds of thousands of complete final deaths of American boys who are alive and joking and having fun while you are doing your planning. You break your heart and your head trying to figure out a way to save one life.
>
> The name given to our invasion plan was Olympic, but I saw nothing godly about the killing of all the people that would be necessary to make that invasion. The casualty estimates called for 750,000 Americans—250,000 killed; 500,000 maimed for life.
>
> I could not worry about what history would say about my personal morality. I made the only decision I ever knew how to make. I did what I thought was right.

During these lectures Dad never forgot the awesome powers of the presidency which clung to him no matter where he went. One day a young man stood up to ask him what he thought of the state's governor. He referred to the governor as "our local

[567]

yokel." Dad responded sharply. He told the boy he should be ashamed of himself for his lack of respect for the high office of governor.

The boy turned pale and sat down. After the lecture was over Dad rushed into the audience, found the young man, shook his hand, and told him that there were no hard feelings, he understood that he was just speaking in an offhand way and intended no disrespect. Dad's sensitivity to what he had done did not stop there. He asked the boy's dean to send him regular reports on the young man's progress in school, and he continued to correspond with him after he left college.

"I realized after I spoke that way," Dad explained to me, "that I had unintentionally humiliated that young man. I was afraid that the memory of my harsh tone might scar his whole life and ruin his reputation among his friends and acquaintances."

Politically, Dad remained intensely interested in the future of the Democratic party. Here he was severely disappointed by the way Adlai Stevenson resumed his Hamlet's role and declined to accept the responsibility which Dad felt he should assume. "His failure to pick up the reins of leadership brought about a period of confusion and drift and factionalism within our party," Dad said. In July, 1955, the two men conferred in Chicago and Dad bluntly urged Mr. Stevenson: "Why don't you announce yourself now as a Presidential candidate, so that we can get a head start? Now is the time to do the necessary advance work that we were prevented from doing in 1952 when you held off until the last moment."

Mr. Stevenson declined to take Dad's advice, and Dad therefore decided to back Averell Harriman for the nomination in 1956. Mr. Stevenson won the nomination, in spite of Dad's prediction—which proved unfortunately accurate—that he would carry fewer states than he did in 1952. Dad campaigned vigorously for him, in spite of his doubts. Even today, whenever anyone mentions Adlai Stevenson's name, Dad will only shake his head and say he was a great Democratic party spokesman but a poor candidate.

In one of their last intimate conversations, Mr. Stevenson said to Dad, "What am I doing wrong?" Dad walked over to the window of their hotel and pointed to a man standing in the entrance of a hotel across the street. "The thing you have got to do is to learn how to reach that man." He was telling him he had to learn how to communicate with the man in the street. Unfortunately for him and the Democratic party, Mr. Stevenson never mastered this difficult art. Eventually, Dad decided that it was just as well that he never won election as President. His indecisiveness might have been a disastrous handicap in the White House.

Politics was not, of course, Dad's only preoccupation during these years. There were some family matters that also interested him. I spent Christmas and New Year's in Independence in 1955 and received a number of rather mysterious telegrams from a man named Clifton Daniel. I had met him at a party in November. I made the mistake of going out to Independence without giving Clifton my phone number, and it was, of course, unlisted and unavailable, even to one of the top editors of *The New York Times*. He worked off his frustration by sending me silly telegrams, which asked questions like "Are you sure it's not Independence, Kansas?" Then he sent me flowers. Mother's eyebrows raised and she asked, "Who is this?"

"A man I met," I said, proving I could be as laconic as any other member of the Truman family.

In January Clifton proposed and I accepted. I called Dad and informed him that he was going to have a newspaperman for a son-in-law. Contrary to the rumors, it did not bother him in the least. But his friends thought it was very funny and kidded the life out of him.

Clifton's first meeting with Dad, about a month later, was almost a disaster. He had come back from Russia the previous fall with a bad case of ulcers—the result of living under the terrific tension which the cold war inflicted on correspondents behind the Iron Curtain. All he could drink was milk. He came by around cocktail time to meet Mother and Dad, and I served drinks to the Trumans and milk to Mr. Daniel. Dad's face fell down to his shoes. I could see him thinking: A newspaperman and he drinks milk! I thought it was funny, and in the best Truman practical joker tradition, absolutely refused to explain it. We did explain eventually, of course, but I let Dad spend a good hour doing mental contortions, first.

Dad tried to be good natured while the preparations for my

wedding swept around him in our house in Independence. He was shunted from one room of the house to another while the women of the family, the neighbors, and assorted house guests, in the usual feminine frenzy, endeavored to prepare the downstairs rooms for the reception after the ceremony. Finally, his native stubbornness acted up. One ritual he did not propose to give up was reading his *New York Times*. He settled down in his chair in the library and began turning the pages.

"Harry, why don't you just go on upstairs," my mother called from the dining room, where she was working on the table. "Vietta has to vacuum the carpet."

"She can sweep around me," Dad announced without looking up from the editorial page, and he wouldn't budge.

As in most families, the son-in-law rapidly achieved more influence with Mother and Dad than the daughter ever had. Particularly with Mother, who can be persuaded to change her mind by Clifton, where I could talk myself blue in the face for a year with no results. There is only one point on which Dad and Clifton disagree. That is on how the news is presented in our papers. Dad insists that it is sometimes slanted by the way pictures are used and by the way stories and pictures are juxtaposed. Clifton insists that there is no intentional slanting on the vast majority of our newspapers. Dad remains unconvinced. I remain studiously neutral.

The next major family event was the birth of our first son. He came very suddenly in June, 1957. I went into labor in the afternoon and headed for the hospital. Clifton telephoned Independence and got Dad. Mother was at her bridge club. Dad took the news very calmly, it seemed to me, for a man who had been saying in the public prints for years that all he wanted was a grandchild (to my frequently expressed annoyance). He did not even bother to telephone Mother at her bridge club. He simply met her on the back porch when she came home and said: "Margaret's in the hospital."

Later in the day, I developed some problems and the doctor decided to perform a Caesarean. Clifton again telephoned Independence and this time got Mother, who was perfectly calm, and even relieved, to hear this news. Where was the grandfather-to-be? Where else—asleep in his bed. Did you think a man who slept through the night of his own election to the presidency would stay awake for a mere grandson?

Clifton Truman Daniel finally arrived just after midnight on June 5. The following day, Dad and Mother were on a train heading east. Every place the train stopped, reporters and well-wishers swarmed aboard to congratulate Dad, as if he were the father. At the hospital, after he saw me and the baby, Dad departed with Clifton, who advised him to wait at the entrance while he captured a taxi. When Clifton returned, he was astonished to discover his father-in-law holding a press conference.

There was a marvelous picture in the *Daily News* of Clifton standing on the outskirts of the crowd, trying in vain to tell Dad that their taxi was waiting. I've often said that it was a good thing Clifton was a working newspaperman and understood the ways of the press. Otherwise I think he might have developed a giant inferiority complex as an ex-President's son-in-law.

In the course of rhapsodizing about his grandson, Dad told the reporters that he had a full head of red hair. This drove me up the wall. The baby had a full head of hair all right, but it was black. For all his emphasis on getting the facts while he was in the White House, the ex-President saw only what he wanted to see when he looked at his grandson. Red hair runs in the Truman family, and he blithely presumed that Truman blood had won its tussle with Daniel blood.

I clashed with reporters while still in my hospital bed. They wanted a picture of the child, and I refused to cooperate. I had made up my mind that my children would not endure the glare of publicity that I had known. I accepted it because I was the President's daughter. But I did not feel that the obligation extended to the grandchildren. Clifton finally worked out a compromise by taking a picture of Mother and Dad looking through the window at the baby, and sending it to *The New York Times* for processing and distribution.

While I was in the hospital, Dad dashed up to Brandeis University to make a speech and came back with sweatshirts for his grandson, all of them big enough for a six-year-old. He also had about a dozen bibs saying, "I'm a little owl from Brandeis."

A few days later I came home. I was the typical nervous mother of a first child. Everything was suspected of being infested with germs. With the second, third, and fourth, such worries were of course abandoned. When we got in the house, Dad asked if he could hold his grandchild.

"You'll have to take off your jacket first," I said sternly. "It may be dirty."

He gave me a very exasperated look, took it off and sat down in a chair. "Do you know how to hold him?" I asked.

"I think I remember," he said sarcastically.

I surrendered my precious bundle to him. Dad sat there for a long time, rocking him back and forth. Although normally Clifton was a screamer, he didn't utter a peep.

"Would you like to give him his bottle?" I asked.

You have never seen any man give a baby back faster in your life. "No," he said, "I won't deprive you of that pleasure."

Obviously, Mr. Ex-President had no intentions of going into the baby-sitting, diaper-changing, bib-and-burping business.

The only time I inveigled either him or Mother into doing anything in this line was about a year after the birth of our second son, William. Clifton and I went to Europe on business. Our trip took us all the way across the continent to Russia. We were gone nine weeks. I had a nurse and a housekeeper staying with the children, but I persuaded Mother and Dad to spend two or three weeks in our apartment to be sure the boys did not get too lonely. Dad had a marvelous time with both of them. They were very active as small boys are, and more than once, they almost wore him out.

One small incident occurred during this visit which showed that even in the canyons of Manhattan, Harry Truman did not forget the lessons he had learned on his Missouri farm. You will remember the story I told about him falling off his pony and his father making him walk home. Three-year-old Clifton had a hobbyhorse which he was very fond of riding too vigorously. One morning at breakfast the horse tipped over and Kif, as we call him, went sprawling. Mother and the nurse both jumped up and rushed toward him. The sight of this feminine consolation immediately started him whimpering.

Dad took charge. "Leave him alone," he said. Then in a very ungrandfatherly voice he said, "Get up. Pick up the horse and get back on." Kif was so startled, he forgot all about crying and obeyed the presidential order. It was a pretty big and heavy hobbyhorse, but he rolled it over and got back on.

Whenever Dad and Mother, or Dad alone, came to New York, they stayed at the Carlyle Hotel. He followed his usual routine, arising at dawn, and taking a 6 A.M. stroll. If he was in town alone, he developed the habit of dropping in on me for breakfast. This created problems until I gave him his own key. My children have inherited their grandfather's habits and insist on getting up by the dawn's early light. The children's schedule and Dad's meshed beautifully. He would arrive at the apartment around seven, sit down in the same chair in the living room, now known as Grandfather's chair, and occupy himself with a book. They would creep downstairs and join him.

One morning I came downstairs and found Kif and Will sitting on the arms of Grandfather's chair, while he read aloud to them.

"Well, good morning," Dad said, putting down the book and implying with one of his looks that I had wasted the better half of the day.

"Hello," I said, yawning and glancing at the title of the book he was reading.

My two sons, whom I had thus far been unable to interest in anything weightier than comic books, had been listening enthralled to the Greek historian Thucydides.

When President and Mrs. John F. Kennedy gave a dinner for my parents, the four of us—Mother, Dad, Clifton, and I—were invited to spend the weekend at the White House. This was very nice of Jack Kennedy and we appreciated it very much. Dad had opposed his nomination in the 1960 convention, but he did it without rancor, simply arguing that JFK was not yet ready for the job. He campaigned for him vigorously, once Jack was the nominee, acting as always on the conviction that this kind of harmony was essential to our two-party system.

Dad accepted the invitation but insisted we would stay in the White House only one night. He knew that longer visits put a strain on the staff as well as on the busy hosts.

For dinner President Kennedy assembled a number of Dad's Cabinet and other high officials in his administration. The President made some witty remarks about how many former Trumanites were working in the White House. They amounted to about 50 percent of the staff.

We dined at the great horseshoe table, decked with the lovely centerpiece President Monroe had commissioned in France, the gold plate, and the gold flatware. The main course was grouse, and each of us was served a small bird of his own. Cheerfully conversing, we began to cut them up. I noticed after a few moments that my knife was simply not penetrating. I pressed a little harder. Still no luck. I noticed Dad was working rather hard on his bird and also getting nowhere. President Kennedy, with true Irish determination, was fighting his to the finish. With a Herculean effort, he actually cut it in two pieces. But the idea of trying to chew, must less digest, such a rubberized item forced him to abandon his efforts there. He looked across the table at Jackie with a very tense mixture of wrath and dismay. I turned to Bobby Kennedy and said, "These White House knives never could cut butter." Bobby broke up.

Mother and Dad, having met similar situations at numerous political banquets, did not so much as hint there was anything wrong. Eventually, the butlers came and took our uneaten grouse away.

After dinner and a concert, we went upstairs with the Kennedys to the family quarters. President Kennedy asked Dad or me or both to play the piano. We said that we would be glad to oblige, if we could find some music. A search of piano benches ensued. The only piece of sheet music turned up was "Once in Love with Mamie."

President Kennedy gave up his hopes of being entertained and told us he was going off to the executive wing to do a few hours' work. He explained to Dad that he was a night worker and late riser. Dad said he was a daytime worker and an early riser. President Kennedy very sensibly said that in that case they had better say good-bye.

The next morning Clifton and I knew that we had to be packed and ready at eight for breakfast in the Lincoln Room. By superhuman effort, we made it, half asleep. Dad was already there, fresh as always.

One of the butlers, who had belonged to the White House staff when we lived there, took care of us. "Nothing has changed,

Ficklin," I muttered to him. "I would like some black coffee, grapefruit, and a glass of ice water."

Dad ate his usual breakfast. By 8:45 we were in the car headed for the Mayflower Hotel, where Dad was to address the ladies of the press at another breakfast. I was faced with a second breakfast, though I have never felt that food should be consumed before 10:00 A.M. Dad cheerfully ate again.

When we finally got upstairs to our hotel room, my telephone was ringing wildly. It was Mrs. Kennedy. "Margaret, what happened?" she asked in genuine distress. "I rushed down at nine o'clock and you had all gone."

"Don't give it another thought," I told her. "My father is an early riser. He said good-bye last night."

"But I thought nine o'clock was early," she said plaintively.

"I couldn't agree with you more," I said, "but I've never been able to prove it to Dad."

About a year after we visited the White House, Dad had a chance to do President Kennedy a favor. As President, Dad had always striven for a balanced budget. President Kennedy became a convert to deficit spending, to pep up the economy. Dad disapproved of this, and he let the reporters know it, during one of his early morning strolls in New York. A plea came from the White House, asking him to soft pedal such talk. Dad sent back the following polite reply. He still believed in a balanced budget but he was a good Democrat, and if the Democratic President of the United States wanted him to stop talking about it, he would shut up, forthwith. He did, too.

Dad was deeply grieved by President Kennedy's assassination. He felt that fate had cut him down before he had a chance to really master the intricacies of the presidency. At the funeral Mass, the Trumans and the Eisenhowers sat in the same pew. Reporters and ex-president watchers immediately started buzzing. They seemed to have forgotten that Ike had visited Dad at the Library in Independence in 1961, to get some pointers on how to set up the Eisenhower presidential library. At that time, there was a spate of "burying the hatchet" cartoons, and much talk about the supposed feud being over. On Dad's part, there never had been a feud. He is simply incapable of holding a grudge long enough to turn it into a feud.

Ike and Mamie offered to share their car with us for the ride to Arlington Cemetery. The two ex-Presidents chatted agreeably en route to that sad final farewell to John F. Kennedy. When I discovered that the Eisenhowers were not planning to stay in Washington, I suggested that they come back to Blair House with us and have something to eat before they went back to Gettysburg. While we were having coffee and sandwiches, a hubbub erupted on the front steps. A sizable tribe of reporters, scenting a story, were demanding to see either or both former chief executives. Neither Dad nor Ike was in the least inclined to oblige them, so guess who got dispatched to deal with them. I scoffed at talk of hatchet burying, and insisted that it was simply a matter of civilized people being hospitable, on both sides.

A year later, Dad flew to Greece at the request of President Johnson to represent the United States at the funeral of King Paul. The party included many old associates from his administration. Though the mission was melancholy, Dad enjoyed being with men he had known and worked with during his White House years. A poker game got going on the plane, and it lasted all night. My husband, Clifton, who was part of the entourage, became very worried. He feared Dad would overtax himself, especially in view of the time change between America and Greece.

"Why didn't you stop him?" I demanded. "After all, he is eighty years old."

"Who me?" Clifton asked, horrified. "Do you think I'm going to tell the former President of the United States, and my father-in-law to boot, to go to bed?"

I had to concede that it wouldn't have done any good, even if Clifton had had the courage.

Dad returned from Greece, flying the Atlantic twice in one week, on the eve of a trip to Florida. He got home at midnight and was up at six as usual and on his way again. His eightieth birthday came soon afterward, and he made a speech at every breakfast, lunch, dinner, and reception given in his honor. This included a visit to the U.S. Senate, where he became the first ex-President to address that body while it was in formal session. After a week of this, he said one night, "You know, I feel tired. I simply can't understand it."

The following year Dad was very pleased when President Lyndon Johnson flew to Independence and signed the Medicare Bill, seated beside him on the stage of the Truman Library auditorium. The bill, President Johnson pointed out, was the culmination of the long struggle for a national health policy which Dad had begun in 1945, as part of the twenty-one-point program that had stunned the complacent conservatives then dominating Congress.

Dad is equally fond of our second set of boys, who came a little later in his grandfatherhood. They are Harrison and Thomas. But he inevitably feels a little closer to Kif and Will, because he has spent more time with them. I have done my best to maintain my standing rule against newspaper publicity, but I have not always succeeded. One day, during a vacation in Florida, Will was photographed walking down a road behind Dad. He was imitating Dad's stride. Moreover, the resemblance between him and Dad was striking. Kif tends more toward the Daniel side of the family. Actually, both Kif and Will were following Dad, but in the photograph the only part of Kif that was evident was his foot. Kif was not too happy about that, especially when Will was presented with a wooden plaque on which a photoengraving of the picture was superimposed.

A few months later Kif and Will were supposed to meet Dad and Mother at Kennedy Airport. On the arrival day Will came down with an earache and to his great dismay couldn't go. Kif made a polite effort to restrain his enthusiasm at being the only youthful ambassador to meet his grandparents, but he was obviously pretty set up about it and took great pains with his appearance. By the time he departed with his father to meet the plane, he looked like an advertisement for Brooks Brothers. The day after the meeting Kif's picture with Dad and Mother and Clifton appeared in the paper. Very pleased with himself, he sauntered into the bedroom and said to Will, "Well, I made the *Tribune* this morning."

All the boys call Dad Grandpa. He has never much liked nicknames, but he tolerates this one. Mother has never liked nicknames either, but she rejoices in the name Gammy and has absolutely no objection to hearing herself called that in public. The mere sight of any one of the five men in my family reduces her to the consistency of a marshmallow. I had expected Dad to welcome the masculine contingent I've accumulated, but it never occurred to

[577]

me that Mother would go off the deep end, even to the extent of offering to serve my husband his breakfast in bed. "Over my dead body!" I cried.

Dad is not the sort of grandfather who gets down on the floor and roughhouses with the children. He treats them with dignity, as if they were men, and they are impressed when he talks or reads to them or tells them stories. "My grandsons respect me," he says, and they do. However, he is perfectly capable of taking their side against mine if there is any justice in it. It is a new experience for me to have Dad on somebody else's side.

During one of Mother and Dad's visits we were vacationing in the country. A stray kitten arrived on our doorstep. Kif and Will immediately fell in love with it and began to pester me to be allowed to keep it. A Bedlington terrier, which came with the house we had rented for the summer, disapproved of the new guest. Although I rarely agreed with the Bedlington, I was in her corner for once. Much to my dismay, Dad upheld Kif and Will. He petted the kitten and said the boys were right.

The Bedlington bided her time until nobody was looking and was on the point of making one mouthful of the tiny thing when the kitten jumped about six feet to the trunk of a big old oak tree, scaled the rough bark like a shot, and got out on the end of the highest limb. There it crouched, yowling piteously, and could not be coaxed to move.

Pandemonium set in. The Bedlington ran round and round the tree trunk, barking fiercely. Kif and Will began to jump up and down and wail that the kitten had to be rescued. "Tie up that dog!" Dad ordered, and somebody undertook to collar the Bedlington. Mr. Arthur Ochs Sulzberger, the publisher of *The New York Times,* a dinner guest (I had planned what I thought would be an especially pleasant and relaxing evening, since we were entertaining my husband's boss), got a ladder out of the garage, climbed the tree, and retrieved the kitten.

I had seen enough of the kitten by now to last me a lifetime and was planning subtle arrangements for its disappearance. But Dad, after applauding Mr. Sulzberger's gallantry in action, expressed great concern for the creature.

"It's had a bad experience," he said to the boys. "We will have to look after it."

"Oh, dear," I murmured. "I thought you liked horses."

"I like cats," Dad informed me, as Kif and Will beamed.

Dad suggested that I go into the house and get a big, soft turkish towel. He instructed me in how the towel should be folded and directed its placement under a chair. "So the kitten will feel secure," he said. "Now, Margaret, go get a bowl of milk."

When I came back with the milk, I plunked it down on the terrace.

"Put it under the chair," Dad said, "on the towel. The kitten is too frightened to eat out in the open."

"But it will just make a big mess," I warned.

"No, it won't," my father said. "Cats are very neat animals."

"But I don't want a kitten," I said. "If we feed it, it will stay."

"We'll get around to that," he said.

It then occurred to me to call our neighbors across the road to find out if they were short a kitten. (The kitten had further irritated me by proving Dad's point and lapping up the milk without spilling a drop.) Our neighbors had, indeed, lost a kitten. I was the only one who was relieved when they came for it.

The boys love to visit their grandfather and grandmother in Independence in the big old house where I was born. They especially like to go there for Christmas, when they are allowed to decorate the tree with all the ornaments I remember from my own childhood and hear stories of Christmases past. In Independence they have a lot of freedom.

All the boys have had a tour of Dad's library, and though I doubt that they completely understand its significance, they are impressed with many of the personal mementos and the importance strangers assign to them. They are becoming more and more aware of the fact that their grandfather has played a very large role in the history of their country.

More recent developments in his grandsons, such as long hair, have startled Dad more than a little. He has swallowed hard and striven to absorb them. But long hair is definitely not one of his preferred styles. The first time he saw a sample of it he did not hesitate to express his opinion. A very friendly young man with shoulder-length blond locks greeted him during one of his walks in Independence. "Good morning, Mr. President," he said.

"Good morning, young man," said Dad without even breaking stride, "you'd look a lot better if you went to a barber."

Ever since he left the White House, Dad has made it a rule not to criticize the foreign policy of any of his successors. He is still convinced that a bipartisan foreign policy is essential to the safety and security of the United States. Once foreign policy is flung into the political arena, the very future of the nation is threatened. Moreover, most of the critics cannot begin to match the President's knowledge of the foreign situation or his global view of the vital interests of the United States. This does not mean that Dad lacks strong opinions on the subject. He simply refuses to voice them in public. He has equally strong opinions on the performances of the Presidents who succeeded him, but he is reluctant to air them, too, for a different reason. He feels that more time must pass before anyone, even an ex-President, can evaluate the performance of a man in the White House.

He remains serenely indifferent to opinions about his own White House days. He is, of course, pleased when he hears that one historian or another, or a group of historians, has rated him as one of the eight or nine greatest Presidents in our history. He is unbothered, and is even amused, by revisionist historians who attempt to paint him as the villain in the cold war. It will take another twenty-five years, he believes, before a genuine perspective can be achieved on the accomplishments of his administration. He is confident, however, that the verdict will be in his favor.

At eighty-eight, Dad remains intensely interested in what is happening around him in the nation. He reads at least two papers a day and is ready and willing to talk politics with anyone who will listen. But he does not feel up to taking on reporters. "The old mind isn't as quick at eighty-eight as it was at sixty," he says with his familiar grin. He is now protected from intrusion by the Secret Service. After President Kennedy's assassination, Congress passed a law providing Secret Service protection for both presidential candidates and ex-Presidents. This has been a tremendous help to Dad, because curiosity seekers and screwballs still show up at the house, and people in their eighties, vigorous as he and Mother are, simply cannot—and should not—cope with such problems.

I asked Dad if he wanted to say anything special, to close this book. He thought for a moment and said that if he had to select one statement to sum up his life in politics, he would choose a speech he made in North Carolina during the 1948 campaign.

It was the only time we invaded the South during those tumultuous weeks. Stirred by the setting, Dad spoke from his heart. He discussed three Southerners who became Presidents of the United States—Andrew Jackson, James K. Polk, and Andrew Johnson. All of them, Dad said, "lived through days when reason was overcome by emotion," and because of this "their acts were misunderstood and misinterpreted. So it is not surprising that the estimates of these men made by their contemporaries have been almost discarded by later generations."

But the thing that made the lives of these Presidents most meaningful to him was the way their policies had aroused the wrath of some sincere and honest men. That, Dad said, was "a serious thing. A President may dismiss the abuse of scoundrels, but to be denounced by honest men, honestly outraged, is a test of greatness that none but the strongest men survive."

There was, he concluded, only one lesson to be drawn from the story of these three Presidents, "Do your duty and history will do you justice."

In this book I have tried to show you how a strong man, whom I happen to love very much, did his duty. I am confident that history will do him justice.

Short excerpts are taken from the following books:

The Journals of David E. Lilienthal, Harper and Row, New
New York, 1964.
A Senate Journal by Allen Drury, McGraw-Hill Book Company, Inc., New York, 1963.

INDEX

Bruenn, Howard, 206
Bulger, Miles, 64, 67, 70
Burnham, D. H., 78
Burns, James MacGregor, 235
Burr, Aaron, 237
Burrus, Florence, 51
Burrus, Rufus, 18
Burton, Harold, 156
Bush, Vannevar, 239
Butterworth, W. Walton, 539
Buxton, Mrs. Ethel Lee, 63
Byrd, Harry, 194
Byrd, Richard E., 250
Byrnes, James, 26, 127, 138–139, 170, 171, 175, 176, 217–218, 220, 221, 223, 239, 249, 252, 253, 262, 266, 271, 275, 276, 279, 282, 296–298, 314–315, 318–319, 359, 426–427
    replaced by Marshall as Secretary of State, 345

Camp David, 334
Camp Meade (Maryland), 140
Camp Wallace (Texas), 140
Canada, Truman's state visit to, 373–374
Canfil, Fred, 280–281, 332
Carol, King (Rumania), 376
Caruthersville, Missouri, annual fair at, 289
Cater, Douglas, 498
Caudle, T. LaMar, 531
Central Intelligence Agency, 449, 506
    creation of, 332
Chambers, Whittaker, 413–414
Chang, John Myun, 461
Chapman, Oscar, 20, 31, 534
Chapultepec (Mexico), 373
Chiang Kai-shek, 275, 300, 301, 409–413, 459, 466, 469, 476–478, 503, 508
Chicago, Illinois, campaign stop in, 36–37
Childs, Marquis, 39

China
    Communist takeover of, 409–413
    U.S. aid to, 411, 412
    U.S. policy toward, 300–301
Chrisman, O. L., 187
Churchill, Mary, see Soames, Mary
Churchill, Sarah, 523
Churchill, Winston, 5, 15–16, 137, 203, 218, 219, 222, 223, 234, 235, 240, 242–243, 247, 251, 253, 262, 498
    attitude toward use of atomic bomb in Japan, 274
    correspondence concerning 1948 Presidential election, 394–395
    defeated in stand for reelection, 277
    Fulton, Mo., speech, 310–313
    Margaret Truman's visit to country home of, 523
    opinion of Truman, 556
    paintings by, 523
    Potsdam Conference, 259–281, 359
    Quebec Conference, 265
    Truman's visit with (1956), 566
    visits U.S., 439, 554–555
Civil rights, Truman and, 391–393
Clark, Bennett, 81, 82, 84, 86, 89, 94, 96, 110, 113, 114, 115, 117, 121–124, 130, 131–132, 177–178, 179, 183–184
Clark, James Beauchamp ("Champ"), 96
Clark, Tom, 139, 253, 325
Clarksburg, West Virginia, campaign speech in, 22
Claunch, Charles, 457
Clay, Henry, 12
Clay, Lucius, 358, 546
Cleveland, Grover, 50
Cleveland, Ohio, campaign speech in, 28–29
Clifford, Clark, 26, 346–347, 349, 350, 353, 354, 408, 438
Coal strike (1946), 321, 324–325
Cochran, John J., 84, 86, 87, 88

Donnell, Forrest, 254, 406
Donnelly, Phil M., 11
Donovan, William, 250
Dorsey, John, 225
Dougherty, Henry L., 92
Dougherty, Jack, 495
Douglas, Lewis, 352
Douglas, William O., 7, 8, 9, 173, 174, 310
Draper, Royal, 15
Drescher, George, 201
Dryden, Millie, 101, 124
Dulles, John Foster, 460, 466–467, 519–520
  election of 1952 and, 540
  Senate race (1949), 540–541
Dun, Angus, 223
Dunlap, Ike B., 83
Dunn, James, 236
Dutra, Mrs. Eurico Gaspar, 376

Eaker, Ira, 263
Early, Stephen, 112, 120, 131, 208, 209, 213, 214, 252, 260
Easley, Harry, 119, 186, 190
Eaton, Charles, 356
Eden, Anthony, 236, 251, 490
Edison, Charles, 126
Eisenhower, Arthur, 54, 165
Eisenhower, Dwight, 54, 242, 260, 334, 423, 575–576
  appointed chief of staff, 421
  conference with MacArthur concerning Korean War, 556
  elected President, 549
  election of 1952 and, 536, 543–549
  Inauguration, 556–557
  Korean War and, 548–549
  meeting with Truman prior to taking office as President, 549–551
  member of Kansas City Club, 566
  President, 563

Presidential aspirations of, 528, 535–536
Presidential campaign (1948) and, 7–8
Supreme Allied Commander in Europe, 505, 510, 511
trip to Korea, 556
Truman's correspondence with, 529–530
Eisenhower, John, 557
Elsey, George, 36, 205, 274, 309, 346, 347, 401, 402, 444, 445–446, 461, 462
Employment Act (1946), 308
Etzanhouser, Mrs., 77
Evans, Tom, 126, 133, 175
Ewing, Oscar, 194, 438
Excelsior Springs, Missouri, 40

Fair Employment Practices Committee, 286, 329
Farley, James, 83, 111, 170
Farrell, Thomas F., 271, 272
Federal Bureau of Investigation, 116
Federal Reserve Board, 444, 445
Feeney, Joe, 443–447
Ferdinand Magellan (presidential car), 1, 2, 26, 27, 29, 434, 558
Fermi, Enrico, 240
Fields, Alonzo, 246, 333–334, 370, 457
Finletter, Thomas, 458
Fitzpatrick, Daniel, 116
"Five percenters," 424–425
Flynn, Edward J., 10, 134, 172, 175, 179, 397
Folliard, Edward T., 495
Foreign aid, 344, 352–357, 411
Foreign Economic Administration, 254
Formosa, 458, 459, 462, 476–478, 503, 504, 508
Forrestal, James, 7, 15, 34, 35, 217, 236, 291, 310, 322, 380, 407–408
  suicide, 408
Fort Leonard Wood, 138
Fox, Joe, 438

Henderson, Leon, 7, 10

Henhouse Hicks Secret Six, 89

Herring, Clyde L., 112

Hersey, John, 492

Hickerson, John D., 458

Hill, Lister, 156

Hillman, Sidney, 151–152, 171, 172, 175, 176, 187

Himmler, Heinrich, 240

Hirohito, Emperor, 283–284

Hiroshima, Japan, atomic bomb attack on, 5, 282

Hiss, Alger, 413–414

Hiss, Donald, 414

Hitler, Adolf, 137, 243, 268, 344, 381

Ho Chi Minh, 433

Hodge, John R., 310

Hodges, Campbell Blackshear, 423

Hoey, Clyde R., 424–426

Hoffman, Anna Rosenberg, 234

Holding companies, 105, 108

Holland, Lou E., 153

Hoover, Herbert, 448, 505, 560
  election of 1952 and, 540

Hope, Bob, 251

Hopkins, Bill, 493

Hopkins, Harry, 152, 174, 222, 240, 252, 253, 255, 263, 266

Horne, Charles Francis, 52

Horton, Drucie Snyder, 159, 402, 403, 442, 536–538

Horton, John Ernest, 442

House Un-American Activities Committee, 413–414, 563

Houston *Herald,* 80

Hughes, Charles Evans, 330

Hull, Cordell, 284

Hume, Paul, 502–503

Humphrey, Hubert, 474

Hungry Horse, Montana, 545

Hunt, James V., 425

Hurley, Patrick J., 300–301

Ibn Saud, King, 298, 327–328

Iceland, U.S. air base in, 314

Ickes, Harold, 8, 37, 125, 146, 172, 251, 290–291, 294

Independence (presidential plane), 374, 457, 483

Independence, Missouri, 39, 40, 41–42, 49, 50, 53

Independence *Examiner,* 62–63, 64, 66, 79, 80, 166

Indianapolis (cruiser), 276

Indiantown Gap, Pennsylvania, 140

Indochina, 433

Insull, Samuel, 92

Insurance companies, 107

Inter-American Conference for the Maintenance of Continental Peace and Security, 374, 375

Interstate Commerce Commission, 105, 120

Iron Curtain, 312, 313

Israel, 299, 386–391

Jackson, Andrew, 581
  equestrian statue of, 81, 89

Jackson, Robert, 139, 210

Jackson, Samuel, 173, 179, 180

Jacobson, Eddie, 61, 62, 257, 387–388, 390

Jagel, Frederick, 341

James, Jesse, 107

Japan
  peace treaty with, 519–520
  unconditional surrender of, 284

Jefferson, Thomas, 237, 535, 561

Jefferson Island, 288

Jenner, William E., 516, 544, 547

Jessup, Philip, 458, 484

Jester, Beauford, 33

Johnson, Andrew, 581

Johnson, Edwin, 417, 418

Lerner, Max, 14
Leviero, Anthony, 438, 495
Lewis, J. Hamilton, 90
Lewis, John L., 143, 147, 304, 321, 324–325, 349
Lewis, Martin, 84
Li Tsung-jen, 412
Liberal party, 37
Lie, Trygve, 478, 479
Lilienthal, David, 8, 248–249, 294, 295, 348–349, 416, 426
  H-bomb and, 417, 418
Lincoln, Abraham, 146, 252, 393
Lincoln University, 128
Lingo, Jane, 159, 442
Lippmann, Walter, 39
List, Eugene, 280, 398
Lloyd, Dave, 446, 530
Lodge, Henry Cabot, 409, 550, 551
Lombardo, Guy, 403
Long, Huey, 101–102
Los Angeles, California, campaign speech in, 30–31
Lovett, Robert M., 388, 405, 534, 552, 553
Lowenthal, Max, 106, 167, 521–522
Loyalty program, 428–429, 474
Lucas, Scott, 178, 179, 180, 181, 475, 490
Luce, Clare Booth, 4, 187
Luce, Henry, 187, 524
Lucey, Charles T., 36
Lupescu, Madame, 376
Lyle, Dorsett W., 72
MacArthur, Douglas, 260, 292–293, 443
  address before Congress following his dismissal, 516–517
  appointment as UN Commander, 476
  conference with Eisenhower concerning Korean War, 556
  Congressional investigation of his dismissal, 517
  election of 1952 and, 540

Korean War and, 4, 56, 458, 459, 460, 462, 464, 466–471, 475–486, 490–495, 497, 503–504, 507–509, 511–518
  meeting with Truman at Wake Island, 483–485
  political ambitions, 476, 484
  relieved of his command, 512–519
MacArthur, Mrs. Douglas, 483, 485
MacLeish, Archibald, 147
Madison, James, 237
Malik, Jacob, 520
Maloney, Francis, 164
Mann, Conrad, 83–84
Mansfield, Mike, 434
Mao Tse-tung, 300, 469, 508
Maragon, John, 424–425
Marks, Ted, 23
Marshall, George C., 148, 236, 261, 263, 273, 407, 492, 493, 502, 511, 513, 514, 557
  China and, 301, 410–411, 412
  Eisenhower and, 544, 547
  farm of, 404
  foreign aid and, 353–357
  McCarthy's attack on, 519
  Palestine question and, 385
  quoted on clash between Truman and MacArthur, 518
  retirement as Secretary of State, 404
  Secretary of Defense, 480, 506
  Secretary of State, 15, 34, 35–36, 345, 357, 374, 375, 388, 389, 390, 405, 406
Marshall, Mrs. George C., 325, 404
Marshall Plan, 401, 405, 409
Martin, Joseph, 210, 287, 513–514
  invites MacArthur to address Congress, 516
Masaryk, Jan, 357
Maschoff, Otto, 95–96
Mason, Lowell B., 93–94, 200
Matthews, Francis, 458
May, George O., 105

[593]

[595]

[599]

Wickard, Claude, 254
Williams, Aubrey, 204
Williamsburg (yacht), 17, 298, 334, 335, 438
Willkie, Wendell, 257
Willoughby, Charles A., 482
Wilson, Charles E., 155, 156, 534
Wilson, Francis M., 79–80, 81, 83
Wilson, Woodrow, 96, 204, 211, 264
  quoted on Congressmen, 346
  Vice Presidency described by, 198
Wilson, Mrs. Woodrow, 194
Winchell, Walter, 422
Windsor, Duke of, 437
Wise, Stephen S., 298, 299, 382
Wogan, M. F., 127

Woodward, Stanley, 380, 423, 453
World War II, 5
  Truman and, 216, 242, 260–285
Wright, Annette, 298
Wright Aeronautical Corporation, 154
Wyatt, Wilson, 10

Yalta Conference, 233–234, 521
Young, Brigham, 78
Young, Harrison (uncle), 54
Young, Solomon (grandfather), 45–46, 135, 256
Young, Truman, 149
Yugoslavia, 247–248

Zimmerman, Bill, 403